# What they're saying about
# Leggetts' Antiques Atlas™

"Antique lovers should check out the **Antiques Atlas,** a listing of more than 15,000 shops in 48 states. The book includes reviews & travel maps."
**Jerry Shriver, USA Today**

"This book certainly fills a void in the antique business."
**Terry Kovel,**
**Kovels on Antiques & Collectibles**

"The **Antiques Atlas** has it all — an exhaustive state-by-state guide to shops, lodging, and even entertainment along with excellent regional maps. How did we ever live without it?"
**New England Antiques Journal**

"It's the perfect gift for a friend who just can't say no to collecting."
**Country Accents Magazine**

"A book that you should spread out on the dining table when you're planning your road trip."
**Maine Antique Digest Staff**

"The **Atlas** makes the entire antique-hunting effort an experience to savor and enjoy."
**Anita Kerba, Antique Trader Weekly**

"This roundup of antiques shops all over the country will be popular with collectors always looking for a new shop to prowl around in."
**Mark Marymont, St. Louis News-Leader**

"There's nothing worse than being somewhere unfamiliar and not knowing where all the antiques in town are. That's why the **Atlas** is so handy."
**Nancy A. Ruhling,**
**Victorian Homes Magazine**

"An ideal travel companion as you hit the road for antiques."
**Ed Klimuska, Lancaster, PA, New Era**

"The bible of unusual and rare articles."
**Fred Petrucelli, Log Cabin Democrat**

"It's a shopper's dream guide."
**Ken Moore, Naples Daily News**

"**Antiques Atlas**: A treasure map, the most complete listing anywhere at this moment."
**Barbara Hertenstein, St. Louis Post-Dispatch**

"The **Atlas** makes life easy for antique hunters. You'll wonder how you ever did without it."
**Ed Conrad, Standard Speaker, PA**

"The most comprehensive guide to antiquing in America."
**Bob Milne, Travelwriter Marketletter**

"Even if you are not into antiques big time, this guide is still most interesting just to have around and look through."
**Edith Smith, The Valdosta Daily Times**

"Up to now, we've had to depend on signs, area brochures and, if we're lucky, state and regional guides to point us toward antiques in unexplored territory. Now some enterprising dealers have come up with a book no collector should leave home without — the **Antiques Atlas**."
**Peggy Welch Mershon,**
**About Antiques, Mansfield News Journal**

"This isn't one (the **Antiques Atlas**) just to browse through at the bookstore, it's one to carry around everywhere you go."
**Shanna Wiggens, Argus Observer**

# Leggetts' Antiques Atlas™

*East*
*2000 Edition*

Kim and David Leggett

Foreword by Ralph and Terry Kovel

THREE RIVERS PRESS
NEW YORK

Published by Three Rivers Press, 201 East 50th Street, New York, New York 10022. Member of the Crown Publishing Group.

Random House, Inc. New York, Toronto, London, Sydney, Auckland
www.randomhouse.com

THREE RIVERS PRESS is a registered trademark of Random House, Inc.

Originally published in different format by Rainy Day Publishing, Inc., in 1997 and by Three Rivers Press in 1999.
Copyright © 1997, 1999 by Kim and David Leggett.

Printed in the United States of America

Library of Congress Cataloging-in-Publication Data
    Leggetts' antiques atlas : 2000 east edition / Kim and David Leggett; foreword by Ralph and Terry Kovel. – Rev. ed.
        p.      cm.
    Originally published in different format by Rainy Day Pub., c1997.

    1. Antique dealers — United States — Directories.   I. Leggett, David.   II. Title.
NK1127.L43   2000
745.1'025'73 — dc21                                      98-34759
                                                         CIP

ISBN 0-609-80490-1 (pbk.)

10 9 8 7 6 5 4 3 2 1

Revised Edition

# Dedication

This book is dedicated to all of those special people who put forth their time, money and talents to make a project of this size happen. A special thanks to Linda Miller, David and Jo Brandon, Frank Bertelt, Kimberly Poland of Mollyockett Antique Market for her hard work in updating the state of Maine, Kitty and Tony Ables, Heart of Country Antiques Shows, the Baird Texas Marketing Alliance, Antique Associations and Chamber of Commerce organizations across America, our editor PJ Dempsey at Crown for her patience and hard work, and Terry Kovel for recommending such a fabulous publisher. We thank you and love you all.

# Contents

# Foreword

Of course, we are always looking for that out-of-the-way shop filled with unrecognized treasures, that $1,000 vase priced at $75. But when does it pay to leave the turnpike and go off into a small town to visit the shops? Local dealers often have brochures listing nearby antiques stores, the farm papers sometimes include a section on shopping for antiques, and the dealers are usually happy to direct us to the next area with stores. But we need more.

The *Leggetts' Antiques Atlas* is the first large national guidebook that recognizes the problems of the out-of-state shopper searching for antiques. It has maps, places to stay, to eat, and a town-by-town guide to the shops and malls. We like to photocopy the pages about the states we plan to be in. That way we have some of the town history, detailed directions, and maps. There are also antiques show schedules so we can try to arrive in a town when the big show is on.

Thank you, Kim and David, for writing this book that helped us out of a very scary night. We were driving in a rural area, no houses in sight, when the fog made it almost impossible to see. Once in a while a street sign was visible. The book listed a phone number for a nearby shop. We hoped the owner lived there and was awake as we called from the car phone to explain our problem. Antiques people are the best! The shop owner talked us along the road and through the fog telling us where to turn. … Thirty minutes later we were at a motel.

We know it is impossible to ever do a complete listing of antiques shops. They open and close daily. The *Leggetts' Antiques Atlas* is as complete as any we have used.

Ralph and Terry Kovel
*Kovels' Antiques & Collectibles Price List*

# Introduction

**E**ven as a child I loved to go "antiquing." Every Friday night my aunt and grandmother would take me along to a little country auction at "Peppermint Pond," where they often purchased incredible antiques at next to nothing prices. To this day my aunt still sleeps in a gorgeous six-foot-long oak bed which she purchased for $20. Not one to be left out of a bargain-hunting shopping excursion, I too purchased a fair amount of jumble and junk along with some "good stuff" (or so I thought). My room became the envy of cousins and friends who came to admire the long, sparkling strands of hippie beads, peace signs, strange-looking incense burners and other '60s memorabilia. Today, 30 years later, I prefer early American painted pieces over the "Partridge Family Does Dixie" look, but one thing has never changed — the intense desire to search and find "pieces of the past."

I was convinced that there were plenty of antiques establishments all across America worth seeking out, but there was simply no handy way to find them. Because I could not find a book that provided such a listing, I resolved to research and write one myself. I am happy to say that most businesses were thrilled to be included in this book. Their personal stories are a testimony to their love and devotion to their business. Within these pages you will find a great mix of "antiquing" possibilities, from the offerings of exclusive antiques markets and group shops to the diverse selections of traditional antiques and collectibles shops and malls. All the antiques shows listed in this book represent only the finest in antique furnishings and very early collectibles. Many of the bed and breakfasts, country inns, and hotels are listed on the National Register of Historical Places and offer exceptional overnight accommodations. You'll also find information on historic towns and suggestions for some very interesting "in-town" side trips to add to your "antiquing" adventures. Should all this shopping make you hungry, I have thrown in a few select dining establishments as well.

If in your travels you happen upon a shop/mall/market/show/auction, etc., that is not included, please call us. We would love to include them in our year 2001 edition. And most important, when visiting any of these businesses, please let them know you read about them in *Leggetts' Antiques Atlas*.

**Happy Hunting!**

**Call us anytime — we would love to hear from you!**

**(615) 599-5406**

**Kim and David Leggett**

# How to Use This Book

1. The listings following the maps are in alphabetical order. Consequently, the numbers appearing on the maps will not be in numerical order.

2. The purpose of the maps is to direct you to a general location using major highways or interstates as references. Secondary highways and streets are intentionally omitted.

3. The directions in this book were submitted to *Leggetts' Antiques Atlas* by the listed business. Neither *Leggetts' Antiques Atlas* nor Crown Publishing Group accepts responsibility for incorrect directions.

4. At the time of publishing, the information in this book was verified to be correct. However, the publisher cannot be responsible for any inconvenience due to outdated or incorrect information.

**NOTE:** *At the time of printing, we were experiencing a large volume of area code changes. If you should reach a number which appears to be disconnected, call the operator to verify if there has been an area code change.*

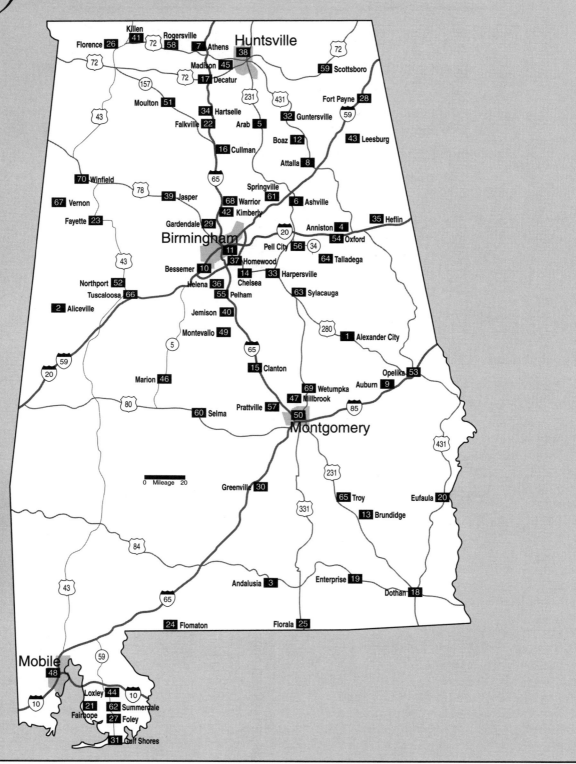

# Alabama

Killen 41
Florence 26
Rogersville
58
Athens 7
38 Huntsville
Madison 45
Madison 72
17 Decatur
59 Scottsboro
157
231
431
Moulton 51
34 Hartselle
32 Guntersville
Fort Payne 28
Falkville 22
Arab 5
59
Boaz 12
43 Leesburg
16 Cullman
Attalla 8
70 Winfield
Springville
61
67 Vernon
39 Jasper
68 Warrior
6 Ashville
35 Heflin
Fayette 23
42 Kimberly
Gardendale 29
Anniston 4
54 Oxford
Birmingham
11
Pell City 56
34
64 Talladega
37 Homewood
Bessemer 10
14 Chelsea
33 Harpersville
Northport 52
Helena 36
Tuscaloosa 66
55 Pelham
63 Sylacauga
2 Aliceville
Jemison 40
Montevallo 49
280
1 Alexander City
5
65
15 Clanton
Opelika 53
Marion 46
Auburn 9
80
69 Wetumpka
60 Selma
47 Millbrook
Prattville 57
50
85
Montgomery
431
231
Greenville 30
65 Troy
Eufaula 20
331
13 Brundidge
84
Andalusia 3
Enterprise 19
43
Dothan 18
65
24 Flomaton
Florala 25
Mobile
48
59
Loxley 44
10
21 Summerdale
10
Fairhope
62
27 Foley
31 Gulf Shores

0 Mileage 20

# Alabama

## 1  ALEXANDER CITY

### Queens Attic Antiques
110 Calhoun St.
256/329-0653

A visit to Queens Attic is like a minitrip to England. That is because for the past 19 years the owner has personally picked and poked throughout the English countryside to bring to you, her customers, a taste of the best England has to offer. She specializes in furniture but a nice collection of smalls can be found as well.

| **Antique Mall of Memories** | **Sara's House Antiques** |
|---|---|
| 1534 Hwy. 280 | 259 Marshall St. |
| 256/234-0963 | 256/329-9468 |

## 2  ALICEVILLE

Nestled snugly along the Sipsey River on the south and the Tennessee Tombigbee Waterway on the west, Aliceville, located in Pickens County, is a hunter, fisherman, camper and boater's paradise. The 234-mile Tenn-Tom Waterway forms ten lakes covering 44,000 acres and each and every acre of water is well stocked with smallmouth, black and stripped bass; bream; catfish and crappie. The Pickensville Campground on Aliceville Lake offers a unique recreational opportunity. The setting on the banks of the waterway is nostalgic of earlier river days, while the modern facilities offer many comforts. The campground is a class-A facility open to campers year-round.

Pilgrimages are a way of life all up and down the waterway and elsewhere in the south. The region has heritage towns where visitors can catch a glimpse of plantation life and architecture. The lovely old antebellum homes are open during the springtime and are well worth the time and small fee sometimes charged for a visit.

During the third weekend in March, Aliceville is host to the annual Dogwood Festival. Of special interest to antiquers is the antique auction and giant flea market. Literally hundreds of antique pieces from the attics of Pickens County are offered for sale on Saturday from 8 a.m. to 10 a.m. Those pieces not sold by 10 a.m. are then auctioned off to the highest bidder. The auction continues until every last item is sold. The friendly bidding competition is a lot of fun and all proceeds go the Pickens County Tourism Committee to be used for fine projects that encourage tourism.

The Aliceville Museum and Cultural Center is a "key player" in the Dogwood Festival. The army operated a World War II prisoner of war camp at Aliceville from Dec. 1942 to Sept. 1945. At the camp, some 6,000 German POWs were held, some from General Erwin Rommel's Afrika Korps. The only thing left of the camp is a huge chimney built by the prisoners. A 50-year reunion in October 1995 brought back together some of the German prisoners and their American guards. The interest of the prisoners, guards, and townspeople generated the idea of the museum housing German artifacts as well as other WWII memorabilia. The museum was established in the old Coca-Cola bottling plant and was dedicated in 1995. It continues to attract hundreds of visitors annually. The museum participates in the Dogwood Festival with a special event such as an excellent display of handmade quilts and a lecture on collecting, care of and storing quilts.

Aliceville is located 50 miles west of Tuscaloosa and 25 miles south of Columbus, Miss. For additional information on historic Aliceville, call the chamber at 205/373-2820.

### Green Gables Antiques
107 Broad St.
205/373-8123

I'm undecided on which is the most interesting; the antique shop or the nice lady who works there. Mrs. Erline Jones runs this privately owned shop belonging to the town historian, Mr. R.R. Johnston, and she sure has some interesting stories to tell. As a matter of fact she was employed during the war at the prisoner of war camp. She saw firsthand the effects of the war and has many stories to tell. In this charming shop you'll find many traditional antiques as well as several oddities. Artifacts of the region are often available there.

### *Great Places to Stay*

### Willowbrooke Bed & Breakfast
205/373-6133 or 205/373-8456

Built in 1911, this grand house was constructed with expert craftsmanship and the finest materials available. The home features over 2,000 square feet of wraparound porches, exquisitely detailed woodwork, high ceilings, lovely antiques and seven coal-burning fireplaces with the original signature mantles still remaining. Most of the original plaster walls still remain in the house. A smokehouse built in the late 1800s still stands in the backyard, but has been converted to a workshop. Guests will enjoy viewing everyday items from yesteryear that will be on display — anything from a bottle of castor oil to *Saturday Evening Post* magazines dating back to the 1920s.

Guests can choose whether to have their breakfast served in the dining room or on one of the wraparound porches. Weather permitting, guests will enjoy their breakfast even more as they view either the town or the lovely gardens landscaped by the owner. The cozy wicker sitting room on the second floor is stocked with magazines and novels for the guests' pleasure.

# Alabama

## The Carriage House
Hwy. 17 & Sanders St.
Carrollton, Ala.
205/367-2220 or 205/367-8161

Built in 1854, the Greek Revival cottage has two matching porticos. Each portico has four columns and double entrance doors with rectangular transoms and sidelights. The house was built by Zachariah Nabors, who became editor of the *West Alabamian* newspaper and was later elected Probate Judge of Pickens County in 1861.

The Carriage House Bed and Breakfast features beautiful period antiques, each room with its own unique feeling. The foyer is of Gothic style with statues. The parlor is musically equipped with a baby grand piano. The dining room will seat 40 guests. The bright and airy sunroom features windows all around and each of the three bedrooms are large and spacious with private baths.

## Myrtlewood Bed & Breakfast
1-800-367-7891 or 205/373-8153

The beautiful woodwork, the Victorian furnishings, the unusual staircase, the stained glass, and the minimuseum including items from the area's history will be of special interest. Suites are available — each including a sitting area, private bath and bedroom. An early continental breakfast or a full plantation breakfast is served in the dining room. Whether it's relaxing on the wide porches, strolling the shady sidewalks, browsing the area antique shops, touring the points of historic interest in the area or enjoying the recreational activities of the Tennessee Tombigbee Waterway, you are sure to enjoy your visit in Aliceville.

### *Great Places to Eat*

## The Plantation House
102 1st Ave. S.E.
205/373-8121

A fine assortment of Southern foods is served including outstanding hors d'oeuvres such as large whole mushrooms and fried green tomatoes. Lunch is served Tues.–Sun. 11–2 and dinner Tues.–Sat. 5–9.

## 3 ANDALUSIA

### Old South Antiques & Collectibles
112 Hillcrest Dr.
334/427-1098
Open: Mon.–Sat. 10–5:30

5,000 square feet of antiques and collectibles. The shop specializes in primitives, Hull, Roseville and Watt pottery.

---

**Loot Antique & Interior Market**
600 River Falls St.
334/222-7841

**Plunder Parlor**
209 E. Three Notch St.
334/222-1549

## 4 ANNISTON

**Mulberry Corner Antiques**
1700 AL Hwy. 21 S.
256/835-3556

**B-Ring Exclusive Inc.**
1928 Cooper Ave.
256/237-8082

**Treasures & Keepsakes**
1900 Wilmer Ave.
256/235-2251

**Anniston Galleries**
906 Noble St.
256/236-3741

**Apple Barrel Antique Mall**
3320 Henry Road
256/237-0091

**Petticoat's**
911 Noble St.
256/235-3944

**Jamie's Antique**
1429 Snow St.
256/831-2830

**Anderson's Antiques**
1130 Snow St.
256/835-9191

**Queens Antiques**
24 W. 13th St.
256/237-3383

### *Nearby Antique Shopping (Ashland)*

## Round the Square Mall
40590 First St. N.
256/354-3513
Open: Mon.–Sat. 9–5
Directions: Located on Hwy. 77 and Hwy. 9, 35 miles from Anniston.

Three buildings and 25 dealers, general mix of antiques, particularly furniture.

## Ashland Antiques
645 Hwy. 31 N.
256/354-3510
Open: Tues.–Sat. 9–5, Sun. 1–5

The shop features 6,000 square feet of antiques.

### *Nearby Antique Shopping (Jacksonville)*

## Puttin on the Ritz
2255 Pelham Road S.
256/435-1999
Directions: 15 miles north of Anniston.

Specialists in vintage jewelry for 25 years. 3,000 to 4,000 pieces available at all times. Visit ebay.com@jmurrayrz@aol.com.

**Country Store Antique Mall**
1964 Cedar Springs Dr.
256/435-6605

### *Great Places to Stay*

### The Victoria: A Country Inn
1604 Quintard Ave.
1-800-260-8781

Queen Anne style built in 1888 — 48 guest rooms.

### 5 ARAB

**Scott's Antiques, Gifts & Accessories**
117 N. Main St.
256/931-2006

**Olde World Antique Gallery**
2330 N. Brindlee Mt. Pkwy.
256/586-2185

**Jean's Antiques**
2893 Hwy. 231
256/586-5007

**Where Memories Linger**
119 Main St.
256/931-2065

**Kelley's Gifts & Antiques**
220 Ruth Road
256/586-4169

**Special Touches**
Hwy. 231 N.
256/498-5504

### 6 ASHVILLE

**Ashville Antiques & Collectibles**
18 Court St. E.
205/594-5970

### 7 ATHENS

Have time to stop and explore a few days in Alabama? Grab your shovels and head for the hills. Rumor has it that an undetermined amount of gold and silver coins are buried in the quaint little Southern town of Athens, Ala. Located in the rolling foothills of the Appalachian Mountains in northern Alabama, Athens is blessed with an abundance of historic homes and sites, many dating back to the mid-1800s. It is here, in this charming historic town, that the story of buried treasures unfolds.

As the Civil War was ending, soldiers loyal to the South collected a large amount of gold and silver coins. The plan was to take the treasure to Montgomery, but Union forces interfered. Near Athens, the wagon carrying the treasure sank in the murky Alabama clay, becoming immobile. While working to free it, the Confederate band was surprised by a small Union patrol. Believing the wagon contained weapons and ammunition, the Union sergeant ordered the wagon unloaded. A skirmish erupted between the two groups. Three of the Yankee soldiers were killed, along with two of the three Confederates. A wounded Union soldier escaped, leaving the Confederate leader — known only as Hansen — behind to defend the treasure. Dumping the treasure in the adjacent bog to conceal it from the Union armies, Hansen made his way to the home of a friend, where he reported his misfortune, along with the general location of the treasure. Hansen was killed shortly afterward by a Union soldier. His friend never recovered the coins.

### Hickory House
2243 U.S. Hwy. 72
256/232-9860
Open: Daily 10–5

The shop features 6,500 square feet of antiques and collectibles. Special features include cast iron banks, period furniture, Tiffany lamps, art glass and vintage quilts.

### Sutton's Furniture 2
12120 U.S. Hwy. 72
256/729-8088
Open: Thurs., Fri., Sat. 9–5
Auctions on occasion (call for dates)

This privately owned shop features 8,000 square feet of fine antiques and collectibles. Mr. Sutton hauls from New York and Pennsylvania so you are sure to find many wonderful American antiques to add to your collection. The auctions are outstanding. A nice collection of unusual antiques is gathered several months prior to the sale.

### S&H Auction
308 Strange St.
256/232-1153 or 256/232-7177
Monthly auctions, usually the last Friday of the month.
Directions: Located 3 miles from the I-65 and U.S. 72 interchange. From I-65, go west on U.S. 72 to Jefferson St., turn north on Jefferson St. and at the fourth light, turn west on Washington St., go 2½ blocks and turn left (south) on Strange St.

Mr. James Sutton has been in the auction business for the past 40 years. I found it most unusual that he and his family were originally from my hometown of Dyersburg, Tenn. The reason they left early in the 20th century is a wild Southern tale indeed. Very amusing but I won't repeat it here.

At the time of this printing I had just received a notice of an upcoming sale so I'll list a few items just to give you an idea of the quality merchandise he brings in: 5-piece mahogany bedroom suite, carved marble-top tables, painted primitive cupboard, primitive baby cradle, Mission oak desk, plantation desk, blanket chest, Berkley & Gay mahogany dresser, Fostoria, crock jugs, pedal cars, and much, much more.

# Alabama

## Regency Antique Mall
1880 Hwy. 72 at Lindsey Lane
256/232-1003
Directions: Located ½ mile east of I-65.

Featuring mantels, Victorian, period and English furniture, chintz china, vaseline glass and estate jewelry.

**Sutton's Antiques**
1010 N. Jefferson St.
256/233-0235

**Athens Antique Mall**
309 S. Marion St.
256/230-0036

**Preston's Antiques Mall**
Located east of I-65 & Hwy. 72
256/233-0813

## 8  ATTALLA

**Days of Old**
418 4th St.
256/538-1950

**Col. John's Auction**
413 4th St. N.W.
256/538-7884

**Memory Lane Antiques**
420 4th St. N.W.
256/538-8594

**Pembroke Antiques**
307 5th Ave.
256/570-0041

**Yesterday's Treasures Antiques**
426 4th St. N.W.
256/538-3111

**Alabama Antiques**
311 5th Ave. N.W.
256/538-0233

**Days Gone By**
328 5th Ave.
205/538-1920

**Gramling Antiques**
419 4th St. N.W.
205/538-2464

**Cellar**
408 4th St. N.W.
256/538-5330

**Hummingbird Antiques**
424 4th St. N.W.
256/570-0205

**Beulah Land Antique Mall**
216 4th St. N.W.
256/538-1585

**Tommorrow's Heirlooms**
428 4th Ave. N.W.
256/538-1958

## 9  AUBURN

**Magnolia Tree**
409 E. Magnolia Ave.
334/821-5211

**Old Timers & Chimers**
223 E. Magnolia Ave.
334/887-0124

**Village Accents**
138 N. Ross St.
334/826-6987

**Village Antiques**
2192 U.S. Hwy. 29 S.
334/826-1960

## 10  BESSEMER

**Bessemer Antique & Design**
506 19th St. N.
205/424-0089

**Consignment World**
1319 9th Ave. N.
205/923-1918

**Gran & Papa's Antiques**
8755 Bluff Ridge Road
205/426-9148

**Rags to Riches**
815 8th St.
205/426-0413

**Sullivan Interiors**
1293 Hueytown Road
205/497-8750

## 11  BIRMINGHAM

### Riverchase Antique Gallery
3454 Lorna Road
205/823-6433
Open: Mon.–Sat. 10–6, Sun. 1–6 (Closed Thanksgiving and Christmas)
Directions: Located at I-459 and Lorna Road, across from the Galleria, only 10 minutes south of Birmingham.

The seasoned veteran, as well as the rookie, loves the thrill of the hunt. To an avid antiquer, the quest for that certain item, be it a Shaker cabinet or a Tiffany lamp, is often as exciting (and treasure-filled) as the find itself.

A fine spot to begin the hunt when traveling near Birmingham, Ala., is Riverchase Antique Gallery. The 146-dealer gallery spans 36,000 square feet for your meandering pleasure. An abundance of furniture in styles such as French, English, Mission, Primitive and Shaker is displayed throughout the gallery. Riverchase Antique Gallery hosts an impressive inventory of bedroom and dining room suites, armoires and sideboards, in addition to many other pieces of fine furniture.

At Riverchase Antique Gallery, the unusual is the norm. Dealers display juke boxes, refurbished telephones, lamps, glassware, china, paints, pottery, toys and collectibles. Is it any wonder the mall was voted "The Best of Birmingham" ten years running?

### Vestavia Antiques and Interiors
700 Montgomery Hwy.
205/979-8740
Open: Mon.–Sat. 10–6, Sun. 1–6

Quality antiques and accessories for the home. Beautiful estate jewelry, china and crystal, represented by professional, well-known dealers.

**Whistle Stop Treasure Shop**
1910 1st Ave. N.
205/951-5500

**Al's Antiques & Used Furniture**
7621 1st Ave. N.
205/836-2270

**Redmont Market Antiques**
2330 7th Ave. S.
205/320-0440

**Peck & Hill Antique Furniture**
2400 7th Ave. S.
205/252-3179

# Alabama

**Lakeview Antiques**
2427 7th Ave. S.
205/323-0888

**Alabama Auction Room Inc.**
2112 5th Ave. N.
205/252-4073

**Wardemond Galleries**
2808 18th St. S.
205/871-0433

**Interiors Market**
2817 2nd Ave. S.
205/323-2817

**Yester Year Antiques & Tea Shop**
587 Shades Crest Road
205/979-4742

**Architectural Heritage**
2807 2nd Ave. S.
205/322-3538

**Antiques by Tommye**
815 Shades Crest Road
205/822-0555

**Carriage Antique Village**
88 Green Springs Hwy.
205/942-8131

**Christopher House Antiques**
2949 18th St.
205/870-7106

**Countrytime**
1408 E. Lake Blvd.
205/841-0420

**Edgewood Antiques**
731 Broadway St. (Rear)
205/870-3343

**Europa Antiques, Inc.**
1820 29th Ave. S.
205/879-6222

**Kings House Antiques & Gifts**
2418 Montevallo Road
205/871-5787

**Little House on Linden**
2915 Linden Ave.
205/879-4186

**Mary Adams Antiques**
1829 29th Ave. S.
205/871-7131

**Old World Market Place**
593 Shades Crest Road
205/823-9007

**Hanna Antiques Mall**
2424 7th Ave. S.
205/323-6036

**5th Avenue Antiques**
2410 5th Ave. S.
205/320-0500

**Antiques & Gardens**
2408 7th Ave. S.
205/252-5549

**Altadena Antiques by Wards**
4704 Cahaba River Road
205/967-8110

**Antique Art Exchange**
361 Summit Blvd.
205/967-1700

**Bridges Antiques**
3949 Cypress Dr.
205/967-6233

**Cahaba Heights Antiques**
3131 Belwood Dr.
205/967-7915

**Christopher Glenn, Inc.**
2713 19th St. S.
205/870-1236

**Bradshaw House Gallery**
2154 Highland Ave. S.
205/933-2121

**E. Earl's Antiques**
585 Shades Crest Road
205/978-7693

**Estate Sales Store**
4244 Cahaba Heights Court
205/969-0904

**Iron Art, Inc.**
2901 Cahaba Road
205/879-0529

**Levy's**
2116 2nd Ave. N.
205/251-3381

**Luke's Antiques & Collectibles**
237 Oxmoor Circle
205/942-9180

**Michael's Antiques**
1831 29th Ave. S.
205/871-2716

**Pump House Antiques**
3279 Cahaba Heights Road
205/967-2855

**Quilted Cat**
63 Church St.
205/871-4741

**Reed Books**
20th St. @ 1st Ave. S. #107
205/326-4460

**Summersfield Antiques**
3961 Crosshaven Dr.
205/969-0914

**On-a-Shoestring**
601 Shades Crest Road
205/822-8741

**Elegant Earth**
1907 Cahaba Road
205/870-3264

**Estate Antiques**
3253 Lorna Road
205/823-7303

**Oak Grove Antiques**
609 Oak Grove Road
205/945-7183

**Antique Mall East**
217 Oporto Madrid Blvd. N.
205/836-1097

**Birmingham Antique Mall**
2211 Magnolia Ave. S.
205/328-7761

**D & G Antiques Interiors**
2233 6th Ave. S.
205/251-8020

**Henhouse**
1900 Cahaba Road
205/918-0505

**Noordermeer Antiques**
731 Broadway St.
205/870-1161

**Royal House**
2805 2nd Ave. S.
205/326-3443

**Re Run Shop Antiques to Junk**
2209 3rd Ave. N.
205/328-3602

**Ruby Ansley Interiors, Inc.**
2806 Petticoat Lane
205/871-8294

**Tricia's Treasures**
1433 Montgomery Hwy. #5
205/822-0004

**Attic Antiques**
5620 Cahaba Valley Road
205/991-6887

**Urban Farmer**
2809 18th St. S.
205/870-7118

**Lamb's Ears Ltd.**
3138 Cahaba Heights Road
205/969-3138

**Antiques & Dreams**
9184 Parkway E.
205/836-2411

**Maryon Allen Co.**
3215 Cliff Road
205/324-0479

**Chinaberry**
1 Hoyt Lane
205/879-5338

**First Avenue Antiques**
7315 1st Ave. N.
205/833-6083

**Interlude**
2415 Canterbury Road
205/870-3376

**Painters Cottage**
15 Dexter Ave.
205/871-3907

## Great Places to Eat

### Ollie's Barbeque
515 University Blvd.
205/324-9485

Memphis, Tenn., has long been recognized as the home of the barbecued pig, but Ollie's Barbeque in Birmingham, Ala., is sitting right on the doorstep.

Since 1926, the McClung family has been serving smoked meat not

# Alabama

only to the hometown crowd, but to folks from as far away as Sacramento, Calif. Their original establishment on Birmingham's south side is gone, but their new pork place on University Boulevard displays a swanky pit built in the middle so customers can see just what it takes to make meat taste this good.

Sliced pork with crunchy edges is the most popular choice. On a plate or piled high in a sandwich, these tender wedges are topped with the McClung family recipe, a vinegar-tomato sauce. A choice of tossed salad, beans, french fries, or coleslaw comes with the meal. If you've saved room for dessert, you're in for a treat of homemade pies (chocolate, coconut, lemon and apple), a yummy end to a great meal!

### *Interesting Side Trips*

### Arlington
331 Cotton Ave. S.W.
205/780-5656
Open: Tues.–Sat. 10–4; Sun. 1–4 (closed Mon. and city holidays)
Directions: Located 1¹⁄₂ miles west of downtown Birmingham on 1st Avenue North, which becomes Cotton Avenue. From I-65 South, take the 6th Avenue North exit; from I-65 North, take the 3rd Avenue North exit. Then follow the signs.

In 1953, this many-times-renovated family home became the property of the City of Birmingham. Arlington is located in Elyton, one of the oldest sections of the city. Incorporated in 1821, Elyton was the first permanent county seat of Jefferson County.

Neither the exact date of Arlington's construction nor the builder's name are known, but construction of the present structure occurred sometime after purchase in 1842 by Judge William S. Mudd. The style of architecture is Greek Revival, easily identified by the central hallways upstairs and down, as well as the symmetry of rooms on either side of the hallways.

Today, the property has been restored to a grandeur reminiscent of its finest era. Arlington possesses an excellent collection of decorative arts, mostly 19th-century American. Additional collections throughout the home have been made available through the generosity of local donors.

### 12  BOAZ

**Downtown Antique Gallery**
102 S. Main St.
256/593-0023
Open: Tues.–Sat. 10–5

Two floors packed with quality antiques and collectibles.

**Sana's Antiques on Main**
111 S. Main St.
256/593-8009

**Gazebo Antique Gallery**
106 Thomas Ave.
256/840-9444

**Almost Antiques**
104 Thomas Ave.
256/593-1412

**Southern Heritage**
285-C U.S. Hwy 431 S.
256/593-1132

**Boaz Antique Mall**
102 Thomas Ave.
256/593-1410

**Adams Antique Mall**
225 E. Mill Ave.
256/593-0406

**Past & Present Consignment Shop**
10306 Hwy. 168
256/593-0505

### 13  BRUNDIDGE

**City Antiques**
108 E. Troy St.
334/735-5164

**Rue's Antique Mall & Deli**
123 S. Main St.
334/735-3125

**Green Star Antique Mall**
126 S. Main St.
334/735-3797

**Green's Antiques**
794 S. Main St.
334/735-2247

**Gingerbread Hall Antiques**
131 S. A. Graham Blvd.
334/735-0224

**Hillside Antiques**
4839 Hwy. 231 N.
334/735-5567

### 14  CHELSEA

**Chelsea Antique Mall**
14569 Hwy. 280
205/678-2151

One of Alabama's largest malls, featuring 22,000 square feet of antiques and collectibles. Visit them at their website at www.bro.net/chelsea.

### 15  CLANTON

**Shadow Antiques**
2309 9th St.
205/755-2050

**The Treasure House**
1000 2nd Ave.
205/755-7205

**Kaye Cee's Flea & Antique Mall**
610 7th St.
205/755-2494

**The Front Porch**
2043 Christian St.
205/280-3656

### 16  CULLMAN

**Yesterdays Antiques & Gifts**
105 2nd Ave. S.W.
256/739-3972
Open: Tues.–Sun. 10–5

Old Paris, pickle castors, bride's baskets, lustres, biscuit jars, epergnes, talking machines, Dresden, R.S. Prussia, flow blue, Roseville.

*Alabama*

**Fireside Antiques**
101 1st Ave.
256/737-5135

Located in the warehouse district. English and American antiques.

**Golden Pond Wholesale Center**
2045 County Road 222
256/739-0850
Open: Mon.–Fri. 9:30–4:30, Sat. 9:30–5, Sun. 1–5
Directions: I-65 to Exit 304 (Goodhope). North 1 mile to County Road 222. Left at First Commercial Bank. Approximately 1½ miles on the left.

Specializing in formal and country furnishings, porcelains, glass and flow blue. They receive containers every three weeks featuring Country French, English and Belgium furniture and accessories.

**Country Village Antiques**
Next to I-65 & U.S. 278
Exit 308
256/739-9500
Open: Thurs.–Mon. 10–5
Directions: Across from the Cullman Flea Market.

10,000 square feet. Lots of furniture.

**Cullman Antique Alley**
500 County Road 1170
256/739-1900

**Nana Attic Antiques**
3701 U.S. Hwy. 278 E.
256/734-0009

**South Wind Antiques**
307 3rd Ave. S.E.
256/737-9800

**Craig's Antiques & Gifts**
220 1st Ave. S.E.
256/734-2252

**Something Olde Something New**
214 2nd Ave. S.E.
256/734-3345

**Brindley Mountain Antiques**
3220 U.S. Hwy. 278 E.
256/737-0700

**Magnolias & Lace**
1716 2nd Ave. N.W.
256/734-9639

**Southern Accents Arch Antiques**
308 2nd Ave. S.E.
256/737-0554

**Plantation Designs**
202 1st Ave. S.E.
256/734-0654

**Antiquities**
308 3rd St. S.E.
256/734-9953

**Margo's Antiques & Gifts**
206 1st Ave. S.E.
256/734-1452

**17 DECATUR**

**Riverwalk Antique Mall**
818 Bank St. N.E.
256/340-0075
Open: Daily 10–5, Sun. 1–5

12,000 square feet of general antique merchandise.

**Parkway Antique Mall**
Hwy. 24 W.
Gordon Terry Pkwy.
256/353-4142

Best selection of Mission furniture in the South.

**Southland Collectibles**
3311 Old Moulton Road
256/350-7272
Open: Mon., Wed., Fri., Sat. 10–5, Sun. 1–5 (closed 2nd and 4th weekends each month)

Furniture, graniteware, coin-operated machines, advertising, old guns, Civil War items, railroad items.

**London's**
114 Moulton St.
256/340-0900

**Sarah's Gifts & Antiques**
302 2nd Ave. S.E.
256/351-1451

**Hummingbird Antiques**
723 Bank St. N.E.
256/355-3704

**Antique Jungle**
219 E. 2nd Ave. S.E.
256/351-6278

**Rhodes Ferry**
502 Bank St. N.E.
256/308-0550

**Inglis House**
814 Bank St. N.E.
256/355-6118

**Sykes Antiques**
726 N.E. Bank St.
256/355-2656

**Nebrig-Howell House Antiques**
722 Bank St. N.E.
256/351-1655

**Eddy Tammy Antiques**
4395 Hwy. 31 S.E.
256/306-0007

**Albany Heritage Antiques**
221 Moulton St.
256/350-3322

**C & W Trading Post**
14 Lee St. N.E.
256/350-9076

**Country Cabin**
211 2nd Ave. S.E.
256/350-9744

# *Alabama*

## 18 DOTHAN

### Alabama Antique Mall & Auction Center
U.S. 231 S. (12½ mi. south of Ross Clark Circle)
334/702-0720 or 1-800-922-0720
Open: Daily Apr.–Sept. 9–6, Oct.–Mar. 9–5

All styles of furniture, large selection of jewelry, gifts, books, kitchenware, lamps, collectibles, reproduction furniture and ironware.

### Old South Antique Mall
1861 Reeves St.
334/794-7568
Open: Mon.–Sat. 10–6, Sun. 1–5:30

42,000 square feet, two floors housing over 100 dealers. McCoy, Watt, Hull, Roseville, Depression glass, Carnival glass, Civil War collectibles, china, silver, crystal, jewelry, clocks, porcelain, toys, books, advertising, linens, quilts, primitives, paintings, prints, all styles of furniture, old Christmas ornaments, Ty Beanie Babies.

### Admiral Possum Face Pee Pot's Antique Warehouse
Open: Mon.–Sat. 10–7
1-800-299-6377
Web site: www.admiralsantiques.com
Directions: Located between Ozark & Newton, Ala., at the north intersection of AL 123 & 134. Easy access to AL Hwy. 231. 11 miles from Dothan or Enterpirse — 6 miles from Ozark or Daleville — 70 miles south of Montgomery.

Largest antique warehouse in the Wiregrass. Direct importers from England and Europe. Wardrobes, buffets, sideboards, beds, pub tables, vanities, secretaries, chairs, dining sets, tea carts, 1800s stained glass windows, cut leaded crystal vases, lamps, knife rests, antique sewing machines, folk art and more.

**Miz Minnie's Antiques**
450 S. Oates St.
334/794-2061

**Wildot, Inc.**
409 S. Oates St.
334/794-8372

**Antique Attic**
5037 Fortner St.
334/792-5040

**Tadlock's Back Room**
1510 Montgomery Hwy.
334/793-5527

**King's Clocks & Antiques**
1015 Headland Ave.
334/792-3964

**Atkinson Antiques**
145 S. St. Andrews St.
334/712-1012

**Today**
107 S. Cherokee Ave.
334/702-7949

**Yesterday & Today's Antiques**
14390 U.S. Hwy. 231 S.
334/677-3504

## 19 ENTERPRISE

**Country Matters & Antiques**
905 E. Park Ave.
334/347-4649

**Special Accents**
102 N. Main St.
334/347-0887

**Country Matters & Antiques II**
1241 Shellfield Road
334/347-4649

**Down Home Antiques**
1308 U.S. 84 Bypass
334/347-1297

**Ronald Evans Antiques**
204 N. Main St.
334/347-4944

**Gaston's Antiques**
528 Glover Ave.
334/347-0285

**Mills House Antiques**
202 N. Edwards St.
334/393-3352

**Memories Antiques**
1304 Boll Weevil Circle
334/308-2503

## 20 EUFAULA

Directions: From Montgomery, U.S. 82 southeast through Union Springs to Eufaula.

Eufaula, Ala., is home to a little more than 13,000 citizens; however, this modest-sized city brags of containing over 700 historic buildings. Situated along the banks of the Chattahoochee River, Eufaula was at one time a prosperous riverport town for planters throughout the states of Alabama, Georgia, and Florida. This town, blossoming in spring with dogwood and azaleas, is blessed with an abundance of antebellum homes characteristic of the deep South. The wealthy families of the 1840s and 1850s put their show of money into the exquisite and lavishly presented homes, churches, and other buildings.

Unlike many of its sister cities whose beauty and grace were interrupted during the Civil War, Eufaula was fortunate that the Confederacy conceded before Union forces could occupy or destroy it. This resulted in the preservation of many hundreds of historic structures. In addition, during the postwar era, many other attractive homes and buildings rose in Eufaula. The tradition of admiration of fine craftsmanship and architecture set the stage for the preservation of these magnificent structures as well. Eufaula is host to the finest 19th-century small-town commercial district. Moreover, guests of the town discover the state's most luxurious and plentiful collection of domestic Italianate architecture. Seth Lore-Irwinton Historic District boasts many of the town's historic homes. Shorter Mansion (1884), Fendall Hall (1860), Holleman-Foy Home (1907), Hart-Milton House (1843) and Kendall Manor offer some of the best examples of Neoclassical and Italianate mansions. Waterford chandeliers, hand-stenciled walls and murals breathe the grace and style of times past within the walls of these homes. Broad Street possesses many of the historic commercial buildings. The Tavern, an inn from the 1830s, later a Confederate hospital, is presently a studio and private home listed on the National Register of Historic Places.

The Eufaula tourism council supplies brochures for walking and driving tours of the homes within the historic district. Although most

homes are private, during Eufaula's Pilgrimage in April, many homeowners open their doors, inviting visitors to enjoy the rooms and family heirlooms inside. The pilgrimage, furthermore, greets guests with open-air art exhibits, tea gardens and concerts. If that's not enough, one of the major antique shows in the state opens during the pilgrimage, occurring each year during the second weekend of April.

**Memory Lane**
106 S. Eufaula Ave.
334/616-0995

**Walker's Antiques**
149 S. Eufaula Ave.
334/687-5362

**Fagin's Thieves Market**
317 S. Eufaula Ave.
334-687-4100

**Martha's Back Room**
2908 S. Eufaula Ave.
334/687-3438

## 21 FAIRHOPE

### Bountiful Home

203 Fairhope Ave.
334/990-8655

Over 1,200 square feet, specializing in painted furniture, American fabrics and designer garden antiques, also a nice selection of Shabby Chic.

### European Treasures

503 N. Section St.
334/990-4050

Nice selection of antique European furniture.

### Ole Bay Antiques

212 Fairhope Ave.
334/928-6650

Offering a broad range of period English, Irish and pine furnishings, as well as Oriental porcelains.

**Bay Antiques & Collectibles**
328 De La Mare St.
334-928-2800

**Yester-Years Antiques**
56 S. Section St.
334/928-6933

**Antique Building Products**
17985 Hwy. 27
334/928-2880

**European Collection**
60 N. Section St.
334/990-3000

**Crown & Colony Antiques Etc.**
15 N. Section St.
334/928-4808

**Fairhope Antique Emporium**
52 S. Section St.
334/928-6290

**Interiors Mart**
122 Fairhope Ave.
334/928-1819

**Joy's Pation**
311 De La Mare St.
334/928-4640

**Past Pleasures Antiques**
19D N. Church St.
334/928-8484

**Silver Market**
19164 Scenic Hwy. 98
334/928-4657

**Antiques & Art**
205 Fairhope Ave.
334/928-1045

**Corner Copia**
9 N. Church St.
334/928-4181

**European Collection**
231 Fairhope Ave.
334/990-3000

**Magnolia Manor**
16 N. Church St.
334/990-3637

### *Nearby Antique Shopping (Point Clear)*

### Ye Old Post Office Antiques

17070 Scenic Hwy. 98
334/928-0108
Directions: 1 mile from Fairhope

Dealer of museum-quality historic antiques and collectibles. Specialists in antique firearms, swords, military, fishing tackle, and early American furniture. Antique firearms repair and restoration available, free verbal appraisals.

## 22 FALKVILLE

### Interstate Antiques Mall

I-65 at Exit 322
205/784-5302
Open: Mon.–Sat. 9–5, Sun. 1–5
Directions: Located on the west side of I-65 on service road.

Offering a few of our favorite things: grandma's china, cozy quilts, heirloom silver, early furniture, quality pristine glass, pottery from the past, vintage linen, warm memories, elusive collectibles and complimentary homemade tea cakes.

## 23 FAYETTE

### Fayette Antique Mall

114 1st St. S.E.
205/932-7423
Open: Mon., Tues., Thurs., Sat. 10–5

3,000 square feet of Roseville pottery, Depression glass, Blue Ridge dinnerware and other smalls.

**Five Points Antique**
1034 Temple Ave. N.
205/932-3050

**Treasures**
114 Temple Ave. N.
205/932-5559

# Alabama

### 24 FLOMATON

**Flomaton Antique Auction**
320 Palafox St.
334/296-3059
Antique auction every six to eight weeks. Call for exact dates.

### 25 FLORALA

**Stateline Mini Mall**
1517 W. Fifth Ave.
334/858-2741
Open: Mon.–Sat. 9:30–5, Sun. 1–5

18,000 square feet, 5 levels, specializing in dolls.

**Arts, Jewelry, Antiques**
1512 W. Fifth Ave.
334/858-4666

Jewelry, old sterling, Roseville, and art.

**Anna's Attic**
1500 W. Fifth Ave.
334/858-7936

3,000-square-foot private shop with a general mix of antiques.

**Past & Present Antiques**
1503 Fifth Ave.
334/858-4016
Open: Daily

Old restaurant converted to an antique shop.

**Gilley's Corner**
1501 W. Fifth Ave.
334/858-4697

**Antique Store–Unique Kountry**
1613 W. Fifth Ave.
334/858-2090

**Sugar Plum Alley**
1513 W. Fifth Ave.
334/858-4298

### 26 FLORENCE

**Bellemeade Antique Mall**
Hwy. 72 E.
256/757-1050
Open: Mon.–Sat. 10–5, Sun. 1–5

Over 13,000 square feet of antiques and collectibles, 40 dealers.

**Antiques on Court**
442 N. Court St.
256/766-4429

**Estate Antique Mall**
3803 Florence Blvd.—Hwy. 72
256/757-9941

**Gifford's Antiques & Gifts**
1201 N. Wood Ave.
256/766-7340

**Collectibles Plus**
702 E. Mobile St.
256/767-6132

**Celestial Antiques**
2909 Florence Blvd.
256/764-8963

**Taylor's Treasures**
3156 Hwy. 17
256/764-7172

**Trinkets & Antiques Shoppe**
533 E. Tuscaloosa St.
256/766-8781

**Memory Lane Antique & Gifts**
Hwy. 43
256/757-0610

### *Nearby Antique Shopping (Leighton)*

**White Oak Antiques**
5570 County Line Road
256/446-5162
Open: Mon.–Fri. 9–5, Sat. 9–1, closed Sun.
Directions: Leighton is 16 miles southeast of Florence.

No reproductions, exclusively antiques. 9,600 square feet of 18th- and 19th-century furniture, bronzes, paintings, porcelains and other quality antiques. Thirty-four years in the business.

### 27 FOLEY

**Hollis "Ole Crush" Antique Mall**
200 S. McKenzie St. (Hwy. 59)
334/943-8154

Located in the historic Ole Crush Bottling Company, this two-level antique mall specializes in a large volume of furniture, nice estate jewelry and quality glassware.

**Old Armory Mall**
812 N. McKenzie St.
334/943-7300

**Southern Belle Antique Mall**
1000 S. McKenzie St.
334/943-8128

**Gift Horse Antique Stalls**
201 W. Laurel Ave.
334/943-7278

**Givens Antique Furniture**
Hwy. 50 Gulf Pkwy. S.
334/955-5227

**Two Torches Antiques**
115 W. Laurel Ave.
334/971-3434

**Gas Works Antique Mall, Inc.**
818 N. McKenzie St.
334/943-5555

**Perdido Antiques, Inc.**
323 S. Alston St.
334/943-5665

**Brown Mule Antique Mall**
8340 Hwy. 59 S.
334/943-4112

**Treasures**
119 W. Orange Ave.
334/943-4033

# Alabama

## 28 FORT PAYNE

### Big Mill Antique Mall
151 8th St. N.E.
256/845-3380
Open: Mon.–Sat. 10–4, Sun. 1–4

Forty dealers located in an 1889 National Historic Old Mill offering a general line of antiques and architectural elements. Deli on the premises serving lunch Mon.–Fri. 11–4.

### The Wizard's Lodge
8th St. S. & Gault Ave.
Open: Weekends only — Sat. & Sun. 9–5

## 29 GARDENDALE

### Gardendale Flea Mall and Antique Center
2405 Decatur Hwy.
205/631-7451
Open: Mon.–Sun. 10–6

Over 150 booths.

**Gardendale Antique Mall**
2455 Decatur Hwy.
205/631-9044

**Baby Boomers Antiques**
753 Main St.
205/631-2781

## 30 GREENVILLE

**Gladys Seay Gallery**
142 Greenville Bypass
334/382-8110

**Graysons**
850 Fort Dale Road
334/382-6262

## 31 GULF SHORES

**Fish House Antiques**
911 S. Gulf Shores Pkwy.
334/948-7701

**Gulf Shores Antique Gallery**
317 Gulf Shores Pkwy. (Hwy. 59)
334/948-5300

### *Nearby Antique Shopping (Orange Beach)*

**Currier Antiques & Fine Art**
22640 Canal Road (Hwy. 180)
334/974-5623

## 32 GUNTERSVILLE

**Spanish House Antiques**
280 Gunter Ave.
256/582-3861

**The House**
732 Gunter Ave.
256/582-0076

**Rust N Dust**
4733 Hwy. 431
256/582-0287

## 33 HARPERSVILLE

### Hen/Son's Antique Mall
917 U.S. 280 W.
205/672-7071

35 dealers offering a general line of antiques and collectibles.

## 34 HARTSELLE

### Hartselle Antique Mall
209 Main St. W.
256/773-0081
Open: Daily 9:30–5, closed Wed. & Sun.

One of the largest malls in the area showcasing 50 dealers; exclusively antiques.

### Jim Norman Antiques & Auctions
101 Main St.
256/773-6878
Open: Tues.–Sat. 10–5

Specializing in fine antique furnishings.

### Emporium at Hickory Crossing
200 Railroad St.
256/773-4972
Open: Mon.–Sat. 10–5

Specialty shops featuring antiques and fine arts.

**Southern Antiques**
103 Railroad St. S.W.
256/773-3923

**Jeanette's Jazzy Jk & Antiques**
115 Railroad St. S.W.
256/773-2299

**Jeff Sandlin's Antiques**
219 Main St. W.
256/773-4774

**Holladay Hill Antiques**
1807 Hwy. 32 N.W.
256/773-0116

**Spinning Wheel Antiques**
206 Main St. W.
256/773-0933

**Heavenly Treasures & Gifts**
221 Main St. W.
256/773-4004

**Country Classic Antiques**
303 Main St. W.
256/773-9559

**Golden Oldies Antiques**
109 Main St. W.
256/773-1508

**Railroad Street Antique Mall**
113 Railroad St. S.E.
256/773-2299

**Annie's Art & Antiques**
934 Hwy. 36 E.
256/773-5331

**Wagon Wheel Antiques**
301 Hwy. 31 N.W.
256/773-1440

**Main Street Antiques**
208 Main St. W.
256/773-2309

# Alabama

**Sweet Peas Antique Gallery**
101 Main St. W.
256/773-7327

**Whistletop Antiques**
215 Main St. W.
256/773-1066

## 35 HEFLIN

### The Willoughby Street Mall
91-A Willoughby St.
205/463-5409
Open: Mon.–Sat. 10–5, Sun. 1–5 (closed New Year's Day, Easter,
Mother's Day, Thanksgiving and Christmas Day)
Directions: From I-20, 70 miles from Atlanta, Ga., or Birmingham,
Ala., Exit 199. Turn north on Hwy. 9. Go 1½ miles to Hwy. 78. Turn
right on 78. Go approximately 3 blocks. Turn right on Coleman St. Go
1 block. Turn left on Willoughby St. Go ½ block. Old red brick high
school building on right.

Back in 1936, The Willoughby Street Mall was the Cleburne County
High School of Heflin, Ala.  The red paint outside is original and the
owners are restoring the building's interior to better represent its school
days.

Today, this 35,000-square-foot mall is filled with a collage of antiques
and collectibles that includes pottery (Hull, Roseville, Shawnee),
Depression glass in a variety of patterns and colors, furnishings from
Victorian to primitive and a list that goes on and on.

If you're in the market for Alabama art, be sure to visit the art gallery
where local artists market their works.

**Colonial Cottage**
758 Ross St.
205/463-7149

## 36 HELENA

**Antique Monger**
5274 Helena Road
205/663-4977

**Our Place Antiques & Things**
Hwy. 261 Main St.
205/620-9361

## 37 HOMEWOOD

**Edgewood Antiques**
731 Rear Broadway St.
205/870-3343

**Little House Art Center**
2915 Linden Ave.
205/879-4186

**Michael's Antiques**
1831 29th Ave. S.
205/871-2716

**Europa Antiques, Inc.**
1820 29th Ave.
205/879-6222

**Frankie Engel Antiques**
4353 Clairmont
205/879-8331

**Carriage Antique Village**
88 Green Springs Hwy.
205/942-8131

## 38 HUNTSVILLE

### Hart Lex Antique Mall
1030 Old Monrovia Road
256/830-4278
Open: Mon.–Sat. 10–7

Alabama's largest antiques mall; 60,000 square feet.

### Packard's Antiques
11595 Memorial Pkwy.
256/883-0181
Open: Mon.–Sat. 10–5, Sun. 1–5

Packard's offers a large selection of furniture and specializes in
primitives and victrolas.

**Cotton Pickin Antiques**
8402 Whitesburg Dr. S.
256/883-1010

**Madison Square Antiques**
1017 Old Monrovia Road
256/430-0909

**Antique Decor**
925 Merchants Walk, #B
256/539-8707

**Red Rooster Antique Mall**
12519 Memorial Pkwy. S.W.
256/881-6530

**Antiques Etc.**
509 Pratt Ave.
256/533-7647

**Haysland Antique Mall**
11595 Memorial Pkwy.
256/883-0181

**Wilma's Antiques**
515 Pratt Ave.
256/536-7250

**Valerie Fursdon, Inc.**
2212 Whitesburg Dr.
256/533-6768

**Railroad Station Antique Mall**
315 N. Jefferson St.
256/533-6550

**Pratt Avenue Antique Mall**
708 N.E. Pratt Ave.
256/536-3117

**Old Town Antique Mall**
820 Wellman Ave. N.E.
256/533-7002

**Kay's Kupboard**
515 Fountain Row
256/536-1415

**Golden Griffin**
104 Longwood Dr. S.E.
256/535-0882

**Gallery Antiques**
209 Russell St. N.E.
256/539-9118

**Darwin Antiques**
320 Church St.
256/539-9803

**Bulldog Antiques**
2338 Whitesburg Dr. S.
256/534-9893

**Ashton Place**
410 Governors Dr. S.W.
256/539-5464

**Antiques, Etc.**
2801 Memorial Pkwy.
256/533-0330

**J. Jones Ltd.**
5000 Whitesburg Dr. S.
256/882-3043

**Jewel Shop**
117 Northside Square
256/534-7384

**Kurt Eklund Inc.**
806 Wellman Ave. N.E.
256/536-7314

**Walker House Antiques**
614 Madison St. S.E.
256/534-0320

**Haysland Antique Mall**
11595 Memorial Pkwy. S.W.
256-883-0181

**Antiques Etc. South**
10300 Baily Cove Road S.E.
256/533-0330

**Village Antiques**
1201 Meridian St. N.
256/539-3254

## 39 JASPER

### The Antique Market
5077 Hwy. 78 E.
256/384-6997
Open: Mon.–Sat. 10–5, closed Sun.

Over 10,000 square feet of vintage jewelry, Moser, Civil War, Indian artifacts and pottery. Tearoom located on the premises.

**Old Town Creek Mall**
59 19th St. E.
256/384-5990

## 40 JEMISON

**Touch of the Past**
120 Old Main St.
205/688-4938

**Farmhouse Antiques**
106 Main St.
205/688-4711

### *Great Places to Stay*

### The Jemison Inn
212 Hwy. 191
205/688-2055
Open: Year-round

Old-time style in a small-town setting describes the Jemison Inn of Jemison, Ala. The intimate inn provides three guest rooms, so reservations are a must to assure you a place to stay. The former family home, built in the 1930s, has been refurbished and now boasts many heirloom antique furnishings. Southern charm and hospitality abound in  this delightful inn. Fresh flowers grace each room. The full breakfast provided to lodgers is accompanied by fresh fruits in season. On fine spring and fall evenings, you can sit on the wraparound porch enjoying an afternoon refreshment, compliments of the inn. A further touch of Southern style is punctuated by turned-down beds and mints on the

**Odds & Ends**
1018 Meridian St. N.
256/539-0500

**Madison Square Antiques**
1017 Old Monrovia Road N.W.
256/430-0909

pillows. The intimate, hospitable charm of the Jemison Inn makes it a great wind-down stop.

**Country Crossroads Antiques**
13181 County Road 42
205/688-5030

## 41 KILLEN

### Hodgepodge Antiques Mall
4225 Hwy. 72
256/757-4010
Open: Mon.–Sat. 10–5, Sun. 1–5, closed Wed.

Located next door to the largest covered flea market in northwest Alabama (Uncle Charlie's), this 13,000-square-foot, 64-dealer mall houses a broad general mix of antiques.

**Victoria Anne Flowers & Antiques**
1289 Hwy. 43
256/757-7600

**J's Antique & Collectible Shop**
213 Hwy. 72
256/757-4552

## 42 KIMBERLY

### Mary Ann's Antiques & Auction
9232 Hwy. 31 N.
205/590-1025

In business since 1989. Antique auction first and third Saturday of the month at 7 p.m.

### Krotzer's Flea Market & G.G. Antiques
9288 Hwy. 31 N.
205/647-6378
Open: Tues.–Sat. 9–5, Sun. 12–5

### Calico & Lace
8711 Hwy. 31 N.
205/647-5513
Open: Fri. 12–5, Sat. & Sun. 9–5

Antiques and just great junque.

## 43 LEESBURG

### *Great Places to Stay*

### "the secret" Bed & Breakfast Lodge
2356 Hwy. 68 W.
205/523-3825
Open: Year-round
Reservations requested
Directions: From I-59 take the Collinsville exit (Exit 205). Follow Hwy. 68 east for about 9 miles. Located on the left side of the street.

"The secret" sits cozily among twelve acres of garden and wilderness atop Lookout Mountain. On a clear day you can see seven cities, including the skyline of Gadsden, the lights of Anniston and the industrial smokestacks of Rome, Georgia. It is perfectly situated on the edge of a mountaintop so the sunrises and sunsets are spectacular.

Carl and Dianne Cruickshank, the owners and innkeepers, found "the secret" almost by accident. "We were looking at possible locations for a bed and breakfast," Diane said. "We had gone all through Etowah and Dekalb Counties one Sunday, and we decided to take a look at this. It was love at first sight."

You might say Carl and Dianne rescued the house from despair. Originally built by People's Telephone Company owner Millard Weaver as a family home, the place had changed owners several times in the years following Weaver's death. It was then empty for a long time. The Cruickshanks came along at the right time while restoration was still possible. Carl performed most of the reconstruction himself.

Today, "the secret" provides a romantic atmosphere throughout the home with such amenities as an enormous central stone fireplace, a 22-foot vaulted living room–dining room ceiling and four spacious guest rooms. The home is furnished throughout with antiques, art, copper, brass, tile and rare woods. The 10-foot Lazy Susan table, from which breakfast is served, has become quite a conversation piece among guests.

In addition to providing breathtaking scenery, the gardens and grounds are also home to two treasured peacocks.

## 44 LOXLEY

**Plunderosa Antiques**
26210 Hwy. 59
334/964-5474

**Flo's Shed Antiques**
5101 Hickory St.
334/964-4696

## 45 MADISON

**Purple Tree Antiques Mall**
29730 U.S. Hwy. 72
256/233-5745

**West Station Antiques**
112 Main St.
256/772-0373

**Tally's Antiques Mall**
7587 Hwy. 72 N.
256/722-7944

**Limestone Flea Market**
30030 Hwy. 72
256/233-5183

## 46 MARION

### Roselane
222 Clements St.
334/683-8310

Wholesale to dealers featuring Federal, Empire, Victorian and primitives.

**Browsabout Antiques & Things**
105 E. Jefferson St.
334/683-9856

**Twink's Antiques & Gifts**
212 Washington St.
334/683-4770

**Pappy's Porch**
106 E. Green St.
334/683-9541

**La Mason**
215 Washington St.
334/683-9131

**Mary Bell Webb Odds & Ends**
311 Washington St.
334/683-0509

**Old Victoria Antiques & Cafe**
216 Washington St.
334/683-2095

**Angel Wings Antiques Mall**
Across from the Courthouse
334/683-4900

**Antiques & Co.**
10001 Washington St.
334/683-4165

## 47 MILLBROOK

### Sisters Antique Emporium
1951 Market St.
334/285-5571

One of the largest antique malls in the area.

## 48 MOBILE

### Mobile Antique Gallery
1616 S. Beltline Hwy.
334/666-6677
Open: Mon.–Sat. 10–6; Sun. 1–6
Directions: Located on the west side service road of I-65 at Exit 1B, one mile north of I-10.

Voted "Best of Mobile" for three consecutive years, Mobile Gallery presents an outstanding market of antiques and collectibles in a 21,000-square-foot gallery. This bustling showplace houses the wares of well over 100 quality antique  dealers offering exquisite furnishings, linens, silver, china, porcelains, Depression-era glassware, antique toys and much, much more. A snack bar is located in the gallery.

# Alabama

**1848 Antiques**
356 Dauphin St.
334/432-1848

**Bentley's**
22S Florida St.
334/479-4015

**Cotton City Antique Mall**
2012 Airport Blvd.
334/479-9747

**Red Barn Antique Mall**
418 Dauphin Island Pkwy.
334/473-9227

**Gallery Old Shell**
1803 Old Shell Road
334/478-1822

**Antoinette's Antiques**
4401 Old Shell Road
334/344-7636

**Yellow House Antiques**
1902 Government St.
334/476-7382

**Prichard Trading Post, Inc.**
616 N. MLK Hwy.
334/452-3456

**Plantation Antique Galleries**
3750 Government Blvd.
334/666-7185

**Kearney Antiques**
1004 Government St.
334/438-9984

**Cobweb**
422 Dauphin Island Pkwy.
334/478-6202

**Dogwood Antiques**
2010 Airport Blvd.
334/479-9960

**E & J Galleries**
1421 Forest Hill
334/380-2072

**Mary's Corner**
2602 Old Shell Road
334/471-6060

**Antique Shop, Inc.**
3510 Cottage Hill Road
334/661-1355

**Criswell's Antiques**
4103 Moffat Road
334/344-4917

**Gemini Shop**
2006 Airport Blvd.
334/478-6695

**Diane's Antiques**
3621 Jarvis Lane
334/645-9300

## Interesting Side Trips

### Oakleigh House Museum
350 Oakleigh Place
334/432-1281
Open: Mon.–Sat. 10–4 (closed legal holidays and Christmas week)
Directions: 2½ blocks south of Government Street between Roper Street and George Street.

Oakleigh Period House Museum and Historic Complex is operated by the Historic Mobile Preservation Society. The 3½ landscaped acres consist of Oakleigh, the city's official antebellum period-house museum, the Cox-Deasy House, and the Archives Building, which also houses the administrative offices of the Society.

Oakleigh, which was begun in 1833 by Mobile merchant James W. Roper, is included in the American Buildings Survey and the National Register of Historic Places. Mr. Roper was his own architect and incorporated unique and practical features into the design of his home. It is beautifully furnished with fine period collections of furniture, portraits, silver, china, jewelry, interesting kitchen implements and toys. The museum gift shop is on the ground floor of Oakleigh.

The Cox-Deasy House, circa 1850, is a contrast to Oakleigh. It is a raised Creole cottage, typical of the modest middle-class city dwellers along the Gulf Coast. It is furnished in simple 19th-century antiques.

Guided tours of Oakleigh and the Cox-Deasy House are conducted by members of the Society.

## 49  MONTEVALLO

**Cedar Creek Antiques**
2979 Hwy. 119 S.
205/665-2446

**The Antique Shop**
615 Main St.
205/665-0775

**Arledge Antiques & Collectibles**
7622 Hwy. 22
205/665-7094

## 50  MONTGOMERY

### SouthEast Antiques & Collectibles
2530 E. South Blvd.
334/284-5711

15,000 square feet of antiques and collectibles.

## Nearby Antique Shopping (Daphne)

### The Daphne Antique Galleria
1699 Hwy. 98 E.
334/625-2200
Open: Mon.–Sat. 10–5:30, Sun. 1–5:30
Directions: 15 minutes from Mobile at Exit 35A off I-10.

Largest antique mall on the Gulf Coast; 15,000 volumes of books, over 175 dealers, snack room, children's play area, husbands' recovery area, RV access.

## Nearby Antique Shopping (Semmes)

### Greenhouse Antiques
8950 Moffett Road
334/649-8884
Open: Tues.–Sat. 10:30–4:30
Directions: 10 miles west of Mobile off Hwy. 98.

Antique furnishings displayed in eight rooms of an historic home.

**Montgomery Antique Galleries**
1955 East Blvd.
334/277-2490
Open: Mon.–Sat. 10–6, Sun. 1–6

20,000 square feet of antiques and collectibles; lamp and crystal repair.

**Eastbrook Flea Market**
425 Colisium Blvd.
334/277-4027
Open: Tues.–Fri. 10–6, Sat. 9–6, Sun. 1–5

Over 50,000 square feet of antiques and collectibles.

**Harmony Antiques**
4323 Hwy. 80
334/271-3334
Open: Tues.–Sat. 9:30–5

Specializing in Vaseline glass, Heisey, Cranberry glass, old Carnival, Cordey, and bride's baskets.

**Nicole Maleine Antiques**
121 N. Goldwiate St.
334/834-8530

**Cottage Hill Antiques**
521 Herron St.
334/265-0450

**Unicorn Shop Antiques**
1926 Mulberry St.
334/834-2550

**Bodiford's Antique Mall**
919 Hampton St.
334/265-4220

**Emily Dearman Antiques**
514 Cloverdale Road
334/269-5282

**Frances Edward's Antiques**
1010 E. Fairview Ave.
334/269-5100

**Louise Brooks Antiques**
1034 E. Fairview Ave.
334/265-8900

**Mulberry House Antiques**
2001 Mulberry St.
334/263-5131

**Old Cloverdale Antiques**
514 Cloverdale Road
334/262-6234

**May-Bell's Corner Antiques**
1429 Bell St.
334/265-3298

**Herron House Antiques**
422 Herron St.
334/265-2063

**Windsor House**
423 Cloverdale Road
334/265-2104

**Yesteryear Antiques**
2908 McGehee Road, #A
334/288-1202

**Fantasy Land Flea Market**
3620 Atlanta Hwy.
334/272-8841

**Antiques in the Courtyard**
514 Cloverdale Rd.
334/262-1560

**Bell Street Brass**
1273 Bell St.
334/262-6345

**E.T.'s Antiques**
549 N. Eastern Blvd.
334/277-7288

**Elegant Junk & Antiques**
1800 W. 5th St.
334/263-5737

**Providence Antiques**
1717 Norman Bridge Road
334/264-1717

**Sara B's Flower & Antique Shop**
1807 W. 4th St.
334/262-6137

**Heirloom Jewelers & Collectibles**
6948 Vaughn Road
334/260-0066

**Sassafras Tea Room & Antiques**
532 Clay St.
334/265-7277

**Seven Sisters Antiques & Gifts**
546 Clay St.
334/262-2660

**Tresses 'n' Treasures**
6565 Narrow Lane Road
334/284-0601

**Martin Antiques**
2015 Mulberry St.
334/265-9004

**Michael Respess Antiques**
1939 Ridge Ave.
334/264-9288

**Once Upon a Time**
2021 Mulberry St.
334/834-2021

**Pickwick Antiques**
3851 Interstate Court
334/279-1481

**Treasure Chest Antiques**
1914 Mulberry St.
334/265-2191

### *Nearby Antique Shopping (Brantley)*

**Conecuh River Antique Mall**
U.S. Hwy. 331
334/527-3267
Directions: South of Montgomery on Hwy. 331, which runs into Florida.

Over 16,000 square feet of antiques and collectibles.

### **51** MOULTON

**The Shelton House Antiques**
2020 Morgan St.
256/974-1444

**Memories Antiques & Ideas**
716 Main St.
256/974-4301

**Blue Willow Antiques & Gifts**
607 County Road 217
256/974-3888

**Town Square Antique Mall**
734 Main St.
256/974-2345

**Heirloom Antiques**
3188 County Road 167
256/905-0602

### **52** NORTHPORT

**Gallery Antiques & Auctions**
5925 Hwy. 43 N.
1-888-333-1398
Open: Mon.–Sat. 10–5, Sun. 1–5, Call for auction dates.

30,000 square feet; specializing in American and Victorian furnishings and accessories and art glass. 30 years in the business.

**Anne Marie's Antiques**
5925 Hwy. 43
1-888-333-1398

**Riverside Antique Market**
1 Bridge Ave.
205/758-6227

**Adams Antiques**
424 Main Ave.
205/758-8651

**Penage, Inc.**
2207 5th St.
205/349-3310

## 53 OPELIKA

**Hwy. 280 Antique Mall**
280 Alabama Hwy. W.
334/821-8540

**Magnolia House**
807 Geneva St.
334/749-9648

**Yesterday's Treasures**
207 N. Third St.
334/749-3918

**Blue Iris Antiques**
400 2nd Ave.
334/745-6756

## 54 OXFORD

Oxford is centrally located between Birmingham and Atlanta, Ga., directly off I-20. Exit 188 from I-20 offers five great antiques malls all within one mile. Over 60,000 square feet of northeast Alabama's finest antiques and collectibles are presented.

**Timeless Treasures Antique Mall**
230 Davis Loop
256/832-0500
Open: Mon.–Sat. 10–6, Sun. 1–6

**Heritage Antique Mall**
1905 U.S. Hwy. 78 E.
256/831-3448
Open: Mon.–Sat. 10–6, Sun. 1–6

**Anderson's Antiques**
1130 Hwy. 78 E.
256/835-9191
Open: Mon.–Sat. 10–5, Sun. 1–5

**Apple Barrel Antiques & Gifts**
1906 U.S. Hwy. 78 E.
256/835-1937
Open: Mon.–Sat. 10–6, Sun. 1:30–5:30

**Jamie's Antique Village**
1429 U.S. Hwy. 78 E.
256/831-2830
Open: Thurs.–Sun. 9–6

## 55 PELHAM

**The Antique Co.**
200 Bearden Road
205/664-1864

**Emporium**
880 Oak Mountain Park Road
205/664-3691

## 56 PELL CITY

### Pell City Auction Company
Hwy. 231 S.
205/525-4100
Directions: 30 miles east of Birmingham, 10 miles south of I-20 from Exit 158.

Auction every Friday night at 7 o'clock, no buyer's premium. Huge auction in an 8,000-square-foot building.

**Kilgroes Antiques**
2212 Third Ave. N.
205/338-7923

**Squirrel's Nest**
604 Hazelwood Dr.
205/338-2440

**Colonial Galleries**
2000 Golf Course Road
205/338-7395

**Landi's Antique Mall**
Hwy. 231 N.
205/338-6255

## 57 PRATTVILLE

**Linda's Antique Mall**
1120 S. Memorial Dr.
334/361-9952

## 58 ROGERSVILLE

### Longs Antique Mall
Hwy. 72 Elgin Crossroads
256/247-0005
Open: Mon.–Sat. 9–5, Sun. 1–5

Architectural items, mantels, bathtubs, hardware, light fixtures, furniture, Coca-Cola items and clocks.

### Ezell's Antiques
Hwy. 101 (Lexington Hwy.)
256/247-5136
Open: Mon.–Sat. 10–7, Sun. 1–5

Stoneware, lamps, oak, walnut and mahogany furniture.

**Rogersville Antique Mall**
104 W. Lee St.
256/247-1491

## 59 SCOTTSBORO

**Gentle Touch**
308 W. Willow St.
256/259-1896

**Scottsboro Antiques**
816 Willow St.
256/574-3921

**Gold Pot Antiques**
143 W. Laurel St.
256/574-1111

**Village Square Antique Mall**
240 S. Broad St.
256/259-0482

## 60 SELMA

**Selma Antique & Art Mall**
1410 Water Ave.
334/872-1663

**Finders Keepers**
106 Broad St.
334/874-6736

**Gordon Antiques**
705 Dallas Ave.
334/875-2400

**R & W Antiques**
1124 Water Ave.
334/872-8265

*Alabama*

*Great Places to Stay*

**Grace Hall B&B**
506 Lauderdale St.
334/875-5744

Antebellum mansion, circa 1857 — six guest rooms.

### 61 SPRINGVILLE

**House of Quilts**
530 Main St. (Hwy. 11)
205/467-6072
Open: Tues.–Sat. 10–5, Sun. 12:30–5

Featuring hundreds of antique quilts; a great source for those hard-to-find Southern quilts.

**Ivy Lane Inc.**
6438 U.S. Hwy. 11
205/467-2400

**S S Juniors Antiques**
U.S. Hwy. 11 (Main St.)
205/467-6772

### 62 SUMMERDALE

**Duncan Ponder Antiques**
207 Hwy. 59
334/989-2100
Open: Mon.–Sat. 9–4
Directions: Approximately 12 miles south of I-10.

Containers of European antiques arrive on a regular basis for wholesale and retail sale. Various styles of furniture from the 1800s through the 1950s. Always a good selection of furniture in stock, including complete bed sets and dining sets.

**Summerdale Antiques**
19445 State Hwy. 59
334/989-7481

**Town Square Antique Mall**
804 Hwy. 59 S.
334/989-6912

### 63 SYLACAUGA

**Antique Attic**
40495 U.S. Hwy. 280
256/249-0903

**The Garage Antique Mall**
110 W. First St.
256/208-7744

**The Cotton Gin**
523 Broadway Ave.
256/245-1588

### 64 TALLADEGA

**White's Antiques**
210 W. Battle St.
256/362-9614
Open: Sat. 9–5 or by appointment

Coca-Cola collectibles, restored vintage machines, straight-sided bottles, button signs, framed cardboard signs, cutouts, trays, toys, restored gas pumps, petroleum signs, restored pedal cars, jukeboxes, old wooden fishing lures and fishing tackle, leather twin gun holsters with rhinestones, plus other collectibles.

**Fuqua Antiques**
107 Court Square W.
256/761-1155

**Golden Era Antiques**
118 Court Square E.
256/362-8878

**Sumthin Ole and Sumthin Nu**
10 Fort Lashley Ave.
256/362-0828

**First Floor Bellevue Antiques**
Hwy. 21
256/362-4928

**Upstairs/Downstairs Antique Mall**
150 Court St. N.
256/362-8390

**Jackie's Antique Shop**
515 North St. E.
256/362-8182

**Townsend's Antiques**
206 Coosa St. W.
256/362-3348

### 65 TROY

**Denim Blues**
Pioneer Village, 4120 Hwy. 231 N.
334/566-1811

**Antique & Quilt Shop**
Pioneer Village, 4120 Hwy. 231 N.
334/566-9040

**Hillside Antiques**
4839 Hwy. 231 N.
334/735-5567

### 66 TUSCALOOSA

**Spiller Antique Mall**
2420 Seventh St.
205/391-0308
Open: Mon.–Sat. 10–6, Sun. 12–5
Directions: Located in historic downtown, built in 1904, renovated in 1991, over 40,000 square feet.

**Hobby Horse Antique Mall**
5500 Old Montgomery Hwy.
205/752-1630

**Eva's Antiques**
5210 University Blvd. E.
205/556-1922

**Sisters Antiques**
517 Greensboro Ave.
205/349-0083

**Boykin Antiques & Decorators**
1109 21st Ave.
205/759-5231

*Alabama*

**Robbie Collection**
2308 Sixth St.
205/750-0501

*Great Places to Stay*

## The Governor's House Bed & Breakfast

Lincoln, Ala.
205/763-2186
Directions: Between Birmingham and Anniston; take Exit 165 from I-20, go two miles south.

The Governor's House Bed & Breakfast was first built as a cottage by former Alabama Governor Lewis Parsons in 1850. Parsons moved the cottage to a new location in favor of a Gothic mansion. However, the cottage was a threat to the expansion of Citizens Hospital and would be destroyed to make way for a parking lot. The Landmarks Foundation of Talladega and the Alabama Historical Commission sought time for its preservation and offered the house free of charge as long as the new owner would move and renovate it.

Many applicants applied to help, but it was Ralph and Mary Sue Gaines who were the first to call. In May 1990, the cottage made headlines as it was partially dismantled and moved to the Gaines' 160-acre farm in Lincoln, Ala. After extensive renovations and modern additions of central heat, air conditioning and ceiling fans, the house still boasts of the original windows and wood floors. Mary Sue also combined many of her family heirlooms from the past, which include kitchen curtains hung on tobacco sticks that came from her great-grandmother's farm and a handmade kitchen cupboard that is gray from age.

The parlor/sitting room opens into the dining room. There is no hallway to speak of. Each of the three bedrooms can be entered through either the adjacent bedroom, or the main room—all can be closed off for privacy. The guest rates for double occupancy range between $75 and $85 per night or you can rent the entire house for a reduced rate. It includes a full country breakfast served at 8:30 (or a continental breakfast if you must leave earlier).

Horse Barn Antique Shop is located on the premises.

## 67 VERNON

### Falkner Antique Mall
Courtsquare
256/695-9841
Open: Mon.–Sat. 10–5, Sun. 1–5

Two levels, 14,000 square feet, 60 dealers.

### Remember When
44848 Hwy. 17
256/695-9655
Open: Mon.–Sat. 9–5, closed Sun.

Specializing in Southern antiques, pottery and art.

## 68 WARRIOR

**Barbara Cooper's Antiques & Collectibles**
133 Louisa St.
205/647-2272

**Currier Antiques**
516 N. Main St.
205/647-8048

**Ice House Antiques**
215 Louisa St.
205/647-0882

**Garden Gate Antiques**
516 N. Main St.
205/647-8048

## 69 WETUMPKA

### The Attic and Great Flea Market
5266 U.S. Hwy. 231
334/567-2666
Open: Mon.–Sat. 10–6, Sun. 1–5

24,000 square feet, over 100 vendors.

**Antiques & Stuff**
2361 U.S. Hwy. 231
334/514-1585

**Blue Ridge Antique Junction**
2341 U.S. Hwy. 231
334/567-6106

## 70 WINFIELD

**Between a Rock & a Hard Place**
Hwy. 78 W.
205/487-2924

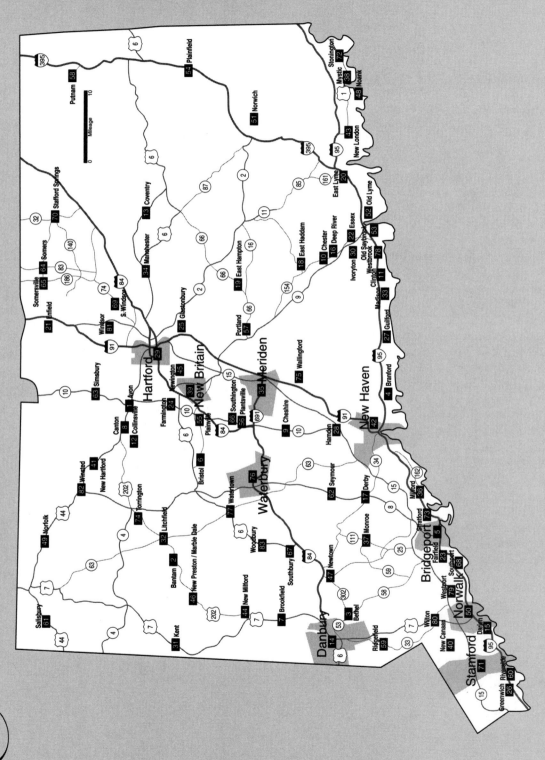

Connecticut

# *Connecticut*

## 1 AVON

**D & W Collectibles**
13 E. Main St.
860/676-2180

**Moosavi Persian Rugs**
45 E. Main St.
860/676-0082

## 2 BANTAM

**Bradford House Antiques**
895 Bantam Road
860/567-0951

**TNT Antiques & Collectibles**
898 Bantam Road
860/567-8823

**Old Carriage Shop Antique Center**
920 Bantam Road
860/567-3234

**Weston Thorn**
940 Bantam Road
860/567-4661

## 3 BETHEL

**Saltbox Antiques**
123 Greenwood Ave.
203/744-6097

## 4 BRANFORD

**Yesterday's Threads Vintage**
206 Meadow St.
203/481-6452

**Oldies but Goodies**
781 E. Main St.
203/488-7230

**Taken for Granite Antiques**
409 Leetes Island Road
203/488-0557

**C & R Antiques**
62 Knollwood Dr.
203/488-9860

**Clock Tower Antiques**
824 E. Main St.
203/488-1919

**Charles Treasures Antiques**
129 Leetes Island Road
203/481-2587

**Stony Creak Antiques**
172 Thimble Island Road
203/488-4802

## 5 BRIDGEPORT

**Sweet Memories**
2714 Fairfield Ave.
203/330-0558

**Tinker's Treasures**
2980 Fairfield Ave.
203/579-4243

**Olivia's Attic**
3004 Fairfield Ave.
203/332-0253

**All That Glitters**
3000 Fairfield Ave.
203/333-5836

**From the Attic**
2142 Fairfield Ave.
203/333-6005

**Park Avenue Curio Shoppe**
1399 Park Ave.
203/333-6896

## 6 BRISTOL

**Collectors Corner**
100 N. Main St.
860/582-1876

**Dave's Antiques**
650 Lake Ave.
860/583-9909

**Lamplighter Antiques**
200 Wolcott Road
860/583-5395

## 7 BROOKFIELD

**Sugar Hollow Antiques**
797 Federal Road
203/775-5111

**Antiques International**
934 Federal Road
203/740-2336

**Old Favorites Antiques**
9 Arrowhead Road
203/775-3744

## 8 CANTON

**Balcony Antiques**
81 Albany Turnpike
860/693-6440

**On the Road Bookshop**
163 Albany Turnpike
860/693-6029

**Canton Green Antique Store**
181 Albany Turnpike
860/693-0008

**Antiques at Canton Village**
Canton Village Route 44
860/693-2715

**Brass Bed Boutique**
125 Albany Turnpike
860/693-0333

**Griffin Brothers & Co.**
10 Front
860/693-9007

**Cob-Web Shop**
20 Dyer Cemetery Road
860/693-2658

**Canton Barn Antiques-Auctions**
75 Old Canton Road (off Route 44)
860/693-0601

**La Falce-Freshier Fine Art**
81 Albany Turnpike
860/693-4478

**Cherrybrook Antiques**
356 Albany Turnpike
860/693-6377

### *Great Places to Stay*

**Special Joys**
41 N. River Road
1-800-750-3979

Discover the ambiance of the old and the new at this Victorian 3-Diamond-AAA-rated B&B that also houses an antique doll and toy shop and museum where treasures of the past blend charmingly with the attractive, sophisticated decor of a small country inn. Modern amenities, flower gardens, a solarium dining area, full breakfast and a relaxed atmosphere add to the comfort of your stay.

## 9 CHESHIRE

**Cartophilians**
430 Highland Ave.
203/272-1143

**Chez Angele**
150 Main St.
203/271-9883

**Granny's Attic**
192 S. Main St.
203/272-8262

**Magnolia Shoppe**
908 S. Meriden Road
203/272-3303

*Connecticut*

Antique Warehouse
403 Dryden Drive
203/271-2014

### 10  CHESTER

**Spiritus Mundi Antiques**
122 Middlesex Ave. (Route 154)
860/526-3406

**One of a Kind Antiques**
21 Main St.
860/526-9736

### *Great Places to Eat*

### Restaurant Du Village
59 Main St.
860/526-5301

Country French cuisine prepared by chef/owners Michael and Cynthia Keller, served in an intimate setting. "Best restaurant in Ct.," *Zagat* and "Best French in State," *Connecticut* magazine. Dinner only. Reservations recommended.

### Mad Hatter Bakery & Cafe
23 Main St.
860/526-2156

Bakery specializing in hearth-baked sourdough breads and old-fashioned pastries. Cafe serves up an eclectic, mostly Mediterranean menu for breakfast, lunch and weekend dinners. Closed Tuesday.

### Inn at Chester
318 W. Main St. (Route 148)
860/526-9541

The Inn at Chester boasts two restaurants: The Post and Beam features fine dining, serving New American cuisine in casual elegance. Dunk's Landing is a comfortable tavern serving lighter fare. Open seven days including Sunday brunch.

### 11  CLINTON

### Wooden Wheelbarrow Antiques & Miller's Antiques
327 E. Main St. (Route 1)
860/669-3533

Wooden Wheelbarrow and Miller's Antiques is a unique antiquing experience inside a Cape Cod-style house. It is two separate businesses with two very knowledgeable owners with a combined 29 years of experience selling antiques. The fellows offer a wonderful line of antique furnishings and one specialty of the shop is the popular Fiestaware. Worth a stop on your antiquing trail.

**Clinton Antique Center**
78 E. Main St.
860/669-3839

**Waterside Antiques & Gifts**
109 E. Main St.
860/669-0809

**John Street Antiques**
23 W. Main St., #A
860/669-2439

**Hey-Day Antiques**
9 Rocky Ledge Drive
860/669-8800

**Antiques on Main Street**
100 E. Main St. (Route 1)
860/664-9163

**Square-Riggers Antique Center**
350 E. Main St.
860/664-9001

**Loft**
59 W. Main St.
860/669-4583

**Clinton Village**
327 E. Main St.
860/669-3350

### *Nearby Antique Shopping (Killingworth)*
### *Killingworth is one mile from Clinton.*

### Country Squire Shoppes
243 Route 80
860/663-3228 or 860/663-3234
Open: Spring, summer and fall, Wed.–Sun. 12–whenever
Call ahead for winter hours.

Housed in an 18th-century country inn, Country Squire Shoppes is much, much more than a collection of antique shops. The shops, all nestled together within 10,000 square feet, are just a sampling of what you are about to experience on your visit. Located within the property is a wonderful restaurant serving international cuisine. Friday  and Saturday nights feature dancing to the sounds of live big bands and Sundays, a treat for singles, features a buffet and singles dance. Additionally, the inn provides overnight accommodations.

### Lewis Scranton Antiques
By appointment
860/663-1060
Directions: Located five miles north of Exit 63 of I-95.

This, by appointment only, shop specializes in upscale early American art and antiques.

# Connecticut

## *Great Places to Stay*

### Captain Dibbell House
21 Commerce St.
860/669-1646
Web site: clintonct.com/dibbell

The Captain Dibble House Bed & Breakfast offers guests the opportunity to experience the warmth and hospitality of a lovingly preserved 1866 Victorian. The house is situated on a historic residential street in a small seacoast town just two blocks from the harbor. Crossing the wisteria covered footbridge leading to the front porch sets the mood. Guests can relax in the spacious parlor in front of the fireplace or on the gazebo after strolling through the gardens or gazing into the water garden. Four comfortable guest rooms are uniquely decorated ranging from the Victorian Captain's Room with its formal furnishings to the casual Garden Room with its painted and stenciled walls, original wood floor and wicker furniture. All are furnished with a mixture of antiques and family heirlooms and have ceiling fans (air conditioners in the summer), private baths and fresh flowers from the gardens. There's a refrigerator stocked with complimentary beverages, afternoon or evening home-baked snacks and hot beverages. Freshly baked savories will tempt you at breakfast and then it's off for a day of exploring quaint towns, antiquing, or enjoying the beach.

## 12 COLLINSVILLE

**The Collinsville Antiques Co.**
1 Main St.
860/693-1011

**Village Green Antiques**
41 Bridge St.
860/693-1972

## 13 COVENTRY

**Coventry Flea Market**
44 Lake
860/742-1993

**Memory Lanes Countryside**
2224 Boston Turnpike, Route 44
860/742-0346

**Ingraham & Co. Antiques**
143 Depot Road
860/742-5447

## 14 DANBURY

**Red White & Blue Antiques**
49 South St.
203/778-5085

**Antiques & Collectibles**
49 South St.
203/791-1275

**Antique Palace Emporium, Inc.**
7 Backus Ave.
203/798-8569

**Antiquity**
66 Sugar Hollow Road
203/748-6244

## 15 DARIEN

**Knock on Wood**
355 Post Road
203/655-9031

**Antiques of Darien**
1101 Boston Post Road
203/655-5133

**Emy Jane Jones Antiques**
770 Post Road
203/655-7576

**Sebastian Gallery**
833 Post Road
203/656-3093

**Windsor Antiques Ltd.**
1064 Post Road
203/655-2330

**Deacons Horse Antiques**
1101 Boston Post Road
203/655-5133

**Catherine Reiss**
1072 Post Road
203/655-8070

**Fred Heintz Antiques**
1101 Post Road
203/656-4393

**Rose Dor**
1076 Post Road
203/655-4668

## 16 DEEP RIVER

**Detour**
Old Piano Factory
860/526-9797

**Irish Country Pine**
246 S. Main St.
860/526-9757

**James E. Elliott Antiques**
453 Winthrop Road
860/526-9455

**Riverwind Antique Shop**
68 Main St.
860/526-3047

**Way We Wore**
116 Main St.
860/526-2944

**Deep River Design**
381 Main St. (Route 154)
860/526-9270

## 17 DERBY

### The Derby Antique Center, Inc.
181 Main St.
203/734-7614
Open: Tues.–Thurs. 10–2, Fri.–Sat. 10–5, closed Sun.–Mon.
Directions: The Derby Antique Center is located on Connecticut Route 34N., 500 feet from Exit 15 North or Route 8 South. Route 8 runs north and south through Connecticut. The shop is on the right side traveling north on Main Street in Derby, which is also Connecticut Route 34 North and South.

There's lots of expertise in antiques here at The Derby for shoppers to draw on as they browse through this large store. Although owner Peter Petrino has had the store only four years himself, he grew up working with the past owner and learned the business inside and out before taking the reins. The former owner also comes back from Florida in the summers to work in the store and greet old, familiar faces. The Derby handles "everything," as Peter says, but seems to get in a lot of musical instruments, besides the furniture, china, collectibles, jewelry, etc.

# *Connecticut*

## 18 EAST HADDAM

**Howard & Dickinson Antiques**
48 Main St.
860/873-9990

**Iron Horse Antiques & Nostalgia**
64 Main St.
860/267-7623

## 19 EAST HAMPTON

Nestled in the south central hills of Connecticut lies the quaint, historic town of East Hampton. Formerly known as Chatham, the area was originally famous for its ship-building and bell industries. Today, the old town center has developed into a cluster of antique shops and eateries making for a pleasant afternoon of antique shopping.

### Old Bank Antiques

66 Main St.
860/267-0790
Open: Wed.–Sun. 10–5, Fri. until 8 p.m., or by appointment
Directions: Route 91 Exit 25 N., connects with Route 2 East, Exit 13, right onto Route 66, left at 3rd light.

Old Bank Antiques is just as its name implies — an old bank. I have always been fascinated with buildings such as these, mostly because they hold something I would like to have—*a lot of money.*

Years ago if you had walked into this "Old Bank," the vaults would have been shut and tightly locked, protecting the loot from bank-robbing bandits who often rode into town. Today, the doors are opened wide, welcoming all to view a different kind of bounty. Displayed within are small antique pieces such as flow blue, Limoges, lamps, sterling, china, music boxes, toys, firearms and art.

Throughout this three-story building, thirty antique dealers offer a distinguished collection of 18th-through 20th-century furnishings and smalls, with over 300 pieces of furniture ready to go in oak, mahogany, pine and wicker. The shop is also one of the few places that always has big tables and *sets* of chairs.

**Antiques at Seventy Main St.**
70 Main St.
860/267-9501

**Past & Present Antiques**
81 Main St.
860/267-0495

**Two Geese & a Gander**
25 E. High St.
860/267-1940

*Nearby Antique Shopping (Colchester)*
*Colchester is 8 miles from East Hampton.*

**A & A Antiques**
48 Kmick Lane
860/537-4828

**N. Liverant & Son Antique Shop**
168 S. Main St.
860/5347-2409

## 20 EAST LYME

**Judy's Unfound Treasures**
180 Boston Post Road #A
860/739-7440

**Country Life Antiques**
55 W. Main St.
860/739-8969

**Book Barn**
41 W. Main St.
860/739-5715

**G-Tiques Antiques**
179 Boston Post Road
860/739-1946

## 21 ENFIELD

**Hazard Antique Center**
287 Hazard Ave.
860/763-0811

**Vernon House Antiques**
9 Moody Road
860/763-1667

## 22 ESSEX

### Bonsal-Douglas Antiques

1 Essex Square
860/767-2282
Open: Tues.–Wed. 10:30–1, Thurs.–Sat. 11–5

Specializing in British and American furniture, European and American paintings, delft.

**Arne E. Ahlberg Antiques**
145 Westbrook Road
860/767-2799

**American Heritage Antiques**
251 Westbrook Road
860/767-8162

**Francis Bealey American Arts**
3 S. Main St.
860/767-0220

**Hastings House**
4 N. Main St.
860/767-8217

**Phoenix Antiques**
10 Main St.
860/767-5082

**Valley Farm Antiques**
134 Saybrook Road
860/767-8555

*Nearby Antique Shopping (Centerbrook)*
*Centerbrook is located 1 mile from Essex.*

**Brush Factory Antiques**
33 Deep River Road
860/767-0845

**Essex Emporium Curious Goods**
19 Deep River Road
860/767-1869

## Connecticut

### *Great Places to Eat*

**Griswold Inn**
36 Main St.
860/767-1776

Famous for meat pies, homemade sausage, fresh seafood and prime rib. World famous marine art collection. Twenty-seven guest rooms.

### 23 FAIRFIELD

**Reminisce with Kathy**
238 Post Road
203/254-0300

**Winsor Antiques**
43 Ruance St.
203/255-0056

**James Bok Antiques**
1954 Post Road
203/255-6500

**Our Place Antiques**
111 Post Road
203/254-3408

### 24 FARMINGTON

**Farmington Lodge Antiques**
185 Main St.
860/674-1035

**Antiq's**
1839 New Britain Ave.
860/676-2670

**Samovar Antiques**
780 Farmington Ave., #F
860/677-8772

### *Great Places to Stay*

**Farmington Inn**
827 Farmington Ave.
860/677-2821

The "quintessential" Farmington Inn is a lovely two-story building of 72 rooms including plush suites, and an inviting, cozy fireplaced lobby decorated in antiques and original paintings. Guests are treated to Victoria's Cafe, the private breakfast room, where a sumptuous daily continental breakfast is served complimentary with an overnight stay.

### 25 GLASTONBURY

**Always Buying Antiques**
By appointment only
860/646-6808

**Black Pearl Antiques**
2217 Main St.
860/659-3601

**Tobacco Shed Antiques**
119 Griswold St.
860/657-2885

**Perfect Finish**
27 Commerce St., #C
860/657-2295

### *Nearby Antique Shopping (Hebron)*
### *Hebron is located 7 miles from Glastonbury.*

**Bland's Antiques**
124 Slocum Road
860/228-3514

**Treasure Factory**
459 Church
860/228-0111

### 26 GREENWICH

**Elaine Dillof Antiques**
71 Church St.
203/629-2294

**Greenwich Ave. Antiques**
369 Greenwich Ave.
203/622-8361

**Guild Antiques**
384 Greenwich Ave.
203/869-0828

**Manderley Antiques**
134 E. Putnam Ave.
203/861-1900

**Rue Fauborg**
44 W. Putnam Ave.
203/869-7139

**Eggplant & Johnson**
58 William St., #A
203/661-5335

**Antan Antiques**
E. Putnam Ave.
203/661-4769

**Fieldstone Antiques**
260 Mill St.
203/531-0011

**Greenwich Antiques-Consignment**
249 Railroad Ave.
203/629-1500

**Eggplant & Johnson**
161 N. Water St.
203/532-0409

**Off the Avenue**
104 Bruck Park Ave.
203/622-7500

**Sophia's Great Dames Vintage**
1 Liberty Way
203/869-5990

**Church Street Antiques**
77 Church St.
203/661-6309

**Henri-Burton French Antiques**
382 Greenwich Ave.
203/661-8529

**Greenwich Antiques**
205 Railroad Ave.
203/629-1700

**Provinces de France**
22 W. Putnam Ave.
203/629-9798

**Hallowell & Co.**
340 W. Putnam Ave.
203/869-2190

**Consign It, Inc.**
115 Mason St.
203/869-9836

**Surrey Collectibles**
563 Steamboat Road
203/869-4193

**French Country Living**
34 E. Putnam Ave.
203/869-9559

**Manor Antiques**
38 W. Putnam Ave.
203/629-0963

**House of Weltz**
522 E. Putnam Ave.
203/661-8244

**Red Studio**
39 Lewis St.
203/861-6525

*Great Places to Stay*

**Stanton House Inn**
76 Maple Ave.
203/869-2110

Built in 1840, the Stanton House Inn is a converted mansion that is now a bed and breakfast inn, located in the prestigious village of Greenwich, Conn. The inn offers elegant surroundings and a satisfying continental breakfast. The 24 guest rooms are bright and cheery, decorated primarily with Laura Ashley–style Waverly fabrics with period antiques and reproductions.

**27 GUILFORD**

**Arne E. Ahlberg Antiques**
1090 Boston Post Road
203/453-9022

**Guilford Antique Center**
1120 Boston Post Road
203/458-7077

**Gustave D. Balacos**
2614 Boston Post Road
203/453-9922

**28 HAMDEN**

**Donald Barese Fine Art**
47 Wakefield St.
203/281-7438

**T. Melillo Antiques**
2373 Whitney Ave.
203/281-3787

**Gallery 4**
2985 Whitney Ave.
203/281-6043

**Mill River Antiques**
3551 Whitney Ave.
203/407-1800

**Nancy Stiner Antiques**
1715 Whitney Ave.
203/248-7682

**Sleeping Giant Antiques**
3551 Whitney Ave.
203/288-4464

**Timeless Furniture II**
1656 Whitney Ave.
203/287-1904

**Unbroken Circle Antiques**
2964 Dixwell Ave.
203/248-3788

**29 HARTFORD**

**The Unique Antique**
Hartford Civic Center
860/522-9094
Open: Mon.–Sat. 10–7:30, Sun. by chance
Directions: Located right in the center of Hartford, the Hartford Civic Center adjoins the Sheraton Hotel. Exit I-91 at the downtown exit. The highrise Sheraton is visible from either I-84 or I-91.

This is the place to stop if you are in the market for very high-end antique and estate jewelry. The Unique Antique is an antique shop in a mall and carries one of the largest selections of antique/estate jewelry in the East. Owner Joanne Douglas brings a lifetime of experience in this field to her shop and customers. She has been in the business for 20 years, but her grandmother was an antique jewelry dealer, and Joanne grew up with an antique store in the house. She gets her stock from sources in New England, mainly through dealers and individuals who bring pieces in to her. If you want anything from "diamonds down to costume," the Unique Antique is a "must."

**Carol's Antiques & Collectibles**
453 Washington St.
860/524-9113

**Bacon Antiques**
95 Maple Ave.
860/524-0040

*Interesting Side Trips*

**The Mark Twain House**
351 Farmington Ave.
860/493-6411
Open: Year-round with peak season and off-season hours.

American author and humorist Mark Twain (Samuel Langhorne Clemens) built a Victorian mansion in Hartford for his family, where they all lived from 1874 to 1891. Now a National Register Historic Landmark (since 1963), the Mark Twain House is a showplace, a museum, a piece of American history and a very rare piece of American decorative art.

Twain wrote seven major works (including *Tom Sawyer, Adventures of Huckleberry Finn, The Prince and the Pauper, Life on the Mississippi*, and *A Connecticut Yankee in King Arthur's Court*) while living in this remarkable High Victorian building. Designed by Edward Tuckerman Potter, the 19-room mansion features an important collection of fine and decorative arts, and the only remaining domestic interiors by Louis Comfort Tiffany and his design firm, Associated Artists. Now restored to its 19th-century glory, the house is a museum and research center with a collection of some 10,000 objects, and offers a full program of literary, musical, family oriented, scholarly, and educational programs.

Mark Twain's Carriage House, also designed by Potter, was home to the Clemenses' coachman and his family, along with horses, carriages and a sleigh. For a time, Twain did his writing in a makeshift study in the Carriage House. The buildings share a lawn with the home of 19th-century author Harriet Beecher Stowe, who was Clemens' neighbor.

*Connecticut*

## 30 IVORYTON

### Great Places to Stay

#### Copper Beech Inn
46 Main St.
860/767-0330
Open: Year-round, except first week of January
Rates: $105–$175

The Copper Beech Inn takes its name from the magnificent copper beech tree that fronts the property, one of the oldest and largest of its kind in Connecticut. The 1880s home was built as an elegant Victorian country cottage, complete with carriage barn, root cellar, and terraced landscaping. Surrounded by turn-of-the-century gardens and native woodlands, the house was rescued from disrepair and vacancy in the 1970s, and restored and opened as the Copper Beech Inn.

The inn has thirteen guest rooms, all with telephones and air conditioning. Four rooms are in the Main House. These have been lovingly restored and decorated with country and antique furnishings. They have old-fashioned baths, kept intact, to lend a note of nostalgia.

There are nine charming, traditional guest rooms in the renovated Carriage House. Several have four-poster or canopy beds. Some of the rooms have soaring cathedral ceilings, in which the original supporting beams have been left exposed. All Carriage House rooms have television, whirlpool baths and also doors leading out onto decks.

An enticing complimentary buffet breakfast — including fresh fruit, homemade pastries, breads, cereal, juice, coffee and tea — is set for all house guests. A plant filled, Victorian-style conservatory offers a delightful spot for an aperitif before dinner, or for quiet moments anytime. Dinner at the Copper Beech Inn is in the hearty, French country style. Fresh flowers, sparkling silver and soft candlelight create an atmosphere of romance and warm elegance. The restaurant has been recognized with the 1998 AAA Four Diamond Award.

The lower Connecticut River Valley is a wonderful place to explore quiet New England countryside, small museums and antique shops. The inn itself has a small gallery offering fine antique Oriental porcelain. The quaint nearby villages of Essex, Old Lyme and Chester are among the most charming in Connecticut. In spring and summer, the area abounds with water-associated activities; there are fine beaches within a 20 minute drive from the inn. The area also enjoys superb theater, including the Ivoryton Playhouse, Goodspeed Opera House and Goodspeed-at-Chester.

## 31 KENT

#### Vivian G. Forrer
Route 7
860/927-3612

Specializing in flow blue, splatterware, Staffordshire, toby mugs.

**Company Store Antiques**
30 Kent Cornwall Road
860/927-3430

**R.T. Facts Garden & Architectural**
22 S. Main St.
860/927-5315

**Foreign Cargo & American Antiques**
Main St.
860/927-3900

**Golden Thistle**
Main St.
860/927-3790

**Harry Homes Antique**
3 Carter Road
860/927-3420

**Kent Antiques Center**
Kent Station Square
860/927-3313

**Main Street Antiques**
8 N. Main St.
860/927-4916

### Nearby Antique Shopping (Cornwall Bridge)
### Cornwall Bridge is located 5 miles N.E. of Kent.

**Brass Bugle Antiques**
Route 45
860/672-6535

**Holmes Antiques**
131 Kent Road
860/672-6427

### Great Places to Stay

#### Chaucer House
88 N. Main St.
860/927-4858

Both of the innkeepers at this beautiful Colonial-style inn are from the same small village in Kent, England. How ironic that they found themselves in Kent, Connecticut. The inn offers three guest accommodations and is within walking distance of antique shops and restaurants.

#### Mavis' Bed and Breakfast
230 Kent Cornwall Road
860/927-4334

Mavis' B&B is a stunning 1860s Greek Revival home with five bedrooms, two of which have fireplaces. The family room has 30x31 ft. beamed ceilings, the dining room overlooks the terrace and rose gardens. There is also a cottage available with dining and kitchen area. Mavis' sits on two acres of property with a fine stream, barn and many plants.

# *Connecticut*

## 32 LITCHFIELD

**Linsley Antiques**
499 Bantam Road
860/567-4245

**Black Swan Antiques**
17 Commons Dr.
860/567-4429

**Thomas M. McBride Antiques**
62 West St.
860/567-5476

**Jeffrey Tillou Antiques**
33 West St.
860/567-9693

**Barry Strom Antiques**
503 Bantam Road
860/567-2747

**Roberta's Antiques**
469 Bantam Road
860/567-4041

**Tyler Antiques**
495 Bantam Road
860/567-0755

## 33 MADISON

**Crescent Antiques**
60 Boston Post Road
203/245-9145

**Mildred Ross**
294 Boston Post Road
203/245-7122

**Kirtland H. Crump Clockmaker**
387 Boston Post Road
203/245-7573

**Madison Trust Antique**
891 Boston Post Road
203/245-3976

**Fence Creek Antiques**
916 Boston Post Road
203/245-0151

**Nosey Goose**
33 Wall St.
203/245-3132

**Friends of Time Antiques**
431 Durham Road
203/245-3580

## 34 MANCHESTER

**Yesterday's Treasures**
845 Main St.
860/646-8855

**Lest We Forget Antiques**
503 E. Middle Turnpike
860/649-8187

**Vintage & Jewels & Collectibles**
190 Middle Turnpike W.
860/645-1525

## 35 MERIDEN

**Dee's Antiques**
600 W. Main St.
203/235-8431

**Fair Weather Antiques**
763 Hanover Road
203/237-4636

## 36 MILFORD

**The Stock Transfer**
554 Boston Post Road
203/874-1333
Open: Tues.–Sat. 10–4
Directions: *From I-95 North*: Take Exit 37 (High St.) and turn right on Route 1. Turn left on Boston Post Road and go ½ block. The shop is on the right. *From I-95 South:* Take Exit 36 (Plains Road) to Route 1. Turn left and go ½ mile. The shop is on the right. *From Merritt Parkway*: Take Exit 54 to the first Milford exit and go to Route 1. Turn right and go ½ block. The shop is on the right in "The Courtyard."

Nanci has been in business for 17 years at The Stock Transfer. With 2,400 square feet of space, it is the largest shop of its kind in the area, and, says Nanci, they carry "everything." Shoppers can find furniture, crystal, china, jewelry, Oriental rugs, paintings and lots more.

**Ray's Antiques**
16 Daniel St.
203/876-7720

**New Beginnings**
107 River St.
203/876-8332

**Antiques of Tomorrow**
93 Gulf St.
203/878-4561

**Something of Bev's**
400 Boston Post Road—Colony Center
203/874-4686

**Geoffrey Flett Antiques**
1027 Bridgeport Ave.
203/874-1698

**Milford Green Antiques Gallery**
22 Broad St.
203/874-4303

**Retro-Active**
30 Broad St.
203/877-6050

**Treasures & Trifles**
580 Naugatuck Ave.
203/878-7045

## 37 MONROE

**Addie's Cottage**
144 Main St.
203/261-2689

**Barbara's Barn**
418 Main St.
203/268-9805

**Strawberry Patch Antiques**
418 Main St.
203/268-1227

**Anna's Antiques & Consignment**
266 Main St., #A
203/452-1866

**Yesteryear's Antiques**
650 Main St.
203/459-9458

## 38 MYSTIC

**Briar Rose Antiques**
27 Broadway Ave.
860/536-4135

**Tradewinds Gallery**
20 W. Main St.
860/536-0119

**Sonny's Toys & Collectibles**
6 Hendel Dr.
860/536-0646

# Connecticut

## Pequot Hotel Bed & Breakfast

Burnett's Corner
711 Cow Hill Road
860/572-0390
Open: Year-round
Rates: $95–$130

It just doesn't seem like stagecoaches ever ran anywhere but the old West — certainly not through New England — but the Pequot Hotel Bed & Breakfast is an authentically restored 1840 stagecoach stop. This stately Greek Revival landmark, located in the center of the Burnett's Corners Historic District, still has its original hardware, moldings and fireplaces. Two of the three guest rooms, all with private baths, have 12-foot-high coved ceilings and Rumford fireplaces. There is a rare book collection in the library, wicker furniture on the screened porch, and two parlors for guests' use. More than 20 acres of trails and woods, open fields, ponds, spacious lawns, and gardens surround the hotel.

## Six Broadway Inn

6 Broadway
860/536-6010
Web site: www.visitmystic.com/sixbroadway

Six Broadway Inn is the only bed and breakfast in the heart of Historic Downtown Mystic. The innkeepers, Jerry and Joan, restored the 1854 homestead to classic Victorian splendor. Guests are invited to enjoy the tranquility of the parlor, the gazebo, and the 5-acre grounds, or to stroll only blocks away to the Mystic Seaport Museum or by the Mystic River. The inn graciously offers sophisticated accommodations with a superb location in a village reminiscent of an era gone by.

## Steamboat Inn

73 Steamboat Wharf
860/536-8300
Web site: www.localnews.com/buspages/steamboa/

Steamboat Inn is Mystic's only waterfront inn. Elegant and intimate accommodations with fireplace, whirlpool baths and continental breakfast. Rooms are directly on the Mystic River in Historic Downtown Mystic, only steps from numerous fine shops and restaurants.

## Mystic Seaport

75 Greenmanville Ave.
860/572-5331
Web site: www.mystic.org
Open: Daily year-round except Christmas Day
Directions: Mystic Seaport is located midway between New York and Boston in Mystic, Conn. Take I-95 to Exit 90. Proceed one mile south on Route 27.

This place is absolutely fascinating! You don't even have to like sailing to be amazed by all the glimpses into our country's history that are preserved here at this private museum. In 1929 three residents of Mystic — Dr. Charles K. Stillman, Edward E. Bradley and Carl D. Cutler — formed the Marine Historical Association, Inc., in order to establish a museum and preserve the rapidly disappearing remnants of America's maritime past. The museum's name was changed in 1978 to Mystic Seaport. So, Mystic Seaport is an indoor/outdoor museum which includes historic ships, boats, buildings and exhibit galleries relating to American maritime history. The exhibit area is located on 17 acres along the Mystic River. Primary emphasis is on the maritime commerce of the Atlantic coast during the 19th century. The village-area architecture, gardens, and demonstrations depict life in a maritime community from 1850 to 1921. Located on an estuary three miles from the open sea, the museum is divided into three main areas: Preservation Shipyard, where museum staff maintain the museum's unique historic ships and small boats, while preserving the traditional skills of wooden shipbuilding; the outdoor Village Exhibits, representing elements of life and work in 19th century New England seaport communities and aboard the ships that sailed from them; and the Gallery Exhibits, presenting fabulous collections of maritime art and artifacts, and special changing exhibitions on important aspects of America's relationship with the sea.

## 39 NEW BRITAIN

**Vintage Shop**
61 Arch St.
860/224-8567

### *Nearby Antique Shopping (Kensington)*
### *Kensington is located 4 miles from New Britain.*

**Gloria's Antiques**
1906 Chamberlain Hwy.
860/828-7865

## 40 NEW CANAAN

**Evans-Leonard Antiques**
114 Main St.
203/966-5657

**Silk Purse**
118 Main St.
203/972-0898

# Connecticut

**Main St. Cellar Antiques**
120 Main St.
203/966-8348

**Sallea Antiques**
66 Elm St.
203/972-1050

**English Heritage Antiques, Inc.**
13 South Ave.
203/966-2979

**Manor Antiques**
110 Main St.
203/966-2658

**Greene Frog**
20 Burtis Ave.
203/972-3841

**New Canaan Antiques**
120 Main St.
203/972-1938

**Courtyard Antiques**
150 Elm St.
203/966-2949

**Elisabeth De Bussy, Inc.**
By appointment only
203/966-5947

**Severed Ties, Inc.**
111 Cherry St.
203/972-0788

## 41  NEW HARTFORD

**Rose Marie**
202 Main St.
860/693-3979

**New Hartford Junction**
510 Main St.
860/738-0689

## 42  NEW HAVEN

**Edwin C. Ahlberg Antiques**
441 Middletown Ave.
203/624-9076

**Antiques Market**
881 Whalley Ave.
203/389-5440

**Second Time Around**
970 State St.
203/624-6343

**Village Francais**
555 Long Wharf Dr.
203/562-4883

**Sally Goodman, Ltd.**
902 Whalley Ave.
203/387-5072

**W. Chorney Antiques**
827 Whalley Ave.
203/387-9707

**Antique Corner**
859 Whalley Ave.
203/387-7200

**Patti's Antiques**
920 State St.
203/865-8496

**Harold's Antiques, Inc.**
873 Whalley Ave.
203/389-2988

## 43  NEW LONDON

**Captain's Treasures**
253 Captains Walk
860/442-2944

## 44  NEW MILFORD

**Chamberlain's Antiques**
469 Danbury Road
860/355-3488

**Accent Antiques**
Church St.
860/355-7707

**Retro**
267 Kent Road
860/355-1975

**This 'n' That Shop**
27 Old State Road
860/350-4001

**Ida's Antiques**
329 Danbury Road
860/354-4388

## 45  NEWINGTON

**Connecticut Antique Wicker**
1052 Main Rear
860/666-3729

**Trellis Antiques & Gifts**
39 Market Square
860/665-9100

**Cricket Hill**
94 Park Lane Road
860/354-8872

**Doll Factory Vintage Clothing**
2551 Berlin Turnpike
860/666-6162

## 46  NEW PRESTON/MARBLE DALE

**Earl Slack Antiques**
Wheaton Road. (Marble Dale)
860/868-7092

**Martell & Suffin Antiques**
1 Main St., #A (New Preston)
860/868-1339

**Room with a View**
13 E. Shore Road (New Preston)
860/868-1717

**Dawn Hill Antiques**
15 E. Shore Road
860/868-0066

**Grampa Snazzy's Log Cabin**
270 Litchfield Turnpike
860/868-7153

**Reece Antiques**
13 E. Shore Road (New Preston)
860/868-9966

**Recherche Studio**
166 New Milford Turnpike
860/868-0281

## 47  NEWTOWN

**McGeorgi's Antiques**
129 S. Main St.
203/270-9101

**Poverty Hollow Antiques**
78 Poverty Hollow Road
203/426-2388

## 48  NOANK

**The Antiquary**
215 Park
860/928-4873

## *Great Places to Stay*

### Palmer Inn
25 Church St.
860/572-9000
Open: Year-round
Rates: $125–$185

On a prime piece of real estate just off Long Island Sound is a soaring, magnificent home that reveals the extravagance and superb craftsmanship of turn-of-the-century architecture. Two miles from Mystic Seaport, shipyard craftsmen built a grand seaside mansion for shipbuilder Robert Palmer in 1906. The house, described by the architects as a "Classic Colonial Suburban Villa," features a hip roof with dormers, a balustrade,

dentil cornices, pilasters, Palladian windows, and a huge portico with two-story Ionic columns. These architectural details remain intact on the outside, while inside guests enjoy and marvel at 13-foot ceilings, a mahogany staircase and beams, brass fixtures, intricate woodwork, stained-glass windows, and original wall coverings, all of which have been restored. The six guest rooms with private baths are filled with family heirlooms and antiques, as well as modern luxuries. Balconies offer views of Long Island Sound, while fireplaces warm the chilly Connecticut winter evenings.

## 49 NORFOLK

### *Great Places to Stay*

**Greenwoods Gate**
105 Greenwoods Road E.
860/542-5439
Web site: www.bbhost.com/greenwoodsgate

The Federal-era architecture of Greenwoods Gate sets the tone for relaxation, warmth and romance. Greenwoods Gate is conveniently located in the picture-perfect village of Norfolk, Conn., one-half mile east of the Village Green. The home has a charming character all its own, having been carefully and lovingly furnished throughout with an eclectic blend of fine antiques, period pieces and collections, all to provide guests with a wondrous country experience.

**Manor House**
69 Maple Ave.
860/542-5690

Treat yourself to an elegant retreat at the Manor House, an 1898 Victorian Tudor estate. Designated Connecticut's most romantic hideaway and included in "10 Best B and Bs" in the country, this historic mansion is described by *Gourmet* as "quite grand with its Tiffany windows." The antique decorated guest rooms are furnished with four-poster, brass, sleigh, spindle or lace-canopy beds, covered with luxurious down comforters. Several rooms have fireplaces, private balconies, a jacuzzi or a deluxe soaking tub. The hearty breakfast includes honey harvested from their own hives, pure local maple syrup and homemade bread. During the day, there is so much to see and do — music festivals, summer theater, antique and craft shops, vineyards, museums, gardens, hiking, biking, water sports, tennis, riding stables, carriage and sleigh rides, alpine and cross-country skiing. They can even arrange an appointment with a massage therapist.

**Mountain View Inn**
67 Litchfield Road, Route 272
860/542-6991

Nestled high in the Berkshire Hills of northwest Connecticut, Norfolk, with its village green, bell towers and postcard landscapes, reflects New England's spirit at its best.

Golf, tennis, fishing, hiking, cross-country and downhill skiing are available nearby. Mountain View Inn, located one-quarter mile south of the Village Green, is a historic Victorian-style, full-service country inn. Individually appointed guest rooms offer spacious, comfortable accommodations filled with period antiques.

## 50 NORWALK

**Pak Trade**
14 Wall St.
203/857-4165

**Old Well Antiques**
135 Washington St.
203/838-1842

**Eagle's Lair Antiques**
565 Westport Ave.
203/846-1159

**Koppels Antique Warehouse**
24 1st St.
203/866-3473

## 51 NORWICH

**Antiques Etc.**
205 Main St.
860/887-0699

**Norwichtown Antique Center**
221 W. Thames St.
860/887-1870

**Rose City Antiques**
33 13th St.
860/886-8414

## 52 OLD LYME

**Antique Associates**
11 Halls Road
860/434-5828

**Treasures**
95 Halls Road
860/434-9338

**Morelock Antiques**
At the Village Shops, Lyme St.
860/434-6333

**Elephant Trunk**
11 Halls Road
860/434-9630

**The Cooley Gallery**
25 Lyme St.
860/434-8807

**Antiques on Lyme**
At the Village Shops, Lyme St.
860/434-3901

### *Great Places to Stay*

**Old Lyme Inn**
85 Lyme St.
1-800-434-5352
Open: Year-round except for first two weeks of January
Rates: $86–$158
Directions: Going south on I-95, take Exit 70 and turn right at the ramp. Going north on I-95, turn left at the ramp, right at the second

light. Follow this road (Route 1) to the second light and the inn is on the left.

Situated on the main street in Old Lyme's historic district, the Old Lyme Inn represents the classic traditions of excellence in dining and lodging that are at the very heart of a small Connecticut town. The original building, constructed around 1850 by the Champlain family, was a 300-acre working farm until the Connecticut Turnpike cut through Old Lyme in the early 1950s. Some guests still remember when the place housed a riding academy in the 1920s, where it is reputed that Jacqueline Bouvier Kennedy Onassis took lessons. Prior to that, around the turn of the century, many of Old Lyme's famous impressionist artists hauled their painting wagons into the beautiful fields and Connecticut woodlands behind the inn. Townspeople also remember lively square dancing in the old barn that burned (only the foundation remains) about 300 yards behind the still-remaining 1850s yellow barn.

When the turnpike arrived, the Champlain family home was sold and became the Barbizon Oaks, named after the Barbizon School for painters that Old Lyme emulated, and the 300-year-old oak tree that still stands on a hill behind the inn. It became a boarding establishment, and survived a major fire that was the beginning of a spiral into disrepair. Its staircase and interior walls disappeared, and it became an Italian restaurant of questionable reputation. When Diana Field Atwood bought it in 1976, the second floor was still charred and the building was ready for demolition. The kitchen, then in the basement, was a hazard to its occupants — including the dead rat found in one of the ovens. The only access to the second floor was up a rickety fire escape supported by a metal milk crate and pulled down with one hand!

But when Diana bought it, she restored the inn to its current beauty. Walls and staircases were rebuilt, marble fireplaces were found and everything was redone from the basement to the attic. Now it offers not only fine dining, but 13 guest rooms with private baths and Empire and Victorian antiques. The inn's facilities include four separate dining rooms and a cocktail lounge, with seating from 2 to 70. In combination with the guest rooms, the inn handles conferences, wedding parties, rehearsal dinners and other special events.

Guests can spend time at the Victorian bar that came out of one of Pittsburgh's oldest taverns. It has never been refinished, retaining its original beveled glass mirrors and scores of dart holes from many games in the past. The mirror over the bar's fireplace was purchased at an auction for $5 — no one else wanted it! The marble mantles in the bar and parlor came from a lady in Wetherfield who had saved them when her family's home was being razed.

Many of the paintings in the inn represent the Old Lyme School of artists who resided up the street at Florence Griswold's home (now the Lyme Historical Society) at the turn of the century. There are also paintings purchased from current artists at Lyme Art Association shows, and some lovely watercolors in the Champlain rooms, from unknown artists of Old Lyme, found at tag sales.

The Empire Room (the main dining room) was an addition to the original building, added around the time of the Barbizon Oak period. The large pier mirror was found in an old Norwich mansion undergoing the wrecker's ball. Curly maple balustrades from an old Pennsylvania home march up the front staircase. Nineteenth-century chestnut paneling covers the walls in the private dining room. In the front hall, the original paintings and stenciling were done by Gigi Horr-Liverant. This type of wall painting was done quite often during the mid-1800s by itinerant artists; they usually painted local scenes, so the inn's wall murals represent several of the old buildings on Lyme St., and going up the stairs, Hamburg Cove in Lyme and Tiffany's Farm, the only remaining working dairy farm, owned by one of Connecticut's former legislators.

Over the years the inn has been awarded multiple prestigious awards and tributes: three star reviews by the *New York Times* on three separate visits; three stars from *Connecticut Magazine;* five stars from the *Norwich Bulletin;* wonderful stories in *Signature, Travel & Leisure, Redbook, Town & Country,* and many more; feature billing in *Bon Appetit* and on a separate cover of the same magazine; feature stories in *Connoisseur, Food & Wine,* and *New York Magazine*. And for three years in a row, the inn's pastry chef won the "Ultimate Chocolate Dessert" contest in Hartford.

## Bee and Thistle Inn

100 Lyme St.
860/434-1667 or 1-800-622-4946
Rates: $75–$210
Directions: By Amtrak from Boston or New York: Train stops at Old Saybrook Station. By car from Boston or Providence: Take I-95 South to Exit 70, turn right off the ramp. The inn is the third house on the left. From New York City: Take the New England Thruway (I-95 North) to Exit 70. At the bottom of the ramp turn left. Take the first right onto Halls Road (Route 1 North) to the "T" in the road and turn left. The inn is the third house on the left. From Hartford: Take I-91 South to Route 9 South to I-95 North. Take Exit 70 and turn left off the ramp. Take the first right onto Halls Road (Route 1 North). Go to the "T" in the road and turn left. The inn is the third house on the left.

The Bee and Thistle is somewhat more formal than many bed and breakfasts, but the effort is worth it. With landscaped and natural areas along the Lieutenant River in the historic district of Old Lyme, the inn states that it is "a return to early American gracious living." The house was built in 1756 for Judge Noyes, very close to the Post Road. Around the turn of the century the Hodgson family moved it back from the road to its present location. They added the lovely sunken garden, the porches and the kitchen area. It remained a private home until the late 1930s, when Henrietta Greenleaf Lindsay found herself a widow with a large house to support. Her friend, Elsie Ferguson, an actress at the Goodspeed Opera House, suggested Henrietta take in boarders. Because it was Elsie's idea, Henrietta named her boardinghouse the Bee and Thistle after the Ferguson clan emblem in Scotland. The logo is still used today.

# Connecticut

Dining is a highlight and a specialty of the house, with appropriate evening dinner attire required and jackets required on Saturdays. But for that little extra effort, guests will enjoy four-star creative American cuisine that has been voted the "Best Restaurant" and "Most Romantic Place" to dine in Connecticut by *Connecticut Magazine* Readers' Choice Poll. Candlelit dining areas showcase the food; wine comes from a large selection; desserts are award-winning — it is an experience many visitors enjoy simply as an evening out. Breakfast is served either on the porches or in the privacy of individual rooms. Luncheon is the chance for the chefs to use their imaginations.

To work off the excesses of the dining room, a walk down Lyme St. leads to historic homes, museums, galleries, fine antique shops, and beautiful private homes. A short drive away are numerous attractions and sites.

## 53  OLD SAYBROOK

### Stephen & Carol Huber
40 Ferry Road
860/338-6809
Web site: www.antiquesamplers.com

Specializing in American sampler embroideries, the shop always has an outstanding selection of samplers and silk embroideries.

**Antiques at Madison**
869 Middlesex Turnpike
860/388-3626

**Corner Cupboard Antiques**
853 Middlesex Turnpike
860/388-0796

**Joseph Goclowski Antiques**
223 Hidden Cove Road
860/399-5070

**Presence of the Past**
488 Main St.
860/388-9021

**Van's Elegant Antiques**
998 Middlesex Turnpike
860/388-1934

**Little House of Glass**
1560 Boston Post Road (Route 1)
860/399-5127

**Weatherbee Hill Antiques**
1340 Boston Post Road (Route 1)
860/388-0442

**Antiques Depot**
455 Boston Post Road
860/395-0595

**Essex-Saybrook Antiques Village**
345 Middlesex Turnpike
860/388-0689

**Old Saybrook Antiques Center**
756 Middlesex Turnpike
860/388-1600

**Sweet Pea Estate Jewelry**
851 Middlesex Turnpike
860/388-0289

**Essex Town Line Antiques Village**
985 Middlesex Turnpike
860/388-5000

**James Demorest Oriental Rugs**
5 Great Hammock Road
860/388-9547

## *Great Places to Eat*

### Cuckoo's Nest
1712 Boston Post Road (Route 1)
860/399-9060

Authentic Mexican and Cajun cuisine, served in an antique-filled barn. Voted "Connecticut's Best Mexican Restaurant" five years in a row. Outside patio. Open 7 days, lunch and dinner.

## 54  PLAINFIELD

**Plainfield Trading Post**
260 Norwich Road
860/564-4115

## 55  PLAINVILLE

**Winter Associates**
21 Cooke St.
860/793-0288

**Fireglow Antiques**
12 W. Main St.
860/793-1600

**March Hare Antiques**
188 W. Main St.
860/747-2526

## 56  PLANTSVILLE

**Village Antique Shop**
61 Main St.
860/628-2498

**Nothing New**
69 W. Main St.
860/276-0143

**Al Judd & Associates**
40 W. Main St.
860/628-5828

**West Main Antiques**
9 W. Main St.
860/620-1124

**Plantsville General Store**
780 S. Main St.
860/621-5225

**G.W.G. Antiques**
758 Main St.
860/620-0244

## 57  PORTLAND

### Robert T. Baranowsky Antiques
66 Marlborough
860/342-2425

Specializing in American folk art, advertising and American antiques.

**Taverin Antiques**
1118 Portland Cobalt Road
860/342-3779

**Tall Tale Antiques**
Portland Cobalt Road
860/342-2444

## 58 PUTNAM

### Riverside Antiques
Bldg. 2A, Suite 101
58 Pomfret St.
860/928-6020
Open: Regular hours Wed.–Sun. 10–5
Apr. 1–Aug.30, Wed.–Sun. 10–5, except Sat. 11–5
Nov. 1–Dec. 23, daily 10–5
Directions: From I-395 take Exit 95. Go right onto Kennedy Drive. At the first traffic light, left onto Pomfret St., 200 yards on the left directly across from WINY radio studio.

Located on the western edge of the extensive Putnam Antiques District, Riverside Antiques is housed in the Wilkinson Mill (Hale Mfg. Co.) ca. 1830, a stone and brick structure formerly used for the manufacture of woolen goods. Riverside Antiques is a co-op featuring more than 20 dealers selling a full range of quality antiques and collectibles, complimented by an on-site clock repair shop.

Riverside Antiques has long been recognized for reasonable prices, product variety, dealer following and handicapped accessibility.

**Grams & Pennyweights**
626 School St. Route 44
860/928-6624

**Grandpa's Attic**
10 Pomfret St.
860/928-5970

**Antiques Marketplace**
109 Main St.
860/928-0442

**Brighton Antiques**
91 Main St.
860/928-1419

**J.B. Antiques**
37 Front St.
860/928-1906

**Antique Corner**
112 Main St.
860/963-2445

**Jeremiah's Antique Shoppes**
26 Front St.
860/963-8989

**Remember When**
80 Main St.
860/963-0422

**Mission Oak Shop**
109 Main St.
860/928-6662

**Palace Antiques**
130 Main St.
860/963-1124

### Nearby Antique Shopping (South Woodstock)

### Scrantons Shops
300 Route 169
860/928-3738

This collection of 75 dealers present their wares in seven rooms of this fun-to-browse shop. The shop offers something for everyone from the serious antiquer to the bargain shopper.

## 59 RIDGEFIELD

### The Red Petticoat Antiques
113 West Lane, Route 35
203/431-9451
Open: Tues.–Sat. 10–5:30, Sun. 12–5:30, closed Mon.

In April 1777, a young girl saved her home (which is now The Red Petticoat Antiques) on West Lane, Ridgefield, from being burned and plundered, and protected a wounded Patriot from being captured, by British soldiers by waving her red petticoat from the window in pretended sympathy with the Tories. The wounded Patriot had an important message to deliver to General George Washington, but was too weak to travel, so the girl sewed the message into the red petticoat and delivered it to Dobb's Ferry. Soon after, Washington expressed his gratitude by sending her some lovely red silk for a new petticoat, hoping it would replace the one she had sacrificed so bravely for her country … or so the story is told.

Continuity and tradition are important parts of the fabric of the Northeast, and The Red Petticoat antique store is built on American history and its own tradition, making it a perfect setting in which to sell historical objects. To begin with, the building itself is a home that was built in 1740, in one of the most beautiful settings in New England. For another, antiques have been sold at the sign of The Red Petticoat for as long as most people can remember. One of the oldest owners and sellers was Florene Maine, who knew and taught people about some of the finest English furniture ever made. After her death, the house remained an antique shop and the present owners, Ralph and Gloria Pershino, bought it. Now the antique selection is much more eclectic, with seven rooms of 18th- and 19th-century antique furnishings, folk art, iron and wicker, ephemera, Oriental rugs, lamps, and fine furniture reproductions by Douglas Dimes.

A specialty of the house is advertising ephemera, which draws a great number of the shop's customers. Many people come to The Red Petticoat just for this. They have customers who are either employed by companies or whose families have started major companies, and the Perschinos call them when particular advertisements come in, usually items from the late 1800s to the early 1900s. A major part of the Perschinos' business is repeat customers, who particularly like to shop at the store for accessories and gifts. They cater to a varied clientele, who either shop by phone, or who come into the store and browse through the room settings. There is a beautiful sunroom filled with antique wicker, a huge fireplace where the old kitchen once was, decked out with tools and iron from the past. There is a staircase leading to a cozy room upstairs, with the entire stairway furnished with Wallace Nutting vintage pictures — seven rooms of 18th- and 19th-century antique furnishings and much more, all in a beautiful country setting in this historical antique house.

**Hunter's Consignments**
426 Main St.
203/438-9065

**Horologists of London Clocks**
450 Main St.
203/438-4332

*Connecticut*

**Consignments by Vivian**
458 Main St.
203/438-5567

**Attic Treasures Ltd.**
58 Ethan Allen Hwy.
203/544-8159

**Route 7 Antiques**
659 Danbury Road
203/438-6671

**Branchville Antiques**
32 Ethan Allen Hwy.
203/544-9940

**Village Emporium**
384 Main St.
203/438-8767

**Silk Purse**
470 Main St.
203/431-0132

**Country Gallery Antiques**
346 Ethan Allen Hwy.
203/438-2535

**Ridgefield Antiques Center**
109 Danbury Road
203/438-2777

**Cromlix Antiques & Consignment**
454 Main St.
203/431-7726

## 60 RIVERSIDE

**Classiques Antiques**
1147 E. Putnam Ave.
203/637-8227

**Maury Rose Antiques**
1147 E. Putnam Ave.
203/698-2898

**Estate Treasures of Greenwich**
1162 E. Putnam Ave.
203/637-4200

## 61 SALISBURY

**Buckley & Buckley**
84 Main St.
860/435-9919

**Salisbury Antiques Center**
46 Library St.
860/435-0424

## 62 SEYMOUR

**Seymour Antique Co.**
26 Bank St.
203/881-2526

**Chrisandra's**
249 West St.
203/888-7223

## 63 SIMSBURY

**Simsbury Antiques**
744 Hopmeadow St.
860/651-4474

**William III Antiques**
21 Wolcott Road
860/658-1121

**Back Fence Collector**
1614 Hopmeadow St.
860/651-4846

**Roxie Taylor Vintage Clothing**
39 E. Weatogue St.
860/658-5141

## 64 SOMERS

**Antiques & Folk Art Shoppe**
62 South Road Route 83
860/749-6197

**Genora's Furn & Antiques**
49 Maple St.
860/749-3650

**Somer House Designs & Antiques**
62 South Road Route 83
860/763-4458

**Oak Tree Antiques**
62 South Road
860/749-5893

## 65 SOMERSVILLE

### *Great Places to Stay*

**The Old Mill Inn Bed & Breakfast**
63 Maple St.
860/763-1473
Rates: $85–$95
Directions: *From the north or south:* Take I-91 to Exit 47E, then proceed east on Route 190 five miles to the Somersville traffic signal. Turn right on Maple St., past the old mill (red brick buildings with a waterfall on the left), to the second house on the left. *From the west:* Take Route 190 east under I-91, then follow the above directions. From the east: Take Route 190 west through Somers, then go 2 miles to the traffic signal, then south to 63 Maple St.

This warm and inviting private home was originally built in the mid-1800s. It was enlarged and renovated 100 years later by an owner of the mill, who raised a family of seven in its gracious rooms. The second-floor guest wing has five bedrooms complete with down comforters, full-size robes and bath sheets, fresh fruit and purified drinking water. There is a quiet, comfortable reading room, a large sun deck, which is perfect for soaking up rays or stargazing by telescope at night. Downstairs is another guest room, a parlor with fireplace, and a dining room with hand-painted walls of flowering shrubs and trees, which merge with a similar vista through the window wall that overlooks a deep expanse of lawn bordered by flowering shrubs and trees. The entire property is surrounded by giant maple trees that open onto the green, and guests can wander down the path through the woods to the private beach on the Scantic River. There, they'll find hammocks, swings, canoes, picnic tables, fishing, bicycles, and a spa for evening soaking of any sore muscles from the day's activities.

Nearby attractions are only minutes away and include antique shops, restaurants, and numerous museums and historic homes. In the immediate area are two golf courses, an equestrian center and a motor speedway.

## 66 SOUTHINGTON

**Memories**
190 Main St.
860/276-8880

**Albert Judd & Associates Antiques**
40 W. Main St.
860/628-5828

**Village Antique Shop**
61 Main St.
860/628-2498

# Connecticut

## 67 SOUTHBURY

**Clarire Bannister Collection**
704 Heritage Village
203/270-6255

**Jefferson Pine Southbury**
Heritage Village Bazaar
203/264-0488

**Lavenders**
123 Southford Road
203/264-2766

**New to You**
134 Main St. S.
203/264-2577

**Salem Antiques**
Heritage Village
203/262-6323

## 68 SOUTHPORT

**Chelsea Antiques**
293 Pequot Ave.
203/255-8935

**Ten Eyck-Emerich**
342 Pequot Ave.
203/259-2559

**Pat Guthman Antiques**
281 Pequot Ave.
203/259-5743

**Pequot Galleries**
340 Pequot Ave.
203/259-7069

## 69 SOUTH WINDSOR

**Treasure Trunk Antiques**
1212 Sullivan Ave.
860/644-1074

**Country Barn Collectibles**
1135 Sullivan Ave.
860/644-2826

**Horace Porter Antique Shop**
16 Shares Lane
860/644-0071

**Time Past**
673 Main St.
860/289-2119

## 70 STAFFORD SPRINGS

**Mallard's Nest**
17 Crystal Lake Road
860/684-3837

**Hometown Collectibles**
107 W. Stafford Road
860/684-5844

## 71 STAMFORD

### Antique & Artisan Center
69 Jefferson St.
203/327-6022
Open: Mon.–Sat. 10:30–5:30, Sun. 12–5
Directions: Traveling north on I-95, take Exit 8, turn right at second light on Canal St. Take first left onto Jefferson St. Antique & Artisan Center is located in second building on the right.

Antique & Artisan Center is housed in a converted historic ice house. Catering to the discriminating shopper, the market is considered to be one of New England's finest. Within 22,000 square feet, over 100 dealers display their wares in spacious room settings. Period and decorative furnishings, exquisite porcelains, glass, silver, art and bronzes are just a sampling of the fine quality pieces you will find here.

### Stamford Antiques Center
735 Canal St.
1-888-329-3546
Open: Mon.–Sat. 10:30–5:30, Sun. 12–5
Directions: *From I-95 South:* Exit 7, left onto Canal St. *From I-95 North:* Exit 8, 2 blocks, turn right onto Canal St.

Owner Debbie Schwartz said her career in the antiques business started in the carriage. "I'm a third-generation antiques dealer. My grandparents sold Tiffany lamps, my parents were called 'second-generation antiques.'" Her mother, Jeri Schwartz, has written a book on antiques, is a columnist for *Country Living* magazine and is a licensed appraiser.

The building, a onetime factory turned antique shop, is an architectural beauty with its pillars and sawtoothed roof featuring hundreds of skylights. The painted honey-colored concrete floors complement the wares of interior designer Gordon McCunis and his associate, Jay, who have taken a booth to display paintings, pillows, fabrics and furnishings.

Outer aisles are filled with chandeliers suspended from the ceiling stretching the length of one aisle into infinity. The center aisle displays showcases of museum-quality antiques such as orientalia, silver, porcelain and collectibles. "We have high end up to Tiffany lamps and then linen for $10," Debbie said. "We display blue and white porcelain, samplers, every single century furniture you can imagine. You name it, we have it. Antiquers can spend the day. This is an antique heaven."

### Steve Newman Fine Arts
112 Revonah Ave.
203/323-7799

Specializing in 19th-century American neoclassic figures, busts and reliefs, garden fountains and figures, decorative arts, fine paintings and furniture.

**Finders Keepers**
22 Belltown Road
203/357-1180

**Good Riddance Girls**
44 Four Brooks Road
203/329-0009

**Anne Corper Country Antiques**
375 Fairfield Ave.
203/359-2818

### 72 STONINGTON

**Stonington Antique Center**
71 Cutler St.
860/535-8373
Open: Tues.–Sun. 10–5
Directions: Exit 91 off I-95. Follow signs to village.

Fifty dealers under one roof.

**Water St. Antiques**
114 Water St.
860/535-1124

**Collections**
119 Water St.
860/535-9063

**Grand & Water Antiques**
135 Water St.
860/535-2624

**Mary Mahler Antiques**
144 Water St.
860/535-2741

**Peaceable Kingdom Antiques**
145 Water St.
860/535-3434

**Orkney & Yost Antiques**
148 Water St.
860/535-4402

**Neil Bruce Eustace**
156 Water St.
860/535-2249

**Pendergast N. Jones**
158 Water St.
860/535-1995

**Quester Maritime Gallery**
77 Main St.
860/535-3860

**Boat House**
109 Water St.
860/535-4714

**Findings**
68 Water St.
860/535-1330

**Church St. Antiques**
5 Church St.
860/572-0457

**Antiques Limited**
530 Stonington Road (Route 1)
860/535-1017

**Second Impression Antiques**
59 Williams Ave.
860/536-4041

### 73 STRATFORD

**4 Seasons Antiques**
427 Honeyspot Road
203/380-2450

**Main St. Antiques**
2399 Main St.
203/377-5086

**Natalie's Antiques**
2403 Main St.
203/377-1483

**Stratford Antique Center**
400 Honeyspot Road
203/378-7754

**Aaron Marcus Antiques**
221 Honeyspot Road
203/377-2231

**Antiques Peddler**
1097 Barnum Ave.
203/375-7543

**New England Attic Treasures**
2410 Main St.
203/378-8612

### 74 TORRINGTON

**Remember When**
66 Main St.
860/489-1566

**Americana Mart**
692 S. Main St.
860/489-5368

**Northwood Antiques**
47 Main St.
860/489-4544

**Wheatfield Antiques**
83 Main St.
860/482-3383

### 75 WALLINGFORD

**Wallingford General Antiques**
202 Center St.
203-265-5567

**Curiosity Shop**
216 Center St.
203/294-1975

**Wallingford Center St. Antiques**
171 Center St.
203/265-4201

**Connecticut Coin Gallery**
428 N. Colony St.
203/269-9888

**Images-Heirloom Linen**
32 N. Colony St.
203/265-7065

**Hunt's Courtyart Antiques**
38 N. Main St.
203/294-1733

**Antique Center of Wallingford**
28 S. Orchard St.
203/269-7130

**Rick's Antiques**
428 N. Colony St.
203/269-9888

### 76 WATERBURY

**Brass City Antiques**
2152 E. Main St.
203/753-1975

**Mattatucks Antiques**
156-158 Meriden Road
203/754-2707

**Century Antiques**
1015 W. Main St.
203/573-8092

*Nearby Antique Shopping (Naugatuck)*
*Naugatuck is 5 miles from Waterbury.*

**Architectural Antiques**
149 Maple St.
203/723-1823

**Joe's Antiques**
160 Church St.
203/723-7012

### 77 WATERTOWN

**Treasures & Trash**
755 Thomaston Road
860/274-2945

**Corner Curio**
413 Main St.
860/945-9611

**Fannie Rose Vintage Clothing**
737 Main St.
860/274-0317

**Things Remembered**
125 Main St.
860/945-6733

### 78 WESTBROOK

**Westbrook Antiques**
1119 Boston Post Road
860/399-9892

**Shops at Tidewater Creek**
433 Boston Post Road
860/399-8399

**Trolley Square Antiques**
1921 Boston Post Road
860/399-9249

**The Source**
374 Essex Road (Route 153)
860/399-6308

**Lovejoy Antiques**
150 Boston Post Road
860/664-9015

**Miller's Antiques**
1420 Boston Post Road
860/299-9254

**Shoreline Antiques**
1411 Boston Post Road
860/399-6522

### 79 WESTPORT

## George Subkoff
260 Post Road E.
203/227-3515

Ultra-quality upscale is about the only way to describe one of the most famous dealers in Manhattan and Connecticut collecting circles. George Subkoff's tony showroom is on Post Road in Westport, just past Main St., across from a picture-postcard New England church. His antiques are not for the faint of heart nor light of wallet. Most are of Continental provenance, with a few early American pieces.

George has been in the business for 35 years, a third-generation antique dealer. He specializes in, as he puts it, "quality, quality, quality" — mostly furniture of the 17th through the mid-19th centuries. A world-renowned dealer who sells to very well-known decorators, George is an avid collector of trompe l'oeil. He often buys privately at auctions and has multiple sources who offer him the select pieces they receive. You never know what you're going to find in his showroom as you browse through the two floors of paintings, lighting fixtures, etc. As George is fond of saying, "Every day is an adventure," whether buying, selling, or hunting.

**Jordan Delhaise Gallery**
238 Post Road E.
203/454-1830

**Family Album**
283 Post Road E.
203/227-4888

**Riverside Antiques Center**
265 Riverside Ave.
203/454-3532

**Leslie Allen: A Home**
3 Kings Hwy. N.
203/454-4155

**Audrey Morgan Interiors**
19 Post Road W.
203/227-1344

**Todburn**
243 Post Road W.
203/226-3859

**Glen Leroux Collections**
68 Church Lane
203/227-8030

**Bungalow**
4 Sconset Square
203/227-4406

**Prince of Wales, Inc.**
1032 Post Road E.
203/454-2335

**Leonce Consignment & Antiques**
1435 Post Road E.
203/254-8448

### *Great Places to Stay*

## The Inn at National Hall
Two Post Road W.
203/221-1351 or 1-800-NAT-HALL
Rates: $195–$475, including breakfast

Neither its sensible name nor its formidable red-brick exterior prepares guests for the delightful mix of whimsy, privacy, history, elegance and luxury that is found in this magnificent 15-bedroom bed & breakfast, with its first-class restaurant, boardroom/conference room and residents' drawing room. The Italianate structure was built in 1873 by Horace Staples, chairman of the First National Bank of Westport, founder of Staples High School and owner/operator of a lumber and hardware business with offices at National Hall and a fleet of commercial sailing vessels. The Saugatuck River was an active waterway in those days and this sailing fleet was berthed alongside National Hall. The building originally housed the First National Bank on the first floor, the local newspaper on the second floor, and the town's meeting hall on the third floor — hence its unofficial name, National Hall.

In 1884 the third-floor public space was converted into classrooms for a short while until Staples High School was completed. The third floor, with its panoramic views of the Saugatuck River, served as the town's location for graduations, dances, and theatrical productions, as well as public meetings. At the turn of the century, the large space was even used for basketball games and other athletic events. National Hall remained the focal point of Westport's business district and social scene until the 1920s. In 1926 the hall was sold for $25,000 (the National Bank had moved by then) and by 1929 the Connecticut State Police maintained offices in the building, sharing it with many of the first tenants. In 1946 the building was renovated and reopened as the Fairfield Furniture Store on all three floors. This business remained for 34 years, closing its doors in 1980.

In 1987 Arthur Tauck, president of Westport-based Tauck Tours, purchased the 120-year-old structure and began its meticulous, five-year, $15 million renovation. Local artists were recruited to do the elaborate stenciling and hand-painted decor throughout the structure. After taking a master class from the renowned English artist Lyn Le Grice, the local artists were assigned individual rooms and areas to work on. San Francisco–based artists John Wullbrandt and Jeff Patch, with Joszi Meskan Associates, supervised the local artists and are personally responsible for the hand-painted decor in several of the rooms, as well as the mural and interior artwork in the restaurant. One of the most notable features — and everybody's favorite — is the tiny elevator decorated with a trompe l'oeil library!

### *Great Places to Eat*

## Coffee An'
343 N. Main St.
203/227-3808

This is the end of the line for donut nuts! Go between 7 and 9 a.m., mingle with the crowds, and watch the regulars at the twin counters on either side of the store and at the seats along the front window. They've got their dunking-sipping-reading-the-paper-routine down to a science — you'd never guess there were so many ways to dunk and eat donuts! And take your appetite — there's no way you can eat just one!

*Connecticut*

The genius responsible for this morning ritual is Derek Coutouras, who starts cooking in the back room every morning at 4 a.m., working at the fry kettles, hanging freshly cooked donuts on dowels to cool, drizzling on the glaze and sprinkling sugar. Up front, Mrs. Coutouras and a team of speed-demon waitresses man the counters and cash register. They can barely keep up with the demand for chocolate, glazed, plain, jelly-filled and powdered-sugar donuts, but the real pièce de résistance is the cinnamon buns — about six inches wide and three inches high, veined with lodes of dark, sweetened cinnamon, with a faintly brittle glaze of sugar — a billowing, yeasty spiral too big for dunking or even picking up whole. It takes half an hour just to work your way through it, washed down with three or four cups of good coffee. To die for!

## 80 WILTON

### Wilton Antiques Shows
Managed by Marilyn Gould
MCG Antiques Promotions, Inc.
10 Chicken St.
203/762-3525

The most exciting antiques venue in the East … where more fine dealers show more notable antiques covering a broader spectrum of the

market and at a range of prices than can be found anywhere. These outstanding shows offer the opportunity for significant buying; making a trip to Wilton is always worthwhile. For a complete listing of show dates and locations call for brochure.

**Connecticut Trading Co.**
Old Ridgefield Road
203/834-5008

**Emelines Heirlooms**
200 Danbury Road
203/834-1148

**Vallin Galleries**
516 Danbury Road
203/762-7441

**Greenwillow Antiques**
26 Cannon Road
203/762-0244

**Escape Design**
436 Danbury Road
203/834-9774

**Old & New Collectibles**
146 Danbury Road
302/762-8359

**Simply Country**
392 Danbury Road
203/762-5275

**Frances Hills Antiques**
1083 Ridgefield Road
203/762-3081

**Forgotten Garden**
643 Danbury Road
203/834-0500

## 81 WINDSOR

**Nadeau's Auction Gallery**
184 Windsor Ave.
860/246-2444

**Patti's Treasures & Antiques**
73 Poquonock
860/687-1682

**Olde Windsor Antique Gallery**
184 Windsor Ave.
860/249-4300

**Great Eastern Antiques Gallery**
184 Windsor Ave.
860/724-0115

### *Great Places to Stay*

### Charles R. Hart House
1046 Windsor Ave.
860/688-5555
Rates: $65 and up
Web site: www.ntplx.net/~harthous
Directions: Take I-91 north or south to Exit 36. Proceed east on Route 178 to Route 159 (7/10 mile). Turn right on Route 159 south, proceed 1/5 mile to Country Lane on the left, enter the first driveway on the left.

Tucked away in Connecticut's oldest town, the Charles R. Hart House was first constructed as a simple farmhouse. It was later added to and embellished with Queen Anne fixtures and appointments. In 1896 Charles R. Hart, a well-known Hartford merchant, carefully restored the house in the Colonial Revival–style by adding luxurious Lincrustra wall coverings, ceramic-tiled fireplaces and an elegant Palladian window. The Hart family maintained ownership until the 1940s, when it became the homestead for a pheasant farm! Today it has been fully restored and furnished with period antiques, including an extensive collection of clocks.

## 82 WINSTED

**Laurel City Coins & Antiques**
462 Main St.
860/379-0325

**Verde Antiques & Books**
64 Main St.
860/379-3135

## 83 WOODBURY

### Wayne Pratt, Inc.
346 Main St. S.
203/263-5676
Open: Daily 10–5, Sun. 12–5

Wayne Pratt, owner of Wayne Pratt Antiques, has long been recognized as one of the most prestigious antique dealers in America and abroad. On occasion, you may find Wayne exhibiting his wonderful "finds" at upscale antique shows across the country. On any other day, you can visit his showroom where you are assured of finding authentic and distinctive pieces of furniture, silver, rugs, art, porcelains, decorative lamps and other antique accessories.

# Connecticut

## David A. Schorsch
American Antiques
244 Main St.
203/263-3131

Specializing in period American antiques.

**Art & Peggy Pappa's Antiques**
113 Main St. S.
203/266-0374

**Gothic Victorian Antiques**
137 Main St. S.
203/263-0398

**Tucker Frey Antiques**
451 Main St. S.
203/263-5404

**Frank Jensen Antiques**
142 Middle Road Turnpike
203/263-0908

**Country Bazaar**
451 Main St. S.
203/263-2228

**Country Loft**
557 Main St. S.
203/266-4500

**British Country Antiques**
50 Main St. N.
203/263-5100

**Woodbury Antiques**
745 Main St. N.
203/263-5611

**Mill House Antiques**
1068 Main St. N.
203/263-3446

**Monique Shay Antiques**
920 Main St. S.
203/263-3186

**Antiques on the Green**
6 Green Circle
203/263-3045

**Joel Einhorn**
819 Main St. N.
203/266-9090

**Eagle Antiques**
615 Main St. N.
203/266-4162

**Madeline West Antiques**
373 Main St. S.
203/263-4604

**Carriage House**
403 Main St. S.
203/266-4021

**G. Sergeant Antiques**
88 Main St. N.
203/266-4177

**Daria of Woodbury**
82 Main St. N.
203/263-2431

**Taylor Manning Antiques**
107 Main St. N.
203/263-3330

**Harold E. Cole Antiques**
Middle Quarter Road
203/263-4909

**Jenny Lynn Shop**
113 Main St. S.
203/263-0284

**Nancy Fierberg Antiques**
289 Main St. S.
203/263-4957

**Rosebush Farm Antiques**
267 Good Hill Road
203/266-9114

**Rosebush Farm Antiques**
289 Main St. S.
203/266-9115

**West Country Antique**
234 Washington Road
203/263-5741

**Grass Roots Antiques**
12 Main St. N.
203/263-3983

*Nearby Antique Shopping (Roxbury)*
*Roxbury is 5 miles southwest of Woodbury.*

## Charles Haber Antiques
Routes 67 & 317
860/354-1031
Open: Thurs.–Sat. 11–5, Sun.1–5
Directions: Minutes from I-84 at Exit 15.

A distinctive selection of 18th- and 19th-century Americana, displayed in Roxbury's historic Phineas Smith House.

### Visiting Historic Lighthouses of Connecticut

Living in a lighthouse ranks right up there with running away to join the circus. Although automation has replaced the jobs of lighthouse keepers, many lighthouses of all shapes and sizes can still be found in Connecticut.

**Old Lighthouse Museum,** Stonington. A photographic journey to other lighthouses is among the exhibits in the Stonington light station on the east side of the harbor. The stone tower and the keeper's house attached to it were built in 1840.

**Sheffield Island Lighthouse,** South Norwalk. The slate-roofed granite lighthouse, on a 53-acre island bird sanctuary, has ten rooms on four levels that you can explore. A picnic area outside and regular ferry service to the island make the adventure even more fun.

Several boat operators, such as Captain John's of Waterford/Old Saybrook, provide harbor tours and visits to lighthouses.

The **New London Ledge Light,** a mile offshore at the entrance to New London's harbor, is among other lighthouses that can be reached by boat. Its beacon and eerie foghorns are automated now, but local legend says that the ghost of an old lighthouse keeper still keeps watch there.

The **New London Light,** at the entrance to the harbor, is the fifth-oldest in the country, dating from 1760. The original building was replaced by the present structure, an 80-foot octagonal tower, in 1801. Its Fresnel lens, now automated, has flashed its warning signals since before the Civil War.

Other lighthouses a short boat ride away from New London are at Great Captain Island, off Greenwich; Penfield Reef, off Fairfield; Stratford Shoal, off Stratford; Southwest Ledge, off New Haven, and Morgan Point, off Noank.

**Avery Point Light,** on the Groton campus of the University of Connecticut, was built in 1941 and was never lit. It services the Coast Guard today as a research and development center, finding ways to make every lighthouse do its job better.

For additional information, call: 1-800-CT-BOUND, 1-800-282-6863.

# Delaware

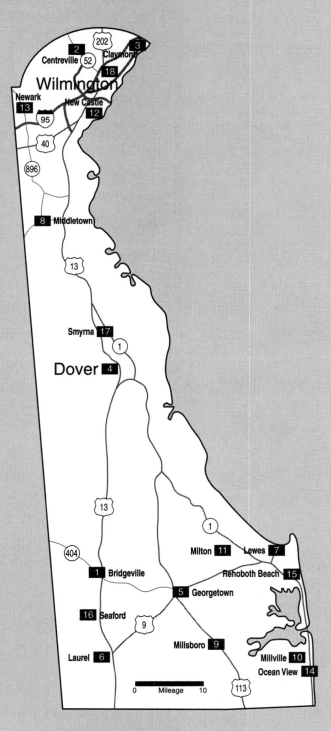

2 Centreville
202
52 Claymont 3
18
Wilmington
Newark
13 New Castle
95 12
40
896
8 Middletown
13
Smyrna 17
1
Dover 4
13
1
Milton 11 Lewes 7
404
Rehoboth Beach 15
1 Bridgeville
5 Georgetown
16 Seaford
9
Millsboro 9
Laurel 6
Millville 10
Ocean View 14
0  Mileage  10
113

# Delaware

## 1 BRIDGEVILLE

**Affordably Yours**
Route 404
302/337-9747

**Arts Antique Alley**
Route 13
302/337-3137

**Bridgeville Emporium**
105 Market St.
302/337-7663

**Pioneer Antiques**
111 Market St.
302/337-3665

## 2 CENTREVILLE

**Twice Nice Antiques**
5714 Kennett Pike R
302/656-8881

**Barbara's Antiques & Books**
5900 Kennett Pike Route 52
302/655-3055

## 3 CLAYMONT

**AAA Claymont Antiques**
2811 Philadelphia Pike
302/798-1771

**Lamb's Loft**
16 Commonwealth Ave.
302/792-9620

## 4 DOVER

**Ancestors, Inc.**
1025 S. Dupont Hwy.
302/736-3000

**Delaware Made**
214 S. State St.
302/736-1419

**Dover Antique Mart**
4621 N. Dupont Hwy.
302/734-7844

**Then Again**
28 W. Loockerman St.
302/734-1844

**Paul's Antique Furniture**
4304 N. Dupont Hwy.
302/734-2280

**Antiques Art & Collectibles**
329 W. Loockerman St.
302/736-0739

**Kilvington Antiques**
103 S. Bradford St.
302/734-9124

**Harmics Antique Gallery**
5409 N. Dupont Hwy.
302/736-1174

**Robert's Antique Lamps**
2035 S. Dupont Hwy.
302/697-3414

**Flamm Antiques**
1958 Mitten St.
302/734-5623

## 5 GEORGETOWN

**Bailey's Bargains**
Route 113
302/856-2345

**Brick Barn Antiques**
Route 9
302/684-4442

**Candlelight Antiques**
406 N. Dupont Hwy.
302/856-7880

**Collector's Corner**
101 E. Market St.
302/856-7006

**Gas Station**
546 N. Dupont Hwy.
302/855-1127

**Georgetown Antiques Market**
105 E. Market St.
302/856-7118

**Passwaters Antiques**
6 Primrose Lane
302/856-6667

**Generations Antiques**
Route 9
302/856-6750

## 6 LAUREL

Front Street is Laurel's oldest street, following an old Indian trail along Broad Creek. The town was plotted in 1802 after the sale of the Indian reservation that had occupied much of the land. The town was named for the abundance of laurel growing in nearby woods. Today it is the site of a rapidly expanding flea market — the largest in Delaware — that complements the traditional farmers' markets and auctions of the region. Laurel is the site of an annual Watermelon Festival.

**O'Neal's Antiques**
Route 13 & 466
302/875-3391

**Delmar Antiques**
Route 13
302/875-2200

**Golden Door**
214 E. Market St.
302/875-5084

**Bargain Carnival**
310 N. Central Ave.
302/875-1662

## 7 LEWES

Settled by the Dutch in 1631, Lewes (pronounced "Lewis") is Delaware's oldest settlement and is located on the Delaware Bay rather than on the Atlantic Ocean. Known for its fishing marinas, Lewes is also the southern terminal of the Cape May–Lewes Ferry that crosses the mouth of the bay between Delaware and New Jersey. Lewes is the site of an enclave of historic buildings and homes, many carefully restored (see Lewes Historical Complex below).

**Heritage Antique Mall**
130 Hwy. One
302/645-2309

**Classic Country Antiques**
Route 9
302/684-3285

**Antique Corner Downtown**
142C Second St.
302/645-7233

**Auntie M's Emporium**
116 W. 3rd St.
302/644-1804

**Auntie M's Emporium**
203B Second St.
302/644-2242

**Art & Antiques**
130 Hwy. One, Booth #8
302/645-2309

**Old & Gnu Antiques**
1503 Hwy. One N.
302/645-8080

**Swan's Nest**
107 Kings Hwy.
302/845-8403

**G. C. Vernon Fine Art**
1566 Hwy. One N.
302/645-7905

**Jewell's Antique & Jewelry**
118 2nd St.
302/645-1828

**Lewes Mercantile Antique Gallery**
109 2nd St.
302/64-7900

*Delaware*

## 8 MIDDLETOWN

**Butler & Cook Antiques**
13 E. Main St.
302/378-7022

**Daniel Bennett Shutt, Inc.**
123 W. Main St.
302/378-0890

**G. W. Thomas Antiques**
2496 N. Dupont Pkwy.
302/378-2414

**MacDonough Antique Center**
2501 N. Dupont Pkwy.
302/378-0485

## 9 MILLSBORO

**Antique Alley**
225 Main St.
302/934-9841

**Millsboro Bazaar**
238 Main St.
302/934-7413

**Antique Mall of Millsboro**
401 W. Dupont Hwy.
302/934-1915

## 10 MILLVILLE

**Hudson's General Store**
Route 26 & Road 348
302/539-8709

**Reflections Antiques**
Route 26
302/537-2308

**Great Expectations**
Route 26
302/537-6539

## 11 MILTON

**His 'n' Hers Lost & Found**
Route 1
302/645-4808

**Jailhouse Art Antiques**
106 Union St.
302/684-8660

**Pete's Antiques**
Route 9
302/684-8188

**Riverwalk Shoppe**
105 Union St.
302/684-1500

## 12 NEW CASTLE

New Castle, on the Delaware River just south of Wilmington, is an undiscovered jewel of the Eastern Seaboard. Cobblestone streets date from the Colonial era, as do the proud homes that line them. "A Day in Old New Castle" is held annually in May, and there are also Christmastime candlelight tours.

New Castle was founded by the Dutch on their way up the Delaware River. It was later settled by the Swedes and then by the British. In 1682, it was the first landing site in North America of William Penn.

**Opera House Antiques**
308 Delaware St.
302/326-1211

**Lynch Antiques/Caroline's Ginger Jar**
1 E. Second St.
302/328-5576

**Yesterday's Rose**
204 Delaware St.
302/322-3001

**Cobblestones**
406 Delaware St.
302/322-5088

**Raven's Nest**
204 Delaware St.
302/325-2510

### *Great Places to Stay*

### William Penn Guest House
206 Delaware St.
302/328-7736

Named in honor of Pennsylvania's Quaker founder, William Penn, this guest house was built in the same year of Penn's arrival in New Castle in 1682. In fact, Penn himself once stayed at the home as an overnight guest. Constructed of brick, this three-story building has been restored to its original architectural features, including wide-planked floors. Three guest rooms are available overlooking the green in the center of town. Revolutionary War sites, walking tours, shopping and dining are within walking distance.

### Armitage Inn
2 the Strand
302/328-6618

The Armitage Inn sets on the bank of the Delaware River only a few feet from the spot where William Penn first stepped into the new world. Built in 1732, the inn includes the main house, a wing, and a garden cottage. It is believed that the inn began life as a one-room dwelling built during the 1600s. The room was incorporated in an expansion in 1732. Within this room is an original brick walk-in cooking fireplace. Guest rooms are historically decorated and furnished with period antiques. Guests are welcome to enjoy the common areas including the parlor, library, screened porch and garden.

## 13 NEWARK

**Chapel Street Antiques**
197 Chapel St.
302/366-0700

**Main Street Antiques**
280 E. Main St.
302/733-7677

**Dee's Antiques & Collectibles**
323 Nonantum Dr.
302/369-3614

**Yesterdays Treasures**
2860 Ogletown Road
302/292-8362

**Austin Brown & Daughter**
201 W. Edgewater Way
302/738-9251

**Olde Tyme Antiques**
294 E. Main St.
302/366-8411

## 14 OCEAN VIEW

**Cinnamon Owl**
Route 26
302/539-1336

**Iron Age Antiques**
10 Central Ave.
302/539-5344

**Miller's Creek Antiques**
Route 26
302/539-4513

**Kennedy's Classics**
41 Atlantic Ave.
302/537-5403

**Seaford Antique Emporium**
323 High St.
302/628-9111

### 15 REHOBOTH BEACH

**Affordable Antiques**
4300 Hwy. One
302/227-5803

**Antiques Village Mall**
221 Hwy. One
302/644-0842

**Garage Sale Antiques**
1416 Hwy. One
302/645-1205

**Stuart Kingston, Inc.**
502 N. Boardwalk
302/227-2524

### *Great Places to Stay*

### Chesapeake Landing Bed and Breakfast

101 Chesapeake St.
302/227-2973

Nestled in a forest of pine and bamboo on the shore of Lake Comegy is Chesapeake Landing. This romantic and secluded setting feels like a mountain retreat or a tropical hideaway but is only steps from the Atlantic Ocean. A sparkling pool, gourmet breakfast, comfy fire, and poolside den contribute to a very special getaway. Sunset refreshments, lakeside dock, and a lifetime of collecting all add to a wonderful experience any time of the year. Four guest accommodations with private baths. $150–$225.

### Lighthouse Inn

20 Delaware Inn
302/226-0407

The Lighthouse Inn is located in the heart of Rehoboth Beach. This wonderful old house was built around the turn of the century and its location is ideal for those who enjoy leaving their car parked and touring the town. The Lighthouse Inn is one-half block from the beach and just blocks from all the fine restaurants and bars. A fabulous breakfast awaits you … the smell of freshly brewed coffee leads you to supreme continental cuisine served on the enclosed porch. Sunday brings a special treat with a hot breakfast consisting of eggs or waffles with topping, Vermont maple syrup, sausage or ham, assorted pastries, bagels, English muffins, cereal, yogurt, fresh fruit and more! The main house has six newly decorated rooms named for cities famous for lighthouses. The inn has a sitting room with fireplace, TV/VCR and a small library of movies. You can relax with your friends at day's end on the enclosed porch or by the fireplace.

### 16 SEAFORD

**Ann's Downtown Antiques**
324 High St.
302/629-0430

**Nelson's Antiques**
125 Pennsylvania Ave.
302/628-0966

### 17 SMYRNA

Smyrna began about 1700 as an English Quaker settlement called Duck Creek Village, one mile north of the current town. The Smyrna Landing wharfs were centers of commerce in the 1800s. Many examples of Federal and Victorian architecture can be found in the town. Smyrna is eight miles west of the Delaware Bay and Bombay Hook Wildlife Refuge.

**A Bit of the Past**
3511 S. Dupont Blvd.
302/653-9963

**Attic Treasures**
2119 S. Dupont Blvd.
302/653-6566

**Eileen Gant Antiques**
5527 Dupont Pkwy.
302/653-8996

**Smyrna Antiques Mart**
3114 S. Dupont Blvd.
302/659-0373

**Tin Sedan**
12 N. Main St.
302/653-3535

**C & J Antiques**
Route 13
302/653-4903

**What Nott Shop**
5786 Dupont Hwy.
302/653-3855

### 18 WILMINGTON

### Sheepish Grin, Inc.

Nancy and Bill Settel
Open: By appointment
302/995-2614
Fax: 302/995-2899

I first met Bill and Nancy at the Heart of Country Show in Nashville, Tennessee. For those of you who read about Sheepish Grin in last year's edition, I had mistakenly called Nancy's husband by the wrong name — George — instead of Bill. I want to set the record straight before the rumors start flying — Nancy was at that time and still is married to Bill. There has been no divorce and remarriage in the family, although Nancy jokingly says that George could be the name of her husband in her next life and that I'm just ahead of my time. Nonetheless, for now it's BILL. And BILL and NANCY are a great team.

They specialize in early painted country furniture and accessories such as old tins, iron, pantry boxes, rag dolls and primitive angels. They also are the manufacturers of the original Colonial Grunge Nubbie Candles (18th-century-looking candles). These candles are fabulous decorator items, and the Settels sell them wholesale to shops all over the world and to folks like me — I have 3 of each scent. (I still think Bill looks like a George.)

# Delaware

## "sweet potato cabin"

antiques and mighty fine folk art
Shop: 302/995-2614
Home: 302/995-1808
Open: By appointment
Directions: One block off I-95.

Nancy and Bill Settel, owners of the Sheepish Grin, have just opened one of the best shops, or should I say "warehouses," for early country furnishings in the U.S. and quiet possibly the world! Okay, so I'm getting a little carried away with that one, but their stuff is so wonderful! Sugar buckets, blanket chests, baskets, cupboards, cabinets and much, much more — most in original paint. An absolute must stop — but don't forget to call first.

**Golden Eagle**
1905 N. Market St.
302/651-3480

**Next to New Shop**
2009 Market St.
302/658-0020

**Brandywine Antiques**
2601 Pin Oak Dr.
302/475-8398

**Wright's Antiques**
802 W. Newport Pike
302/994-3002

**Merrill's Antiques**
100 Northern Ave.
302/994-1765

**Twice Nice Antiques**
5714 Kennett Pike
302/656-8881

**Brandywine Trading Co.**
804 Brandywine Blvd.
302/761-9175

**Impulse Antiques**
216 Main St. (Stanton)
302/994-7737

**Bellefonte Shoppe**
901 Brandywine Blvd.
302/764-0637

**Willow Tree**
1605 E. Newport Pike
302/998-9004

**Brandywine Treasure Shop**
1913 N. Market St.
302/656-4464

**Holly Oak Corner Store**
1600 Philadelphia Pike
302/798-0255

**Country Corner**
641 W. Newport Pike
302/998-2304

**Doyle Antiques**
601 S. Maryland Ave.
302/994-1424

**Resettlers Inc.**
5801 Kennett Pike
302/658-9097

**Barbara's Antiques & Books**
5900 Kennett Pike
302/655-3055

**Browse & Buy**
1704 Philadelphia Pike
302/798-5866

**Jackson-Mitchell, Inc.**
5718 Kennett Pike
302/656-0110

**Brandywine Resale Shop**
900 Brandywine Blvd.
302/764-4544

**La Femme Mystique Boutique**
Trolley Square Shopping Center
302/651-9331

## *Great Places to Stay*

**Darley Manor Inn**
3701 Philadelphia Pike
(Claymont Community)
302/792-2127,  or 1-800-824-4703
Web site: www.dca.net/darley/

The Darley Manor Inn located at 3701 Philadelphia Pike in Wilmington, Del., was once the home of America's most famous illustrator, Felix Darley. This 1790s Historic Register home features six suites decorated in classic Colonial antiques and reproductions. The North-South Writers' Suite features Civil War–period antiques and collectibles, including the porch rail from the Confederate White House in Richmond, Va. Additional suites are the Dickens or Cooper Room, overlooking the gardens and  lawn; the Darley Suite, named for the famous illustrator; the Irving Suite, located on the third floor and overlooking the backyard; and the Wren's Suite, the most private and largest of all the suites, providing a cozy fireplace and separate sitting room.

Situated in the beautiful wine country of Delaware, nearby Interstates 495, 95 and Route 202 give quick and easy access to Winterthur, Longwood Gardens, Brandywine Art Museum, Historic Philadelphia, good restaurants and great antique shopping.

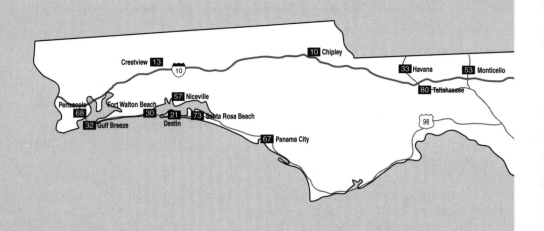

Crestview 13
10 Chipley
33 Havana
53 Monticello
80 Tallahassee
57 Niceville
Pensacola 68
Fort Walton Beach
30
21 73 Santa Rosa Beach
32 Gulf Breeze
Destin
67 Panama City
98

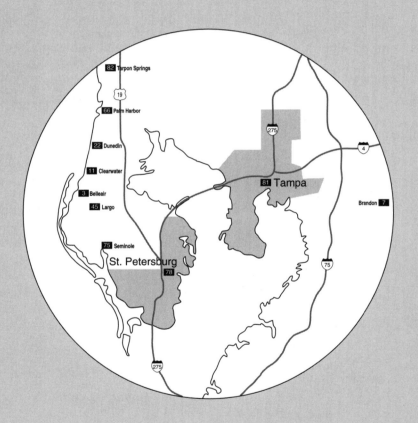

82 Tarpon Springs
19
66 Palm Harbor
275
4
22 Dunedin
11 Clearwater
81 Tampa
3 Belleair
45 Largo
Brandon 7
75 Seminole
St. Petersburg
78
75
275

*Florida*

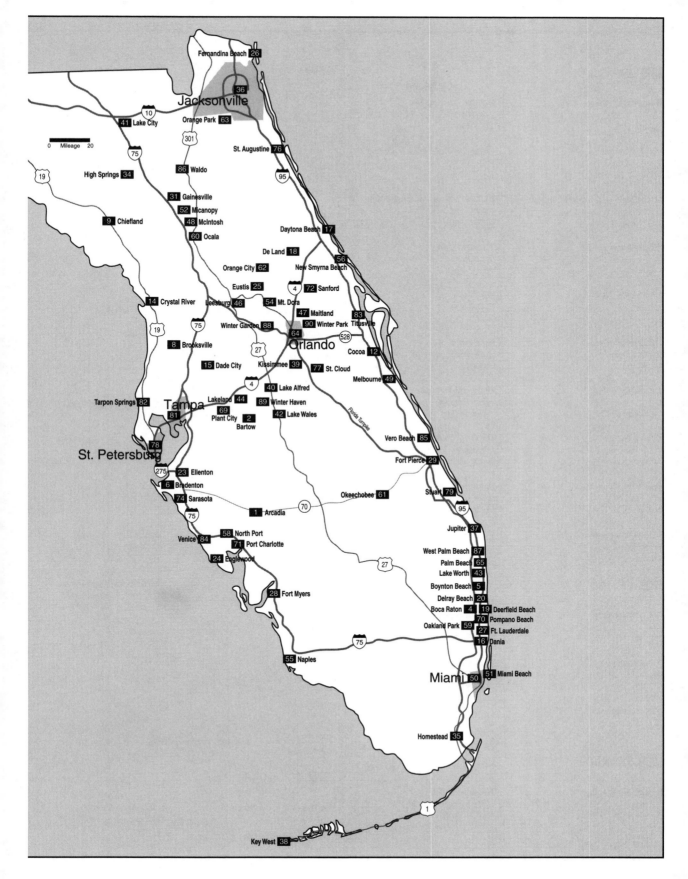

# 1　ARCADIA

**Townsend Antiques**
5 E. Oak St.
941/494-2137

**Maddy's Antiques**
101 W. Oak St.
941/494-2500

**Glacier Melt—Antiques & Unusuals**
114 W. Oak St.
941/993-4489

**Hidden Treasures**
33 W. Magnolia Hwy. 70
941/491-0060

**The Crested Duck**
121 W. Oak St.
941/491-8600

**The Collectors Addict**
109 W. Oak St.
941/993-2228

**Arcadia Tea Room**
117 W. Oak St.
941/494-2424

**Make It Yours**
37 W. Magnolia
941/494-6006

**Mainstreet Memories**
133 W. Oak St.
941/993-9300

**Kingston Antiques**
142 S. Monroe Ave.
941/491-5477

**Hitching Post Antiques**
24 W. Oak St.
941/993-9963

**Orange Blssm & Picket Fence Antqs.**
15 S. Polk Ave.
941/491-0008

**Old Opera House Mus. Antq. Mall**
106 W. Oak St.
941/494-7010

**Forgotten Things**
132 W. Oak St.
941/491-0053

**Mary's Attic**
12 W. Oak St.
941/993-2533

**My Friend & Me**
110 W. Oak St.
941/993-4438

**Three Amish Shoppe & More**
12 N. Desoto Ave.
941/993-4151

**The Corner Store**
2 W. Oak St.
941/993-2001

**Veranda Antiques**
305 W. Oak St.
941/993-0455

# 2　BARTOW

**Dolene's Downtown**
290 E. Main St.
941/534-3311

**Philip's Antiques**
330 E. Main St.
941/533-2365

**Bartow Antiques**
280 S. Wilson Ave.
941/534-1094

**Apple Blossom**
318 E. Main St.
941/534-1717

**Yates Antiques**
875 E. Main St.
941/533-7635

# 3　BELLEAIR

**Belleair Bluffs Antiques**
428 Indian Rocks Road N.
813/586-1488

**Treasures & Dolls**
518 Indian Rocks Road N.
813/584-7277

**Collum Antiques**
580 Indian Rocks Road N.
813/581-6585

**Royal Crown Antiques Etc.**
562 Indian Rocks Road N.
813/584-6525

**Encore Events**
562 E. Indian Rocks Road N.
813/585-7242

**Neil's Furniture/Antique Shop**
568 Indian Rocks Road N.
813/586-3232

**Jean's Locker Collectibles**
596 Indian Rocks Road N., #17A
813/585-8460

**Back Door Antiques**
596 Indian Rocks Road N.
813/581-2780

**Victoria's Parlour**
596 Indian Rocks Road N.
813/581-0519

**Music Box**
784 Indian Rocks Road N.
813/581-1359

**Provence Art & Antiques**
2620 Jewell Road
813/581-5754

**Posh Pineapple Antiques**
560 Indian Rocks Road N.
813/586-3006

**Merndale Antiques**
562D Indian Rocks Road N.
813/581-1100

**Lejan's Antqs. at Remember When**
570 Indian Rocks Road N.
813/586-7515

**Antiques & Specialities**
566 Indian Rocks Road N.
813/584-4370

**Elaine's Antiques**
596 Indian Rocks Road N.
813/584-6143

**Antiques & Design**
560 Indian Rocks Road N.
813/584-8843

**Belleair Coins**
730 Indian Rocks Road N.
813/581-6827

**Jewel Antiques Mall**
2601 Jewel Road
813/585-5568

# 4　BOCA RATON

**Village Rose**
7044 Beracasa Way
561/750-7070

**Art Nouveau Antiques**
6000 A Glades Road #168
561/347-2885

**C-Trois & Co**
2831 N. Federal Hwy.
561/347-1169

**Maybe Shop Antiques**
221 E. Palmetto Park Road
561/392-5680

**Country Pine**
161 N.W. 11th St.
561/368-8470

**Country Tyme Antiques**
672 Glades Road
561/391-7749

**Find a Deal Antiques Gallery**
2621 N. Federal Hwy.
561/362-9022

**Unusual Usuals**
2831 N. Federal Hwy.
561/367-6083

**Luigi's Objects D'Art Gallery**
6018 S.W. 18th St., Suite C9
561/394-4968

# 5　BOYNTON BEACH

**A & B Antiques & Collectibles**
2951 S.W. 14th Place
561/731-2213

**Consignment Shoppe**
411 E. Boynton Beach Blvd.
561/736-8767

# Florida

**Mrs. Hilda's Antique Shop**
524 E. Ocean Ave.
561/735-0333

**Red Tag Furnishings**
531 Ocean Ave.
No Phone Listed

**Pat's Accents**
528 E. Ocean Ave.
561/374-9040

**Treasures & Antiques**
640 E. Ocean Ave.
561/364-1272

## 6 BRADENTON

**Leach-Wells Galleries Antiques**
316 12th St. W.
941/747-5453

**Antiques on the Avenue**
2931 Manatee Ave. W.
941/749-1360

**Dotty's Depot**
1421 12th Ave. W.
941/749-1421

**George M. Hicks Antiques**
5206 Manatee Ave. W.
941/749-1866

## 7 BRANDON

**Nostalgia Station Antiques**
514 Limona Road
813/681-5473

**Somewhere in Time**
720 W. Lumsden Road
813/684-0588

**About Antiques**
728 W. Lumsden Road
813/684-2665

**Cottage Corner Antiques**
616 N. Parsons Ave.
813/654-2193

**Victoria's Attic Antiques**
714 W. Lumsden Road
813/685-6782

**Remember When Antiques**
408 N. Parsons Ave.
813/654-8323

**Sweet Memories Antiques**
608 N. Parsons Ave.
813/685-3728

**American Country Antiques**
745 Sandy Creek Dr.
813/681-9592

## 8 BROOKSVILLE

Brooksville, originally known as Melendez and then Benton, is a wonderful city of hills, ranging in elevation from 175 to 274 feet. Coupled with its condensed area (2.77 square miles) and its long history of successful planters, growers, and cattlemen, Brooksville is more a reflection of the "Old South" than other west coast towns. Its Southern background is reflected in its name, honoring South Carolina Congressman Preston Brooks, who is best noted for hitting abolitionist Senator Charles Sumner on the head with his cane.

**Barnette's Antique Mall**
2 N. Broad St.
352/544-0910

**Hillhouse Antiques**
406 E. Liberty St.
352/796-8489

**Red Rooster Antiques & Collectibles**
838 E. Jefferson St.
352/799-4636

**Antiques at the Corner**
10431 Broad St.
352/796-7518

**Cabin Creek Antiques**
770 E. Jefferson St.
352/799-8770

**Old World Antiques**
31 S. Main St.
352/796-2729

### Great Places to Stay

### Verona House
201 S. Main St.
1-800-355-6717
Web site: www.bbhost.com/veronabb

Verona House is a 1925 Sears and Roebuck catalog house in the Historic Downtown area of Brooksville. With picturesque tree-lined streets and rolling hills, Brooksville, unlike most of Florida, has many hills and canopied streets with large oak trees. Located in a small Southern town of 7,500 people and "a quiet getaway from the fast pace of city life," your hosts Bob and Jan Boyd will extend Southern hospitality and share with you the historical background of their town. There are four guests rooms decorated in cherished pieces, a fireplace and hot spa. Each morning enjoy Jan's fresh-baked casserole and muffin or bread, accompanied with fruit and juice. Canoeing, horseback riding, golf, tennis, antique stores, coffee houses and Roger's Christmas House are nearby. Special weekends are scheduled around local antique, craft and entertainment festivals.

### Interesting Side Trips

At Liberty and Saxon Avenue is the famous Roger's Christmas House, 103 Saxon Avenue. Mary Roger's Christmas gift shop has grown into an amazing complex of houses filled with decorations, displays, and attractions.

## 9 CHIEFLAND

**Kip's Trading Post**
914 N. Young Blvd. (U.S. 19)
352/493-1083

**Elaine's Treasure House**
1708 N. Young Blvd.
352/493-1306

## 10 CHIPLEY

### Historic Chipley Antique Mall
1368 N. Railroad Ave.
850/638-2535

Historic Chipley was settled in the 1880s as a railroad town and was named for Colonel Chipley, who built the railroad across the panhandle of Florida. The center of town is known as the Historic District and boasts vintage storefronts and meticulously restored buildings dating back to the 1800s.

This beautifully resurrected area is home to Historic Chipley Antique Mall. The mall is located in what once was the town mercantile store. The owners have restored the front of the building to resemble its appearance in a 1907 photograph.

Within this 10,000-square-foot mall over 50 dealers display an array of antiques and collectibles including Depression glass, pottery, flow blue

# *Florida*

and other fine porcelains as well as quality furnishings from several styles and eras.

The mall promotes special events throughout the year such as dealer day sales. This has become a very popular occasion among the many customers who frequent the mall. It's that one special day when the customer can deal one-on-one with the booth operator. Guest speakers often frequent the mall and Harry Rinker, distinguished author and lecturer, has been among the celebrity guests. Don't be surprised when you drop in to find the staff decked out in vintage attire.

## 11 CLEARWATER

**Able Antiques**
1686 Clearwater Largo Road
813/581-5583

**Pack Rat Corner**
617 Cleveland
813/443-2721

**Iron Gate Antiques**
703 Court St.
813/443-4730

**Antique Pine Imports**
13585 49th St. N.
813/572-0956

**Banyan Tree's Trunk**
1775 Clearwater Largo Road
813/587-0799

**Singletree Antiques**
1411 Cleveland
813/447-1445

**Savoy Antiques**
924 N. McMullen Booth Road
813/726-1111

## 12 COCOA

**Country Life**
313 Brevard Ave.
407/639-3794

**Antiques & Old Lace Mall**
1803 N. Cocoa Blvd.
407/631-5787

**Past Gas Co.**
308 Willard St.
407/636-0449

**Forget-Me-Not**
404 Brevard Ave., #A
407/632-4700

**Gould's Old Time General Store**
307 Delannoy Ave.
407/632-2481

## 13 CRESTVIEW

**Yesteryear's Attic**
1407 Ferdon Blvd. S.
850/682-9296

**Pappy T's**
388 Main St. N.
904/689-2323

## 14 CRYSTAL RIVER

**Heritage Antiques Mall**
103 N.W. U.S. Hwy. 19
352/563-5597

**Trader Jack's Antiques**
706 S.E. U.S. Hwy. 19
352/795-5225

**Crystal River Antiques**
756 N.E. U.S. Hwy. 19
352/563-1121

## 15 DADE CITY

**Ivy Cottage**
14110 7th St.
352/523-0019

**Church Street Antiques**
14117 8th St.
352/523-2422

**Sugarcreek Antiques**
37846 Meridian Ave.
352/567-7712

## 16 DANIA

**Mark First Antique Guns**
1 N. Federal Hwy.
954/925-0856

**Antique Jewels by Paula**
3 N. Federal Hwy.
954/926-1060

**Gallery Picture Frames, Inc.**
3 N. Federal Hwy.
954/920-2086

**Linda's Antique Collectibles**
3 N. Federal Hwy.
954/920-2030

**Michael T. Pye**
3 N. Federal Hwy.
954/922-5467

**Crown Antiques**
10 N. Federal Hwy., #A
954/923-4764

**Memorable Moments Antiques**
15 N. Federal Hwy.
954/929-7922

**Cameo Antiques**
18 N. Federal Hwy.
954/929-0101

**Collectomania**
19 N. Federal Hwy.
954/926-7999

**Dania Antique & Jewelry Arcade**
19 N. Federal Hwy.
954/925-9400

**Glass Antique or Not**
19 N. Federal Hwy.
954/925-7667

**Cobblestone Alley Antiques**
657 Citrus Ave.
352/795-0060

**Remember When Antique Mall**
14129 7th St.
352/521-6211

**Corner Emporium**
14136 8th St.
352/567-1990

**Antique Center of Dania, Inc.**
3 N. Federal Hwy.
954/922-5467

**E & F Antiques & Collectibles**
3 N. Federal Hwy.
954/929-3119

**Goldie Kossow Antiques, Inc.**
3 N. Federal Hwy.
954/921-5569

**Madeleine France's Past Pleasures**
3 N. Federal Hwy.
954/921-0022

**Murray's Antiques**
3 N. Federal Hwy.
954/921-0470

**Lorraine's Collectibles**
13 N. Federal Hwy.
954/920-2484

**Rose Antiques**
17 N. Federal Hwy.
954/921-0474

**Athena Gallery**
19 S. Federal Hwy.
954/921-7697

**Daddy's Antiques & Collectibles**
19 N. Federal Hwy.
954/920-4001

**Doe's Treasures**
19 N. Federal Hwy.
954/923-3081

**Jackie's Fine Things**
19 N. Federal Hwy.
954/456-5655

**Antique Tony's & Furniture**
24 N. Federal Hwy.
954/920-4095

**Tamara's Treasures**
25 N. Federal Hwy.
954/927-1040

**The Garden Path**
27A N. Federal Hwy.
954/929-7766

**Aries Antiques**
47 N. Federal Hwy.
954/923-2239

**Grand Central Station**
47 N. Federal Hwy.
954/925-8181

**Davidson Antiques**
53 N. Federal Hwy.
954/923-8383

**Royal Red Antiques**
56 N. Federal Hwy.
954/925-6111

**Allison Jaffee Antiques**
60 N. Federal Hwy.
954/923-3939

**Antique Galleries Mall**
60 N. Federal Hwy.
954/920-2801

**Iris Fields of Dania**
60 N. Federal Hwy.
954/926-5658

**Scintillations Antiques Ltd.**
67 N. Federal Hwy.
954/921-8325

**Gordon's of London**
71 N. Federal Hwy.
954/927-0210

**Ambiance Antiques & Design**
19 N. Federal Hwy., Booth #7
954/925-9400

**A to Z Antiques**
11 N. Federal Hwy.
954/927-2707

**Barbra's Place, Inc.**
249 S. Federal Hwy.
954/927-8083

**Dick's Toys & Collectibles**
3 N. Federal Hwy.
954/922-5467

**Dania Antique Emporium**
25 N. Federal Hwy.
954/927-1040

**Pyewackett's Antiques**
26 N. Federal Hwy.
954/926-7975

**Attic Treasures**
32 N. Federal Hwy.
954/920-0280

**Audrey Arovas Antiques**
47 N. Federal Hwy.
954/920-0706

**Memory Lane**
52 N. Federal Hwy.
954/922-0616

**Beaudet Antiques**
56 N. Federal Hwy.
954/922-5040

**English Accent Antiques**
57 N. Federal Hwy.
954/923-8383

**Antique Fancies**
60 N. Federal Hwy.
954/929-4473

**Celia & Louis Kleinman Antiques**
60 N. Federal Hwy.
954/920-2801

**F & N Antiques**
63 N. Federal Hwy.
954/923-3910

**Wilburn's, Inc**
68 N. Federal Hwy.
954/922-3188

**Hattie's Antiques & Collectibles**
3 N. Federal Hwy.
954/929-4290

**Antiquety Farms Antiques**
6 N.W. 1st Ave.
954/925-0402

**Aunty Q's, Inc.**
27 N. Federal Hwy.
954/925-3446

**Connie's Place**
3 N. Federal Hwy.
954/922-5467

**Friendly Shoppers**
3 N. Federal Hwy.
954/922-5467

**Gary Slade**
47 N. Federal Hwy.
954/925-8181

**J. J. Haag, Ltd.**
3 N. Federal Hwy.
954/922-5467

**Murray's Antiques**
3 N. Federal Hwy.
954/921-0470

**House of Hirsch Antiques**
75 N. Federal Hwy.
954/925-0818

**Maurizio's Antiques**
8 N. Federal Hwy.
954/929-9954

**Talya's Antiques**
3 N. Federal Hwy.
954/923-6512

## 17 DAYTONA BEACH

### Bus Station Antique Mall
138 Ridgewood Ave.
904/239-0330
Directions: ¹/₂ block south of International Speedway Blvd.

Over 35 dealers offering a large selection of antiques and collectibles.

**Arlequin Antiques**
122 S. Beach St.
904/252-5498

**AAAB As Antiques**
114 S. Beach St.
904/252-1040

**Bagwell's Flowers & Antiques**
909 S. Ridgewood Ave.
904/257-4423

**Bagwell's Flowers & Antiques**
312 S. Peninsula Dr.
904/252-7687

**Browse About Shop**
6296 S. Ridgewood Ave.
904/322-6900

**Daytona Flea & Antique Market**
1425 Tomoka Farms Road
904/252-1999

**House of Gamble Antique Mall**
1102 State Ave.
904/258-2889

**Jerry's Antiques**
1311 Center Ave.
904/252-8952

**Kay's Antiques**
522 Seabreeze Blvd.
904/252-1656

**Let's Talk Antiques**
140 N. Beach St.
904/258-5225

**Maxwell Galleries**
228 Carswell Ave.
904/238-0076

**My Nanna's Antiques**
2008 Schultz Ave.
904/239-5992

**Olde Loved Things**
900 Ridgewood Ave.
904/252-7960

**Silver Coast**
222 E. Intl. Speedway Blvd.
904/252-5775

### *Great Places to Stay*

### Live Oak Inn
444 S. Beach St.
1-800-831-1871

Live Oak Inn stands where Mathias Day founded Daytona. Two carefully restored houses — both listed on the National Register of Historic Places (1871-81) — are among Florida's top-ten historic inns, and are the cornerstone of Daytona's historic district. Each of Live Oak Inn's 12 rooms celebrates one of the people or events which helped shape Florida's history. All rooms have private baths and either Jacuzzi or Victorian soaking tubs.

## 18   DE LAND

**Cratina's Frameshop & Antiques**
108 S. Woodland Blvd.
904/736-8392

**Rivertown Antique Mall**
114 S. Woodland Blvd.
904/738-5111

**Sylva's Antiques**
428 S. Woodland Blvd.
904/734-4821

**Estate Furniture**
114 N. Woodland Blvd.
904/740-1104

**Outhouse Antiques**
1765 N. Woodland Blvd.
904/736-1575

**Muse Book Shop**
112 S. Woodland Blvd.
904/734-0278

**De Land Antq. Mall/Temple of Time**
142 S. Woodland Blvd.
904/740-1188

**Angevine & Son**
2999 S. Woodland Blvd.
904/734-6347

**Our Hearts in the Country**
136 N. Woodland Blvd.
904/736-4528

**Florida Victorian Architecture**
112 W. Georgia Ave.
904/734-9300

## 19   DEERFIELD BEACH

### A Moment in Time Antiques & Collectibles
3575 W. Hillsboro Blvd.
954/427-7223
Open: Tues.–Sat. 10:30–5:30
Directions: From I-95 go to Hillsboro Blvd., then head west to Powerline Road in the Shoppes of Deer Creek.

Shellee grew up in the art business. Her dad was a third-generation art dealer, so it was only natural that she follow in his footsteps. In her shop, the art is carefully blended with a selection of other wonderful things. Her exquisite taste and flair for decorating are evident throughout this beautifully arranged store. In settings reminiscent of *Country Living* magazine, you'll find country, early American and painted furniture accented with pottery, copper pots, old tools, washboards and other old iron and rustic pieces. If you're not into country, there are plenty more offerings of Limoges, Royal Dalton, vintage jewelry and such.

### Hillsboro Antique Mall & Tea Room
1025 E. Hillsboro Blvd.
954/571-9988
Open: Mon.–Sat. 10–6, Sun. 12–5
Directions: 2 miles east of I-95 at Exit 37.

South Florida's largest antique mall featuring over 250 dealers.

**Absolutely Fabulous**
337 S.E. 15th Terrace
954/725-0620

**Antiques Unusual**
100 S. Federal Hwy.
954/421-8920

**Cove Cottage Antiques, Inc.**
1645 S.E. 3rd St.
954/429-0408

**Joyce M. Dudley Antiques**
839 S.E. 9th St.
954/428-8500

## 20   DELRAY BEACH

**Martha T. Bartoo**
430 E. Atlantic Ave.
561/279-0399

**Antique Buying Center**
1201 N. Federal Hwy.
561/379-7360

**Finders Keepers Antiques**
88 S.E. 4th Ave.
561/272-7160

**Estate Galleries**
1201 N. Federal Hwy.
561/276-0029

**Second Chance Emporium**
2101 N. Federal Hwy.
561/276-6380

**Antiques Plus**
130 N. Federal Hwy.
No Phone Listed

## 21   DESTIN

**Smith's Antique Mall**
12500 Emerald Coast Pkwy.
904/654-1484

**Antiques on the Harbor**
202 Hwy. 98 E. (near the Harborwalk)
904/837-6463

**Clements Antiques of Florida**
9501 U.S. Hwy. 98 W.
904/837-1473

## 22   DUNEDIN

**P. Kay's Downtown**
359 Scotland St.
813/734-1731

**Cindy Lou's**
330 Main St.
813/736-3393

**The Highlands**
362 Scotland St.
813/547-1637

**Vyctoria's**
365 Main St.
813/736-0778

## 23   ELLENTON

### Old Feed Store Antique Mall
4407 Hwy. 301
941/729-1379
Open: Mon.–Sat. 10–5 (closed Sun.)
Directions: From I-75, take Exit 43. Go west 9/10 mile on Hwy. 301. Turn left on 45th Ave.

You'll never guess where this shop got its name. Okay, so I gave you a hint. Somewhere in the early to mid-1920s, the Old Feed Store Antique Mall was just as its name implies, the old feed store in Ellenton. Today, you'll find no evidence of grains, seeds or beans. What you will find are 65 dealers displaying a wide selection of oak, mahogany and walnut furnishings, exquisite glass and crystal items, jewelry, mirrors, china and much more.

(The Gamble Plantation, a historic mansion and grounds is located approximately 200 yards from the mall.)

*Florida*

## 24 ENGLEWOOD

**Rujean's Collectibles Past & Present**
Corner Route 41 & Biscane Dr.
941/426-5418

**Linda's Charming Choices**
145 W. Dearborn St.
941/474-1230

**The Paisley Pelican Artisan & Antique Mall**
447-449 W. Dearborn St.
941/473-2055

**Coins, Jewelry & Antiques**
140 N. Indiana Ave. (S.R. 776)
941/475-4740

**A Bull in a China Shop**
395 W. Dearborn St.
941/474-5004

## 25 EUSTIS

**Cowboys**
120 N. Bay St.
352/589-1449

**Merry's Silver Vault**
32 S. Eustis St.
352/589-4321

**Old South Antique Mall**
320 S. Grove St.
352/357-5200

**Palm Village Shoppes**
100 E. Magnolia Ave.
352/589-7256

**Ye Olde Kracker House**
517 E. Orange Ave.
352/357-3291

## 26 FERNANDINA BEACH

One of America's few remaining unspoiled island paradises, Amelia Island is the southernmost of the chain of Atlantic-coast barrier islands that stretch from North Carolina to Florida. Its rich history, thirteen miles of uncrowded beaches, lush, natural setting, moss-covered oaks, unparalleled golf, boating, and fishing, stunning sunrises and sunsets, and friendly "locals" make it more than just a place for antiquing.

Birthplace of the modern shrimping industry, Fernandina Beach, located near the north end of the island, hosts its annual "Isle of Eight Flags Shrimp Festival" the first weekend of May. The event attracts hundreds of artists, artisans, and craftsmen from across the country — and more than 150,000 visitors — each year.

**Yesterday's Child**
14 N. 4th St.
904/277-0061

**Fleur De Lis**
14 S. 2nd St.
904/261-1150

**Eight Flags Antique Warehouse**
21 N. 2nd St.
904/277-7006

**Country Store Antiques**
219 S. 8th St.
904/261-2633

**Plantation Shop**
4828 First Coast Hwy.
904/261-2030

**Amelia Island Antique Mart**
1105 S. 8th St.
904/277-3815

### *Great Places to Stay*

**Addison House**
614 Ash St.
1-800-943-1604

The Addison House, located in the historic district of Fernandina Beach on beautiful Amelia Island, is a stunning circa-1876 home. The guest rooms feature private porches, and whirlpool tubs. Each afternoon beverages and homemade goodies are offered on the veranda overlooking the courtyard. The island offers the perfect getaway and the innkeepers, the Gibson family, are dedicated to providing a special place to stay. Special arrangements can be made for romantic desserts, picnic lunches, anniversary or honeymoon packages.

**Bailey House**
28 S. 7th St.
904/261-5390

Built in 1895 in historic Fernandina Beach on Amelia Island, the Bailey House, a Queen Anne Victorian home, is listed on the National Register of Historic Places. The wraparound porch, turrets, widow's walk, stained glass, heart pine floors, grand staircase, and six fireplaces all contribute to the charm. All five bedrooms, entrance hall, parlor and the dining room are decorated with authentic period furnishings.

### *Great Places to Eat*

**1878 Steak House**
"Authentic 19th-century atmosphere"
12 N. 2nd St.
904/261-4049

**Beech Street Grill**
"A *Jacksonville* magazine top 25 selection"
801 Beech St.
904/277-3662

**Brett's Waterway Cafe**
"A tradition in the making"
1 S. Front St. — at the foot of Centre St.
904/261-2660

# Florida

**The Cafe**
"At the Ritz-Carlton"
4750 Amelia Island Pkwy.
904/277-1100

**Captain Van's Seafood**
"Fresh-cooked seafood"
1214 Beech St.
904/261-5581

**The Crab Trap**
"Serving Fernandina Beach for over 15 years"
31 N. 2nd St.
904/261-4749

**DJ's Seafood Restaurant**
"Dining inside & out"
3199 S. Fletcher Ave.
904/261-5711

**Down Under Restaurant**
"Fernandina's freshest seafood with a spectacular view of the Intercoastal"
A1A at the Intercoastal Waterway — under the bridge
904/261-1001

**The Florida House Inn**
"Serving the Florida traveler since 1857"
22 S. 3rd St.
904/261-3300

**The Golden Grouper Cafe**
"Fresh seafood — grilled, broiled, baked & fried"
5 S. 2nd St.
904/261-0013

**The Grill at the Ritz Carlton**
"Florida's only AAA five diamond restaurant"
4750 Amelia Island Pkwy.
904/277-1100

**Horizon's Continental Cuisine**
"Continental cuisine — casual elegance"
803 Ash St.
904/321-2430

**Island Bar-B-Q**
"Lewis Williams' original"
2045 S. Fletcher Ave.
904/277-3894

**Kabuki Japanese Steakhouse & Sushi Bar**
"Where the show is good … and the food is great!"
18 N. 2nd St.
904/277-8782

**The Marina Restaurant**
"A 10-time *News-Leader* 'Best of the Best' selection"
18 N. 2nd St.
904/261-9976

**Pompeo's**
"Italian continental cuisine and seafood restaurant"
302 Centre St.
904/261-7490

**Shakespeare's Kitchen**
"A coffee house"
316 Centre St. (Upstairs)
904/277-2005

**Slider's Oceanfront Restaurant & Lounge**
"The seaside inn"
1998 S. Fletcher Ave.
904/261-0954

**The Southern Tip**
"A *Jacksonville* magazine top 25 selection"
A1A at Palmetto Walk Shopping Village
904/261-6184

## 27 FORT LAUDERDALE

**Carl Stoffer's Antiques**
3699 N. Dixie Hwy.
954/564-9077

**Gemini Antiques**
4117 N. Dixie Hwy.
954/563-9767

**Jim's Antiques Ltd.**
1201 N. Federal Hwy.
954/565-6556

**June Sharp Antiques**
3000 N. Federal Hwy.
954/565-8165

**Lilywhites Antiques & Interior**
3020 N. Federal Hwy.
954/537-9295

**Down East Antiques**
3020 N. Federal Hwy.
954/566-5023

**Malouf Tower Antiques**
2114 S. Federal Hwy.
954/523-5511

**Teddy Bear Antiques**
4136 S.W. 64th Ave.
954/583-7577

*Florida*

| | |
|---|---|
| **Antiques Limited**<br>2125 S. Federal Hwy.<br>954/525-3729 | **Glausiers Antiques**<br>2130 S. Federal Hwy.<br>954/524-3524 |
| **Las Olas Arts & Antiques**<br>611 E. Las Olas Blvd.<br>954/527-2742 | **Coo-Coo's Nest**<br>1511 E. Las Olas Blvd.<br>954/524-2009 |
| **Lomar Collectibles**<br>3291 W. Sunrise Blvd.<br>954/581-1004 | **Victorian Reflections, Inc.**<br>1348 Weston Road<br>954/389-4498 |
| **Perry & Perry**<br>3313 N.E. 33rd St.<br>954/561-7707 | **Nostalgia Mall**<br>2097 Wilton Dr.<br>1-888-394-7233 |

### *Great Places to Stay*

## Caribbean Quarters

3012 Granada St.
954/523-3226

Nestled just a few yards from the heart of Fort Lauderdale's famous promenade and beach, this exquisite setting offers a very high degree of comfort and service that would enchant the most discerning of travelers. The interior setting boasts 16-inch pillow-top mattresses with well-ventilated rooms, decorated in light shades of pastels and Caribbean colors, and comfortable wicker and rattan furnishings. Built in 1939 and totally renovated in 1998, this superior, luxury bed and breakfast captures the romantic charm of a bygone era. The small, intimate, three-story property embraces all the southern Florida and Caribbean architectural qualities for which southern Florida was famous for in the late '30s and early '40s. All units are nonsmoking, fully air-conditioned and have private bathrooms, direct-dial phones with duel jacks for computers or fax machines, remote-controlled color TV with VCR, guest movie library, coffee maker and daily maid service. Some units offer private balconies, living room and full kitchen facilities. The tropical courtyard features a hot tub/Jacuzzi, sun deck, patio, barbeque grills, shuffleboard, Ping-Pong table, darts and numerous other games. An extended continental breakfast is so extensive that a menu is required.

## 28  FORT MYERS

| | |
|---|---|
| **Old Times Antiques**<br>1815 Fowler St.<br>941/334-7200 | **Yesterday & Today**<br>1609 Hendry St.<br>941/334-6572 |
| **Flowers to Fifties**<br>2229 Main St.<br>941/334-2443 | **Margie's Antique Market Place**<br>2216 Martin Luther King Blvd.<br>941/332-3321 |
| **Heartland Antiques**<br>12680 McGregor Blvd.<br>941/482-3979 | **Valerie Sanders Antiques**<br>12680 McGregor Blvd.<br>941/433-3229 |

| | |
|---|---|
| **Blough's Antiques**<br>12680 McGregor Blvd., #3<br>941/482-6300 | **Era Antiques**<br>12691 McGregor Blvd.<br>941/481-8154 |
| **Bayview Collectibles & Antiques**<br>12695 McGregor Blvd.<br>941/432-0988 | **Absolutely the Best Antique Empor.**<br>12695 McGregor Blvd., #1<br>941/489-2040 |
| **Judy's Antiques**<br>12710 McGregor Blvd.<br>941/481-9600 | **George Brown Antiques**<br>12710 McGregor Blvd.<br>941/482-5101 |
| **Tit for Tat This & That**<br>12717-2 McGregor Blvd.<br>941/489-3255 | **Laura's Aura**<br>2218 1st St.<br>941/334-6633 |
| **Pappy Antique 'n' Good Junque**<br>1079 N. Tamiami Trail<br>941/995-0004 | **Bea's Antique Shop**<br>1535 N. Tamiami Trail<br>941/995-0130 |

## 29  FORT PIERCE

| | |
|---|---|
| **Frederick's Antiques**<br>2872 N. U.S. Hwy. 1<br>561/464-0048 | **Red Rooster Attic**<br>3128 N. U.S. Hwy. 1<br>561/466-8344 |
| **Treasure Coast Antique Mall**<br>4343 N. U.S. Hwy. 1<br>561/468-2006 | **Red Barn Antiques Mall**<br>4809 N. U.S. Hwy. 1<br>561/468-1901 |
| **Antiques Etcetera**<br>211 Orange Ave.<br>561/464-7300 | **Olde Town Antique Mall**<br>116 N. 2nd St.<br>561/468-9700 |

## 30  FORT WALTON BEACH

| | |
|---|---|
| **King Arthur Classics**<br>30 Eglin Pkwy. S.E.<br>904/243-9197 | **Rose Harbor Interiors**<br>85A Eglin Pkwy. N.E.<br>904/664-0345 |
| **Garden Gate Antique Mall**<br>85B Eglin Pkwy. N.E.<br>904/664-0164 | **Fran's Treasure Trove**<br>167 A&B Eglin Pkwy. N.E.<br>904/243-2227 |
| **Willow Tree**<br>169B Elgin Pkwy. N.E.<br>904/243-4991 | **Abrams Antiques**<br>86 N. Eglin Pkwy.<br>904/664-0770 |
| **Bailey's Antiques**<br>136 Miracle Strip Pkwy.<br>904/244-2424 | **Darby Mitchell Antiques**<br>158 Miracle Strip Pkwy.<br>904/244-4069 |
| **White Sands Antiques**<br>161 Miracle Strip Pkwy.<br>904/243-6398 | **Country Junkshun**<br>1303 Beverly St.<br>904/864-4735 |
| **Abrams Antique Cottage**<br>147 Hollywood Blvd. N.E.<br>904/664-0011 | **Rose Garden Antiques**<br>151 A Elgin Pkwy.<br>904/243-2268 |
| **Fort Walton Beach Antique Mall**<br>167 Miracle Strip Pkwy. S.E.<br>904/243-6255 | **Magnolia Tree**<br>151 Eglin Pkwy. S.E.<br>904/244-2727 |

**Village Emporium**
149 Hollywood Blvd. N.E.
904/302-0111

**Li'l Darlings by JW**
100 Beal Pkwy. S.W.
904/244-2551

### 31  GAINESVILLE

**Browse Shop**
433 S. Main St.
352/378-5121

**Reruns**
807 W. University Ave.
352/336-0063

**My Mother's Place**
2441 N.W. 43rd St., #24A
352/376-4580

### 32  GULF BREEZE

### Kensington Market

4335 Gulf Breeze Pkwy.
850/934-3552

An upscale market featuring fine antiques and collectibles.

### 33  HAVANA

### Havana's Cannery

115 E. 8th Ave.
850/539-3800
Open: Wed.–Sun. 10–6, Fri. & Sat. 10–10

A 30,000-square-foot antique and collectible marketplace.

**Antique Center**
104 N. Main St.
850/539-0529

**Berry Patch**
117 6th Ave.
850/539-6988

**H & H Antiques**
302 N. Main St.
850/539-6886

**Antiques & Accents**
213 N.W. 1st St.
850/539-0073

**My Secret Garden**
127 E. 7th Ave.
850-539-8729

**McLauchlin House**
201 W. 7th Ave.
850/539-0901

**Hallway Annex**
110 E. 7th Ave.
850/539-8822

**Sticks 'n' Stitches**
108 E. 7th Ave.
850/539-8070

**Kudzu Plantation**
102 E. 7th Ave.
850/539-0877

**Antique Center**
104 N. Main St.
850/539-0529

### 34  HIGH SPRINGS

In 1883 the Savannah, Florida, and Western Railroad was extended from Live Oak to Gainesville and a post office and railroad station were established under the name of Santaffey, which was the common spelling of the nearby Sante Fe River. In 1888 the name was changed to High Springs and in the next few years the town prospered as a result of phosphate mining in the area. In 1893 the town was incorporated and the railroad completed its connection to Tampa. The community of High Springs was built and prospered because of the honest hard work of men and women who toiled on the railroad, in the mines, and in the fields.

In cooperation with the University of Florida, High Springs is now involved in the restoration of her downtown area. The two adjacent buildings which now house the Great Outdoors Trading Company and Cafe were restored in 1986. Built circa 1895, the trading company building was generally known as the Old Opera House. The bottom floor housed many different mercantile firms over the years and the top floor was where stage performances, silent movies, and dances were held. The cafe building was originally built as a barber shop circa 1915. (See the Great Outdoors Trading Company and Cafe listed under Great Places to Eat.)

**Bus Stop Antiques**
205 N.W. Santa Fe Blvd.
904/454-2478

**Burch Antiques Too**
60 N. Main St.
904/454-1500

**High Springs Antiques Center**
145 N. Main St.
904/454-4770

**Sophie's Antiques & Gifts**
215 N. Main St.
904/454-2022

**Wisteria Corner Antique Mall**
225 N. Main St.
904/454-3555

**Main St. Antique Mall**
10 S. Main St.
904/454-2700

**Palm Springs Antiques**
220 S. Main St.
904/454-5389

**Platz Antiques & Collectibles**
625 S. Main St.
904/454-4193

**Victorian Village**
1700 U.S. 441 S.
904/454-1835

**The Painted Lady Antiques**
30 N.E. 1st Ave.
904/454-5511

**Wendy's Treasure Chest**
280 N.E. 1st Ave.
904/454-0408

**Aristocratic Attic**
5 N.W. 1st Ave.
904/454-1496

**Apple Creek Mercantile**
55 N.W. 1st Ave.
904/454-2178

**Heartstrings**
65 N.W. 1st Ave.
904/454-4081

**A Step in the Past**
75 N.W. 1st Ave.
904/454-5389

### *Great Places to Stay*

### Grady House

420 N.W. 1st Ave.
904/454-2206

Built in 1917, the Grady House served as lodging for railroad workers at a time when the railroad was a major industry in High Springs. The name, derived from a long-standing High Springs family, was also home to many young married couples in the High Spring area. Today, this historic home is owned by innkeepers Ed and Diane Shupe. Ed's primary interest is art. He is especially proud of the Honeymoon Suite, which houses his collection of classic nudes. Diane enjoys cooking. The breakfast menu includes homemade scones, banana bread, herbed eggs and cheese grits. Fresh fruit is always included. She is also a CPA, so she tells the guests that she is the "bean counter" and Ed is the artist. She loves to read and dabbles in writing. She hopes to write a novel someday.

## The Rustic Inn
3105 S. Main St.
904/454-1223

Indulge yourself in solitude at the Rustic Inn nestled on a 10-acre ranch-style setting. Enjoy a stroll along the nature trails, take a dip in the pool, play cards, games, or just curl up and read a book from the library. Enjoy magnificent sunsets from the comfort of a rocking chair on the front porch. The Rustic Inn offers six rooms, each of which carries out an endangered-species theme.

### *Great Places to Eat*

## Great Outdoors Trading Company & Cafe
65 N. Main St.
904/454-2900

Try the oatmeal pancakes for breakfast, or maybe French toast with real maple syrup — just two of the many special treats offered here. For lunch choose from the extensive menu and daily chef's specials. The cafe offers a range of salads and vegetarian dishes for non—meat eating friends.

For dinner the atmosphere is casual, comfortable, and candlelit. Evening specials include dishes such as tofu Bombay, Mediterranean chicken or steak cooked the chef's very special way. At the end of a fabulous meal try a sinful homemade dessert with gourmet coffees or teas.

Once a week a musician plays for dinner and on weekends live music is heard in the "Old Opera House" upstairs. Before you leave be sure to visit the Great Outdoors Trading Company store where you'll find maps and guides, rock candy, chocolate, British candy, jams and jellies … even a kayak!

## 35 HOMESTEAD

**Bayleaf Peddler**
813 N. Homestead Blvd.
305/247-9200

**Albury Road Antiques**
115 N. Krome Ave.
305/242-1366

**Renaissance Interiors**
69 N.W. 4th St.
305/247-5283

**Book Nest**
115 N. Krome Ave.
305/242-1366

**Forever Antiques**
115 N. Krome Ave.
305/248-0588

**Yesterday's Memories**
115 N. Krome Ave.
305/247-0191

**Jo Crafton Antiques**
123 N. Krome Ave.
305/245-1700

**Cam's Antiques**
140 N. Krome Ave.
305/245-3320

**Autumn Leaf Cottage**
229 N. Krome Ave.
305/246-3513

**Cobblestone Antiques**
501 N. Krome Ave.
305/245-8831

**Ages Ago**
102 S. Krome Ave.
305/245-7655

**Sian San Antiques & Collectibles**
115 N. Krome Ave.
305/246-8010

**Time Line Vintage Clothing**
115 N. Krome Ave.
305/248-6511

**Crouse's Homestead Antiques**
137 N. Krome Ave.
305/247-5555

**Jacobsen's Antiques & Collectibles**
144 N. Krome Ave.
305/247-4745

**Roby's Antiques & Collectibles**
229 N. Krome Ave.
305/246-3513

**Antique Clocks & Gifts**
1316 N. Krome Ave.
305/247-9555

## 36 JACKSONVILLE

## Carriage House Antique Mall
8955 Beach Blvd.
904/641-5500
Open: Mon.–Sat. 10–6, Sun. 12–6
Directions: Located on Beach Blvd. at Southside Blvd.

Carriage House Antique Mall offers visitors that "Jack-of-all-trades" atmosphere with its spectrum of items and services. Once inside the mall, you can roam through aisles of glassware, including decanters, goblets, china, crystal, and depression pieces. A wide selection of collectibles and gifts are also housed within the mall.

## Bayard Country Store
U.S. Hwy. 1 S.
904/262-2548
Open: Thurs.–Sun. 10–5
Directions: 3 miles south of I-295 on U.S. Hwy. 1, halfway between Jacksonville and St. Augustine.

This three-story, 11,000-square-foot, 1905 hotel is now the home to over 20 dealers of antiques and collectibles.

## Avonlea Antiques
11260 Beach Blvd.
904/645-0806

Largest antique mall in the region, featuring the wares of 180 dealers within 100,000 square feet. Everything under the Florida sun in antiques, fine art and collectibles. Tearoom on the premises.

**Tappin Book Mine**
705 Atlantic Blvd.
904/246-1388

**Antique House**
1841 Dean Road
904/721-0886

**Somewhere in Time Antiques**
1341 University Blvd. N.
904/743-7022

**Springfield Antiques**
1755 N. Pearl St.
904/355-2897

**Little Shop of Antiques**
2010 Forbes St.
904/389-9900

**Ina's Antiques**
3572 Saint Johns Ave.
904/387-1379

**Frontier**
5161 Beach Blvd.
904/398-6055

**Uncle Davey's Americana**
6140 St. Augustine Road
904/730-8932

**White House Antiques**
214 4th Ave. S.
904/247-3388

**China Cat Antiques**
226 4th Ave. S.
904/241-0344

**Orange Tree Antiques**
4209 St. John Ave.
904/387-4822

**Interiors Market**
5133 San Jose Blvd.
904/733-2223

**Don's Antiques**
5121 San Jose Blvd.
904/739-9829

**Gallery of Antiques**
7952 Normandy Blvd., #1
904/783-6787

**Audrey's Attic at Five Points**
1036 Park St.
904/355-8642

**Olde Gallery**
3921 Hendricks Ave.
904/396-2581

**Canterbury House Antiques**
1776 Canterbury St.
904/387-1776

**Antiques Are Forever**
2 Independent Dr.
904/358-8800

**Judy Judy Judy**
1633 San Marco Blvd.
904/396-1537

**Grandma's Things**
5814 St. Augustine Road
904/739-2075

**Olde Albert's**
5818 St. Augustine Road
904/731-3947

**Shop of M. Miller**
1036 Park St.
904/384-3724

**Mary's Antiques**
597 S. Edgewood Ave.
904/389-1212

**Antique Wooden Horse**
6323 Phillips Hwy.
904/739-1008

**Annie's Antiques**
9822 Beach Blvd.
904/641-3446

**Lovejoy's Antique Mall**
5107 San Jose Blvd.
904/730-8083

---

*Great Places to Stay*

## Cleary-Dickert House
1804 Copeland St.
903/387-4003
Web site: members.aol.com/idjo/index.htm

Upon arrival at this stately mansion, you will be greeted by the owners — Joseph Cleary, who prides himself on being a true Englishman and his wife, the ebullient Southern lady Betty Dickert. Join them in getting acquainted in the warm, flower-decked porch overlooking the St. Johns River. Each suite (one award winning) consists of a separate sitting room, private bedroom and bath. Relax, have some tea, enjoy the warm and inviting atmosphere and smell the freshly cut flowers. In keeping with English tradition, each suite has facilities for a late night beverage. Join Betty and Joe in the formal dining room each morning for a delicious breakfast. The food varies from Southern to English gourmet recipes, complete with an assortment of breads and jams. If privacy is desired, breakfast may be served in your suite, upon request. An authentic English tea is brewed and served in the afternoon. Wine and cheese is also served.

## House on Cherry Street
1844 Cherry St.
904/384-1999

The House on Cherry Street is a beautiful Colonial home situated on the St. Johns River, decorated with period antiques, Oriental rugs, tall case clocks, a large decoy collection, baskets, pewter and numerous other unique collectibles. The home is a true "antiquers" dream getaway. Four guest bedrooms have woven coverlets and canopied beds, one twin room with private bath and three queen rooms with private baths, each with a sitting-room area.

## 37 JUPITER

**Axe Antiques**
275 AH A 1A (SR811)
561/743-7888

**Patricia Ann Reed Fine Antiques**
126 Center St., Suite B-7
561/744-0373

## 38 KEY WEST

**Wanted Store**
1219 Duval St.
305/293-9810

**Joseph's Antiques**
616 Greene St.
305/294-9916

**Commodore Antiques**
500 Simonton St.
305/296-3973

**Sam's Treasure Chest**
518 Fleming St.
305/296-5907

**China Clipper**
333 Simonton St.
305/294-2136

**Just Good Stuff**
1100 White St.
305/293-8599

*Florida*

## Blue Parrot Inn

916 Elizabeth St.
1-800-231-BIRD
Web site: blueparrottinn.com

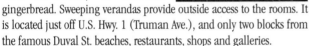

Key West and the Florida Keys are the only car-accessible islands of the Caribbean and the 3-hour drive from Miami is absolutely amazing: the Gulf on one side of the road and the ocean on the other. It is also the perfect setting for the Blue Parrot Inn which has been located in the heart of "Historic Downtown" Key West since 1884.

The inn is a relaxed, friendly home reflecting classic Bahamian charm with an overlay of Victorian gingerbread. Sweeping verandas provide outside access to the rooms. It is located just off U.S. Hwy. 1 (Truman Ave.), and only two blocks from the famous Duval St. beaches, restaurants, shops and galleries.

Morning comes with its own clean, tropical sweetness as you awaken to the sounds of Mozart, heliconia and softly whooshing palm fronds. Freshly brewed coffee and homebaked muffins are served by the pool. Evenings offer fond memories of paintbox sunsets and walks down Old Town lanes and historic alleys under the spell of a tropical moon. And after everything, the quiet comfort of the Blue Parrot Inn awaits where sweet dreams are only a prelude to an even sweeter tomorrow.

## Heron House

512 Simonton St.
1-800-294-1644
Web site: www.heronhouse.com

Heron House is a bit of a half-breed — it possesses all of the charm of a Key West guesthouse, while at the same time, it is operated with all the professionalism of a small luxury hotel. It consists of four historical buildings with 23 rooms total. One of the oldest homes was built in 1856 and represents one of the few remaining examples of "Conch Architecture" in Key West, and is in fact, the oldest house on Simonton Street. The innkeepers Fred Geibelt and Robert Framarin have gone out of their way to bypass the ordinary at this fabulous Key West getaway.

Stained glass transoms above beautiful French doors invite you into your accommodations, where cool tile floors, granite baths and custom "signature walls" in teak, oak or cedar await. Private decks and balconies merge with private gardens to allow interior and exterior spaces to blend. Multilevel decks provide areas to sun, to lounge, or to just enjoy the beauty of your surroundings.

You should not miss a stroll through the tropical gardens and take in the beauty of the hand-grown, rare orchids set amid the trees.

## William Anthony House

P.O. Box 107
1-800-613-2276
Web site: www.WmAnthonyHse.com

This beautifully renovated historic inn is the winner of two awards for preservation and new construction. Four luxury suites, one with separate bedroom, and two guest rooms are available. Suites have sitting and dining areas. A spa, lovely gardens and pond, porches and decks offer the opportunity to relax and appreciate the warm Florida weather.

## 39  KISSIMMEE

**Euro Classics**
3645 Old Dixie Hwy.
407/846-2122

## 40  LAKE ALFRED

| **Biggar Antiques** | **Potpourri Antiques** |
|---|---|
| 140 W. Haines Blvd. | 144 W. Haines Blvd. |
| 941/956-4853 | 941/956-5535 |
| **Picket Fence** | **Barn Antiques** |
| 135 E. Pierce St. | State Road 557 |
| 941/956-3471 | 941/956-1362 |

## 41  LAKE CITY

## Webb's Antique Mall

I-75 at Exit 80
904/758-9280
Open: Mon.–Sun. 9–6

Florida's largest antiques mall, with over a half mile of showcases filled with rare collectibles. Over 150,000 square feet of fine antique furniture and smalls.

## Marion St. Mini-Mall

315 Marion St.
904/752-3550
Open: Mon.–Sat. 10–5

A large selection of coins and stamps, over 100,000 old picture postcards, 15,000 back-issue comics, 3,000 old phonograph records, sports cards, non–sports cards.

| **Britannia Antiques** | **Nancy's Antiques** |
|---|---|
| Hwy. 90 | 412 N. Marion St. |
| 904/755-0120 | 904/752-0272 |

**Remember When**
420 N. Marion St.
904/755-6007

**Antiques Antiques**
4447 U.S. Hwy. 90, Suite 1
904/758-4744

## 42 LAKE WALES

**Inglenook Antiques & Collectibles**
3607 Alt. 27 N.
941/678-1641

**Liberty Antiques**
130 E. Park Ave.
941/678-0730

**Bruce's Antiques**
201 N. Scenic Hwy.
941/676-4845

## 43 LAKE WORTH

**Mickey's Antiques**
12 S. J St.
561/582-7667

**P & G Antiques**
702 Lake Ave.
561/547-6326

**Tuesday Gallery**
705 Lake Ave.
561/586-1180

**Yesterday's Antique Mall**
716 Lake Ave.
561/547-3816

**Antique Palace**
808 Lake Ave.
561/582-8803

**Heritage Antiques**
621 Lake Ave.
561/588-4755

## 44 LAKELAND

**Agape Antique Center**
243 N. Florida Ave.
941/686-6882

**Celebration Gallery**
1037 S. Florida Ave., #106
941-686-9999

**Peacock Antiques**
234 N. Kentucky Ave.
941/686-7947

**The Pink Magnolia**
202 Duval St.
904/752-4336

**Bittersweet Memories**
113 E. Park Ave.
941/676-4778

**Once Upon a Tyme Antiques**
201 N. Scenic Hwy.
941/676-0910

**Wisteria Cottage**
229 E. Stuart, Suite 11
941/676-6730

**Ada's Olde Towne Antique Mall**
25 S. J St.
561/547-1700

**Lake Avenue Antiques**
704 Lake Ave.
561/586-1131

**Hawkins Antiques & Art**
712 Lake Ave.
561/582-4215

**Roussos & Sons Antiques**
801 Lake Ave.
561/585-2100

**Carousel Antiques Center**
813 Lake Ave.
561/533-0678

**Silver Cloud Shop**
701 N. Florida Ave.
941/687-4696

**Somewhere in Time — Nonstalgia**
1715 S. Florida Ave.
941/688-9472

**A. Keslinger Antiques Complex**
244 N. Kentucky Ave.
941/683-4444

**Sissy's Gallery**
314 N. Kentucky Ave.
941/687-6045

**Bubba's Country Store**
3720 County Line Road
941/647-5461

**Roger A. Cheek Gallery**
218 E. Pine St.
941/686-5495

**Reflections of the Past**
215 Traders Alley
941/682-0349

## 45 LARGO

**Nearly New Shop**
623 W. Bay Dr.
813/586-2196

**Details**
1260 W. Bay Dr.
813/585-6960

**Country Village**
11896 Walsingham Road
813/397-2942

## 46 LEESBURG

### Morning Glori Antique Mall
1111 S. 14th St. (Hwy. 27)
352/365-9977
Open: Mon.–Sat. 10–6, Sun. 12–4

Located in over 7,500 square feet of nostalgia comfort, features 60 dealers offering antique furniture, pottery, art, quilts, jewelry, paper and lots of primitives.

### Smith's Antiques
717 W. Main St.
352/787-1102

French, traditional and Art Deco furnishings, loads of glassware, china, chandeliers, Quimper and select period pieces.

**Leesburg Antique Mall**
403 W. Main St.
352/323-3396

**Mademoiselle Antiques**
1406 W. Griffin Road
352/787-3351

**Mary's Treasure Chest**
2300 W. Main St.
352/326-3181

**My Cottage Garden**
327 N. Kentucky Ave.
941/688-9686

**Frog Pond**
3403 Providence Road
941/858-1979

**Casey Lynn Antiques**
214 Traders Alley
941/682-2857

**Time & Again**
814 W. Bay Dr.
813/586-3665

**Brenda's Styling**
39 Clearwater Largo Road
813/582-9839

**T & T Antiques**
12790 66th St. N.
813/531-8072

**Victorian Rose**
415 W. Main St.
352/728-8388

**Ruth's Antiques**
1223 W. Main St.
352/787-7064

**Curiosity Shop**
1310 N. Shore Dr.
352/365-6555

**Almost Antiques**
125 W. Main St.
352/315-9929

**Reminisce Antiques**
1012 W. Main St.
352/326-8322

### 47 MAITLAND

**Cranberry Corners**
203 E. Horatio Ave.
407/644-0363

**Pence & Pound House**
630 S. Maitland Ave.
407/628-4911

**Bestenwurst Antiques**
145 S. Orlando Ave.
407/647-0533

**Halley's Antiques Mall**
473 S. Orlando Ave.
407/539-1066

### 48 McINTOSH

**Creekside Antiques/Collectibles**
Hwy. 441 & Ave. E
352/591-4444

**Book Barn/O. Brisky's**
Hwy. 441 & Ave. F
352/591-2177

**Fort McIntosh Armory**
Hwy. 441 & Ave. G
352/591-2378

**Harvest Village**
22050 N. U.S. Hwy 441
352/591-1053

### 49 MELBOURNE

**Hometown Expressions**
712 E. New Haven Ave.
407/676-0692

**Born Again**
724 E. New Haven Ave.
407/768-8442

**Melbourne Antique Mall**
806 E. New Haven Ave.
407/951-0151

**Finders Keepers**
809 E. New Haven Ave.
407/676-5697

**Antiques Anonymous**
811 E. New Haven Ave.
407/724-5666

**Effie's Antiques & Collectibles**
819 E. New Haven Ave.
407/728-7345

**Red Lion Antiques**
821 E. New Haven Ave.
407/726-8777

**Eclectibles Unlimited**
825 E. New Haven Ave.
407/768-9795

**Just for You**
829 E. New Haven Ave.
407/768-2636

**Helen's Antique & Modern**
847 E. New Haven Ave.
407/723-8830

**Age of Elegance**
932 E. New Haven Ave.
407/728-8870

**Antique Mall & Collectibles**
3830 W. New Haven Ave.
407/727-1761

**Antique Connection**
568 W. Eau Gallie Blvd.
407/255-1333

**Betty's Antiques**
2001 Melbourne Court
407/951-2258

### *Nearby Antique Shopping (Grant)*
### *Grant is located 12 miles south of Melbourne.*

**River Breeze Antiques Mall**
5910 U.S. 1
407/726-6919
Open: Mon.–Sun. 10–5

There are 250 dealers inside this 19,000-square-foot mall with an array of antiques from A to Z. Well worth the stop.

**Mom's Antiques**
5680 U.S. 1
407/733-5536
Open: Mon.–Sun. 10–5

Old house with over 15 quality dealers.

**Grant Antique Mall**
5900 U.S. 1
407/726-6778
Open: Mon.–Sun. 10–5

5,000-square-foot mall with a little of everything in the way of quality merchandise.

### 50 MIAMI/NORTH MIAMI

**Aunt Hattie's Attic**
10828 N.E. 6th Ave.
305/751-3738

**Echoes of the Past Antiques**
12325 N.E. 6th Ave.
305/895-8462

**Len's 7th Ave. Antiques**
4950 N.W. 7th Ave.
305/754-5601

**Manetta's Antiques**
5531 S.W. 8th St.
305/261-8603

**J R Antiques**
5987 S.W. 8th St.
305/264-6614

**Harris Antique Shop**
8747 N.W. 22nd Ave.
305/693-0110

**Gloria's Place**
2231 S.W. 22nd St.
305/285-2411

**Antiques Paradise**
2371 S.W. 22nd St.
305/285-7885

**Escala Antiques & Gifts**
2385 S.W. 22nd St.
305/857-9955

**Ralph's Antiques**
3660 S.W. 22nd St.
305/441-1193

**Hidden Place**
1092 S.W. 27th Ave.
305/644-0469

**Arenas Antiques**
1131 S.W. 27th Ave.
305/541-0900

**Antique Center**
2644 S.W. 28th Lane
305/858-6166

**Charlotte's International**
2650 S.W. 28th Lane
305/858-9326

**ITO**
2685 S.W. 28th Lane
305/856-1361

**Antiques & Gifts by Roses**
6350 S.W. 40th St.
305/667-8703

**Well Design**
6550 S.W. 40th St.
305/661-1386

**Robin's Nest Antiques**
6703 S.W. 40th St.
305/666-7668

**Antiques & Tribal**
7165 S.W. 47th St., #B319
305/661-1094

**Suarez Graciela**
7209-7217 S.W. 48th St.
305/667-3431

**Pine Mine**
7262 S.W. 48th St.
305/663-4432

**Dietel's Antiques**
2124 S.W. 67th Ave.
305/266-8981

**1800's Antiques & Accessories**
4666 S.W. 72nd Ave.
305/668-9777

**Drummond of Perth Antiques**
4691 S.W. 72nd Ave.
305/665-3345

**Antiques & Country Pine**
4711 S.W. 72nd Ave.
305/665-7463

**Malina's Victorian Country**
4836 S.W. 72nd Ave.
305/663-0929

**Ideas & More, Inc.**
4467 S.W. 75th Ave.
305/265-8538

**Joylot Antiques**
921 N.E. 79th St.
305/754-9136

**Golden Era Antiques**
1640 N.E. 123rd St.
305/891-1006

**Dietel's Antiques**
6572 Bird Road
305/666-0724

**Twery's, Inc.**
160 N.E. 40th St.
305/576-0564

**Nostalgiaville**
6374 S.W. 40th St.
305/669-1608

**Beall's Antiques & Collectibles**
6554 S.W. 40th St.
305/663-2103

**Old Paris**
7125 S.W. 47th St.
305/666-7008

**Gloria Allison Antiques**
7207 S.W. 48th St.
305/666-3900

**Antiquario Fine Furniture**
7219 S.W. 48th St.
305/663-8151

**Gilbert's Antiques, Inc.**
7265 S.W. 48th St.
305/665-2006

**Ceramic by Design**
4664 S.W. 72nd Ave.
305/663-5558

**British Connection Antiques**
4669 S.W. 72nd Ave.
305/662-9212

**Bonnin Ashley Antiques, Inc.**
4707 S.W. 72nd Ave.
305/667-0969

**General Consignment**
4762 S.W. 72nd Ave.
305/669-0800

**General Consignment**
4215 S.W. 75th Ave.
305/261-3200

**Eclectique**
6344 Bird Road
305/666-7073

**F. & D. Lopez — Del Rincon Art**
803 82nd St.
305/861-5997

**Tania Sante's Classic**
6556 Bird Road
305/662-4975

**A & J Unique Antiques**
2000 Biscayne Blvd.
305/576-5170

**Spencer Art Gallerie**
4441 Collins Ave.
305/532-7577

**Alhambra Antiques Center**
3640 Coral Way
305/446-1688

**Oldies but Goodies**
17842 S. Dixie Hwy.
305/232-5441

**B & H Antiques**
12777 W. Dixie Hwy.
305/899-0921

**Victoria's Armoire Country**
4077 Ponce De Leon Blvd.
305/445-3848

**Olde Tyme Shoppe**
1549 1/2 Sunset Dr.
305/662-1842

**Valerio Antiques**
2901 Florida/Coconut Grove
305/448-6779

**Midori Gallery Antique**
3170 Commodore Plaza
305/443-3399

**Alba Antiques**
3656 Coral Way
305/443-5288

**Ye Olde Cupboard**
17844 S. Dixie Hwy.
305/251-7028

**Washington Square Antiques**
19090 W. Dixie Hwy.
305/937-0409

**Stone Age Antiques**
3236 N.W. South River Dr.
305/633-5114

**Antiques & Art**
10143 S.W. 79th Court
305/663-3224

### 51 MIAMI BEACH

**Collectors Art Gallery**
730 Lincoln Road
305/531-4900

**Bolero**
1688 Meridian Ave.
305/534-3759

**Circle Art & Antiques**
1014 Lincoln Road
305/531-1859

**Senzatempo**
815 Washington Ave.
305/534-8882

### 52 MICANOPY

**Smiley's Antique Mall**
I-75 at Exit 73, CR 234
352/466-0707
Open: Mon.–Sun. 9–6
Directions: 8 miles south of Gainesville off I-75, Exit 73.

    Longer than a football field, voted "Best of Best" mall in Florida. Need we say more?

**The Shop**
Cholokka Blvd.
352-466-4031

**Among the Ivy**
Cholokka Blvd.
352/466-8000

**House of Hirsch Too Antiques**
209 E. Cholokka Blvd.
352/466-3774

**Chateau Des Antiques**
Cholokka Blvd.
352/466-4505

**Delectable Collectibles**
Cholokka Blvd.
352/466-3327

**Baytree Antiques, Inc.**
Cholokka Blvd.
352/466-3946

**Sun Glo Farm Antiques**
16319 S.E. County Road 234
352/466-3037

**Antique Alley**
110 Cholokka Blvd.
352/466-0300

**Elena's Antiques**
206 E. Cholokka Blvd.
252/466-4260

**Micanopy Country Store**
108 Cholokka Blvd.
352/466-0510

**Savino's Antiques**
203 Cholokka Blvd.
352/466-3663

**Roberts Antiques**
208 Cholokka Blvd.
352/466-3605

## 53  MONTICELLO

### Southern Friends Antique Mall

I-10, Exit 33 (U.S. Hwy. 19)
904/997-2559
Open: Mon.–Sat. 10–6, Sun. 1–6
Directions: From I-10, take Exit 33 (U.S. Hwy 19).

The name suggests true Southern hospitality. Southern Friends Antique Mall opened its doors in March 1997 and has done a wonderful job of filling this 7,500-square-foot store with quality antiques. No reproductions or crafts are accepted by the 50 dealers who work to create an authentic representation of glassware, pottery, porcelain, quilts, linens, books, clocks and more. For you Civil War buffs, Southern Friends has a nice offering of Civil War memorabilia as well.

**Bush Baby**
280 N. Cherry St.
904/997-6108

**Mister Ed's**
Hwy. 27
904/997-5880

**Rosewood Flowers & Antiques**
Hwy. 19
904/997-6779

**Court House Antiques**
205 E. Washington St.
904/997-8008

## 54  MOUNT DORA

Mount Dora is described as a bustling village in the rolling hills of Central Florida overlooking lovely Lake Dora. Known for the historic Lakeside Inn, it's filled with nineteen antique stores, twenty-two specialty gift shops and stylish boutiques. You can enjoy a sandwich at a sidewalk deli, fajitas in a parrot-filled cafe, high tea in an English garden or gourmet meals in several fine restaurants.

Tour the town on a trolley or buggy ride, cruise the Dora Canal, walk Palm Island, swing at Gilbert Park, play tennis, shuffleboard or just enjoy a park bench.

Listed by *Money Magazine* as one of the three best places in the United States to retire, Mount Dora is less than an hour from Walt Disney World, Sea World and Universal Studios. It is located on Hwy. 441 just 30 minutes northwest of Orlando or 30 minutes west of Sanford on Hwy. 46.

**Mt. Dora Antique Mall**
315 N. Donnelly St.
352/383-0018

**Baker Street Gallery**
110 E. 5th Ave.
352/383-4199

**Caroline's Antiques**
331 N. Donnelly St.
352/735-4003

**Corner Nook Antiques**
426 N. Donnelly St.
352/383-9555

**Old Village Antiques**
439B N. Donnelly St.
352/383-1820

**My Secret Garden**
404B N. Donnelly St.
352/735-0995

**Southern Exotic Antiques**
116 W. 5th Ave.
352/735-2500

**Cottage Artwork & Antiques**
605 N. Donnelly St.
352/735-2700

**Rosecreek Antiques & Gifts**
418 N. Donnelly St.
352/735-0086

**Stairway to the Stars**
411 Donnelly St.
352/383-9770

**Purple Pineapple**
317 N. Donnelly St.
352/735-2189

**Oliver Twist Antique Furniture**
404 N. Donnelly St.
352/735-3337

**Verandah Antique Galleries**
427 N. Donnelly St.
352/735-0330

**Olde Bostonian Antiques & Gifts**
442 N. Donnelly St.
352/383-3434

**Wild Rose Antique Mini Mall**
140 E. 4th Ave.
352/383-6664

**Renninger's Antique Center**
20651 U.S. Hwy. 441
352/383-8393

**Courtyard Antiques**
142 E. 4th Ave.
352/735-1915

**Di Antiques**
122 E. 4th St.
352/735-1333

**Old Town Bookshop**
127 W. 5th Ave.
352/383-0878

### *Great Places to Stay*

### Farnsworth House

1029 E. Fifth Ave.
352/735-1894

Built in 1886, the Farnsworth House is only ten blocks away from one of the best antiquing areas in Florida. Three suites are available in the main house and two theme efficiencies are located in the carriage house. After a full day of antiquing and exploring the quaint, historic town of Mt. Dora, guests can relax on the screened porch overlooking a beautifully landscaped yard.

### Magnolia Inn

347 E. Third Ave.
1-800-776-2112
Web site: magnolia.cde.com

The Magnolia Inn features true Southern hospitality and charm at its finest. Relaxation and romance are found at this inn where guests can escape the hectic life outside this one-acre estate in downtown Mt. Dora. Lounge in a hammock by the garden wall, swing under the majestic magnolia, unwind in the gazebo spa, or curl up with a good book in the chaise longue. Park at the inn and walk to many antique shops, boutiques, bookstores, tearooms, and exceptional restaurants found along flower-box-lined streets. Perhaps you would like a romantic evening carriage ride, a historic trolley tour, hot-air balloon ride, or boat ride. Fishing, water sports, tennis, golf, and nature trails are all available nearby. Guest rooms are beautifully decorated and each has its own private bath. Breakfast is included and varies daily. Eggs Benedict, gourmet blueberry french toast, and citrus pancakes are some of the favorites. Only thirty minutes from many Orlando attractions, but the uniqueness of Mt. Dora and the pampering you receive at the Magnolia Inn might keep you from the big-city activities!

### Mount Dora Historic Inn

221 E. 4th Ave.
1-800-927-6344
Web site: www.lcia.com/clients/inn/

Re-live the elegance of the past at the lovely Mount Dora Historic Inn. Nestled in a secluded setting in romantic downtown Mount Dora, the inn is only twenty-five minutes from Orlando. Enjoy the gracious hospitality, authentic period antiques, and relaxed atmosphere of this charming bed and breakfast. Originally built in the late 1800s as a downtown merchant's home, the inn has been lovingly restored to its original beauty by the proprietors, Lindsay and Nancy Richards. The efforts of their labor of love have resulted in a memorable ambiance of warmth and embraceable character. The Mount Dora Historic Inn features fine, beautifully appointed rooms with private baths, each decorated with individuality, and an emphasis on complete guest comfort and tranquillity. From the hearty breakfast to the nightly turn-down service, you will be welcomed to the return of a bygone era.

**Lakeside Inn**
3rd & Alexander
352/383-4101

**Christopher's Inn**
539 Liberty Ave.
352/383-2244

**Seabrook B&B**
644 N. Donnelly St.
352/383-4800

**Simpson's B&B**
441 N. Donnelly St.
352/383-2087

**Upper Room**
3rd & Donnelly St.
352/735-5203

**Darst Victorian Manor**
485 Old Hwy. 441
352/383-4050

### *Great Places to Eat*

### A Taste of Home

411 N. Donnelly St.
352/735-1717
Sandwiches, soups and more

### Gable's Restaurant & Lounge

322 N. Alexander St.
352/383-8993
Fine dining

### Goblin Market

321b N. Donnelly St. (in alley)
352/735-0059
Casual dining

### La Cremerie

425 N. Donnelly St.
352/735-4663
Ice cream, coffee, cappuccino

### Park Bench Restaurant

116 E. 5th Ave.
352/383-7004
Gourmet, featuring seafood

### Sinfully Sweet

633 N. Baker St.
352/735-1926
Chocolate, ice cream, yogurt

### Windsor Rose English Tea Room

144 W. 4th Ave.
352/735-2551

### *Interesting Side Trips*

### Antique Extravaganza

Renninger's Twin Markets
Call 352/383-8393 for exact dates
January, February, Novmber

### Annual Mount Dora Antiques Show and Sale

Downtown Mount Dora
Contact Clay Oliver at 352/735-3337 for exact dates.
March

### Antique Fair

Renninger's Twin Markets
Call 352/383-8393 for exact dates.
April, May, June, July, August, September, October

*Florida*

## 55 NAPLES

**Lovejoy Antiques**
960 2nd Ave. N.
941/649-7447

**Antiques — Glenna Moore**
465 5th Ave. S.
941/263-4121

**Baldwin's at Fifth**
604 5th Ave. S.
941/263-2234

**Naples Trading Co.**
810 6th Ave. S.
941/262-0376

**Ivy House Antiques**
639 8th St. S.
941/434-9555

**Margie's Antiques**
153 10th St. S.
941/262-3151

**Catherine's Collectibles, Inc.**
255 13th Ave. S.
941/262-4800

**Barney's Island Antiques**
348 Capri Blvd.
941/394-2848

**Granny's Attic**
1971 County Road 951
941/353-0800

**Debbie's Monkey Business**
2033 Pine Ridge Road, #3
941/594-8686

**Rocking Horse Antiques**
950 3rd Ave. N.
941/263-6997

**Gabriel's South**
555 5th Ave. S.
941/643-0433

**Thompson-Strong Antiques**
605 5th Ave. S.
941/434-6434

**Yahl Street Antique Mall**
5430 Yahl St.
941/591-8182

**Bailey's Antiques & Country**
606 9th St. N.
941/643-1953

**Antique Guild**
183 10th St. S.
941/649-0323

**Recollections New & Old**
639 8th St. S.
941/649-1954

**Lovejoy Antiques**
950 Central Ave.
941/649-7447

**Wizard of Odds II**
4584 Mercantile Ave.
941/261-4459

**Black Bear Cove, Inc.**
1661 Trade Center Way
941/598-1933

## 56 NEW SMYRNA BEACH

**Victoria Station**
402 Canal St.
904/426-8881

**Coronado Antiques**
512 Canal St.
904/428-3331

**Jeff's Antiques**
507 S. Dixie Freeway
904/423-2554

**New Smyrna Antiques**
419 Canal St.
904/426-7828

**Kelly's Country Store**
569 Canal St.
904/428-2291

**Lion D'or Antiques**
511 N. Orange St.
904/428-1752

## 57 NICEVILLE

**Steven's Yesterday's Furnishings**
98 Nathey @ Hwy. 85 N.
904/678-6775

**Little Ole Lady Trading Post**
314 Bayshore Dr.
904/678-7424

**Gee Gee's Antiques**
1209 N. Partin Hwy. 285
904/678-2689

## 58 NORTH PORT

**Rujan's Antiques & Collectibles**
13640 Tamiami Trail
941/426-5418

## 59 OAKLAND PARK

**C. Strange Antiques**
3277 N. Dixie Hwy.
954/565-6964

**Yesteryear's Today**
3689 N. Dixie Hwy.
954/568-0362

**Affordable Treasures**
1051 N.E. 45th St.
954/938-4567

**The Early Attic**
119 Jones Ave.
904/678-9089

**Antique Exchange**
3493 N. Dixie Hwy.
954/564-3504

**Vintage Fabrics & Etc.**
3500 C N.E. 11th Ave.
954/564-4392

## 60 OCALA

**Gwen's Antiques**
4700 S. Hwy. 441
352/840-0747
Open: Mon.—Sat. 10:30—4:30, Sun. 12—4:30

A fine selection of old toys, jewelry, primitives, pottery, furniture, bottles and glass.

**Stuf 'n' Such**
1310 Hwy. 484
352/245-7744

**Ocala Antique Mall**
3700 S. Pine Ave.
352/622-4468

**Antique Attic**
507 S.E. Fort King St.
352/732-8880

**A Corner of Yesterday**
521 S.E. Fort King St.
352/622-1927

**ABS Antiques Co.**
4185 W. Hwy. 40
352/351-1009

**Camellia House Antiques**
1317 S.E. Fort King St.
352/629-8085

**Antique Emporium Inc.**
6500 S. Pine Ave.
352/351-1003

## 61 OKEECHOBEE

**Peddlers Cove**
216 S.W. 4th St.
941/467-1939

**Fort Drum Antique Mall**
30950 Hwy. 441 N.
941/763-6289

**My Other House**
10017 Hwy. 441 N.
941/357-3447

**Curiosity Shop**
118 S.E. Park St.
941/467-6411

# *Florida*

**Silver Spoon**
401 S.W. Park St.
941/763-0609

## 62 ORANGE CITY

**Curiosity Corner Furniture & Antiques**
746 N. Volusia Ave.
904/775-3122

**Orange City Mighty Mall**
747 N. Volusia Ave.
904/775-1666

**Antiques & Things**
1427 S. Volsia Ave.
904/775-4900

## 63 ORANGE PARK

**Victoria's Timely Treasures**
835 Park Ave.
904/269-0907

**Old Towne Antiques**
2020 Carnes St.
904/269-2318

## 64 ORLANDO

### Butterpat's
2439 Edgewater Dr.
407/423-7971

A beautiful display of antiques and fine collections awaits those who visit Butterpat's Antiques. The warmth and charm of the shop is created from the gathering of all the wonderful collections assembled by the owners. Not your ordinary array of antiques and collections, Butterpat's specializes in the rare and exquisite. Among the selections, you'll find Majolica, mercury glass, English lusters, Coors, "Rosebud" pottery, McCoy, Quimper, papier mâché, unusual wooden boxes, and my favorites — architectural details and garden ornaments.

**Swanson's Antiques**
1217 N. Orange Ave.
407/898-6050

**Penny Edwards Antiques**
1616A N. Orange Ave.
407/896-2499

**William Moseley Gallery**
1221 N. Orange Ave.
407/228-6648

**Troy's Treasures**
1612A N. Orange Ave.
407/228-6648

**Designer House, Inc.**
1249 N. Orange Ave.
407/895-9060

**Fee Fi Fauk**
1425 N. Orange Ave.
407/895-9060

**Antique Exchange**
1616 N. Orange Ave.
407/896-3793

**Marge Leeper Collection**
1618 N. Orange Ave.
407/894-2165

**A & T Antiques**
1620 N. Orange Ave.
407/896-9831

**Flo's Attic**
1800 N. Orange Ave.
407/895-1800

**Allison's Antiques**
1804 N. Orange Ave.
407/897-6672

**Jack Lampman Antiques**
1810 N. Orange Ave.
407/897-1144

**Rock & Roll Heaven**
1814 N. Orange Ave.
407/896-1952

**1817 Antiques**
1817 N. Orange Ave.
407/894-6519

**DeJavu Vintage Clothing**
1825 N. Orange Ave.
407/898-3609

**Golden Phoenix**
1826 N. Orange Ave.
407/895-6006

**A. J. Lillun Antiques**
1913 N. Orange Ave.
407/895-6111

**Red's Antiques & Collectibles**
1827 N. Orange Ave.
407/894-6519

**Victorian Gallery**
1907 N. Orange Ave.
407/896-9346

**Pieces of Eight Antique Emporium**
2021 N. Orange Ave.
407/896-8700

**Corner Cupboard**
4797 S. Orange Ave.
407/857-1322

**B's Antiques**
1214 N. Mills Ave.
407/894-6264

**Millie's Glass & China Shop**
5512 Edgewater Dr.
407/298-3355

**Backstreet Bodega**
817 Virginia Dr.
407/895-9444

**Apple Core Antiques & Gifts**
3327 Curry Ford Road
407/894-2774

**Antique Shop by Flo's Attic**
310 E. New Hampshire St.
407/894-0607

**Antiques Arcade**
1806 N. Orange Ave.
407/898-2994

**Two Timer**
1815 N. Orange Ave.
407/894-4342

**Floraland**
1808 N. Orange Ave.
407/898-2301

**D L Times Two Antiques**
1827 N. Orange Ave.
407/894-6519

**Backstreet Bodega**
1909 N. Orange Ave.
407/895-9444

**Oriental Unlimited & Antiques**
2020 N. Orange Ave.
407/894-2067

**Back Street**
2310 N. Orange Ave.
407/895-1993

**White Wolfe Cafe & Antiques**
1829 N. Orange Ave.
407/895-9911

**Annie's Antique Alley**
2010 N. Orange Ave.
407/896-0433

**Bangarang**
2309 N. Orange Ave.
407/898-2300

**And So On**
1807 N. Orange Ave.
407/898-3485

**College Park Antique Mall**
1317 Edgewater Dr.
407/839-1869

**Virginia Rose**
542 Virginia Dr.
407/898-0552

**Laughing Gargoyle Antiques**
322 W. Colonial Dr.
407/843-8070

**Antique Mall**
361 E. Michigan St.
407/849-9719

**Em's Attic**
1530 S. Primrose Dr.
407/896-0097

*Florida*

Orlando Antique Exchange
420 W. 27th St.
407/839-0991

Myrtee B's Antiques
321 Ivanhoe Blvd. N.
407/895-0717

Antique Cottage
903 Harrison Ave.
850/769-9503

Shady Oaks Antiques
3706 W. Hwy. 98
850/785-3308

## 65  PALM BEACH

**Deco Folies**
210 Brazilian Ave.
561/822-8960

**Island Trading Co.**
105 N. County Road
561/833-0555

**Art & Antiques**
117 N. County Road
561/833-1654

**Rose Pennm, Inc.**
301 S. County Road
561/835-9702

**Kofski Antiques**
315 S. County Road
561/655-6557

**F. S. Henemader Antiques**
316 S. County Road
561/835-9237

**R.J. King & Co.**
6 Via Parigi
561/659-9029

**Lars Bolander Ltd.**
375 S. County Road
561/832-2121

**Bellon Antiques**
309 Peruvian Ave.
561/659-1844

**Fleur-De-Lis Antiques**
326 Peruvian Ave.
561/655-2295

**Christian Du Pont Antiques, Inc.**
353 Peruvian Ave.
561/655-7794

**Vilda B. De Porro**
211 Worth Ave.
561/655-3147

**Spencer Gallerie**
240 Worth Ave.
561/833-9893

**Meissen Shop**
329 Worth Ave.
561/832-2504

**L'Antiquaire**
329 Worth Ave.
561/655-5774

**Yetta Olkes Antiques**
332 S. County Road
561/655-2800

**Brighton Pavillon**
340 Worth Ave.
561/835-4777

**Devonshire**
340 Worth Ave.
561/833-0796

**Barzina**
66 Via Mizner
561/833-5834

**Galerie Haga Antiques**
2 Via Parigi
561/833-2051

## 66  PALM HARBOR

**Generations Antiques**
1682 Alt. 19 N.
813/787-0067

**Miss B's Antiques & Collectibles**
1710 Alt. 19 N.
813/787-0388

**Cierra-Jordan Antique & Gift**
1026 Florida Ave., Suite C
813/781-0305

**The Gift Connection**
1001 Omaha Circle
813/781-0103

## 67  PANAMA CITY

### Ron's Antique Place

3213 Hwy. 98
850/769-6911
Open: Wed.–Sat. 10–5, Sun. 1–5

**The Eclectic Emporium**
2113 E. 3rd. St.
850/914-9114

**Elegant Endeavors**
2609 E. Business 98
850/769-1707

**Sentimental Treasurers of the Past**
18400 Panama City Beach Pkwy.
850/233-1224

**Antique Mall**
Hwy. 77
850/271-9810

**J & M Doll Castle & Collectibles**
1700 Bayview Ave.
850/872-0092

## 68  PENSACOLA

### 9th Avenue Antique Mall

380 9th Ave.
850/438-3961
Open: Mon.–Sat. 10–6, Sun. 12–6

Over 10,000 square feet of jewelry, baskets, pottery, paintings, old toys, stained glass, sterling, china, crystal, advertising, quilts, vintage clothing, rugs and American and European furniture.

### The Muse

2226 Palafox
850/432-8825
Open: Mon.–Fri. 11–5, Sat. 10–4

Fine art, antiques, ceramics and ideas.

### Little Audrey's Antiques

6508 W. Jackson St.
850/453-8108
Open: Mon.–Sat. 10–6

Over 20 dealers presenting a general mix of antiques and collectibles.

### Poor Richard's Antiques

2015-2019 N. T St.
850/434-0880

This 6,000-square-foot showroom features antiques from France, Belgium, the Netherlands and Germany.

*Florida*

### Jackson Hill Antiques
9th & E. Jackson St.
850/470-0668
Open: Mon.–Sat. 10–5
Directions: Take Exit 4 off I-10 on 110 S. Then take Exit 2, turn left, go to 9th Ave. Then right two blocks.

A fabulous selection of American, European and Chinese antiques, porcelain, pottery and painted furniture.

### Unique Antiques
3622 Barrancas Ave.
850/457-7871
Open: Tues.–Sat. 10–5

Antiques, furniture, glassware, china and perfume bottles.

| | |
|---|---|
| **American Antique Mall**<br>2019 N. T St.<br>850/432-7659 | **Turn of the Century Antiques**<br>2401 N. T St.<br>850/434-1820 |
| **Heirlooms**<br>2706 N. T St.<br>850/438-2279 | **Burch Antiques**<br>3160 N. T St.<br>850/433-5153 |
| **Burch Antiques**<br>2410 N. T St.<br>850/433-5153 | **This Ole House**<br>712 S. Palafax St.<br>850/432-2577 |
| **Hamilton House Antiques**<br>4117 Barrancas Ave.<br>850/456-2762 | **Warehouse Antiques**<br>60 S. Alcaniz St.<br>850/432-0318 |
| **Ragtime Antiques**<br>3113 Mobile Blvd.<br>850/438-1232 | **Dusty Attic**<br>1113 N. 9th Ave.<br>850/434-5568 |
| **Baily Attic**<br>9204 N. Davis Hwy.<br>850/478-3144 | **Lind House Estate Jewelers**<br>217 S. Alcaniz St.<br>850/435-3213 |
| **East Hill Antique Village**<br>805 E. Gadsden St.<br>850/435-7325 | **Cleland Antiques-Seville Square**<br>412 E. Zarragossa St.<br>850/432-9933 |
| **L.L. Sloan Antiques**<br>115 S. Florida Blanca St.<br>850/434-5050 | **Status Symbol**<br>698 Hindberg, Suite 106<br>850/432-6614 |

### Nearby Antique Shopping (Milton)
*Milton is approximately 15 miles east of Pensacola.*

### Antique Mall of Milton
6776 Caroline St.
850/626-2912
Open: Tues.–Sat. 10–5, Sun. 1–5

### Blackwater River Antique Mall
7060 Hwy. 90 E.
850/626-4492
Open: Mon.–Sat. 9:30–5

One of the most unique shops on the Gulf Coast, this 7,500-square-foot mall features fine antique furniture and collectibles along with primitives and costume jewelry.

### 69 PLANT CITY

Plant City is located 24 miles east of Tampa and 10 miles west of Lakeland. Just off I-4, take Exit 13, then follow Wheeler St. to downtown, or take Exit 12 to U.S. 92 east into downtown.

### The Olde Village Shoppes Mini Mall and Le Bistro Cafe
108 S. Collins St.
813/752-3222
Open: Tues.–Sat. 10–5:30, closed Sun. & Mon.

It takes a person of great vision to take an old, dilapidated building and turn it into a thing of beauty. That is just what Victoria Hawthorne has accomplished. She saw beyond the crumbling bricks, broken windows and littered interior. Hawthorne envisioned an enclosed European-style shopping village. She and her husband purchased the historic building in 1996 and began the work to fulfill her dream. The results are spectacular.

The quaint shops are connected by a red-brick walkway with overhead ceilings painted sky blue with big puffy clouds. All the shops have European facades or are a part of a beautiful English garden with a bubbling fountain. The 56 shops are filled with such eclectic treasures as stained glass pieces, antique Victorian lamps, *Gone with the Wind* memorabilia, paintings, fine antique furnishings, glassware, vintage jewelry, imported tiles from around the world and porcelain dolls, just to name a few. Le Bistro Cafe gives shoppers a respite from the day's hectic pace. Chef Christopher, trained at the American Culinary Art Institute, prepares fresh soups, sandwiches, salads and seafood. Catering is available, as well as high tea, by reservation.

Vickie Hawthorne's dream to promote the revival of downtown Plant City is off to a remarkable start. Take some time to discover for yourself The Olde Village Shoppes and enjoy the beautiful surroundings of historic Plant City.

Dale Gardner contributed to this story.

### Miss Vicki's
113 S. Collins St.
813/757-0282

Art and antiques and artists' lofts.

*Florida*

## Abbie's Corner
101 E. Arden Mays Blvd.
813/719-3348

Specializing in American dinnerware and Depression glass.

**Annie Marie & Co.**
2201 Thonotosassa Road
813/759-6473

**The Outpost**
101 N. Thomas St.
813/752-3354

**Heritage**
102 S. Evers St.
813/759-2758

**Antiques & More**
105 S. Evers St.
813/719-6336

**Mayo Bargain Shop**
111 S. Evers St.
813/687-4814

**Frenchman's Market**
102 N. Collins
813/754-8388

**Aunt Nellie's Antiques**
107 N. Collins
813/707-9160

**Antiques & Collectibles**
120 N. Collins
813/759-2828

**Herban Cowboy**
109 E. Reynolds St.
813/719-8345

## 70 POMPANO BEACH

**Heritage Clock Shop**
713 E. Atlantic Blvd.
954/946-4871

**Antique Market Place**
721 E. Atlantic Blvd.
954/943-6221

**Emporium Antiques**
1642 E. Atlantic Blvd.
954/946-0120

**Memories**
2692 E. Atlantic Blvd.
954/785-1776

**Purnie's Antiques**
25 N. Ocean Blvd.
954/941-6154

## 71 PORT CHARLOTTE

**Port Charlotte Gold & Silver**
2221D Tamiami Trail
941/629-3745

**Westchester Gold Fabricators**
3361A Tamiami Trail
941/625-0666

**Visions Unlimited**
3750A Tamiami Trail
941/625-6418

## 72 SANFORD

**Arts & Ends**
116 E. 1st St.
407/330-4994

**Granny Squares**
118 E. 1st St.
407/323-3919

**Granny's on Magnolia**
201 E. 1st St.
407/322-7544

**Junk Exchange**
118 Palmetto Ave.
407/330-7748

**Two Doves & a Hound Antiques**
205 E. 1st St.
407/321-3690

**Antiques Etc.**
205 E. 1st St., Suite C
407/330-1641

**Yester Years**
205 E. 1st St., #A
407/323-3457

**Bennington & Bradbury Antiques**
210 E. 1st St.
407/328-5057

**Somewhere in Time**
222 E. 1st St.
407/323-7311

**Delilah's**
301 E. 1st St.
407/330-2272

**Sanford House, Inc.**
616 W. 1st St.
407/330-0608

**Sanford Antiques**
700 W. 1st St.
407/321-2035

**Helen's Den**
205 N. Palmetto Ave.
407/324-3726

**Park Avenue Antique Mall**
1301 S. Park Ave.
407/321-4356

**The Rusty Duck**
303 E. 1st St.
407/323-2900

## 73 SANTA ROSA BEACH/GRAYTON BEACH/SEASIDE/ SEAGROVE BEACH

**Bayou Arts & Antiques**
105 Hogtown Bayou Lane
904/267-1404

**Martha's Plantation Shop**
1727 S. County Hwy. 393
904/267-2944

**Gunby's**
4415 Scenic Route 30-A E.
904/231-5958

**Grandma's Stuff**
35 Musset Bayou Road
904/267-1999

**Ole Outpost**
687 S. Church St.
904/267-2551

**Tidewater Antiques**
Emerald Coast Plaza, Suite 33
904/267-9599

**Hogtown Landing**
Hwy. 393 N. & Cessna Park
904/267-1271

**Tea Tyme Antiques**
Hwy. C-30A & Tanglewood Dr.
904/267-3827

**"S" House Antiques**
3866 W. Hwy. C-30A & Satinwood
904/267-2231

**Fernleigh, Ltd.**
Hwy. C-30A (Seaside Town Center)
904/231-5536

## 74 SARASOTA

### Mark of Time
24 S. Lemon Ave.
1-800-277-5275
Open: Mon.–Thurs. 10:30–5:30, Fri. 11–4, Sat. 10–2
Directions: Traveling on I-75, take Exit 39 onto Fruitville Road (SR 780), going west for 5 miles into downtown. Turn left onto Lemon Avenue, and proceed through two stop signs and a traffic light. The shop is on the right.

Located in the heart of Sarasota's antique district, Mark of Time specializes in rare antique clocks. The shop recently acquired a Ferdinand

# Florida

Lapp Centennial clock, circa 1876. This one-of-a-kind clock and cabinet was created by Ferdinand Lapp especially for the Centennial International Exhibit in Philadelphia. Mark of Time also offers expert clock and watch repair. Antique furnishings and accessories are available along with the many fine selections of clocks.

**Bargain Box Consignment Shoppe**
4406 Bee Ridge Road
941/371-1976

**Miller's Antiques**
970 Cattleman Road
941/377-2979

**Alley Cat Antiques**
1542 4th St.
941/366-6887

**Shadow Box**
1520 Fruitville Road
941/957-3896

**Sarasota Antiques & Upholstery**
1542 Fruitville Road
941/366-9484

**Queen Anne's Lace Antiques**
2246 Gulf Gate Dr.
941/927-0448

**Design Shop**
34 S. Lemon Ave.
941/365-2434

**A World Coin & Jewelry Exchange**
1564 Main St.
941/365-5415

**Hartman, William**
48 S. Palm Ave.
941/955-4785

**Kevin L. Perry, Inc.**
127 S. Pineapple Ave.
941/366-8483

**Beverly's Antiques & Collectibles**
510 S. Pineapple Ave.
941/953-6887

**Creative Collections**
527 S. Pineapple Ave.
941/951-0477

**Jack Vinale's Antiques**
539 S. Pineapple Ave.
941/957-0002

**Yesterday's Browse Box**
2864 Ringling Blvd.
941/957-1422

**Daddy Franks**
907 Cattleman Road
941/378-1308

**Talk of the Town**
4123 Clark Road
941/925-3948

**Treasures & More**
1466 Fruitville Road
941/366-7704

**Li Lou**
1522 Fruitville Road
941/362-0311

**Dotty's Accents & Antiques**
1555 Fruitville Road
941/954-8057

**Sanders Antiques**
22 N. Lemon Ave.
941/366-0400

**A. Parker's Books**
1488 Main St.
941/366-2898

**Rosie O'Grady's Antqs. & Fine Gifts**
32 S. Palm Ave.
1-800-793-4193

**Apple & Carpenter Gallery Fine Art**
64 S. Palm Ave.
941/951-2314

**New England Antiques**
500 S. Pineapple Ave.
941/955-7577

**Sarasota Trading Co.**
522 S. Pineapple Ave.
941/953-7776

**Orange Pineapple**
533 S. Pineapple Ave.
941/954-0533

**Avenue Antiques**
606 S. Pineapple Ave.
941/362-8866

**Antiques & Collectibles Vault**
1501 2nd St.
941/954-4233

**Bacon & Wing**
1433 State St.
941/371-2687

**Remember Gallery**
1239 S. Tamiami Trail
941/955-2625

**British Pine Emporium**
4801 S. Tamiami Trail
941/923-7347

**Antiques and Country Pine**
5201 S. Tamiami Trail
941/921-5616

**Franklin Antiques & Collectibles**
3512 N. Lockwood Ridge Road
941/359-8842

**Crissy Galleries**
640 S. Washington Blvd., Suite 150
941/957-1110

**Yellow Bird of St. Armands, Inc.**
640 S. Washington Blvd., Suite 230
941/388-1823

**Steven Postan's Antiques**
2305 Whitfield Park Dr.
941/755-6063

**Cherubs of Gold**
2245 Ringling Blvd.
941/366-0596

**Raymond's Second Hand World, Inc.**
5624 Swift Road
941/925-7253

**Caroline's Used Furniture & Antqs.**
4511 S. Tamiami Trail
941/924-7066

**Shah Abba's Fine Oriental Rugs**
4801 S. Tamiami Trail
941/366-6511

**Coral Cove Antique Gallery**
7272 S. Tamiami Trail
941/927-2205

**Methuselah's Antiques**
322 S. Washington Blvd.
941/366-2218

**Robert A. Blekicki Antiques**
640 S. Washington Blvd.
941/365-4990

**Century Antiques**
3626 Webber St.
941/921-0056

**Coco Palm Gallery Art & Antiques**
1255 N. Palm Ave.
941/955-1122

**Franklin Antiques & Collectibles**
3512 N. Lockwood Ridge Road
941/359-8842

## 75 SEMINOLE

## Cobweb Antiques

7976 Seminole Blvd.
813/399-2929
Open: Mon.–Sat. 10–5, closed Mon. May–September
Directions: Traveling on I-275, take Exit 15; go west on Gandy Blvd. (becomes Park Blvd.) to Seminole Blvd. (Alt. 19). Turn right onto Seminole Blvd. Drive two blocks north. Make a left into Temple Terrace. Located on the northwest corner of Seminole Blvd. and Temple Terrace.

Cobweb Antiques is one of those "have all," "do all," "be all" kind of shops. They carry antique furniture, pottery, jewelry, watches, clocks, china, silver, books, postcards, prints, paintings, mirrors, lamps, linens, vintage clothing, antique firearms and related items. And if that weren't enough, they do estate liquidations, appraise firearms, real estate and antique automobiles. I wonder if these guys ever take a vacation.

**The Fox Den**
6020 Seminole Blvd.
813/398-4605

**Vintage Antiques**
6920 Seminole Blvd.
813/399-9691

**Cobwebs Antiques**
7976 Seminole Blvd.
813/399-2929

**Evon's Antiques**
7480 90th St.
813/391-3586

**Adams Emporium**
8780 Seminole Blvd.
813/397-7938

**The Hen Nest**
5485 113th St. N.
813/398-1470

## 76 ST. AUGUSTINE

St. Augustine, America's oldest city, is a time capsule capturing nearly 500 years of fascinating history. Located on the uppermost Atlantic coast of Florida, the city exudes a playful charm with a refreshing mixture of antiquated romance, youthful vibrance and Southern sweetness. St. Augustine was founded in 1565 and is the oldest continuously occupied European settlement in the continental United States. Evidence of the magic and mystery spanning five centuries in St. Augustine is revealed in more than sixty historic sites, including massive forts, missions and living history museums. Just minutes from historic downtown lie the beaches of Anastasia Island, which stretch along 24 miles of sun-swept shores. There you will find the waves sprinkled with water enthusiasts sailing, surfboarding and windsurfing. Incredibly fresh seafood and global delicacies are served in more than 150 eateries in St. Augustine. Options range from waterfront restaurants and shrimp shacks to gourmet bistros and turn-of-the-century Victorian mansions. The strong Minorcan heritage makes spicy tastes such as pilau and datil pepper sauce savory specialities. St. Augustine is truly a place where history comes alive.

### Antique Warehouse

6370 N. U.S. 1, Bldgs. 4 & 5
904/826-1524
Open: Mon.–Sat. 10–5

Five thousand square feet presenting an eclectic gathering of antique and custom pine, French and English furniture from 1860 to 1960. Wrought iron, architectural goods and English floor lamps.

### Tropical Rattan

3905 U.S. Hwy. 1 S.
904/797-7544

A large selection of oak, mahogany, walnut, cherry and pine furniture, glassware, clocks and radios.

### Lovejoy's Antique Mall

1302 Ponce de Leon (U.S. 1)
904/826-0200

An outstanding display of Civil War, jewelry, antique toys, vintage clothing, nautical and antiques and collectibles.

### The Antique Market

"Old England Tours"
1974 S.R. 16 (1 mi. from I-95)
904/824-9394
Open: 10–5, closed Sun.

Antiques and collectibles for the dealer trade. English, French, Central European, American, Asian. Furniture, china, linens, architectural and the unexpected. Accompanied European antique buying tours, shipping.

### St. Augustine Antique Emporium

62 San Marco Ave.
904/829-0544
Open: Mon.–Sat. 10–5, Sun. 11–5

Something for every collector! Over 33 quality dealers and merchandise ranging from country kitchen collectibles, silver and gold jewelry, paper weights, cameras, furniture and much more.

### Center Aisle Books, Etc.

56 San Marco Ave.
904/827-0203
Open: Daily 10:30–5

Offering art, antiques, vintage furniture, custom mosaic tile pieces and 15,000 rare and out-of-print books. Multiple experienced dealers invite you to come in.

### Askew Antiques

1000 Ponce De Leon Blvd.
904/808-7222
Open: Daily 11–6

Specializing in Italian, French and English; antiques, large chandeliers, decorative furniture and accessories. No Depression glass.

### Vin-Tiques

56 Charlotte St.
904/829-0841
Open: Thurs.–Mon. 10:30–5, July–August by appointment

Experience the adventure: antique European pine furniture, china and glass, antique and European linens, worldwide artifacts and regional art. Specializing in old wood boxes, cabinets and iron pieces.

## Museum of Weapons & Early American History

81-C King St.
904/829-3727
Open: Daily 9:30–5

Unique Civil War relics, lithographs, newspapers, documents, discount books, reproduction swords and fine art.

## John Bouvier Maps & Prints

11-D Aviles St.
904/825-0920
Open: 10–5, closed Tues. & Wed.

Antique maps, prints and books, Floridiana. Old city maps, road maps, battle plans, railroad and geological maps, nautical charts, maps back to 1600s.

## By-Gone Days

9-C Aviles St.
904/824-5536
Open: Fri.–Mon. 11–5

Specializing in American art pottery: Roseville, Weller, McCoy, etc. Glass and kitchenware from the Depression era and the '40s, '50s and '60s.

## Punch Jones

4 Anastasia Blvd.
904/824-9878
Open: Mon.–Fri. 9–5, (Sat. & Sun. by chance)

Eclectic mix of 19th- and 20th-century furniture. Textiles, prints, architectural elements. Garden accessories. Design service available including custom design furniture.

## Timeless Treasures

213 Anastasia Blvd.
904/827-9997
Open: Tues.–Sat. 12–7, Sun. 2–7

Timeless Treasures specializes in antiques, furniture, jewelry, frames and prints — almost everthing — at thrift store prices!

## Sea Bridge Landing

912 Anastasia Blvd.
904/824-3358
Open: Thurs.–Sat. 11–5, or by appointment

Antique decorating treasures, ethnic folk art, paintings, French and Oriental porcelains, unique bird cages, trunks, Oriental rugs, rarieties!

## Conch House Antiques

600 Anastasia Blvd.
904/825-1255

## All Precious & Pleasant Riches

203 S. Ponce De Leon Blvd.
904/824-3156

## San Marco Antique Mall

63 San Marco Ave.
904/824-9156

## Ravenswood Antiques

81 San Marco Ave.
904/824-1740

## Second Time Around Antiques

Lightner Antique Mall
904/825-4982

## Barclay-Scott Antiques

4 Rohde Ave.
904/824-7044

## Wolf's Head Books

48 San Marco Ave.
904/824-9357

## Country Store Antiques

67 San Marco Ave.
904/824-7978

## First Encounter Antiques

216 San Marco Ave.
904/823-8855

### *Great Places to Stay*

## Carriage Way Bed & Breakfast

70 Cuna St.
1-800-908-9832
Web site: www.carriageway.com

Carriage Way is a beautifully restored 1883 Victorian home in the heart of the St. Augustine historic district. It is within walking distance of the waterfront, shops, restaurants and historic sites. The rooms are decorated with antiques and reproductions. Private baths have showers or antique claw-foot tubs. The atmosphere is leisurely and casual. Complimentary beverages, newspaper, cookies, and a full gourmet breakfast is offered. Roses, fruit and cheese tray, gourmet picnic lunch, carriage rides and sweetheart packages can be arranged especially for you.

## Casa de la Paz Bayfront Bed & Breakfast

22 Avenida Menendez
1-800-929-2915
Web site: www.oldcity.com/delapaz

In keeping with the Flagler era, Casa de la Paz graces St. Augustine's bayfront and historic district with its elegant Mediterranean architecture. It is centrally located to all sites, fine restaurants, shopping and miles of ocean beach. Each guest room is distinctive in style and furnishings and is reminiscent of the early 1900s. All have a queen or king bed, cable TV, phone and private bath. From your room or veranda you will enjoy views of passing boats on Matanzas Bay or the beautiful, walled Spanish garden courtyard. Awake to the fragrant aromas of a freshly baked breakfast and specially blended coffee. A delicious full breakfast typically includes a savory quiche, muffins or cakes, fresh fruit and homemade apple butter.

## Casa de Solana

21 Aviles St.
904/824-3555

A lovingly renovated colonial home in the heart of St. Augustine's historical area, within walking distance of restaurants, museum and quaint shops. There are four antique-filled guest accommodations. All are suites, some with fireplaces, others with balconies that overlook the beautiful garden, and others have a breathtaking view of Matanzas Bay. All have private baths.

## Casa de Suenos B&B

20 Cordova St.
1-800-824-0804

Casa de Suenos Bed and Breakfast, the "House of Dreams," is a beautiful turn-of-the-century Mediterranean home built during Florida's Golden Age. It is located on the romantic carriage route, still traveled today by horse-drawn carriages. You'll be just steps from charming shops, fine restaurants and fascinating landmarks. Six lovely rooms, including two suites (each with a private bath), feature special touches such as terry robes, decanters of sherry and fresh flowers. Several rooms have relaxing whirlpool baths. Casa de Suenos' exquisite rooms and suites are decorated with quality antiques and objets d'art. There is a gorgeous Honeymoon/Anniversary Suite and a "Dream Suite." Enjoy sumptuous, full breakfasts in the lovely, bay-windowed dining room. During weekends and holidays you'll be serenaded by a guitarist.

## Old Mansion Inn

14 Joyner St.
904/824-1975

This historic mansion home is on the National Register of Historic Sites. Constructed in 1872, it is the oldest and most architecturally significant structure in the area. Conveniently located opposite the Visitors Center and within walking distance of all historic sites, attractions and fine restaurants. An English-style breakfast is served in the formal dining room of the mansion.

## St. Francis Inn

279 St. George St.
1-800-824-6062
Web site: www.stfrancisinn.com

Located in St. Augustine's restored historic district, the inn is rich in Old World charm and modern comforts. Built in 1791, it is constructed of coquina limestone, which is made up of broken shells and coral. The entrance faces a courtyard containing lush banana trees, bougainvillea, jasmine and other exotic flora. Two courtyards, several balconies, porches and patios are perfect places for guests to read, write or paint. Each accommodation in this Spanish Colonial home is unique; all have private baths, antiques or quality reproductions, several have fireplaces, two-person whirlpool tubs and kitchenettes. A two bedroom, two bath cottage (formerly the slave quarters and later the cookhouse for the main building) is ideal for a family or couples. Inn guests enjoy a hearty, complimentary breakfast, private parking, complimentary admission to the nation's oldest house, use of inn bikes and swimming pool.

## The Cedar House Inn

79 Cedar St.
1-800-233-2746
Open: Year-round. Reservations taken from 10–8:30 daily
Directions: *From the north:* On I-95 S, take SR 16 (Exit 95) east to U.S. 1 (Ponce de Leon Blvd.). Turn right and go to the third traffic light. Turn left on King Street and go through two traffic lights. Turn right on next street (Granada St.) and go one block to Cedar Street. Turn right. The inn is the 2nd house on the left. *From the south:* On I-95 N, take SR 207 (Exit 94) east to U.S. 1 (Ponce de Leon Blvd.). Turn left and go to the second traffic light. Turn left on King Street and go through two traffic lights. Turn right on the next street (Granada St.) and go one block to Cedar Street. Turn right. The inn is the 2nd house on the left.

The Cedar House Inn is located in St. Augustine, the oldest town in the United States. Built in 1893, this Victorian inn has been characterized by family lore and love. As a remembrance to Russ and Nina Thomas' grandparents, each of the six guest rooms are named in their honor. Additionally, the rooms are decorated with family heirlooms and memorabilia from the particular grandparent's life. Tess's Room, often called the "angel room" by guests, was named for Russ's maternal grandmother. During the 1920s, she was an actress on early radio, the cofounder of the first Girl Scout troop in Paterson, N.J., and known to many as an "angel." "Tess's room reflects her life and love of people," explains Russ. It is often requested by new brides and grooms.

On one such occasion, a honeymoon couple booked the suite for a one night's stay between their wedding reception and their departure for the Bahamas the next day. They arrived late at night and departed early, apparently never needing to use the key nor ever having glanced at the key's name tag. Departing in a rush, they forgot to turn in the key. For the next week, Russ and Nina joked about how Tess's key was on a honeymoon.

Meanwhile, on the islands, the honeymooners were in quite a state of dismay. It seems upon checking into their hotel the groom had slipped the room key into his pocket. When they reached the room, try as he might, the key he took out of his pocket wouldn't open the door. He and his bride promptly marched down to the hotel lobby, confronted the desk clerk and displayed the offending key. With one glance, the clerk explained that that was not his hotel's key and asked, "Who is Tess," anyway? Which

# *Florida*

is exactly what the bride wanted to know: "And who is Tess??!!" Fortunately, after a few embarrassing moments, the groom fished into his other pocket, found the real hotel key, unraveled the mystery, and saved his new marriage.

## 77　ST. CLOUD

**A & D Antiques & Collectibles**
1032 New York Ave.
407/891-0331

**Caesar's Treasure Chest**
1116 New York Ave.
407/892-8330

**Troy's Treasures**
1037 New York Ave.
407/957-0588

**Forget Me Not Antiques**
1122 10th St.
407/892-7701

## 78　ST. PETERSBURG

### Karen's Place
9999 Gandy Blvd.
813/576-0764
Open: Mon.–Sat. 10–5

Specializing in antique furniture; pub tables, chair sets, armoires, sideboards, hall stands, dining and bedroom sets.

### Antiques Exchange
2535 Central Ave.
813/321-6621
Open: Mon.–Sat. 10–5, Sun 12–5

The ultimate antique experience, a full city block of over 100 dealers.

**Nana's Other Place**
260 1st Ave. N.
813/827-0813

**Rosemary's Antiques**
770 4th Ave. N.
813/822-1221

**4th Street Antique Arcade, Inc.**
1535 4th St. N.
813/823-5700

**Dessa Antiques**
2004 4th St. N.
813/823-5006

**Patty & Friends Antiques**
1225 9th St. N.
813/821-2106

**Memory Lane**
2392 9th St. N.
813/896-1913

**Nana's Place**
428 4th St. N.
813/823-4015

**B & G Antiques**
1018 4th St. N.
813/823-2452

**Sunken Gardens Antique Gallery**
1825 4th St. N.
813/822-5117

**More Friends Antiques**
1219 9th St. N.
813/896-5425

**Person's Antiques Too**
1250 9th St. N.
813/895-1250

**Suzette's Antiques**
3313 W. Maritana Dr.
813/360-2309

**Main House Antique Center**
4980 38th Ave. N.
813/522-2492

**Bennie's Barn**
3700 58th Ave. N.
813/526-4992

**Tudor Antiques**
601 Central Ave.
813/821-4438

**Stuart Galleries**
647 Central Ave., #1
813/894-2933

**Jackie's Place**
657 Central Ave.
813/544-1844

**Hauser Antiques**
7204 Central Ave.
813/343-5511

**Blue Bear Antiques**
7214 Central Ave.
813/345-8851

**Antique Shoppe**
7223 Central Ave.
813/341-1199

**Antique Depot**
2835 22nd Ave. N.
813/327-0794

**Beach Drive Antiques**
134 Beach Dr. N.E.
813/822-3773

**Napier's Antique Hardware & Supplies**
4498 49th Ave.
813/528-2687

**Gas Plant Antique Arcade**
1246 Central Ave.
813/895-0368

**Carrousel Antiques**
7033 46th Ave. N.
813/544-5039

**Ma's Glass Barn**
5822 60th Ave. N.
813/546-2459

**Elephant Trunk**
627 Central Ave.
813/823-2394

**David Ord Antiques & Fine Art**
649 Central Ave.
813/823-8084

**Urbana**
665 Central Ave.
813/824-5669

**Burr Antiques**
7214 Central Ave.
813/345-5727

**Cappy's Corner Antiques**
7215 Central Ave.
813/345-4330

**Harpies' Bazaar**
7240 Central Ave.
813/343-0409

**Park Street Antique Center**
9401 Bay Pines Blvd.
813/392-2198

**Abbey Road Antiques**
1581 Canterbury Road N.
813/345-6852

**Pink House of Collectibles**
1515 4th St. N.
813/894-2746

**Echo Antiques**
1209 Central Ave.
813/898-3246

### *Great Places to Stay*

### Bay Shore Manor Bed & Breakfast
635 12th Ave. N.E.
813/822-3438
Email: baymanor@aol.com

The Bay Shore Manor is one of the oldest buildings in the old northeast neighborhood located across from Northshore Park and the beach. The Bay Shore Manor opened for business in 1928 and is now hosted by the German Gross family. Each suite is nicely furnished and has its own bath. On hot summer days you'll love to sit outside and look to the bay. Guests are served a delicious German-style breakfast that consists of coffee,

*Florida*

tea, milk, orange juice, homemade bread and rolls, butter, cold cuts, cheese, honey, marmalade, eggs and cereal.

## 79  STUART

**Pastimes Furniture**
2380 N.W. Bay Colony Dr.
561/335-0590

**A Certain Ambiance**
522 Colorado Ave.
561/221-0388

**Partners Antique Mall**
6124 S.E. Federal Hwy.
561/286-6688

**Collections**
53 S.W. Flagler Ave.
561/288-6232

**Partners Mall**
6124 S. East Federal Hwy.
561-286-6688

**Custom Woods**
650 N.W. Buck Henry Way
561/692-0702

**Beckoning Antiques**
614 Colorado Ave.
561/288-5044

**Time Will Tell**
3 S.W. Flagler Ave.
561/283-6337

**Bon Bon Antiques**
2681 S.E. Ocean Blvd.
561/288-0866

## 80  TALLAHASSEE

**Grant's Collectibles**
2887 W. Tharpe St., #C
850/575-2212

**Killearn Antiques**
1415 Timberland Road
850/893-0510

**Country Collection**
1500 Apalachee Pkwy.
850/877-0390

**Early American Antiques**
2736 Pecan Road
850/385-2981

**Old World Antiques**
929 N. Monroe St.
850/681-6986

**Primrose Antiques**
7820 Tennessee St.
850/575-1436

### *Nearby Antique Shopping (Panacea)*
### *Panacea is 31 miles south of Tallahassee.*

## Antiques & Art
49 Blue Crab Lane
850/984-5139
Web site: straubart.com

Specializing in fine art. The Straubs exhibit at upscale antique shows nationwide.

## 81  TAMPA

## Gaslight Antiques
3616 Henderson Blvd.
813/870-0934
Open: Mon.–Sat. 10:30–5, Sun. 12–4

Three huge buildings, 11 showrooms featuring more fine American and European furniture under one roof than the largest market in England, France or Italy. Museum quality antiques and interior design service available.

**Paris Flea**
3115 W. Bay to Bay Blvd.
813/837-6556

**L'Exquisite Antiques**
3413 W. Bay to Bay Blvd.
813/837-8655

**Cox/Feivelson**
3413 W. Bay to Bay Blvd.
813/837-8655

**A Silver Chest**
203 S. Dale Mabry Blvd.
813/228-0038

**Flo's Antiques**
4301 W. El Prado Blvd.
813/837-5871

**Tureville Antiques**
4303 W. El Prado Blvd., #A
813/831-0555

**Antique & Art by Patty**
4305 W. El Prado Blvd., #A
813/832-6129

**Frantiques**
1109 1/2 W. Waters Ave.
813/935-3638

**The Antique Room**
4119 S. Macdill Ave.
813/835-8613

**Decades Ago-Go**
1514 E. 7th Ave.
813/248-2849

**Grandma's Attic**
1901 N. 13th St.
813/247-6878

**Hunter's Find Antiques**
3224 W. Bay to Bay Blvd.
813/251-6444

**Your Treasures**
3413 W. Bay to Bay Blvd.
813/837-8655

**Neta Winders**
3901 W. Bay to Bay Blvd.
813/839-0151

**Antique Mall of Palma Ceia**
3300 S. Dale Mabry Blvd.
813/835-6255

**Larry R. Engle Antiques**
4303 W. El Prado Blvd.
813/839-0611

**Grandma's Place**
4305 W. El Prado Blvd.
813/839-7098

**Ceia Palma Porcelain & Art**
1802 S. Macdill Ave.
813/254-7149

**South Macdill Antique Mall**
4004 S. Macdill Ave.
813/832-3766

**Cracker House**
4121 S. Macdill Ave.
813/837-2841

**Uptown Threads**
1520 E. 8th Ave.
813/248-5470

**Lorene's Antiques & Collectibles**
9840 Angus Dr.
813/249-0901

# Florida

**Antique Mall of Tampa**
1102 E. Busch Blvd.
813/933-5829

**Floriland Antique Center**
9309 N. Florida Ave.
813/935-9257

**Smith's Trading Post**
1781 W. Hillsborough Ave.
813/876-2292

**Timeless Treasures**
2305 W. Linebaugh Ave.
813/935-8860

**Brushwood**
3006 W. Swann Ave.
813/873-8022

**Red Rooster Antiques**
6420 N. Central Ave.
813/238-2615

**Greg's Unique Antiques**
708 E. Grove Ave.
813/977-1990

**Boyd Clocks**
937 S. Howard Ave.
813/254-7862

**Huckleberry's Cottage Antiques**
3808 W. Neptune St.
813/258-0707

## 82  TARPON SPRINGS

Turn-of-the-century street lights, brick streets and sidewalks, towering oaks, the beautiful Anclote River, historic bayous, recreational parks, and beaches on the Gulf of Mexico are just a few of the many sights that greet you when you enter Tarpon Springs by vehicle or boat. Located in the center of town is the Tarpon Springs Downtown Historic District, listed on the National Register of Historic Places. This seven-block area features buildings from the late 1800s that house shops, art galleries, restaurants, and music venues that proudly welcome visitors from all over the world.

**Angelic Antiquities & Accents**
104 E. Tarpon Ave.
813/942-8799

**Carter's Antique Asylum**
106 E. Tarpon Ave.
813/942-2799

**Through the Looking Glass Antiques**
132 E. Tarpon Ave.
813/942-2851

**Antiques Forever**
143 E. Tarpon Ave.
813/938-0078

**Court of Two Sisters**
153 E. Tarpon Ave.
813/934-9255

**Vintage Department Store**
167 E. Tarpon Ave.
813/942-4675

**Beehive**
104 E. Tarpon Ave.
813/942-8840

**Antiques on the Main, Inc.**
124 E. Tarpon Ave.
813/937-9497

**Menzer's Antiques**
134 E. Tarpon Ave.
813/938-3156

**Victorian Ivy**
151 E. Tarpon Ave.
813/942-6080

**Tarpon Avenue Antiques**
161 E. Tarpon Ave.
813/938-0053

## Great Places to Stay

### Bed and Breakfast on the Bayou
976 Bayshore Dr.
813/942-4468

You'll love your stay at this beautiful contemporary home situated on a quiet bayou. Fish for a big old red or watch the blue herons and pelicans nesting in a bird sanctuary behind the B&B. Go for a swim in your hosts solar-heated pool or soak your cares away in a whirlpool spa. Then take a stroll through the famous sponge docks or do some antiquing in town. The inn is located just minutes from a white sandy beach with breathtaking sunsets.

### Fiorito's East Lake Bed & Breakfast
421 Old East Lake Road
813/937-5487

Just off a quiet road that runs along Lake Tarpon's horse country, this meticulously maintained home on two and a half acres offers respite for the visitor. The guest room and bath are decorated in tones of blue, enhanced with beautiful accessories. Fresh fruit, cheese omelet, homemade bread and jam, and a choice of beverage is served on the tree-shaded, screened terrace. The hosts will be happy to direct you to the Greek sponge docks in Tarpon Springs for deep-sea fishing, golf courses, beaches and great restaurants which abound in the area.

### Heartsease
272 Old East Lake Road
813/934-0994

You'll find plenty of "heartsease," meaning peace of mind and tranquillity at this beautiful guest suite. Wicker and pine furniture and a green and rose color scheme create a light and airy feeling. Amenities include a private entrance, minikitchen with a microwave, stocked with breakfast goodies, a color TV and private bath. The suite overlooks the pool and tennis courts. Pluck an orange or grapefruit from a tree and then settle in the gazebo, an ideal place to relax. Only twenty miles from Busch Gardens and five miles from the beach.

## 83  TITUSVILLE

**C.C.'s Antique Mall**
4547 S. Hopkins Ave.
407/383-2204

**Banana Alley – 1913 Shop**
106 Main St.
407/268-4282

**Crow's Nest**
4521 S. Hopkins Ave.
407/383-1007

**Dusty Rose Antique Mall**
1101 S. Washington Ave.
407/269-5526

*Florida*

**Linger Awhile Antiques & Gifts**
326 S. Washington Ave.
407/268-4680

**River Road Mercantile**
342 S. Washington Ave.
407/264-2064

## 84 VENICE

**Buttercup Cottage**
227 Miami Ave. W.
941/484-2222

**Albee Antiques**
602 E. Venice Ave.
941/485-0404

**Treasures in Time**
101 W. Venice Ave.
941/486-1700

## 85 VERO BEACH

**Red Barn Antiques**
5135 N. U.S. Hwy. 1
561/778-9860

**Gaslight Collectibles**
6235 U.S. Hwy. 1
561/569-0033

**Company Store & Antique Mall**
6605 N. U.S. Hwy. 1
561/569-9884

**Antique Alley**
1171 Commerce Ave.
561/569-5068

**Olde Towne Antiques**
1708 Old Dixie Hwy.
561/778-5120

**Antique Time**
3600 69th St.
561/567-0900

## 86 WALDO

**Waldo Antique Village**
17805 N.E. U.S. Hwy. 301
352/468-3111

**Red Barn of Waldo**
455 S.W. 3rd Way
352/468-2880

**Casa Las Brujas Antiques**
State Road 24
352/468-2709

**Laura's Antiques & Collectibles**
State Hwy. 24
352/468-2016

**Past Reflections**
250 N. Main St.
352/468-2528

## 87 WEST PALM BEACH

### Boomerang Modern

3301 S. Dixie Hwy.
561/835-1865
Open: Tues.–Sat. 11–5 and by appointment
Directions: On I-95, take Exit 50 (Southern Blvd.). Go east 1 mile to South Dixie Hwy. Then go north ½ mile to Boomerang Modern located on the left.

Boomerang Modern offers mid-20th century style and design, with the largest collection of blond, streamlined Heywood Wakefield furniture in the Southeast. Early and rare pieces designed by Gilbert Rhode, Leo Jiranek and the renowned streamline automotive designer Count Alexis de Sakhnoffsky, are featured.

Also offered are decorative objects and accessories by leading artisans

and designers of the mid-twentieth century, along with funky '50s lamps, ceramics and glass.

**Tinson Antique Galleries & Appraisers**
718 S. Dixie Hwy.
561/833-0700

**Argosy**
1913 S. Dixie Hwy.
561/832-5753

**Cassidy's Antiques**
3621 S. Dixie Hwy.
561/655-2313832-8017

**Antique Row's Little House**
3627 S. Dixie Hwy.
561/833-1552

**Bittersweet of Palm Beach, Inc.**
3630 S. Dixie Hwy.
561/655-2313

**Land's End Antiques**
3634 S. Dixie Hwy.
561/833-1751

**James & Jeffrey Antiques**
3703 S. Dixie Hwy.
561/832-1760

**Cashmere Buffalo**
3709 S. Dixie Hwy.
561/659-5441

**E. Nelson Antiques**
3715 S. Dixie Hwy.
561/659-4726

**Old-Timers Antique Mall**
3717 B Dixie Hwy.
561/832-5141

**Lu Lu's Stuff**
3719 S. Dixie Hwy.
561/655-1529

**Dennis Joel Fine Arts**
3720 S. Dixie Hwy.
561/835-1991

**Brass Scale**
3721 S. Dixie Hwy.
561/832-8410

**Art Lane's Time and Again**
3725 S. Dixie Hwy.
561/655-5171

**Elephant's Foot**
3800 S. Dixie Hwy.
561/832-0170

**John Cantrell & Margaret**
7729 S. Dixie Hwy.
561/588-8001

**Michael Maclean Antiques & Estate**
3803 S. Dixie Hwy.
561/659-0971

**Greta S. Decorative Antiques**
3803 ½ S. Dixie Hwy.
561/655-1533

**Floral Emporium**
3900 S. Dixie Hwy.
561/659-9888

**Time Worn Treasures**
4211 S. Dixie Hwy.
561/582-8064

**Real Life Antiques**
5105 S. Dixie Hwy.
561/582-8064

**Deco Don's**
5107 S. Dixie Hwy.
561/588-2552

**R. B. Antiques**
5109 S. Dixie Hwy.
561/533-5555

## 88 WINTER GARDEN

**Shirley's Antiques**
12900 W. Colonial Dr.
407/656-6406

**Winter Garden Country Store**
403 S. Dillard St.
407/656-0023

**Trailside Antiques**
12 W. Plant St.
407/656-6508

**Page's Pastiques, Inc.**
741 Tildenville School Road
407/877-3845

**Antiques**
1075 S. Vineland Ave.
407/656-5166

## 89 WINTER HAVEN

**Classic Collectibles & Antiques**
279 W. Central Ave.
941/294-6866 or 1-800-287-6866

**Antique Mall Village**
3170 U.S. Hwy. 17 N.
941/293-5618

**Joan Alach Antiques**
326 W. Central Ave.
941/293-8510

**Robert Holley Antiques & Gifts**
318 W. Central Ave.
941/299-3131

**Mimi's Bargain Corner**
3240 Dundee Road
941/324-5275

## 90 WINTER PARK

**Per Se Antiques & Collectibles**
116 E. Park Ave.
407/628-5231

**Antique Buff**
334 Park Ave. N.
407/628-2111

**Mimi's Antiques**
535 Park Ave. N.
407/645-3499

**Carol's Antiques & Collectibles**
171 E. Morse Blvd.
407/645-2345

**Our Antiques Market**
5453 Lake Howell Road
407/657-2100

**Orange Tree Antiques Mall**
853 S. Orlando Ave.
407/644-4547

**American Antiques**
1500 Formosa Ave.
407/647-2260

**Chintz & Co.**
515 Park Ave. N.
407/740-7224

**Ferris-Reeves Galleries**
140 E. Morse Blvd.
407/647-0273

**Ginger's Antiques**
2695 W. Fairbanks Ave.
407/740-8775

**Winter Park Antique Mall**
2335 Temple Trail
407/628-5384

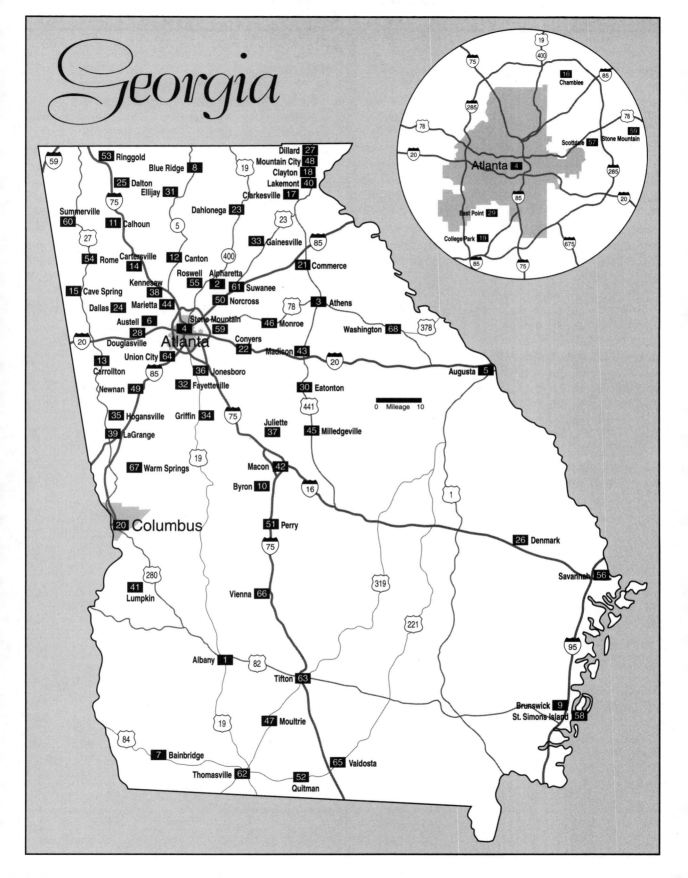

# Georgia

Dillard 27
Mountain City 48
Clayton 18
Lakemont 40
Clarkesville 17

53 Ringgold
Blue Ridge 8
19
25 Dalton
Ellijay 31
Dahlonega 23
23

59

Summerville 60
27
11 Calhoun
5
33 Gainesville
23
85

54 Rome
Cartersville 14
12 Canton
400
21 Commerce

15 Cave Spring
Kennesaw 38
Roswell 55
Alpharetta 2
61 Suwanee

Dallas 24
Marietta 44
50 Norcross
78
3 Athens

Austell 6
Stone Mountain 59
46 Monroe
Washington 68
378

28
Conyers 22
Madison 43

Douglasville
Atlanta 4 64
20

13
Union City
36 Jonesboro
Augusta 5

Carrollton
85
32 Fayetteville
30 Eatonton

Newnan 49
441

35 Hogansville
Griffin 34
45 Milledgeville

39 LaGrange
Juliette 37

67 Warm Springs
19
75

Macon 42
1

Byron 10
16

20 Columbus
26 Denmark

51 Perry
75

280
Savannah 56

41 Lumpkin
Vienna 66
319

221

95

Albany 1
82

Tifton 63

Brunswick 9
St. Simons Island 58

19
47 Moultrie

84
7 Bainbridge
65 Valdosta

Thomasville 62
52 Quitman

0  Mileage  10

## Atlanta (inset)

19
75
400
16 Chamblee
85
285
78
78
59
Scottdale 57
Stone Mountain
20
Atlanta 4
85
285
20
East Point 29
675
College Park 19
85
75

## 1 ALBANY

**Treasure House Antiques**
800 N. Slappey Blvd.
912/436-9874

**Bennett's Home Place**
910 N. Slappey Blvd.
912/436-0040

**Cottage Antiques**
526 Pine Ave.
912/435-7333

## 2 ALPHARETTA

## Queen of Hearts Antiques

700 N. Main St.
678/297-7571
Open: Mon.–Sat. 10–6, Sun. 12–5

Newest and largest antique mall in Alpharetta. Featuring fabulous selection of antiques and collectibles.

## Historic Crabapple Antique Village

For information call 770/475-4545
Open: Mon.–Sat. 10–5, Sun. 1–5
Directions: Historic Crabapple is located 25 miles north of Atlanta off GA-400; 5 miles north of Roswell/Crabapple Road.

Home of six fine antique shops housing over 40 antique dealers specializing in 18th- and 19th-century antiques, porcelains, early painted primitives, capel braided rugs, select reproductions and folk art.

The shops are housed in restored mercantile shops, Southern homes and a circa-1860 cotton gin.

**Old Milton Antique Mall**
27 S. Main St.
770/752-0777

**Main St. Antiques**
53 S. Main St.
770/663-1355

**A Flea Antique**
222 S. Main St.
770/442-8991

**Murf's Applecart Market**
735 Mayfield Road
770/740-0308

**Crabapple House Antiques**
765 Mid Broadwell Road
770/343-9454

**Crabapple HomePlace Antiques**
12680 Crabapple Road
770/475-2799

**Crabapple Corners**
790 Mayfield Road
770/475-4545

**Laura Ramsey Antiques**
220 S. Main St.
770/475-2085

**Sweetapple Antiques Crabapple**
780 Mayfield Road
770/663-6555

**Shops of the Gin**
780 Mayfield Road
770/475-3647

## 3 ATHENS

One of Athens' most cherished landmarks is a unique failure. The double-barreled cannon was cast at the Athens Foundry in 1862 to the specifications of John Gilleland, a local house builder.

Each barrel was to be loaded with a cannonball connected to the other by an eight-foot chain. When fired, the balls were supposed to separate, pull the chain taut and sweep across the field, mowing down Yankees.

A contemporary reported that when test-fired, the projectile "had a kind of circular motion, plowed up an acre of ground, tore up a cornfield, mowed down saplings, then the chain broke sending the two balls in opposite directions. One of the balls killed a cow in a distant field, while the other knocked down a chimney on a log cabin." The observers "scattered as though the entire Yankee army had been turned loose in that vicinity" (end of quote).

Athens displays its unusual weapon in a special park on the City Hall lawn, with the cannon pointing north, "just in case."

Another beloved landmark is the "tree that owns itself," perched atop a hill approached by a cobblestone street.

**Antiques Etc.**
10 Huntington Road, #3B
706/354-7863

**Archipelago Antiques**
1676 S. Lumpkin St.
706/354-4297

**Young's Antiques**
1379 Prince Ave.
706/353-6997

**Jingles**
1737 S. Lumpkin St., #B
706/549-6843

**Swap Shop**
1739 Lexington Road
706/613-6037

**Sam's Antiques**
1957 W. Broad St.
706/548-3764

**Stolls Studio**
135 Towns Grocery Road
706/549-4263

## 4 ATLANTA

## Cheshire Antiques

1859 Cheshire Bridge Road
404/733-5599
Open: Daily 11–7, closed Christmas & Thanksgiving
Directions: Located 1 mile from I-85. Take Monroe Drive or Lenox Road Exit, go 2 blocks north from Pedmont Road. Located in the shopping center.

Within 7,000 square feet of space, 35 dealers offer exceptional, sought-after items such as Hull, Fostoria, Fiesta, Roseville, McCoy and fine porcelains and glassware. In addition, the shop has dealers who specialize in toys, sterling and exquisite glassware.

## Historic Lakewood Antique Market
Lakewood Fairgrounds
404/622-4488
Open: Second weekend every month
Directions: I-75/85 to Exit 88, east to Lakewood Fairgrounds

Atlanta's oldest and largest antiques market. Over 1,500 dealers inside.
Thousands of dealers outside.

## Scott's Antique Market
Atlanta Expo Center
Open: Second weekend of every month
Directions: 3 miles east of Atlanta airport on I-285 at Exit 40

2,400 indoor booths, thousands of dealers outside.

**Turnage Place Antiques**
3097 Piedmont Road
404/239-0378

**Irish Country Pine Ltd.**
511 E. Paces Ferry Road
404/261-7924

**Now & Again**
56 E. Andrews Dr.
404/262-1468

**Reed Savage Antiques**
110 E. Andrews Dr.
404/262-3439

**Toby House**
517 E. Paces Ferry Road
404/233-2161

**Providence**
1409 N. Highland Ave.
404/872-7551

**Allan Arthur Oriental Rugs**
25 Bennett St.
404/350-9560

**Bittersweet Antiques**
45 Bennett St.
404/351-6594

**Interiors Market**
55 Bennett St.
404/352-0055

**John Eric Riis Designs Ltd.**
875 Piedmont Ave. N.E.
404/881-9847

**Peurifoy Antiques**
2300 Peachtree Road, Suite C103
404/355-3319

**Buckhead Antiques**
3207 Early St.
404/814-1025

**Jeff Littrell Antiques & Interiors**
178 Peachtree Hills Ave.
404/231-8662

**Plantation Shop**
96 E. Andrews Dr.
404/841-0065

**Regals Antiques**
351 Peachtree Hills Ave.
404/237-4899

**Antiques Etc.**
1044 N. Highland Ave.
404/874-7042

**Boomerang**
1145 Euclid Ave.
404/577-8158

**Beaman Antiques**
25 Bennett St.
404/352-9388

**H. Moog Antique Porcelains**
2300 Peachtree Road, Suite B 105
404/351-2200

**Jacqueline Adams Antiques**
2300 Peachtree Road, Suite B-110
404/355-8123

**Nottingham Antiques**
45 Bennett St.
404/352-1890

**Robuck & Co. Antiques**
65 Bennett St.
404/351-7173

**Shelton Antiques**
2267 Peachtree Road N.E.
404/351-5503

**J. Michael Stanley**
2265 Peachtree Road N.E.
404/351-1863

**Woodward & Warwick**
45 Bennett St.
404/355-6607

**Anne Flaire Antiques**
900 Huff Road N.W.
404/352-1960

**Bull & Bear Antiques**
1189 Howell Mill Road N.W.
404/355-6697

**Howell Mill Antiques**
1189 Howell Mill Road N.W.
404/351-0309

**O'Callaghan Antiques**
1157 Foster St. N.W.
404/352-2631

**Robert Mixon Antiques**
1183 Howell Mill Road N.W.
404/352-2925

**Acquistions**
631 Miami Circle N.E.
404/261-2478

**Antique Paintings**
631 Miami Circle N.E.
404/264-0349

**Bobby Dodd Antiques**
695 Miami Circle N.E.
404/231-0580

**Granny Taught Us How**
1921 Peachtree Road
404/351-2942

**Milou's Market**
1927 Cheshire Bridge Road N.E.
404/892-8296

**Pine & Design Imports**
721 Miami Circle N.E.
404/266-3741

**Thames Valley Antiques**
631 Miami Circle N.E.
404/262-1541

**Williams Antiques**
699 Miami Circle N.E.
404/231-9818

**Stalls at Bennett Street**
116 Bennett St.
404/352-4430

**Walker McIntyre Antiques**
2300 Peachtree Road, Suite B101
404/352-3722

**House of Treasures**
1771 Centra Villa Dr. S.W.
404/752-7221

**Atlanta Antiques Exchange**
1185 Howell Mill Road N.W.
404/351-0727

**Garwood House Ltd.**
1510 Ellsworth Industrial Blvd. N.W.
404/892-7103

**Pine Cottage**
1189 Howell Mill Road N.W.
404/351-7463

**Provenance**
1155 Foster St. N.W.
404/351-1217

**Another Time — Antiques**
1382 Dresden Dr. N.E.
404/233-2500

**Antique Collections**
1586 Piedmont Road N.E.
404/875-0075

**Freeman Galleries & Graham Antqs.**
631 Miami Circle N.E. #15
404/237-0599

**Canterbury Antiques Ltd.**
660 Miami Circle N.E.
404/231-4048

**Dearing Antiques**
709 Miami Circle N.E.
404/233-6333

**Out of the Attic Antiques**
1830 Cheshire Bridge Road N.E.
404/876-0207

**Red Baron's Private Reserve**
631 Miami Circle N.E.
404/841-1011

**Twickenham Gallery, Inc.**
631 Miami Circle, Suites 24 & 26
404/261-0951

**Antiquities Historical Gallery**
3500 Peachtree Road N.E.
404/233-5019

*Georgia*

**Sandy Springs Galleries**
233 Hilderbrand Dr. N.E.
404/252-3244

**The Levison & Cullen Gallery**
2300 Peachtree Road, Suite C101
404/351-3435

**Designer Antiques Ltd.**
25 Bennett St.
404/352-0254

**A Cherub's Attic**
2179 Cheshire Bridge Road N.E.
404/634-9577

**Act 2**
3070 Cambellton Road S.W.
404/629-9966

**Architectural Accents**
2711 Piedmont Road N.E.
404/266-8700

**Back to Square One**
1054 N. Highland Ave. N.E.
404/815-9970

**Consignment Shop**
1185 Howell Mill Road N.W.
404/351-6025

**Century Antique Rugs**
727 Miami Circle N.E.
404/816-2412

**Gables Antiques**
711 Miami Circle N.E.
404/231-0734

**English Accent Antiques**
22 Bennett St. N.W.
404/351-9433

**Joseph Konrad Antiques**
693 Miami Circle N.E.
404/261-3224

**Red Barons Antiques**
6450 Roswell Road N.E.
404/252-3770

**Antiques of Vinings**
4200 Paces Ferry Road N.W., #230
770/434-1228

**20th Century Antiques**
1044 N. Highland Ave.
404/892-2065

**Gallery Momoyama**
2273 Peachtree Road
404/351-0583

**A Flea Antique II**
1853 Cheshire Bridge Road N.E.
404/872-4342

**Antiquish Things**
3734 Roswell Road N.E.
404/261-0911

**Atlanta Camera Exchange**
2793A Clairmont Road N.E., #203
404/325-9367

**Big Chandelier**
484 14th St. N.W.
404/872-3332

**Cache Antiques**
1845 Cheshire Bridge Road N.E.
404/815-0880

**Davis & Fille Ltd. Antiques**
1151 Foster St. S.W.
404/352-5210

**Designer Antiques Ltd.**
25 Bennett St. N.W.
404/352-0254

**Jane Marsden Antiques**
2300 Peachtree Road N.W., #A102
404/355-1288

**Mayfair Antiques**
631 Miami Circle N.E.
404/816-4532

**Tara Antiques**
2325 Cheshire Bridge Road N.E.
404/325-4600

### Great Places to Stay

## Gaslight Inn
1001 St. Charles Ave. N.E.
404/875-1001
Web site: www.gaslightinn.com

This extravagantly decorated B&B inn has been featured in *Better Homes & Gardens* magazine and on CNN's *Travel Guide* show. *Frommer's Official Guide to Atlanta* lists the inn among the "Best Bets"

and says that "the most exquisite interior is found at the Gaslight Inn." Located in Atlanta's Virginia-Highland neighborhood and within walking distance of numerous restaurants, antique shops, galleries, and theaters, this inn is an oasis with a spectacular Southern-style walled garden. Other amenities include antique-glass light fixtures, six working fireplaces and detached carriage-house rooms.

### The Woodruff B&B
223 Ponce de Leon Ave.
1-800-473-9449
Email: RSVP@mindspring.com

Atlanta's Woodruff Bed and Breakfast is centrally located in midtown adjacent to many fine restaurants, cultural activities, and convention centers. This 1900s house abounds with original antiques, hardwood floors and stained glass windows. The Woodruff's history may make you smile or make you blush. Bessie Woodruff, along with a staff of fine young ladies, once operated a licensed massage parlor rumored to have catered to some of Atlanta's finest politicians.

### Ansley Inn
253 15th St.
1-800-446-5416

Built in 1907 as the home of famous Atlanta clothier George Muse, the Ansely Inn is a landmark in Ansley Park. It is within walking distance of the Atlanta Botanical Garden, Symphony Hall and the High Museum of Art. While close to midtown Atlanta office buildings, the inn is situated among other stately homes on a quiet tree-lined residential street. The inn offers the amenities normally found in much larger properties with the personal attention found only in the very best.

### Great Places to Eat

### Mary Mac's Tea Room
224 Ponce de Leon Ave. N.E.
404/876-1800

There seems to be something inversely proportional in the more of a lack of sophistication and elegance, to the more enjoyable and tasty cooking of food. Such is the case at Mary Mac's in Atlanta. It's a lunchroom with no frills and low prices where you write your own order for the waitress to pick up. But it is one of the tops in regional cuisine in the South. They even have a dessert called Carter Custard, made with peanuts and named after a well-known Georgia resident!

Mary Mac's is most noted for its fast service, fried chicken, and vegetables. Once you are seated at one of the plain laminated tables, you check the day's menu (printed on pastel paper), then write your order on a tiny pad. The waitress flies by, grabs the order, and is instantly back

*Georgia*

with the food! Do order the fried chicken, and eat as many different vegetables as you can get down. It is a breathtaking, belt-tightening experience.

## 5  AUGUSTA

**Antique World Mall, Inc.**
1124 Broad St.
706/722-4188

**Broad Street Antique Mall**
1224 Broad St.
706/722-4333

**Attic Antiques**
2301 Peach Orchard Road
706/793-1839

**Antiques & Furnishings**
1421 Monte Sano Ave.
706/738-4400

**Riverwalk Antique Depot**
505 Reynolds St.
706/724-5648

**Antique Market**
3179 Washington Road
706/860-7909

**Antiques & Stuff, Inc.**
4471 Columbia Road, #4
706/863-7195

**Charleston Street Antiques**
1423 Monte Sano Ave.
706/738-6298

**Merry's Trash & Treasures**
1236 Broad St.
706/722-3244

**Marketplace Antiques**
1208 Broad St.
706/724-6066

**Downtown Antique Mall**
1243 Broad St.
706/722-3571

**Quaint Shop**
1918 Central Ave.
706/738-7193

**Aunt Sissy's Antiques**
421 Crawford Ave.
706/736-0754

**Ann Spivey Antiques**
2611 Central Ave.
706/733-5889

**Antique Gallery of Augusta**
2055 Walton Way
706/667-8866

**Consignment Shop**
1421 Monte Sano Ave.
706/738-1340

**Days Gone By**
1401 Monte Sano Ave.
506/667-8579

### Great Places to Stay

**Azalea Inn**
312-316 Greene St.
706/724-3454
Web site: www.theazaleainn.com

Discover the Azalea Inn and enjoy turn of the century charm in this restored Victorian bed and breakfast. The inn provides upscale Victorian accommodations and elegance, presented with a personal touch. King and queen guest suites feature fireplaces, private baths with large Jacuzzi tubs, and 11-foot ceilings. The elegant decor includes antiques and period-style furnishings.

**The Partridge Inn**
2110 Walton Way
1-800-476-6888

The Partridge Inn is Old South indeed, offering charming white wicker, potted palms, and sunny porticoes for pure lyric. The Veranda Bar & Grill sings its own praise of the inn's glorious past, offering a quarter mile of covered verandas for comfortable, unique dining. Wall-to-wall sepia and black-and-white photographs, comfortable rattan, and overstuffed couches provide an atmosphere of relaxation and the comforts of home.

**Perrin Guest House Inn**
208 Lafayette Dr.
1-800-668-8930

The Perrin place is an old cotton plantation home established in 1863. The plantation's original tract has long since become the Augusta National, home of the Masters, while the three acres of the home place remain a little spot of magnolia heaven. For guests, Perrin offers ten beautifully appointed bedrooms featuring fireplaces, Jacuzzi, period antiques and gracious surroundings. Treat yourself to the pleasure of a front porch rocker or the comfort of a cozy parlor.

## 6  AUSTELL

**Grapevine**
2787 Bankhead Hwy.
404/944-8058

Specializing in Blue Ridge dinnerware; largest selection in the area.

**Whistle Stop Antiques**
2809 Bankhead Hwy.
404/739-8366

**Antiques & More**
4434 Powder Springs Road, #B
404/439-6605

**Ramona's Antiques & Things**
2805 Bankhead Hwy.
404/941-2993

**Wishful Thinking**
5850 Bankhead Hwy.
404/745-1194

**Busters Antiques**
6289 Bankhead Hwy.
404/944-7844

## 7  BAINBRIDGE

In Bainbridge you can picnic on the banks of the Flint River, shop quaint antique shops, dine in the Famous Jack Wingate Restaurant on Lake Seminole, and stay in a fine bed and breakfast.

**The Carousel House**
709 Calhoun St.
912/246-7022

**Jewels & Junk Antiques**
1204 Dothan Road
912/246-2518

*Georgia*

**Veranda Antiques**
218 E. Shotwell St.
912/246-8999

**Mi Mi's Mini Flea Market**
603 N. Miller Ave.
912/246-0013

**Tapestry Antiques**
420 1/2 E. Shotwell St.
912/243-7325

**The Coach House Antiques**
915 Albany Road
912/246-4153

**The Dusty Rose**
1314 Dothan Road
912/243-1777

### Great Places to Stay

**The Gilded Cage Bed & Breakfast**
722 S. West St.
912/243-2040

**The White House Bed & Breakfast**
320 Washington St.
912/248-1703

## 8   BLUE RIDGE

**Sammy's Antiques**
662 E. Main St.
706/632-3991

**Blue Ridge Antiques**
631 E. Main St.
706/632-7871

**Blue Ridge Antique Mall**
285 Depot St.
706/632-5549

**Main Street Antiques**
631 E. Main St.
706/632-7788

## 9   BRUNSWICK

## Fizzwhistle Antiques

4738 New Jesup Hwy.
912/261-1125
Directions: 3/4 mile east of I-95, Exit 7-A

Collectibles, folk art, art glass, Steuben, advertising, pottery, garden iron and furniture.

## Downtown Antique & Collectibles Mall

1208 Gloucester St.
912/264-2322
Open: Mon.–Sat. 10–6
Directions: Located in historic downtown Brunswick

Over 8,000 square feet of furniture, glassware, silver, pottery, pictures and quilts.

**Miss Milley's Antiques/Tea Room**
1709 Reynolds
912/265-5300

**Loves Antiques**
1508 Bay St.
912/265-9221

**Victorian Place**
1412 Gloucester St.
912/265-3175

**Hildergard's Antiques**
1515 Newcastle St.
912/265-8378

**Piddlers**
1505 Martin Luther King
912/265-0890

**Carriage Trade**
1529 Newcastle St.
912/261-0507

**Wisteria Lane**
211 Gloucester St.
912/261-2210

**Brown's Antiques**
1527 Norwich St.
912/265-6099

## 10   BYRON

## Big Peach Antique & Collectibles Mall

Hwy. 49 — Exit 46 at I-75
912/956-6256

40,000 square feet, over 200 dealers, 90 showcases.

**Lord Byron Antiques & Collectibles**
100 W. Heritage Blvd.
912/956-2789

**Little Peach Antiques & Gifts**
Hwy. 49
912/956-4222

## 11   CALHOUN

## Calhoun Antique Mall

1503 Red Bud Road N.E.
706/625-2767
Open: Mon.–Sat. 10–6, Sun. 1–5
Directions: From I-75, take Exit 130

80 dealers, over 10,000 square feet of antiques and collectibles.

**Ridley's Antiques**
209 S. Wall St.
706/629-8684

**Magnolia House**
309 Belwood
706/625-2942

**Showcase Antiques**
1017 Hwy. 53 East S.E.
706/602-1233

**Sam's Antiques**
3051 U.S. 41 Hwy. S.W.
706/629-6856

**Wall Street Trading**
117 S. Wall St.
706/625-0011

## 12   CANTON

**Beaver's Antiques**
370 E. Marietta St.
770/720-2927

**Chamberhouse**
145 W. Main St.
770/479-2463

**Cherokee Antiques**
210 Lakeside Dr.
770/345-2989

## 13   CARROLLTON

**Antiques & Stuff**
4552 Carrollton Villa Rica Hwy.
770/832-1855

**Antique Mall**
106 Adamson Square
770/832-2992

**Linda's Antiques**
269 Cross Plains Hulett Road
770/836-8051

**Cotton Gin Antiques**
4640 E. Hwy. 166
770/834-3196

**Carrollton Antique Mall**
109 City Hall Ave.
770/832-0507

**Ben's Antiques & Collectibles**
4098 N. Hwy. 27
770/832-8050

## 14 CARTERSVILLE

**Antiques Downtown**
9 E. Main St.
770/382-1744

**Ruff's Antiques**
525 Hwy. 61 S.E.
770/387-0084

## 15 CAVE SPRING

**County Roads Antique Mall**
19 Rome Road
706/777-8397

**411 Antiques & Uniques**
22 Alabama St.
706/777-0411

## 16 CHAMBLEE

### Eugenia's Authentic Antique Hardware
5370 Peachtree Road
770/458-1677 or 1-800-337-1677
Fax: 770/458-5966
Open: Mon.–Sat. 10–6

This is a store that should be invaluable to anyone who buys antiques. Eugenia's specializes in one-of-a-kind, hard-to-find hardware items. But what sets them apart is that all their hardware is authentic—no new pieces or reproductions. Owners Eugenia and Lance Dobson search out every piece, and clean and polish everything they buy for the store. They carry an extensive line of authentic antique door hardware, both interior and exterior, dating back to the 19th century, primarily 1840–1960. Here is just a short list of some of the items Eugenia's carries.

• Bath and powder-room accessories: soap, cup and toothbrush holders, towel bars, faucets, cast-iron claw feet, wire soap baskets, cabinet latches and hinges.

• Furniture hardware: handles, pulls and knobs in Hepplewhite, Queen Anne, arts and crafts, Art Deco, Victorian, Colonial, Eastlake, Art Nouveau, Chippendale.

• Door hardware, both interior and exterior: thumb-latch entry sets, glass rosette sets, Victorian cast-iron dead bolts, mortise locks, rim locks, elbow locks, door plates.

• Other accessories: sconces, door knockers, mechanical door bells, curtain/drapery tie-backs, hooks, letter slots, finials, switch/receptacle

**Oak Mountain Mall**
2093 S. Hwy. 16
770/838-0037

**Cartersville Antique Mall**
1277 Joe Frank Harris Pkwy. S.E.
770/606-0035

**Spring Place Antiques**
1329 Joe Frank Harris Pkwy. S.E.
770/387-1345

**Appletree Antiques**
24 Broad St.
706/777-8060

plates, pocket door hardware, brass bed finial balls, trunk/chest hardware, casters, decorative wrought iron pieces, old keys, door stops.

• Fireside shop: andirons, fire sets, fire fenders, fire screens, cast-iron grates.

**A Little Bit Country Antiques**
5496 Peachtree Road
770/452-1726

**Pennsylvania John's**
5459 B Peachtree Road
770/451-8774

**24 Carat Antiques**
5360 Peachtree Industrial Blvd.
770/451-2224

**Blue Max Antiques**
5180 Peachtree Industrial Blvd.
770/455-3553

**Cannon Mall Antiques**
3509 Broad St.
770/458-1662

**Blanton House Antiques**
5449 Peachtree Road
770/458-1453

**Rust & Dust Co.**
5486-92 Peachtree Road
770/458-1614

**Moose Breath Trading Co.**
5461 Peachtree Road
770/458-7210

**End of the Row Antiques**
5485 Peachtree Road
770/458-3162

**The Cameo Estate Jewelry**
3535 Broad St.
770/457-9925

**Antique Asylum**
5356 Peachtree Road
770/936-0510

**Chamblee Antique Row**
3519 Broad St.
770/455-4751

**Murphy's Antiques**
5180 Peachtree Industrial Blvd.
770/451-6143

**Metropolitan Artifacts**
4783 Peachtree Road
770/986-0007

**Happy Happy Shoppe**
5498 Peachtree Road
770/458-8700

**Way We Were Antiques**
5493 Peachtree Road
770/451-3372

**Antique City**
5180 Peachtree Industrial Blvd.
770/458-7131

**Atlanta Antq. Center & Flea Market**
5360 Peachtree Industrial Blvd.
770/458-0456

**Antique Haus**
3510 Broad St.
770/455-7570

**Broad Street Antique Mall**
3550 Broad St.
770/458-6316

**Helen's Antiques & Collectibles**
5494 Peachtree Road
770/454-9397

**Biggar Antiques**
5576 Peachtree Road
770/451-2541

**Liza's Cafe**
2201 American Industrial Blvd.
770/452-7001

**Baby Jane's**
5350 Peachtree Road
770/457-4999

**Atlanta Vintage Books**
3660 Clairmont Road N.E.
770/457-2919

**Great Gatsby's**
5070 Peachtree Industrial Blvd.
770/457-1905

**Townsend Fine Antique Clocks**
3524 Broad St.
770/986-8981

**24 Carat Antiques**
5180 Peachtree Industrial Blvd.
770/451-2224

*Georgia*

## 17  CLARKESVILLE

**Barbara's Antiques**
Hwy. 197
706/947-1362

**Wonders' Antiques**
On The Square - Washington St.
706/754-6883

**Once Upon a Time Co.**
On The Square - 1440 N. Washington
706/754-5789

**Mustang Village Antiques**
6357 State Hwy. 17
706/754-3179

**Dixie Galleries Antiques**
1404 Washington Square
706/754-7044

**Parker Place Antiques & Gifts**
On The Square - Washington St.
706/754-5057

**Nostalgia Antiques & Collectibles**
On The Square - 1417 Washington St.
706/754-3469

## 18  CLAYTON

**Berry Patch Antiques**
Hwy. 441 N.
706/782-7216

**Second Hand Rose Antiques**
Charlie Mountain Road
706/782-1350

**Rhonnettes**
W. Savannah St.
706/782-6963

**Timpson Creek Millworks**
Hwy. 76 W.
706/782-5164

**Heritage Antiques**
Hwy. 441 S.
706/782-6548

**Mountain Peddlers**
E. Savannah St.
706/782-4633

**Shiloh Post Cards**
Main St.
706/782-4100

### *Great Places to Eat*

## Green Shutters Tea Room
Old Hwy. 441, south of Clayton
706/782-3342

If you've never experienced the utter delight and pure pleasure of eating great food in the absolute quiet of the real, undisturbed country, then take a break and eat at the Green Shutters Tea Room. Hidden in the mountains of northern Georgia, this little jewel has been serving three meals a day for the past 40 or so years.

Get there early and enjoy breakfast on the back porch overlooking a meadow with a split-rail fence, and watch the sunrise slowly paint the dewy grass with tiny jewels of light while the rooster crows. Eat crisp-crust biscuits slathered in homemade jelly and honey fresh from the hive, crispy pan-fried country ham, grits swimming in butter, eggs any way you like and steaming hot coffee.

Stop for lunch or dinner in the indoor dining room, and sink into crunchy fried chicken, country ham, biscuits, and all the Southern-style vegetables you can imagine. Everything is served country/family style, in bowls that are passed whenever needed. Green Shutters is open from

the day school closes until the day school starts, or until it gets too cold, so call first to see if they're cooking.

## 19  COLLEGE PARK

**Mu Mac Antiques**
3383 Main St.
404/768-6121

**Sarah's Antiques**
2815 Roosevelt Hwy.
404/761-2881

**Good & Plenty Antiques**
3827 Main St.
404/762-5798

**Royal Touch Antiques**
3395 Main St.
404/669-9525

**Gallen's Antiques**
1682 Virginia Ave.
404/761-5166

## 20  COLUMBUS

**Beaver's Antiques**
1409 Warm Spring Road
706/327-2123

**Granny's Thrift Shop**
308 10th St.
706/324-3378

**English Patina**
1120 10th Ave.
706/576-4300

**The Tea Caddy**
1231 Stark Ave.
706/327-3010

**Keeping Room**
4518 Reese Road
706/563-2504

**Peaches & Cream**
1443 17th St.
706/327-7485

**Farmhouse Furniture**
3808 River Road
706/323-4325

**Scavengers**
1147 Brown Ave.
706/324-3539

**That Added Touch of Columbus**
1103 13th St.
706/327-2330

**Glass Porch Antiques**
3852 Gentian Blvd.
706/569-7777

**Charles & Di Antiques**
7870 Veterans Pkwy.
706/324-3314

### *Nearby Antique Shopping (Phenix City, Ala.)*
### *Phenix City is across the river from Columbus.*

## Zeke's Antique Mall
1921 Crawford Road
334/297-5011
Open: Tues.–Sat. 10–5

Specializing in primitive antiques and architectural elements.

*Georgia*

## 21 COMMERCE

### *Great Places to Stay*

#### The Pittman House
81 Homer Road
706/335-3823

Built by rural mail carrier T. C. Pittman in 1890, this stunning home is located in northeast Georgia about one hour from anything important in the northeast Georgia mountains. You can visit college campuses, attend major sporting events, fish to your heart's content, golf on championship golf courses (3 or 4 in the immediate area), and antique at many shops in the area. There are many discount shops in the shopping malls five minutes away.

## 22 CONYERS

**Collector's Choice**
908 Commercial St. N.E.
770/388-9434

**Conyers Antique Junction**
939 Railroad St. N.W.
770/922-5445

**Horse Crazy**
936 Center St. N.E.
770/860-1966

## 23 DAHLONEGA

**Do-Drop-In Antiques**
87 N. Chestatee St.
706/867-6082

**Golden Memories Antiques**
8 Public Square
706/864-7222

**Rockhouse Market Place**
Hwy. 52 E. & Rockhouse Road
706/864-0305

**Quigley's Antiques & Rare Books**
103 N. Chestatee St. N.W.
706/864-0161

### *Great Places to Stay*

#### Stanton Storehouse
78 Meaders St. N.
706/864-6114

Situated two blocks from the historic courthouse and public square, the inn is a short stroll to all the downtown attractions and restaurants. The inn's three suites are situated on the second floor of this folk Victorian storehouse built in 1884. A full gourmet breakfast is served each morning and afternoon tea may be enjoyed in the Rose and Herb Garden. Claw-foot and whirlpool tubs, fireplace, English and American antique furnishings, and original hand-finished heart of pine floors complete the decor.

### *Great Places to Eat*

#### The Smith House
84 S. Chestatee
706/864-3566

The Smith House is a first-come, first-served, no-holds-barred kind of place; no reservations are accepted, and on weekends the place is packed. It's an elbow-to-elbow type of atmosphere, with communal tables, shared by whomever is fortunate enough to get a seat! Pay one price and eat all you want. There is no menu, no choices. Everything that the kitchen has prepared that day is brought to the tables in large serving dishes, and it's a constant passing game. You can always count on fried chicken, bolstered either by Brunswick stew or catfish and hush puppies, plenty of Southern-style vegetables and warm breads.

The history of the Smith House began before the Civil War, during Georgia's gold rush—yes, I mean Georgia! This Southern love affair with the golden stuff attracted prospectors from all over America, one of whom was wealthy Vermonter Captain Frank Hall. Hall staked a claim just east of Dahlonega's public square, and struck a fashionably rich lode. Dahlonega authorities, so the legend goes, would not allow their town's heart to be stripped open, so the stubborn Yankee decided if he couldn't have the wealth, nobody could. He promptly built an ostentatious mansion, complete with carriage house and servants' quarters, right on top of the vein! In 1922, long after Captain Hill's feud with Dahlonega had ended, Henry and Bessie Smith bought the house to operate it as an inn. For $1.50 travelers got a room and three meals! Mrs. Smith was a sensational cook, and praise for her culinary creations soon spread far and wide, especially about her fried chicken, country ham and fresh vegetables. When Fred and Thelma Welch took over ownership in 1946, the Smith House became known for its family-style offerings. Today, although the rooms have been spruced up a little, the food has not changed. It's still old-fashioned north Georgia cooking. As of yet, nobody has tried to dig up Captain Hall's gold.

## 24 DALLAS

#### Estate Antiques
210-216 Main St.
770/443-0751
Open: Mon.–Sat. 10–5

7,000 square feet of oak, Victorian, Empire, French, Art Deco, primitive, Roseville, Watt, Shawnee, Hull, McCoy, Murano, Nippon, Heisey, toby mugs, Jewel Tea, bottles, Coke advertising, clocks, Depression glass, old coins and much, much more.

*Georgia*

## Log Cabin Antiques
101 Holder Road
770/445-1317
Open: Thurs.–Sat. 10–5, Sun.–Wed. by chance
Directions: 1 mile east of Dallas off East Memorial Dr.

Specializing in country and primitives; pie safes, cupboards, Hoosier cabinets, rope beds, crocks, Amish rockers, quilts and churns.

**The Country House**
255 E. Memorial Dr.
770/445-7060

**Somewhere in Time**
213 Main St.
770/445-7555

## 25 DALTON

**Jot M Down Store**
311 N. Glenwood Ave.
706/226-2872

**Simply Outrageous**
114 W. Cuyler St.
706/272-4744

## 26 DENMARK

### 67 Antique Mall
6700 Hwy. 67
912/839-2757
Open: Mon.–Sun. 10–6
Directions: From I-16 take Exit 26, go north 2/10 of a mile

Featuring 40 dealers with a large selection of antiques. Several dealers specialize in stained glass, china, Currier & Ives and art pottery.

## 27 DILLARD

**Appalachian Trader**
Hwy. 441
706/746-5194

**Olde Feed Store Mall**
1093 Franklin St.
706/746-6525

**Black Rock Antiques**
Hwy. 441
706/746-2470

**Yesterday's Treasures**
6 Depot St.
706/746-3363

**Pine Cone Antiques of Dillard**
Hwy. 441
706/746-2450

**Stikeleathers**
Hwy. 441
706/746-6525

**Treasures Old & New Antiques**
Hwy. 441
706/746-6566

**Village Peddler**
Hwy. 441
706/746-5156

## 28 DOUGLASVILLE

**The Trading Post**
4233 Bankhead Hwy.
Tues.-Sat. 11-6

**Homespun Country Antiques**
6118 Fairburn Road
770/949-1020

**Your Cup of Tea**
5848 Bankhead Hwy.
770/489-7908

**Antiques by the Square**
6674 Broad St.
770/577-9075

**Antiques of Klint Chestnut**
6722 Broad St.
770/920-6722

### *Nearby Antique Shopping (Lithia Springs)*

### White House Antiques
3803 Temple St.
770/944-8181
Open: Tues.–Sat. 10–5

Specializing in American, Victorian and primitive furnishings.

## 29 EAST POINT

**Dragon's Lair**
1605 White Way
404/762-7020

**Amazing Grace Elephant Co.**
1613 White Way
404/767-2423

**Sara Goen's Antiques**
1603 White Way
404/762-1234

## 30 EATONTON

Welcome to Eatonton and Putnam County, home of Brer Rabbit and the Uncle Remus Tales. As you drive through the tree-lined streets, you will witness some of the most unique styles of antebellum architecture in the South, or you might even catch a glimpse of Sylvia, the ghost that occupies Panola Hall, the former home of Dr. Benjamin Hunt. Eatonton is proud of the many people it has produced. Two of the most famous are Joel Chandler Harris, creator of the Uncle Remus Tales; and Alice Walker, author and Pulitzer Prize winner for her book *The Color Purple*.

**Fox Hunt Antiques**
109 N. Jefferson Ave.
706/485-6402

**Crystal Palace Flea Market**
1242 Madison Road
706/485-9010

## 31 ELLIJAY

**East Towne Antiques**
715 River St.
706/636-1931

**Victorian Attic**
40 N. Main St.
706/636-3700

**Cartecay Trading Post**
Big Creek Road
706/635-7009

**Old Hotel Antique Mall**
11 North Ave.
706/276-2467

**Antiques & More**
6 River St.
706/635-7738

**Ole Harpers Store**
3 miles out 52 W.
706/276-7234

**Coosawattee Mini Mall**
215 S. Main St.
706/636-4004

*Georgia*

## 32 FAYETTEVILLE

**Brannon Antiques**
165 W. Lanier Ave.
770/461-9160

**Fayette Collectibles**
105 E. Stonewall Ave.
770/460-6979

**Attic Treasures Antiques**
235 S. Glynn St.
770/460-8114

## 33 GAINESVILLE

**Antiquities in Time**
330 Bradford St. N.
770/534-3689

**Antiques & Uniques**
2145 Cleveland Road
770/536-1651

**Brickstore Antiques**
1744 Cleveland Road
770/532-8033

**Queen City Antiques**
112 Bradford St. N.E.
770/535-8884

**Gainesville Antique Gallery**
131 Bradford St.
770/532-4950

**Fourth Colony Antique Shop**
5170 Browns Bridge Road
770/536-6423

**Antique Nook**
1740 Cleveland Road
770/536-0646

**Curiosity Shop**
2714 Old Cornelia Hwy.
770/536-7088

**Stuff Antiques**
4760 Dawsonville Hwy.
770/889-8183

## 34 GRIFFIN

**Dovedown Antique Mall**
315 W. Solomon St.
770/412-6121

**J. Newton Bell Jr. Antiques, Inc.**
417 S. 6th St.
770/227-2516

**Nearly New Store**
1003 W. Taylor St.
770/229-8397

**Treasures Antiques & Furniture**
233 N. Hill St.
770/228-0053

**Complements**
522 W. Solomon St.
770/229-2561

**Solomon House Antiques**
103 N. 13th St.
770/229-5390

**Country Cottage**
1975 Atlanta Road
770/227-0476

## 35 HOGANSVILLE

**Ray Cheatham's Enterprises**
304 E. Main St.
706/637-6227

**Liberty Hill Antiques**
301 S. Hwy. 29
706/637-5522

## 36 JONESBORO

**Jonesboro Antique Shoppe**
203 N. Main St.
770/478-4021

## 37 JULIETTE

In Juliette the primary color is green, as in *Fried Green Tomatoes*. They are now served hot at the Whistle Stop Cafe, the actual film location of the movie. Other notable stops include the Piedmont Wildlife Refuge, Lake Juliette and the 1847 Jarrell Plantation Historic Site.

**Garments Praise & Antiques**
McCrackin Road
912/994-0011

**Southern Grace**
420 McCrackin St.
912/994-0057

## 38 KENNESAW

**By-Gone Treasures**
2839 S. Main St.
770/428-2262

**Kennesaw Mountain Military**
1810 Old Hwy. 41
770/424-5225

**Garner's Antiques**
2950 Moon Station Road
770/428-6481

**Big Shanty Antique Mall**
1720 N. Roberts Road
770/795-1704

## 39 LaGRANGE

**BJ's Quiet Country Barn**
29 Old Hutchinson Mill Road
706/845-7838

**B. A. Evans Home House**
2106 Hamilton Road
706/882-1184

**Lemon Tree Shoppes**
204 Morgan St.
706/882-5382

**Main Street Antique Mall**
130 Main St.
706/884-1972

## 40 LAKEMONT

### The Lakehouse on Lake Rabun
Lake Rabun Road
706/782-1350
404/351-5859
Open: Fri., Sat., and Sun. 11–6 May 1–Oct. 30, closed winter months
Directions: From Clayton, Ga., go south on Hwy. 441 approximately 4 miles to Wiley Junction. Turn sharp right and go 50 yards to old Hwy. 441. Turn left and go approximately 1 mile to Alley's store in Lakemont. Continue approximately 1/4 mile to a fork in the road. Take the right fork (Lake Rabun Road) and go approximately 2 miles to The Lakehouse antique shop (on the left across from the historic Rabun Hotel).

The Lakehouse antique shop on beautiful Lake Rabun in the northeast Georgia mountains is a multidealer shop with two floors of antiques and mountain (rustic) furniture. The shop specializes in Adirondack furnishings for the mountain cabin and lake home. They also carry a line of mountain twig furnishings by Buz Stone. Bamboo fly rods, outboard motors, old camp paddles, blankets, birchbark items along with local folk ark and paintings complete the inventory at this unique mountain shop.

## 41  LUMPKIN

### Nana's Nook

South side of Court House Square
912/838-4131
Open: Tues.–Sat. 11–5, Sun. by chance and closed Mon.
Directions: Nana's Nook is located on the south side of the Court House Square, Lumpkin, Ga. Lumpkin is 35 miles south of Columbus, Ga., on U.S. 27.

Nana's Nook, owned and operated by Dolores Harris and Gina Mathis, a mother and daughter team, has no consignors or dealers. It was a life-long dream of Dolores (Nana) to own an antique shop when she retired after having taught 30 years of elementary school music. Daughter Gina talked her into opening the shop. Their goal is to have affordable antiques and collectibles for everyone's taste and budget. The two have decorated the shop as you would your own home and have been complimented numerous times by customers on its "at home" feel and "no dust" atmosphere. While visiting Lumpkin, be sure to enjoy the other shops and tourist sights such as Westville Historic Village and Providence Canyon State Park. The town of Lumpkin offers two great places to eat, Dr. Hatchett's Drugstore Museum and Michele's Country Cooking Buffet.

| **Browse-a-Bout** | **Town Square Antiques** |
|---|---|
| Broad St. | 104 Broad St. |
| 912/838-6793 | 912/838-0400 |

### *Interesting Side Trips*

### The Village of Westville

Intersection of U.S. 27 and GA. 27
912/838-6310
Open: Tues.–Sat. 10–5, Sun. 1–5

Westville is a functioning living-history village of relocated, authentically restored original buildings and landscape. The Village of Westville realistically depicts Georgia's preindustrial life and culture of 1850 for your educational benefit.

Stroll down the streets and watch craftsmen at work producing items for their neighbors in the village. Hear the clang of the blacksmith's hammer and anvil, and smell the gingerbread and biscuits cooking on the stove and fireplace. Try your hand at making seasonal crafts, such as candles, syrup, and soap. Here, your family will "glimpse the forgotten dreams" of 150 years past.

## 42  MACON

Welcome to America's dream town, historic Macon, your southernmost stop on Georgia's Antebellum Trail. Founded in 1823 on the banks of the Ocmulgee River, Macon is a dream town for those looking for a wealth of antebellum treasures. Wide avenues, created by Macon's original town planners, lead you through what has been called "a city in a park." In fact, Macon was designed to resemble the ancient gardens of Babylon, providing for large parks and garden squares. Today, some 200,000 Yoshino cherry trees throughout the city make Macon the cherry blossom capital of the world!

### Village Antique Mall

2390 Ingleside Ave.
912/755-0075
Email: vam2@mindspring.com
Open: 7 days a week until 6. Extended hours at Christmas.
Directions: Located only three minutes from I-75 in the heart of Georgia. Northbound, take Exit 52, cross 41 South, turn left onto 41 North, turn right at the 5th traffic light (Rogers Ave.), go to the next traffic light and turn left onto Ingleside Avenue. You will find Village Antique Mall at the end of the block on the left. From Exit 54 southbound, go to second traffic light and turn right onto Ingleside Avenue. They will be on the left after the first traffic light at the end of the block.

Specializing in pieces rarely found in the area, Village Antique Mall offers the discriminating shopper items from the arts and crafts era, such as Stickley, Limbert, Van Briggle and Niloak. Twenty-five expert antique dealers specialize in fine china, oil paintings, '30s & '40s mahogany furnishings as well as period pieces offered by Sherwood Antiques. Considered by its customers to be one of the finest antique malls in the middle Georgia area, this shop prides itself on offering only the finest in true antiques and collectibles.

Dealer of quality-care products for your antiques: Howard's Products, Kramer's Antiques Improver, Bri-Wax and more.

| **Eclectic Era Antique Place** | **Exmoor Antiques** |
|---|---|
| 1345 Hardeman Ave. | 2370 Ingleside Ave. |
| 912/746-1922 | 912/746-7480 |
| **Catherine Callaway Antiques** | **McLean Antiques** |
| 3164 Vineville Ave. | 2291 Ingleside Ave. |
| 912/755-9553 | 912/745-2784 |
| **Yellow House Antiques** | **Mallard Nest Antiques** |
| 2176 Ingleside Ave. | 5860 Bankston Lake Road |
| 912/742-2777 | 912/788-8606 |
| **Kennington's Antiques** | **Amals Antiques** |
| 5296 Riverside Dr. | 3108 Vineville Ave. |
| 912/477-1422 | 912/746-1878 |
| **Antiques & Nostalgia** | **Attic Treasures** |
| 612 Poplar St. | 2989 Columbus Road |
| 912/746-8668 | 912/742-6072 |
| **Colonial Collection** | **Edwards House** |
| 1346 Hardeman Ave. | 2376 Ingleside Ave. |
| 912/746-1922 | 912/741-9825 |

**Kathryn's Fine Furniture**
623 Cherry St.
912/755-8700

**Purple Door**
6394 Zebulon Dr.
912/477-7170

**Old Mill Antique Mall**
155 Coliseum Dr.
912/743-1948

### 43 MADISON

**Old Madison Antiques**
184 S. Main St.
706/342-3839

### 44 MARIETTA

## DuPre's Antique Market
17 Whitlock Ave.
770-428-2667

Over 90 dealers in a 14,000-square-foot showroom at the historic Marietta Square. Featuring antique furniture, clocks, jewelry, Depression glass, primitives, art, garden items and much more. The market also has an in-house clock repair shop. For more information on DuPre's and to view hundreds of pictured items for sale, visit their web site at www.antiqnet.com/dup.

**Railway Antiques & Design Center**
472 N. Sessions St. N.W.
770/427-8505

**Keeping Room**
77 Church St.
770/499-9577

**Southern Traditions Antiques**
93 Church St.
770/428-6005

**Willow Antiques**
105 Church St.
770/426-7274

**Mountain Mercantile**
115 Church St.
770/429-1889

**Trading Memories**
686 Roswell Road
770/421-9724

**Payne Mill Village Antiques**
342 Rose Ave.
912/741-3821

**Steve Popper Gift & Antique**
1066 Magnolia Dr.
912/743-2234

**Attic Treasures Antiques**
121 S. Main St.
706/342-7197

**Antique Accents**
67 Church St.
770/426-7373

**Hill House Antiques**
85 Church St.
770/425-6169

**Heather's Neste**
95 Church St.
770/919-8636

**Mountain Mercantile**
107 Church St.
770/429-1663

**Antique Store of Marietta**
113 Church St.
770/428-3376

**Back Home Antiques**
1450 Roswell Road
770/971-5342

**A Classy Flea**
1355 Roswell Road
770/579-2555

**Abe's Antiques**
1951 Canton Road
770/424-0587

**Papa's Antiques**
721 Roswell St. N.E.
770/590-0109

**Ari's I Antiques**
19 Powder Springs St.
770/425-0811

**Antiques & Interiors**
685 Johnson Ferry Road
770/565-7903

**Antique Corner**
110 S. Park Square
770/428-4294

**Antiquity Mall**
815 Pine Manor
770/428-8238

**My Favorite Things**
1355 Roswell Road, #200
770/992-7589

### 45 MILLEDGEVILLE

**J & K Fleas Antiques**
2937 N. Columbia St.
912/454-3006

**Sugartree**
1045 N. Jefferson St. N.E.
912/452-7914

**Carolyn's Antiques**
1415 Vinson Hwy. S.E.
912/453-9676

**Marietta Antiques Exchange**
1505 Roswell Road
770/565-7460

**Water Spaniel Collectibles**
7 Whitlock Ave.
770/427-0277

**Lamps of Yesteryear, Inc.**
5 Powder Springs St.
770/424-6015

**Juniper Tree Collectibles & Antqs.**
15 W. Park Square
770/427-3148

**Victoria's Garden**
21 W. Park Square
770/419-0984

**Antiques on the Square**
146 S. Park Square
770/429-0434

**Elizabeth Cottage**
825 Church St. Extd.
770/424-6818

**Jean's Antique Shop**
2205 Irwinton Road
912/452-1550

**Browsing Barn**
169 Sparta Hwy. N.E.
912/452-7740

*Great Places to Stay*

## Maras Tara
330 W. Greene St.
912/453-2732

Straight from the pages of *Gone with the Wind*, this beautiful 171-year-old home boasts massive columns on three sides. With over 5,000 square feet of finished space, the Maras Tara has two parlors, a library and is filled with pre–Civil War antiques. Conveniently located in the center of the historic district.

*Georgia*

## 46 MONROE

**Primitive Touch**
136 N. Broad St.
770/267-9799

**Picket Fence**
120 N. Broad St.
770/267-3350

**Marvin's Antiques**
104 Walker St.
770/267-2271

**Road Side Bargain Shop**
2183 Hwy. 78 N.W.
770/267-6227

**Green Leaf Consign. & Flea Market**
530 S. Madison Ave.
770/267-0952

**Walton County Flea Market**
216 Davis St.
770/267-9927

## 47 MOULTRIE

**Olde Harmony Antiques**
15 2nd Ave. S.E.
912/985-5679

**Southland Country Antiques**
123 1st St. S.E.
912/985-7212

**Sid's**
112-114 1st St. N.E.
912/985-8300

**R & R Antiques**
4246 Tallokas Road
912/985-3595

**Southland Antiques & Gifts**
120 1st St. S.E.
912/890-2092

## 48 MOUNTAIN CITY

**Lana's Country Store**
Hwy. 441 - Depot St.
Seasonal Shop

**Blue Antler**
Hwy. 441 - Depot St.
706/746-7381

**Rocking Horse Antiques**
Hwy. 441 - Depot St.
706/746-6979

## 49 NEWNAN

### Rockin' B Antiques
Hwys. 34 & 154
770/253-8730
Open: Mon.–Sat. 10–6, Sun. 12–6
Directions: 4 miles south of I-85 and Hwy. 154. 1½ miles south of
Thomas Crossroads.

10,500 square feet, 62 booths plus glass cases.

**Homespun Heart**
50 Farmer St.
770/253-0480

**Green Door**
53 Southerland Dr.
770/251-9993

**Amelia's Collectibles**
182 Jefferson St.
770/251-6467

**RJ's Antiques & Collectibles**
17 Augusta Dr.
770/251-0999

**Three Crowns Antiques Ltd.**
733 E. Hwy. 34
770/253-4815

**Jefferson House Antiques & Gifts**
51 Jefferson St.
770/253-6171

## *Great Places to Stay*

### The Old Garden Inn
51 Temple Ave.
706/304-0594

The Old Garden Inn is a neoclassic Greek Revival mansion located in one of five historic districts of Newnan. While housed in a wonderful old home, the innkeeper's focus is always the relaxation and comfort of each guest. The atmosphere is casual while the surroundings are serene and elegant. The cozy guest rooms offer bubbles, lotions, and romantic candles.

## 50 NORCROSS

**Georgia Antique Center & Market**
6624 Dawson Blvd.
770/446-9292

**Antiques Market**
6 Jones St.
770/840-8365

**Pride of Dixie Antique Market**
1700 Jeurgens Court
770/279-9853

## 51 PERRY

**Antiques from the Shed**
1139 Macon Road
912/987-2469

**Rainbow's End**
1126 Macon Road
912/987-0994

**Perry Antique Mall**
351 Gen. C. Hodges Blvd.
912/987-4001

**The Front Porch Antique Mall**
1127 Macon Road
912/988-9035

## 52 QUITMAN

**Backward Glance**
111 E. Screven St.
912/263-4430

**Blair's Flowers & Gifts**
110 W. Screven St.
912/263-8902

**Coin Quest**
113 E. Screven St.
912/263-8083

**Quitman Antique Mall**
101 E. Screven St.
912/263-4808

**Bank of Antiques**
108 S. Lee St.
912/263-5537

**Bargain Place**
401 E. Screven St.
912/263-4120

**Keeping Room Antiques**
313 E. Screven St.
912/263-4411

**McCord's Antiques**
311 E. Screven St.
912/263-9004

*Georgia*

### *Great Places to Stay*

## Malloy Manor Bed & Breakfast

401 W. Screven St.
912/263-5704 or 1-800-239-5704
Rates: $55–$85
Directions: Go west on U.S. Hwy. 84 off I-75 at the Quitman, Ga., exit, about halfway between Atlanta and Orlando.

Malloy Manor is the place to go to experience a unique blend of Victorian elegance and Old South hospitality! At this three-story, 1905 Victorian home listed on the National Register of Historic Places, you can literally stop and smell the roses, or any other flowers for that matter, because this city is situated in the middle of a "fragrance zone." Quitman is Georgia's camellia city; Valdosta, Georgia's azalea city, and Thomasville, Georgia's rose city.

You can imagine yourself in pre–Civil War times enjoying the balmy days on the large wraparound porch outfitted with rockers and a swing, or gliding gracefully through the entrance that features leaded glass in sidelights and transom, with more leaded glass sidelights in the upper sitting room. All the staircases, wainscoting and moldings are original, and each room holds not only antiques and lace curtains but a working fireplace! The parlor features a wind-up Victrola, and the music room houses an old upright piano. Three suites are available, each with sitting room and private bath. There is also a pair of rooms that share a sitting room and bath. Gourmet lunches and dinners are served next door at the Booth House restaurant, in a restored Victorian home.

Antiquers can explore all of Quitman—the entire town is on the National Historic Register!—and there are multiple antique shops and fascinating old homes. The Brooks County Cultural Arts Museum, open every afternoon, features local artistry and Civil War and local artifacts.

## 53  RINGGOLD

## Gateway Antiques Center

4103 Cloud Springs Road
706/858-9685
Open: Daily 9–8
Directions: Last exit in Georgia or first exit south of Chattanooga, I-75 Exit 142 — 200 yards on right.

Gateway Antiques Center, appropriately named for its location in Georgia, is a whopping 40,000-square-foot wonderland of antiques and collectibles. Considered by some to be the South's largest antique mall (I certainly won't argue that), the store has 300 dealers, 400 showcases and a true sampling of every antique imaginable. The mall specializes in offering a large variety of smalls for the traveler.

**Autumn Oak Antique Mall**
383 Bandy Lane
706/965-7222

**Joel's Antiques**
4192 Bandy Road
706/965-2097

**Huskey's Antiques**
3218 Boynton Dr.
706/937-4881

**Barn Gallery Antiques**
Alabama Road
706/935-9044

**My Favorite Things**
7839 Nashville St.
706/965-8050

**Golden Oak Gallery**
5546 Boynton Dr.
706/86602526

## 54  ROME

## Antique Mall

1943 Broad St.
706/234-5667
Open: Mon.–Sat. 10–6, Sun. 1–5

Over 100 dealers offering a general line of antiques and collectibles.

## Rare Cargo

239 Broad St.
706/290-9010

Over 5,000 square feet of fine antiques and collectibles.

**Apple Cart Antiques**
1572 Burnett Ferry Road
706/235-7356

**Heritage Antique Mall**
174 Chatillon Road
706/291-4589

**Northside Antiques**
1203 Calhoun Ave.
706/232-6161

**Three Rivers Antique Shop**
109 Broad St.
706/290-9361

**Chisholm & Thomason Ltd.**
14 E. 3rd Ave.
706/234-0533

**Skelton's Red Barn Antiques**
10 Burton Road
706/295-2713

**Antique Musique**
2358 Old Kingston Hwy.
706/291-9230

**Masters Antiques**
241 Broad St.
706/232-8316

**Smart Shop**
1943 N. Broad St.
706/234-5667

**Grandpa's Attic**
516 Shorter Ave.
706/235-8328

**West Rome Trading Post**
1104 Shorter Ave.
706/232-3525

## 55  ROSWELL

### Roswell Antique Gallery

10930 Crabapple Road (Crabapple Square Shopping Center)
770/594-8484 or 1-888-JACK-NIX
Fax: 770/594-1511
Open: Daily Mon.–Sat. 10–6, Sun. 1–6, closed Thanksgiving Day and
Christmas Day
Directions: Located 2⁸/₁₀ miles west of Hwy. 400 at the intersection of
Crabapple Road and Crossville Road (next to Van Gogh's Restaurant).

Are you looking for something a little different in the way of an
antiquing experience? Roswell Antique Gallery will be worth your stop.

The gallery has 30,000
square feet, 240 quality
dealer spaces, and plenty of
room outside to accom-
modate even the most
lavish traveler's bus-sized
recreational vehicle. What
makes the gallery unique is
the focus on quality and
the assurance that the
merchandise is period
antique — no repro-
ductions are allowed. If
questionable, a product's
authenticity is judged by three impartial experts before being added to
the inventory, giving the customer a quality selection dating prior to the
1950s.

Boasting "something for everyone" would be appropriate for the
Roswell Antique Gallery. They offer a concession area, a Kid's Korner
with a television, and a "husband recovery area" for men whose wives
cannot bear to leave before visiting every square foot of the gallery.

**Arts & Antiques**
938 Canton St.
770/552-1899

**Roswell Clock & Antique Co.**
955 Canton St.
770/992-5232

**Moss Blacksmith Shop**
1075 Canton St.
770/993-2398

**Elizabeth's House**
1072 Alpharetta St.
770/993-7300

**Shops of Distinction**
11235 Alpharetta Hwy.
770/475-3111

**Victorian Dreams**
944 Canton St.
770/998-9041

**Mulberry House Antiques**
1028 Canton St.
770/998-6851

**Corner Collections**
1132 Canton St.
770/641-9422

**Historic Roswell Antique Market**
1207 Alpharetta St., #C
770/587-5259

**Irish Antique Shop**
679 Atlanta St.
770/998-3499

**Smith's Antiques & Consignments**
1154 Alpharetta St.
770/518-9689

**European Antiques**
938 Canton St.
770/552-1899

**Cotton Blossom**
944 Canton St.
770/642-2055

## 56  SAVANNAH

**Alex Raskin Antiques**
441 Bull St.
912/232-8205

**A Second Chance**
3326 Skidaway Road
912/236-4576

**Arthur Smith Antiques**
1 W. Jones St.
912/236-9701

**Bozena's European Antiques**
230 W. St. Julien St., #A
912/234-0086

**Contents**
205 W. River St.
912/234-7493

**Jere's Antiques**
9 N. Jefferson St.
912/236-2815

**Kenneth Worthy Antiques, Inc.**
319 Abercorn St.
912/236-7963

**Historic Savannah Antique Market**
220 W. Bay St.
912/238-3366

**Memory Lane Antiques & Mall**
230 W. Bay St.
912/232-0975

**Old Arch Antiques & Collectibles**
235 W. Boundary St.
912/232-2922

**Pinch of the Past**
109 W. Broughton St.
912/232-5563

**V & J Duncan Antique Maps**
12 E. Taylor St.
912/232-0338

**D & B Collection**
408 Bull St.
912/238-0087

**Treasure Trove**
3301 Waters Ave.
912/353-9697

**Alexandra's Antique Gallery**
320 W. Broughton St.
912/233-3999

**Antique Alley**
121 E. Gwinnett St.
912/236-6281

**Blatner's Antiques**
347 Abercorn St.
912/234-1210

**Carriage House Antiques**
135 Bull St.
912/233-5405

**Japonica**
13 W. Charlton St.
912/236-1613

**Jimmie's Attic Antiques**
14 C Bishop Court
912/236-9325

**Carson Davis Ltd.**
7 W. Charlton St.
912/236-2500

**Melonie's**
202 E. Bay St.
912/231-1878

**Mulberry Tree**
17 W. Charlton St.
912/236-4656

**Once Possessed Antiques**
130 E. Bay St.
912/232-5531

**Scrooge & Marley Antiques**
230 Bull St.
912/236-9099

**Willows**
101 W. Broughton St.
912/233-0780

**Seventh Heaven Antique Mall**
3104 Skidaway Road
912/355-0835

**Olde Savannah Estates**
3405 Waters Ave.
912/351-9313

Fiesta & More
224 W. Bay St.
912/238-1060

17 South Antiques
4401 Ogeechee Road
912/236-6333

Peddler Jim's Antiques
39 Montgomery St.
912/233-6642

Junk House Antiques
5950 Ogeechee Road
912/927-2354

Attic Antiques
224 W. Bay St.
912/236-4879

Cobb's Galleries
417 Whitaker St.
912/234-1582

Southern Antiques & Interiors
28 Abercorn St.
912/236-5080

Yesterday Today & Tomorrow
1 W. Victory Dr.
912/232-3472

## Great Places to Stay

### Ballastone Inn and Townhouse

14 E. Oglethorpe Ave.
1-800-822-4553

This antebellum mansion, circa 1838, has 24 guest rooms/suites with private baths (some have whirlpools) and is furnished with period antiques. Continental breakfast-plus served in room, bar or courtyard. Four blocks from Savannah riverfront. Recommended by *New York Times, Brides, Glamour, Gourmet* and *Conde Nast Traveler.*

### Eliza Thompson House

5 W. Jones St.
1-800-348-9378

Located on Jones Street, the most beautiful street in Savannah according to *Southern Living Magazine*, this lovely Federal-style inn has twenty-three large guest rooms beautifully restored with antiques, heart of pine floors, fireplaces and one of the most stunning courtyards in the city. An extended continental breakfast and wine and cheese reception is offered , plus dessert and coffee in the late evening.

### Foley House Inn

14 W. Hull St.
1-800-647-3708

Located on Chippewa Square, where *Forrest Gump* was filmed, this inn has 19 spacious rooms, beautifully appointed with period furniture, fireplaces, color TV; some rooms have oversized whirlpool baths. Continental breakfast served in your room, courtyard or in the stunning lounge. Nearby golf and tennis can be arranged.

### The Forsyth Park Inn

102 W. Hall St.
912/233-6800

This Queen Anne Victorian mansion, circa 1893, has a wide veranda overlooking a beautiful historic park. The inn focuses on lovely architectural details such as antique marble, fireplaces, carved oak floors and a grand staircase.

### The Gastonian

220 E. Gaston St.
1-800-322-6603

This 1868 historic inn is furnished with English antiques, operating fireplaces and in-room Jacuzzi baths with showers. Fruit and wine is served upon arrival; nightly turn-down is provided with cordials and sweets. Full, hot sit-down breakfast; sundeck with hot tub.

### The Grande Toots Inn

212 W. Hall St. at Tattnall
1-800-835-6831

One of Savannah's newest Victorian inns, located two blocks from beautiful Forsythe Park. This charming 1890s mansion is well located for guests exploring historic Savannah. It has been lovingly restored and is elegantly furnished to offer luxurious lodging. Breakfast each morning; tea and cordials in the afternoon. Private garden and verandas.

### Hamilton-Turner Inn

330 Abercorn St.
1-888-448-8849
Email: homemaid@worldnet.att.net

One of the finest examples of Second French Empire style of architecture in the United States, this inn has fourteen luxurious bedrooms and suites furnished with Empire, Eastlake and Renaissance Revival–period antiques. Several have working fireplaces and balconies overlooking Lafayette Square in the heart of the historic district. A full Southern breakfast and afternoon tea await guests.

### Jesse Mount House

209 West Jones St.
912/236-1774

Built in 1854, this beautiful Georgian town house is decorated with antiques and artwork from around the world. The Jesse Mount House offers modern comforts with historic charm.

## Kehoe House

12 Habersham St.
1-800-820-1020

A magnificent Victorian mansion located in the heart of the historic district. Restored to its full turn-of-the-century perfection as a European-style inn, this combination of luxurious guest rooms and gracious public spaces offers a unique experience in timeless elegance and personalized service.

## Lion's Head Inn

120 E. Gaston St.
1-800-355-LION

A stately 19th-century home in quiet neighborhood within walking distance to all attractions and amenities. Each guest room is exquisitely appointed with four-poster beds, private baths, fireplaces, TVs, and telephones. Enjoy a deluxe continental breakfast, turn-down service and wine and cheese reception.

## Park Avenue Manor

107-109 W. Park Ave.
912/233-0352

Park Avenue Manor is a restored 1879 Victorian bed & breakfast graced with charm and beauty that beacons the professional and reserved traveler. This pristine inn is furnished with antiques, period prints, porcelains, and has the ambiance of true Southern living. The inn, adjacent to Forsyth Park, is ideally located to shopping, dining and the business district.

## 57  SCOTTDALE

**Old Mill Antiques**
3240 E. Ponce de Leon Ave.
404/292-0223

**Yesterday's Antiques**
3252 E. Ponce de Leon Ave.
404/292-3555

**Grandma's Treasures**
3256 E. Ponce de Leon Ave.
404/292-6735

## 58  ST. SIMONS ISLAND

**Low Country Walk**
1627 Frederica Road
912/638-1216

**Antiques & Interiors Inc.**
1806 Frederica Road
912/638-9951

**Shaland Hill Gallery**
3600 Frederica Road
912/638-0370

**J. Atticus**
3600 Frederica Road
912/634-0606

**D'Amico's**
208 Redfern Village
912/638-2785

**Frederica Antiques**
10 Sylvan Dr.
912/638-7284

**Sainte Simone's**
536 Ocean Blvd.
912/634-0550

**Island Annex**
545 Ocean Blvd.
912/638-4304

**One of a Kind**
320 Mallory St.
912/638-0348

**Village Mews**
504 Beachview Dr.
912/634-1235

**Mimi's Antiques & Gifts**
3600 Frederica Road
912/638-5366

**Olde World Antiques**
3600 Frederica Road, #14
912/634-6009

**Peppercorn Collection**
276 Redfern Village
912/638-3131

## 59  STONE MOUNTAIN

**Country Manor Antiques**
937 Main St.
770/498-0628

**C.M. Becker Ltd. Antiques**
1100 2nd St.
770/879-7978

**Paul Baron's Antiques**
931 Main St.
770/469-8476

**Remember When Collectibles**
6570 Memorial Dr.
770/879-7878

**Stone Mountain Relics, Inc.**
968 Main St.
770/469-1425

## 60  SUMMERVILLE

Soon after retiring as a Baptist preacher in 1965, the Reverend Howard Finster received instructions from the Lord to convert the swampland surrounding his lawnmower and bicycle repair shop in Summerville into "Paradise Garden." Working with cast-off materials, Finster created sculpture illustrating Scriptural messages, sidewalks embedded with glass and tools, edifices composed of bicycle parts and bottles, and a "Wedding Cake" chapel. He also began to paint in response to God's instructions. His distinctive sermon art combines visual imagery with texts from the Bible and other sources.

Now one of America's most popular self-taught artists, Finster's works came to the world's attention through exhibitions, as well as a 1980 *Life* magazine article that included his work.

The National Endowment for the Arts recognized Finster's work with a 1982 Visual Artist Fellowship in Sculpture, which he used to enhance his Paradise Garden. Since then, the garden has become a popular site for art lovers, tourists and advocates of self-taught artists. In October 1994, Finster made several major pieces from the garden available to the High Museum of Art in Atlanta to ensure their long-term preservation.

*Georgia*

## Cherokee Antique Market

132 S. Commerce St.
706/857-6788
Open: Daily Mon.–Sat. 10–5, Sun. 1:30–5
Directions: *From the north*: 40 miles south of Chattanooga, Tenn., on U.S. Hwy. 27. Exit I-75 at Ringgold (Exit 140). Go south on Georgia 151 to U.S. 27. *From the south*: 25 miles north of Rome, Ga., on U.S. Hwy. 27. Exit I-75 at Adairsville (Exit 128). Follow Georgia 140 west to U.S. 27, then north to Summerville. The store is located at the junction of U.S. Hwy. 27 and Georgia Hwy. 48 in Summerville.

In the heart of Confederate territory, Cherokee Antique Market deals in rare Civil War documents and antiques, as well as flow blue, Majolica, and other fine porcelains. A nice selection of fine furniture, primitives, linens, books and collectibles are also available at the 6,400-square-foot store featuring 16 dealers.

**TLC Antiques**
5 N. Commerce St.
706/857-6723

### 61 SUWANEE

**Early Attic Antiques**
4072 Suwanee Dam Road
770/945-3094

**Pierce's Corner Antiques**
597 Main St.
770/945-0111

### 62 THOMASVILLE

**Thomasville Antique Mall**
132 S. Broad St.
912/225-9231

**Firefly Antiques**
125 S. Broad St.
912/226-6363

**Kelly's Flea Market**
210 W. Jackson St.
912/225-9054

**Collector's Corner**
326 S. Broad St.
912/228-9887

**James S. Mason Antiques**
309 W. Remington Ave.
912/226-4454

**Town & Country Antiques**
119 S. Madison St.
912/226-5863

**Times Remembered**
209 Remington Ave.
912/228-0760

**Brass Ring**
124 S. Stevens St.
912/226-0029

**Ross' Woodshop**
Hwy. 319 S.
912/226-8786

**Southern Traditions**
302 Gordon St.
912/227-0908

### *Great Places to Stay*

**Serendipity Cottage**
339 E. Jefferson St.
1-800-383-7377
Web site: www.bbhost.com/serendipity

Step back to a slower, gentler time when Victorian ladies and gentlemen enjoyed evenings on welcoming porches with white wicker furniture and large potted ferns. This 4,600-square-foot home, located in a quiet, convenient, residential area, offers the best of both worlds — a combination of days past and present (all updated comforts).

### 63 TIFTON

**Sue's Antique Mall**
I-75 at Exit 23
912/388-1856

Offering the "real McCoy," absolutely no reproductions in this 10,000-square-foot antique mall.

**Judy's Antiques & Collectibles**
332 S. Main St.
912/387-8591

**Carey Antiques & Furniture**
506 S. Main St.
912/386-8914

**Things**
511 S. Main St.
912/382-7726

### 64 UNION CITY

**Robinson's Antiques**
6425 Roosevelt Hwy.
770/964-6245

### 65 VALDOSTA

**Joli Antiques**
1006 Slater St.
912/244-0514

**Martha's Antiques**
1915 Baytree Place
912/241-8627

**Odds & Ends Antique**
1919 Baytree Place
912/244-6042

**Landmark**
1110 N. Patterson St.
912/247-2534

**Worth Keeping Antiques**
1809 Remonton
912/241-7633

## 66 VIENNA

### Exit 36 Antique Mall
1410 E. Union St.
912/268-1442

Over 10,000 square feet, featuring walnut, mahogany, heart pine, primitives and unique English pieces.

**Olde Shoppe Upstairs**
108 A Union St.
912/268-9725

**Vienna Antiques**
101 N. 7th St.
912/268-2851

**Joel's Antiques & Collectibles**
215 N. 6th St.
912/268-2919

## 67 WARM SPRINGS

"It was the best holiday I ever had" Franklin D. Roosevelt said, upon returning from Warm Springs, Ga., in March 1937. President Roosevelt made Warm Springs world famous when he became a regular visitor and built his home, the Little White House, there. He was often seen riding around Meriwether County in his little blue roadster. Even before Roosevelt's day, visitors came seeking the warm mineral springs which were believed to have curative powers.

### Antiques & Crafts Unlimited Mall
Santa Fe Art Gallery
Alternate 27
706/655-2468
Web site: www.users.dircon.co.uk/~andyc/ANTIQUES
Open: Daily 9–7 April–October, 9–6 November–March, closed Christmas Day

Located two miles north of Warm Springs, Ga., on U.S. Hwy. 27A, Antiques & Crafts Unlimited Mall is open year-round for your shopping pleasure. There are 114 shops, including the Santa Fe Art Gallery. You will find a wide variety of antiques & collectibles including quality furniture, Depression glass, elegant glass, collectibles of all kinds, plus a few quality crafts.

The Sante Fe Art Gallery is located inside Antiques & Crafts Unlimited Mall. You will be able to view and purchase art by regional artist Arthur Riggs. His work is unique and much sought after. Don't miss this art gallery when you are in the area. Also you will find art by Roberta Geter in the Santa Fe Art Gallery. Roberta is a young, budding artist, who is proving to be very talented.

You will also find art located elsewhere in the building by Roberta Jacks of Monroe, La. Roberta has a unique style of her own. You must see her art to really appreciate it.

**Llewellyn's**
5634 Spring St.
706/655-2022

## 68 WASHINGTON

**Colonial Antiques**
721 E. Robert Toombs Ave.
706/678-2635

**Carl's Antiques & Collectibles**
722 E. Robert Toombs Ave.
706/678-2225

**Heard House Gallery**
32 E. Robert Toombs Ave.
706/678-3604

**Veranda**
10 Broad St.
706/655-2646

**Sunny Daze Antique & Gift Shop**
4151 Lexington Road
706/274-3286

**Ye Olde Lamplighter**
222 E. Robert Toombs Ave.
706/678-2043

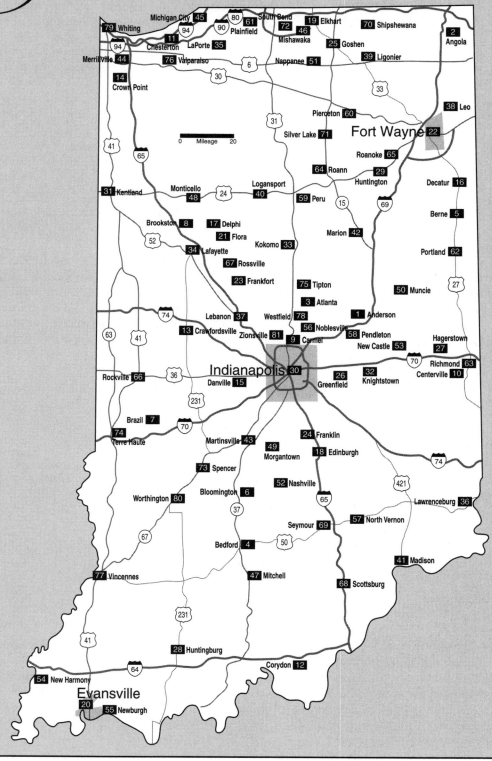

# Indiana

Michigan City `45`
`79` Whiting
`80` Plainfield
South Bend
`72`
`19` Elkhart
`70` Shipshewana
`2` Angola
`11`
`94`
`90`
Mishawaka
`46`
Chesterton
LaPorte `35`
`25` Goshen
Merrillville `44`
`94`
`76` Valparaiso
Nappanee `51`
`39` Ligonier
`14`
Crown Point
`6`
`30`
`33`
`38` Leo
`31`
Pierceton `60`
Fort Wayne `22`
Silver Lake `71`
`41`
`65`
Roanoke `65`
`31` Kentland
Monticello
`48`
`24`
`64` Roann
`29`
Huntington
Decatur `16`
Logansport
`40`
`59` Peru
`69`
Berne `5`
Brookston `8`
`17` Delphi
`15`
`52`
`21` Flora
Kokomo `33`
Portland `62`
`34` Lafayette
Marion `42`
`27`
`67` Rossville
`23` Frankfort
`75` Tipton
`50` Muncie
`3` Atlanta
`74`
Lebanon `37`
Westfield `78`
`1` Anderson
`13` Crawfordsville
`63`
`41`
Zionsville `81`
`56` Noblesville
`58` Pendleton
Hagerstown
`9` Carmel
New Castle `53`
`27`
`70`
Richmond `63`
Rockville `66`
`36`
Indianapolis `30`
`32`
Centerville `10`
Danville `15`
`26`
Knightstown
Greenfield
`231`
Brazil `7`
`70`
`74`
Terre Haute
Martinsville `43`
`24` Franklin
`49`
`18` Edinburgh
`74`
Morgantown
`73` Spencer
`52` Nashville
`421`
Worthington `80`
Bloomington `6`
`65`
Lawrenceburg `36`
`67`
`37`
Seymour `69`
`57` North Vernon
Bedford `4`
`50`
`77` Vincennes
`47` Mitchell
`41` Madison
`68` Scottsburg
`231`
`41`
`28` Huntingburg
`64`
Corydon `12`
`54` New Harmony
Evansville
`20`
`55` Newburgh

0 Mileage 20

# Indiana

## 1 ANDERSON

**Jerry's Junkatique**
509 E. 8th St.
765/649-4321

**Harold's Hideaway**
2023 Lindberg Road
765/642-7880

**Anderson Antique Mall**
1407 Main St.
765/622-9517

**Abby's**
1231 Meridian St.
765/642-8016

**Antiques by Helen Marie**
909 Raible Ave.
765/642-0889

### Great Places to Stay

## Plum Retreat

926 Historic W. Eighth St.
765/649-7586

Innkeepers John and Marilyn Bertacchi have a philosophy: "Come to the Plum Retreat as strangers, leave as friends. We love sharing this beautiful home and enjoy telling about its history and the life of the previous owners. But more than that, we enjoy people and chatting with them about their lives and pampering our guests to make their stay as pleasant as possible."

The architectural style is Victorian, circa 1892. This peaceful getaway is decorated in wonderful antiques and has three guest rooms available.

## 2 ANGOLA

**Angola Mini Mall**
109 W. Gale St.
219/665-7394

**Olde Towne Mall**
101 W. Maumee St.
219/665-9920

**Then & Now Mini Mall**
200 W. Maumee St.
219/665-6650

**Angola Antique Depot**
208 W. Maumee St.
219/665-2026

**Angola Antique Depot**
611 W. Maumee St.
219/665-2026

## 3 ATLANTA

## The Wooden Indian Antiques

115 W. Main St.
765/292-2722
Open: Summer (April–December, Sat.–Wed. 11–5), winter (January–March, Fri.–Sun. 12–5), other times by chance or appointment
Directions: Located in downtown Atlanta next to the railroad tracks. Atlanta is 5 miles south of Tipton on State Route 19 and 12 miles north of Noblesville on State Route 19. U.S. 31 is 5 miles west of Atlanta. The road to Atlanta from U.S. 31 is 20 miles north of I-465 (on north edge of Indianapolis) and 20 miles south of Kokomo.

As you might have surmised, the Wooden Indian Antiques shop specializes in wood. They stock from 800 to 1,000 pressed-back chairs and although they are not always in pristine condition, choices are limitless. There is something for everyone, including the do-it-yourselfer. They also do chair caning, a disappearing art.

The next time someone asks, "It that chair taken," you can tell them, "Yes, but there are many, many more where that one came from at the Wooden Indian Antiques."

## 4 BEDFORD

## Brown Hen Antique & Craft Mall

Route 11, Box 646
812/279-9172
Open: Mon., Thurs., Sat. 10–5, Fri. 10–6, Sun. 12–5
Directions: Located three miles south of 16th St. in Bedford on Hwy. 37/50 just south of Hickory Hill Restaurant & Dalton's RVs

Brown Hen Antiques & Craft Mall definitely has something to cackle about. The "old" Brown Hen Mall was leveled by a tornado in 1991; however, hanging over the check-out counter was a large painting of a brown hen. An inspection of damage found the shop completely gone, but the brown hen survived with only minor damage. Today, this "brown hen" has a place of honor in the new Brown Hen shop, which offers an eclectic array of antiques and collectibles.

**Pandora's Box Antique Mall**
3300 W. 16th St.
812/275-6534

## 5 BERNE

**Berne Antique Mall**
105 W. Water St.
219/589-8050

**Karen's Treasures**
444 E. Main St.
219/589-2002

**Pandora's Box**
Stone City Mall F-6
812/275-6534

## 6 BLOOMINGTON

## The Garret

403 W. Kirkwood
812/339-4175
Open: Mon.–Wed., Fri. & Sat. 9–6; Thurs., Sun. by appointment or chance
Directions: Hwys. 37, 45, 48 and 446 all go into Bloomington. Go to the Court House Square in downtown. One street south is Kirkwood (also called 5th St.). The Garret is 2 blocks west on the corner of Kirkwood and Madison.

*Indiana*

The Garretts have been in the antiquing business nearly 40 years and, according to them, their shop is "simply the largest, oldest, and most diversified shop in the area." The three floors of this unique shop house not only a world of wonderful antiques, but a rock and mineral shop as well. The specialties of the Garret are lighting and furniture.

**Cowboys & Indians**
110 E. Kirkwood Ave.
812/323-1013

**Grant St.**
213 S. Rogers St.
812/333-6076

**Odds & Olds**
2524 S. Rogers St.
812/333-3022

**Bloomington Antique Mall**
311 W. 7th St.
812/332-2290

**Elegant Options Antique Gallery**
403 N. Walnut St.
812/332-5662

**Different Drummer**
2964 E. 2nd St.
812/337-1776

### Great Places to Stay

## Quilt Haven
711 Dittemore Road
812/876-5802

This quaint New England saltbox home is nestled in some of Indiana's finest woodlands but less than 15 minutes from downtown Bloomington.

Fall asleep to a cricket's lullaby, and awaken to the trill of a titmouse or a glimpse of a pileated woodpecker making his rounds. The three antique-filled guest rooms are beautifully decorated and each displays a collection of the innkeeper's hand-sewn quilts. A full gourmet breakfast is served each morning.

## 7 ■ BRAZIL

**Brazil Antique Mall**
105 E. National Ave.
812/448-3275

**Crestline Antiques**
531 E. National Ave.
812/448-8061

**Stuff 'n' Things Antiques**
U.S. Hwy. 40 E.
812/448-3861

**His & Hers**
RR 12
812/448-3153

## 8 ■ BROOKSTON

**Rolling Wheels Antiques & Collectibles**
8136 West St. Road 26
765/379-2649

## 9 ■ CARMEL

**Matty's Antiques**
210 W. Main St.
317/575-6327

**Heritage of Carmel**
250 W. Main St.
317/844-0579

**Acorn Farm Country Store**
15466 Oak Road
317/846-6257

**Antique Emporium**
1055 S. Range Line Road
317/844-8351

## 10 ■ CENTERVILLE

## The Oak Leaf
205 W. Main St.
765/855-2623

Specializing in antique art, especially antique paintings and furniture.

## The Tin Pig Antiques
130 W. Main St.
765/855-5313

Specializing in country furnishings and accessories.

**Tom's Antique Center**
117 E. Main St.
765/855-3296

**Now & Then Antiques**
139 E. Main St.
765/855-2806

**Wheeler's Antiques**
107 W. Main St.
765/855-3400

**Webb's Antique Mall**
200 Union St.
765/855-2489

## 11 ■ CHESTERTON

**Antiques 101**
101 Broadway
219/929-1434

**Kathy's Antique Shop**
530 Indian Boundary Road
219/926-1400

**Yesterday's Treasures Antique Mall**
700 Broadway
219/926-2268

**Russ & Barb's Antiques**
222 W. Lincoln Ave.
219/926-4937

**Emma's Antiques & Gifts**
428 S. Calumet Road
219/929-4427

### Great Places to Stay

## Gray Goose Inn
350 Indian Boundary Road
219/926-5781

The Gray Goose Inn sits on 100 wooded acres overlooking a private lake. The decor is Williamsburg with a mixture of antiques, fine reproductions, tapestries and fine prints. Guest rooms are tastefully decorated from Shaker, 18th-century English, French Country and English Victorian. A gourmet breakfast is served in the dining room overlooking the lake, where guests can enjoy the wildlife such as Canada geese and ducks. Walking trails ring the lake for nature lovers.

# Indiana

## 12 CORYDON

**Griffin Building Antique Mall**
113 E. Beaver St.
812/738-3302

**John's Try'Al**
110 N. Elm St.
812/738-1924

**Red Barn Antique Mall**
215 Hwy. 62 W.
812/738-2276

### Great Places to Stay

## Kinter House Inn

101 S. Capitol Ave.
812/738-2020
Fax: 812/738-7430
Open: Year-round

All the elements which made Kinter House Inn the finest hotel in Corydon are still preserved today. The current owners have restored this three-story brick Italianate to its 1873 grandeur.

## 13 CRAWFORDSVILLE

**Cat's Meow**
4030 State Road 32 E.
765/362-0053

**Fireside Antique Mall**
4035 State Road 32 E.
765/362-8711

**Cabbages & Kings**
124 S. Washington St.
765/362-2577

## 14 CROWN POINT

**Gard Gallery Antiques**
700 N. Sherman St.
219/663-0547

**Dan's Antiques**
8703 E. 109th Ave.
219/663-4571

**Antique Shoppe**
Old Courthouse Shops
219/663-1031

**Antique Mall of Crown Point**
103 W. Joliet St.
219/662-1219

## 15 DANVILLE

## Danville Antique Mall

132 W. Main St.
317/745-1774
Open: Mon.–Sat. 10–5, Sun. 12–5

Fine porcelain and glass, primitives, quilts, pottery, used and rare books, Victorian and oak furniture.

## Heritage Antique Mall

Route 36
317/539-4233
Open: Tues.–Sat. 10–5, Sun. 12–5

Antiques and collectibles; large selection of furniture.

## 16 DECATUR

## 2nd at Court Street Antiques

140 S. 2nd St.
219/724-8019
Open: Mon.–Sat. 10–6, first Sun. 10–6

Primitives, pottery, textiles, firearms, glass and furniture.

## Red Duck Antiques

132 N. 2nd St.
219/728-2643

Quilts, primitives, country furniture and smalls.

**Family Tree Antiques**
618 Adams St.
219/728-2880

**Memories Past Antique Mall**
111 E. Jefferson St.
219/728-2643

**Aumann's Antique Mall**
208 W. Monroe St.
219/724-7472

**Town House Antiques**
222 N. 2nd St.
219/724-2920

**Yvonne Marie's Antique Mall**
152 S. 2nd St.
219/724-2001

## 17 DELPHI

Delphi is at the center of a circle that encompasses several cities, each filled with unique shops. On leaving Delphi in any direction within a 20-mile radius, the antiquer will encounter at least 20 locations. The cities within the circle have organized a co-op to promote themselves, a membership that is growing and includes shops within or between the cities of Flora, Brookston, Rossville, Monticello and Delphi.

Each city within the co-op recognizes the others' ability to draw a crowd. Monticello is home of the famous Indiana Beach; Brookston has an annual popcorn and apple festival; Rossville has a summer's-end festival with roads closed and street vendors in operation. Flora has an annual pork producer cook-off, with a old car "cruise in," oldies music, and a lot of activity. The area also has the Wabash and Erie Canal digs every summer. Visit the area. You'll be a satisfied antiquer.

**J&B Furniture Store**
113 S. Washington St.
765/564-9204

**Delphi Antique Mall**
117 Washington St.
765/564-3990

**Lil' Bit of Country**
125 S. Washington St.
765/564-6241

**Teddy's Emporium**
115 E. Main St.
765/564-3742

**Crouch's Victorian Antiques**
404 E. Main St.
765/564-4195

**Town Square Mall**
110 W. Main St.
765/564-6937

**Times Past Antiques & Art**
124 S. Main St.
765/564-6317

**Linda's Treasure Trove/Ruby's Cttge.**
1816 N. Wells
765/564-3649

### 18 EDINBURGH

**Edinburgh Antiques, Crafts & Collectibles**
101 W. Main Cross
812/526-0054

**Back in Time Antiques**
126 E. Main Cross
812/526-5409

**Pac Rats**
109 W. Main Cross
812/526-8891

### 19 ELKHART

**Caverns of Elkhart**
111 Prairie Court
219/293-1484

**Elkhart Antique Mall**
51772 State Road 19
219/262-8763

### 20 EVANSVILLE

**Different Things**
2107 W. Franklin St.
812/423-3890

**Em Siler Antiques**
513 N. Green River Road
812/476-2656

**Lori's Antiques**
12747 N. Green River Road
812/867-7414

**American & European Antiques**
402 N. Main St.
812/421-1720

**1001 Antiques**
711 N. Main St.
812/422-0291

**Bill's Antiques**
601 E. Virginia St.
812/422-0810

**Franklin Street Antique Mall**
2123 W. Franklin St.
812/428-0988

**Puckett's Treasures & Collectibles**
Washington Square Mall
812/473-2988

**A. King's Antique Shoppe**
504 N. Garvin St.
812/422-5865

**Daylight Country Store**
12600 N. Green River Road
812/867-6932

**Pack Rat**
305 N. Main St.
812/423-7526

**Walkway Mall**
518 Main St.
812/421-9727

**Rick Tremont Antiques**
608 S.E. 2nd St.
812/426-9099

**Paxson's Antiques**
1355 Washington Ave.
812/476-6790

**Inside Out**
12747 N. Green River Road
812/867-7414

**The Tuesday Shop**
7521 Old State Road
812/867-6332

**Whispering Hills Antiques**
10600 Hwy. 65
812/963-6236

### *Great Places to Stay*

### River's Inn Bed and Breakfast
414 S.E. Riverside Dr.
812/428-7777 or 1-800-797-7990
Fax: 812/421-2902
Open: Year-round

Built in 1866 and furnished throughout with fine antiques and collectibles, this three-story Italianate home overlooks the Ohio River. Third-floor rooms have balconies from which you can view the river or the beautiful gardens below. Johnny Walker potato pie is often served at breakfast.

### 21 FLORA

### Bill's Clockworks
Repair and sales of antique clocks
8 W. Columbia St. (Hwy. 18)
219/967-4709 or 1-888-742-5625
Web site: www.qklink.com/clockworks
Open: Mon.–Fri. 9–6, Sat. 9–5
Directions: *From Chicago (I-65 S):* Take Exit 188 (SR 18 Brookston/Fowler). Turn east through Brookston and Delphi, go approximately 26 miles, at second four-way flasher on right in center of Flora. *From Indianapolis west side (I-70) or points south (I-65N):* North on I-165 to Exit 72 (SR 26 Lafayette/Rossville). Turn right (east) through Rossville to SR 75 (approximately 17 miles), turn left (north), go 8 miles to Flora & SR 18. Turn right, located just before next flasher in center of town. *From Indianapolis/NE side or from points east (I-70 and I-74):* Take I-465 to Exit 27 (U.S. 421 N. Frankfort/Zionsville). Turn north on U.S. 421, go approximately 48 miles to SR 18, turn left (west) on SR 18 to Flora, 7 miles (U.S. 421 turns into SR 29 at SR 28, continue north on SR 29). *From Ft. Wayne/Michigan/Northern Ohio:* Take I-69 S. to Exit 64 (SR 18 Marion). Go West on SR 18 approximately 55 miles.

Owner Bill Stoddard has had a lifelong interest in clocks. When he was a small boy, his grandfather, who had a small clock collection, showed Bill how to wind and regulate clocks. At the age of eight he acquired his first timepiece and so began his love for collecting. Bill and his mother, while cleaning out an attic, discovered a broken Waterbury octagon-lever wall clock, ca. 1880. Several years later, he saved up money mowing lawns and had the clock repaired.

Throughout his teen years, Bill's love for collecting clocks grew. In April 1991 Bill opened his own clock shop in his home in Indianapolis.

By 1995 Bill had moved to Flora where he opened shop in the former Rainbow Cafe. He enjoys repairing many different types of clocks, particularly early American weight-driven ones. Bill says he enjoys his work because he gets to repair each clock, treating it as if it were his own, enjoying it while it's in the shop, then seeing the smile on the customer's face when their timepiece is clean, shiny and repaired. And the best part is that he gets paid for doing something he truly loves.

**Wertz Antiques**
IN 18 W. of IN 75
291/967-3056

## 22 FORT WAYNE

**Aaron's Oriental Rug Gallery**
1217 Broadway
219/422-5184

**Candlelight Antiques**
3205 Broadway
219/456-3150

**Baxter's on Broadway Antique Mall**
1115 Broadway
219/422-6505

**Old House Galleries**
701 Columbia Ave.
219/424-3737

**Karen's Antique Mall**
1510 Fairfield Ave.
219/422-4030

**Nature's Corner Antique Mall**
2305 Spy Run Ave.
219/493-5236

## 23 FRANKFORT

**John's Toys & Antiques**
4160 N. County Road O.E.V.
765/659-9017, or 659-3519

## 24 FRANKLIN

**Jeri's Antiques**
56 E. Jefferson St. #C
317/738-3848

**Lighthouse Antique Mall**
62 W. Jefferson St.
317/738-3344

**Peddler's II**
90 W. Jefferson St.
317/736-6299

**Town Square Antiques**
104 W. Jefferson St.
317/736-9633

**Countryside Antiques**
4251 N. State Road 135
317/422-9206

## 25 GOSHEN

## Carriage Barn Antiques

1100 Chicago Ave.
219/533-6353
Open: Mon.–Fri. 9:30–5, Sat. 9:30–4
Directions: From 80/90 Indiana Toll Road, Exit 101 at Bristol. Turn south on State Road 15 to Goshen. Go right (west) on U.S. 33 to K.F.C. (Indiana Avenue). Turn right and continue for 2½ blocks to the old Bag Factory. Park behind the log house. Look for arched entry into brick building.

Looking for a piece of furniture like "Grandma" used to own? Unless Grandma is 125–225 years old, you're not likely to find it here in the Carriage Barn. Their circa 1780–1890 furniture is displayed in room settings with appropriate accessories and quilts.

Fine replica tin, copper, and brass lighting accentuate these fine old furnishings. If you are a true antique enthusiast, you can't help but feel a pang for the past as you browse through this truly unique antique haven.

## Goshen Antique Mall

107 S. Main St.
219/534-6141
Open: Mon.–Sat. 10–5

Country furniture, yellowware, tinware, original paint, Adirondack and pine furniture.

## Mustard Seed Antiques

1100 Chicago Ave.
219/534-6475

Specializing in country antiques and primitives.

### *Great Places to Stay*

## Front Porch Inn

320 S. Fifth St.
219/533-4258

This 1800s Italianate Victorian home is located in Goshen's historic district near downtown shopping, churches and government offices. If your interest is bicycling you will enjoy the location on the city's greenway, which winds its way through the town from Goshen College to many parks, along the Mill Race, and downtown. Guest rooms are spacious and newly decorated. Located in Amish country, a short drive from Shipshewana, Middlebury and Nappanee.

## Indian Creek Bed & Breakfast

20300 CR 18
219/875-6606

This new Victorian-style home is filled with family antiques and collectibles and has been lovingly decorated throughout. The guest rooms, named after the innkeeper's grandchildren, have either queen or full-size beds, private baths and each is uniquely different. Indian Creek is within driving distance of the beach and Shipshewana Flea Market.

# Indiana

## 26  GREENFIELD

**Carriage House Antiques**
210 Center St.
317/462-3253

**Red Ribbon Antiques**
101 W. Main St.
317/462-5211

**Bob's Antiques**
113 W. Main St.
317/462-8749

**Sugar Creek Antique Mall**
2244 W. U.S. Hwy. 40
317/467-4938

**Reflections of Time**
14 W. Main St.
317/462-3878

**J.W. Riley's Emporium**
107 W. Main St.
317/462-5268

**The Red Rooster**
1001 W. Main St.
317/462-0655

## 27  HAGERSTOWN

**As the Crow Flies**
98 E. Main St.
765/489-4910

**Main Street Antiques Uniques**
96 E. Main St.
765/489-5792

**Found Treasures of Hagerstown**
51 E. Main St.
765/489-5335

**Zachary's Antiquities**
61 E. Main St.
765/489-5335

## 28  HUNTINGBURG

### Mulberry Tree Antiques and Collectibles

4625 S. State Route 162
812/482-1822
Open: Wed.–Sun. 10–5, Mon.–Tues. by appointment
Directions: Traveling I-64, take Exit 63 north approximately 7 miles.
The Mulberry Tree is centrally located in the county, ½ mile north of
State Highways 162 and 64, 5 miles north of Ferdinand, 5 miles south
of Jasper, or 5 miles east of Huntingburg.

This shop's "claim to fame" is their quality antiques and excellent
dealers. Mulberry Tree is owner-operated and friendly, providing two good
reasons to stop in for a visit!

**Parker House Antiques**
307 E. 4th St.
812/683-5352

**Goodthings**
517 E. 4th St.
812/683-4815

**Country Corner**
3rd & Geiger St.
812/683-4849

**Locker Antiques**
314 E. 4th St.
812/683-4149

**B-K Antiques**
507 E. 4th St.
812/683-2534

**Antique Boutique**
3582 S. 75 W.
812/683-2850

**Green Tree Antiques**
312 E 4th St.
812/683-4448

**Yesterdays Antiques & Collectibles**
320 E. 4th St.
812/683-4422

**Enchantingly Yours**
330 E. 4th St.
812/683-5437

**Judy Ann's Antiques**
S.E. Corner 4th & Main
812/683-4993

**Gene's Antiques**
330 4th St.
812/683-4199

**Lamb's 'n' Ivy**
421 E. 4th St.
812/683-5533

## 29  HUNTINGTON

**S & B Antiques & Collectibles**
434 N. Jefferson St.
219/356-1302

## 30  INDIANAPOLIS

### Colonial Antiques

5000 W. 96th St.
317/873-2727
Open: Fri.–Sat. 10–5, other days by appointment
Directions: Take I-465 north to Michigan Road (Exit 421). Exit north
and go 1 block to 96th St. Colonial Antiques is 1 mile west on the right.

Once, not long ago, architectural treasures were destroyed, falling prey
to the wrecking ball in order to build society's latest needs—a new high
rise, a service station, a grocery store, or even a cement parking lot. Today
these treasures are sought after and salvaged by decorators, builders and
collectors. Colonial Antiques specializes in these unique, mostly one-of-
a-kind finds including lighting, mantels, hardware and more.

### Manor House Antique Mall

5454 U.S. 31 S.
317/782-1358
Web site: inct.net/manorhouseantiques
Directions: U.S. 31 S., ½ mile south of I-465 at Exit 2B.

20,000 square feet of quality antiques and collectibles displayed
throughout sixty rooms and glass showcases.

### Allisonville Antique Mall

6230 N. Allisonville Road
317/259-7318
Open: Mon.–Sat. 10–8, Sun. 12–5

American art, decoys and furniture.

### Books, Antiques & More

1048 Virginia Ave.
317/636-1595
Open: Mon.–Sat. 10–6, Sun. 12–5

Specializing in books, collectible ephemera. Dealer discounts.

# Indiana

## Colby Antiques
1111 E. 61st St.
317/253-2148
Open: Tues.–Sat. 10–4

18th- and 19th-century and continental furniture.

## Southport Antique Mall
2028 E. Southport Road
317/786-8246
Open: Mon.–Sat. 10–8, Sun. 12–5

One of the Midwest's largest antique malls.

**Bluemingdeals Antiques & Jazzy Junk**
4601 N. College Ave.
317/924-4765

**Margie's Menagerie**
4905 N. College Ave.
317/931-1400

**Neat Antiques & More**
4907 N. College Ave.
317/921-1916

**Recollections Antiques**
5202 N. College Ave.
317/283-3800

**Barn Village Antiques**
5209 N. College Ave.
317/283-5011

**A Rare Find Gallery**
4040 E. 82nd St. #10C
317/842-5828

**D.T. Hollings Antiques, Inc.**
1760 E. 86th St.
317/574-1777

**Find's Antiques**
1764 E. 86th St.
317/571-1950

**North Indy Antique Mall**
7226 E. 87th St. #E
317/578-2671

**Sayger Antiques**
711 E. 54th St.
317/251-1936

**Hope's Shop**
116 E. 49th St.
317/283-3004

**Trash to Treasures**
5505 N. Keystone Ave.
317/253-2235

**Abe's Attic Treasures**
1431 S. Meridian St.
317/636-4105

**Midland Arts & Antiques**
907 E. Michigan St.
317/267-9005

**Red Barn Galleries**
325 E. 106th St.
317/846-8928

**Blue Sun Gallery**
922 E. Westfield Blvd.
317/255-8441

**Antique Centre**
3422 N. Shadeland Ave.
317/545-3879

**Antiques 'n' More**
3440 N. Shadeland Ave.
317/542-8526

**Antique Mall**
3444 N. Shadeland Ave.
317/542-7283

**Quality Antiques**
1105 Shelby St.
317/686-6018

**Nostalgia**
7501 Somerset Bay #B
317/926-0097

**Southport Antique Mall, Inc**
2028 E. Southport Road
317/786-8246

**Indianapolis Downtown Antiques**
1044 Virginia Ave.
317/635-5336

**Mobile Merchant**
1052 Virginia Ave.
317/264-9968

**Fountain Square Antique Mall**
1056 Virginia Ave.
317/636-1056

**D & D Antique Mall**
6971 W. Washington St.
317/486-9760

### *Great Places to Stay*

## Tranquil Cherub
2164 N. Capitol Ave.
317/923-9036

This 95-year-old Greek Revival home has four guests rooms, each with private bath and unique charm. Guests often wander through the antique-filled rooms, enjoy the 1914 player piano or relax with a good book in the upstairs sitting room. Breakfast is served in the beautiful dining room near the fire. Weather permitting, you may eat on the outside deck overlooking the garden and koi ponds.

## 31 KENTLAND

**Pastyme Peddlers**
210 & 213 N. 3rd St.
219/474-9306

**Dad's Trash & Treasures**
506 E. Seymour St.
219/474-3231

## 32 KNIGHTSTOWN

## Knightstown Antique Mall
136 W. Carey St.
765/345-5665
Open: Mon.–Sat. 10–5, Sun. 12–5

Located in an old furniture factory complex. Three buildings of furniture, cast iron, toys, banks, advertising, pottery, stoneware, primitives and Depression glass.

**Lindon's Antique Mall**
32 E. Main St.
765/345-2545

**Nostalgia Nook**
6 E. Main St.
765/345-7937

**The Glass Cupboard**
115 E. Main St.
765/345-7572

**J. W. Riley's Emporium**
121 E. Main St.
765/345-7480

### *Great Places to Stay*

## Main Street Victorian
130 W. Main St.
765/345-2299

This Victorian cottage offers a unique decor with a romantic ambiance. Lace, stained-glass windows and soft light complete the three guest rooms, each decorated in beautiful colors and antique furnishings. The cottage is located within "Antique Alley," making it a perfect place to rest after a full day of antiquing.

# Indiana

## Old Hoosier House

7601 S. Greensboro Pike
1-800-775-5315

Central Indiana's first and favorite country bed and breakfast, the Old Hoosier House is ideally suited for sightseeing and shopping Indiana's "Antique Alley." The architectural style is Victorian, ca. 1836, and is furnished in antique decor throughout. Four guest rooms are available; breakfast is included, as well as afternoon tea.

## 33 KOKOMO

**White Bungaloo Antique Mall**
906 S. Main St.
765/459-0789

**C & L Antiques**
841 S. Main St.
765/452-2290

**Ol' Hickory & Lace Antiques**
913 S. Main St.
765/452-6026

**Wild Ostrich Antiques**
929 S. Main St.
765/452-3990

**Roninger's Then & Now Store**
4410 S. 00 EW
765/453-0521

**Cricket Box**
907 S. Main St.
765/459-8790

**Treasure Mart Mall**
3780 S. Reed Road
765/455-9855

## 34 LAFAYETTE

### Buck's Collectibles & Antiques

310 S. 16th St.
765/742-2192
Open: Mon.–Sat. 10–5
Directions: Enter Layfayette either on Interstate 65 or State Road 52. If entering on Interstate 65, exit on State Road 26 West. Travel west on State Road 26 (which is South Street) after crossing State Road 52. Travel South Street until the 5-points intersection before South Street heads downtown. At the 5-points intersection turn left onto 16th Street and the antique mall will be on the right side of the corner of 16th Street and Center Street.

Buck's Collectibles & Antiques is filled to the brim with antiques and collectibles, which include primitives, Coca-Cola, antique dolls, collector dolls, antique furniture, pottery, occupied Japan, monon and nickle-plate railroad, advertising, Keen Kutter tools, antique tools, and case knives supplied by a mix of 45 dealers from around the greater Lafayette area. This antique mall is definitely a must stop if you are interested in browsing or purchasing the unique and unusual.

**Leonard's Antiques & Books**
1324 N. 14th St.
765/742-8668

**Pack Rat Antiques**
424 Main St.
765/742-7490

**Alley Gifts & Collectibles**
638 Main St.
765/429-5758

**Lee-Weises Antiques**
1724 N. 9th St.
765/423-2754

**Koehler Bros. General Store**
3431 State Road 26 E.
765/447-2155

**Antique Mall of Lafayette**
800 Main St.
765/742-2469

**Chesterfield Antiques & Collectibles**
210 N. 6th St.
765/742-2956

**Lamb & Heart Americana**
3433 State Road 26 E.
765/447-1863

## 35 LaPORTE

The city of LaPorte is brimming with a rich historical heritage. Start here for the antique tour of LaPorte County; follow the tour with a visit to the LaPorte County Historical Society Museum. Housed in the LaPorte County Courthouse, the museum displays everything from a 1,000-piece antique firearms collection to old musical instruments to re-created shops and offices. Don't leave town until you've followed LaPorte's Stroll Along the Avenues walking tour of historic homes and elegant architecture. The Door Prairie Museum, south of LaPorte, displays a distinguished collection of automobiles spanning 100 years.

**Corner Cupboard**
108 Lincolnway
219/326-9882

**It's a Wonderful Life**
708 Lincolnway
219/326-7432

**Walnut Hill Antiques**
613 Michigan Ave.
219/326-1099

**Coachman Antique Mall**
500 Lincolnway
219/326-5933

**Antique Junction Mall**
711 Lincolnway
219/324-0363

## 36 LAWRENCEBURG

**Shumways Olde Mill Antiques**
232 W. High St.
812/537-1709

**Livery Stable Antique Mall**
318 Walnut St.
812/537-4364

## 37 LEBANON

### Bits & Pieces

210 W. Washington St.
765/482-1823
Open: Tues.–Sat. 11–6, Sun. 12–5

Depression glass, McCoy, Roseville, cut glass, cranberry glass, toys and dolls.

**Cedars of Lebanon Antiques**
126 W. Washington St.
765/482-7809

*Indiana*

## 38  LEO

**Leo Antique Exchange**
11119 Grabill Road
219/627-2242

**Shades of Country**
51004 State Road 1
219/627-2189

**Cellar Antique Mall**
15004 A State Road 1
219/627-6565

## 39  LIGONIER

**Creative Visions**
115 S. Cavin St.
219/894-3449

**Mad Hatter Antiques**
254 W. U.S. Hwy. 6
219/894-4995

## 40  LOGANSPORT

**A-1 Preowned Items**
112 Burlington Ave.
219/739-2121

**Yesteryear Antiques & Collectibles**
525 E. Market St.
219/753-7371

**Cluttered Closet**
811 Burlington Ave.
219/753-5196

**Market Street Antiques**
222 E Market St.
219/735-0131

**Homewood Antiques**
1075 N. State Road 25
219/722-2398

## 41  MADISON

### Old Town Emporium

113 E. Second St.
812/273-4394
Web site: www.antiqnet.com/sommerfeld
Open: Mon.–Sat. 10–5, Sat. 12–5

Located in an 1820s Federal home with a period kitchen. Direct importers of 18th-, 19th- and 20th-century English, American and Dutch.

**Carita's Antique Shoppe**
108 W. Main St.
812/265-6606

**Jefferson Street Antique Mall**
200 Jefferson St.
812/265-6464

**The Purple Strawberry**
326 Mulberry St.
812/265-9090

**Broadway Antique Mall**
701 Broadway St.
812/265-6606

**Wallace's Antiques**
125 E. Main St.
812/265-2473

**D & J Antiques & More**
313 Mulberry St.
812/265-2324

**Main Cross Antiques**
630 W. Main St.
812/273-5378

**Snicklefritz Antiques**
128 E. Main St.
812/273-0646

**Lumber Mill Antique Mall**
721 W. 1st. St.
812/273-3040

**Antiques on Main**
129 E. Main St.
812/265-2240

**Best Friends**
133 E. Main St.
812/265-5548

**Antiques Etc.**
224 E. Main St.
812/273-6768

**Madison Antique Mall**
401 E. 2nd St.
812/265-6399

**Main Street Antique Mall**
210 E. Main St.
812/273-5286

**507 Antiques**
507 Jefferson St.
812/265-2799

**Eban Sommerfeld Antiques**
118 E. Main St.
812/265-2026

### *Great Places to Stay*

### Main Street B&B

739 W. Main St.
1-800-362-6246

Main Street Bed and Breakfast is a graceful, classic Revival home built in 1843 and located in Madison's historic district. This charming accommodation has three tastefully decorated, spacious guest rooms, all with private baths. While there is an atmosphere of elegance in the home and its furnishings, the mood is relaxed and friendly. A delicious full breakfast awaits guests in the morning. Restaurants, shops, historic homes, and the Ohio River are all within walking distance.

### Schussler House Bed and Breakfast

514 Jefferson St.
812/273-2068 or 1-800-392-1931
Open: Year-round
Rates: $75–$120

The Schussler House was built in 1849 for Charles Schussler, a local physician who used the residence for his office and home.

Today, this Federal and Greek Revival–style home is an elegant bed and breakfast featuring antique and reproduction furniture throughout the three guest rooms and common areas. A gourmet breakfast is served in the dining room.

## 42  MARION

### Hummel Hill Antiques

2210 N. Huntington Road
765/668-7488
Open: Mon.–Sat. 10–6, Sun. 12–5

Specializing in Civil War memorabilia.

**Jake's Antiques**
1440 Winona
765/664-9765

**Ol' Hickory & Lace**
913 S. Main St.
765/452-6026

# Indiana

## 43 MARTINSVILLE

**Emporium**
110 N. Main St.
765/349-9060

**Gateway Collectibles**
96 E. Morgan St.
765/342-8983

**Morgan County Auction & Flea Mkt.**
128 N. Main St.
765/342-8098

**Creative Accents, Inc.**
166 E. Morgan St.
765/342-0213

## 44 MERRILLVILLE

**Carriage House**
420 W. 73rd Ave.
219/769-2169

## 45 MICHIGAN CITY

### The Antique Market

3707 N. Frontage Road
219/879-4084
Open: Mon.–Sat. 10–5, Sun. 12–5, closed major holidays
Directions: Take I-94 to Exit 34B and U.S. Highway 421 North. Go 1 block to stoplight and turn right, then take another quick right onto Frontage Road.

Easily accessible from I-94 and Hwy. 142, The Antique Market with its more than 85 dealers is one of the few remaining markets or malls that has not conformed by adding crafts and reproductions to its line of antiques and collectibles. If you are a true antique enthusiast, you will enjoy shopping among the fine old treasures.

**Road House Antiques**
3900 W. Dunes Hwy.
219/878-1866

**E.T. World Antiques**
7326 Johnson Road
219/872-9002

**Stocking Bale Antiques Mall**
227 W. 7th St.
219/873-9270

**Mona's Treasure Chest**
4496 Wozniak Road
219/874-6475

**Days Gone By Antiques**
10673 W. 300 N.
219/879-7496

## 46 MISHAWAKA

**Antiques Etc.**
110 Lincoln Way E.
219/258-5722

**Pack Rat Pat's**
3005 Lincoln Way E.
219/259-5609

**Interiors Etc.**
301 Lincoln Way E.
219/259-7717

**Ed's Collectables**
126 N. Main St.
219/255-5041

## 47 MITCHELL

**Ma Nancy's Antiques**
609 W. Main St.
812/849-2203

**Persimmon Tree Antiques**
619 W. Main St.
812/849-5300

**Checkerberry**
615 W. Main St.
812/849-3784

**Mitchell Antique Mall**
706 W. Main St.
812/849-4497

## 48 MONTICELLO

**Beth's Antiques**
12355 N. Upper Shore Dr.
219/583-3002

**Blossom Station**
101 W. Broadway
219/583-5359

**Turquoise 'n' Treasures**
400 W. Fisher
219/583-8413

**Inntwinned Inn Time**
U.S. 421 S.
219/583-5133

**Uptowne Antiques Mall**
134 Main St.
219/583-5359

**Main Street Antiques Mall**
127 N. Main St.
219/583-2998

**Creative Clutter**
2702 W. Shafer Dr.
No phone listed

## 49 MORGANTOWN

**Morgantown Antiques**
49 E. Washington St.
812/597-0412

**Yesterday's Antique & Auction Service**
149 W. Washington St.
812/597-5525

**Miller's Antiques**
Route 1 Box 5A
812/597-6024

## 50 MUNCIE

**Off-Broadway Antique Mall**
2404 N. Broadway Ave.
765/747-5000

**Walker Antiques**
4801 E. Memorial Dr.
765/282-0399

## 51 NAPPANEE

Imagine yourself leisurely driving over scenic country back roads and broad, flat prairie lands, past picturesque farms, stopping for handmade quilts and crafts. All this and more quietly awaits you in northern Indiana Amish country. Take the Heritage Trail, a 90-mile loop through the heart of mid-America, which is even easier to enjoy with a self-guided tour complete with map, guidebook and audio-cassette tape with directions. Between the towns of Middlebury, Shipshewana, and Nappanee you'll sense the influence of one of the largest Amish settlements in the United States. To receive a full listing of accommodations and attractions along the trail or make lodging reservations, call Northern Indiana Amish Country at 1-800-860-5957.

*Indiana*

## Borkholder Dutch Village

71945 C.R. 101
219/773-2828
Fax 219/773-4828
Open: Mon.–Sat. 10–5 winter, 9–5 summer
Directions: Located 1/4 mile north of U.S. 6, 1 1/2 miles west of State Rd. 19; or 13 miles east of U.S. 31, then 1/4 mile north off U.S. 6.

In 1987, Freeman Borkholder, owner of Borkholder American Vintage Furniture, decided to purchase a facility to showcase the local crafts and antiques for which Nappanee is well known. He bought, believe it or not, high-rise chicken houses, completely renovated them, and created Borkholder Dutch Village. It is an authentic country-style marketplace, complete with a flea market, an arts and crafts mall, a restaurant, antique mall, events center and village shops.

The Dutch Village is open six days a week (see hours above) and a huge antique auction is held every Tuesday at 8 a.m. At the auction and throughout the antique mall, you can find quality furniture, including bedroom and dining room suites, dry sinks, roll-top desks, iceboxes, hall trees, buffets and more. And you can add a taste of the past to your life with antique dinnerware, jewelry, dolls, vintage clothes—and more!

Stroll through the arts and crafts mall, where you'll find quilts, wood carvings, shelving, dolls, framed artwork, knitted and crocheted items, new and used household goods, floral arrangements and many other hand-crafted items.

For lunch, visit the Dutch Kitchen, where you can indulge in a soda-fountain treat, like a Green River or a phosphate, enjoy a homemade lunch and top it off with Amish Apple Dumplings or another scrumptious dessert.

**Antiques on Sixth Antique Mall**
26358 Market St.
219/773-7755

**AAA Antique Shop**
Hwy. 6 W.
219/773-4912

**Antiques on the Square**
106 S. Main St.
219/773-5770

**Amishland Antique Mall**
106 W. Market St.
219/773-4795

**Si's Son-Dan Antiques**
110 S. Main St.
Mon.-Sat. 9:30-4:30

**Main Street Antiques Mall**
160 N. Main St.
219/773-5158

**Nappanee Antique Mall**
156 S. Main St.
219/773-3278

## 52 NASHVILLE

**Lee's Antiques**
S. Jefferson #45 A
812/988-1448

**Grandma Had One Antique Center**
216 S. Van Buren St.
812/988-1039

**Brown County Antique Mall II**
3288 E. State Road 46
812/988-1025

## Great Places to Stay

## Allison House Inn

90 S. Jefferson
812/988-0814

In the early 1900s, the rolling hills and spectacular fall colors of this time-forsaken area brought many artists from far and wide who were inspired by its beauty. Turning the country village of Nashville into an artist's colony, T. C. Steele and other award-winning Impressionist artists, dubbed the "Hoosier Group," were among the first to discover this artists' haven.

Nashville is still known as the home of artists. In galleries and shops you will find everything from fine paintings and pottery to weavings, stained glass, and charming country crafts. But don't stop there—this town has nearly 350 quaint shops selling not only art, but antiques, fine clothing and great souvenirs. A buggy or trolley ride can get you around the town to complete your shopping. Hearty country food has made Nashville famous. You can enjoy such wonderful treats as fried biscuits and apple butter. In 1868, Frank Taggart built the dry goods store which is now Nashville's oldest commercial building, housing Hobnob Corner at 17 W. Main St., a restaurant featuring fresh, hearty homemade fare. Enjoy a collection of Hohenberger photos in an old-time drugstore setting boasting a swatch of wallpaper from the 1890s.

In a town full of history, the Allison House (built in 1883) stands as a fine example of this charming scenic area. An American flag floats from its staff on the porch of the inn, pots of geraniums sit on wicker tables and firewood is stacked beside the door. "Neighborliness is contagious," says innkeeper Tammy Galm as she serves breakfast on a deck screened by pole beans. The Galms figured rightly that inn lovers would appreciate this small-town setting. After they purchased the house in 1985, they completely gutted and rebuilt the building, more than doubling its original size. There are five guest rooms newly remodeled and individually decorated with an emphasis on comfort and charm.

A full breakfast is served each morning. Fortified with calories, shoppers can work them off in search of antiques, a cornhusk doll or perhaps a ceramic pig with a red bandana.

## 53 NEW CASTLE

**Imperial Antique Mall**
1318 Broad St.
765/521-7418

**Recollections & Collections**
1431 Broad St.
765/531-8960

**Raintree Antique Emporium**
1331 Broad St.
765/529-7548

**St. Clair's Trash to Treasures**
111 N. 6th St.
765/521-8218

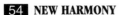
*Indiana*

## 54 NEW HARMONY

**New Harmony Antique Mall**
500 Church St.
812/682-3948

**Donna Smith's Heirlooms, Etc.**
527 Church St.
812/682-5027

**Antiques Showrooms in the Mews**
531 Church St.
812/682-3490

**Treasure Trove**
514 S. Main St.
812/682-4112

### *Great Places to Stay*

### Raintree Inn Bed and Breakfast

503 West St.
1-888-656-0123
Web site: www.raintree-inn.com

In New Harmony, one of Indiana's most unique and historic communities, a late Victorian mansion has been reborn as a premier bed and breakfast establishment dedicated to providing quality service and excellent accommodations. Raintree Inn's magnificent interiors and furnishings are just part of its appeal. Whether your interests are in history, shopping, art, theater, relaxation or a romantic getaway, innkeepers Scott and Nancy McDonald will help you get the most out of your New Harmony experience. Tastefully furnished guest rooms, each with large comfortable beds and private baths combine with a sumptuous full breakfast to insure that your visit to New Harmony is both pleasant and memorable.

## 55 NEWBURGH

**Rivertown Antiques**
1 W. Jennings St.
812/853-2562

**Generations**
218 W. Jennings St.
812/853-7270

**Little Red Barn Antiques**
10044 W. State Route 662
812/853-8096

**Country Gentleman Antiques**
103 State St.
812/858-9544

## 56 NOBLESVILLE

### Noblesville Antique Mall

20 N. Ninth St.
317/773-5095
Open: Mon.–Sat. 9–6, Sun. 12–6

Located on the courthouse square in historic downtown Noblesville, this large three-floor mall offers a wide range of antiques and collectibles. A large library and a "ruff room" is also located on the premises.

**Durwyn Smedley Antiques**
853 Conner St.
317/776-0161

**Olde House Antiques**
293 S. 8th St.
317/773-6951

**Lazy Acres Antiques**
77 Metsker Lane
317/773-7387

**Noblesville Emporium**
950 Logan St.
317/773-4444

**Bound to Be Found Antiques**
74 N. 9th St.
317/776-1993

## 57 NORTH VERNON

**Country Corner Market**
4250 N. State Hwy. 7
812/346-1095

**Olde Store Antiques**
162 E. Walnut St.
812/346-1925

**Cornett's**
246 E. Walnut St.
812/346-8995

**North Vernon Antique Mall**
247 E. Walnut St.
812/346-8604

## 58 PENDLETON

### Heritage Antique Mall

231 S. Pendleton Ave.
765/778-4726
Open: Daily 1–5

Trunks, textiles, glassware, furniture and pottery.

**Bob Post Antiques**
104 W. State St.
765/778-7778

**Pendleton Antique Mall**
123 W. State St.
765/778-2303

## 59 PERU

**Annie's Attic**
57 N. Broadway
765/473-4400

**Peru Antique Mall**
21 E. Main St.
765/473-8179

## 60 PIERCETON

**Beebe's Antique Shop**
Downtown Pierceton
219/594-2244

**Old Theater Antique Mall**
103 N. 1st St.
219/594-2533

**Antiques at the Sign of the Gas Light**
130 N. 1st St.
219/594-2457

**Curiosity Shop**
112 S. 1st St.
219/594-2785

**Gregory's Antiques**
306-308 N. 1st St.
219/594-5718

**Antique Town Mall**
107-109 N.1st St.
219/594-9665

**Huntington House Antiques**
123 N. 1st St.
219/594-5074

## 61 PLAINFIELD

**Gilley's Antique Mall**
5789 E. U.S. Hwy. 40
317/839-8779

**Avon Antiques**
7673 E. U.S. Hwy. 36
317/272-4842

**Little Dave's Everything Store**
10107 W. Washington
317/839-6040

**Haunted Bridge Antique Mall**
184 N. State Road 267
317/272-6956

## 62 PORTLAND

**Farmstead Antiques**
Hwy. 275
219/726-4930

**Carlson's Antiques**
212 N. Meridian St.
219/726-7919

## 63 RICHMOND

### Terry Harkleroad Antiques

1110 Sylvan Nook Drive
765/966-5353
Open: Hours by appointment

Country furniture, folk art, quilts, garden and architectural antiques.

**Scott Lure Co. & Trading Post**
1449 E. Chester Road
765/935-5091

**Foster's E Street Gallery**
825 N. E St.
765/935-9055

**Ft. Wayne Furniture Store**
193 Fort Wayne Ave.
765/966-9372

**The Silhouette Shop**
126 S. 4th St.
765/935-7887

**Top Drawer Antique Mall**
801 E. Main St.
765/939-0349

**John's**
823-825 Promenade
765/962-0214

**Kate's Furniture**
131 Richmond Ave.
765/966-5246

**At the Garden Gate**
111 S. 3rd
765/939-0777

## 64 ROANN

**Covered Bridge Merchandise Co.**
165 N. Chippewa Road
765-833-7473

**Mom & Pop's Jazzy Junk**
175 N. Chippewa Road
765/833-2233

**Royal Attic Design**
180 N. Chippewa St.
765/833-5333

**Roann Antique Mall**
200 N. Chippewa St.
765/833-6242

## 65 ROANOKE

### Antiques from BC at Lonsdale

10979 N. Roanake Road
219/672-9744
Open: Daily 10–5, by chance and any time by appointment
Directions: Just 7 miles south of I-69, take Exit 102 to Hwy. 24 South until you reach 1100 North, then turn right and go to the next corner. The shop is located in the front of the school building.

Located in a 1915 school building, this shop specializes in quality country and formal furniture dating from the 18th to the 20th century.

Additionally, they offer decorative paintings and accessories to enhance your home.

## 66 ROCKVILLE

**Covered Bridge Mall**
115 S. Jefferson St.
765/569-3145

**Rockville Antique Mall**
411 E. Ohio St.
765/569-6873

**Aunt Patty's Antiques**
U.S. Route 36
765/569-2605

**Bart's Corner**
Walker Ramp Road
765/344-6112

## 67 ROSSVILLE

**Back Through Time Antiques Mall**
9 W. Main St. (at flasher)
765/379-3299

**Pappy's Rossville Antique Mall**
54 E. Main St.
765/379-9000

**Rolling Wheels**
8136 West St. Road 26
765/379-2649

## 68 SCOTTSBURG

**Country Cousins Antiques**
Hwy. 31 S.
812/752-6353

**Scottsburg Antique Mall**
4 N. Main St.
812/752-4645

## 69 SEYMOUR

**Broadway Antiques**
219 N. Broadway St.
812/522-9538

**Remember When Antiques**
317 N. Broadway St.
812/522-5099

**Lucille's House of Antiques**
603 S. Chestnut St.
812/522-5541

**Crossroads Antique Mall**
311 Holiday Square
812/522-5675

## 70 SHIPSHEWANA

**Log House Country Store**
255 Depot
219/768-4652

**Berry's Hitching Post**
250 E. Middlebury
219/768-7862

**Fisher's Antiques**
155 Morton
219/768-4213

**Haarer's Antiques**
165 Morton
219/768-4787

### *Nearby Antique Shopping (Middlebury)*
### *Middlebury is located ten minutes from Shipshewana.*

### Main St. Antique Mall

511 S. Main St.
219/825-9533
Open: Mon.–Sat. 8–5:30

Quilts, old toys, tools, iron, antiques and collectibles.

*Indiana*

**Unique Antique Mall**
106 Wayne St.
219/825-1900

### 71 SILVER LAKE

**Attic Antiques**
107 N. Jefferson
219/352-2744

**D & J Antiques**
102 S. Jefferson
219/352-2400

**Twin Lakes Antiques**
7208 W. State Road 114
219/982-2939

### 72 SOUTH BEND

## Unique Antique Mall

50981 U.S. Route 33 N.
219/271-1799

Country primitives, oak, walnut, cherry furniture, clocks, flow blue, glassware, and Belleek.

**Thieves Market Mall**
Crossroad Shopping Center
219/273-1352

**Anthony's Antiques**
1606 W. Ewing Ave.
219/287-8180

**A-Antiques Ltd**
1009 N. Frances St.
219/232-1134

**Antiques & Things**
2210 Huron
219/282-2550

**Light Owl Antiques**
529 Lincoln Way W.
219/287-1184

**Victorian Galleries**
2011 Miami St.
219/233-3633

**AAA Quality Antiques**
1763 Prairie Ave.
219/232-1099

**Dixie Way South Antiques**
63760 Rt. 31
219/291-3931

**Antique Avenue Mall**
52345 U.S. Route 31 N.
219/272-2558

### *Great Places to Stay*

## The Book Inn

508 W. Washington
219/288-1990
Fax 219/234-2338
Web site: members.aol.com/bookinn/
Directions: Exit 77 off the I-80/90 toll road.

Built by Martha and Albert Cushing in 1872, this home was one of the earliest residences in the historic district of South Bend. Cushing was a local businessman with interests in several enterprises, including a drug- and bookstore at 101 North Michigan Street. The house is listed as an outstanding example of Second Empire architecture by the Indiana Historic Site Preservation Committee. Sometimes called French Victorian, the mansard roof with ornamental arched dormer windows creates an impression of massive elegance. The entry doors with double-leaf wood and applied decoration reportedly won first place for design at the 1893 Columbian Exposition in Chicago.

Inside you will find 12-foot ceilings and hand-hewn, irreplaceable butternut woodwork that welcome you into this elegant mansion. The Book Inn has been a designer showcase and every room offers comfortable bed and breakfast accommodations. The five sleeping rooms all have private bathrooms.

The Book Inn is located in the historic West Washington district of downtown South Bend. The original owners, the Cushings, must have watched in wonder when Clement Studebaker built his home, Tippecanoe Place, right next door in 1888. Studebaker's 40-room "feudal castle" is now an elegant restaurant where you can explore the mansion and enjoy a wonderful meal.

*"High ceilings, large comfortable beds with beautiful linens, lovely antique furnishings, picture books, novels, cozy reading chairs, fresh flowers, lush terry robes, private bath — everything I could possibly want. The entire house, from the well-stocked library and kitchen to the dining room set with crystal, linen, great coffee, and tasty breakfast fare, is a weary traveler's dream. Peggy and John made me feel welcome, relaxed and pampered."*

Suzanne Peck (Guest)
*America's Favorite Inns, B&Bs & Small Hotels*

### 73 SPENCER

**River Valley Sales**
27 E. Franklin St.
812/829-4948

**Hillside Cottage and Antiques**
870 W. Hillside Ave.
812/829-4488

**Maxine's**
56 E. Jefferson
812/829-6369

**Spencer Antique Mall**
165 S. Main St.
812/829-0785

**Robinson House Galleries**
3 N. Montgomery
812/829-9558

### 74 TERRE HAUTE

There's something for everyone in Terre Haute! Enjoy a walking tour through the lovely Farrington Grove Historical District, near downtown Terre Haute, where over 800 homes offer visitors a wealth of historic architectural detail and colorful histories.

Take a step back even further in time at the new Native American Museum located on the east side of Terre Haute in Dobbs Park. This museum lets you explore Native American cultures through exhibits, programs, and a Native American heirloom garden.

*Indiana*

**Hoosier Antiques & Clocks**
1630 S. 3rd St.
812/238-0562
Open: Mon.–Sat. 10–5, Sun. by chance or appointment
Directions: Traveling I-70 exit at U.S. 41 (Exit 7) and proceed 1²/₁₀ miles north on 3rd St. Turn right at either Hulman St. or Osborne St. Parking is at the rear off the alley. Traveling U.S. 40, drive 1²/₁₀ miles south of the courthouse at Wabash Avenue and 3rd St. In Terre Haute, 3rd St. is U.S. 41 and Wabash is U.S. 40.

Hoosier Antiques & Clocks is located in a charming, shingled cottage built in the early 1900s. The shop carries a general line of antiques and collectibles and specializes in antique clocks. All clocks are in running condition.

**Swank Antiques**
1126 N. 8th St.
812/235-7734

**E. Bleemel Flour & Feed**
904 Poplar St.
812/232-2466

**Ancient Tymes Antiques Mall**
1600 S. 3rd St.
812/238-2178

**Gatherings**
1429 S. 25th St.
812/234-8322

**Granny's Daughter**
11746 S. U.S. Hwy. 41
812/299-8277

**North Side Collectables**
2323 Lafayette Ave.
812/466-9091

**Anderson Antiques**
1612 S. 3rd St. (U.S. 41)
812/232-2991

**Kasameyer Antiques & Collectibles**
5149 S. U.S. 41 (7th & 41)
812/299-1672

**Antiques Crafts & Things**
137 W. Honey Creek Pkwy.
812/232-8959

**Lowry's Antiques**
1132 Poplar St.
812/234-1717

**Antiques, Inc.**
2000 S. 3rd St.
812/235-4829

**Shady Lane Antique Mall**
9247 S. U.S. Hwy. 41
812/299-1625

**Nancy's Downtown Mall**
600 Wabash Ave.
812/238-1129

**Colonial Antiques**
Farmersburg, S. on U.S.41
812/696-2600

**Antiques, Tim Weir**
1641 S. 25th St.
812/234-6515

**75 TIPTON**

**Dezerland**
114-116 S. Main St.
765/675-8999

**Tipton Antique Center**
114-116 S. Main St.
765/675-8993

**Foster's Last Stand**
122 N. Main St.
765/675-3391

**76 VALPARAISO**

**Sydow Antiques**
153 W. Lincolnway
219/465-1777

**Valparaiso Antique Mall**
212 E. Lincolnway
219/465-1869

**Accents, Etc.**
202 E. Lincolnway
219/464-3739

**77 VINCENNES**

**Yesteryear**
305 Main St.
812/882-2459

**Old Town Attic Antiques**
1804 Washington Ave.
812/882-0903

**Hitching Post**
1717 Washington Ave.
812/882-9372

**78 WESTFIELD**

**Antiques Galore & More**
110 E. Main St.
317/867-1228

**Jonathan Westfield Co.**
120 N. Union St.
317/896-3566

**Westfield Antique Mall**
800 E. Main St., Hwy. 232
317/867-3327

**Welcome House Antiques, Etc.**
202 E. Main St.
317/867-0077

**R. Beauchamp Antiques**
16405 Westfield Blvd.
317/897-3717

**79 WHITING**

**Granny's General Store**
1309 Community Court
219/659-7538

**Just Little Things**
1600 119th St.
219/659-3438

**Blue Ribbon Antiques**
1858 Indianapolis Blvd.
219/659-4502

**80 WORTHINGTON**

**Carriage House Antiques**
318 S. Jefferson St.
812/875-3219

**81 ZIONSVILLE**

**Brown's Antique Shop**
315 N. 5th St.
317/873-2284

**Sow's Ear**
76 S. Main St.
317/873-2785

**Zionsville Antiques**
75 N. Main St.
317/873-1761

**Indiana Folkart & Antiques**
120 S. Main St.
317/873-4424

*Indiana*

**Captain Logan**
150 S. Main St.
317/873-9999

**Helen Kogan Antiques**
195 S. Main St.
317/873-4208

### *Great Places to Stay*

## Brick Street Inn

175 S. Main St.
317/873-9177
Email: www.Brickstinn@aol.com

Capture the essence of Midwestern hospitality and country living at Brick Street Inn, a historic five-room circa-1865 home. The style is relaxed, which means all the comforts with a casual attitude. The attention to detail is not just how it looks, but how it feels … cozy, romantic, friendly, the inn is a secret that unfolds. Rooms feature down comforters, fluffy robes and an eclectic mix of new and old furnishings. Your hosts provide fresh flowers, mouth-watering goodies and a gourmet breakfast. Set in historic Zionsville, which quietly borders metropolitan Indianapolis, the inn is privy to some of the best shopping and dining in central Indiana.

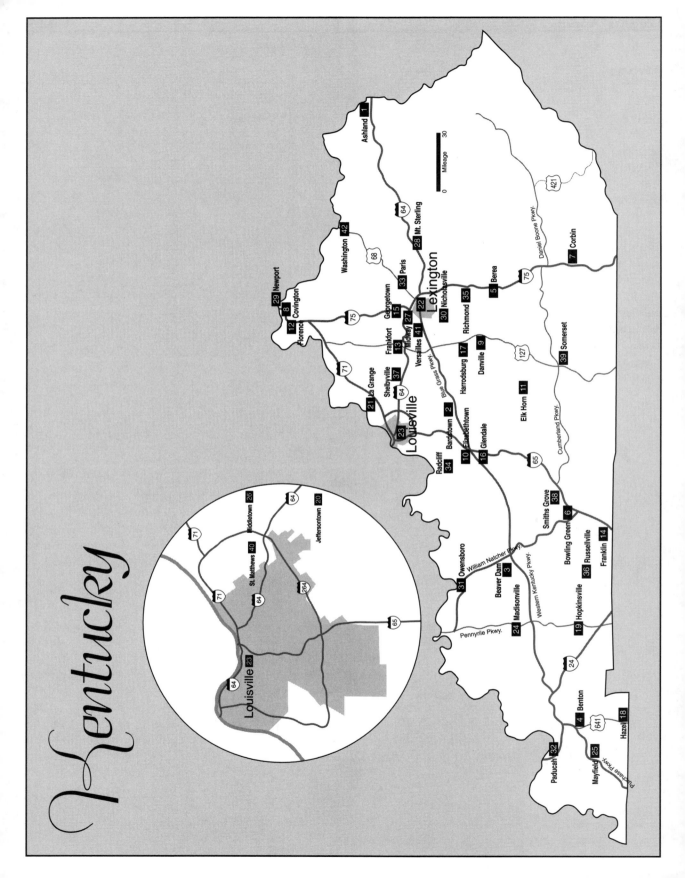

## 1 ASHLAND

**Tunnel Hill Antique Shoppe**
1827 6th St.
606/324-6880

**Miners Coins & Antiques**
830 29th St.
606/325-9425

**Vintage Hall**
By Appointment Only
606/329-1173

**Treasured Possessions**
1430 Winchester Ave.
606/324-4798

## 2 BARDSTOWN

**Town and Country Antiques**
118 N. 3rd St.
502/348-3967

**Scarlett's Fever**
Appointment Only
502/349-9211

### *Great Places to Stay*

### Arbor Rose Bed & Breakfast

209 E. Stephen Foster Ave.
1-888-828-3330

The Arbor Rose is a late Victorian-style home thoroughly renovated in 1993. The original structure was built in 1820 and contains five fireplaces, some of which were designed by Alexander Moore, master craftsman of My Old Kentucky Home. Five guest suites all have private baths. Homemade cookies and beverages are available at all times in the common area, as well as TV, phone, fax and a computer hook-up. Located in historic Bardstown, the Arbor Rose provides easy accessibility to shopping and all the local attractions. Each room comes with a full "Country Gourmet" breakfast and, weather permitting, it is served on the garden terrace by a pond stocked with Japanese koi and a garden complete with hummingbirds.

### Jailer's Inn

111 W. Stephen Foster Ave.
502/348-5551 or 1-800-948-5551
Open: February–December, closed January

Ever wondered what it would be like to spend a night or two in jail? Well you can—sort of—if you stay at the Jailer's Inn in Bardstown! This 1819 building (listed on the National Register) was originally built as a jail, with prisoners housed above and the jailer living below. In 1874 prisoners were moved to a new jail built right behind this old one, and the old building became the jailer's official permanent residence. Believe it or not, both buildings were used for the original purposes until 1987! The complex was then declared the oldest operating jail in the state of Kentucky. Now the 1819 building has been completely renovated into six individually decorated guest rooms filled with antiques, original rugs and heirlooms. Guest quarters range from the Victorian Room and the Garden Room to the former women's cell, which is decorated in prison black and white and features two of the original bunk beds plus a more modern waterbed. One room even has a Jacuzzi. Guests are treated to a filling continental-plus breakfast and refreshments.

### Kenmore Farms

1050 Bloomfield Road
1-800-831-6159

Kenmore Farms was established in the 1860s as the Victorian residence at a prominent Kentucky horse farm. This stately home features antiques throughout, oriental rugs, and gleaming wood, from the poplar floors to the cherry stairway. The decor and Southern hospitality creates a relaxing and enjoyable atmosphere. Within driving distance of Derby Museum and Churchill Downs, Keeneland Racetrack, Kentucky Horse Park and the Shaker Village at Pleasant Hill.

### The Mansion Bed & Breakfast

1003 N. Third
502/348-2586

The home was placed on the National Register of Historic Places in 1979, described in the nomination as a "truly dignified, aristocratic and striking example of Greek Revival architecture." Overnight guests at the Mansion are treated to a deluxe continental breakfast served in the dining room on china, silver and crystal. The Mansion also boasts a rich history. The home is on the site where the first Confederate flag, the "Stars and Bars," was raised in Kentucky.

## 3 BEAVER DAM

Ohio County is older than the Commonwealth of Kentucky and was named for the Ohio River, which was originally its northern boundary. It is the fifth-largest county in Kentucky—located 23 miles south of Owensboro, 40 miles north of Bowling Green, 100 miles southwest of Louisville, and 90 miles north of Nashville, Tenn.

**Downtown Antique Mall**
103 N. Main St.
502/274-4774

**Casey's Antiques & Collectibles**
116 N. Main St.
No Phone Listed

**Past & Presents Antiques**
930 N. Main St.
502/274-3360 or 502/274-7124

**Reflections**
340 S. Main St.
502/274-7980

**Knob Hill Antiques**
282 Knob Hill Road
502/274-3065

**Pat's Antiques & Collectibles**
Hwy. 269 off Hwy. 231
502/274-3076

**Beaver Dam Auction**
200 E. 3rd
502/274-3349

**Papa's Playhouse**
724 Buttermilk Lane
502/274-7558

**Central Park Antiques**
Jefferson St. (McHenry)
502/274-7200

## 4  BENTON

### The Benton Antique Exchange
1026 Main St.
502/527-5062
Open: Mon.–Sun. 10–5

Specializing in furniture and special requests. Importing from England, shipments arriving monthly.

**Answer**
321 Main St.
502/527-1078

**Antiques Et Cetera**
1026 Main St.
502/527-7922

**Benton Antiques & Collectibles**
103 W. 13th St.
502/527-5424

**The Strawberry Patch**
2391 U.S. Hwy. 68 W.
502/527-8186

**The Antique Mall**
600 Main St.
502/527-2085

**Treasured Memories**
1207 Main St.
502/527-0039

**Twin Lakes Antique Mall**
6953 U.S. Hwy. 641 N.
502/362-2218

## 5  BEREA

**McCray's Antiques**
408 Chestnut St.
606/986-2520

**Bay Window Antiques**
436 Chestnut St.
606/986-2345

**Bratcher's Antiques & Lamp Repair**
438 Chestnut St.
606/986-7325

**Todd's Antique Mall**
7435 Hwy. 21 E.
606/986-9087

**Howard's Antique Mall**
573 Mount Vernon Road
606/986-9551

**Chestnut Street Antique Mall**
420 Chestnut St.
606/986-2883

**Something Olde**
437 Chestnut St.
606/986-6057

**Place in Time**
440 Chestnut St.
606/986-7301

**Impressions of Berea**
116 McKinney Dr.
606/986-8177

**Teresa's Antiques & Art Gallery**
702 Prospect St.
606/986-9147

## 6  BOWLING GREEN

**River Bend Antique Mall**
315 Beech Bend Road
502/781-5773

**Werner-Lowe Ltd.**
1232 U.S. 31 W. Bypass
502/796-2683

**Greenwood Mall**
Scottsville Road
502/781-9655

**Daniel's Wicker**
2125 Bill Dedmon Road
502/842-6926

**Timeless Treasures**
5521 Russellville Road
502/781-3698

### *Great Places to Stay*

### Bowling Green B&B
3313 Savannah Dr.
502/781-3861

This lovely brick two-story home, furnished with antiques, sits next to a woods and is a comfortable walk to a charming duck pond. Relax by the fireside in winter in the comfortable den with books, TV, video or organ. In summer enjoy the covered patio or walk the pleasant, safe streets. Western Kentucky University, restaurants, shopping and entertainment are all nearby. The hosts are a chemistry professor and retired nurse and teacher who enjoy people, travel and photography.

## 7  CORBIN

### Past Times Antique Mall, Inc.
135 W. Cumberland Gap Pkwy.
606/528-8818
Open: Mon.–Sat. 9–6, Sun. 11–6
Directions: From I-75: take Exit 29 East. At the first traffic light make a right turn. Past Times is located behind Burger King and Super 8 Motel.

Past Times houses some interesting things in its 14,000 square feet of space. Its 95 booths hold the general consignment of furniture, primitives, collectibles, etc., with a great deal of glassware, plus railroad and mining memorabilia, plus a very active trade in antique knives, period safety razors, etc.

**Meadow Land Antiques & Collectibles**
3475 Cumberland Falls Hwy.
606/523-2803

## 8  COVINGTON

### The World's Largest Outdoor Sale
August 14–17, 19–22

Covington is the northern starting point . . . and the roadside bargains extend south to Alabama! Pack a lunch and hop in the car for this 450-mile shopping adventure. 513/357-MAIN.

**Sentimento Antiques & Collectibles**
525 Main St.
606/291-9705

**Philadelphia Street Antiques**
526 Philadelphia St.
606/431-6866

## 9  DANVILLE

History abounds in the picturesque community of Danville, 35 miles southwest of Lexington. The Rhodes House (305 North Third, where

*Raintree County* was filmed in 1956) is just one of the 50 sites on the city's walking tour. The visitor center is in the beautiful Greek Revival McClure-Barbee House (304 South Fourth, Monday through Friday, 9 to 4, 1-800-755-0076). Danville's internationally recognized Great American Brass Band Festival is in mid-June.

Ten constitutional conventions took place at Constitution Square State Historic Site (134 South Second) between 1784 and 1792. The park includes the original pre-1792 post office (the first west of the Alleghenies), Governor's Circle, and replica meetinghouse, courthouse and jail. You'll also see the 1817 Fisher's Row houses, now an art gallery; and the Historical Society Museum in the Watts-Bell House featuring a great collection of vintage clothing.

**Leigh & Company Estate Liquidators**
128 & 130 S. 4th St.
606/236-2137

**Antique Mall of Historic Danville**
158 N. 3rd St.
606/236-3026

**Annie's Loft**
By appointment only
606/236-6735

## 10 ELIZABETHTOWN

Elizabethtown, 35 miles south of Louisville, has a wealth of American history including ties to Abraham Lincoln's family. The walking tour on Thursdays (free, June through September, 7 p.m.) has costumed characters from the town's past such as Carrie Nation, General George Custer and Sarah Bush Lincoln.

Around the corner is the 1825 Brown-Pusey House, the town's first haven for travelers. This stately Georgian Colonial building housed General Custer and his wife in the 1870s.

**Back Home**
251 W. Dixie Ave.
502/769-2800

**Irene's Antiques**
407 E. Dixie Ave.
502/737-2552

**Addington Antiques**
711 W. Park Road
502/769-6456

**Buckboard Antiques**
125 Hillsdale Drive
502/737-0589

**Heartland Antique Mall**
1006 N. Mulberry
502/737-8566

**Touch of the Past Antiques**
9 Houchens Plaza
502/765-2579

**Goldnamers**
210 N. Main St.
502/766-1994

**Elizabethtown Antique Mall**
516 N. Main St.
502/769-3959

## 11 ELKHORN

**Piece of the Past**
466 Elkhorn
502/465-3171

## 12 FLORENCE

**Heirloom Antique Gallery**
6614 Dixie Hwy.
606/371-5566

**Kelly's Antiques**
7610 U.S. 25
606/371-0303

## 13 FRANKFORT

Frankfort, chosen the state capital in 1792, is nestled among the rolling hills of the Bluegrass in a beautiful Kentucky River valley. Much of Kentucky's history has been written here—old frontiersman Simon Kenton pleaded for relief from taxes, Henry Clay practiced his oratory, former Vice President Aaron Burr was charged with treason—the stories go on and on.

**Button Box**
123 Brighton Park Blvd.
502/695-7108

**Ron-Jo's Antiques & Collectibles**
227 Broadway St.
502/223-5466

**Poor Richard's Books**
233 W. Broadway St.
502/223-8018

**Old Capitol Antiques**
239 W. Broadway St.
502/223-3879

**Treadle Works**
333 W. Broadway St.
502/223-2571

**Rail Fence Antiques**
415 W. Broadway St.
502/875-5040

**Gift Box**
1500 Louisville Road
502/223-2784

## 14 FRANKLIN

A surveyor's mistake created the Kentucky-Tennessee "Triangular Jag," a small piece of land that forms Simpson County's southern border. The muddy waters of legal ownership made the area a safe place for duelists to avoid the law. The Sanford Duncan Inn, six miles south of Franklin, was a popular overnight stop for guests such as General Sam Houston before meeting at nearby Linkumpinch to settle their "gentlemanly disputes."

Franklin's downtown historic district includes the Simpson County Archives & Museum in the old jailer's residence, with wall drawings left by Civil War soldiers held prisoner here (free, Monday–Friday, 206 North College, 502/586-4228).

**Strickly Country Antique Mall**
5945 Bowling Green Road
502/586-3978

**Main St. Antiques & Collectibles**
207 N. Main St.
502/586-6104

**Two Sisters Antiques**
Walmart Shopping Center
502/586-0099

**Heritage Antique Mall**
111 W. Washington St.
502/586-3880

**P.J.'s General Store**
205 W. Cedar St.
502/586-8340

**Classic Image**
101 W. Cedar St.
502/586-8886

*Kentucky*

**Country Cottage**
1037 N. Main St.
502/586-6742

## 15 GEORGETOWN

Located just north of the crossroads of I-75 and I-64, Georgetown was founded in 1790 by the Baptist minister Elijah Craig. The Reverend Craig is perhaps best known for his world-famous invention, bourbon whiskey.

Today, Georgetown is a blend of old and new. Noted for its profusion of historic houses and perhaps the finest antique shopping in the state, it is also one of Kentucky's fastest growing communities and the American home of Toyota's Camry, Avalon, and Sienna production facility. From mid-July to mid-August, Georgetown is also host to the Cinncinnati Bengals training camp.

Georgetown offers beautiful horse farms, Irish fieldstone fences, the meandering Elkhorn and Eagle Creeks and rolling fields of tobacco and cattle. You'll find small, quaint communities like Stamping Ground and Sadieville. Elkhorn Creek, the inspiration for Walt Whitman's "Leaves of Grass," offers both canoeists and fishermen a rewarding and relaxing experience.

Georgetown and Scott County offer a complete range of overnight accomodations (more than 800 rooms) from clean and affordable motels to antique bed and breakfasts. All of this, plus you are just five minutes from the world-famous Kentucky Horse Park.

Georgetown and Scott County are host to numerous craft shows and other events. For additional information, contact Georgetown/Scott County Tourism Commission, 401 Outlet Center Dr., Suite 240, Georgetown, KY 40324 or call the commission at 1-888-863-8600 (Email: gtown@mis.net or www.georgetownky.com).

**Den of Antiquity**
100 W. Main St.
502/863-7536

**Pooh's Place**
122 E. Main St.
502/867-3930

**Trojan Antiques Gallery**
130 N. Broadway St.
502/867-1823

**The Vault Antique & Collectible Mall**
201 E. Main St.
502/863-2728

**Kollector's Corner**
1365 Lexington Road
502/863-5829

**Central Kentucky Antique Mall**
114 E. Main St.
502/863-4018

**Georgetown Antique Mall**
124 W. Main St.
502/863-9033

**Wyatt's Antique Center**
149 E. Main St.
502/863-0331

**Gretchen's Antiques**
119 S. Broadway St.
502/863-2538

**Cox's Collectibles**
Hwy. 62 (Oxford)
502/863-1407

**Olde Barn Antiques**
222 N. Broadway St.
502/863-2013

**The Wee Shop**
3830 Cynthia Road
502/863-0841

**Oxford Antiques**
Hwy. 62 (5 mi. east of Georgetown)
502/863-3965

### *Great Places to Stay*

**Blackridge Hall**
4055 Paris Pike
502/863-2069 or 1-800-768-9308
Rates: $89–$159

This Southern Georgian-style mansion situated on five acres in the heart of horse country exemplifies the high style and elegant living of a true Kentucky horse farm. Blackridge Hall's grand entry looks out upon

the rolling bluegrass landscape. It is surrounded by horse farms and is just an eight-minute drive from the Kentucky Horse Park and twenty minutes from Keeneland, Lexington and Rupp Arena. For the antique shopper, there's Midway, a community known for its antique shops, as well as numerous quaint antique shops in Georgetown. Nearby are the Factory Stores of American Outlet Mall, and the Toyota Motor Co., which offers tours of its plant.

Blackridge Hall, built on a ridge which has a view of the Lexington lights at night, was completed in 1991 and features 10,000 square feet of living space.

Five guest suites/rooms are available and all have names which indicate their decor. The Colonial Williamsburg master suite is a large, plush suite with Jacuzzi, fireplace, living room and sitting area. The Fox and Hound and Thoroughbred guest rooms both have private baths.

Guests will love the tiled sunroom and the elegant formal dining room, where proprietor Jim D. Black serves breakfast on fine china, with sterling flatware and crystal stemware. The furnishings throughout the house are 18th- and 19th-century antiques and reproductions and include rice-carved queen-size beds.

## 16 GLENDALE

Don't miss the charming historic register community of Glendale, 7 miles south of Elizabethtown off I-65, Exit 86. Antique malls, shops and a country store line the street bisected by the L & N railroad crossing. Enjoy great food at the Whistle Stop, 502/369-8586, or the Depot, 502/369-6000. Most shops are open Tuesday through Saturday 11–6. The annual Glendale Crossing Festival is in October.

## Side Track Shops
212 E. Main St.
502/369-8766
Open: Tues.–Sat. 11–9

Twenty unique shops under one roof. Specializing in Blue Ridge pottery.

## A Step Back Antiques
College St.
502/369-6122

Specializing in Derby items, trunks and Hoosier cabinets.

| | |
|---|---|
| **Log Cabin Antique Shop**<br>101 Jaggers Road<br>502/369-6001 | **Ivy Gate**<br>1 block off Main St.<br>502/369-6343 |
| **Crow's Nest**<br>138 Main St.<br>502/369-6060 | **Sisters**<br>1 block off Main St.<br>502/369-8604 |
| **Through The Grapevine**<br>1 Block off Main St.<br>502/369-7925 | **Bennie's Barn**<br>434 E. Main St.<br>502/369-9677 |
| **Glendale Antique Mall**<br>103 W. Railroad Ave.<br>502/369-7279 | **Ramona's Antiques**<br>122 E. Railroad Ave.<br>502/369-9652 |

## 17  HARRODSBURG

Once a frontier territory, Harrodsville was founded in 1774 as the first permanent English settlement west of the Allegheny Mountains. On the walking and driving tours, spanning more than 200 years of history, you'll pass by stately pre–Civil War homes, churches and businesses representing various architectural styles. Morgan Row, 220-232 S. Chiles, is the oldest row house standing in Kentucky. While on Main, don't miss a stroll through Olde Towne Park, which features a cascading fountain.

A highlight of the historic community is Beaumont Inn, built on the site of the Greenville Springs Spa. It was constructed in 1845 as one of the South's most prestigious girls schools. Since 1919, it has operated as a country inn under four generations of the same family.

## North Main Center Antique Mall
520 N. Main St.
606/734-2200
Open: Mon.–Sat. 10–5, Sun. 1–5, closed Wed.

Owner Nena Inden has loved antiques since she was a teenager, so what better business to get into than owning an antique store? She has over 22,000 square feet filled with Victorian pieces, primitives, china, glassware, '50s collectibles, jewelry, silver, old prints, frames, and children's toys.

But the real treat would be to see Nena and husband Christian's home, fabulous Ashfeld Manor. This 1891 stone mansion, complete with a four-story tower, is about 8,000 square feet of breathtaking Old-World craftsmanship and opulence. Every room is made of a different wood, with hand-carved fireplaces, French chandeliers, and original wainscotting.

| | |
|---|---|
| **Old Kentucky Restorations**<br>122 W. Lexington St.<br>606/734-6237 | **Granny's Antique Mall**<br>1286 Louisville Road<br>606/734-2327 |
| **Main Street Antiques**<br>225 S. Main St.<br>606/734-2023 | **Tomorrow's Another Day**<br>117 Poplar St.<br>606/734-9197 |
| **J. Sampson Antiques & Books**<br>107 S. Main St.<br>606/734-7829 | **The Antique Mall of Harrodsburg**<br>540 N. College St. (Hwy. 127)<br>606/734-5191 |

### *Great Places to Stay*

## Canaan Land Farm Bed and Breakfast
4355 Lexington Road
1-800-450-7307

Located off Highway 68, near Shakertown, Canaan Land Farm B&B is a working sheep farm where guests can enjoy a variety of barnyard animals.

Canaan Land, circa 1795, is on the National Register of Historic Places and is also designated a Kentucky Historic Farm. In 1995, a historic log house was restored on the property, giving the B&B six rooms with private baths, and three working fireplaces. Amenities include antiques, feather beds, large pool, hot tub, and hammocks in the shade. Peaceful, secluded and romantic.

## 18  HAZEL

Easily reached by antique hounds in four states (Tennessee, Kentucky, Arkansas and the Missouri bootheel), Hazel is western Kentucky's oldest and largest antique shopping district. Located on U.S. Highway 641 at the Kentucky-Tennessee state line just east of the fabulous Land Between the Lakes, this tiny turn-of-the-century community has been transformed into an antique shopper's heaven. Almost all the storefronts are now antique shops or malls, offering a smorgasbord of antiques and collectibles.

There are several annual festivals and open houses in Hazel targeted for antique lovers.

• Freedom Fest — July 4 with decorations, fireworks, and special deals on antiques throughout town.

• Hazel's Celebration — Oct. 4, an old-time country street festival. Hazel's population is 500; this festival draws 8,000! There's food, entertainment, art, cloggers, even the winning lottery ticket is drawn here!

• Christmas Open house (sponsored by the Antique Dealer's Association) — Saturday after Thanksgiving, all the shops in town have refreshments, decorations and carolers.

## Miss Bradie's Antiques and Christmas
304 Dees St. (Dees and Main)
502/492-8796
Open: Daily except Thanksgiving Day and Christmas Day, Mon.–Sat. 10–5, Sun. 12:30–5

Here's a good stop for early Christmas shoppers. Miss Bradie's specializes in antiques and decorative accessories and also features a year-round Christmas room. Owner Jo McKinley is an authorized dealer for Christopher Radko glass ornaments, Old World Christmas, Annalee Dolls and Boyds Bears. Indulge your shopping habit and get those pesky Christmas shopping chores out of the way at the same, enjoyable time!

## Ginger's Antiques and Refinishing
310 Main St., P.O. Box 37
502/492-8138
Open: Mon.–Sat. 10–4:30, Sun. 1–4:30

Among the many antique shops in Hazel is Ginger's. They offer not only the wares of 12 dealers, but folks can visit Ginger's 3rd Floor Candy Store. The candy store is like an old-fashioned general store, with big glass jars full of Mrs. Burton's Gourmet candy, lots of jams and jellies, different kinds of honey, and all the luscious things that used to fascinate kids in an old-fashioned candy store! They also have a soda fountain in the candy store, so shoppers can quench their thirst after all that buying!

## Miss Martha's Antiques
302 Main St.
502/492-8145
Open: Daily 10–4:30

Bill Price has been offering a general variety of antiques, including primitives, kitchen collectibles and furniture, to the public for 14 years. During these years, he has had the opportunity to see and hear lots of funny stories from his customers and shoppers. Here's one of the stories he has to tell:

"Two ladies came into my shop several years ago late on a Saturday afternoon. They had spent the day at the Heart of Country Show in Nashville and had decided to come to Hazel on their way home. They had obviously had a good time and had probably stopped somewhere for a lunch that had included a couple of Bloody Marys. One of the ladies immediately began picking up items and talking about how much cheaper things were here than at the show (naturally!). She began making a pile of things on my checkout counter. She would put something on the counter then go back for more. Each time she put something in her pile, her friend would say, 'Oh, Roger's gonna kill you!' The first lady would find something else she wanted and her friend would say, 'Oh, Roger's gonna kill you!' This went on for a while, and after about three or four of these comments, the happy shopper stopped and looked at her friend. 'Listen,' she said, 'When I first started going out on these shopping trips, Roger used to worry about how much money I had with me or whether or not I had the checkbook with me. Later, he'd be nervous if I went out and took the credit card with me. Now when I get home, the only thing Roger asks is, "Is anybody shipping anything?" '

## Country Collectibles
Main St., P.O. Box 258
502/492-8121
Open: Tues.–Sat. 10–4:30, Sun. 1–4:30, closed Mon.

This collection cache offers the shopping public Victorian furnishings, primitives and glassware.

## Hazel Antique Mall & Flea Market
Route 2, Box 169AAA
502/492-6168
Open: Mon.–Sat. 8–5

An all-purpose, well-rounded antique shop and flea market, the mall is located approximately 2 miles north of Hazel's antique district on U.S. Highway 641.

## Horse's Mouth Antiques
308 Main St., Box 207
502/492-8128
Open: Daily 10–4:30

The name of the shop makes you grin, but if you're into crystal, silver, china, old kerosene lamps and Aladdin lamps, you won't want to miss this stop!

## Decades Ago Antique Mall
317 Main St.
502/492-8140
Open: Year-round Mon.–Sat. 10–4:30, Sun. 1–4:30

Decades Ago—it sounds like the beginning of a bedtime story, doesn't it? It is a multidealer mall with more than 90 exhibitors plus showcases filled with wonderful antiques and collectibles.

# Kentucky

## Memory Lane Antiques

P.O. Box 155
502/492-8646
Open: Daily Mon.–Sat. 10–4:30, Sun. 1–4:30

For the past two years Larry Elkins' mall has offered 25 booths that carry a variety of furniture, glass, collectibles, primitives and other items, catering to both the individual shoppers and to dealers.

## Tooters Antique Mall

209 3rd St.
502/492-6111
Open: Daily Mon.–Sat. 10–4:30, Sun. 1–4:30 (winter) and Mon.–Sat. 10–5:30, Sun. 1–4:30 (summer)

Snacks and drinks are available when you take a break from strolling through this 8,000-square-foot, multidealer mall with showcases and more than 40 booths.

## Retro-Wares

306 Main St., P.O. Box 251
502/492-8164
Open: Daily Mon.–Sat. 10:30–4:30, Sun. 1–4:30

Situated in the heart of Hazel's antique district, this is the place to find those neat chrome and vinyl retro things. The shop specializes in mid-century furnishings and art deco, with a large collection of costume jewelry, limited edition Barbies, and fashion flashbacks.

## Idle Hour Antiques

Main St., P.O. Box 42
502/492-8180
Open: By appointment or by chance

Idle Hour Antiques is another Hazel shop that specializes in Victorian furnishings and collectibles.

## 19 HOPKINSVILLE

**Hopkinsville Antique Mall**
1010 S. Main St.
502/887-9363

**Country Boy Stores**
Newstead Road
502/885-5914

**Aunt Mary's Antiques**
2180 Madisonville Road (Hwy. 41)
502/885-9623

**The Snoop Shop**
Main St.
502/889-0360

**Quidas Antiques**
1301 E. 9th St.
502/886-6141

**Forget-Me-Nots Antiques**
110 E. 6th St.
502/885-5556

**Butler's Antiques**
601 E. 17th St.
502/889-9603

## 20 JEFFERSONTOWN

**Madge's Antiques**
3515 Chenowith Run Road
502/266-5622

## 21 LaGRANGE

**Heirlooms**
110 E. Main St.
502/222-4149

**Primrose Antiques**
123 E. Main St.
502/222-8918

**Iron Horse Antiques**
119 E. Main St.
502/222-0382

**Three Peas in Pod**
125 E. Main St.
502/222-2139

## 22 LEXINGTON

## Boone's Antiques of Kentucky, Inc.

4996 Old Versailles Road
606/254-5335
Open: Mon.–Sat. 8:30–5:30
Directions: From Highway 75: Follow all the signs to the airport, then pass the entrance on Man-of-War. Stay on Highway 60 West. Boone's is located on Highway 60 West, 1½ miles from the airport, ¾ mile from Keeneland Race Track. From Highway 64: Take Highway 60 East when approaching Castle. Go to the top of the hill to the caution light, then right on Old Versailles Road.

Boone's offers 27,000 square feet of English, French and American antiques. They carry everything from furniture and rugs to porcelains and unusual accent pieces.

**Pless Antiques**
247 N. Broadway St.
606/252-4842

**Country Antique Mall**
1455 Leestown Road
606/233-0075

**Heritage Antiques**
380 E. Main St.
606/253-1035

**Mike Maloney Antiques**
303 Southland Dr.
606-275-1934

**Cowgirl Attic**
220 Walton Ave.
606/225-3876

**Blue Grass Antique Market**
760 Winchester Road
606/258-2105

**Gift Box**
171 N. Lowry Lane
606/278-2399

**Lexington Antique Gallery**
637 E. Main St.
606/231-8197

**O'Loves Collectible Antiques**
410 W. Vine St. #149
606/253-0611

**Blue Grass Bazaar**
246 Walton Ave.
606/259-0303

**Clock Shop**
154 W. Short St.
606/255-6936

## 23 LOUISVILLE

Some people call it "Louaval," others say "Louieville," but regardless of how you pronounce it, you'll find plenty of things to see and do in Kentucky's largest city. Louisville is a blend of restored historic sites and sparkling new structures, fine arts and architecture, horses and sports, and more park acreage than any other city in the country.

The excitement in Louisville comes to a fever pitch each year during the Kentucky Derby Festival, one of the country's largest civic celebrations, beginning with the "Thunder over Louisville" fireworks extravaganza and ending with the "Run for the Roses," the one and only Kentucky Derby (April 19 through May 5, 502/584-6383).

Louisville is a treat for antique shopping. The largest malls are Den of Steven, Joe Ley Antiques, and Louisville Antique Mall.

### St. James Court Art Show
Held each October
For more information and show dates, call: 502/635-1842

Historic Old Louisville marks the spot for this treasure hunting adventure also known as one of the largest outdoor art shows in the nation! Explore tree-lined streets of this grand old Victorian neighborhood to unearth a king's ransom of trinkets and treasures. This one is more than a must see, it's a must BE!

**Tin Horse Antiques**
1040 Bardstown Road
502/584-1925

**Alines Antiques**
1130 Bardstown Road
502/473-0525

**Steve Tipton**
1327 Bardstown Road
502/451-0115

**David R. Friedlander Antiques**
1341 Bardstown Road
502/458-7586

**All Booked Up**
1555 Bardstown Road
502/459-6348

**Century Shop**
1703 Bardstown Road
502/451-7692

**Swan Street Antique Mall**
947 E. Breckinridge St.
502/584-6255

**Archibald Geneva Galleries**
1044 Bardstown Road
502/587-1728

**As Time Goes By**
1310 Bardstown Road
502/458-5774

**Discoveries**
1315 Bardstown Road
502/451-5034

**Charmar Galleries**
2005 Frankfort Ave.
502/897-5565

**Another Antique Shop**
1565 Bardstown Road
502/451-5876

**Steve White Gallery**
945 Baxter
502/458-8282

**Architectural Salvage**
618 E. Broadway
502/589-0670

**Antiques on Broadway**
821 Broadway
502/584-4248

**Louisville Antique Mall**
900 Goss Ave.
502/635-2852

**Red Geranium Shop**
1938 Harvard Dr.
502/454-5777

**Jan's Antique Shop**
704 Lyndon Lane
502/426-0828

**Antique Galleries**
8601 W. Manslick Road
502/363-3326

**Joe Ley Antiques**
615 E. Market St.
502/583-4014

**Annie's & Mine**
12123 Old Shelbyville Road
502/254-9366

**Red Barn Mall**
12125 Old Shelbyville Road
502/245-8330

**Holland House**
129 D Saint Matthews Ave.
502/895-2707

**2023 Antiques**
2023 Frankfort Ave.
502/899-9872

**Henderson Antiques**
2044 Frankfort Ave.
502/895-6605

**John Henry Sterry Antiques**
2144 Frankfort Ave.
502/897-1928

**Bittner's**
731 E. Main St.
502/584-6349

**Highland Antiques**
940 Baxter Ave.
502/583-0938

**Zigafoos Antiques & Beyond**
1287 Bardstown Road
502/458-2340

**Forevermore**
1734 Bonnycastle Ave.
502/473-0021

**Isaacs & Isaacs**
3937 Chenoweth Square
502/894-8333

**Kathryn's**
1008 Goss Ave.
502/637-7479

**Candyjack's Antique Store**
703 Lyndon Lane
502/429-6420

**Madalyn's Antiques**
8026 New LaGrange
502/425-9700

**Towne House Antiques**
612 E. Market St.
502/585-4456

**Middletown Antiques**
11509 Old Shelbyville Road
502/244-1780

**Pieces of Olde Antiques**
11405 Old Shelbyville Road
502/244-3522

**Schumann Antiques**
4545 Taylorsville Road
502/491-0134

**Annie's Attic**
3812 Frankfort Ave.
502/897-1999

**Scott F. Nussbaum Antiques**
2023 Frankfort Ave.
502/894-9292

**Elizabeth's Timeless Attire**
2050 Frankfort Ave.
502/895-5911

**Nanny Goat Strut Antiques**
638 E. Market St.
502/584-4417

**Baxter Ave. Antitque Mall**
623-625 Baxter Ave.
502/568-1582

**Hanna's Place Antiques**
1126 Bardstown Road
502/589-3750

**Antiques at the Loop**
1940 Harvard Dr.
502/584-4248

**J.C. & Co. Dreamlight**
1004 Barret Ave.
502/456-4106

*Kentucky*

**Frances Lee Jasper Rugs**
1330 Bardstown Road
502/459-1044

**Children's Planet**
1349 Bardstown Road
502/458-7018

**The Weekend Antiques**
2910 Frankfort Ave.
502/897-1213

**Attic Treasures**
600 Baxter Ave.
502/587-9543

**The Eclectic Jones**
1570 Bardstown Road
502/473-0396

**Annie's Attic**
12410 Shelbyville Road
502/244-0303

**Mary Lou Duke**
2916 Frankfort Ave.
502/893-6577

**Louisville Visual Art Association**
3005 River Road
502/896-2146

### Great Places to Stay

## Inn at the Park Bed and Breakfast
1332 S. 4th St.
1-800-700-7275
Web site: www.bbonline.wom/ky/innatpark

You will find this 7,400-square-foot restored Victorian mansion nestled in among other equally beautiful homes in the Historic Preservation District of Old Louisville. Inn at the Park boasts a grand, sweeping staircase, 12½-foot ceilings, crown moldings, fireplaces and private stone balconies. Relax in an atmosphere of a bygone era and enjoy mouth-watering breakfasts, leisurely walks in Central Park, adjacent to the inn, and romantic, fireside evenings.

## Rocking Horse Manor Bed and Breakfast
1022 S. 3rd St.
1-888-HOR-SEBB
Web site: www.bbonline.com/ky/rockinghorse

Built in 1888, the Rocking Horse Manor B&B is one of the finest Victorian mansions in "Old Louisville." It has all the elegance of a bygone era plus all the modern conveniences for today's traveler. Take a step back in time with a visit to the parlor or library, or if you choose, use the third-floor sitting area equipped with a minioffice for those who can't leave work behind. If a romantic getaway is your plan, choose the room with a cast wrap queen-size bed and whirlpool for two. Awaken each morning to a wonderful full gourmet breakfast offering homemade breads, quiches, fresh fruits and muffins.

## Aleksander House Bed & Breakfast
1213 S. First St.
502/637-4985

Aleksander House is a gracious in-town Victorian Italianate home built in 1882. It is centrally located in historical Old Louisville near shops, restaurants, museums and many attractions. The three-story brick

building is completely restored and is listed on the National Registry of Historic Landmarks. Inside are 14-foot ceilings, original hardwood floors, light fixtures, stained glass and fireplaces. The walls of the spacious dining room are lined with French toile paper and prints of 19th-century French Impressionists. Sumptuous breakfasts are served along with specially blended coffees, an assortment of fine teas, homemade granolas, muffins and jams. Two sweeping staircases lead to the second- and third-floor guest rooms, each uniquely decorated with eclectic or period furnishings with fine linen and comforters.

### 24 MADISONVILLE

**Ole House Antique Mall**
343 E. Center St.
502/821-4020

**Country Store Antiques & Crafts**
455 S. Madison Ave.
502/825-1556

**Kesterson's Antiques**
502 Hall St.
502/821-7311

### 25 MAYFIELD

**Mayberry Antique Mall**
114 W. Broadway St.
502/247-1979

**Remember When Antiques**
200 S. 6th St.
502/247-7228

**Sarah's Grapevine**
112 W. Broadway St.
502/247-9034

**Country Corner**
Hwy. 97/Sedalia Road
502/247-9361

**Collector's Shop**
104 W. South St.
502/247-1706

### 26 MIDDLETOWN

**Annie's Attic**
12410 Shelbyville Road
502/244-0303

### 27 MIDWAY

**Gordon H. Greek Antiques**
204 N. Gratz St.
606/846-4336

**D. Lehman & Sons**
100 Winter St. N.
606/846-4513

**Midway Antiques Gallery**
138 E. Main St.
606/846-5669

### 28 MT. STERLING

**Monarch Mill Antiques**
101 S. Maysville St.
606/498-3744

**Mt. Sterling Antique Mall**
16 E. Main St.
606/498-5868

**Smokehouse Antiques**
310 E. Main St.
606/498-7585

# Kentucky

## 29 NEWPORT

**R & L Collectibles & Etc.**
602 Monmouth St.
606/431-2230

**Peluso Antique Shop**
649 York St.
606/291-2870

**471 Antique Mall**
901 E. 6th St.
606/431-4753

## 30 NICHOLASVILLE

**Antiques on Main**
221 N. Main St.
606/887-2767

**Coach Light Antique Mall**
213 N. Main St.
606/887-4223

## 31 OWENSBORO

**Spend a Buck Galleries**
210 Allen St.
502/685-5025

**Peachtree Galleries Antiques**
104 W. 2nd St.
502/683-6937

**Plantation Antiques**
113 E. 2nd St.
502/683-3314

**Downstairs Attic Country Store**
2753 Veach Road
502/684-1819

**Second Avenue Antiques**
109 E. 2nd St.
502/683-0308

**Peachtree Galleries**
105 W. 2nd St.
502/926-1081

**Owensboro Antique Mall**
500 W. 3rd St.
502/684-3003

**Antiques & Collectibles**
724 W. 2nd St.
No Phone Listed

## 32 PADUCAH

### Michael Stewart Antiques
136 Lone Oak Road
502/441-7222
Open: By chance or appointment
Directions: From I-24 take Exit 7. Travel east on Lone Oak Road 1¹/₂ miles. The shop is located on the right side of the street, a half block before Broadway.

Michael Stewart specializes in 18th- and 19th-century furniture, paintings, books, maps and accessories. The shop handles primarily English and American furniture, and occasionally French. Civil War and 19th-century maps, 19th-century American and European paintings, and leather-bound 19th-century books, either in complete sets or single volumes, are found here.

### American Harvest Antiques
632 N. 6th St.
502/442-4852
Open: Wed. 10–5 and Sat. 10–4 or anytime by appointment
Directions: Traveling I-24: Take Exit 4. Travel east approximately 5 miles toward historic downtown Paducah. Turn left on North 6th Street. American Harvest is located at the end of the block on the corner of North 6th and Park Avenue.

This interesting arrangement was originally a four-dealer group that has now, unfortunately, had to become three because of one member's health. The four women who started the shop have all been dealers and friends for many years, traveling and buying together all over the region. They decided to open the shop together because their tastes and ideas are similar and because, as one said, "We just love it!"

Lisha Holt, Sharon Clymer and Brenda Jones, along with retired member/dealer Wilma Becker, opened American Harvest Antiques in historic downtown Paducah in an old grocery building. They also have the historic shotgun house next door filled with antiques. These ladies specialize in early American country furniture and accessories — from large pieces on down — with original paint or surface.

### Farmer's Daughter Antiques
6330 Cairo Road
502/444-7619 or 502/443-5450
Open: Wed.–Sat. 10–5, Sun. 1–5, closed Mon.–Tues.
Directions: From I-24 take Exit 3 onto Highway 305 South. The shop is just 1¹/₂ miles from I-24 on Cairo Road.

This cutely named shop holds 2,400 square feet of browsing pleasure for all who stop to look around. Noted for its wide variety of quality antiques such as oak and country furniture, kitchen wares, tools, old toys, fishing collectibles, decoys, quilts, linens, advertising memorabilia and more. Jane's love for "old things" is evident in her creative design of displays throughout the store. This is a "must stop" for the decorator who loves country furnishings and accessories at a reasonable price.

### Chief Paduke Antiques
300 S. 3rd
502/442-6799
Open: Mon.–Sat. 10–5, Sun. 12–5

Over 11,000 square feet of antiques and collectibles. Located in the historic North Carolina and St. Louis Railroad depot.

### American Quilter's Society National Show and Contest
Held in April each year.
For more information call: 502/898-7903

More than $80,000 in prizes draws the best quilters and their heirlooms to this national competition. Exhibits and workshops complete this quilt-crazy festival in Paducah, home of the museum of the American Quilter's Society.

# Kentucky

Antiques Cards & Collectibles, Inc.
203 Broadway St.
502/443-9797

Broadway House Antiques
229 Broadway St.
502/575-9025

Market Antiques & Collectibles Shop
401 Jefferson St.
502/443-6480

Sherry & Friends Antique Mall
208 Kentucky Ave.
502/442-4103

Shirley's Antiques
217 Kentucky Ave.
502/444-7599

Anthony Barnes Antiques
111 Market House Square
502/442-1891

Wood Whittlers
201 Ohio
502/443-7408

Things Unique & Antique
133 S. 3rd St.
502/575-4905

Vick's Attic
133 S. 3rd St.
502/575-4905

Giller Antiques
405 Jefferson
502/444-6786

The Rose Antiques
215 Broadway St.
502/443-2483

Cynthia's Playhouse & Antiques
218 Broadway St.
502/442-5770

Grandma & Grandpa's Treasures
200 Kentucky Ave.
502/443-6505

Once upon a Time Antiques
212 Kentucky Ave.
502/443-1062

D. Beverly Johnson
2201 Kentucky Ave.
502/443-1034

Market Square Antiques
113 Market House Square
502/444-9253

Affordable Antiques, Inc., II
933 S. 3rd St.
502/442-1225

Fleur de Lis Antiques
219 Kent Ave.
502/443-6103

Marshall's Antiques
113 N. Second
502/442-2052

Lamon's Antiques
1616 S. Sixth St.
502/443-7225

## Great Places to Stay

### The 1857's Bed and Breakfast
127 Market House Square
502/444-3960 or 1-800-264-5607
Rates: $65–$85

This three-story, friendly brick Victorian home offers everything needed for a complete and secluded weekend getaway. Listed on the National Register of Historic Places, the first floor holds Cynthia's Ristorante. Two guest rooms and a bath are on the second floor, and the third floor holds a family room and game room with hot tub and billiard table. All this is located in the downtown historic district, with antique stores, carriage rides, a quilt museum, lots of restaurants, and the Market House Cultural Center within walking distance. Guests may choose to book the entire second floor with private bath, if they want true privacy.

## 33 PARIS

Loch Lea Antiques
410 Main St.
606/987-7070

Antiques Arts & Collectibles
627 Main St.
606/987-0877

Green Apple Gift Shop
600 Main St.
606/987-7512

Fairbanks Antiques
Main St.
606/987-0877

## 34 RADCLIFF

### Buried Treasure Antiques
400 N. Dixie Blvd.
502/352-0600
Open: Tues.–Sat. 10–5, Sun. 12–5
Directions: From the Interstate, exit 102 off I-65 onto Joe Prather Hwy. (313 W.). Drive 8⁷/₁₀ miles to the stoplight, turn right onto Dixie Hwy. Located 3³/₁₀ miles from the light on the right.

Buried Treasure had its beginnings in a tiny three-room basement in 1992, which it quickly outgrew. On September 8, 1998, the mall moved to the old roller rink, (you can still see the hardwood skating floor), with over 12,500 square feet of glassware, furniture, toys, Derby glasses, salt and peppers, character collectibles, pottery, cookie jars, books and more.

Radcliff Antique Mall
509 S. Dixie Hwy.
502/351-5155

Somewhere in Time Antiques & Cafe
332 N. Dixie Hwy.
502/352-0055

The Red Brick Cottage
776 S. Dixie Hwy.
502/351-1224

## 35 RICHMOND

Historic Richmond, off I-75 south of Lexington, has a variety of attractions to enjoy. This was Daniel Boone's site for his wilderness outpost, the birthplace of Kit Carson, and home of the fiery abolitionist Cassius Marcellus Clay. Civil War buffs will want to take the Battle of Richmond driving tour (1-800-866-3705). And, along the way, stop at the 1780 Valley View Ferry on Kentucky 169.

Lena's Antiques
2047 Berea Road-U.S. Hwy. 25
606/623-4325

Gift Box
139 N. Keeneland Dr.
606/624-0025

Memories Antiques
401 North St.
606/625-0909

Waterstreet Mall
129 S. 1st St.
606/625-1524

Olde Tyme Toys
209 W. Main St.
606/623-8832

Country Porch Antiques
2529 Doylesville Road (Union City)
606/625-0851

**Old Country Store**
Ashland Ave.
606/625-1275

## 36  RUSSELLVILLE

For a community of its size, Russellville boasts the largest historic district in Kentucky. The Southern Bank of Kentucky at Sixth and Main was the site of the first documented bank robbery by Jesse James, with a reenactment each October during the Logan County Tobacco Festival.

The Bibb House Museum, a circa-1822 Georgian mansion, was built by Major Richard Bibb, an early abolitionist and Revolutionary War officer. The collection of antebellum antiques includes Belter and Duncan Phyfe originals (183 West 8th, 502/726-2508).

Check out Libby's Family Entertainment, eight miles west on U.S. 68. Friday night is the Country Jamboree, while Saturday night's "Live at Libby's" show is syndicated to more than 65 radio stations in the United States and Canada.

### Diamond D Auction

208 N. Bethel St.
502/726-7892
Call for auction dates

David and I first heard about the Diamond D Auction from Leon Tyewater (a great auctioneer with a wife who can really cook). We were stuck in Nashville, Tenn., for a few days so we decided to check out this little country auction which was only an hour's drive away. It's one of those "sleeper" auctions. You know the kind—when you walk in and at first glance you see nothing—then about 30 minutes into the sale something pops up that you can't live without! I was sitting there minding my own business when out of the blue the most wonderful cupboard crossed the auction block. An authentic Tennessee piece from Piney Flats with its original dark oak finish, yellow paint inside, complete with perfect rat holes, and old glass doors— a true "virgin." Of course I bought it! For $550 wouldn't you?

**Russellville Antique Mall**
141 E. 5th St.
502/726-6900

**Russellville Flower Shop**
104 S. Franklin St.
502/726-7608

**Betty's Antiques**
103 Bethel Shopping Center
502/725-8222

**Shaker Museum**
S. Union (U.S. 68)
502/453-4167
Open: March–December 15, Mon.–Sat. 9–5, Sun. 1–5

The Shaker Museum at South Union, 15 miles east of Russellville on U.S. 68, is the site of the last western Shaker community (1807–1922). The 1824 Centre House showcases the fine craftsmanship of this inventive communal group with hundreds of original artifacts. Have lunch at Shaker Tavern, 502/542-6801, Tuesday through Saturday from 11:30 a.m. to 2:00 p.m.; Sunday and dinner by reservation; also a bed and breakfast. Events include the Shaker Festival in late June.

## 37  SHELBYVILLE

You'll find a charming area of antique and specialty shops amid the late-Victorian, National Register downtown district at I-64, Exit 35, between Louisville and Frankfort. Shelbyville is home to world-renowned Wakefield-Scearce Galleries, located within the historic Science Hill buildings, with an outstanding inventory of English and European antiques (Washington Street, 502/633-4382).

The area is also known for wonderful regional restaurants. There's Science Hill Inn, 502/633-2825; the Claudia Sanders Dinner House, originally operated by the Colonel, at 3202 Shelbyville Road/U.S. 60 West, 502/633-5600; and the Old Stone Inn in Simpsonville, once a stagecoach inn, on U.S. 60 East, 502/722-8882.

**Country Cottage Collectibles**
137 Frankfort Road
502/633-5341

**Main St. Antique Mall**
514 Main St.
502/633-0721

**Antiques for You Mall**
528 Main St.
502/633-7506

**Tam Antiques**
610 Main St.
502/633-3106

**Old Mill Shop Antiques**
117 7th St.
502/633-2733

**Shelbyville Antique Mall**
524 Main St.
502/633-0720

**Corner Collectibles & Antiques**
629 Washington St.
502/633-4838

**Something Unique**
By appointment only
502/633-3621

## 38  SMITHS GROVE

**Smiths Grove Antique Mall**
604 S. Main St.
502/563-4921

**The Corner Cupboard**
133 S. Main St.
502/563-6221

**Pony Express**
105 S. Main St.
502/563-5130

**Ye Olde Bank Antiques**
108 E. First St.
502/563-9313

# Kentucky

**Wright House Antiques Etc.**
124 First St.
502/563-9430

**Anytime Antiques**
133 N. Main St.
502/563-9111

**Martin's Antiques**
Hwy. 68-80
502/563-2575

**Wanda's Antiques & Collectibles**
131 N. Main St.
502/563-6444

**Village Grove Antiques**
135 N. Main St.
502/563-9100

**Cotton Corner**
Main St.
502/563-4607

## 39 SOMERSET

**North 27 Antique Mall**
3000 N. Hwy. 27
606-679-1923

**Pitman Creek Antique Mall**
6940 S. Hwy. 27
606/561-5178

**Somerset Antique Mall**
209 E. Market St.
606/679-4307

**Cumberland Antique Mall**
6494 S. Hwy. 27
606/561-8622

**Gift Box Uniques, Inc.**
207 E. Market St.
606/679-8041

## 40 ST. MATTHEWS

**Elaine Claire**
211 Clover Lane
502/895-0843

**Sarah Few McNeal Co.**
2866 Frankfort Ave.
502/895-2752

## 41 VERSAILLES

**Irish Acres**
4205 Fords Mill Road
606/873-6956

**Olde Towne Antique Mall**
161 N. Main St.
606/873-6326

**Mason Antiques**
408 Lexington Road
606/873-4792

**Farm House Antiques & Gifts**
175 N. Main St.
606/873-0800

### *Great Places to Stay*

## Rose Hill Inn
233 Rose Hill
1-800-307-0460

Rose Hill Inn is a two-story Kentucky Gothic mansion on three acres within walking distance of downtown Versailles. The home was built about 1820 and it is rumored that both Confederate and Union troops used the manor during the Civil War. The first floor has 14-foot ceilings and original woodwork. Fireplaces warm the atmosphere and coffee, tea and treats are always available. All bedrooms are invitingly furnished and have private baths. One has a Jacuzzi tub/shower, one a claw-foot tub and the cottage (the original summer kitchen) has been updated to include two full-size beds, kitchen and bath. Smells from the morning's breakfast call you to the dining room for a delicious meal, either at a table for two or conversing with other guests at the larger dining table. Afterward, some time on the front porch is always a favorite.

## 42 WASHINGTON

**House of Three Gables**
2027 Old Main St.
No Phone Listed

**Peiis**
2029 Old Main St.
606/759-5533

**Strawberry Patch Antiques & Gifts**
2109 Old Main St.
606/759-7001

**Phyllis Antique Lamp & Dollhouse**
2112 Old Main St.
606/759-7423

**Alice's Antiques & Jewels**
2028 Old Main St.
606/564-4877

**Iron Gate**
2103 Old Main St.
606/759-7074

**Washington Hall Antiquities**
2111 Old Main St.
606-759-7409

**1790 Row House Mall**
2117 Old Main St.
606-759-7025

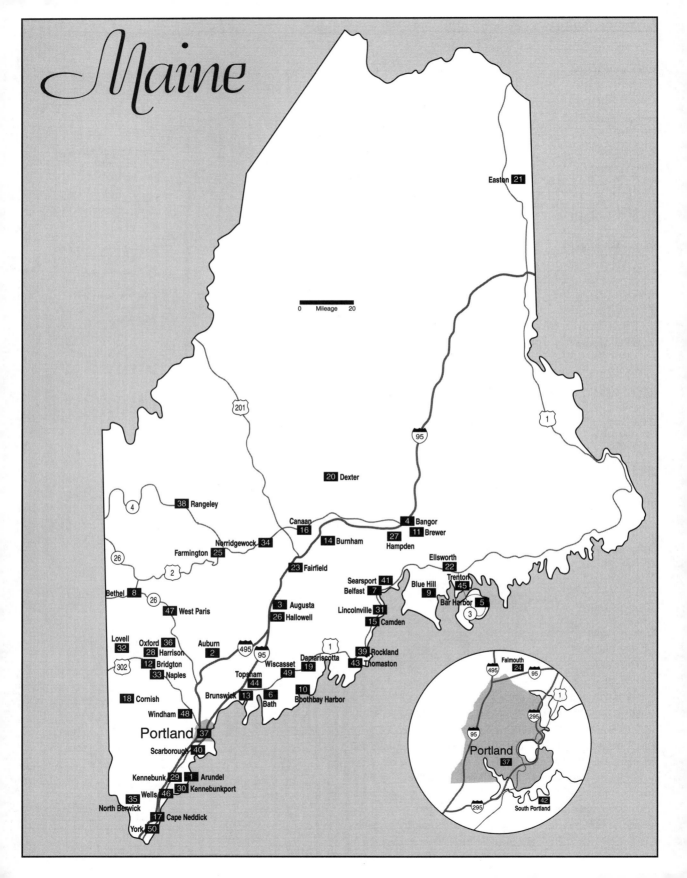

# Maine

0 Mileage 20

Easton 21

Dexter 20

Rangeley 38

Canaan 16

Bangor 4
Brewer 11

Norridgewock 34

Burnham 14

Hampden 27

Farmington 25

Fairfield 23

Ellsworth 22

Searsport 41
Belfast 7

Blue Hill 9

Trenton
45

Bethel 8

Augusta 3

Lincolnville 31

Bar Harbor 5
3

West Paris 47

Hallowell 26

Camden 15

Lovell 32

Oxford 36
Harrison 28

Auburn 2

Rockland 39
Thomaston 43

Bridgton 12

Damariscotta 19

Naples 33

Wiscasset 49

Cornish 18

Topsham 44

Boothbay Harbor 10

Windham 48

Brunswick 13
Bath 6

Portland 37

Scarborough 40

Kennebunk 29 1 Arundel

30 Kennebunkport

Wells 46

North Berwick 35

York 50 17 Cape Neddick

Falmouth 24

Portland 37

South Portland 42

# Maine

## 1 ARUNDEL

**Arundel Antiques**
1713 Portland Road
207/985-7965

**Rose's Antiques**
Route #1
207/799-7828

**The Front Porch Antiques**
21 Old Post Road
207/985-1233

**Nothing New Antiques**
2796 Portland Road (Route 1)
207/286-1789

**Auntie Em's**
Route #1
207/985-7975

## 2 AUBURN

### Orphan Annie's Antiques

96 Court St.
207/782-0638
Open: Mon.–Sat. 10–5, Sun. 12–5
Directions: Take Exit 12 off the Maine Turnpike. Go left after the exit three miles into town. At the third stoplight, turn right onto Court St. The shop is down four blocks on the right, across from the county courthouse.

For lovers of art glass, this is a shop you don't want to miss! Owner Dan Poulin has been in the antique business for 20 years, the last ten dealing primarily in art glass. This shop is full of such jewels as Tiffany, Stuben, Quezal, Imperial and numerous other styles in American glass; French glass pieces by Galle, Daum Nancy, D'Argental, Loetz; and Czech glass. He specializes in art glass from the 1890s to the 1930s, getting most of the glass from private sources and some at auction.

The shop also offers over 100 pieces of Roseville, vintage clothing, and a three-story warehouse filled to the brim with antique furnishings.

**Rower J. Morin & Son, Inc.**
195 Turner St.
207/782-7511

### *Nearby Antique Shopping (Lewiston)*
*Lewiston is 4 miles east of Auburn.*

### Alice's Attic

829 Main St. (Route 202)
207/784-7193

Quaint shop located in an 1830s Victorian home. Offering carnival and Depression glass, McCoy, Roseville, Nippon, Noritake, crystal. Also, estate jewelry, full line of furniture, music boxes, dolls, primitives and country collectibles.

### *Nearby Antique Shopping (Turner)*
*Turner is 12 miles north of Auburn.*

### Northland Antiques & Collectibles

Route 4
207/225-2466

Offering a nice selection of jewelry, dolls, sports items, glassware and furniture.

### *Nearby Antique Shopping (Greene)*
*Greene is located 9 miles north of Auburn*
*and 5 miles north of Lewiston.*

### Cutter Brook Antique Mall

Route 202
207/946-5264

Primitives, country and decorative items, pottery, milk bottles and a general line of antiques and collectibles.

### Wilbur's Antiques

11 Key Hill Road
207/946-5711

Large barn of country and Victorian furniture, clocks, Roseville, lamps, Depression glass, white ironstone and cut glass. If you are traveling from a distance, phone ahead.

## 3 AUGUSTA AREA

### Borssen's Antiques

Route 135 (Belgrade)
207/495-2013
Directions: Belgrade is 11 miles S.E. of Augusta.

Thirty-three years in business, specializing in country furniture, pottery, baskets, oak and Victorian furniture.

### Lakeside Antiques Mall

Route 202 (East Winthrope)
207/377-2616
Directions: East Winthrope is 4½ miles west of Augusta.

Forty dealers and two floors of antiques.

*Maine*

## Witts End Country Store
Route 133 (Wayne)
207/897-7170
Directions: Wayne is 24 miles west of Augusta.

Global vintage textiles; lace, blankets, vintage character clothing from Napoleon to Elvis, costume jewelry, movie posters and kitsch and clutter. Worth the trip, but they are hard to find so call ahead for specific directions. He is always open.

## Riverside Antiques
907 Riverside Dr. (Route 201)
207/621-0994

Specializing in dolls, doll accessories, linens, glass and jewelry.

## Yesteryear's Treasures
Off Route 27 (Summer Haven Road, Sidney)
207/622-7980

Country furniture, baskets, spinning wheels, advertising items and canning jars.

### *The next four shops are on, or just off, Route 3, close to one another (10 to 15-minute drive).*

## Fifi's Finely I Found It — Salvage Co.
Route 3/202 N. Belfast Ave.
207/623-0434

House parts, flooring, tin ceilings, doors, porch rockers, lampshades, hundreds of shutters and antique furniture.

## Meader's Stony Brook Antiques
Route 3/202 N. Belfast Ave.
207/623-0076

Country and Victorian furniture, cupboards, Depression glass, stoneware, lanterns, trunks and tools.

## Ron Reed Antiques
Route 3 (South China)
207/445-3551

Cottage pine furniture, cupboards, period furniture, lighting, yellowware, pottery and odd objects. Wholesale/retail shop and warehouse. Call ahead.

## Carl F. Rau Antiques
Route 32 (South China)
207/445-2315
Directions: The shop is located 200 yards off Route 3 on Route 32, Windsor Road.

A real antique shop. Specializing in early American country furniture, both refinished and in original paint. Also yelloware, spongeware, hooked rugs, samplers, paintings and early country accessories.

### 4 BANGOR

**Alcott Antiques**
30 Central St.
207/942-7706

**Maritime International**
89 Central St.
207/941-8372

**Dave's Furniture Co.**
100 Central St.
207/942-5291

**Ireland's Antiques**
650 Main St.
207/945-5902

### 5 BAR HARBOR

**Bar Harbor Antiques**
128 Cottage St.
207/288-3120

**Olde Stuffe & Things**
7 Everard Court
207/288-2203

**Shaw Antiques**
204 Main St.
207/288-9355

**Super's Junkin Co.**
Town Hill Route 102
207/288-5740

**Albert Meadow Antique**
10 Albert Meadow
207/288-9456

### *Great Places to Stay*

## Bar Harbor Inn
Newport Dr.
1-800-248-3351

Built as a private club in 1887, the Bar Harbor Inn was designed by Boston architect William Ralph Emerson. The inn rests on an estate-style, seven-acre property, in the center of the historic village of Bar Harbor. The main inn is tastefully decorated in the traditional inn style with many rooms featuring views of Frenchman's Bay. The Oceanfront Lodge has 64 deluxe rooms with oversized beds and private balconies directly overlooking the ocean.

## Black Friar Inn
10 Summer St.
207/288-5091

The Black Friar Inn is a uniquely restored Victorian home surrounded by a perennial flower garden. Mantels, bookcases, windows and finely

# Maine

crafted woodwork from turn-of-the-century "cottages" on Mount Desert Island shape every part of the inn. Seven romantic guest rooms are tastefully furnished with period antiques. Fine linens dress the beds and each room has a private bath. During the months of May, June and September the innkeepers offer professional guided trips on some of the most beautiful trout and salmon waters in the state of Maine.

## Breakwater 1904
45 Hancock St.
1-800-238-6309

In 1904, John Innes Kane, the great grandson of John Jacob Astor, built a magnificent "summer cottage" and named it "Breakwater." Located on over four acres of lush lawns, beautiful gardens, and natural woods, this oceanfront English Tudor estate was completely renovated and restored to its original grandeur in 1991, and placed on the National Historic Register on March 26, 1992. The inn features six guest chambers, eleven working fireplaces and nine spacious common areas.

## The Canterbury Cottage
12 Roberts Ave.
207/288-2112
Web site: www.acadia.net/canterbury

A small bed and breakfast with comfortable, tastefully decorated rooms on a quiet side street within easy walking distance to in-town and harbor activities. Owners share a lifetime of island knowledge with guests while breakfast is served in the dining room.

## Castlemaine Inn
39 Holland Ave.
1-800-338-4563

Castlemaine Inn is nestled on a quiet side street in the village of Bar Harbor, only minutes from the magnificent Acadia National Park and within easy reach of galleries, shops and restaurants. The inn has 12 charming rooms and four comfortable suites. Rooms have queen canopy beds, queen four-poster beds or king-size beds. Many rooms have fireplaces and private balconies. All rooms have private baths.

## Cleftstone Manor
92 Eden St.
1-888-288-4951
Web site: www.acadia.net/cleftstone

The Cleftstone Manor is an 1884 Victorian mansion featuring sixteen guest rooms, each with a private bath. The inn is furnished with Victorian antiques and period pieces, creating an atmosphere reminiscent of the turn of the century.

## Hatfield Bed & Breakfast
20 Roberts Ave.
207/288-9655

Hatfield Bed & Breakfast is located on a quiet side street in Bar Harbor, two blocks from the center of town and two and one half blocks from the waterfront. The inn is only minutes from beautiful Acadia National Park and the Nova Scotia ferry terminal. Hatfield's eclectic mix of antique and country decor and the unpretentious, down-home hospitality of innkeepers Jeff and Sandy Miller bring true meaning to the term "relaxed atmosphere." Jeff and Sandy serve up a full, hearty breakfast.

## The Holland Inn
35 Holland Ave.
207/288-4804
Web site: www.downeast.net/com/holland

The 1895 Holland House is the only in-town traditional Maine farmhouse B&B. Offering five recently restored rooms with private baths, each one illuminates the gracious simplicity and comfort of a county farm. The generous yards and gardens surrounding the inn fill each window with light and a fresh summer breeze. Relax on the sun porch or under the shaded maples in the backyard. Stroll to the town pier or your favorite restaurant. Your hosts Evin and Tom will treat you with friendly down-east hospitality and endless activities to fill your days. Cottages also available.

## Inn at Canoe Point
Route 3, Eden St.
207/288-9511
Web site: www.innatcanoepoint.com

This secluded waterside inn is situated among the pines on two acres tucked into a quiet cove. Located only moments away from lively Bar Harbor and next door to the unspoiled natural attractions of Acadia National Park. Situated directly on Frenchman's Bay, you can walk among the trees, sit on the rocks and watch the boats sail by, or relax in front of the granite fireplace and enjoy the views of the sea and mountains. From a surrounding deck you can look out over the ocean and listen to the roaring surf.

## Stratford House Inn
45 Mount Desert St.
207/288-5189

The Stratford House Inn is one of the few remaining summer "cottages" that amplify the grand and elegant life of Bar Harbor at the turn of the century. Built in 1900 by the noted Boston book publisher Lewis A. Roberts, the Stratford House Inn is styled with the romantic charm of an English Tudor manor. The inn boasts 10 beautifully decorated bedrooms, each with its own individual charm and style. In the mornings, guests are treated to a continental breakfast in the elegant dining room.

### The Maples Inn

16 Roberts Ave.
207/288-3443
Web site: www.acadia.net/maples

Enjoy classic tranquility in this 1903 Victorian inn, located on a quiet tree-lined street near downtown Bar Harbor. Stroll to the water's edge, just two blocks away. All five guest rooms, and two room suites with fireplaces, have down comforters and all rooms are designed in a traditional decor. Some of the inn's breakfast entrees have been featured in *Gourmet* and *Bon Appetit* magazines and have recently been published in the inn's own cookbook called *Cats Can't Cook*, written by Bailey the Wonder Dog.

### Twin Gables Inn

P.O. Box 282
207/288-3064

At Twin Gables Inn, you can experience all the natural delights of Acadia National Park while enjoying the country comfort and charm of a completely restored 100-year-old inn. Each of the six cheerful guest rooms provides a private bath and some have beautiful mountain and ocean views. Share good conversation with other guests during the "forget about lunch" breakfast from a menu that includes the house specialty … raspberry pancakes.

### 6　BATH

East of Brunswick along Coastal Route One is the shipbuilding city of Bath. Here is the site of Bath Iron Works, which produces many vessels for the United States Navy and the Merchant Marine. It is an impressive sight to see such massive ships under construction. Spectators can get a bird's-eye view from the Route One Carlton Bridge, which spans the mighty Kennebec River.

Bath is the business hub for many nearby resort areas along the Kennebec. Its downtown business district features wonderful brick sidewalks and street lamps reminiscent of the 19th century, while old sea captains' and shipbuilders' homes line the avenues. Visitors will also find a waterfront public park and several specialty and antique shops.

Between 1862 and 1902, Bath was the nation's fifth largest seaport, and nearly half of the United States' wooden sailing vessels were built here. During that era, more than 200 private shipbuilding firms flourished along a four-mile stretch of waterfront, producing large numbers of vessels. Exhibits describing the Maine shipbuilding traditions are displayed at the Maine Maritime Museum on the banks of the Kennebec

in Bath. The museum is a must for travelers interested in our nautical heritage.

| | |
|---|---|
| **Brick Store Antiques**<br>143 Front St.<br>207/443-2790 | **Countryside Antiques & Books**<br>170 Front St.<br>207/442-0772 |
| **Cobblestone & Co.**<br>176 Front St.<br>207/443-4064 | **Pollyanna's Antiques**<br>182 Front St.<br>207/443-4909 |
| **Front Street Antiques**<br>190 Front St.<br>207/443-8098 | **Atlantic Coast Antiques**<br>Sanford Road<br>207/443-9185 |
| **Timeless Treasures Antiques**<br>104 Front St.<br>207/442-0377 | **Trifles Antiques**<br>42 High St.<br>207/443-5856 |

***Great Places to Stay***

### The Galen C. Moses House

1009 Washington St.
207/442-8771
Web site: www.bnbcity.com/inns/20028
Email: galenmoses@clinic.net.
Open: Year-round
Rates $65–$95
Directions: Take the Maine Turnpike (I-95) to Exit 6A (I-295). After Portland, I-295 rejoins I-95. Continue to Exit 22 (Route 1, Brunswick and Bath). Entering Bath, stay right for the last exit before the bridge (marked "Historic Bath") and proceed to Washington St. Turn left and drive 6 blocks to 1009 Washington, which is on the right.

The historic town of Bath offers both remarkable antique shopping and an incredible bed & breakfast. In 1994 former antique dealers James Haught and Larry Kieft moved from the antique business (but who really ever gets "out" of antiques!) into the bed and breakfast field — and they did it with a bang! They purchased the 1874 Galen C. Moses House and immediately made it the talk of the town.

The house was designed by Francis Fassett for Galen C. Moses (1835–1915) and redesigned in 1901 by John Calvin Stevens, one of Fassett's apprentices. The vernacular Italianate has an interior that is both Victorian and Colonial Revival. There are so many original, unique touches and finishes that I can't begin to list them all, but I will give you just a taste of what's in store when you visit: stained glass windows, elaborately carved mantels, window seats, arched windows, claw-foot tubs, and on the third floor, a full movie theater (vintage 1930s) complete with a projection booth and sixteen tiered seats facing a makeshift stage. During World War II, officers from the Brunswick Navel Air Station were invited to view movies (some of them supposedly "blue") as part of the local effort to build moral.

The three guest rooms, all with private baths, are upstairs (second floor) and continue the uniqueness of the house. The Victorian Room has bay windows and a white marble fireplace. The Moses Room holds an antique washstand and the original plaster frieze on all four walls. The Vintage Room has been furnished with oak and walnut pieces of the period which compliment the 1874 built-in washstand. And if all this doesn't overdose you on antiques, there are eight antique shops within blocks of the house, plus six antique shows per year in Bath.

Wait. There's more! Besides the rooms filled with antiques and the elegant gardens, the house contains a number of spirits other than the sherry served at 5 p.m.! The ghosts are friendly and seem to make their presence felt on a regular basis. A full breakfast is served each morning, and the fare depends entirely on the cook's mood. Juice, coffee and muffins are always available for early risers or late sleepers, but the full meal can range from fresh fruit and blueberry pancakes to mushroom quiche or sour cream and chive omelets. It's an adventure all the way at the Moses House in Bath!

### 7 BELFAST

Once a prosperous shipbuilding center, Belfast exhibits more than its share of exquisite Federal and early Victorian sea-merchants' mansions, many of them now operated as gracious inns and bed and breakfasts. White clapboard, aged brick, gingerbread trim, large lawns and enormous overarching oaks, elms and maples give the town a stately air. The charm is complimented by the "all-of-a-piece" flow of late-19th-century brick shopfronts down Main St. to the bay and the attractive and neatly maintained Waterfront Heritage Park.

**Anna's Antiques**
Route 1
207/338-2219

**Hall Hardware Co.**
Searsport Ave., U.S. Route 1
207/338-1170

**Kendrick's Collectibles**
213 N. Port Ave.
207/338-1356

**Landmark Architectural Antiques**
108 Main St.
207/338-9901

**Apex Antiques**
208 High St.
207/338-1194

### 8 BETHEL

**Farmhouse Antiques**
Route 26
207/824-2686

**Bennett's Antiques**
21 Mechanic St.
207/824-2336

**Far East Antiques**
162 Main St.
207/824-2997

**Playhouse Antiques**
46 Broad St.
207/824-3170

*Nearby Antique Shopping (West Paris)*
*West Paris is 13 miles east of Bethel.*

**Mollyockett Marketplace Antique Center**
For information see West Paris, #47

*Nearby Antique Shopping (Locke Mills)*
*Locke Mills is 10 miles from Bethel.*

**Mt. Mica Rarities**
Route 26
207/875-2030

Antiques and collectibles, especially costume and estate jewelry with a fine selection of Maine gemstone jewelry such as tourmaline, amethyst, aqua and garnet.

*Nearby Antique Shopping (Hanover)*
*Hanover is 8 miles east of Bethel.*

**Oxford County Antiques & Collectibles**
**Top Hat Antiques**
Route 2
207/364-8321

A large 80-by-100-foot shop full of fine antiques and country items.

**Lyons' Den Antiques**
Route 2
207/364-8634

40-by-110-foot barn, two floors of glass, china, primitives, clocks, furniture, paintings, rugs and bed rugs.

*Nearby Antique Shopping (East Andover)*
*East Andover is 15 miles from Bethel off Route 2.*

**Birches Antiques**
East Andover Road
207/392-2211

Large barn full of country and Victorian furniture, Roseville, carnival and Depression glass, Fiesta and lots more.

# Maine

**Connie's Antiques**
190 Lincoln Ave.
207/364-3363

*Nearby Antique Shopping (Roxberry)*

**Yankee Gem Co.**
Route 17
207/364-4458

Two floors in a large barn full of furniture, glass, painting, tins, and a general line of antiques. In business for over 40 years.

## 9 BLUE HILL

**Anne Wells Antiques**
Route 172
207/374-2093

**Liros Gallery**
Main St.
207/374-5370

**Emerson Antiques**
Main St.
207/374-5140

**Blue Hill Antiques**
8 Water St.
207/374-8824

**Thomas Hinchcliffe Antiques**
Route 176
207/326-9411

**Belcher's Antiques**
Water St.
207/374-5769

*Nearby Antique Shopping (Deer Isle)*
*Deer Isle is 16 miles south of Blue Hill.*

**Parish House Antiques**
Route 15
207/348-9964

**Belcher's Antiques**
Reach Road
207/348-9938

## 10 BOOTHBAY HARBOR

**Bay Street Studio East Side**
2 Bay St.
207/633-3186

**Palabra Shops**
85 Commercial St.
207/633-4225

**Marine Antiques**
43 Townsend Ave.
207/633-0862

**Opera House Village Antiques**
Townsend Ave.
207/633-6855

**Sweet Woodruff Farm**
Route #27
207/633-6977

**Albert Meadow Antiques**
8 McKown
207/633-3021

## Great Places to Stay

### Anchor Watch
3 Eames Road
207/633-7565
Web site: www.maineguide.com/boothbay/anchorwatch

Lighthouse beacons, lobster boats, rock shores and fir trees on many islands provide the view this inn is famous for. Bedrooms are set among lots of fir, maple and oak trees making the rooms sunny in winter, and cool in summer with lots of leaf color in fall. Boating, hiking on Monhegan Island and other land preserves and shopping are popular activities; and of course, restaurants feature excellent food prepared by many award-winning chefs. Lobsters are abundant and can be consumed picnic style while watching the boats bring in their catch or in a fancy restaurant with Newburg sauce. Rooms at the Anchor Watch are comfortable and cheerful, and decorated with quilts and stenciling. The kitchen and social rooms have pine floors, pleasing blue and white colors, a cozy fireplace and lots of windows facing the water. The side lawn slopes to the water and the pier provides sunbathing, fishing or even swimming. Breakfast is an enjoyable experience as you join others from around the world, or take a tray to the deck or your room. The delicious full breakfast includes lots of fresh fruit, granola, hot egg casserole and muffins or breads. Coffee lasts as long as the guests linger over fascinating conversations. Within an hour's drive are white sandy beaches, the famous L. L. Bean and shopping malls of Freeport, Pemaquid Point Lighthouse and Museum, Owl's Head Light, Maine Maritime Museum, and the Farnsworth Art Gallery.

### Five Gables Inn
Murray Hill Road
1-800-451-5048
Web site: www.maineguide.com/boothbay/5gables

Taking its name from the prominent windowed gables along its front, the Five Gables Inn sits on a sloping lawn overlooking Linekin Bay and East Boothbay, a quiet shipbuilding village. Once a 22-room, three-bath hotel, the stately structure underwent a tasteful remodeling that reduced the rooms to 16, all with private baths. Five have working fireplaces. Furnishings are traditional with uncluttered country details. A gourmet buffet breakfast is prepared by the owner/chef.

### Harbour Towne Inn on the Waterfront
71 Townsend Ave.
1-800-722-4240
Web site: www.acadia.net/harbourtowneinn

Harbour Towne Inn, the finest B&B on the waterfront, combines the convenience of village lodging coupled with the charm of a country inn.

*Maine*

The inn is a handsomely refurbished Victorian townhouse with spectacular penthouse lodging available. Deluxe continental breakfast is served.

## Jonathan's Bed and Breakfast

15 Eastern Ave.
207/633-3588

Jonathan's is situated on the edge of a lovely woods, a short walk to the harbor, abounding in shops, boating, fishing and restaurants. After a hearty breakfast of fresh fruit, homemade muffins and special entree, the hosts will help guests plan a day of sightseeing throughout the beautiful coastal region. Return in late afternoon to cool harbor breezes on the deck, and sherry or lemonade, or, in wintertime, hot tea and a roaring fire in the parlor.

## 11 BREWER

### Center Mall

39 Center St.
207/989-9842
Web site: www.metiques.com/catalog/centermall.html
Open: Daily 10–5

12,000 square feet on three levels of antiques and collectibles displayed by 56 dealers.

### My Brother Her Sister

53 Center St.
207/989-0300
Open: Mon.–Sun. 10–5

Large antique mall featuring advertising items, cast iron, country antiques and collectibles and formal furnishings.

### *Nearby Antique Shopping (East Holden)*
### *East Holden is 7 miles east of Brewer.*

### Country Store Antiques

Bar Harbor Road (Route 1)
207/843-7449
Open: Mon.–Sat. 10–5

Specializing in formal period antiques; Chippendale, Hepplewhite, Federal, Queen Anne, American country and accessories of all periods.

## 12 BRIDGTON

**Hidden Brook Antiques**
North High St. (Route 302)
207/647-5241

**Fair Exchange Group**
62 Main St.
207/647-2220

**Wales & Hamblen Antique & Gift Center**
134 Main St.
207/647-3840

**Paper Chase Antiques & Collectables**
Route 37
207/647-2230

**Wells Antiques**
31 Main St.
207/647-2548

**The Lamp and Shade Shop**
95 Main St.
207/647-5576

**"Wee 3" Antiques**
Route 117 (Off Route 302)
207/647-2102

## 13 BRUNSWICK

### Cabot Mill Antiques

14 Main St.
207/725-2855
Open: Mon.–Sun. 10–5

Over 15,000 square feet and 140 dealers featuring a large selection of antiques displayed inside a restored 1820s mill on the scenic Androscoggin River.

**Robbin's Antique & Art Gallery**
343 Bath Road
207/729-3473

**Days Antiques**
153 Park Row
207/725-6959

**Waterfront Flea Market**
14 Main St.
207/729-0378

**Dionne's Antique Shop**
92 Merrymeeting Road
207/725-4263

**Antiques at 184 Pleasant**
184 Pleasant St.
207/729-8343

### *Great Places to Stay*

### Bethel Point Bed & Breakfast

Bethel Point Road 2387
207/725-1115

Peaceful oceanside comfort in a 150-year-old house furnished with antiques. Perfect view of islands and ocean birds while you watch seals at play and lobster boats at work. Opportunity for ocean swimming and shoreline walks to explore and find treasures from the sea. Easy drive to area specialties such as Bowdoin College, Popham Beach, L.L. Bean and local restaurants featuring seafood delicacies.

*Maine*

**14　BURNHAM**

### Houston-Brooks Auctioneers

Horseback Road
207/948-2214 or 1-800-254-2214
Fax: 207/948-5925
Directions: Off of I-95, take Exit 37 and take a right off the ramp. Follow the road 1 ½ miles to Clinton Village. Take a right on Route 100 and follow for 7 miles to Burnham. Take a right at the store (signs are posted) and go 3 ²/₁₀ miles to the four corners. Take a right (signs are posted here, too) and the auction hall is the next place on the left.

Among the best-known auction houses in New England, Houston-Brooks is a family business that has been auctioning antiques for 27 years. Auctioneer and co-owner Pamela Brooks is one of the few practicing women auctioneers in the state. She's been at it 20 years herself, learning the art from working with her dad, who started the company. The auctions pull lots of customers from all over the region, especially from New England, upstate New York and Canada. Auctions are held every Sunday, and they offer a wide range of antique furniture, glass, collectibles, art and other items. According to Pam, they always have odd pieces come through. She says that the worst part of holding a weekly auction is that it's like running a never-ending race; you sell everything on Sunday and then wonder if you're going to have anything come in for the next week!

**15　CAMDEN**

Slightly larger than Kennebunkport — Camden's population is right at 4,000 — Camden is one of those rare places that is so stereotypically picturesque that it really looks "postcard perfect." Harbors, sailboats, softly mellowed houses, tree-lined streets and roads with dappled sunlight, breathtaking views around each bend in the road — this is Camden.

This is also sailboat country, and to really get a feel for the area, every visitor must spend at least a couple of hours out on Penobscot Bay. There are a variety of cruise options on both schooners and motor vessels, with trips running from just an hour to all day. If you are staying more than a little while, overnight, three-day and six-day cruises of the Maine coast are available on classic windjammers. You can also take weekend and weeklong courses in sailing and earn a certificate that says "learned to sail in Maine."

When you shop, you'll find many more hand-loomed sweaters and handcrafted jewelry than you will T-shirts. And the food is not to be missed — all of the famous Maine fare, from lobsters, scallops and mussels to clams, haddock, salmon and swordfish. Here's a most interesting and refreshing end note: Camden has no fast-food franchises! So it really is "postcard perfect"!

**Downshire House Clocks**
49 Bayview St.
207/236-9016

**Hard Alee**
51 Bayview St.
207/236-3373

**Star Bird**
17 Main St.
207/236-8292

**Schueler Antiques**
10 High St.
207/236-2770

### *Great Places to Stay*

### A Little Dream

66 High St.
207/236-8742
Web site: www.obs-us.com/obs/english/books/chesler/ne/05/bnb/meb122.htm

Sweet dreams and little luxuries abound in this lovely white Victorian with wicker and flower-filled wraparound porch. Set on two acres of rolling lawns and lovely perennial gardens, it overlooks two small castles with distant views of Penobscot Bay. Noted for its lovely breakfast, beautiful rooms, and charming atmosphere, A Little Dream's English-Country-Victorian decor has been featured in *Country Inns Magazine*, and in *Glamour*'s "40 Best Getaways Across the Country." Located in the historic district, just a few minutes from shops and harbor, it is listed on the National Register of Historic Places. All rooms have special touches such as imported soaps and chocolates.

### Castleview by the Sea B&B

59 High St.
1-800-272-8439

Located on the waterside of the oceanview section of Camden's historic district, this gorgeous inn offers spectacular glass-walled views of Camden's only two castles and the sea, right from your bed! Count the stars across the bay and wake up to bold Maine coast views. Enjoy the bright and airy charm of classic 1856 cape architecture, wide pine floors, beams, claw-foot tubs, skylights, ceiling fans and stained glass. Private balconies.

### Edgecombe-Coles House

64 High St.
1-800-528-2336

Edgecombe-Coles House is a classic example of a 19th-century summer home. Situated on a quiet hillside overlooking Penobscot Bay, it offers an escape from summer's traffic. A lovely private place, Edgecombe-Coles House is a short walk from Camden's picturesque harbor with its fine restaurants, shops and recreational facilities. Visitors can view the ocean from the front porch or drive less than a mile to Camden Hills State Park, where there are miles of uncrowded hiking trails.

## Swan House
49 Mountain St.
1-800-207-8275
Web site: www.swanhouse.com

Swan House is a small, intimate inn nestled at the foot of scenic Mt. Battie. This 1870 Victorian offers a private haven in a lovely, quiet setting. With its location in the residential village, away from the busy, nonstop Rte. 1 traffic, Swan House could be considered one of Camden's best-kept secrets. A short walk down the hill leads to the picturesque harbor, unique and interesting shops and excellent restaurants. Swan House offers six tastefully decorated guest rooms, all with private baths. A delicious breakfast is served on the glass-enclosed front porch. Relax and unwind in one of the parlors or discover the shaded gazebo — a perfect place to catch up on a favorite book. For the outdoor enthusiast, hike the many trails of Camden Hills State Park, one of which starts directly behind the inn and leads to Mt. Battie's summit.

## The Victorian by the Sea
P.O. Box 1385
1-800-382-9817

By the Sea, by the sea, by the beautiful sea, is a century-old Queen Anne Victorian restored to its original charm with spacious rooms, queen-size beds, private baths, waterviews, and fireplaces. Decorated in period decor, the inn provides a quiet atmosphere in a unique country setting. Relax on the beautiful porch and enjoy spectacular views of the gardens, the ocean, and the islands off the coast. Wake up to a full country breakfast to start off your day. Off Route 1 and 300 feet from the shore.

## Windward House Bed & Breakfast
6 High St.
207/236-9656

Windward House is located on historic High Street in the picturesque seacoast village of Camden, the "jewel of the Maine coast," where the mountains meet the sea. This beautifully restored 1854 Greek Revival home has eight tastefully decorated guest rooms, all with queen beds and private baths. Located within one block of harbor, village, shops and restaurants.

## 16 CANAAN

## Canaan's Specialty Shop
Corner Oak Pond Road & Route 2
207/474-8529

Aladdin lamps, shades, parts and repair. Coca-Cola, Pepsi, milk and other bottles, brass and copper, signs, cast iron, old coins and license plates. Much, much more.

## Allan Soll Architectural Antiques
Route 2
207/474-5396

Maine's largest selection of stained glass windows, doors, pedestal sinks, mantels and lighting. A large selection of Victorian furniture and accessories.

## Drake/Haiss Antiques
Route 2
207/474-5753

Specializing in antique buttons, vintage sewing items, kerosene lanterns, Hull and Roseville pottery.

### *Nearby Antique Shopping (Corinna)*
### *Corinna is 21 miles north of Canaan.*

**Dee's Group Shop**
Route 7
207/278-2500

## 17 CAPE NEDDICK

## The Barn at Cape Neddick
Route 1
207/363-7315
Open: Mon.–Sun. 10–5

Displays of 75 dealers offering a nice variety of American country and period furniture. A great selection of folk art and unique decorative items.

**Columbary Antiques**
RR 1
207/363-5496

**Cranberry Hill Antiques**
RR 1
207/363-5178

**Gold Bug**
Route 1 & Clarke Road
207/351-2707

# Maine

***Nearby Antique Shopping (Ogunquit)***
***Ogunquit is located 2 miles northeast of Cape Neddick.***

## Blacksmith's Antique Mall
116 Main St. (Route 1)
207/646-9643
Open: Mon.–Sun. 9–4:30, closed Wed.

A large 65-dealer shop known for quality antiques at fair prices. Weekend dealer market in annex.

**The Pommier Collection**
94 Shore Road
207/646-5573

## 18  CORNISH

**Plain & Fancy**
Route 25/Main St.
207/625-3577

**The Smith Company**
Route 25
207/625-6030

**Cornish Trading Company**
Route 25/Main St.
207/625-8387

**Lily's Fine Flowers & Antiques**
Route 25
207/625-2366

**Maple Street Antiques & Collectibles**
25 Maple St., Route 25
207/642-3116

## 19  DAMARISCOTTA

Damariscotta is a classic Maine coastal village nestled along the eastern side of the Damariscotta River.

Oyster-shell heaps, some reaching 30 feet in height, attest to this area being a centuries-old sanctuary for native American people. During the mid-1800s, Damariscotta was home to Metcalf and Norris, pioneer clipper ship builders. From their yards came the *Flying Scud*, famous for her 76-day passage to Melbourne.

**1839 House**
370 Bristol Road
207/563-2375

**Patricia Anne Reed Fine Antiques**
148 Bristol Road
207/563-5633

**Loon's Landing Antiques**
Courtyard Shops
207/563-8931

**Arsenic & Old Lace**
Main St.
207/563-1414

**Cooper's Red Barn**
Waldoboro Road
207/563-3714

**Bunker Hill Antiques**
Route #213
207/563-3167

***Nearby Antique Shopping (Nobleboro)***
***Nobleboro is 5 miles north of Damariscotta.***

**Wayside Tearoom House**
163 Route #1
207/563-3622

**Adelaide's Antiques**
63 Route #1
207/563-6693

## 20  DEXTER

**The Gray Barn Antiques**
59 Maple St.
207/924-6419

**Adrienne's Attic**
Shore Road
207/924-6923

**Creations Past Antiques & Flea Market**
2 Church St.
207/924-3974

## 21  EASTON

## Memory Lane Antiques & Collectibles
Station St.
207/488-3663
Directions: 7 miles from Presque Isle off Route 10.

Specializing in quality oak, walnut and mahogany furniture, clocks, dolls, vintage clothing, crocks and kitchen collectibles.

## Joe's Antiques & Collectibles
Main St.
207/488-6811

Primitives, stepback cupboards, toy trains, flow blue, carnival glass, porcelain, tin and architectural items.

## 22  ELLSWORTH

**Mill Mall Treasures**
Bangor Road, Route 1A
207/667-8055

**His & Her's Antiques**
Bucksport Road
207/667-2115

**Eastern Antiques**
52 Dean St.
207/667-4033

**Sandy's Antiques**
111 Oak St.
207/667-5078

**Big Chicken Barn Books &Antiques**
RR 3
207/667-7308

**Finest Finds Antiques**
140 Water St.
207/667-1808

## 23  FAIRFIELD

## Fairfield Antiques Mall
Route 201
207/453-4100
Open: Mon.–Sun. 9–5
Directions: 2 ½ miles north of I-95 at Exit 36 on Route 201 (Skowhegan Road)

Over 24,000 square feet of antiques and showcase collectibles. The largest antique mall in Maine.

*Maine*

## Julia-Poulin Antiques
199 Route 201
207/453-2114

Two large barns full of early furniture and accessories. A wholesale/retail shop.

## Connor-Bovie House Antiques
22 Summit St.
207/453-4919

Staffordshire, blue and white transfer, flow blue, Leeds, pearlware, Derby, soft paste, Torquay, Dresden, Paris, Rose Medallion, Canton, Kangxi and children's china.

## Autumn's Antiques
Route 201
207/453-9024

Specializing in antique lumber, windows, doors and lots of architectural salvage.

### *Nearby Antique Shopping (Benton)*

**Beane's Antiques**
58 River Road
207/453-6790

**C & G Antiques**
435 River Road
207/453-2248

## 24 FALMOUTH

## Mortimer's Antiques
Off Route #88
207/781-3562
Directions: Call ahead.

General line of antiques with a concentration in black memorabilia, hooked and braided rugs, baskets and folk art.

**Scottish Terrier Antiques**
89 Hillside Ave.
207/797-4223

**Port 'n' Starboard Gallery**
53 Falmouth Road
207/781-4214

**Gerald Bell Antiques**
124 Gray Road
207/797-9386

## 25 FARMINGTON

## The Old Barn Annex Antiques
30 Middle St. #3
207/778-6908

Always presenting outstanding quality and exceptional antiques. If you can't visit them in Maine, be sure to watch for The Old Barn Annex Antiques on exhibit at finer antique shows.

## Cobweb Corner Collectibles
Route 5
207/778-9744

Specializing in 1920s through 1940s kitchenware and American dinnerware with a large selection of Fire King, Depression glassware, cookbooks, mixing bowls and much, much more.

**Maple Ave. Antiques**
23 Maple Ave.
207/778-4850

**Mary Lovejoy Antiques**
26 Anson St.
207/778-4487

**Audrey B. Bergeron**
4 Sunset Ave.
207/778-4749

**Blackberry Farm Antiques**
Town Farm Road
207/778-2035

**Antiques**
Route 4, 71 N. Main St.
207/778-6358

**Frost Antiques**
Route 4
207/778-3761

**Antique Tools from Powder House Hill**
Route 1
207/778-2946

### *Nearby Antique Shopping (Winslow)*
### *Winslow is 4 miles north of Farmington.*

## Ed Welch Antiques
Route 201
207/872-5849

Featuring furniture by Herman Miller, Charles Eames, Knoll International and other American designers. Medical and dental antiques including tools, books, charts and instruments from the 1600s through the 1930s. In addition the shop offers folk art, paintings, Civil War and spectacles.

*Nearby Antique Shopping (New Vineyard)*
*New Vineyard is 10 miles northwest of Farmington.*

### The Fred O. Smith Line
Main St.
207/778-4177

Various antique and aged wood furniture. The shop specializes in its own line of antique-style furniture and will custom build your choice. A convenient stop when en route to Sugarloaf, U.S.A., or to the Rangeley Lake region.

*Nearby Antique Shopping (New Portland)*
*New Portland is a 20-minute drive from Farmington.*

**Nora West Antiques**
Route 27
207/628-2200

### 26 HALLOWELL

### Acme Antiques
165 Water St.
207/622-2322

20th-century wacky tac, old tin, '50s memorabilia, antiques and collectibles.

### Johnson-Marsano Antique Jewelry
172 Water St.
207/623-6263

Specializing in antique jewelry from the Victorian to Art Deco, Bakelite, Taxco and sterling. Hand-colored photos by Nutting, Sawyer and Davidson.

### Dealer's Choice Antique Mall
108 Water St.
207/622-5527

60 showcases, glass, porcelain, sterling, Indian items, country and Victorian.

### James H. Lefurgy Antiques & Books
168 Water St.
207/623-1771

American furniture, Native American art, nautical antiques, toys and folk art.

### Josiah Smith Antiques
181 Water St.
207/622-4188

American and British glass and ceramics, art, art pottery and a large collection of Japanese pottery.

### Manny's Antiques
202 Water St.
207/622-9747

A large collection of early antiques and collectibles.

### Newsom & Berdan's Antiques
151 Water St.
207/622-0151

Specializing in period furniture and early accessories including folk art.

### Jayhawk Antiques & Collectibles
163 Water St.
207/622-7675

Group shop featuring '30s, '40s and '50s furniture, pottery, glass, china, bottles, Steiff toys and clock radios.

*Nearby Antique Shopping (Farmingdale)*

### Clark's Antiques
Route 201-415 Main Ave.
207/622-0592

Flow blue, blue onion, blue willow, Limoges and English china, Roseville, Weller, McCoy, art glass, paintings and more.

*Nearby Antique Shopping (Gardiner)*

### McKay's Antiques
75 Brunswick Ave.
207/582-4671

Over 20,000 pieces of glass and china; cut, early pattern, Nippon, Noritake, ironstone, crystal, Blue Willow, Depression and sets of dishes. Also tin, iron, brass, copper, crocks, baskets and paintings.

*Maine*

## 27 HAMPDEN

The shops listed in this town carry a large selection of country antiques, Victorian furniture, glassware from all eras, all types of pottery, kitchen collectibles and oak, walnut and mahogany furniture.

**The What Not Shoppe**
586 Main Road N.
207/942-3607

**Chesley Farm Antiques**
336 Main Road S.
207/862-3866

### *Nearby Antique Shopping (Winterport)*
### *Winterport is 5 miles SE of Hampden.*

**Peter & the Baldwin Sisters**
Old County Road
207/223-4732

**Lavender & Old Lace**
1103 N. Main St.
207/223-4703

## 28 HARRISON

**Camp David Antiques**
Main St.
207/583-6797

**Hermitage Antiques**
Main St.
207/583-2821

**Village Antiques**
Main St.
207/583-6046

**Aged to Perfection Antiques**
3 Winslow St.
207/583-2776

**"Mr. Oak"**
Main St.
207/583-4206

## 29 KENNEBUNK

**Heritage House Antiques**
10 Christensen Lane
207/967-5952

**Rivergate Antique Mall**
RR 1
207/985-6280

**Antiques on Nine**
75 Western Ave. (Route 9)
207/967-0626

**Victorian Lighting**
29 York St.
207/985-6868

**Paper Collectibles**
58 Portland Road
207/985-0987

**Chocolate Tree Antiques**
54 York St.
207/985-7779

### *Nearby Antique Shopping (Alfred)*
### *Alfred is 9 miles from Kennebunk.*

## De Wolfe & Wood

Waterboro Road
207/490-5572

Specializing in Shaker artifacts, furniture and general antiques.

**Shiretown Antiques Center**
Route 202
207/324-3755

A wide selection of antiques exhibited by 40 dealers.

### *Nearby Antique Shopping (Hollis)*

**Sharon's Shed Antiques**
Follow signs from 202/4
207/727-3714

Large barn and shed of furniture, tribal arts, pottery, rugs and baskets.

### *Great Places to Stay*

**Arundel Meadows Inn**
P.O. Box 1129
207/985-3770
Web site: www.biddefoRoadcom/arundel-meadows-inn/

This old farmhouse located two miles north on Route 1 from the center of Kennebunk, combines the charm of antiques and art with the comfort of seven individually decorated bedrooms with sitting areas—two are suites, three have fireplaces, some have cable television, and all have private bathrooms. Full homemade breakfasts and afternoon teas are prepared by co-owner Mark Bachelder, a professionally trained chef.

## 30 KENNEBUNKPORT

Kennebunkport, with its little population of just 1,100, offers something for just about everyone, but especially for those who love the sea and a little seclusion. Scattered among its beaches, harbors, boatyards, rocky coasts, manicured streets, quaint shops and historic churches are the magnificent homes of 18th- and 19th-century sea captains, shipbuilders and wealthy summer residents. Many of these homes are now bed and breakfasts; indeed, few towns can match Kennebunkport for number, variety, and quality of its inns and the experience of the town's innkeepers. There are also several restored seaside hotels from another era that dot the scenic landscape of the town.

If you want a good introduction to the history of the Kennebunks (the name of the townsfolk), visit the Brick Store Museum. The museum shop features quality reproductions and books on local history and crafts. Another way to visit the area's past is to tour White Columns, a gracious Greek Revival mansion (1851–1853) with original furnishings that is maintained by the Kennebunkport Historical Society.

There's all sorts of things to do and see around Kennebunkport. Many of the historic buildings on Dock Square and elsewhere now house galleries and artists' studios, as well as many interesting little shops. The

# Maine

Seashore Trolley Museum has a collection of over 225 trolleys from around the world, and offers a three-mile ride on an antique electric trolley. And all visitors should take at least one offshore excursion and indulge in whale-watching, sightseeing and cruising. There's also canoeing, golfing, cross-country skiing, hiking or biking.

| | |
|---|---|
| **Old Fort Inn**<br>8 Old Fort Ave.<br>207/967-5353 | **Antiques USA**<br>RR 1<br>207/985-7766 |
| **Times Past & Past Times**<br>11 Pier Road<br>207/967-0266 | **Arundel Antiques**<br>1713 Portland Road<br>207/985-7965 |
| **Antiques Workshop**<br>64 North St.<br>207/967-5266 | **Anna Benjamin Antiques**<br>Old Limerick Road<br>207/985-2312 |
| **Antiques Kennebunk Port**<br>Route #9, Lower Village<br>207/967-8033 | **Old Fort Inn & Antiques**<br>Old Fort Ave.<br>207/967-5353 |

## *Great Places to Stay*

### 1802 House B&B Inn

15 Locke St.
1-800-932-5632
Web site: www.bbhost.com/1802inn

This 19th-century inn is situated along the 15th fairway of the Cape Arundel Golf Club. Like so many New England homes, the inn has been added to over the years. The second story was added just after the turn of the nineteenth century. The structure was converted into an inn in 1977 and since that time, the original barn was converted to a gourmet kitchen and guest dining room. The six guest rooms are located in the original part of the house, each configured and decorated differently, each offering a fireplace or a double whirlpool tub, and some rooms offer both. The luxurious three-room suite provides the ultimate in comfort and privacy.

### Captain Lord Mansion

P.O. Box 800
207/967-3141
Web site: www.captainloRoadcom

The Captain Lord Mansion was built during the War of 1812 as an elegant private residence and is situated at the head of a sloping green overlooking the Kennebunk River. Large guest rooms, luxurious appointments, oversize antique four-poster beds and gas fireplaces create a true haven for romantic and celebratory escapes. A three-course breakfast is served "family style" giving lots of opportunity to share with fellow travelers. Awarded both AAA 4 Diamonds and Mobil 4 Stars. Many "quiet season" events and activities. Walk to shops, galleries and restaurants. River-view rooms.

### Inn at Harbor Head

41 Pier Road
207/967-5564

The nostalgia of a bygone era lingers in this picturesque fishing village. Your artist/innkeeper has beautifully decorated the rambling shingled inn with various sculptures, marine paintings, Oriental carpets, antique furniture and handpainted murals on guest room walls. Beautifully appointed beds are king or queen. The library is perfect for reading or watching ocean and harbor activities, while a stroll past the gardens will take you to the water's edge.

### Maine Stay Inn & Cottages

34 Main St.
1-800-950-2117
Web site: www.mainstayinn.com

Maine Stay is a beautiful 1860 Victorian inn with an Italianate hip roof, accentuated by a Queen Anne–period flying staircase, wraparound porch, bay windows, and masterful architectural detail. The Maine Stay offers a variety of accommodations, from suites in the main house to delightful one-bedroom cottages, some with fireplace and separate kitchens. Cottage guests may have a breakfast basket delivered to their door. The living room is a comfortable place to sit and meet fellow travelers.

### The Captain Jefferds Inn

5 Pearl St.
1-800-839-6844
Web site: www.captainjefferdsinn.com

Hospitality abounds in this gracious 1804 Federal-style mansion. Originally built by Daniel Walker, the property was given as a wedding present to his daughter Mary, and her husband, Captain William Jefferds, in 1805. Each of the 16 guest rooms are named, designed and decorated in the spirit of Pat and Dick Bartholomew's favorite places. The Italian suite has a king-size verdigris iron bed, fireplace and indoor water garden. Other rooms in the inn include the Charleston, the Chatham, the Adare and the Monicello. Six have fireplaces, all have private baths and are furnished with antiques and period reproductions. Each morning a full, gourmet breakfast is served by candlelight in front of a warm fire or, in the summer months, on the sunny terrace overlooking the gardens. Located in Kennebunkport's magnificent historic district, within easy walking distance to many fine shops, restaurants and galleries.

## The Waldo Emerson Inn
207/985-4250
Web site: www.bbhost.com/waldoemersoninn

 This interesting inn has had several famous owners. The original Dutch grambrel was constructed by Waldo Emerson in 1753 and is the oldest remaining house in Kennebunk. Waldo, great-uncle of Ralph Waldo Emerson, the poet/essayist, made a tidy profit building clipper ships on the river behind the house. It was inherited, through marriage, by Theodore Lyman, who made a fortune building ships on the site and added the enormous addition in 1784 as a wedding gift for his second wife. Theodore sold the home in 1804 to build the now-famous Lyman Estate and Greenhouses in Waltham, Massachusetts. The house was purchased by John Bourne, father of fifteen children, one of whom was George Washington Bourne, the builder of the famous "Wedding Cake House" next door. The inn is a wonderful recollection of the past. You enter directly into the 245-year-old keeping room, with its hand-hewn oak timbers hung with dried flowers, pewter, and copper. During your stay, please stop by Mainely Quilts, innkeeper Maggie Carver's shop in the carriage house. You will likely find her working on her latest creation. Her heirloom-quality quilts and wall hangings, often taking hundreds of hours to create, grace homes all over the world.

### 31 LINCOLNVILLE

**Beach House Antiques**
RR 1
207/789-5323

**Country Patch Antiques**
RR 1
207/763-4069

**Blue Dolphin Antiques**
164 Atlantic Hwy.
207/338-3860

**Deer Meadows**
RR 1
207/236-8020

**Painted Lady**
RR 1
207/789-5201

**Andrews & Andrews**
71 Cross St.
207/338-1386

### *Nearby Antique Shopping (Northport)*

**Blue Dolphin Antiques**
RR 1
207/338-3860

**Ellen Katona & Bob Lutz**
RR 1
207/338-1444

**Sign of the Owl Antiques & B&B**
243 Atlantic Hwy.
207/338-4669

### 32 LOVELL

**Kezar Five Antiques**
Route 5, Lovell Village
207/925-6292

**Hartmart Stamps & Antiques**
Main St.
207/925-6525

**Lovell Village Trading Company**
Route 5, Lovell Village
207/925-6848

### 33 NAPLES

**Antique Revival & Ice Cream Parlor**
Route 302 & 35
207/693-6550

**Picture Perfect**
Corner Route 302 & 114
207-693-6365

**Naples Gallery**
Route 302
207/693-6084

**Sudbury Schoolmarm Antiques**
Route 302
No phone listed

**Old Fishing Stuff, Etc.**
Route 302
207/693-5000

**The Scottish Trader**
Route 302
207/693-5019

### 34 NORRIDGEWOCK

**Black Hill Antiques & Collectibles**
Main St.
207/634-5151

### *Nearby Antique Shopping (Skowhegan)*
### *Skowhegan is 13 miles north of Norridgewock.*

**Hilltop Antiques**
55 E. Front St.
207/474-3972

 Selling to the trade only. Supplying a fresh-picked load every week from private homes in the area. In business for the past thirty years. Anything from country to Victorian furniture to lamps, clocks, rugs, sporting, tools and paintings.

**David Jewell Antiques**
34 Turner Ave.
207/474-9676

### 35 NORTH BERWICK

**Brick House Antiques**
Corner Route 9 & Main St.
207/676-2885
Open: Daily

 Located seven miles from Wells and Ogunquit, Brick House Antiques is literally a treasure trove of hand-picked antiques. Reverse-painted lamps, Bohemian glass, Art Nouveau, fine porcelain, quality furniture, steins and objects of art are some of the things that may be found in one of Maine's finest antique shops.

### 36 OXFORD

**Kall Us Antiques**
Route 26
207/743-9788

**Meetinghouse Antiques**
Route 26
207/539-8480

**Undercover Antique Mall**
Route 26
207/539-4149

### *Nearby Antique Shopping (Norway)*
*Norway is 10 miles northwest of Oxford.*

**Brookside Antique Shop**
260 Main St.
207/743-0979

**Arsenault's Antiques**
18 Tannery St.
207/743-9133

### *Nearby Antique Shopping (Welchville)*

## Meetinghouse Antiques
Junction Routes 26 & 121
207/539-8480

Offering two floors of fine antiques and country furnishings.

### *Great Places to Stay*

## The Inn at Little Creek
Route 121
207/539-4046 or 1-888-539-4046
Open: Year-round
Rates: $35–$75
Directions: Take the Maine Turnpike to Exit 11 (Gray) to Route 26 North. Travel approximately 30 minutes to OxfoRoad. Take Route 121 South. The inn is located in the village of OxfoRoad.

This bed & breakfast truly stands out from all the others. It was started only two years ago by Ken Ward and Diane Lecuyer, and already has repeat guests from around the world.

What sets it apart is that it is furnished in a Native American/ Southwestern flavor, complete to the serving of buffalo meat and Native American teas for breakfast. And all this is tucked away in the southwestern end of Maine!

Running a B&B has been a dream of Ken's since he was 18 years old. When he and Diane decided to open the inn, they spent a year traveling around the country, visiting B&Bs, to see just what was available. They knew they wanted something totally different so, since Diane is part Native American, they decided to include her heritage as the main focus of their B&B.

Although Diane is associated with the Iroquois Nation of the Northeast, they used the Southwestern feel because most non–Native Americans only know that side of the culture. The inn is furnished in the soft, muted pastel palette of the Southwest that is familiar to most people (as opposed to the harsher, more vivid palette that is also part of the Southwestern culture). But they have not focused on any specific tribes, using instead artifacts and accessories from all over North America. In this way, they use their B&B to help educate people about Native Americans in general.

They are not yet selling Native American artifacts and antiques, but may in the future.

As to where one obtains buffalo meat in Maine? Well, surprise, there are two buffalo ranches in the state, one of which is conveniently near the inn and is operated by a friend of Ken and Diane's. Diane is the cook and prepares all the buffalo-meat dishes. The Native American teas are brought in from the Dakotas and served to the inn's guests for breakfast.

Although the Inn at Little Creek is new on the B&B scene, it has already established a following and is certainly a welcome addition and change of pace. So visit Ken and Diane and soak up a little culture and history while you relax in the "wilds" of Maine.

## 37 PORTLAND

**Shipwreck & Cargo Co.**
207 Commercial
207/775-3057

**Seavey's**
249 Congress St.
207/773-1908

**Anna's Used Furniture & Collectibles**
612 Congress St.
207/775-7223

**Antiques at Zinnias**
662 Congress St.
207/780-6622

**Venture Antiques**
101 Exchange St.
207/773-6064

**F. O. Bailey Co.**
141 Middle St.
207/774-1479

**West Port Antiques**
8 Milk St.
207/774-6747

**Geraldine Wolf Antique Jewelry**
26 Milk St.
207/774-8994

**Magpies**
610 Congress St.
207/828-4560

**Nelson Rarities, Inc.**
1 City Center #8
207/775-3150

**O'Brien Antiques**
38 High St.
207/774-0931

**Tucker's Furniture & Antiques**
255 Congress St.
207/761-0719

**Andrew Nelson & Co.**
1 City Center, #8
207/775-1135

**Westport Antiques**
8 Milk St.
207/774-6747

**Portland Antique Center**
382 Commercial
207/773-7052

**Renaissance Antiques**
382 Commercial
207/879-0789

**Venture Antiques**
101 Exchange St.
207/773-6064

**Polly Peter's Antiques**
26 Bracket St.
207/774-6981

### *Great Places to Stay*

## Inn at St. John
939 Congress St.
1-800-636-9127

The Inn at St. John is a most unique 100-year-old inn noted for its European charm and quiet gentility, centrally located in Portland, just a

*Maine*

short walk to the Old Port Waterfront and Art District. Built in 1897, the inn offers tastefully decorated rooms with traditional and antique furnishings.

## 38 RANGELEY

Access Rangeley by traveling Route 4 out of Farmington.

The next three shops offer an outstanding selection of early country, oak, walnut and pine furniture, fishing collectibles, glassware and more.

**Gearsyl Antiques**
Route 4
207/864-5784

**Hayshaker Antiques**
Corner of Main & Allen St.
207/864-3765

**Blueberry Hill Antiques**
Dallas Road
207/864-5647

## 39 ROCKLAND

### Rockland Antique Marketplace
25 Rankin St.
207/596-9972
Web site: www.mint.net/rocklandantiques
Open: Daily 9–5

Over 100 dealers offering 10,000 square feet of quality antiques and collectibles.

### Pennyroyal Antiques
23 Oak St.
207/594-4400
Open: Daily 11–4

Featuring Maine Indian baskets, quilts, cut glass, advertising, black collectibles, sporting and nautical items and much, much more.

**Katrin Phocas Ltd. Antiques**
19 Main St.
207/236-8654

**Hall Antiques**
432 Main St.
207/594-5031

**Mainly Paper**
474 Main St
207/596-0077

**Early Times Antique Center**
Route (90) in Rockport
207/236-3001

**Antique Treasures**
Midway on Route 90
207/596-7650

**Jordan's Antiques**
187 Pleasant St.
207/594-5529

**Old County Clock**
269 Rankin St.
207/594-1455

**Mermaid Antiques**
256 Main St.
207/594-0616

### Nearby Antique Shopping (Washington)

### Luce's Bargain Shop
Route 220 (2 miles off Route 17)
207/845-2420

Large barn full of antique furniture and collectibles.

## 40 SCARBOROUGH

### Centervale Farm Antiques
200 U.S. Route One at Oak Hill
207/883-3443 or 1-800-896-3443
Open: Year-round 10–5 (Nov.–June closed Mon.)
Directions: Maine Turnpike, Exit 6, then take Route 1 north. 6 miles south of Portland via 295.

Delight in this New England barn filled with country antiques, furniture, paintings, rugs, lamps plus all sorts of accessories. An addition connected to the barn extends the wonderful selection to include porcelain, glassware, silver, toys, and up to and beyond "you-name-it."

**A Scarborough Fair Antiques**
264 U.S. Route 1
207/883-5999

**Top Knotch**
14 Willowdale Road
207/883-5303

**Cliff's Antique Market**
RR 1
207/883-5671

**Widow's Walk**
20 Black Point Road
207/883-8123

## 41 SEARSPORT

### Pumpkin Patch Antiques
RR 1
207/548-6047
Open: Daily 9:30–5

Maine's most imaginative group shop, with 26 professional dealers offering 18th- and 19th-century American, good music, good humor, complete services, and usually a Maine coon cat to welcome you.

**Searsport Antique Mall**
RR 1
207/548-2640

**The Galloping Beggar**
15 Elm St.
207/548-6532

**Hart-Smith Antiques**
190 E. Main St.
207/548-2412

**Antiques at the Hillman's**
362 E. Main St.
207/548-6658

**Primrose Farm Antiques**
RR 1
207/548-6019

**Hobby Horse Antiques**
RR 1
207/548-2981

# *Maine*

## Great Places to Stay

### Brass Lantern Inn
81 W. Main St.
1-800-691-0150

Sunlight pours through the windows of this beautiful sea captain's home nestled at the edge of the woods on a rise overlooking Penobscot Bay. The inn is furnished with a combination of antiques, reproductions and contemporary furniture. Ornate woodwork, marble fireplaces and tin ceilings enhance the inn's ambiance. Guests awake to the smell of freshly ground coffee and homemade bread or muffins. A full gourmet breakfast is served in the formal dining room. Blueberry pancakes and maple syrup are one of the favorites.

### Old Glory Inn
Route 1 (89 W. Main St.)
207/548-6232

Old Glory Inn, a colonial sea captain's home, was built prior to 1830 on land acquired by the Gilmore family in 1784. Constructed of brick and set on two acres, the inn is a fine example of New England architecture. The "Captain's Suite" plus two additional guest rooms, each with a private bath, allow you to enjoy the beach. Breakfast is included and served in the keeping room. Country antiques and artist-made Santas are available in the shop on the premises.

### Watchtide "B&B by the Sea"
190 W. Main St.
1-800-698-6575
Web site: www.agate.net/~watchtyd/watchtide.html

This circa-1795 early American New England Cape home is situated on three and a half oceanside acres with a magnificent view of Penobscot Bay. Once owned by General Henry Knox, this home has hosted many Presidential wives and was often frequented by Eleanor Roosevelt. A fan which belonged to Mary Todd Lincoln is one, of many, of the collections of this estate. Angels to Antiques Gift Shoppe is located in the adjacent barn with guest discounts.

## 42 SOUTH PORTLAND

**Mulberry Cottage**
45 Western Ave.
207/775-5011

**G.L. Smith Antiques Art Collectibles**
378 Cottage Road
207/799-5253

**Brass House Antiques**
580 Main St.
207/773-7662

## 43 THOMASTON

Located on the St. George River is Thomaston, once an important port and home to many prominent sea captains. Beautiful homes still exist to mark the rich heritage of the town. General Henry Knox, chief-of-staff and Secretary of War for President George Washington, once resided in Thomaston. Today a replica of his mansion, Montpelier, offers visitors a chance to see the home as it was in the days when it housed the general's family.

### David C. Morey American Antiques
103 Main St.
207/354-6033 or 207/372-6660
Open: Wed., Fri. & Sat. 10–5 or by appointment anytime

Honoring the American craftsmen, David C. Morey Antiques presents 18th-century American country furnishings and accessories in this 2,000-square-foot shop.

**Wee Barn Antiques**
4 1/2 Georges St.
207/354-6163

**Ross Levett Antiques**
111 Main St.
207/354-6227

**Anchor Farm Antiques**
184 Main St.
207/354-8859

**The Rose Cottage**
187 Main St.
207/354-6250

## 44 TOPSHAM

**Red Schoolhouse Antiques**
8 Middlesex Road
207/729-4541

**Affordable Antiques**
49 Topsham Fair Mall, #21
207/729-7913

**Lisbon Road Antiques**
1089 Lewiston Road
207/353-4094

## 45 TRENTON

### Tiffany's of Trenton Antiques
Junction of Route 230 & Route 3
207/667-7743
Web site: www.downeast.net/com/tiffany
Open: Wed.–Sun. 10–5

One of the largest shops in the area; three floors of quality furnishings diversely displayed.

**Sherman's Antiques**
Route 230 Bayside Road
207/667-2910

*Maine*

## 46 WELLS

### Reed's Antiques & Collectibles
U.S. Route 1
207/646-8010 or 1-800-891-2017
Open: Daily 10–5
Directions: Exit 2, ME Turnpike, left on Route 1

In two short years Reed's has become known as the number-one multi-dealer shop in Maine for quality antiques and collectibles. Open year-round, seven days a week, this customer-friendly store has merchandise ranging from Meissen to Mickey Mouse, Sevres to Star Wars, neolithic artifacts to Nouveau art. Whether you are shopping for a personal treasure, a choice resale item or a special gift, you're sure to find it at Reed's. Come join the thousands of other satisfied customers from all over the world who have made Reed's their must-stop shop. When a Maine native says "This is the best shop in New England" they must be doing it right!

### MacDougall-Gionet Antiques & Associates
U.S. Route One; 2104 Post Road
207/646-3531
Open: Daily 9–5, closed Mon.

Known as New England's most exciting period-antiques center, MacDougall-Gionet's sixty quality dealers pack the barn full of names such as Hepplewhite, Chippendale and Sheraton. Here you will find items such as camphorwood chests, tavern tables, a Pennsylvania dower chest in original salmon and smoked paint, an original mustard and stenciled dressing table, a turquoise-inlaid secretary desk and the list goes on. Stop in and see for yourself the marvelous inventory of fine antiques.

### Maine Coast Antiques
1784 Post Road
207/641-2962
Open: Mon.–Sun. 10–5

Housed in an authentic 1840s post and beam barn. Three stories of antique furnishings and collectibles.

### Wells General Store
2023 Post Road
207/646-5533

The store is set in a 200-year-old barn with two floors of quality antiques and collectibles.

**1774 House Antiques**
Route #1
207/646-3520

**R. Jorgensen Antiques**
502 Post Road, Route #1
207/646-9444

**Bomar Hall Antiques & Collectibles**
1622 Post Road
207/646-4116

**Peggy Carboni Antiques**
1755 Post Road
207/646-4551

**Wells Antique Mart**
RR 1
207/646-8153

**Wells Union Antique Center**
1755 Post Road
207/646-6996

**Riverbank Antiques**
Route #1
207/646-6314

**Old Art & Antiques**
Route #1
207/646-6996

**Country Mouse D & A**
2077 Sanford Road
207/646-7334

## 47 WEST PARIS

### Mollyockett Marketplace Antique Center
255 Bethel Road, Route 26 (at junction of Route 219)
207/674-3939
Open: Mid-May–mid-Oct. daily 10–5, mid-Oct.–mid-May Fri.–Mon. 10–4

Best find in western Maine for the antique lover or browser. Huge two-story group shop loaded with antiques: pedal cars and toys, oak, pine, Victorian and period furniture, Parrish and other prints and art and books, jewelry, glass and china, Old Ivory, flow blue, Depression glass, Fiesta, Limoges, Roseville, Majolica, McCoy, silver and pewter, rugs, linens, quilts and vintage clothing,  tins and bottles, advertising, primitives and baskets, skis and snowshoes, lanterns and clocks.

**Antique Shop**
Route 26
207/674-3241

**Red Beard's Antiques**
11 Gary St. (S. Paris)
207/643-6287

## 48 WINDHAM

### The Barn
71 Route 115
207/892-9776
Open: Mon.–Fri. 9–5, Sat. 10–5

Specializing in kerosene lamp parts and shades.

**Antiques at the Grange**
18 Old Route 202
207/892-5873

*Maine*

### Nearby Antique Shopping (East Baldwin)
### *East Baldwin is located 16 miles from Windham.*

## Chadbourne Homestead Antiques
School St.
207/787-2689

Over 2,500 square feet of antiques and collectibles.

### *Nearby Antique Shopping (Gray)*
### *Gray is 7 miles north of Windham.*

**The Barn on 26 Antique Center**
Route 26
207/657-3470

### *Nearby Antique Shopping (South Casco)*
### *South Casco is located 13 miles from Windham.*

**Antiques at S. Casco**          **Varney's Volume**
Route 302                          Quaker Ridge Road
207/655-5034                       207/655-4605

## 49  WISCASSET

Wiscasset is an inspiring community for artists and writers, as well as shoppers and sightseers. Located on the west bank of the Sheepscot River at the western edge of Lincoln County, the town's attractions include two decaying four-masted schooners which were beached along the banks of the Sheepscot in 1932. *Luther Little* and *Hester*, as they are called, were built during World War I and saw active service during the 1920s as cargo vessels.

Other points of interest in this charming town are the distinguished and stately mansions which used to belong to sea captains and shipping merchants. Several of these are open to the public during the summer months. Scenic boat rides and train trips leave from the waterfront area to provide unique views of coastal wildlife and marvelous vistas.

## Parkers of Wiscasset Antiques
Coastal Route One
207/882-5520
Open: Daily 9–5; after Columbus Day, 10–4
North and South Buildings open April–December

A dream come true; two buildings filled to overflowing with anything you might desire in the antique line. You will find folk art, toys, early pottery, Quimper, country and primitives, furniture, quilts and rugs, paintings, Indian jewelry as well as the unusual — Irish lace baby bonnet, 18th-century iron toaster, early brass trivet and human hair art in a frame are just a few of the recent offerings. If you're looking for the ordinary as well as the unique, we recommend you visit Parkers of Wiscasset Antiques.

**Marston House American Antiques**
Main St.
207/882-6010

**Two at Wiscasset**
Main St.
207/882-5286

**Maine Antiques**
RR 1
207/882-7347

**Wiscasset Bay Gallery**
Water St.
207/882-7682

**Margaret Ofslager**
Main St.
207/882-7082

**Portside Antiques**
Main St.
207/882-6506

**Patricia Stauble**
Main St.
207/882-6341

**Nonesuch House Antiques**
1 Middle St.
207/882-6768

**Maine Trading Post**
RR 1
207/882-7400

**Wm. Dykes Antiques**
Route #1
207/882-6381

**Wizard of Odds & Ends**
7 Main St.
207/882-7870

**Part of the Past**
Water St.
207/882-7908

## 50  YORK

## York Antiques Gallery
Route 1
207/363-5002
Open: Daily 10–5 year-round
Directions: Easy access from I-95, just 9/10 of a mile north from the Yorks, Ogunquit Exit (last exit before toll).

Intrigue and artistry are the hallmarks of the collection found at York Antique Gallery. Showcased in this multiple dealer shop are 18th- and 19th-century country and formal furniture in addition to accessories. Shoppers will also discover a surprising assortment of other goods including textiles, paintings/prints, nautical items, decoys/hunting, advertising, folk art, Indian, military/fire, as well as out of print reference books.

## Marie Plummer & John Philbrick
44 Chases Pond Road
207/363-2515

Offerings of exceptional quality and a unique display of early antiques makes this shop grandly unique. Just a sampling of the superior items available are: ca. 1780 New England pine pipe box, an 18th-century Westwald jug, and an 18th-century New England maple rope bed.

*Maine*

## Bell Farm Antiques
RR 1
207/363-8181
Open: Mon.–Sat. 10–5, Sun. 12–5

A fine quality group shop featuring 2 floors of country antiques, art, silver, Steiff toys, early glass and china.

## Rocky Mountain Quilts
130 York St.
207/363-6800
Open: Mon.–Sun. 10–5

Over 350 antique quilts from 1750 to 1940; folk art to early chintz. Antique quilt and textile restorer.

**Maritime Antiques**
935 U.S. Route 1
207/363-4247

**Olde Stuff Shop**
RR 1
207/363-4517

**York Village Crafts Antiques & Gifts**
211 York St.
207/363-4830

**Orr-iginils Antiques**
470 York St.
207/363-4761

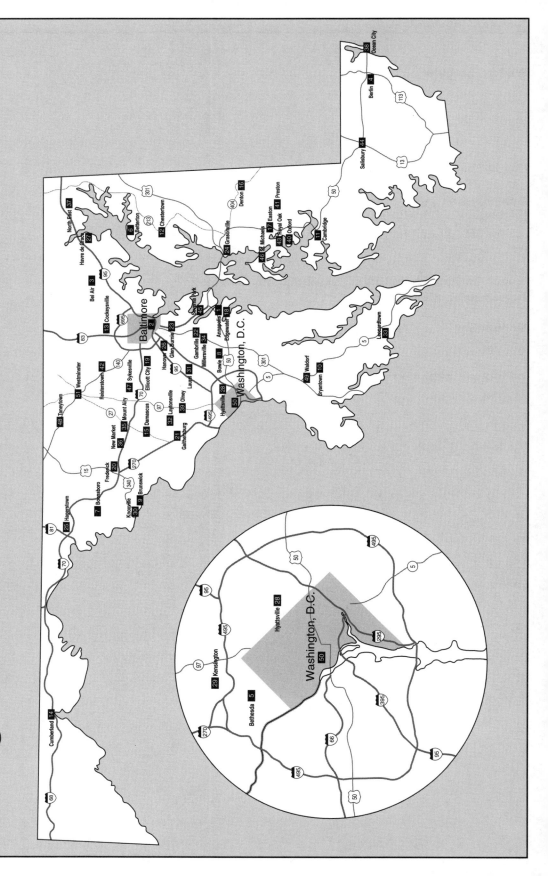

# 1 ANNAPOLIS

Founded in 1649, Annapolis is often referred to as a "museum without walls," for the number of historic homes and buildings that have been restored and are open to the public. The city has served as Maryland's state capital since 1694, and was the nation's capital from November 1783 to August 1784.

## DHS Designs
86 Maryland Ave.
410/280-3466

Deep in the heart of the Loire Valley lie some of France's most cherished treasures. Those who have traveled there know that there is something very special, very different about this

region and its homes. It is as if one is transported to another dimension, unique in its charm and atmosphere with warmth and hospitality, a sense of continuity. The country house, or chateau, speaks of forests and hunting, families, music and gardening—all that we associate with the pleasures of country life.

Royal grandeur and merchant wealth produced the Loire Valley castles and neoclassic mansions. The variety of riches throughout this region is seemingly inexhaustible, but to be able to share a part of this history is a rare opportunity. DHS Designs offers a collection of exquisitely carved period French limestone mantels from these manor houses. Dating from the 16th to the 19th centuries, the styles range from Renaissance to Romantic. These works of art, hand-carved of local limestone by the artisans of the courts, are for a discerning few who won't settle for reproductions.

**AA West Annapolis Antiques**
14 Annapolis St.
410/268-8762

**Country Finds**
103 Annapolis St.
410/267-9366

**Clockmaker Shop**
1935 Generals Hwy.
410/266-0770

**Baldwin & Claude Antiques**
47 Maryland Ave.
410/268-1665

**Sixth Street Studio**
422 6th St.
410/267-8233

**Third Millennium Designs**
57 Maryland Ave.
410/267-6428

**Walnut Leaf Antiques**
62 Maryland Ave.
410/263-4885

**Maryland Ave. Antiques**
82 Maryland Ave.
410/268-5158

**Ron Snyder Antiques**
2011 West St.
410/266-5452

**Annapolis Antique Gallery**
2009 West St.
410/266-0635

## Great Places to Stay

### The Gatehouse Bed & Breakfast
249 Hanover St.
410/280-0024

Overlooking the U.S. Naval Academy in Annapolis, the Gatehouse Bed & Breakfast is a towering, three-story Georgian home, offering elegant accommodations.

The Gatehouse provides five luxuriously appointed guest rooms: four with queen-size beds and private baths, and one with double bed and shared bath. Fresh flowers, bath amenities, and down-soft robes are provided in each room. Full breakfast is served daily.

### Jonas Green House B&B
124 Charles St.
410/263-5892
Web site: www.bbhost.com/ighouse

This charming old home, dating from the 1690s and early 1700s, is one of Annapolis' two oldest residences. It was the home of Jonas Green and his wife, Anne Catherine Green. Jonas was a colonial printer and patriot, from 1738 until his death in 1775. The home has been continuously occupied by their family ever since. The current owners are Jonas' five great-grandsons. Much of the original house fabric survives. It still maintains its original floor, fireplace surrounds, and old cooking fireplace.

# 2 BALTIMORE

A 14-block area in eastern Baltimore, fronting on the Patapsco River with the deepest harbor in the area, this active post is one of the original communities that joined "Baltimore Town" to become the city of Baltimore.

The first settlers came in 1724, and the grid plan was laid out by Edward Fell in 1761. Many of the cobblestone streets retain their English-inspired names, including Thames and Shakespeare. Fells Point's famed shipyards produced the renowned Baltimore clippers used as privateers, along with frigates and sloops used by the Continental Navy. The Broadway Market, along with scores of charming antiques shops and restaurants, still welcomes visitors from foreign lands—as well as locals intent on shopping or dining.

## Antique Amusements
## A-1 Jukebox & Nostalgia Co.
208 S. Pulaski St.
410/945-8900 or 1-888-694-9464
Web site: members.aol.com/jukeboxusa/
Open: Mon.–Fri. 10–5 and some Sat., closed on Sun. From 5:30–8:30

Mon.-Fri., they offer customers in-home service and installation for the items they sell.

Directions: Located one mile west of Oriole Park at Camden Yards in west Baltimore. *From Oriole Park:* Take Lombard St. (it's one way west) 1 mile to Pulaski Street and turn left 1 ½ blocks, on the right side. *From Interstate 95 northbound or southbound:* Take Exit 50 North to Wilkens Ave. and turn right. At the 5th traffic light turn left onto South Pulaski Street. 2 blocks north on the left side.

Antique Amusements A-1 Jukebox & Nostalgia Company has been in business for 18 years selling and servicing jukeboxes. If you have a jukebox to sell they also buy jukeboxes. They will even rent a jukebox to you for your next party or company event. Their inventory consists of new compact disc Wurlitzer jukeboxes and Original Seeburg jukeboxes from the '50s, '60s, and '70s. It's interesting to know that more 45 R.P.M. records (the 7-inch singles with the big hole) are currently being made now than at any time in the past because so many folks are purchasing new Wurlitzer and original jukeboxes for their homes and businesses. Their $4.95 "Singles" record catalog lists 10,000 45 R.P.M. records, and on any given order they can supply at least an 80 percent fill. They carry many replacement parts for Wurlitzer and Seeburg jukeboxes and all of the repair and parts manuals including schematics for Rock-Ola, Rowe/Ami, Seeburg, and Wurlitzer jukeboxes. They also carry a complete line of classic-style diner booths, chairs, stools, and tables. Some of the most unique items include: Edison Cylinder Machines from the turn of the last century (they actually reproduce sound by playing a wax cylinder); reproduction barber poles which light up and rotate, (made of glass and metal just like the originals); reproduction metal signs (very limited production) mostly soft drink signs, some with thermometers; and a line of stained glass hanging light fixtures (top quality). Antiques Amusements A-1 Jukebox & Nostalgia Company currently occupies 5,000 square feet of space in a five-story brick building known as the Cambridge Building. They are planning to move the entire business operation to Howard County, Md., soon.

If you would like to see color pictures of their unique and beautiful items, please visit their web site at members.aol.com/jukeboxusa/. The web site has taken the place of the old catalog, which they no longer use. Domestic and worldwide shipping is available. Visa, Mastercard, and personal checks in U.S. dollars are accepted.

**The Karmic Connection**
508 W. Broadway
410/558-0428

**Along the Way, Ltd.**
1719 Aliceanna St.
410/276-4461

**Saratoga Trunk**
1740 Aliceanna St.
410/327-6635

**Constance**
1709 Aliceanna St.
410/563-6031

**Auntie Qs**
1721 Aliceanna St.
410/276-7660

**Velveteen Rabbit**
20 Allegheny Ave.
410/583-1685

**Portebello Square, Inc.**
28 Allegheny St.
410/821-1163

**Memory Lane Antiques**
607 S. Broadway
410/276-0865

**Oh! Susanna**
620 S. Broadway
410/327-1408

**A Squirrel's Nest**
313 Eastern Blvd.
410/391-3664

**Modest Rupert's Attic**
919 S. Charles St.
410/727-4505

**Olde Touch**
2103 N. Charles St.
410/783-1493

**Thompson's Antiques**
430 Eastern Blvd. (Essex)
410/686-3107

**Reginald Fitzgerald Antiques**
1704 Eastern Blvd.
410/534-2942

**Sunporch Antiques**
6072 Falls Road
410/377-2904

**American Pie**
1704 Fleet St.
410/276-0062

**Davids-Gans Co., Inc.**
910 W. 36th St.
410/467-8159

**R & H Antiques**
1720 Fleet St.
410/522-1621

**Antique Man**
1731 Fleet St.
410/732-0932

**Angela R. Thrasher Antiques**
833 N. Howard St.
410/523-0550

**Three Rag Picker Collection**
5722 Harford Road
410/254-0033

**DJ's Antiques & Collectibles**
7914 Harford Road
410/665-4344

**Collectors Item**
4903 Belair Road
410/483-2020

**Off Broadway Antiques**
614 S. Broadway
410/732-6522

**Hattie's Antiques & Collectibles**
726 S. Broadway
410/276-1316

**Craig Flinner Gallery**
505 N. Charles St.
410/727-1863

**Silver Mine**
1023 N. Charles St.
410/752-4141

**Sabina & Daughter**
1637 Eastern Ave.
410/276-6366

**Ramm Antiques & Collectibles**
811 Eastern Blvd.
410/687-5284

**John's Art & Antiques**
1733 Eastern Blvd.
410/675-4339

**Antique Toy & Train World**
3626 Falls Road
410/889-0040

**J & M Antiques**
1706 Fleet St.
410/732-2919

**The Bowery of Antiques**
1709 Fleet St.
410/732-2778

**Mystery Loves Company**
1730 Fleet St.
410/276-6708

**In the Groove Antiques**
1734 Fleet St.
410/675-7174

**Old Treasure Chest**
3409 Greenmount Ave.
410/889-0540

**Valley Gun**
7719 Harford Road
410/668-2171

**Dusty Attic**
9411 Harford Road
410/668-2343

**Hamilton House Antiques**
865 N. Howard St.
410/462-5218

**Cross Keys Antiques**
801 N. Howard St.
410/728-0101

**Dubey's Art & Antiques**
807 N. Howard St.
410/383-2881

**Thaynes Antiques**
823 N. Howard St.
410/728-7109

**Heritage Antiques**
829 N. Howard St.
410/728-7033

**E.A. Mack Antiques, Inc.**
839 N. Howard St.
410/728-1333

**Wintzer Galleries**
853 N. Howard St.
410/462-3313

**Sindler Fine Arts & Antiques**
809 Howard St.
410/728-3377

**Connoisseurs Connection**
869 N. Howard St.
410/383-2624

**L.A. Herstein & Co.**
877 N. Howard St.
410/728-3856

**Antique Warehouse at 1300**
1300 Jackson St.
410/659-0663

**Collectiques**
1806 Maryland Ave.
410/539-3474

**French Accents**
3600 Roland Ave.
410/467-8957

**A & M Antique & Modern Jewelry**
708 N. Rolling Road
410/788-7000

**Heirloom Jewels**
5100 Falls Road, #14
410/323-0100

**Antique Exchange, Inc.**
318 Wyndhurst Ave.
410/532-7000

**Gaines McHale Antiques**
836 Leadenhall St.
410/625-1900

**Antiques at 805**
805 N. Howard St.
410/728-8419

**Antique Treasury**
809 N. Howard St.
410/728-6363

**Cuomo's Antiques & Interiors**
871 N. Howard St.
410/383-9195

**Imperial Half Bushel**
831 N. Howard St.
410/462-1192

**Amos Judd & Son, Inc.**
841-843 N. Howard St.
410/462-2000

**Drusilla's Books**
859 Howard St.
410/225-0277

**Yakov's Antiques**
861 N. Howard St.
410/728-4517

**Harris Auction Galleries, Inc.**
875 N. Howard St.
410/728-7040

**Regency Antiques**
893 N. Howard St.
410/225-3455

**Antique Furniture Co.**
3524 Keswick Road
410/366-2421

**Nostalgia Too**
7302 N. Point Road
410/477-8440

**Turnover Shop, Inc.**
3547 Chestnut Ave.
410/366-2988

**Grrreat Bears**
1643 Thames
410/276-4429

**Mel's Antiques**
712 S. Wolfe St.
410/675-7229

**Alex Cooper Oriental Rugs**
908 York Road
410/828-4838

**Consignment Galleries, Inc.**
6711 York Road
410/377-3067

**Keepers Antiques**
222 W. Read St.
410/783-0330

**Christie's Fine Art**
100 W. Road, #310
410/832-7555

**Early Attic Furniture**
415 E. 32nd St.
410/889-0122

**Michael's Rug Gallery**
415 E. 33rd St.
410/366-1515

**Another Period in Time**
1708 Fleet St.
410/675-4776

**Mt. Vernon Antique Flea Market**
226 W. Monument St.
410/523-6493

**S. Balser Paintings, Prints & Books**
By appointment only
410/484-0880

*Great Places to Stay*

**Gramercy Mansion Bed & Breakfast**
1400 Greenspring Valley Road
1-800-553-3404
Web site: www.angelfire.com/md/gramercy/

Gramercy, a majestic Tudor-style mansion and estate, situated on 45 acres in Maryland's Greenspring Valley, provides an Olympic-size pool, tennis court, extensive woodland trails, Honeybrook Stream, a working organic farm, and classic flower gardens. In addition to five spacious public rooms with fireplaces, the mansion offers antiques, Oriental carpets, artwork, high ceilings, a stunning grand staircase, chandeliers and a serene outdoor terrace. Railroad magnate Alexander Cassatt, brother of Impressionist painter Mary Cassatt, presented this historic house as a wedding present to his daughter. Later occupants included the Brewster family, descendants of Benjamin Franklin, and the Koinonia Foundation, a predecessor of the Peace Corps. The Carriage House and Gramercy Mansion are also available for weddings, meetings, seminars and parties.

**Betsy's Bed & Breakfast**
1428 Park Ave.
410/383-1274

An elegant home in the architecturally significant downtown neighborhood of Bolton Hill, this four-story "petite estate" overlooks a quiet tree-lined street with a brass rail and white marble steps. Inside you will marvel at the high ceilings with medallions, carved marble mantels, and a center staircase that rises to a skylight. Throughout the house, the expansive walls are hung with handsome brass rubbings, family heirloom quilts and coverlets.

## 3 BEL AIR

**Country Schoolhouse Antiques**
1805 E. Churchville Road
410/836-9225

**Back Door Antiques**
106 N. Main St.
410/836-8608

**Antiques Bazaar**
117 N. Main St.
410/836-7872

**Bel Air Antiques, Etc.**
122 N. Main St.
410/838-3515

**Oak Spring Antiques**
1321 Prospect Mill Road
410/879-0942

## 4 BERLIN

**Something Different**
2 S. Main St.
410/641-1152

**Brass Box**
27 N. Main St.
410/641-1858

**Sassafrass Station**
111 N. Main St.
410/641-0979

**Stuart's Antiques**
5 Pitts St.
410/641-0435

**Findings**
104 Pitts St.
410/641-2666

## 5 BETHESDA

### Grapevine of Bethesda

7806 Old Georgetown Road
301/654-8690
Open: Tues.–Sat. 10–5
Directions: Located in downtown Bethesda at the intersection of Old
Georgetown Road, Wilson Lane, Arlington and St. Elmo. Store has
Georgetown entrance and Wilson Lane parking.

Timothy Albrecht has always had a personal interest in antiques and
tableware. He can remember collecting at the age of 10. Tim applied for
a position at the Grapevine at the age of 16 and was turned down. Today,
he owns the store now known as the Grapevine of Bethesda.

The Grapevine of Bethesda consigns and sells antiques, Persian rugs,
and oil paintings. The store specializes in French and Continental
furniture pieces as well as tableware. Most merchandise is dated between
1850 and 1920. You can find anything from place plates to finger bowls
at the Grapevine. You can find most place settings of 12 pieces and the
shop carries English and Continental porcelain. Beautiful oil paintings
can also be bought or consigned here. Many of these paintings can be
researched for history or an auction trail.

The Grapevine has been in existence for 50 years. Past owners had
impeccable qualities of honesty and fairness, traits which are carried on
today. First owned by Linda Gore, a very distant relative of Al Gore, the
shop was located on Brookville Road and then moved to Bethesda. Ms.
Gore owned the business for 23 years before selling to the second owner,

Mrs. Grant. Timothy Albrecht is the third owner and has operated this
highly reputable business for three years.

This unique shop is located on the
corner of Wilson Road and Old
Georgetown Road in the heart of
Bethesda. There is a storefront window
with an entrance at each street side.
Cafe Bethesda, a French cooking
school, is located next door (and is
known as one of the best 50 restaurants
in Washington, D.C.).

Most of the Grapevine's clientele are
individuals interested in fine art or who
spend a lot of time entertaining.
Diplomats, high society, and world
travelers often shop at this reputable
antique store. Many of the Grapevine's
clientele bring pieces for consignment due to liquidation or the
accumulation of fine pieces acquired from a heritage.

The Grapevine of Bethesda is a member of ADAM, Maryland Antique
Association, an affiliate of the Maryland Retail Association. Benefits of
membership in the association, says Mr. Albrecht, are the "opportunities
to share notes with other antique dealers and members, and the advantage
of buying pieces among themselves."

Approximately every two months, the Grapevine of Bethesda hosts a
workshop called "The Art of Entertaining." Clients are invited to listen to
knowledgeable speakers talk on subjects such as Russian porcelain,
English porcelain or style and tableware.

Mr. Albrecht's future goal for his antique business is to fine tune his
collection and services; learn more about his fine collectibles; and to
continue to look for quality merchandise and fine pieces that his clientele
are searching for. His long-term goal is to become a professional appraiser.

When asked what he enjoys most about his business, Mr. Albrecht says
"the interesting people—most of whom are mature, well-traveled
individuals who often have tales to tell of their travels and the pieces they
bring in for consignment." Mr. Albrecht says that "Washington is a
wonderful city, offering a large variety of collectibles and antiques."

Timothy Albrecht loves history and is a collector himself. His interest
and love for collecting is reflected in the fine quality pieces his store offers.

**Cordell Collection Furniture**
4922 Cordell Ave.
301/907-3324

## 6 BETTERTON

### Great Places to Stay

**Lantern Inn**
115 Ericsson Ave.
410/348-5809
Open: Year round
Directions: Off of Maryland 213 between Chestertown and Galena. Turn north on Still Pond Road (Maryland 292) to Betterton's Beach. Left 2 blocks to inn.

The inn was constructed in 1904 and is located in a small Victorian resort town. Thirteen guest rooms reflect the heyday of Betterton when excursion boats brought vacationers from Baltimore and Philadelphia. A large front porch offers relaxation in the beautiful surroundings. The inn is conveniently located near Dixon's Furniture Auction and many fine antique shops.

## 7 BOONSBORO

**Fitz Place**
7 N. Main St.
301/432-2919

**Antique Partners**
23 S. Main St.
301/432-2518

**Auction Square Antiques & Collectibles**
7700 Old National Pike
301/416-2490

## 8 BOWIE

**Bets Antiques & Uniques**
8519 Chestnut Ave.
301/464-1122

**Fabian House**
8519 Chestnut Ave.
301/464-6777

**House of Hegedus**
8521 Chestnut Ave.
301/262-4131

**Welcome House**
8604 Chestnut Ave.
301/262-9844

**Keller's Antiques**
8606 Chestnut Ave.
301/805-9593

**Olde Friends & Memories**
13006 9th St.
301/464-2890

**Treasure House Antiques**
13010 9th St.
301/262-2878

## 9 BRUNSWICK

**Antiques 'n' Ole Stuff**
2 E. Potomac St.
301/834-6795

**Jimmy Jake's Antique Center**
24 W. Potomac St.
301/8334-6814

## 10 BRYANTOWN

### Great Places to Stay

**Shady Oaks of Serenity Bed and Breakfast**
7490 Serenity Dr.
1-800-597-0924 or 301/932-8864
Open: Year-round
Directions: For specific directions to Shady Oaks of Serenity, please call the innkeeper who will provide specific directions from your location.

Shady Oaks of Serenity is a Georgia Colonial Victorian situated on three acres and surrounded by trees. This secluded home is off the beaten path, yet within a 45-minute drive of the nation's capital and Annapolis, Md., home of the U.S. Naval Academy. Just down the road is the Amish country with antiques and unique shops, several historic churches, the renowned Dr. Mudd Home and Gilbert Run Park, a favorite county stop. Also, this retreat may be of interest to small groups of 25 or less for meetings.

Decorated with various themes, each room has a private bath and king-size bed for a peaceful night's rest. Visitors are welcome to gather in the family room, the front porch or enjoy an evening on the deck. Kathy and Gene cordially invite you to be a guest in their home and visit their historic county. The morning brings fresh coffee, homemade muffins or breads and a variety of fresh fruit.

## 11 CAMBRIDGE

Established in 1684 as a port on the Choptank River, Cambridge has a rich history as a shipbuilding center, mill town, Civil War "underground railroad" stop, and internationally known packing and canning center. The historic district reflects the commercial and economic history of the town, with fascinating 18th- and 19th-century Georgian and Federal buildings clustered in the 100 and 200 blocks of High Street. Large mansion houses are located on Mill, Oakley and Locust Streets (many in the Queen Anne and Colonial Revival styles), while rhythmic rows of modest gable-front homes dating from the turn of the century are found along Vue de L'eau, West End, Willis and Choptank Streets. Skipjacks and other sailing vessels are often seen on scenic Cambridge Creek.

**Heirloom Antique Gallery**
419 Academy St.
410/228-8445

**Packing House Antique Mall**
411 Dorchester Ave.
410/221-8544

**Bay Country Antique Co-Op**
415 Dorchester Ave.
410/228-3112

**Jones Antiques**
518 High St.
410/228-1752

**A J's Antiques Mall**
2923 Ocean Gateway
410/221-1505

**Artwell's Mall**
509 Race St.
410/228-0997

**Another Man's Treasure**
114 Belvedere Ave.
410/228-4525

## 12 CHESTERTOWN

The county seat of Kent County was created in 1706 and designated as one of Maryland's official ports in 1707. This river town had grown elegant, prosperous and daring by the 1770s. Residents angry over the Boston Port Act staged their own tea party—in broad daylight—against the British brigantine *Geddes* in 1774. This daring event is reenacted each June as the Chestertown Tea Party. Chestertown is a wonderful place to explore on foot, and visitors may stroll past Federal town houses, Georgian mansions, a stone house supposedly constructed from a ship's ballast and many fine antiques and specialty shops. Chestertown is also home to Washington College, which was chartered in 1782 and named after George Washington with his expressed consent.

| | |
|---|---|
| **Crosspatch** | **Red Shutters** |
| 107 S. Cross St. | 337 High St. |
| 410/778-3253 | 410/778-6434 |
| **Seed House Gallery** | **Childrens Exchange** |
| 860 High St. | 306 Park Row |
| 410/778-2080 | 410/778-1467 |

**Chestertown Antique & Furniture Center**
6612 Churchill Road (Route 213)
410/778-5777

### *Great Places to Stay*

## Brampton
25227 Chestertown Road
410/778-1860
Email: brampton@friendly.net

The Brampton Bed & Breakfast is one of the finest inns on Maryland's Eastern Shore. Built in 1860 as a plantation house, Brampton still retains nearly all of its original details. The 35 acres of grounds that surround Brampton with century-old trees and boxwood plantings provide a quiet, pastoral setting for a peaceful escape. The historic bed & breakfast inn is tucked between the Chester River and the Chesapeake Bay, just one mile south of historic Chestertown. You can pass the time antiquing, shopping, bird watching, crabbing, hunting, fishing and horseback riding, or just relax on one of the front porch swings. All rooms are spacious and well appointed with beautiful period furnishings.

## Inn at Mitchell House
8796 Maryland Pkwy.
410/778-6500

Nestled on ten rolling acres, surrounded by woods and overlooking Stoneybrook Pond, this historic manor house, built in 1743, greets you with warmth and affords a touch of tranquillity. The five-bedroom inn with parlors and numerous fireplaces provides a casual and friendly atmosphere. Depending upon the season, you may be awakened in the morning by birdsong or migrating geese. At sunset, sighting white-tailed deer, red fox, or a glimpse of a soaring eagle add to the scene.

## Lauretum Inn
954 High St.
1-800-742-3236

Lauretum Inn sits atop a tree-graced knoll on six acres in Chestertown. A long, winding lane invites you to the inn and reveals a stunning example of 19th-century Queen Anne Victorian architecture. The original owner, U.S. Senator George Vickers (1801–1879), lovingly built this gracious country manor and called it "Lauretum Place." Lauretum features a delightful screened-in porch, charming rooms, fireplaces, and the pleasant company of other guests.

## 13 COCKEYSVILLE

| | |
|---|---|
| **Cuomo's Interiors & Antiques** | **Abundant Treasures Gallery** |
| 10759 York Road | 10818 York Road |
| 410/628-0422 | 410/666-9797 |
| **Pack Rat** | **Hunt Valley Antiques** |
| 10834 York Road | 10844 York Road |
| 410/683-4812 | 410/628-6869 |
| **Bentley's Antiques Show Mart** | **Alley Shoppes** |
| 10854 York Road | 10856 York Road |
| 410/667-9184 | 410/683-0421 |
| **Decorative Touch** | **Corner Cottage Antiques** |
| 11008 York Road | 11010 York Road |
| 410/527-1075 | 410/527-9535 |

**Kendall's Antique Shop**
3417 Sweet Air Road
410/667-9235

## 14 CUMBERLAND

| | |
|---|---|
| **Historic Cumberland Antique Mall** | **Yesteryear** |
| 55 Baltimore St. | 62 Baltimore St. |
| 301/777-2979 | 301/722-7531 |
| **Ye Olde Shoppe** | **Auntie's Antiques & Collectibles** |
| 315 Virginia Ave. | 328 Virginia Ave. |
| 301/724-3537 | 301/724-3729 |
| **Goodwood Old & Antique Furniture** | **Queen City Collectibles** |
| 329 Virginia Ave. | 28 N. Centre St. |
| 301/777-0422 | 301/724-7392 |

## 15 DAMASCUS

**Appleby's Antiques**
24219 Ridge Road
301/253-6980

**Bea's Antiques**
24140 Ridge Road
301/253-6030

**Flo's Antiques**
28314 Kemptown Road
301/253-3752

## 16 DENTON

**Attic Antiques & Collectibles Mall**
24241 Shore Hwy.
410/479-1889

**Denton Antique Mall**
24690 Meeting House Road
410/479-2200

## 17 EASTON

**Windsor Gallery**
21 Goldsborough St.
410/820-5246

**Camelot Antiques Ltd.**
7871 Ocean Gateway (Route 50)
410/820-4396

**Delmarva Jewelers**
210 Marlboro Ave.
410/822-5398

**Stock Exchange Antq. & Consignment Mall**
8370 Ocean Gateway (Route 50)
410/820-0014

**Chesapeake Antique Center—The Gallery**
29 S. Harrison St.
410/822-5000

**Picket Fence Antiques**
218 N. Washington St.
410/822-3010

**Lanham Merida Antiques & Interiors**
218 N. Washington St.
410/763-8500

**Oxford Antiques & Art Gallery**
21-A N. Harrison St.
410/820-0587

**Tharpe House Antiques & Decorative Arts**
30 S. Washington St.
410/820-7525

**Wings Antiques**
7 N. Harrison St.
410/822-2334

**Wye River Antiques**
23 N. Harrison St.
410/822-3449

**Sullivan's Antique Warehouse**
28272 Saint Michaels Road
410/822-4723

**Foxwell's Antiques & Collectibles**
7793 Ocean Gateway (Route 50)
410/820-9705

**American Pennyroyal**
5 N. Harrison St.
410/822-5030

**Easton Maritime Antiques**
27 S. Harrison St.
410/763-8853

**Kathe & Company**
20 S. Harrison St.
410/820-9153

**Antique Center of Easton**
Ocean Gateway (Route 50)
410/820-5209

**Tabot Antiques**
218 N. Washington St.
410/476-5247

**The Flo-Mir**
23 E. Dover St.
410/822-2857

## Ashby 1663
27448 Ashby Dr.
410/822-4235

Situated on an Eastern Shore peninsula, Ashby 1663 defines tranquillity. The 23-acre waterfront estate features crape myrtle, magnolia, oak and tulip trees. Guests are greeted by sounds of nature including bobwhites, mockingbirds and waterfowl. Each of the guest rooms includes a private bath and may feature a fireplace, whirlpool tub or deck. A full breakfast, evening cocktails and use of the lighted tennis court, heated pool, exercise room, canoe and paddle boat are complimentary.

## Gross' Coate Plantation 1658
11300 Gross Coate Road
1-800-580-0802

Built in 1760 by William Tilghman, Gross' Coate is a unique part of American history. A fine example of Georgian architecture, it is extremely romantic, comfortable, and extraordinarily beautiful. The historic mansion and its dependencies, framed by emerald lawns and immense trees, beckon guests to 18th-century plantation life at its finest. The plantation is located along the scenic banks of the Wye River as it converges with Gross' Creek and Lloyd Creek.

## 18 EDGEWATER

**Rafters Antique Mini-Mall**
1185 Mayo Road
410/798-1204

**Londontown Antiques**
1205 Mayo Road
410/698-6192

## 19 ELLICOTT CITY

Unique and well-preserved, this 19th-century mill town on the Patapsco River has sloping streets and sturdy granite buildings reminiscent of English industrial towns. Ellicott City was a summer destination for Baltimore residents and notable visitors who came by train, including Robert E. Lee and H. L. Mencken. Antiques shops, specialty boutiques and restaurants are abundant in this small town.

**American Military Antiques**
8398 Court Ave.
410/465-6827

**Antique Depot**
3720 Maryland Ave.
410/750-2674

**Halls Antiques & Collectibles**
8026 Main St.
410/418-9444

**Maxine's Antiques & Collectibles**
8116 Main St.
410/461-5910

**A. Caplans Antiques**
8125 Main St.
410/750-7678

**Ellicott's Country Store**
8180 Main St.
410/465-4482

**Cottage Antiques**
8181 Main St.
410/465-1412

**Catonsville Village Antiques**
787 Oella Ave.
410/461-1535

**Rebel Trading Post**
3744 Old Columbia Pike
410/465-9595

**Shops at Ellicott Mills**
8307 Main St.
410/461-8700

**Historic Framing & Collectibles**
8344 Main St.
410/465-0549

**Oella Flea Market**
787 Oella Ave.
410/461-1535

**Wagon Wheel Antique Shop**
8061 Tiber Aly
410/465-7910

## 20 FREDERICK

Antique hunters and history lovers will find much to enjoy in Frederick. The city had a role in the Revolutionary War, War of 1812 and Civil War. Much of the historic district includes businesses and residences in and around the original 1745 city grid, with Market Street the north-south axis and Patrick Street the east-west axis. A wealth of commercial, residential, public and religious structures in the architectural styles spanning two centuries contribute to this historic and culturally significant city.

### Off the Deep End
712 East St.
301/698-9006
Open: Mon.–Sat., 10–7; Sun., 10–6
Directions: *From Washington, D.C.:* From Interstate 270 to Maryland Route 15 N., take 7th St. (East) Exit. Proceed to the stop sign at East St. Take a left onto East St. for ½ block. The shop is located on the right. *From Baltimore:* Interstate 70 W. to Route 15 N. Then proceed as above. *From Pennsylvania:* Maryland Route 15 S. to 7th St. (East) Exit. Then proceed as above.

With over 3,000 square feet of space, a wide array of antique furniture and accessories are on display. Antique toys, collectibles, vintage clothing, plus intriguing '50s memorabilia and "bizarre" items form a part of this massive collection. You will also want to browse through the over 14,000 old and used books in stock.

**Warehouse Antiques**
47 E. All Saints St.
301/663-4778

**Brass & Copper Shop**
13 S. Carroll St.
301/663-4240

**Cannon Hill Place**
111 S. Carroll St.
301/695-9304

**Catoctin Inn & Antiques**
3619 Buckeystown Pike
301/831-8102

**The Consignment Warehouse**
35 S. Carroll St.
301/695-9674

**Carroll St. Mercantile**
124 Carroll St.
301/620/4323

**Gaslight Antiques**
118 E. Church St.
301/663-3717

**Collage Antiques**
7 N. Court St.
301/694-0513

**Eastside Antiques**
221 East St.
301/663-8995

**Antique Galleries**
3 E. Patrick St.
301/631-0922

**J & T Antiques**
29 E. Patrick St.
301/698-1380

**Family's Choice Antiques**
Route 15 & Biggs Ford Road
301/898-5547

**Old Glory Antique Market Place**
5862 Urbana Pike
301/662-9173

**Antique Station**
194 Thomas Johnson Dr.
301/695-0888

**Homeward Bound**
313 E. Church St.
301/631-9094

**Antique Imports**
125 East St.
301/662-6200

**Emporium at Creekside Antiques**
112 E. Patrick St.
301/662-7099

**Carroll Creek Antiques, Etc.**
14 E. Patrick St.
301/663-8574

**Craftworks Antiques**
55 E. Patrick St.
301/662-3111

**Flea Factory**
Route 15 & Biggs Ford Road
301/898-5052

**Frederick's Best**
307 E. 2nd St.
301/698-1791

### *Great Places to Stay*

### The Turning Point Inn
3406 Urbana Pike
301/874-2421 or 301/831-8232
Rates: $75 weekdays, $85 weekends
Open: Year-round

Shaded by four acres of trees and gardens, this exquisite antique-filled bed and breakfast country inn offers a delightful spot for a getaway or special occasion. With five spacious bedrooms having private baths, guests find additional comfort in the large living and dining room. A basket of fruit greets each guest, as well as the full country breakfast. Tuesday–Friday, lunch and dinner is served.

## 21 GAITHERSBURG

**Emporium of Olde Towne**
223 E. Diamond Ave.
301/926-9148

**Becraft Antiques**
405 S. Frederick Ave.
301/926-3000

**Peking Arts, Inc.**
7410 Lindbergh Dr.
301/258-8117

**Old Town Antiques**
223 E. Diamond Ave.
301/926-9490

**Yesteryear Antique Farms, Inc.**
7420 Hawkins Creamery Road
301/948-3979

**Days of Olde Antiques**
710 State Route 3 Northbound
410/987-0397

**Julia's Room**
9001 A Warfield Road
301/869-1410

**Gaitherburg Antiques**
5 N. Summit Ave.
301/670-5870

**Gate House Antiques**
21125 Woodfield Road
301/869-4480

**Griffith House Antiques**
21415 Laytonsville Road
301/926-4155

## 22 GAMBRILLS

**Holly Hill Antiques**
382 Gambrills Road
410/923-1207

**Days of Olde Antiques**
710 Maryland Route 3 N.
410/987-0397

## 23 GLEN BURNIE

**Rosies Past & Present**
7440 Balt Annapolis Blvd.
410/760-5821

**Neatest Little Shop**
7462 Balt Annapolis Blvd.
410/760-3610

**Curiosity Unlimited, Inc.**
7450 Balt Annapolis Blvd.
410/768-8697

**Fourth Crane Antiques**
310 Crain Hwy. S.
410/760-9803

## 24 GRASONVILLE

**Going Home Unique Gift Antiques**
3017 Kent Narrow Way S.
410/827-8556

**Enchanted Lilly**
4601 Main St.
410/827-5935

**Dutch Barn Antiques**
3712 Main St.
410/827-8656

**Eastern Bay Trading Co.**
4917 Main St.
410/827-9286

## 25 HAGERSTOWN

### A & J Antiques
20154 National Pike
301/745-4757
Open: Mon.–Sun. 10–5, closed Wed.

Specializing in advertising as well as offering a general line of antiques and collectibles.

**Halfway Antiques & Collectibles**
11000 Bower Ave.
301/582-4971

**Ravenswood Antique Center**
216 W. Franklin St.
301/739-0145

**Antique Crossroads**
20150 National Pike
301/739-0858

**Beaver Creek Antique Market**
40 East Ave.
301/739-8075

**Country Village of Beaver Creek**
20136 National Pike
301/790-0006

**Country Lanes**
326 Summit Ave.
301/790-1045

### Great Places to Stay

### Beaver Creek House
20432 Beaver Creek Road
301/797-4764

Comfort, relaxation, and hospitality await you at this turn-of-the-century country Victorian home, located in the historic area of Beaver Creek, Md. Choose from five guest rooms, and enjoy a country breakfast served on the spacious wraparound screen porch or in the elegantly appointed dining room. Stroll through the country garden, or linger by the fish pond and gaze at the mountain. Nearby are the National Historic parks of Antietam and Harper's Ferry.

### Lewrene Farm Bed & Breakfast
9738 Downsville Pike
301/582-1735

This authentic 125-acre farm offers lodging in a charming turn-of-the-century farmhouse. The grounds provide a forest to stroll through, a gazebo to relax in, and a platform swing. Local attractions include Antietam Battlefield, Harper's Ferry, Fort Frederick, and the Appalachian Trail. In the winter, skiing is available at the nearby Whitetail Resort.

### Sundays Bed & Breakfast
39 Broadway
1-800-221-4828
Web site: www.sundaysbnb.com

This elegant 1890 Queen Anne Victorian home is situated in the historic north end of Hagerstown. Relax in any of the many public rooms and porches or explore the many historic attractions, antique shops, golf courses, museums, shopping outlets, and ski areas that are nearby. You'll experience special hospitality and many personal touches at Sundays. A full breakfast, afternoon teas and desserts, evening refreshments, fruit baskets, fresh flowers, special toiletries, and late-night cordial and chocolate are just some of the offerings at Sundays.

### Wingrove Manor Inn
635 Oak Hill Ave.
301/797-7769
Web site: www.interaccess.com/wingrovemanor/index.html

The Wingrove Manor is a beautifully restored bed and breakfast minutes from the Antietam Battlefield and Whitetail Ski Resort. Relax in wicker rockers stretched across a large Southern porch surrounded by 23 white columns, ceramic-tile floors, and beauty that is breathtaking. Inside, you will enjoy marble fireplaces, winding staircase, crystal chandeliers, and white towering columns all reflecting the home's lineage.

## 26   HANOVER

### AAA Antiques Mall, Inc.
2659 Annapolis Road
Routes 295 & 175 (between Severn & Jessup)
410/551-4101

Be prepared to spend the day at Maryland's largest antiques mall offering over 58,000 square feet of quality, affordable antiques and collectibles.

You will find plenty of fine furniture from all periods as well as glassware from the brilliant, depression and elegant periods. The mall also offers a fine selection of art glass and pottery. If you are in the market for military, movie, black memorabilia or any number of yesterday's treasures, this is the place to be.

Located only minutes from Baltimore and Washington, AAA Antiques Mall, Inc. offers plenty of free parking and welcomes bus tours (wheelchair accessible — wheelchair on premises). If you need more information or require overnight accommodations, please feel free to call the mall at 410/551-4101.

## 27   HAVRE DE GRACE

**Eclections**
101 N. Washington St.
410/939-4917

**Investment Antiques & Collectibles**
123 Market St.
410/939-1312

**Street's Uniques**
2132 Pulaski Hwy.
410/273-6778

**Wonder Back Antiques**
331 N. Union Ave.
410/939-6511

**Washington Street Books & Antiques**
131 N. Washington St.
410/939-6215

**Franklin St. Antiques & Gifts**
464 Franklin St.
410/939-4220

**Splendor in Brass**
123 Market St.
410/939-1312

**Bank of Memories**
319 Saint John St.
410/939-4343

**Golden Vein**
408 N. Union Ave.
410/939-9595

### Great Places to Stay

### Currier House Bed & Breakfast
800 S. Market St.
1-800-827-2889
Web site: www.currier-bb.com

Currier House is located in the heart of Havre De Grace's historic residential district and overlooks the juncture of the Chesapeake Bay and the Susquehanna River. The original portion of the house that now forms the dining room and an upstairs bedroom and bath dates from the 1790s.

The house was first occupied by the Currier's in 1861. Over the years, the house was enlarged and modernized. Its decor now reflects Havre De Grace's late historical period when the town was a regional recreational center that attracted waterfowl hunters and horsemen who wagered at the local track.

## 28   HYATTSVILLE

**Anna's Antiques & Bits & Pieces**
5312 Baltimore Ave.
301/864-5953

**Maryland Precious Metals**
By appointment only
301/779-3696

**Ellington's**
1401 University Blvd. E.
301/445-1879

## 29   KENSINGTON

**Barrington Antique**
10419 Fawcett St.
301/949-1994

**Jantiques**
10429 Fawcett St.
301/942-0936

**Kensington Station Antiques**
3730 Howard Ave.
301/946-0222

**Pen Haven**
3730 Howard Ave.
301/929-0955

**ABS Consignment & Collectibles**
3734 Howard Ave.
301/946-9646

**Sally Shaffer Interiors**
3742 Howard Ave.
301/933-3740

**Pritchard's**
3748 Howard Ave.
301/942-1661

**Dianes Antiques**
3758 Howard Ave.
301/946-4242

**Antique Scientific Instruments**
3760 Howard Ave.
301/942-0636

**Antiques and Uniques**
3762 Howard Ave.
301/942-3324

**Paul Feng Antiques**
3786 Howard Ave.
301/942-0137

**Phyllis Van Auken Antiques, Inc.**
10425 Fawcett St.
301/933-3772

**James of Kensington**
3706 Howard Ave.
301/933-8843

**Nancy T.**
3730 Howard Ave.
301/942-8446

**Villa Accents**
3730 Howard Ave.
301/942-7944

**Oriental Antiques by Susan Akins**
3740 Howard Ave.
301/946-4609

**Jill Americana & Co.**
3744 Howard Ave.
301/946-7464

**Antique Market II**
3750 Howard Ave.
301/933-4618

**Mariea's Place**
3758 Howard Ave.
301/949-2378

**Kensington Antique Market Center**
3760 Howard Ave.
301/942-4440

**Antique Market**
3762 Howard Ave.
301/949-2318

**European Antiques**
4080A Howard Ave.
301/530-4407

**Ambiance Galleries Ltd.**
4115 Howard Ave.
301/656-1512

**Paris-Kensington**
4119 Howard Ave.
301/897-4963

**Gonzales Antiques**
4130 Howard Ave.
301/564-5940

**Lighting by Estate Gallery Antiques**
4217 Howard Ave.
301/493-4013

**Furniture Mill, Inc.**
4233 Howard Ave.
301/530-1383

**Time Frames**
10408 Montgomery Ave.
301/929-8419

**All Books Considered**
10408 Montgomery Ave.
301/589-2575

**Lionel Buy, Sell, Repair**
3610 University Blvd. W.
301/949-5656

**Sparrows**
4115 Howard Ave.
301/530-0175

**Onslow Square Antiques**
4125-4131 Howard Ave.
301/530-9393

**Great British Pine Mine**
4144 Howard Ave.
301/493-2565

**Chelsea & Co.**
4218 Howard Ave.
301/897-8886

**Victoria Antiques**
4265 Howard Ave.
301/530-4460

**For Cats Sake, Inc.**
10513 Metropolitan Ave.
301/933-5489

**International Parade**
10414 Montgomery Ave.
301/933-1770

**Potomac Trade Post & Antique Guns**
3610 University Blvd. W.
301/949-5656

**Red Barn Antique Shops**
6860 Olney Laytonsville Road
301/926-3053

### 33  LEONARDTOWN

**Maryland Antiques Center**
593 Jefferson St.
301/475-1960

**Antiques on the Square**
337 N. Washington St.
301/475-5826

### 34  MILLERSVILLE

**Arundel Way Antiques**
1004 Cecil Ave.
410/923-2977

**Red Barn Antiques**
241 Najoles Road
410/987-2267

### 35  MOUNT AIRY

**Trading Post Antiques**
13318 Glissans Mill Road
301/829-0561

**Country House**
309 N. Main St.
301/829-2528

### 36  NEW MARKET

Located on the old National Pike, New Market's Main Street was an important stop for 19th-century travelers headed west and for cattle drivers going to the eastern markets. Though the town was laid out in 1788 and patrolled by Confederate forces during the Civil War, it has survived the years well enough to be a largely intact rural town with many early buildings restored for combined use as antiques shops and homes. Unique buildings include the Prosser House, Ramsburg House and Fehr-Schriss House.

**Comus Antiques**
#1 N. Federal St.
301/831-6464

**Before Our Time**
1 W. Main St.
301/831-9203

**Fleshman's Antiques**
2 W. Main St.
410/775-0153

**John Due Antiques**
13 W. Main St.
301/831-9412

**Jo's Antiques**
21 W. Main St.
301/831-3875

**Shaws of New Market**
22 W. Main St.
301/831-6010

**Victorian Jewelry**
33 Main St.
301/865-3083

**Arlene's Antiques**
41 W. Main St.
301/865-5554

**C.W. Wood Books**
42 W. Main St.
301/865-5734

**Glen Moore & Violet**
45 W. Main St.
301/865-3710

**Main Street Antiques**
47 W. Main St.
301/865-3710

**1812 House**
48 W. Main St.
301/865-3040

**Tomorrow's Antiques**
50 W. Main St.
301/831-3590

**Mr. Bob's**
52 W. Main St.
301/831-6712

### 30  KNOXVILLE

**Schoolhouse Antiques**
847 Jefferson Pike
301/620-7470

**Garrett's Mill Antiques**
1331 Weverton Road
301/834-8581

### 31  LAUREL

**Antique Center**
8685 Cherry Lane
301/725-9174

**Dark Horse Antiques Mall**
8687 Cherry Lane
301/953-1815

**Antique Alley**
99 Main St.
301/490-6500

**David's Antiques & Gifts**
353 Main St.
301/776-5636

**Main Street Corner Shoppe, Inc.**
401 Main St.
301/725-3099

**Geary's Antiques**
508 Main St.
301/725-7733

**L & L Antiques & Gifts**
512 Main St.
301/725-7539

**Antique Market**
9770 Washington Blvd. N.
301/953-2674

### 32  LAYTONSVILLE

**Griffith House Antiques**
21415 Laytonsville Road
301/926-4155

**Ludington's Antiques**
21520 Laytonsville Road
301/330-4340

**Browsery Antiques**
55 W. Main St.
301/831-9644

**Thomas Antiques**
60 W. Main St.
301/831-6622

**Antiques Folly**
105 W. Main St.
301/607-6513

**R.P. Brady Antiques**
3 E. Main St.
301/865-3666

**Smith's Tavern Antiques**
Main & Fifth St.
301/865-3597

**Mimi's Antiques**
3 Strawberry Alley
301/865-1644

**Iron Bell**
59 W. Main St.
301/831-9589

**Village Tea Room & Antique Shop**
81 W. Main St.
301/865-3450

**Finch's Antiques**
122 W. Main St.
301/685-3926

**Thirsty Knight Antiques**
9 E. Main St.
301/831-9889

**Rossig's Frame Shop**
1 N. Strawberry Alley
301/865-3319

**Grange Hall Antiques**
1 8th Alley
301/865-5651

### Great Places to Stay

## National Pike Inn
9 W. Main St.
301/865-5055
Open: Year-round

Located on Main Street amid antique shops, this 1796–1804 Federal-style inn offers five guest rooms decorated with individual themes. The large Federal sitting room surrounds guests in comfort. For a private outdoor retreat, step into the enclosed courtyard. The Colonial dining room is the location for the hearty morning breakfast. Create a memory in New Market.

## 37   NORTH EAST

**JB's Collectibles**
32 S. Main St.
410/287-0400

### Great Places to Stay

## The Mill House
102 Mill Lane
410/287-3532
Open: Year round

A tidal creek authenticates the early-1700s Mill House, which is filled with antique furnishings. Guests can take strolls through the spacious lawn, or settle back before the crackling fire in the parlor. Also, antique shops and restaurants are within an easy walk.

## 38   OCEAN CITY

**Bookshelf, Etc.**
8006 Coastal Hwy.
410/524-2949

**GG's Antiques**
9 Somerset St.
410/289-2345

**Edgemoor Antiques**
10009 Silver Point Lane
410/213-2900

**Brass Cannon**
204 S. Saint Louis Ave.
410/289-3440

### Great Places to Stay

## Inn on the Ocean
10th St. and the Ocean
1001 Atlantic Ave.
1-888-226-6223

Inn on the Ocean is a perfect blend of elegance, hospitality and quiet graciousness. All rooms are magnificently decorated for luxury and comfort. From the wraparound oceanfront veranda you can watch the waves and world go by. In winter, a fireplace welcomes you in the living room. Expanded continental breakfast, afternoon refreshments, bicycles, beach equipment and health-club facilities are complimentary.

## 39   OLNEY

**Briars Antiques**
4121 Briars Road
301/774-3596

**Hyatt House Antiques**
16644 Georgia Ave.
301/774-1932

**Liz Vilas Antiques**
16650 Georgia Ave.
301/924-0354

**Barry Rogers**
16650 Georgia Ave.
301/570-0779

**Olney Antique Village**
16650 Georgia Ave.
301/570-9370

**Jimmy's Village Barn**
16650 Georgia Ave.
301/570-6489

**Nicco's Antiques**
16650 Georgia Ave.
301/924-3745

## 40   OXFORD

**Americana Antiques**
111 S. Morris St.
410/226-5677

**Donald D. Donahue, Sr.**
111 S. Morris St.
410/226-5779

**Vintage Shop**
202 S. Morris St.
410/226-5712

**Anchorage House Antiques**
Oxford Road
410/822-8978

**Oxford Salvage Co.**
301 Tilghman St.
410/226-5971

## 41 PRESTON

### Country Treasures
208 Main St.
410/673-2603
Open: Mon.–Sun. 10–5

George and Carol Meakin have been professional antique dealers for several years, presenting their unique country antiques at major antique shows as well as in their fabulous shop. If you are into country antiques this is the shop for you. Painted finishes are their speciality. Additionally, the shop offers a variety of architectural elements to blend with your country or formal motif. I highly recommend shopping with George and Carol.

## 42 REISTERSTOWN

**Curiosity Shoppes**
17 Hanover Road
410/833-3434

**Now 'n' Then**
208 Main St.
410/833-3665

**New England Carriage House**
218 Main St.
410/833-4019

**Derby Antiques**
222 Main St.
410/526-6678

**Relics of Olde**
222 Main St.
410/833-3667

**Things You Love Antiques**
234 Main St.
410/833-5019

**Margie's Antiques & Dolls**
237 Main St.
410/526-5656

**Tina's Antiques & Jewelry**
237 Main St.
410/833-9337

## 43 ROYAL OAK

**Bellevue Store**
5592 Poplar Lane
410/745-5282

**Oak Creek Sales**
25939 Royal Oak
410/745-3193

## 44 SALISBURY

**Henrietta's Attic**
205 Maryland Ave.
410/546-3700

**Springhill Antiques**
2704 Merritt Mill Road
410/546-0675

**Peddlers Three**
Old Quantico Road
410/749-1141

**Holly Ridge Antiques**
1411 S. Salisbury Blvd.
410/742-4392

## 45 SEVERNA PARK

**Antiques in the Park**
540 Balto Anap Blvd.
410/544-2762

**Taylor Antiques**
557 Balton Anap Blvd.
410/647-1701

**Memory Post Antique Boutique**
Riggs Ave.
410/315-9610

**Anatiue's Market Place**
4 Riggs Ave.
410/544-9644

**Adair & Halligan**
5 Riggs Ave.
410/647-0103

## 46 ST. MICHAELS

St. Michaels began in 1778 as a planned development backed by a Liverpool merchant firm, and was small but firmly established by the end of the Revolutionary War. Surrounded by tributaries of the Chesapeake Bay, St. Michaels is a delightful waterfront town and easy to explore on foot. Historic buildings span a period of two centuries, with many Federal-period houses built in the early 19th century, including the Cannonball House, the Old Inn and the Kemp House. Many restaurants, specialty shops, bed and breakfasts, and inns welcome visitors to the town. The harbor has been developed into a marina, but commercial watermen also use it, as they have for generations.

**Freedom House Antiques**
121 A S. Fremont St.
410/745-6140

**Hodgepodge**
308 S. Talbot St.
410/745-3062

**Nina Lanham Ayres Antiques**
401 S. Talbot St.
410/745-5231

**Sentimental Journey Antiques**
402 Talbot St.
410/745-9556

**Pennywhistle Antiques**
408 S. Talbot St.
410/745-9771

**Saltbox Antiques**
310 S. Talbot St.
410/745-3569

### *Great Places to Stay*

### Wades Point Inn on the Bay
Wades Point Road
1-888-923-3466
Web site: www.wadespoint.com

This country bed and breakfast inn overlooking Chesapeake Bay is ideal for those seeking country serenity and the splendor of the bay. All rooms enjoy a water view. The inn's 120 acres of fields and woodland, a dock for fishing and crabbing, and the ever-changing view of boats, birds and water lapping the shoreline provide a peaceful setting for relaxation and recreation. Interesting shops and fine dining, the famed Chesapeake Bay Maritime Museum and other attractions are nearby.

## 47 SYKESVILLE

**Alexandra's Attic**
7542 Main St.
410/549-3095

**All Through the House**
7540 Main St.
410/795-6577

**Village Antique Shoppe**
7543 Main St.
410/795-0556

**Clocks & Collectibles**
7311 Springfield Ave.
410/549-1147

**TLC Creations**
7615 Main St.
410/549-1425

**Yesterday Once More**
6251 Sykesville Road
410/549-0212

## 48 TANEYTOWN

**Margaret J. Maas**
202 E. Baltimore St.
410/756-2480

## 49 WALDORF

**Country Connection**
2784 Old Washington Road
301/843-1553

**Heritage Designs**
3131 Old Washington Road
301/932-7379

**Madatic's Attic**
3141 Old Washington Road
301/645-6076

## 50 WASHINGTON, D.C.

### Amaryllis Vintage Company, Inc.

4922 Wisconsin Ave.
202/244-2211
Open: Daily 11–7
Directions: Traveling I-495, take Exit 33. Travel south on Connecticut Ave. to Fessenden St. (approximately 3 1/2 miles). Turn right on Fessenden. Go to Wisconsin Ave., turn left on Wisconsin, the shop is 1/2 block on the right.

With pieces from the 1840s to 1940s, this shop carries furniture and accessories. The most popular furnishing styles include Empire, Mission and Art Deco. Mirrors, lamps, rugs, paintings and jewelry add to the selection. Bridal registry, gift certificates, and local delivery are available. A 90-day-same-as-cash credit line can be established for qualified applicants.

### Dunnan's, Inc.

3209 O St. N.W.
202/965-1614
Open: Daily 11–4
Directions: Located in historic Georgetown off Wisconsin Ave.

With hundreds of antique items and accessories, this historic Georgetown shop offers a wide selection and variety. Furniture, lamps, memorabilia, advertising, in addition to jewelry, collectibles and art, make up the eclectic array of wares. Inventory varies as a result of frequent deliveries.

**Antiques on the Hill**
701 N. Carolina Ave. S.E.
202/543-1819

**Tiny Jewel Box**
1147 Connecticut Ave. N.W.
202/393-2747

**Antiques Anonymous**
2627 Connecticut Ave. N.W.
202/332-5555

**Mission Possible**
5516 Connecticut Ave. N.W.
202/363-6897

**Mom & Pop Antiques**
3534 Georgia Ave. N.W.
202/722-0719

**Dalton Brody Ltd.**
3412 Idaho Ave. N.W.
202/244-7197

**Logan's Antiques**
3118 Mount Pleasant St. N.W.
202/483-2428

**Two Lions Antiques**
621 Pennyslvania Ave. S.E.
202/546-5466

**Justine Mehlman Antiques**
2824 Pennsylvania Ave. N.W.
202/337-0613

**Rooms & Gardens**
3677 Upton St. N.W.
202/362-3777

**Proud American (Georgetown)**
1529 Wisconsin Ave. N.W.
202/625-1776

**Julie Walters Antiques**
1657 Wisconsin Ave. N.W.
202/625-6727

**Rooms with a View**
1661 Wisconsin Ave. N.
202/625-0610

**Blair House Antiques**
1663 Wisconsin Ave. N.W.
202/338-5349

**VIP Antiques**
1665 Wisconsin Ave. N.W.
202/965-0700

**China Gallery & Gifts**
2200 Wisconsin Ave. N.W.
202/342-1899

**Consignment Galleries**
3226 Wisconsin Ave. N.W.
202/364-8995

**Amaryllis Vintage Co., Inc.**
4922 Wisconsin Ave. N.W.
202/244-2211

**Chevy Chase Antique Center**
5215 Wisconsin Ave. N.W.
202/364-4600

**Antiques & Gifts Boutique**
5300 Wisconsin Ave. N.W.
202/237-2060

**Ruff & Ready Furnishings**
1908 14th St. N.W.
202/667-7833

**Brass Knob**
2311 18th St. N.W.
202/332-3370

**Retrospective, Inc.**
2324 18th St. N.W.
202/483-8112

**Uniform**
2407 18th St. N.W.
202/483-4577

**Cherishables**
1608 20th St. N.W.
202/785-4087

**Old Print Gallery, Inc.**
1220 31st St. N.W.
202/965-1818

**Adam A. Weschler & Son**
909 E St. N.W.
202/628-1281

**Janis Aldrige, Inc.**
2900 M St. N.W.
202/338-7710

**Cherub Antiques Gallery**
2918 M St. N.W.
202/337-2224

**Susquehanna Antiques Co., Inc.**
3216 O St. N.W.
202/333-1511

**Kelsey's Kupboard**
3003 P St. N.W.
202/298-8237

**Adams Davidson Galleries, Inc.**
By appointment only
202/965-3800

**Washington Doll House & Toy Mus.**
5236 44th St. N.W.
202/363-6400

**Antique Textile Resource**
1730 K St. N.W., Suite 317
202/293-1731

**Frank Milwee**
2912 M St. N.W.
202/333-4811

**Michael Gett's Antiques**
2918 M St. N.W. (Georgetown)
202/338-3811

**Second Store Books & Antiques**
2000 P St. N.W.
202/659-8884

**Affrica**
2010 R St. N.W.
202/745-7272

### Great Places to Stay

## Morris-Clark Inn

1015 L St., N.W.
202/898-1200
Rates $115–$185
Year-round accommodations

Built in 1864 and the only area inn listed independently in the National Register of Historic Places, it originally stood as two detached Victorian mansions. One presents an ornate Chippendale porch topped by a mansard roof. 1980s restoration united the structures creating an elegant small hotel. Original interior features include 12-foot-high mahogany-framed mirrors and elaborately carved marble fireplaces. All rooms offer Victorian, neoclassical, or country decor. *Gourmet* has featured the inn's well-respected restaurant.

## Adams Inn

1744 Lanier Place, N.W.
202/745-3600
Year-round accommodations

This three-story townhouse built in 1908 nestles among antique shops in the surrounding blocks. Guest rooms have individual and distinctive home-style furnishings and accessories. Public rooms include breakfast room, parlor, and television lounge. A seat amid the flowers of the garden patio, or taking in the view from the front porch, enhance each stay. Refreshments are complimentary.

### Interesting Side Trips

## Washington Dolls' House & Toy Museum

5236 44th St. N.W.
202/244-0024
Open: Tues.–Sat. 10–5; Sun. 12–5
Directions: One block west of Wisconsin Avenue between Jenifer and Harrison Streets.

The Washington Dolls' House and Toy Museum began as a private collection belonging to doll-house historian Flora Gill Jacobs. Her extensive antique collection of doll houses, toys and games were researched and dated; all are representative of either the architecture, decorative arts, or social history of the time of their creation.

### 51 WESTMINSTER

**Seven East Main St.**
7 E. Main St.
410/840-9123

**White's Bicycles**
10 W. Main St.
410/848-3440

**Westminster Antique Mall**
433 Hahn Road
410/857-4044

**Locust Wines & Antiques**
10 E. Main St.
410/876-8680

**Ain't That a Frame**
31 W. Main St.
410/876-3096

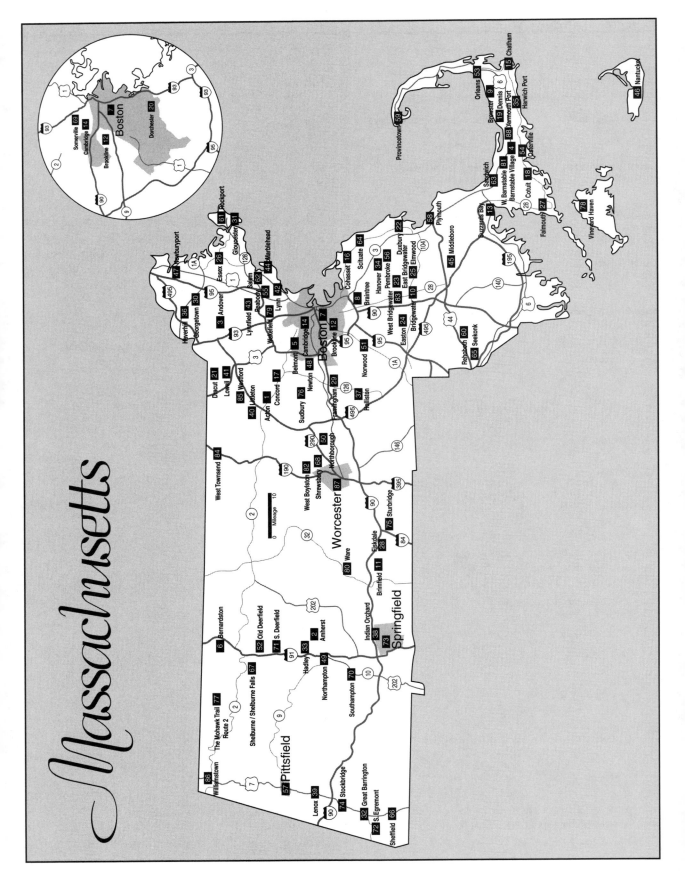

# *Massachusetts*

## 1 ACTON

**Seagull Antiques**
481 Great Road
978/263-8260

**Encores Antiques**
174 Great Road
978/263-1515

## 2 AMHERST

### Black Walnut Inn

1184 N. Pleasant St.
413/549-5649
Fax: 413/549-5149
Open: Year-round
Rates: $95–$125
Directions: *Traveling north on I-91:* Take Exit 19 (Amherst) onto
Route 9 East. Go 4 ⁶/₁₀ miles and turn left (Staples will be on your
right) onto Route 116 North. Go 3 miles to the first traffic light and
turn right onto Route 63 (Meadow Street). The next light is North
Pleasant St. and Black Walnut Inn is the brick house on the right.
*Traveling south on I-91:* Take Exit 24, turn right onto Route 5;
continue for 1 mile. Turn left on Route 116 South for 6 miles. Turn left
at the first Amherst light onto Route 63 (Meadow Street). The next
light is North Pleasant Street and Black Walnut Inn is on the right.

The Black Walnut Inn, a stately 1821 Federal-style brick house shaded
by tall black walnut trees, stands on the corner of North Pleasant and
Meadow Streets in Amherst, just a few minutes from the campuses of
Amherst College and the University of Massachusetts. Although the double
doors, crowned with a large fan window, give the house an imposing
facade, inside you'll find coziness and comfort. Each guest room is
furnished with a mix of antiques and period-piece reproductions, all
distinctive in size, furnishings, and history. Touches like the turn-of-the-
century mulberry color chosen for the Mulberry Room, cherry Windsor-
style and sleigh beds, antique dressing tables, a spinning wheel, a cast-
iron canopy bed, original wood wainscotting, exposed post and beam
and fine wood floors all add rich, historical detail to an already historic
house. A full breakfast, including homemade muffins and jams and fresh
squeezed orange juice is genially served by hosts Edd and Marie Twohig,
who also offer guests tea, coffee and goodies from 2–8 p.m. on request.
The barn that goes with the Black Walnut Inn is the last one in western
Massachusetts of the scientific agricultural design.

**Kay Baker's Antiques**
233 N. Pleasant St.
413/549-4433

**Main St. Antiques & Books**
321 Main St.
413/256-0900

**Grist Mill Antiques**
Route 116 — S. Amherst
413/253-5296

**Amherst Glass & Antiques**
754 Main St.
413/253-9574

**Amherst Antiques Center**
308 College St.
413/253-1995

## 3 ANDOVER

**Andover Antiques, Inc.**
89 N. Main St.
978/475-4242

**Rose Cottage Antiques**
68 Park St.
978/475-6214

**Necessities**
185 N. Main St.
978/475-7992

**Bider's Antiques**
6 Park St.
978/475-8336

**Limoges Antiques**
20 Post Office Ave.
978/470-8773

**Collen's**
68 Park St.
978/474-8983

**New England Gallery, Inc.**
350 N. Main St.
508/475-2116

## 4 BARNSTABLE VILLAGE

### Beech Wood

2839 Main St., Route 6A
1-800-609-6618 or 508/362-6618
Email: bwdinn@virtualcapecod.com
Web site: www.virtualcapecod.com/market/beechwood/
Directions: For specific directions to Beech Wood, please call the
innkeepers who will be happy to provide directions from your location.

Sometimes you dream about getting away from it all—whiling away
a summer afternoon with a glass of lemonade out on the porch, or
relaxing in front of the fireplace with a mug of hot chocolate. Beech
Wood is the place where these
fantasies become reality.

A tall hedge shields the gabled-
roofed Victorian from Main Street,
making it a peaceful respite. Two
sprawling beech trees embrace the
grounds, and a wide porch wraps
around three sides of the house; a perfect spot for lounging, or even
making friends with the resident golden retrievers, Hobbes and Star.

Innkeepers Debbie and Ken Taugot have made sure that the inn is as
comfortable as it is pretty. The seven guest rooms are each strikingly
different, from the elegant Rose Room with its canopy bed and fireplace,
to the airy Lilac Room with its claw-foot bathtub, to the cozy third-floor
Garrent Room with its brass bed.

If you want to find out a bit more about the Cape Cod area on your
visit, head down to the inn's parlor, where you will find an ample guide
to local restaurants, information on sightseeing, and able advice from
Debbie and Ken. There's plenty to do in Barnstable, but the highlight is
really antiquing. There are dozens of shops, craft stores, and the like just
a stone's throw away from Beech Wood.

If you'd rather stay put, play croquet or badminton on Beech Wood's
broad lawn or treat yourself to a few quiet moments on the porch swing.

But before you decide, don't forget about breakfast. Each morning, guests are served a bountiful breakfast in the dining room. Start with muffins or breads, followed by fresh fruit and a hearty entree.

It is here that guests gather for spirited conversation, to plan their days, or just slowly ease into the morning. And midday brings a respite of afternoon tea, with beverages and treats the civilized way. Beech Wood will feel like your home away from home.

**Esprit Decor**
3941 Main St. (Route 6A)
508/362-2480

**Harden Studios**
3264 Main St. (Route 6A)
508/362-7771

**Salt & Chestnut**
651 Main St. (Route 6A)
503/362-6085

**Village Antiques**
3267 Main St. (Route 6A)
508/362-6633

## 5 BELMONT

**Fancy That**
4 Trapelo Road
617/489-3497

**Cross & Griffin**
468 Trapelo Road
617/484-2837

**Antiques by Olde Mystic**
367 Trapelo Road
617/489-4147

**In Place**
3 Bartlett Ave.
617/489-4161

**Belmont Antique Exchange**
243 Belmont St., #A
617/484-9839

**As Time Goes By**
97 Trapelo Road
617/489-3212

**Consignment, Etc.**
352 Trapelo Road
617/489-4077

## 6 BERNARDSTON

**Carriage Barn Antiques**
Route 5, 727 Brattleboro Road
413/648-9406

## 7 BOSTON

**Devonia Antiques**
43 Charles St.
617/523-8313

**George Gravert Antique**
122 Charles St.
617/227-1593

**Bradstreet's Antiquarins**
51 Charles St.
617/723-3660

**Regency Antiques**
70 Charles St.
617/742-3111

**Eugene Galleries**
76 Charles St.
617/227-3062

**Antiques at 80 Charles**
80 Charles St.
617/742-8006

**Elegant Findings Antiques**
89 Charles St.
617/973-4844

**Upstairs Downstairs Antiques**
93 Charles St.
617/367-1950

**Towne & Country Home**
99B Charles St.
617/742-9120

**Antiques at 99 Charles**
99A Charles St.
617/367-8088

**Boston Antique Co-op I**
119 Charles St.
617/227-9810

**Boston Antique Co-op II**
119 Charles St.
617/227-9811

**Marika's Antique Shop**
130 Charles St.
617/523-4520

**Danish Country**
138 Charles St.
617/227-1804

**Stephen Score**
73 Chestnut St.
617/227-9192

**Charles River St. Antiques**
45 River St.
617/367-3244

**Buddenbrooks Fine & Rare Books**
31 Newbury St.
617/536-4433

**Small Pleasures**
142 Newbury St.
617/267-7371

**Marcoz Antiques**
177 Newbury St.
617/262-0780

**Nostalgia Factory**
51 N. Margin St.
617/236-8754

**Autrefois Antiques**
125 Newbury St.
617/424-8823

**Gallagher-Christopher Antiques**
84 Chestnut St.
617/523-1992

**Newbury St. Jewelry & Antiques**
255 Newbury St.
617/236-0038

**Brookline Village Antiques**
1 Design Center Place, Suite 325
617/734-6071

**Akin Lighting Company**
28 Charles St.
617/523-1331

**Streamline Antiques**
1162 Washington St.
617/298-3326

**Commonwealth Antiques**
121 Charles St.
617/720-1605

**Alberts-Langdon, Inc.**
126 Charles St.
617/523-5954

**Antiques on Tremont**
550 Tremont St.
617/451-3329

**Camden Co.**
211 Berkeley St.
617/421-9899

**Cameron Adams Antiques**
37 River St.
617/725-1833

**Comeno's Fine Arts**
9 Newbury St., #2
671/262-9365

**Cove Hollow Antiques**
138 St. James Ave.
617/266-7850

**David L. O'Neal Antiquarian**
234 Clarendon St.
617/266-5790

**Howard Chadwick**
40 River St.
617/227-9261

**Hyacinth's**
91 Charles St.
617/367-0917

**India Antiques & Musical Instruments**
279 Newbury St.
617/266-6539

**Jerry Freeman, Ltd.**
211 Berkleley St.
617/236-4945

**JMW Gallery**
144 Lincoln St.
617/338-9097

**Lannan Ship Model Gallery**
540 Atlantic Ave.
617/451-2650

**Machine-Age Corp.**
354 Congress St.
617/482-0048

**Polly Latham Antiques**
96 Charles St.
617/723-7009

**Shreve Crump & Low Co.**
330 Boylston St.
617/267-9100

**Newbury Galleries**
18 Arlington St.
617/437-0822

**S. W. Alan Antiques**
131 Charles St.
617/720-7808

**Twentieth Century Ltd.**
73 Charles St.
617/742-1031

### *Great Places to Eat*

## No Name Restaurant
15 ½ Fish Pier
617/338-7539

It's places like No Name Restaurant that you look for in every city you visit. Because you know that not only will you have a delightful dining experience, but the trip and the atmosphere alone will create memories that bear retelling over and over. No Name is the name. There is no sign outside; none is needed. It started years ago as a luncheonette with a counter and a few tables, strictly for wharf workers. But word got around about its inexpensive, simple, fresh seafood, and No Name expanded. There is still a dingy luncheonette counter for single diners, but most tourists are seated in the new, paneled dining room with nautical decor and harbor view. Tables are crowded and communal. Customers yell out their orders, and waiters yell back and practically toss food from the kitchen. Start with the fish chowder—nothing but fish! Main course choices are scrod, sole, bluefish, scallops, clams or salmon. Side orders are homemade tartar sauce and fresh-cut slaw with a light, milky dressing. For dessert there's strawberry-rhubarb or blueberry pie, plain or a la mode. Very straightforward, very New England!

### 8 BRAINTREE

**Second Thoughts Antiques**
871 Washington St.
781/849-6750

**Antiques & Things**
826 Washington St.
781/843-4196

**Out of the Wood**
230 Quincy Ave.
781/356-5030

### 9 BREWSTER

**William Baxter Antiques**
3439 Main St.
508/896-3998

**Monomoy Antiques**
3425 Route 6A
508/896-6570

**Pflock's Antiques**
598 Main St.
508/896-3457

**Heirloom Antiques**
2660 Main St.
508/896-2080

**Mark Lawrence**
1050 Main St.
508/896-8381

**Gaskill Antiques**
134 Main St.
508/385-6663

**Breton House Antiques**
1222 Stoney Brook Road
508/896-3974

**Donald B. Howes Antiques**
1424 Main St.
508/896-3502

**Homestead Antiques**
2257 Main St. (Route 6A)
508/896-2917

**Pink Cadillac Antiques**
3140 Main St. (Route 6A)
508/896-4651

**Shirley Smith & Friends**
2926 Main St. (Route 6A)
508/896-4632

**Kings Way Books & Antiques**
774 Main St. (Route 6A)
508/896-3639

**Eve's Place**
564 Main St.
508/896-4914

**Barbara Grant Antiques & Books**
1793 Main St.
508/896-7198

**Kingsland Manor Antiques**
440 Main St.
508/385-9741

**Huckleberry's Antiques**
2271 Main St. (Route 6A)
508/896-2670

**Punkhorn Bookshop**
672 Main St. (Route 6A)
508/896-2114

### 10 BRIDGEWATER

**Antiques Etc.**
1278 Bedford St.
508/697-3005

**Fond Memories**
34 Central Square
508/697-5622

**Harvest Hill Antiques**
450 Plymouth St.
508/697-7160

**Pandora's Box**
10 Broad St.
508/697-8185

**Central Market**
27 Central Square
508/697-2121

**Hidden Treasures**
50 Central Square
508/697-2828

**Old Dutch Cottage**
1 Broad St.
508/697-1586

**Hatfield House Antiques**
136 Birch St.
508/697-5869

### 11 BRIMFIELD

## Brimfield Antiques & Collectibles Show
The Granddaddy of Them All!
May, July, September
Call 413/245-9329 for dates

The Brimfield "Strip" is a quarter of a mile long — and what a piece of land it is! All adjacent to one another are 23 major fields offering both antique and collectible buyers the opportunity to select millions of items from any style and period. It's the only place on earth where you can find both the familiar and unfamiliar in gizmos and gadgets, furniture, folk art, pottery, war memorabilia, garden decor, graniteware, books, toys, scores of glassware and other stuff! This monumental phenomenon started as a small show of about 60 to 75 dealers in 1959. Within a few short years it had grown to become the largest antique and collectible show in the world. And it certainly is not uncommon to find folks from around the world at Brimfield. Antiquers from countries such as Germany, England, Australia, and Canada (just to name a few) are seen throughout the week examining and purchasing the wonderful wares.

If you are a serious antiquer who loves the thrill of the hunt you must make plans to attend the Brimfield shows.

Submitted by Bob Brown
Author of *Brimfield: The Collector's Paradise*

**Sturbridge Road Antiques**
109 Sturbridge Road
413/245-6649

## 12 BROOKLINE

**Turnip & Brig's**
313 Washington St.
617/232-9693

**Erinn's Antiques**
185 Corey Road
617/734-4522

**Autrefois Antiques**
130 Harvard St.
617/566-0113

**Antique Company**
311 Washington St.
617/738-9476

**Cypress Trading Post**
146 Cypress St.
617/566-5412

**Gurari Antique Prints**
91 Marion St.
617/864-0404

**Vintage Jewelry, Gifts, Antiques**
1382 Beacon St., #B
617/739-3265

## 13 BUZZARDS BAY

**Heirlooms Etc.**
95A Main St.
508/759-1455

**Grey Goose**
95C Main St.
508/759-3055

**Brier Rose Antiques**
95B Main St.
508/759-5588

**Lost Engine Antiques**
14 Allston
617/254-4678

**Antiquers III**
171 Harvard St., #A
617/738-5555

**A Room with a Vieux Antiques**
200 Washington St.
617/277-2700

**Appleton Antique Lighting**
195 Harvard St.
617/566-5322

**Dreaming of Vieux**
214 Washington St.
617/277-6200

**Towne Antiques**
256 Washington St.
617/731-3326

**Almost Antiques**
89 Main St.
508/759-2111

**Marketplace**
61 Main St.
508/759-2114

## 14 CAMBRIDGE

**European Country Antiques**
146 Huron Ave.
617/876-7485

**James & Devon Booksellers**
12 Arrow St.
617/868-0752

**Cambridge Antique Market**
201 Monsignor O'Brien Hwy.
617/868-9655

**Harvard Antiques**
1654 Massachusetts Ave.
617/354-5544

**City Lights Antique Lighting**
2226 Massachusetts Ave.
617/547-1490

**Antiques on Cambridge Street**
1076 Cambridge St.
617/234-0001

**Hurst Gallery**
53 Mount Auburn St.
617/491-6888

## 15 CHATHAM

**Spyglass**
618 Main St.
508/945-9686

**Agnes of Cape Cod**
Balfour Lane 17C
508/945-4099

**Aquitain Antiques**
35 Cross St.
508/945-9746

**Archer Antiques**
595 Main St.
508/945-7500

**Bayberry Antiques**
300 Orleans Road (Route 28)
508/945-9060

**House on the Hill Antiques**
17 Seaview St. (at Main St.)
508/945-2290

## 16 COHASSET

**3 A Antiques Center**
130 Chief Justice Cushing Hwy.
781/383-9411

**Easy Chairs**
375 Huron Ave.
617/491-2131

**Penny Scale Antiques**
1353 Cambridge St.
617/576-6558

**Sadye & Co.**
182 Massachusetts Ave.
617/547-4424

**Offshore Trading Co.**
1695 Massachusetts Ave.
617/491-8439

**All & Everything**
2269 Massachusetts Ave.
617/354-8641

**Consignment Galleries**
2040 Massachusetts Ave.
617/354-4408

**Justin Tyme**
91 River St.
617/491-1088

**Amazing Lace**
726 Main St.
508/945-4023

**Carol's Antiques & Collectibles**
1278 Main St.
508/945-1705

**Rose Cottage Antiques**
1281 Main St.
508/945-3114

**Bob's Antiques**
1589 Main St.
508/945-4606

**Chatham Antiques**
1409 Main St. (Route 28)
508/945-1660

**1736 House Antiques**
1731 Main St. (Route 28)
508/945-5690

**Victoria's by the Sea**
87 Elm St.
781/383-2087

# Massachusetts

**Reflections**
808 Jerusaleum Road
781/383-6465

**Green Gage Plum**
819 Chief Justice Cushing Hwy.
781/383-1778

**Carousel Antiques**
93 Ripley Road
781/383-9654

## 17 CONCORD

**Upstairs Antiques**
23 Walden St.
978/371-9095

**North Bridge Antiques**
45 Walden St.
978/371-1442

**Soft Antiques**
1/2 Main St.
978/369-8870

## 18 COTUIT

**Acorn Acres Antiques**
4339 Route 28
508/428-3787

**Remember When**
4015 Route 28 Falmouth Road
508/428-5650

**Antiques of Tomorrow**
45 Main St.
508/428-6262

**Isaiah Thomas Books & Prints**
4632 Route 28
508/428-2752

## 19 DENNIS/DENNISPORT

## Main Street Antique Center

691 Route 28 (Dennisport)
508/760-5700
Directions: To reach this truly unique shop on the Cape take Route 6 to Exit 9 (Route 134), proceed south on Route 134 and go 2 miles to Route 28. Turn left on Route 28, go 1 3/10 miles.

Main Street Antique Center is located in the heart of Dennisport Village on old Cape Cod. The perfect setting for selling antiques, Richard or Vince (the shopkeepers) are always on hand to help with any questions you might have regarding their full line of antiques and collectibles.

In the beginning, Main Street Antiques was a moderate-size shop of 50 dealers, mostly exhibiting in cases. In 1997 the shop moved next door

**Lilac House Antiques**
26 S. Main
781/383-2598

**Cohasset Antiques**
Route 3A
781/383-6605

**Country House Antiques**
818 Chief Justice Cushing Hwy.
781/383-1832

**Ford Crawford Antiques**
1/2 Main St.
978/369-8870

**Concord Antiques**
32 Main St. D/Stairs
978/369-8218

**Sow's Ear Antique Co.**
4698 Route 28 & 130
508/428-4931

**Cotuit Antiques**
4404 Route 28 Falmouth Road
508/420-1234

**1849 House**
809 Main St.
508/428-2258

**Paper Junction**
215 Main St.
508/428-8061

to a larger building increasing to 126 dealers from eight states. Americana to interesting smalls can be found in the spacious new area. All merchandise is beautifully presented, focusing on quality and diversity. Conveniently located along Route 28, the shop is easy to get to from Route 6 and Route 134. Additional antique shops are located nearby.

**Red Lion Antiques**
601 Main St.
508/385-4783

**Antiques 608**
608 Main St.
508/385-2755

**Johanna**
606 Main St.
508/385-7675

**Audrey's Antiques**
766 Main St. (Route 6A)
508/385-4996

**Gloria Swanson Antiques**
632 B Main St.
508/385-4166

**Second Hand Rose**
668 Main St. (Dennisport)
508/394-6620

**Lilac Hedge Antiques & Home Furniture**
620 Main St. (Route 6A)
508/385-0800

**Leslie Curtis Antiques & Design**
838 Main St. (Route 6A)
508/385-2931

**East Dennis Antiques**
1514 Main St. (Route 6A)
508/385-7651

**Recollections**
623 Main St. (Route 6A)
508/385-7504

**Village Peddler Antiques**
601 Main St.
508/385-7300

**Antiques Center of Cape Cod**
243 Main St.
508/385-6400

**Old Town Antiques**
593 Main St.
508/385-5202

**Dovetail Antiques**
543 Main St. (Route 6A)
508-385-2478

**Antiques Center Warehouse**
243 Main St. (Route 6A)
508/385-5133

**Side Door**
103 Main St. (Dennisport)
508/394-7715

**The Cape Cod Galleries**
632 Main St. (Route 6A)
508/385-5436

**Southside Antique Center**
691-A Route 28
508/394-8601

**Webfoot Farm Antiques**
1475 Main St. (Route 6A)
508/385-2334

## 20 DORCHESTER

**Avenue Antiques**
863 Dorchester Ave.
617/265-7100

**Time Traders Antiques**
857 Dorchester Ave.
617/288-9000

**Darkhorse Antiques**
2297 Dorchester Ave.
617/298-1031

**Streamline Antiques**
1162 Washington St.
617/298-3326

# *Massachusetts*

## 21 DRACUT

**James McKenna Antique Clocks**
16 Hovey St.
978/937-8283

## 22 DUXBURY

**Gordon & Genevieve Deming Antiques**
125 Wadsworth Road
781/934-5259

**Wickham Books**
285 Saint George St.
781/934-6955

**Folk Art Antiques**
447 Washington
781/934-7132

**Simon Hill Antiques**
453 Washington St.
781/934-2228

**Duxbury Antiques**
285 St. George St.
781/934-2127

## 23 EAST BRIDGEWATER

**Elmwood Antiques & Country Store**
734 Bedford St.
(Intersection of Routes 106 and 18)
508/378-2063
Open: Tues.–Sat. 11–5, Sun. 12–5
Directions: Travel I-95 to Route 24 South. Take Exit 16, Route 106 East to Route 18. Elmwood Antiques is on the corner of Routes 106 and 18.

A 10-dealer group shop, Elmwood Antiques & Country Store offers mail order service from the U.S. to Europe. They carry a variety of items, including advertising, furniture, glass, china, Royal Doulton, Disney collectibles, toys, trains, dog collectibles, Coca-Cola memorabilia, military items and prints. While visiting, be sure to see their 132-year-old working post office.

**Attic Treasures**
582 West St.
508/378-7510

**Red House Antiques**
355 Bedford St.
No phone # available

**Hartman House Antiques**
334 Bedford St.
508/378-7388

**Antiques at Forge Pond**
35 N. Bedford St.
508/378-3057

**Victorian Gardens & Books**
76 N. Bedford St.
No phone listed

**Ye Olde Tyme Shoppe**
280 N. Bedford St.
508/378-3222

## 24 EASTON

**Barbara Bailey Antiques**
143 Washington St.
508/238-9770

**Orchid Antiques**
593 Turnpike St.
508/238-6146

## 25 ELMWOOD

**Mrs. Swifts & Moore**
741 Bedford St.
508/378-9383

## 26 ESSEX

Essex is a mecca for antiques hunters. But be warned: You'll find it impossible to resist the enticing aroma of fried clams that pervades the main street. Local restaurants pay homage to the tasty bivalve, which was first cooked here.

**White Elephant's Shop**
32 Main St.
978/768-6901

**Chebacco Antiques**
38 Main St.
978/768-7371

**Main Street Antiques**
44 Main St.
978/768-7039

**A.P.H. Waller & Sons**
140 Main St.
978/768-6269

**Ro-Dan Antiques**
67 Main St.
978/768-3322

**Annex Antiques**
69 Main St.
978/768-7704

**Emmons & Martin Antiques**
2 Martin St.
978/768-3292

**Howard's Flying Dragon Antiques**
136 Main St.
978/768-7282

**Westerhoff Antiques**
144 Main St.
978/768-3830

**Neligan & Neligan**
144 Main St.
978/768-3910

**North Hill Antiques**
155 Main St.
978/768-7365

**Ellen Neily Antiques**
157 Main St.
978/768-6436

**L.A. Landry Antiques**
164 Main St.
978/768-6233

**Susan Stella Antiques**
166 Main St.
978-768-6617

**Antiques & Elderly Things**
199 Western Ave.
978/768-6328

**Essex Antiques & Interiors**
235 John Wise Ave.
978/768-7358

**Friendship Antiques**
John Wise Ave.
978/768-7334

**J. E. Rider Antiques**
164 Main St.
978/768-7441

**Joshua's Corner Antiques**
2 Southern Ave.
978/768-7716

**South Essex Antiques**
166 Eastern Ave.
978/768-6373

## 27 FALMOUTH

### Hewins House Bed & Breakfast
20 Hewins St., Village Green
508/457-4363 or 1-800-555-4366
Best time to call is 9–7 daily
Open: Year-round
Directions: Take Route 28 south to Falmouth. Route 28 veers to the left at "Queens Byway" and becomes Main Street Falmouth. Make the left at "Queens Byway." (There is a pillar with a "Keep Right" sign in the middle of the road.) The next right is Hewins St., and Hewins House is right on the corner of Route 28 and Hewins.

Built around 1820 by John Jenkins, a wealthy merchant and sea captain, Hewins House today remains much as it was in the 19th century. The Federal-era building, home of some of Falmouth's most prominent families, features wide pine floors, the original staircase, and a black-and-white floor cloth in the foyer that was made by current owner, Mrs. Albert Price, who also planned the formal gardens and restored a side porch to provide access to the garden area. Within easy walking distance are downtown shopping, restaurants, antique stores, tourist attractions, and a free shuttle that goes to the ferry docks that service Martha's Vineyard.

**The Village Barn**
606 Route 28A
508/540-3215

**Chrisales Country Home**
550 W. Falmouth Hwy.
508/540-5884

**Antiquarium**
204 Palmer Ave.
508/548-1755

**Aurora Borealis Antiques**
104 Palmer Ave.
508/540-3385

**Enseki Antiques**
73 Palmer Ave.
508/548-7744

**Antiques in West Falmouth**
634 Route 28A
508/540-2540

**Beach Rose**
35 N. Main St.
508/548-1012

## 28 FISKDALE

### Commonwealth Cottage
*See Sturbridge #75*

**Faxon's Antique Shows**
60 Mount Dan Road
508/347-3929

## 29 FRAMINGHAM

**Framingham Centre Antiques**
931 Worcester Road (Route 9)
508/620-6252

**Wex Rex Collectibles**
Tropical Isle Plaza (Route 9 E.)
508/620-6181

## 30 GEORGETOWN

**A.F. Scala Antiques**
28 W. Main St.
978/352-8614

**Elmwood Antiques**
22 E. Main St.
978/352-9782

**Sedler's Antique Village**
51 W. Main St.
978/352-8282

**Puddle Duck**
10 E. Main St.
978/352-4655

## 31 GLOUCESTER

**Tally's Trading Post**
108 Eastern Ave.
978/283-8662

**Jer-Rho Antiques**
352 Main St.
978/283-5066

**Salt Island Antiques**
269 Main St.
978/283-2820

**Beauport Antiques**
43 Main St.
978/281-4460

**Main St. Art & Antiques**
124 Main St.
978/281-1531

## 32 GREAT BARRINGTON

### The Coffman's Country Antiques Market
Jennifer House Commons
Stockbridge Road, Route 7
413/528-9282
Open: Daily 10–5
Directions: Located in the southwestern Berkshires, Coffman's is located on Route 7 between Great Barrington and Stockbridge.

A feast for serious, upscale antique lovers, Coffman's Country Antiques Market hosts over 100 quality antique dealers in room settings on three floors. Known for its distinctive, authentic American country antiques, Coffman's handles only merchandise produced before 1949 and only the upper end.

**Elise Abrams Antiques**
11 Stockbridge Road
413/528-3201

**Snyder's Store**
945 Main St.
413/528-1441

**Memories**
306 Main St.
413/528-6380

**Emporium Antique Center**
319 Main St.
413/528-1660

**Le Perigord**
964 S. Main St. (Route 7)
413/528-6777

**Bygone Days**
969 Main St.
413/528-1870

**Reuss Antiques Gallery**
420 Stockbridge Road (Route 7)
413/528-8484

**Red Horse Antiques**
117 State Road
413/528-2637

**Carriage House**
389 Stockbridge Road
413/528-6045

**Paul & Susan Kleinwald, Inc.**
578 S. Main St. (Route 7)
413/528-4252

# Massachusetts

**Donald McGrory Oriental Rugs**
24 Railroad St.
413/528-9594

**The Kahn's Antique & Estate Jewelry**
38 Railroad St.
413/528-9550

**Corashire Antiques**
Route 7 & 23 @ Belcher Square
413/528-0014

**Mullin-Jones Antiquities**
525 S. Main St. (Route 7)
413/528-4871

**The Country Dining Room Antiques**
178 Main St. (Route 7)
413/528-5050

**Reeves Antiques**
420 Stockbridge Road
413/528-5877

## 33 HADLEY

**Hadley Antique Center**
Route 9
413/586-4093

**North Hadley Antiques**
Route 47 - 399 River Dr.
413/549-8776

## 34 HANOVER

**La Petite Curiosity Antiques**
195 Washington St.
978/829-9599

**Lloyd Antiques**
140 Broadway
978/826-9232

## 35 HARWICH/HARWICHPORT

**Mews Antiques at Harwichport**
517 Main St.
508/432-6397

**A London Bridge Antiques**
9 Pleasant Lake Ave. (Route 124)
508/432-6142

**Barn at Windsong**
243 Bank St.
508/432-8281

**Harwich Antique Center**
10 Route 28
508/432-4220

**Diamond Antiques & Fine Art**
103 Main St. (Route 28) W. Harwich
508/432-0634

**Old Cape Antiques**
1006 Main St. (Route 28) S. Harwich
508/432-8885

**Syd's A & J**
338 Bank St. (Harwich)
508/432-3007

## 36 HAVERHILL

**Graham & Sons Antiques**
420 Water St.
978/374-8031

**Tom's Place**
4 Auburn St.
978/373-3820

**Elmwood Antiques**
229 Kenoza Ave.
978/374-7778

**Antique World**
108 Washington St.
978/372-3919

**Parker's Antiques**
110 River St.
978/373-2332

**Paul Martin Antiques**
266 River St.
978/521-0909

## 37 HOLLISTON

**Yankee Picker**
86 Church Rear
508/429-9825

**Wilder Shop**
400 Washington St.
508/429-4836

**Antiques Plus**
755 Washington St.
508/429-9186

**Holliston Antiques**
798 Washington St.
508/429-0428

## 38 INDIAN ORCHARD

**Cat's Paw Antiques**
45 Parker St.
413/543-5254

**Tri-Town Antiques**
524 Main St.
413/543-5020

**Cabotville Collectors**
8 1/2 Parker
413/543-6095

**Oldies from the Estate**
10 Parker St.
413/543-6065

**Sherman Alden Antiques**
520 Main St.
413/543-1820

## 39 LENOX

**Charles L. Flint Antiques**
56 Housatonic St.
413/637-1634

**Stone's Throw Antiques**
51 Church St.
413/637-2733

**Past & Future**
38 Church St.
413/637-2225

### *Great Places to Stay*

## Seven Hills Country Inn

40 Plunkett St.
413/637-0060 or 1-800-869-6518
Open: Year-round
Directions: Take Exit 2 off I-90 (Massachusetts Turnpike) and follow Route 20 West for approximately 3 miles. You will see a blue sign on the right that says "Seven Hills." That sign will be pointing to the left, which is Plunkett Street. Seven Hills Inn is 1 mile down Plunkett Street on the left.

Not just a fair-weather haven, Seven Hills Inn works year-round to customize just about anything for vacations, banquets, weddings, business retreats and conferences. Furnished with care-worn antiques, and boasting hand-carved fireplaces, leaded glass windows and high ceilings, nothing has changed since the inn was originally built and known as Shipton Court, one of the original Berkshire cottages. The inn is comprised of 15 manor house and 37 terrace house guest rooms, including 3 handicapped accessible ones, on 27 acres in the heart of the Berkshires. There's also a 60-foot swimming pool and two hard-surface tennis courts. Ideally situated to take advantage of the Bershires' seasonal and cultural activities and scenery, Seven Hills Inn is surrounded with such offerings as fall foliage festivals, cider pressings, hayrides, downhill and cross-country skiing, historic homesites and museums. Tanglewood and Jacobs Pillow Dance Theatre are nearby, and next door is the Edith Wharton estate, home of Shakespeare and Company.

## 40 LITTLETON

**Van Wyck's Antiques**
325 Great Road
978/952-2878

**Upton House Antiques**
275 King St.
978/486-3367

**Sunflower Antiques**
537 King St.
978/486-0606

**Littleton Antiques**
476 King St.
978/952-0001

**Hamlet Antiques**
161 Great Road
978/952-2445

**Flowers & Spice & Everything**
2 Mannion Place
978/486-3687

**Blue Cape Antiques**
620 Great Road
978/486-4709

**Frederic Gallery**
510 King St.
978/486-9183

## 41 LOWELL

**Whitney House Antiques**
913 Pawtucket St.
978/458-0044

**Hank Garrity Antiques**
331 Broadway St.
978/453-6497

**Vintage Co.**
17 Shattuck St.
978/453-9096

## 42 LYNN

**Diamond District Antiques**
9 Broad St.
781/586-8788

### *Great Places to Stay*

## Diamond District Bed & Breakfast

142 Ocean St.
781/599-4470 or 1-800-666-3076
Fax: 781/599-2200
Directions: Located about 8 ½ miles north of Boston and Logan
International Airport, near the intersection of Routes 1A and 129.

Just 300 feet off of a 3½-mile stretch of beach, the Diamond District
Bed & Breakfast offers guest rooms with private baths, ocean swimming,
walking and biking paths, and business services. Recently listed on the
National Register as a historic district, the inn is a 1911 Georgian-style
mansion with 17 rooms, sitting on one half acre in Boston's North Shore,
also known as Lynn's "Diamond District." Once the private estate of P. J.
Harney, a Lynn shoe manufacturer, the original house plans and
specifications remain with the house, as do some original fixtures.
Features include a three-story staircase, established gardens, hardwood
floors, antiques and Oriental rugs, an 1895 rosewood Knabe concert grand
piano, and a custom-made Chippendale dining room table and chairs.

## 43 LYNNFIELD

**B & D Antiques & Collectibles**
451 Broadway
781/598-4653

## 44 MARBLEHEAD

## Wicker Unlimited

108 Washington St.
781/631-9728
Open: Mon.–Sat. 10–5, Sun. Noon–6
Directions: Take Route 128 North from Massachusetts Turnpike (I-95)
about 20 miles to Route 114 East (Exit 25A Marblehead). Go east on
114 through Salem into Marblehead (Route 114 East becomes
Pleasant Street). Follow Pleasant Street all the way to end "T"
intersection. Turn left on Washington Street and look to your right.
The store can be seen in old town. From 128 to Marblehead is 6 miles.

Marla Segal bought her first piece of wicker at the ripe old age of 15.
The purchase of that single wicker rocker inspired her to the point of
hopeless infatuation. After serving several years as an apprentice at a
Boston firm, where she learned to repair wicker, Marla decided to open
up her own shop. She quickly earned the reputation as an honest and
knowledgeable dealer. Today, she supplies both veteran and new collectors
with wicker she acquires from all parts of the country. "I try to match the
lifestyle of the person to the right piece of wicker," she explains.

However, Marla's interests are unlimited, so a full array of American
antiques and collectibles is also found in Wicker Unlimited. Quilts, Fiesta,
Roseville, Limoges, linens, rugs, and even garden tools are just a small
sampling of what might be available. Country pine, mahogany, oak or
walnut—it's always a surprise to see what has been discovered in some
of the great, old New England estates that surround the area.

**Calico**
92 Washington St.
781/631-3607

**Old Town Antique Co-op**
108 Washington St.
781/631-9728

**Heeltapper Antiques**
134 Washington St.
781/631-7722

**Marblehead Antiques**
118 Pleasant St.
781/631-9791

**Honest Ladies—Good Buy**
120 Pleasant St.
781/631-7555

**Antiquewear—Buttons**
82 Front St.
781/639-0070

**Evie's Corner**
96 Washington St.
781/639-0007

**Sack's Antiques**
38 State St.
781/631-0770

## 45 MIDDLEBORO

**Sam's Antique Centre**
51 Centre St.
508/947-9550

**Middleboro Antiques Co.**
11 N. Main St.
508/947-1844

# Massachusetts

**Christina's Antiques**
19 S. Main St.
508/947-5220

**Barewood**
282 W. Grove St.
508/947-4482

## 46 NANTUCKET

### Nantucket Island

Step off the ferry or the plane and you're in another world. Thirty miles off Cape Cod, this crescent-shaped island retains a quiet charm found in past days when whaling ships made the island haven their home. You'll find lots to explore on foot or on bicycle: unspoiled beaches and the solitary lighthouses, peaceful byways and lanes, historic mansions, and open-air farmers' stands.

Nantucket Town abounds with elegant restaurants and antiques, craft and specialty stores. Sea captains' houses line the cobblestone streets. The Whaling Museum, a former spermaceti factory, now overflows with artifacts and memorabilia from the island's once-thriving industry. Whale-watching trips, deep-sea fishing charters, and numerous excursion boats leave from Straight Wharf.

The island's magic continues year-round. In late April, the Daffodil Festival features millions of yellow flowers planted by islanders as a celebration of spring.

### Wayne Pratt, Inc.

28 Main St.
508/228-8788
(Seasonal)

Offering the discriminating shopper the opportunity to purchase antiques of exceptional quality and design. When traveling in Connecticut, be sure to visit their 3,000-square-foot showroom located in Woodbury.

**Weeds**
14 Centre St.
508/228-5200

**Nantucket House Antiques**
1 S. Beach St.
508/228-4604

**Frank Sylvia Jr. Antiques**
0 Washington St.
508/228-2926

**Antiques Depot**
14 Easy St.
508/228-1287

**Forager House Collection**
20 Center St.
508/228-5977

**Milady's Mercantile**
21 S. Main St.
508/946-2121

**Celtic Pine**
118 Orange St.
508/228-6866

**Jewelers Gallery of Nantucket**
21 Center St.
508/228-0229

**Sylvia**
6 Rays Court
508/228-0960

**Modern Arts**
67 Old South Road
508/228-2358

**Gallery at 4 India**
4 India St.
508/228-8509

**Manor House Antiques**
31 Center St.
508/228-4335

**Nantucket Country**
38 Center St.
508/228-8868

**Val Maitino Antiques**
31 N. Liberty St.
508/228-2747

**Letitia Lundeen Antique**
34 Center St.
508/228-8566

**Nina Hellman**
48 Center St.
508/228-4677

**Tonkin of Nantucket Antiques**
33 Main St.
508/228-9697

### *Great Places to Eat*

### Atlantic Cafe

15 S. Water St.
508/228-0570

Atlantic Cafe is one of those kinds of eating places where anybody can go at any time and feel comfortable, because it really doesn't matter how you look. They have a huge menu of all-American food, and eventually everyone you know will come in. You can bring the kids, the in-laws, the weekend guests, all in shorts, or grunge clothes, or whatever—it doesn't matter!

### Jared Coffee House

29 Broad St.
508/228-2400

Jared Coffee House is a legend and a landmark in Nantucket—one of those "see and be seen" places. The formal dining room serves breakfast and dinner (steaks, fish, stuffed shrimp and desserts). An informal pub serves lunch and dinner (fish and chips, tuna, burgers, etc.). A must-do tourist destination.

## 47 NEWBURYPORT

**Newburyport Estate Jewelers**
7 State St.
978/462-6242

**Flukes & Finds & Friends**
37 State St.
978/463-6968

**Sam's Treasured Memories**
39 Water St.
978/462-0024

**Seacoast Antiques**
115 Merrimac St.
978/463-3106

**Pleasant Village Antiques**
40 Pleasant St.
978/463-8605

**Olde Port Book Shop**
18 State St.
978/462-0100

**Lady Di's Antiques**
21 Water St.
978/462-5858

**Annex**
49 Water St., #R
978/462-8212

**Shandell Antiques**
12 Federal St.
978/463-0681

## 48 NEWTON

**Marcia & Bea**
1 Lincoln St.
617/332-2408

**Sonia Paine Antiques Gallery**
373 Boylston St.
617/566-9669

**Give & Take Consignments**
799 Washington St.
617/964-4454

**Dining Room Showcase**
833 Washington St.
617/527-8368

**Antique Gallery—Eugene O'Neill**
381 Elliot St.
617/965-5965

**Antique Nook**
381 Elliot St.
617/969-1060

**Antique Treasures**
381 Elliot St.
617/965-8141

**Belle Maison**
51 Langley Road
617/964-6455

**Consignment Galleries**
1276 Washington St.
617/965-6131

**Eric's Antiques**
381 Elliot St.
617/332-3744

**Madeleine C. Scanlon Antiques**
381 Elliot St.
617/964-8853

**Marcy's Antiques Ltd.**
381 Elliot St.
617/244-3237

**Ruth Feldman Antiques**
381 Elliot St.
617/527-7121

**Shirley Van Antiques**
381 Elliot St.
617/969-1846

**Steve's Antique Shop**
381 Elliot St.
617/969-2403

**Tactile**
381 Elliot St.
617/527-4938

**Touch of Glass**
381 Elliot St.
617/527-4865

**Acorn Antiques**
289 Elliot St.
617/527-8511

## 49 NORTHAMPTON

**Antiques Corner**
5 Market St.
413/584-8939

**Antique Center of Northampton**
9 1/2 Market St.
413/584-3600

**American Decorative Arts**
3 Olive St.
413/584-6804

**Up in the Attic**
11 Market St.
413/587-3055

**C. J. Sprong & Co.**
300 Pleasant St.
413/584-7440

**Family Jewels**
56 Green St.
413/584-0613

**Collector**
11 Bridge St.
413/584-6734

## 50 NORTHBOROUGH

**Tins & Things**
28 Main St.
508/393-4647

**Elegant Junk**
94 Main St.
508/393-8736

**Bell Tower Antiques**
56 W. Main St.
508/393-5477

**Cyrus Gale Antiques**
20 Main St.
508/393-7300

## 51 NORWOOD

**Norwood Antiques & Restorations**
483 Washington St.
781/769-9198

**Wise Owl**
637 Washington St.
781/769-5255

**Brenda's Antiques**
644 Washington St.
781/762-3227

**Applegate Antiques**
721 Washington St.
781/769-8892

**Norwood Trading Post**
1182 Washington St.
781/762-2186

## 52 OLD DEERFIELD

In *Historic Deerfield: An Introduction*, the author describes a setting of long ago:

"Deerfield is a beautiful ghost, haunted by the drama and violence of its early history as well as by more recent spirits who have witnessed the joys and sorrows of life in a small New England town over 300 years ago. Unlike other ghosts, Deerfield is no disembodied spirit eluding our sight and grasp. The town retains material evidence of Native American habitations from several millennia, the 17th-century English town plan of compact village and broad meadows, 18th- and 19th-century houses filled with the relics of hearth and home that reveal to us so many intimate details of life in early New England. Twenty-four of the houses along The Street in Deerfield were here when revolution broke out against England in 1775. Another 23 buildings had been erected before 1850. Their contents date from the time of Deerfield's first English settlement in 1669 to the flourishing of the Arts and Crafts movement in the early 20th century."

In 1952 Mr. and Mrs. Henry N. Flynt, wanting to assure the future of the village of Deerfield, incorporated Historic Deerfield, Inc. (then known as the Heritage Foundation) to preserve Deerfield, open its old houses to visitors, and use the buildings and their collections to foster education in and understanding of the American past.

When the Flynts founded Historic Deerfield in 1952, they had four houses open to the public in which they attempted to offer visitors a view of life in Deerfield in the Colonial and early national periods. Although they had acquired a few choice antiques for display in these buildings, most of their furnishings were country pieces.

In the 1950s their collection grew under the influence of antiques dealers, museum curators, and fellow collectors. They turned increasingly to high style furniture and began to form special collections of early American silver, English ceramics and Chinese export porcelain, and textiles, needlework, and costume. By the end of the decade the Flynts and Historic Deerfield had become widely recognized for the national importance of these collections.

They are displayed in sympathetic settings in six historic buildings along The Street.

Today, Historic Deerfield offers workshops, lecture series, antiques forums, summer archaeological excavations and educational programs for students and visitors of all ages.

Daily guided museum tours and walking tours through the village highlight Deerfield and America's history for tourist and travelers from all over the world.

Among the accommodations for dining and lodging is the 1884 Deerfield Inn. The inn has 23 guest rooms, three dining rooms, a coffee shop and full-service bar. There are facilities on the premises for weddings, private parties and small business meetings. The inn is open throughout the year. (413) 774-5587.

All in all, there is plenty to see. Thirteen museum houses dating from 1720 to 1850 display more than 20,000 objects made or used in America from 1600 to 1900. Highlights of the collections include American furniture with special emphasis on the Connecticut River Valley; English and Chinese ceramics; American and English silver; and American and English textiles.

For further information, call (413) 774-5581.

— *Contributed by* Southern Antiques Magazine, *May 1995*

### 5 & 10 Antique Gallery

Routes 5 & 10 (Old Deerfield)
413/773-3620
Web site: antiques510.com
Open: Daily 10–5, Jan.–May, closed Wed.
Directions: Exit 26 off I-91, 2A East, right at Dunkin' Donuts, right at first light, 1¼ mile on Routes 5 & 10. Exit 24 off I-91, 7 miles north on Routes 5 & 10, 1 mile north of Historic Deerfield, Mass.

The 5 & 10 Antique Gallery is a bit of history within itself. The shop has provided quality antiques for the past 20 years. Featuring two levels of 18th-, 19th- and early 20th-century furnishings, fine porcelain, china, glassware, silver, linens, primitives, toys, dolls, books, antique reference books, Sotheby catalogs, tools, kitchenware, and showcases of smalls and collectibles all within the beautiful setting of Old Deerfield.

**Lighthouse Antiques**
Routes 5 & 10
No phone listed

### 53  ORLEANS, EAST ORLEANS, SOUTH ORLEANS

**Lilli's Antique Emporium**
Route 6 A
508/255-8300

**Continuum**
7 Route 28
508/255-8513

**Countryside Antiques**
6 Lewis Road
508/240-0525

**East Orleans Antiques**
204 Main St.
508/255-2592

**Antique Center of Orleans**
34 Main St.
508/2240-5551

**Pleasant Bay Antiques, Inc.**
540 Chatham Road (Route 28)
508/255-0930

### 54  OSTERVILLE

**A. Stanley Wheelock Antiques**
870 Main St.
508/420-3170

**Farmhouse**
1340 Main St.
508/420-2400

### 55  PEABODY

**Chuck Watts Antiques**
18 Main St.
978/532-7400

### 56  PEMBROKE

**Magic Garden Antiques**
74 Congress
781/826-7930

**North River Antiques Center**
236 Water St.
781/826-3736

**Endless Antiques**
95 Church St.
781/826-7177

### 57  PITTSFIELD

**Greystone Gardens**
436 North St.
413/442-9291

**Potala**
148 North St.
413/443-5568

**Craftsman Auctions**
1485 W. Housatonic St.
413/448-8922

**The Clock Shop at Pleasant Bay**
403 S. Orleans Road
508/240-0175

**Hollyhocks**
891 Main St.
508/420-0484

**Good Riddance Antiques**
95 Church St.
781/826-8955

**Red Lion Antiques**
95 Church St.
781/829-8782

**Memory Lane Antiques**
446 Tyler St.
413/499-2718

**Fontaine Auction Gallery**
1485 W. Housatonic St.
413/448-8922

### *Interesting Side Trips*

### Hancock Shaker Village

413/443-0188 or 1-800-817-1137

Hancock Shaker Village is located in western Massachusetts in the heart of the Berkshires. It is at the junction of Routes 20 and 41, west of Pittsfield. Convenient to the Massachusetts Turnpike, Taconic State

# *Massachusetts*

Parkway and New York Thruway, it is a one-hour drive from Albany and a three-hour drive from New York or Boston. The village is located near Tanglewood, the Norman Rockwell Museum, Clark Art Institute and many other major cultural attractions.

The Shakers' "City of Peace" beckons you to discover the way of life of America's most successful communitarian society. Now a living history museum, the village was an active Shaker community from 1790 to 1960.

Members held all property in common and practiced celibacy, equality and separation of the sexes, and pacificism as they sought to create "heaven on earth." Putting their "hands to work and hearts to God," the Shakers created a society based in spirituality but rich in practicality and ingenuity. Discover their unique approach to life and the remarkable fruits of their labors at Hancock Shaker Village.

Explore the extraordinary 1826 round stone barn, the remarkable 1830 communal brick dwelling, and eighteen other restored buildings which span three centuries. From the early water-powered laundry and machine shop to the heated 1916 automobile garage, you will marvel at Shaker design, workmanship, inventiveness and efficiency. Envision the Shakers worshiping in ecstatic dance and song in the sparse simplicity of the 1793 meetinghouse. Learn about 20th-century Shaker life amid the worldly decor and comforts of the Trustees' office and store.

Appreciate Shaker industriousness as you watch artisans and farmers at work. Chat with gardeners as they harvest herbs, vegetables, and seeds in the heirloom gardens.

Try a spinning wheel, loom, or quill pen in the Discovery Room. Enjoy a candlelight dinner in the quiet of the matches, sheep shearing and harvest activities. Explore Shaker archaeological sites. Savor the order and tranquility of the "City of Peace."

## 58 PLYMOUTH

**Dillon & Co. English Country**
12 North St.
508/747-2242

**Chiltonville Antiques**
40 State Road
508/746-2164

**Antique House**
184 Water St.
508/747-1207

**Thyme Collections Center**
15 Main St.
508/746-6970

**North Plymouth Antiques**
398 Court St.
508/830-0127

**Plymouth Antiques Trading Co.**
8 Court St.
508/746-3450

**Village Braider**
48 Sandwich St.
508/746-9625

## *Interesting Side Trips*

### Plimoth Plantation
Plimoth Plantation Hwy.
Accessible via Route 3
508/746-1622

It's places like Plimoth Plantation and other living history museums that let us know just how remarkable our ancestors really were. Plimoth Plantation offers a chance to see Plymouth as it was when America's most famous immigrants, the Pilgrims, first colonized the New World. It also gives an in-depth look into the lives of the Wampanoag Indians, on whose land the Pilgrims settled. Key parts of the museum are the 1627 Pilgrim Village, where people represent actual Pilgrims in everyday life and settings, like house building, food preparation and gardening; the Carriage House Crafts Center, where you can watch period goods being reproduced using materials and tools like those of the 17th century; Hobbamock's Wampanoag Indian Homesite, where Native Americans describe the effects of the colonists' arrival on their own ancestors and how the events continue to affect their people today. Some of the staff are in native attire, and the area itself is a re-creation of one family's homesite. Don't forget to check out the *Mayflower II*, a reproduction of the ship that brought the Pilgrims to Plymouth, located on the waterfront adjacent to Plymouth Rock.

## 59 PROVINCETOWN

**Provincetown Antique Market**
131 Commercial St.
508/487-1115

**Scott Dinsmore Antiques**
179 Commercial St.
508/487-2236

**Small Pleasures**
359 Commercial St.
508/487-3712

**Alan's Attic**
194 Commercial St.
508/487-4234

**Emporium Antiques**
220 Commercial St.
508/487-1948

**Sagamore Antiques**
Corner Route 6A & Westdale Park
508/888-5186

**West End Antiques**
146 Commercial St.
508/487-6723

**Clifford-William Antiques**
225 Commercial St.
508/487-4174

**Remembrances of Things Past**
376 Commercial St.
508/487-9443

**194 Memory Lane**
194 Commercial St.
508/487-4234

**Julie Heller Gallery**
2 Gosnold St.
508/487-2169

## 60 REHOBOTH

**Madeline's Antiques**
164 Winthrop St.
508/252-3965

**Mendes Antiques**
Route 44 - 52 Blanding Road
508/336-7381

# *Massachusetts*

**Sleepy Hollow Antiques**
309 Winthrop St.
508/252-3483

## 61  ROCKPORT

**Hanna Wingate of Rockport**
11 Main St.
978/546-1008

**Rockport Trading Co.**
67 Broadway
978/546-8066

**Ye Olde Lantern Antiques**
28 Railroad Ave.
978/546-6757

## 62  SALEM

**Filigree & Fancy Antiques**
4 Wharf St.
978/745-9222

**Asia House**
18 Washington Square
978/745-8257

**Pickering Wharf Antiques**
71-73 Wharf St.
978/740-6734

**Salem Antiques**
266 Canal St.
978/744-7229

## 63  SANDWICH

**Sandwich Antique Center**
131 Route 6A
508/833-8580

**May Pope Lane**
161 Old Kings Hwy
508/888-1230

**Brown Jug**
155 Main St.
508/833-1088

**Nodding Violet**
25 Jarves
508/888-7756

**Horsefeathers Antiques**
454 Route 6A, E. Sandwich
508/888-5298

**Old Time Shop**
379 Route 6A (E. Sandwich)
508/888-2368

**Wooden Keyhole**
582 Winthrop St.
508/336-7475

**Woodbine Collection**
35 Main St.
978/546-9324

**Rockport Quilt Shoppe**
2 Ocean Ave.
978/546-1001

**Burke Antiques**
11 Central
978/744-2242

**AAA Olde Naumkeag Antiques**
1 Hawthorne Blvd.
978/745-9280

**Union Street Antiques**
1 E. India Square Mall
978/745-4258

**Paul Madden Antiques**
16 Jarves St.
508/888-6434

**H. Richard Strand Antiques**
2 Grove St./Town Hall Square
508/888-3230

**Coco Plum Garden Antique**
18 Liberty St.
508/1-888-9001

**Ezra Weston**
433 St. 6A, E. Sandwich
508/833-2228

**Keepers of the Past**
198 Old King's Hwy.
508/888-8278

**Shawme Pond Antiques**
13 Water St. (Route 130)
508/888-2603

## 64  SCITUATE

**Quarter Deck**
206 Front St.
781/545-4303

**Echo Lake Antiques**
165 Front St.
781/545-7100

**Quarter Deck**
51 Cole Pkwy.
781/544-3301

**Needful Things Antiques**
161 Front St.
781/544-0299

## 65  SEEKONK

**Antiques at Hearthstone House**
15 Fall River Ave. (Route 114A)
508/336-6273

**Consignment Barn**
394 Fall River Ave.
508/336-3228

**Lost Treasures Antiques**
1460 Fall River Ave.
508/336-9294

**Grist Mill Country Store**
879 Arcade Ave.
508/336-8232

**Bittersweet Memories**
642 Fall River Ave.
508/336-9300

**Leonard's Antiques & Reproductions**
600 Tauton Ave.
508/336-8585

## 66  SHEFFIELD

**David M. Weiss**
Main St. (Route 7)
413/229-2716

**Corner House Antiques**
Main St. (Route 7)
413/229-6627

**Frederick Hatfield Antiques**
99 S. Main (Route 7)
413/229-7986

**Saturday Sweets**
755A N. Main St. (Route 7)
413/229-0026

**Greenhouse Antiques**
182 First Parish Road
781/545-1964

**Gatherings**
131 Front St.
781/545-7664

**Bird in Hand Antiques**
157 Front St.
781/545-1728

**Vinny's Antiques Center**
380 Fall River Ave.
508/336-0800

**Ruth Falkinburg Doll Shop**
208 Taunton Ave.
508/336-6929

**County Squire Antiques**
1732 Fall River Ave.
508/336-8442

**Amanda Lynn's Antiques**
640 Fall River Ave.
508/336-5205

**John George Antiques**
370 Tauton Ave.
508/336-6057

**Darr Antiques & Interiors**
28 S. Main St. (Route 7)
413/229-7773

**1750 House Antiques**
S. Main St. (Route 7)
413/229-6635

**Anthony's Antiques**
102 Main St. Rear (Route 7)
413/229-8208

**Centuryhurst Berkshire Antiques**
Main St. (Route 7)
413/229-3277

*Massachusetts*

**Cupboards & Roses**
Main St. (Route 7)
413/229-3070

**Kuttner Antiques**
Main St. (Route 7)
413/229-2955

**Jenny Hall Antiques**
Route 7
413/229-0277

**Classic Images Art & Antiques**
527 Sheffield Plain
413/229-0033

**North Main Street Antique**
655 Route 7
413/229-9029

**Ole T J's Antique Barn**
Main St. (Route 7)
413/229-8382

**Berkshire Gilder's Antiques**
15 Main St. (Rte 7)
413/229-0113

**Dovetail Antiques**
Route 7
413/229-2628

**Le Trianon**
1854 N. Main St. (Route 7)
413/528-0775

**May's Everything Shop**
655 Route 7
413/229-2037

### 67 SHELBURNE/SHELBURNE FALLS

**Shea Antiques**
69 Bridge St.
413/625-8353

**Rainville Trading Post**
251 Main St.
413/625-6536

**Yankee Pastime Antiques**
Route 112 N. Colrain Road
413/625-2730

**Charlemont House Gallery**
6 State St.
413/625-2800

**Merry Lion**
6 State St.
413/625-2800

**Strawberry Field**
1204 Mohawk Trail
413/625-2039

**Orchard Hill Antiques**
108 Colrain Road
413/625-2433

**Amstein's Antiques**
46 Crittendon Hill Road
413/625-8237

**Blacksmith Shoppe**
44 State St.
413/625-6291

**Shelburne Country Shop**
Mohawk Trail
413/625-2041

### 68 SHREWSBURG

**The Antique Center of Shrewsburg**
510 Boston Turnpike Road (Route 9)
508/845-9600

### 69 SOMERVILLE

**Londontowne Galleries**
380 Somerville Ave.
617/625-2045

**Warped Collectibles**
236 Elm St.
617/666-3129

**Karma Antiques**
248 Beacon St.
617/864-5875

### 70 SOUTHAMPTON

**Southampton Antiques**
172 College Hwy. (Route 10)
413/527-1022
Fax: 413/527-6056
Open: Sat. 10–5, appointments welcome, closed August

Meg and Bruce Cummings offer the largest selection of authentic antique American oak and Victorian furniture in New England — no reproductions, no imports and authenticity guaranteed. They have three large barns with five floors of merchandise for customers to browse through, sigh over, touch, examine and take home.

Instead of having a store catalog, they offer customers a custom-made video for $25, designed to meet particular specifications and needs. Each video is individually made and includes price quotes, style description, condition, approximate age and dimensions.

"We focus on high style American Victorian walnut, rosewood, mahogany, and turn-of-the-century oak," say the Cummings. "Furniture found in our barns is in three categories: 'as found' original varnish, superb original finish and refinished. We are very proud of our refinished product and feel that our refinishing process has reached a quality second to none."

Among the pieces regularly offered by the Cummings are curio cabinets, hall trees, desks, wicker, swivel chairs, bedroom suites, lockside chests, conference tables, clocks, bookcases, lamps, side-by-sides, library tables, beds, roll-top desks, Victorian sofas, marble-top furniture, sets of chairs, and square and round dining tables. Their specialties include Victorian Renaissance Revival, turn-of-the-century oak and Victorian Rococo.

### 71 SOUTH DEERFIELD

**Yesterdays Antique Center**
Routes 5 & 10
413/665-7226

**House of the Ferret**
Routes 5 & 10
413/665-0038

**Antiques at Deerfield**
Routes 5 & 10
No Phone Listed

**Antiques by Sandra Pavoni**
Routes 5 & 10
413/665-0511

### 72 SOUTH EGREMONT

**Red Barn Antiques**
72 Main St.
413/528-3230

**Howard's Antiques**
Hillsdale Road (Route 23)
413/528-1232

# *Massachusetts*

**The Splendid Peasant Ltd.**
Route 23 at Sheffield Road
413/528-5755

**Geffner/Schatzky Antiques**
Route 23
413/528-0057

## 73 SPRINGFIELD

**Fancy That**
699 Sumner Ave.
413/739-5118

**Lady in Red Antiques**
712 Sumner Ave.
413/734-6100

**A-1 Antique Store**
752 Sumner Ave.
413/732-6855

**Tri-Towne Collectibles**
524 Main St.
413/543-5020

**Prestige Antiques**
435 White St.
413/739-2190

**Cat's Paw Antiques**
45 Parker St.
413/543-5254

**Antiques on Boland Way**
1500 Main St.
413/746-4643

**Susan T's Antiques**
705 Sumner Ave.
413/827-8910

**Patti's Antiques & Treasures**
532 Main St.
413/543-8484

## 74 STOCKBRIDGE

**Greystone Gardens**
The Mews
413/298-0113

**John R. Sanderson Rare Books**
8 W. Main St.
413/298-5322

### *Great Places to Stay*

## Inn at Stockbridge

P.O. Box 618, Route 7 N.
413/298-3337
Open: Year-round
Rates: $75–$225
Directions: On Route 7, 1 ½ miles north of Stockbridge Center. Off the Massachusetts Turnpike, take Exit 2, Route 102 West to Route 7 North. Travel Route 7 North for 1 ¼ miles.

Graciously operated by Alice and Len Schiller, the Inn at Stockbridge offers eight guest rooms with private baths, including two suites. Settled on 12 secluded acres, the Colonial Revival-style home, complete with Georgian detailing and classical columns, has remained structurally unchanged since its construction in 1906 as a vacation home for a Boston attorney. Each morning a full breakfast is served on a grand mahogany table set with china, silver, crystal, linen and lighted candles. Often after a refreshing dip in the pool, guests are treated to afternoon wine and cheese, and can spend a quiet evening browsing the inn's extensive library.

### *Interesting Side Trips*

## Charles H. Baldwin & Sons

1 Center St.
W. Stockbridge
413/232-7785
Open: Tues.–Sat. 9–5, occasionally open Sun.

As a counterpoint to overindulged chocoholics, West Stockbridge offers a vanilla lover's nirvana. In the tiny storefront of Charles H. Baldwin & Sons, vanilla connoisseurs can see vanilla being made according to the methods used by the Baldwin family since 1888. The shop itself dates back to the late 1700s; the oak barrels in which the extract is aged, over 100 years. The whole place smells like, well, vanilla. Shoppers can watch family members draw the spice from the casks into gallon jugs, then use the vintage, soldered-steel measuring cup with a spring-operated siphon to pour the fragrant brandy-colored liquid into tiny bottles, which are capped and labeled by hand. In the rear of the store is the "laboratory," where more family members blend almond, anise, peppermint and lemon extracts or their special vanilla sugar. Purchases are rung up on a 19th-century cash register, and money is kept in a 100-year-old safe that opens with an antique brass key. A true piece of "living history."

## 75 STURBRIDGE

## Showcase Antique Center, Inc.

Route 20
At the Entrance to Old Sturbridge Village
508/347-7190
Merchandise listings faxed back 24 hrs.: 508/347-2400
Web site: www.showcaseantiques.com
Email: showcase@hey.net
Open: Mon., Wed.–Sat. 10–5, Sun. 12–5, closed Tues.
Extended hours during Brimfield Antique Shows
Directions: Located on Route 20 in Sturbridge, just one mile west from Exit 9 off I-90 (Massachusetts Turnpike) and from Exit 3B off I-84.

Linking history and the future through modern technology, Showcase Antique Center offers not only the physical, visual delight of strolling through selections of 180 showcase dealers, but modern conveniences of worldwide shopping, 24-hour fax, answering machine, email, web site cyber store on the Internet and merchandise listings faxed back 24 hours a day.

Located at the entrance to Old Sturbridge Village, the selections feature art glass, sterling, jewelry, paintings, toys, primitives, advertising, art, pottery, Royal Bayreuth, tools, china, Shaker, medical, Indian, furniture and much, much more. Some of the items most recently found at Showcase Antique Center were a Dedham pottery crab plate, Vienna bronze hunter on horseback with dogs, milk glass phrenological of George Washington in cast-iron frame with a milk glass inkwell, Bavarian clothes cabinet with original floral design, pictorial Navajo mat made by Lorretta Chee, "Salisbury Cathedral" oil on canvas and a sterling kettle on a stand, signed Alexander Clark Co., London.

**Fairground Antique Center**
362 Main St.
508/347-3926

**Antique Center Sturbridge**
426 Main St.
508/347-5150

**Sturbridge Antique Shops**
200 Charlton Road
508/347-2744

**This & That**
446 Main St.
508/347-5183

**Airport Antiques**
22 New Boston Road
508/347-3304

## *Great Places to Stay*

### The Wildwood Inn Bed & Breakfast
121 Church St.
413/967-7798 or 1-800-860-8098
Open: Year-round
Rates: $50–$80

The Wildwood Inn Bed & Breakfast is located very near Sturbridge. For specific information see Ware, #80.

### Commonwealth Cottage
11 Summit Ave.
508/347-7708
Open: Mon.–Sun. all year
Rates: $85–$145
Directions: *From Massachusetts Turnpike (I-90):* Take Exit 9 to Route 20 West toward Brimfield. After passing the intersection of Route 148 on the right, take the next left onto Commonwealth Avenue. At the "Heritage Green" sign, veer left and you'll see Commonwealth Cottage straight ahead. *From I-84 East:* Take Exit 3B (Route 20 W/Palmer). Follow Route 20 West and proceed as before. *From Brimfield:* Follow Route 20 East into Sturbridge. Make a right onto Commonwealth Avenue, then proceed as above. (Be careful—Commonwealth Avenue appears quickly. Just after the sign for 630 Main Street in front of the gray building of shops on the left, and a yellow clapboard house on the right.)

Sitting on a knoll surrounded by 200-year-old maple trees, almost in the heart of Sturbridge's attractions, is the charming Queen Anne Victorian

home known as Commonwealth Cottage. Lovingly run by Wiebke and Bob Gilbert, the Commonwealth is comfortably furnished with period pieces and family hand-me-downs. A variety of guest rooms is available, most with queen-sized beds and private bath. Each room has its own personality, like the M&M Room, named after both Wiebke and Bob's grandmothers and furnished with many of their cherished belongings. Or Uncle Sam's baroque-themed room, and Mr. Bigelow's Room, named after Bob's dad and filled with lots of greens, wicker and an actual picket fence for the queen headboard. In addition to a sumptuous breakfast, complete with the house's own jams and jellies, guests are treated to afternoon tea.

## *Interesting Side Trips*

### Old Sturbridge Village
Route 20 W.
508/347-3362
Web site: www.osv.org
Directions: Route 20, Sturbridge, Massachusetts, Exit 2 off I-84 (after 7 p.m. use Exit 3B) Exit 9 off the Massachusetts Pike.

Old Sturbridge Village is another amazing piece of living history. It is an extraordinary outdoor museum that brings to life a working community of the 1830s, down to the smallest details. The largest history museum in the Northeast, Old Sturbridge is a re-created community on

over 200 acres, with more than 40 restored structures, carefully relocated from as far away as Maine. The museum concept was conceived by a member of the Wells family in 1936 as the families of Albert B. and Joe Cheney Wells tried to decide what to do with both men's extensive collections of furniture, tools, utensils, paperweights, glassware, and 19th-century clocks. After several interruptions, including a hurricane and World War II, the museum opened to the public in 1946. In the ensuing 50 years the museum has grown and developed, been redefined and researched. Each exhibit and program is meticulously grounded in historical research, which provides a clearer understanding of the region's past.

By exploring the museum, visitors can experience daily life in an early 19th-century country village in New England — from the rustic farmhouse kitchen to the elegant parlor in the finest house on the village common, from the blacksmith shop to a rural printing office and bookstore, examining along the way home furnishings and decorative arts, costume and dress, food and cooking utensils, and implements and devices of all sorts. By choosing to re-create the life and times of the 1830s, the museum founders have chosen a transitional era in New

# *Massachusetts*

England when life was changing from an agrarian society to an industrial one, when water and steam power was replacing man and animal power, when exploration was increasing through better mass transportation, and the Northeast was moving into the industrial age. The exhibits show these changes in New England: farming with its seasonal tasks and customs; women's lives and their households; mill neighborhoods with their sawmills and gristmills; artisans and rural industry; the center village, more attuned to changes emanating from the cities; community events; and the story of Old Sturbridge Village itself, which celebrated its 50th anniversary in 1996 and is a major force in the field of historic preservation and restoration.

## 76   SUDBURY

**Flashback Furnishings**
88 Boston Post Road
978/443-7709

**Sudbury Art & Antiques**
730 Boston Post Road
978/443-0994

**Pairs of Chairs, Etc.**
345 Boston Post Road
978/443-3363

**Smith & Jones, Inc.**
12 Clark Lane
978/443-5517

## 77   THE MOHAWK TRAIL

For an antidote to the hectic pace of modern life, travel the back roads of the northwest corner of Massachusetts, where you'll find charming villages, swimming holes, and covered bridges. The Mohawk Trail, now Route 2, began as a Native American trail, was widened by the early settlers, then was developed as America's first scenic automobile route. The trail is most spectacular in autumn, when the trees turn to brilliant crimsons, oranges and yellows.

A fragrant stop is Shelburne Falls, where the Bridge of Flowers, an old trolley bridge, is planted with masses of blossoms.

## 78   VINEYARD HAVEN/MARTHA'S VINEYARD

Once you've experienced the Vineyard's charm, you'll find it hard to leave. New England's largest island has soft sandy beaches, pine forests, rolling hills and moors, and a number of delightful towns.

Oak Bluffs is famous for its Methodist campground with brightly painted Victorian gingerbread cottages, built in the mid-1800s as a religious retreat. The town also features the Flying Horses, the oldest working carousel in America. Vineyard Haven is a picturesque turn-of-the-century community and a year-round ferry port. Edgartown, once a prosperous whaling port, is now a yachting center filled with stately mariners' homes. The town's Old Whaling Church is a performing arts center. All three towns have bistros, boutiques, and galleries.

Head "up island" and you'll discover the classic New England town of West Tisbury and the rolling hills of Chilmark. At the outermost point of the island are the dramatic color-streaked clay cliffs of Gay Head National Monument.

**C. W. Morgan Maine Antiques**
Beach Road
508/693-3622

**Chartreuse**
State Road
508/696-0500

**Early Spring Farm Antiques**
93 Lagoon Pond Road
508/693-9141

**Summer Old Summer New**
76 Main St.
508/693-8333

**Bramhall & Dunn**
19 Main St.
508/693-6437

**Pyewacket's Flea Circus**
63 Beach Road
508/696-7766

**All Things Oriental**
Beach Road
508/693-8375

### *More shopping in Martha's Vineyard's Oak Bluffs*

**Now & Then Shop**
176 Circuit Ave.
508/696-8604

**Federal House Antiques**
469 New York Ave.
508/693-8602

**Pik-Nik Antiques at Four Gables Inn**
New York Ave.
508/696-8384

**Tuckernuck Antiques**
101 Tuckernuck Ave.
508/696-6392

### *More shopping in Martha's Vineyard's West Tisbury*

**Hull Antiques**
Edgartown Road
508/693-5713

**Forget-Me-Not Antiques**
State Road
508/693-1788

**M. M. Stone**
527 State Road
508/693-0396

**The Granary Gallery**
The Red Barn Emporium
508/693-0455

### *More shopping in Martha's Vinyard's Menemsha*

**Over South**
Basin Road
508/645-3348

### *More shopping in Martha's Vinyard's Edgartown*

**Vintage Jewelry**
Main St.
508/627-4509

**Past & Presents**
37 Main St.
508/627-3992

**Arbor Antiques**
222 Upper Main St.
508/627-8137

**Past & Presents**
12 N. Water St.
508/627-6686

**Great Places to Eat**

**The Black Dog Tavern**
Beach St., Vineyard Haven Harbor
508/693-9223
**The Black Dog Bakery**
Water St., Vineyard Haven Harbor
508/693-4786

Home of the Black Dog T-shirt, the Black Dog Bakery offers "only the best" breads, pies, cookies and more, while the Black Dog Tavern offers an eclectic menu of fresh seafood, pasta salads, and American ethnic thrown in.

## 79 WAKEFIELD

**Iron Horse Antique Gallery**
951 Main St.
781/224-1188

**Back Track Antiques**
239 North Ave.
781/246-4550

## 80 WARE

**The Wildwood Inn Bed & Breakfast**
121 Church St.
413/967-7798 or 1-800-860-8098
Open: Daily
Rates: $50–$80
Directions: From Massachusetts Turnpike (I-90): Take Exit 8. Turn left off the exit ramp onto Route 32 North. Follow Route 32 North for 8 miles to junction Route 32 North and Route 9 East. (A movie theater is in front of you.) Take a right onto Routes 32 North and 9 East. At the second light, take a left onto Church Street. (If you reach the fire station, you missed the left turn!) Wildwood Inn is on the right, ³/₄ mile up Church Street, across from the Highland Street sign.

Midway between Boston and the Berkshires, near the southern gateway to New England, the town of Ware is located right on Highways 9 and 32, two of the beautiful foliage routes of New England, and just a short ride from Exit 8 of the Massachusetts Turnpike.

Waiting to greet you in Ware is a homey, 1880 Victorian inn furnished with American primitive antiques, handmade heirloom quilts, and early cradles. Located on a maple tree–canopied street lined with stately Victorian homes, Wildwood Inn offers a wraparound porch for lazing away the afternoon, or two landscaped acres for strolling. You can even wander the adjacent 100-acre park, or canoe, bike or ski nearby. The Brimfield Antique Market is a 20-minute drive on "no traffic" back roads. It's also an easy drive to the Five College area, Old Sturbridge or Deerfield, Yankee Candle Complex, the Basketball Hall of Fame, or beautiful Quabbin wilderness. Seven of the nine guest rooms have private baths, and there is a two-bedroom suite with bath and parlor.

## 81 WEST BARNSTABLE

**Bird Cage, Inc.**
1064 Main St.
508/362-5559

**Salt & Chestnut**
651 Route 6A
508/362-6085

**Maps of Antiquity**
1022 Route 6A
508/362-7169

## 82 WEST BOYLSTON

**Robert & Co. Antiques**
271 W. Boylston St.
508/835-6550

**West Boylston Antiques**
277 W. Boylston St.
508/835-8853

**Wexford House Gifts**
9 Crescent St.
508/835-6677

**Yankee Heritage Antiques**
44 Sterling St. (Junction 12 & 110)
508-835-2010

**Obadiah Pine Antiques**
160 W. Boylston St.
508/835-3806

## 83 WEST BRIDGEWATER

**Upstairs Downstairs Antiques**
118 S. Main St.
508/586-2880

**One Horse Shay Antiques**
194 S. Main St.
508/587-8185

**America's Attic**
221 W. Center St.
508/584-5281

**Cherry Lane Antiques**
26 W. Center St.
508/559-0359

**West Bridgewater Antiques**
220 S. Main St.
508/580-5533

**Armen Amerigion Antiques**
223 W. Center St.
508/580-1464

**Carriage House Antiques**
102 W. Center St.
508/584-3008

**West Bridgewater Antiques**
165 W. Center St.
508/584-9111

## 84 WEST TOWNSEND

**Delaney Bros. Clocks**
435 Main St.
978/597-8340

**Hobart Village Antique Mall**
445 Main St.
978/597-0332

**Antique Associates at W. Townsend**
473 Main St.
978/597-8084

## 85 WESTFORD

**Antiques**
301 Littleton Road
978/392-9944

**Westford Valley Antiques**
434 Littleton Road
978/486-4023

**Wolf's Den Antiques**
139 Concord Road RM. 225
978/692-3911

# *Massachusetts*

## 86 WILLIAMSTOWN

**Saddleback Antiques**
Route 7 S.
413/458-5852

**Greenbrier**
Route 7
413/458-2248

**Village Flowers Country Store**
Route 43, 112 Water St.
413/458-9696

**The Amber Fox**
622A Main St. (Route 2)
413/458-8519

**The Library Antiques**
70 Spring St.
413/458-3436

**Collectors Warehouse**
105 North St.
413/458-9686

## 87 WORCESTER

**Ragtime Ann-tiques**
70 James St.
508/752-6638

**A & A Antiques**
276 Plantation St.
508/752-6567

**Collector's Corner**
1 Greenwood
508/754-2062

**Encore Consignment Shop**
417 Park Ave.
508/757-8887

**Pastiche**
113 Highland St.
508/756-1229

## 88 YARMOUTH PORT

**Design Works**
159 Main St.
508/362-9698

**Nickerson's Antiques**
162 Main St.
508/362-6426

**Ryan Cooper Maritime Antiques**
161 Main St.
508/362-0190

**King's Row Antiques**
175 Main St.
508/362-3573

**Minden Lane Antiques**
175 Main St.
508/362-0220

**Lookout Farm Antiques**
175 Main St.
508/362-0292

**Constance Goff Antiques**
161 Main St.
508/362-9540

**Crooks Jaw Inn**
186 Main St.
508/362-6111

**Stephen H. Garner Antiques**
169 Main St. (Route 6A)
508/362-8424

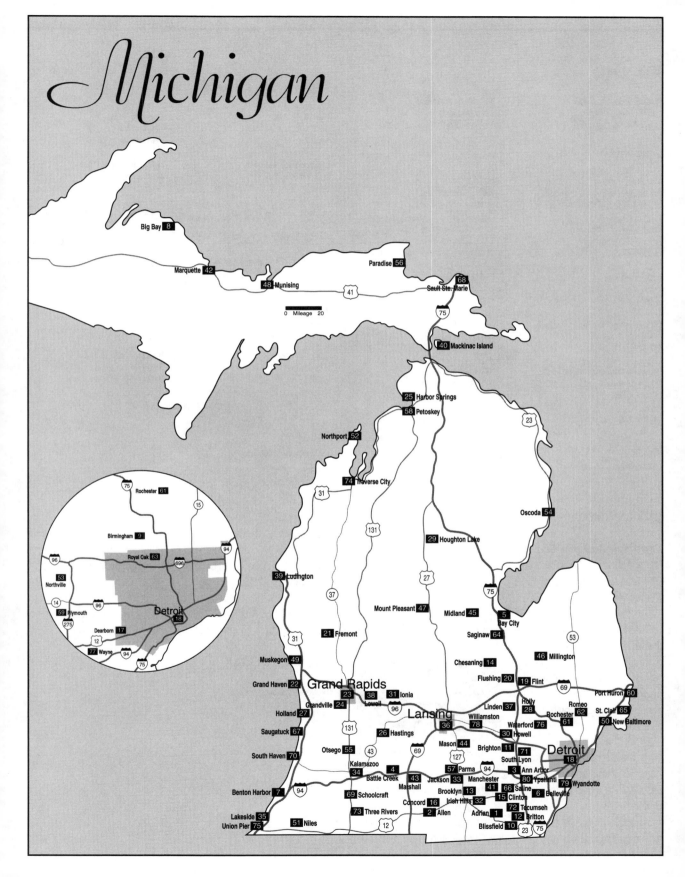

# Michigan

## 1 ADRIAN

**Birdsall Depot Antiques**
4106 N. Adrian Hwy.
517/265-7107

**Marsh's Antique Mall**
136 S. Winter St.
517/263-8826

## 2 ALLEN

**Michiana Antiques**
100 W. Chicago Road
517/869-2132

**Hand & Heart Antiques**
109 W. Chicago Road
517/869-2553

**Sandy's Simple Pleasures**
109 W. Chicago Road
517/869-2875

**Allen Old Township Hall**
114 W. Chicago Road
517/869-2575

**Andy's Antiques**
118 W. Chicago Road
517/869-2182

**Peddlar's Alley**
164 W. Chicago Road
517/869-2280

**Olde Chicago Pike Antiques Mall**
211 W. Chicago Road
517/869-2719

**A Horse of Course**
106 Prentiss
517/869-2527

**Greentop Country Antique Mall**
8651 W. Chicago Road
517/869-2100

**Allen Antique Mall**
9011 W. Chicago Road
517/869-2788

**Capital Antiques**
U.S. Hwy. 12
517/869-2055

**Antique East Side Mall**
237 E. Chicago Road
517/869-2039

**Chicago Pike Antiques**
211 W. Chicago Road
517/869-2719

**Grandpa's Attic Antiques**
222 E. Chicago Road
517/523-2993

## 3 ANN ARBOR

### Ann Arbor Antiques Market

Margaret Brusher, Promoter
5055 Ann Arbor Saline Road
734/662-9453

Thirty years ago, Margaret Brusher was a pioneer in the antique market, holding her first show at the local Ann Arbor Farmer's Market with 68 dealers participating. Nowadays, the monthly market draws over 350 dealers and a national (sometimes international) clientele.

So why has Ann Arbor stood the test of time? First is Brusher's tough standards of authenticity, with every item guaranteed. Second, the market has shown a tendency to change as the antiques market in general changes.

Where once booth after booth was filled with country furniture and related accessories, desirous at the time, today's Ann Arbor represents variety and quality, irrespective of style or period to reflect the diversity of the customer. (For show dates, call the number listed above).

**Rage of the Age**
314 S. Ashley St.
734/662-0777

**Treasure Mart**
529 Detroit St.
734/662-1363

**Past Presence Antiques**
303 S. Division St.
734/663-2352

**Antiques Market Place**
210 S. 1st St.
734/913-8890

**Antelope Antiques & Coins**
206 S. 4th Ave.
734/663-2828

**Graces Select Antiques**
122 S. Main St.
734/668-0747

**Arcadian Too Antiques & Collectibles**
322 S. Main St.
734/994-8856

**Maple Ridge Antiques**
490 S. Maple Road
734/213-1577

**Antique Mall of Ann Arbor**
2739 Plymouth Road
734/663-8200

**Kaleidoscope Books**
217 S. State St.
734/995-9887

**Lotus Gallery**
1570 Covington Dr.
734/665-6322

**Dixboro General Store**
5206 Plymoth Road
1-800-DIXBORO

### *Great Places to Stay*

**Woods Inn**
2887 Newport Road
734/665-8394
Rates: $50–$60

Here's a place to relax in the Michigan woods. The Woods Inn is an 1859, two-story wood and stone Early American home with four spacious guest rooms, plus an ample kitchen, dining room, parlor and large screened porch filled with wicker furniture. There are three acres of pine and hardwoods for guests' strolling pleasure, complete with sprawling gardens, a barn, and one of the few remaining smokehouses in Michigan. The inn is filled with Early American pieces and period collections of ironstone, colored art glass, and Staffordshire figurines.

## 4 BATTLE CREEK

**Old Beckley School Antiques**
3019 B Dr. N.
616/979-1842

# Michigan

## 5 BAY CITY

### Bay City Antiques Center
1010 N. Water St.
517/893-0251
Web site: www.antiquecenteronline.com
Open: Mon.–Sat. 10–5, Sat. 12–5
Directions: I-75 Exit 162A to downtown Bay City. Left at first light after river, then north six blocks to Third St. Then left one block to Water St.

Voted #1 antique mall in Michigan by AAA readers. Michigan's largest; a full city block of antiques on three floors along the historic river in downtown Bay City.

| | |
|---|---|
| **Mid-Michigan Retail Sales**<br>614 Garfield Ave.<br>517/893-6537 | **Everybody's Attic**<br>606 E. Midland St.<br>517/893-9702 |
| **Owl Antiques**<br>703 E. Midland St.<br>517/892-1105 | **Hen in the Holly**<br>110 3rd St.<br>517/895-7215 |
| **Little House**<br>924 N. Water St.<br>517/893-6771 | **Downtown Antiques Market**<br>1020 N. Water St.<br>517-893-0251 |

## 6 BELLEVILLE

**Antiques on Main**
430 Main St.
313/699-8285

## 7 BENTON HARBOR

| | |
|---|---|
| **Good Old Times Antiques**<br>3076 E. Napier Ave.<br>616/925-8422 | **Antique Exchange**<br>4823 Territorial Road<br>616/944-1987 |

## 8 BIG BAY

### *Great Places to Stay*

### Big Bay Point Lighthouse Bed & Breakfast
3 Lighthouse Road
906/345-9957

Lighthouses have this mysterious pull and fascination for just about everybody, so imagine the thrill of staying in a lighthouse that's a B & B! In 1986, the two-story brick building and its adjoining 60-foot-high square light tower at Big Bay Point were adapted to a bed and breakfast. It is now an 18-room inn with seven guest rooms (five with private bath) and a common living room with a fireplace, a dining room, a library, and a sauna in the tower. Not only do guests get great accommodations and a really nice place to poke around, but they can also go up in the tower and see the original 1,500-pound third order Fresnel lens — the second largest ever used on the Great Lakes.

## 9 BIRMINGHAM

| | |
|---|---|
| **Watch Hill Antiques**<br>330 E. Maple Road<br>248/644-7445 | **Cece's**<br>335 E. Maple Road<br>248/647-1069 |
| **Lesprit**<br>336 E. Maple Road<br>248/646-8822 | **Patrick Vargo Antiquarian**<br>250 Martin St.<br>248/647-0135 |
| **Chase Antiques**<br>251 E. Merrill St.<br>248/433-1810 | **Cowboy Trader**<br>251 E. Merrill St.<br>248/647-8833 |
| **Leonard Berry Antiques**<br>251 E. Merrill St.<br>248/646-1996 | **O'Susannah**<br>570 N. Woodward Ave.<br>248/642-4250 |
| **Merwins Antiques Gallery**<br>588 N. Woodward Ave.<br>248/258-3211 | **Chelsea Antiques Ltd.**<br>700 N. Woodward Ave.<br>248/644-8090 |
| **Troy Corners Antiques**<br>251 E. Merrill St.<br>248/594-8330 | **Classic Country Antiques**<br>2277 Cole St.<br>248/258-5140 |
| **La Belle Provence**<br>185 W. Maple Road<br>248-540-3876 | **Madelines Antique Shop**<br>790 N. Woodward Ave.<br>248/644-2493 |
| **Hagopian World of Rugs**<br>850 S. Woodward Ave.<br>248/646-1850 | |

## 10 BLISSFIELD

### Williams Crossroads Antiques & Collectibles
10003 Route 223
517/486-3315
Open: Mon.–Sat. 10–6, Sun. 11–6

Large selection of antique furniture and collectibles; china, glassware, jukeboxes, and railroad memorabilia.

| | |
|---|---|
| **Blissfield Antiques Mall**<br>103 W. Adrian St.<br>517/486-2236 | **J & B Antiques Mall**<br>109 W. Adrain St.<br>517/486-3544 |
| **Triple Bridge Antiques**<br>321 W. Adrian St.<br>517/486-3777 | **Memories on Lane St.**<br>104 S. Lane<br>517/486-2327 |
| **Greens Gallery of Antiques**<br>115 S. Lane<br>517/486-3080 | **Estes Antiques Mall**<br>116 S. Lane<br>517/486-4616 |

# *Michigan*

## 11 BRIGHTON

**Nostalgia Days Gone By Antiques**
116 W. Main St.
810/229-4710

**Mill Pond Antique Galleries**
217 W. Main St.
810/229-8686

**Entre Nous Antiques**
323 W. Main St.
810/229-8720

**Hidden Treasures**
7925 Winans Lake Road
810/231-7777

**The Quaker Shop**
210 Hyne St.
810/231-3530

## 12 BRITTON

**Britton Village Antiques**
126 E. Chicago Blvd.
517/451-8129

**McKinney's Collectibles**
108 E. Chicago Blvd.
517/451-2155

**YesterYears Antiques**
208 E. Chicago Blvd.
517/451-8600

## 13 BROOKLYN

**Pine Tree Centre Antique Mall**
129 N. Main St.
517/592-3808

**Memory Lane Antique Shop**
12939 South M-50
517/592-4218

**Brooklyn Depot Antiques**
207 Irwin St.
517/592-6885

## 14 CHESANING

**Fancy That Antiques & Uniques**
324 W. Broad St.
517/845-7775 or 1-800-752-0532
Fax: 517/845-4190
Open: April–December Mon.–Sat. 10–6, Sun. 12–5, January–March
weekends Sat. 11–5, Sun. 12–5, or by appointment
Directions: From I-75/U.S. 23, the shop is located north of Flint,
Michigan. Use Exit 131, which is M-57. Head west 18 miles on M-57.
Located 2 miles east of M-52 on M-57, and 21 miles east of U.S. 27. 30
miles from Flint and Saginaw and 40 miles from Lansing.

Nothing but true antiques are allowed in the multilevel Fancy That
Antiques & Uniques. No reproductions will be found among the crystal,
china, silver, toys or two large cases of jewelry. You can also browse through
art glass that includes Tiffany, French Cameo, Moser, Lotton and Loetz;
cut glass and perfume bottles; American art pottery like Roseville and
Rookwood; country primitives, quilts, linens, European porcelains and
Nippon. An interesting and unique service that this shop offers is atomizer
repairs — those squeezy bulbs on the ends of perfume bottles that squirt
out the good-smelling stuff! The shop also offers appraisal services.

## 15 CLINTON

**First Class Antique Mall**
112 E. Michigan Ave.
517/456-6410

**Turn of the Century Light Co.**
116 W. Michigan Ave.
517/456-6019

**Wooden Box**
141 W. Michigan Ave.
517/456-7556

**Oak City Antiques**
1101 W. U.S. Hwy. 12
517/456-4444

**The Rose Patch Antiques**
162 W. Michigan Ave.
517/456-6473

## 16 CONCORD

**The Antique Cellar**
102 S. Main St.
517/524-8675

**Fuzzy's Old Toys & Antiques**
12123 M-60
517/524-9027

**King Road Granary**
12700 King Road
517/524-6006

**Mother 'n' Sons Antiques**
119 M-60
517/524-8017

## 17 DEARBORN

**A & D Antiques & Oriental Rugs**
13333 Michigan Ave.
313/581-6183

**Retro Image Co.**
14246 Michigan Ave.
313/582-3074

**Village Antiques**
22091 Michigan Ave.
313/563-1230

**Michelangelo Woodworking**
1660 N. Telegraph Road
313/277-7500

**Howard Street Antiques**
921 Howard St.
313/563-9352

## 18 DETROIT

**Marketplace Gallery**
2047 Gratiot Ave.
313/567-8250

**Dumouchelle Art Galleries Co.**
409 E. Jefferson Ave.
313/963-6255

**Relics**
10027 Joseph Campau St.
313/874-0500

**Antique & Resale Shop**
4811 Livernois Ave.
313/898-1830

**Park Antiques**
16235 Mack Ave.
313/884-7652

**In-Between**
16237 Mack Ave.
313/886-1741

**Another Time Antiques**
16239 Mack Ave.
313/886-0830

**Xavier's**
2546 Michigan Ave.
313/964-1222

**Michigan Ave. Antiques**
7105 Michigan Ave.
313/554-1012

**Mikes Antiques**
11109 Morang Dr.
313/881-9500

**Mingles**
17330 E. Warren Ave.
313/343-2828

**Detroit Antique Mall**
828 W. Fisher Freeway
313/963-5252

# *Michigan*

**New World Antique Gallery**
12101 Grand River Ave.
313/834-7008

## 19 FLINT

**Sue's Antiques**
G3106 N. Center Road
810/736-0800

**Reminisce Antique Gallery**
3124 S. Dort Hwy.
810/744-1090

**Westwood Antiques & Gifts**
4123 W. Coldwater Road
810/785-1300

## 20 FLUSHING

**Trudy's Antiques**
113 N. McKinley Road
810/659-9801

**Antique Center R&J Needful Things**
G6398 W. Pierson Road
810/659-2663

## 21 FREMONT

**Brass Bell Antique Mall**
48 W. Main St.
616/924-1255

**Rolling Ladder Antique Mall**
10 W. Main St.
616/924-0420

## 22 GRAND HAVEN

### Carriage House Antiques

122 Franklin Ave.
616/844-0580
Open: Tues.–Sat. 11–5, Sun. 1–5, closed Mon., closed January &
February
Directions: From U.S. Hwy. 31, travel west on Franklin in downtown
Grand Haven. Parking and entrance in rear.

This quaint shop is located in a restored 1892 carriage house. The
owners have been in the antiques business for 20 years so experience is a
plus for shopping here. Specializing in true antiques from the 1830s to
the 1930s, this two-story, 2,000-square-foot shop offers quilts, linens, estate
jewelry, glassware and a large selection of Victorian and country
furnishings.

**Whims and Wishes**
216 Washington Ave.
616/842-9533

**West Michigan Antique Mall**
13279 168th Ave.
616/842-0370

## 23 GRAND RAPIDS

### Yarrington Antiques

6718 Old 27th St.
616/956-6800
Open: Tues.–Fri. 12:30–5:30, Sat. 10–5

Quaint shop filled with art, pottery, pattern and depression glass,
porcelain, buttons, medalwares, and unusual antiques.

**Antiques by the Bridge**
445 Bridge St. N.W.
616/451-3430

**Bygones**
910 Cherry S.E.
616/336-8447

**Heartwood**
956 Cherry St. S.E.
616/454-1478

**Classic Woods Refinishing**
966 Cherry St. S.E.
616/458-3700

**Turn of the Century Antiques**
7337 S. Division Ave.
616/455-2060

**Scavenger's Hunt**
210 E. Fulton St.
616/454-1033

**Nobody's Sweetheart Vintage**
953 E. Fulton St.
616/454-1673

**Marlene's Antiques & Collectibles**
1054 W. Fulton St.
616/235-1336

**Perception**
7 Ionia Ave. S.W.
616/451-2393

**Mary's Used Furnishings**
732 Leonard St. N.W.
616/774-8792

**Ms. Doll's Gifts & Collectibles**
150 Madison Ave. S.E.
616/336-8677

**Home Sweet Home**
2712 Kraft S.E.
616/949-7788

**Cherry Hill Antique Emporium**
634 Wealthy St. S.E.
616/454-9521

**Plaza Antique Mall**
1410 28th St.
616/243-2465

**Scavenger Hunt Too**
2 Jefferson Ave. S.E.
616/454-9955

**Brooknelle Antiques**
4600 Knapp St. N.E.
616/363-3687

**Marlene's Antiques & Collectibles**
1054 W. Fulton St.
616/235-1336

**Village Antiques & Lighting**
1334 Burton St. S.W.
616/452-6975

## 24 GRANDVILLE

**Sherrie's Antiques**
3948 20th St. S.W.
616/249-8066

## 25 HARBOR SPRINGS

**TLC Summer Place Antiques**
811 S. Lake Shore Dr.
616/526-7191

**Huzza**
136 E. Main St.
616/526-2128

**Joe De Vie**
154 E. Main St.
616/526-7700

**Lesprit**
195 W. Main St.
616/526-9888

**Pooter Olooms Antiques**
339 State St.
616/526-6101

**Elliott & Elliott**
292 E. 3rd St.
616/526-2040

## 26 HASTINGS

**Carlton Center Antique Market**
2305 E. Carlton Center Road
616/948-9618

**Davals Used Furniture & Antiques**
2020 Gun Lake Road
616/948-2463

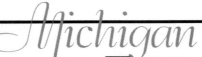

**Hastings Antique Mall**
142 E. State St.
616/948-9644

## 27  HOLLAND

**Dutch Colonial Inn**
560 Central Ave.
616/396-3664

**Nob-Hill Antique Mall**
A1261 Graafschap Road
616/392-1424

**Twig's**
184 S. River Ave.
616/392-2775

**Tulip City Antique Mall**
3500 U.S. Hwy. 31
616/786-4424

**Antiques & Etc.**
383 Central Ave.
616/396-4045

**Possessions Gifts & Antiques**
287 Howard Ave.
616/395-8207

**Stonegate Antiques & Gifts**
1504 S. Shore Dr.
616/335-3646

**Brick House Antiques**
112 Waukazoo Dr.
616/399-9690

### *Great Places to Stay*

### Dutch Colonial Inn Bed and Breakfast
560 Central Ave.
616/396-3664
Open: Year-round
Directions: From Chicago: Take I-196 North to Exit 44. Follow Business 196 to U.S. 31 (Muskegon). From U.S. 31, veer left on Central Avenue (1st stoplight). The inn is 1 1/4 miles on the right. From Detroit: Take I-94 to U.S. 131 North, turn onto M-89 toward Allegan. Continue on M-89 to M-40. M-40 becomes State Street in Holland. Continue north on State Street until 23rd Street. Turn left from 23rd Street to Central Avenue. From Grand Rapids: Take I-196 to Exit 52. Follow 16th Street west turning left onto Central Avenue.

What was once a wedding gift in 1928 is today a bed and breakfast inn offering Dutch hospitality. The decor is eclectic from Victorian country to 1930s chic. The inn offers five guest suites (one a cozy hideaway), whirlpool tubs for two, a common area with fireplace and an open porch for relaxing.

## 28  HOLLY

**Battle Alley Arcade Antiques**
108 Battle Alley
810/634-8800

**Holly Crossing Antiques**
219 S. Broad St.
810/634-3333

**Home Sweet Home**
101 S. Saginaw St.
810/634-3925

**Balcony Row**
216 S. Broad St.
810/634-1400

**Water Tower Antiques Mall**
310 S. Broad St.
810/634-3500

**Holly Antiques on Main**
118 S. Saginaw St.
810/634-7696

## 29  HOUGHTON LAKE

**Macvicar Antiques**
9103 W. Houghton Lake Dr.
517/422-5466

**Antique Mall**
418 Shelden Ave.
906/487-9483

## 30  HOWELL

**Adams Antique Mall**
203 E. Grand River Ave.
517/546-5360

**Lake Chemung Oldies**
5255 W. Ri Circle
517/546-8875

**Egnash Antiques & Auctions**
202 S. Michigan Ave.
517/546-2005

**Victorian Gardens**
128 E. Sibley St.
517/546-6749

## 31  IONIA

### Grand River Antiques
7050 S. State Road
616/527-8880
Open: Daily 10–5
Directions: When traveling I-96, Exit 367. Drive 1/4 mile north on M-66 to the light. Grand River Antiques is across from the Corner Landing Restaurant.

Any day of the week antique hounds can visit the 20-plus dealers at Grand River Antiques. Housed in an old fresh-fruit market, everything offered is authentic; no reproductions are allowed. There is a large collection of furniture, country primitives, vintage clothing, glassware and advertising collectibles. And Art Perkins, who owns Grand River Antiques along with wife Marcia, restores old trunks.

**Ionia Antique Mall**
415 W. Main St.
616/527-6720

**Checkerboard Antiques**
524 W. Lincoln Ave.
616/527-1785

**Fire Barn Antiques**
219 W. Washington St.
616/527-2240

## 32  IRISH HILLS

### Artesian Wells Antique Mall
18707 W. Toledo Road
517/547-7422

Specializing in antique furniture, advertising, primitives, books and lamps as well as art glass, clocks, fine art, jewelry, pottery, Royal Doulton, Tiffany, trunks, Winchester and reference books.

**The Enchanted Schoolhouse**
14012 U.S. Route 12
517/592-4365

**Gateway Antiques**
2519 W. U.S. Route 12
517/456-4532

**Irish Hills Antiques**
10600 U.S. Route 12
517/467-4646

**Muggsie's Antiques**
12982 W. U.S. Route 12
517/592-2659

### 33 JACKSON

**Jackson Antique Mall**
201 N. Jackson St.
517-784-3333

**The Antique Shop**
340 Otsego
517-787-2033

**The Camp Gallery**
109 W. Washington
517/780-0606

**Treasurable Finds**
145 N. Jackson St.
517/768-1120

**Ann's Copper, Brass & Glass**
218 S. Mechanic St.
517/782-8817

### 34 KALAMAZOO

**Kalamazoo Antiques Market**
120 N. Edwards St.
616/226-9788
Open: Mon.–Sat. 11–6, Sun. 1–5
Directions: From U.S. 131, take Exit 36 or 38 East to downtown. From I-94, take Exit 78 North to downtown. Once in downtown, take Michigan Avenue to Edwards (behind Wendy's).

In the early 1890s the Kalamazoo Antiques Mall was a carriage maker's shop. Today it holds the wares of 32 dealers who offer a broad selection of high quality antiques from Victorian to early country along with a great array of collectibles.

This is a "must stop" since the market is located next to an architectural salvage shop, two garden shops, and is near two antique shops and three microbreweries and only one block from the famous Kalamazoo Downtown Mall. Stay at the Radisson Hotel and rest up for two or three days of shopping.

**JP's Coins, Collectibles & Antiques**
420 S. Burdick St.
616/383-2200

**Alamo Depot**
6187 W. D Ave.
616/373-3886

**Emporium**
313 E. Kalamazoo
616/381-0998

**Souk Sampler**
4614 W. Main St.
616/342-9124

**Wild Goose Chase**
4644 W. Main St.
616/343-5933

**Crosstown Collectibles**
7616 E. Michigan Ave.
616/385-1825

**Red Wagon Antiques**
5348 N. Riverview Dr.
616/382-5461

**Warehouse Distributors**
6471 Stadium Dr.
616/372-1175

**Aldon Antiques**
608 Summer St.
616/388-5375

**Aaron & Associates**
824 S. Westnedge Ave.
616/342-8834

**Attic Trash & Treasures**
1301 S. Westnedge Ave.
616/344-2189

**Heritage Architectural Salvage**
150 N. Edwards St.
616/385-1004

### 35 LAKESIDE

**Lakeside Antiques**
14876 Red Arrow Hwy.
616/469-7717

**Rabbit Run Antiques & Interiors**
15460 Red Arrow Hwy.
616/469-0468

### 36 LANSING

**Antique Connection**
5411 S. Cedar St.
517/882-8700

**Tom's Furniture & Antiques**
319 E. Grand River Ave.
517/485-8335

**Classic Arms Company**
1600 Lake Lansing Road
517/484-6112

**Pennyless in Paradise**
1918 E. Michigan Ave.
517/372-4526

**Slightly Tarnished — Used Goods**
2006 E. Michigan Ave.
517/485-3599

**Triola's**
1114 E. Mt. Hope Road
517/484-5414

**Unique Furniture Store**
1814 S. Washington Ave.
517/485-8404

**Mid-Michigan Mega Mall**
15487 U.S. Hwy. 27
517/487-3275

**Airport Antiques**
5124 N. Grand River Ave.
517/886-9795

### 37 LINDEN

**Thimbleberry Antiques**
100 W. Broad
810/735-7324

**Linden Emporium**
115 N.E. Bron Ave.
810/735-7987

**Tangled Vine**
131 N.E. Bron Ave.
810/735-4611

### 38 LOWELL

**Cranberry Urn Antique Shop**
208 E. Main St.
616/897-9890

**Flat River Antique Mall**
210 W. Main St.
616/897-4172

**Main Street Antiques**
221 W. Main St.
616/897-5521

*Michigan*

## Great Places to Stay

### McGee Homestead Bed & Breakfast
2534 Alden Nash N.E.
616/897-8142
Open: Mar. 1–Dec. 31
Rates: $38–$58
Directions: Take Exit 52 off I-96 North. Go 7 miles through Lowell to Bailey Dr. turn left. At Alden Nash, turn right for 2 miles to McGee Homestead.

This 1880s brick farmhouse (just like Grandma's) is set on five acres and surrounded by orchards. There is a big ol' barn filled with petting animals, making it a great place to stay if you have children.

The guest area of the bed and breakfast has its own entrance, sitting room with fireplace, parlor and small kitchen. Four spacious guest rooms are individually decorated with antiques and all have private baths. A big country breakfast with eggs fresh from the McGee farm is served each morning.

There is a golf course next door, the largest antique mall in Michigan five miles away and it's only 18 miles to Grand Rapids.

### 39  LUDINGTON

### Cole's Antiques Villa
322 W. Ludington Ave.
616/845-7414
Open: (March–April & Nov.–Dec.) Fri.–Sat. 10–5, Sun. 1–5; (May–Aug.) Mon.–Sat. 10–6, Sun. 12–5
Directions: *Going north on U.S. 31:* From McKegon, exit for Old U.S. 31, turn left on Old U.S. 31 (Pere Marquette Road), follow to the intersection of U.S. 10. Turn left (west), head toward Lake Michigan. Go straight through downtown Ludington (3 stoplights, 1 block apart). Cole's Antiques Villa is 2 blocks ahead on the right, just before House of Flavors Restaurant. *Coming south on U.S. 31:* from Traverse City, go west on U.S. 10 at Scottsville junction. *Coming from the east:* Take U.S. 10 straight west to downtown Ludington and follow the previous direction.

This group of dealers offers a great selection of furniture, glassware, china, pottery, quilts, linens, paper products, jewelry, fishing and military memorabilia, advertising collectibles, country decoratives, tools and kitchenware. They also hold two antiques shows and sales each year: one on the third weekend in October at the West Shore Community College, and another the first weekend in February at Lands Inn.

### Antique Store
127 S. James St.
616/845-5888

### Sunset Bay Antiques
404 S. James St.
616/843-1559

### Country Charm Gifts & Antiques
119 W. Ludington Ave.
616/843-4722

### Christa's Antiques & Collectibles
1002 S. Madison St.
616/845-0075

### Sandpiper Emporium
809 W. Ludington Ave.
616/843-3008

### Washington Antiques
102 2nd St.
616/843-8030

### 40  MACKINAC ISLAND

## Great Places to Stay

### Haan's 1830 Inn
Huron St.
906/847-6244
Rates: $80–$120
Open: Mid–May to mid–November
(Winter address: 3418 Oakwood Ave., 708/526-2662)

According to a survey conducted under the National Historic Preservation Act of 1966, Haan's 1830 Inn is the oldest example of Greek Revival architecture in the Northwest Territory. It is the oldest building used as an inn in the state of Michigan. Each of the seven guest rooms (five with private bath) is furnished with antiques from the mid-19th century and artifacts from the island's fur-trading period. The inn has been featured in numerous publications, including the *Chicago Tribune* and *Innsider*. It is located only a short distance from Mackinac Island's downtown area, old Fort Mackinac, and the ferry docks.

### 41  MANCHESTER

### Manchester Antique Mall
116 E. Main St.
313/428-9357

### Raisin Valley Antiques
201 E. Main St.
313/428-7766

### Eighteenth Century Shoppe
122 W. Main St.
313/428-7759

### 42  MARQUETTE

### Collector Lower Harbor Antiques
214 S. Front St.
906/228-4134

### Antique Village
2296 U.S. Hwy. 41 S.
906/249-3040

### Summer Cottage
810 N. 3rd St.
906/226-2795

### Fagans
333 W. Washington St.
906/228-4311

### 43  MARSHALL

### Marshall House Center
100 Exchange St.
616/781-7841

### McKee Monument & Mercantile
200 Exchange St.
616/781-8921

**J.H. Cronin Antique Center**
101 W. Michigan Ave.
616/789-0077

**Keystone Antiques**
110 E. Michigan Ave.
616/789-1355

**Little Toy Drum Antiques**
135 W. Michigan Ave.
616/781-9644

**Pineapple Lane Antiques**
209 W. Michigan Ave.
616/789-1445

**Finders Keepers Antiques**
858 E. Michigan Ave.
616/789-1611

**Olde Homestead Antique Mall**
15445 N Drive N.
616/781-8119

**Hildor House Antiques**
105 W. Michigan Ave.
616/789-0009

**Smithfield Banques**
117 E. Michigan Ave.
616/781-6969

**J & J Antiques**
206 W. Michigan Ave.
616/781-5581

**Heirlooms Unlimited**
211 W. Michigan Ave.
616/781-1234

**Cornwells Turkeyville USA**
15 1/2 Mile Road
616/781-4293

## 44 MASON

**Art & Shirley's Antiques**
1825 S. Aurelius Road
517/628-2065

**Carriage Stop**
208 Mason
517/676-1530

**Mason Antiques District**
111-208 Mason
517-676-9753

**Old Mill Antiques Mall**
207 Mason
517/767-1270

**Front Porch**
208 Mason
517/676-6388

## 45 MIDLAND

**Michigan Antique Festival**
2156 Rudy Court
517/687-9001

Antique show and sale, collectible market, memorabilia, oddities and folk art, 1,000 outside and inside vendors — May, July and September. Call for exact dates.

**Big Jim's Antiques**
4816 Bay City Road
517/496-0734

**Dad's Antiques**
3004 S. Poseyville Road
517/835-7483

**Linda's Cobble Shop**
2900 Isabella St.
517/832-9788

**Corner Cupboard**
2108 E. Wheeler St.
517/835-6691

## 46 MILLINGTON

**Millington Antique Co-op**
8549 State St.
517/871-4597

**Millington Antique Depot**
8484 State St.
517/871-3300

## 47 MOUNT PLEASANT

**Riverside Antiques**
993 S. Mission St.
517/773-3946

**Mount Pleasant Antique Center**
1718 S. Mission St.
517/772-2672

## 48 MUNISING

**Bay House**
111 Elm Ave.
906/387-4253

**Old North Light Antiques**
M 28 E.
906/387-2109

## 49 MUSKEGON

**Downtown Muskegon Antique Mall**
1321 Division, Suite 10
616/728-0305
Open: Mon.–Sat. 11–6, Sun. 1–6
Directions: Exit U.S. 31, west on Laketon, one block west of Henry St. turn right on Division. Located at the corner of Division and Western, across the street from Muskegon Lake.

Downtown Muskegon Antique Mall is now bigger and better! Their new location in the old Shaw Walker Industrial Building offers 12,000 square feet with 40 dealers displaying a general line of antiques and collectibles. Quality "pickings" arrive daily as excited dealers fill their booths to the brim with treasures for your selecting!

**Old Grange Mall**
2783 E. Apple Ave.
616/773-5683

**Home Town Treasures**
3117 Heights Ravenna Road
616/777-1805

**Kensington Antiques**
2122 Lake Ave.
616/744-6682

**Airport Antique Mall**
4206 Grand Haven Road
616/798-3318

**Country Peddler**
2542 W. Bard Road
616/766-2147

**Memory Lane Antique Mall**
2073 Holton Road
616/744-8510

**Mandy's Antiques**
1950 E. Laketon Ave.
616/777-1428

## 50 NEW BALTIMORE

**Charlotte's Web Antiques**
36760 Green St.
810/725-7752

**Days Gone By**
50979 Washington St.
810/725-0749

**Heritage Square Antique Mall**
36821 Green St.
810/725-2453

**Washington Street Station**
51059 Washington St.
810/716-8810

# Michigan

## 51 NILES

**Michiana Antique Mall**
2423 S. 11th St.
616/684-7001

**Bookouts Furniture**
2439 S. 11th St.
616/683-2960

**Yankee Heirlooms**
211 N. 2nd St.
616/684-0462

**River City Antique Mall**
109 N. 3rd St.
616/684-0840

**Pickers Paradise Antique Mall**
2809 S. 11th St.
616/683-6644

**Antiques and More**
2429 S. 11th St.
616/683-4222

**Niles Antique Mall**
220 Front St.
616/683-6652

**Four Flags Antique Mall**
218 N. 2nd St.
616/683-6681

**Old Time Outfitters, Ltd.**
16 S. 12th St.
616/683-3569

## 52 NORTHPORT

**Grandma's Trunk**
102 N. Mill St.
616/386-5351

**5th St. Antiques**
211 N. Mill St.
616/386-5421

**Bird 'n' Hand**
123 Nagonaba Ave.
616/386-7104

**Heathman Antiques & Finery**
210 Mill St.
616/386-7006

**Back Roads Antiques & Collectibles**
116 S. Nagonaba Ave.
616/386-7011

**Cobweb Treasures Antiques**
393 S. West
616/386-5532

## 53 NORTHVILLE

### The Barn Antiques
48120 W. 8 Mile Road
248/349-0117
Open: Tues.–Sat. 10–5, Sun. 12–5

Specializing in intricate glass, unique lamps, beautiful furniture and a wide variety of primitives in a barn rebuilt in the 1920s on a historic farmstead property dating from 1827.

**Knightsbridge Antique Mall**
42305 W. 7 Mile Road
248/344-7200

## 54 OSCODA

**McNamara Antique Mall**
2083 N. U.S. Hwy. 23
517/739-5435

**Antique Mall**
4239 N. U.S. Hwy. 23
517/739-4000

**Ryland Company**
2091 N. U.S. Hwy. 23
517/739-0810

**Wooden Nickel Antiques**
110 E. Park Ave.
517/739-7490

## 55 OTSEGO

**Otsego Antique Mall**
114 W. Allegan St.
616/694-6440

**Heritage Antique Mall**
621 Lincoln Road
616/694-4226

**Harry J's**
123 W. Allegan St.
616/694-4318

**Mercantile**
504 Lincoln Road
616/692-3630

## 56 PARADISE

### *Interesting Side Trip*

### Village of Sheldrake, near Paradise
Directions: Go west on Route 28 through Hiawatha National Forest, turn north on Route 123. Or take the scenic route along the shore of Lake Superior. From Paradise, Sheldrake can be reached by taking the Whitefish Point Road north.

Although Sheldrake is on the Michigan Historic Register, the village is no longer on the map. It's on Whitefish Bay, four miles north of Paradise, which is 60 miles north and west of Sault Sainte Marie, the largest town on Michigan's Upper Peninsula. Sheldrake is an old logging village that once had about 1,500 people and about 150 buildings. Now only about a dozen buildings are still standing, and they are owned by Brent Biehl, an entrepreneur from Detroit who moved his family to Sheldrake in the 1960s and who has developed a small manufacturing plant for wood products that employs a dozen people. Biehl, his wife, and their six grown children have been, for the most part, the only year-round residents of the village, although they have renovated some of the wooden houses and do summer rentals.

Actually, that statement should be qualified: the Biehl family is the only live, year-round family in the village. Everybody else is a ghost! And there seem to be lots of them, mostly former residents. There's the old sea captain who stands on the dock, wearing a cap and cape, smoking a pipe. There's the retired city engineer from Detroit who sits in a chair on the front porch of his old house and who turns on the lights in the house in the winter when nobody's home. There's the dark, bearded logger who used to walk through the older parts of one house and sit on the couch so people renting the house could see him. The ghost often opened and closed doors and walked around, but never did anything else.

The Biehls themselves have seen so many ghosts over the past 30 years that they have become rather blasé about the whole situation. Figures appear and disappear regularly, voices are heard, pictures fall off walls, bathroom faucets turn on for no visible reason, smells of food cooking waft through the houses — "Just the garden variety poltergeist things," says Biehl.

*Michigan*

## 57 PARMA

### Cracker Hill Antique Mall
1200 Norton Road
517/531-4200

Primitives, furniture, glassware, granite, tools, paintings and collectibles.

## 58 PETOSKEY

**Jedediah's Antiques & Collectibles**
422 E. Mitchell St.
616/347-1919

**Joseph's World Art & Antiques**
2680 U.S. 31 S.
616/347-0121

**Joie De Vie**
1901 M 119
616/347-1400

**Longton Hall Antiques**
410 Rose St.
616/347-9672

### *Great Places to Stay*

### Stafford's Perry Hotel
Gaslight District, Bay at Lewis
616/347-4000 or 1-800-456-1917
Directions: *From Detroit or the Upper Peninsula:* Take I-75 to the Indian River Exit, then take M-68 west to U.S. 31 and turn south. *From Chicago:* Follow I-94 to I-96 and then pick up U.S. 131 at Grand Rapids. U.S. 131 ends at Petoskey's northwest side.

The Perry Hotel opened in 1899 to the rave reviews of the thousands of summertime visitors who flocked to northern Michigan for its clean air, water and relaxing atmosphere. The Perry was built next to the downtown train depot, and many Perry guests spent the afternoons on the large front porch greeting friends and relatives as they arrived at the station. The hotel is now filled with antiques and reproductions that reflect the grandeur of the Edwardian era. Just out the back door is the Gaslight District, which has all manner of art studios, antique galleries and shops, or, for the more athletic, just 20 minutes away is world-class skiing, golf, boating, cross-country trails and beaches.

### Stafford's Bay View Inn
2011 Woodland Ave.
616/347-2771 or 1-800-258-1886
Fax: 616/347-3413
Web site: stafford @freeway.net or http://innbook.com/staffbay.html

Just a mile north of Petoskey, and owned and operated by the same Stafford family as the Perry Hotel in downtown Petoskey, is the Bay View Inn. Built in 1886, it is one of only three locations in the nation where guests can participate in a Chatauqua: a summertime educational program that includes lectures, concerts, plays, musicals, various spiritual speakers and Sunday church services. Encased in a sprawling, elegant, airy building, all 31 guest rooms have been decorated with Victorian antiques, wallpapers, quilts and modern amenities such as whirlpool tubs, fireplaces and private balconies overlooking the bayside gardens. The entire inn is filled with antiques, and with the staff dressed in period costumes, it's like walking back in time.

## 59 PLYMOUTH

**Uptown Antiques**
120 E. Liberty St.
313/459-0311

**In My Attic**
157 W. Liberty St.
313/455-8970

**Memory Lane Antiques**
336 S. Main St.
313/451-1873

**Upstairs Downstairs Antiques**
149 W. Liberty St.
313/459-6450

**Plymouth Antiques Mall**
198 W. Liberty St.
313/455-5595

**Robin's Nest Antique Mall**
640 Starkweather St.
313/459-7733

## 60 PORT HURON

**Antique Collectors Corner**
1603 Griswold St.
810/982-2780

**Yesterday's Treasures**
4490 Lapeer Road
810/982-2100

**Citadel Antique Gallery**
609 Huron Ave.
810/987-7737

**Wooden Spool**
2513 10th Ave.
810/982-3390

## 61 ROCHESTER

**Antiques by Pamela**
319 S. Main St.
248/652-0866

**Tally Ho!**
404 S. Main St.
248/652-6860

**Watch Hill Antiques**
329 S. Main St.
248/650-5463

**Chapman House**
311 Walnut Blvd.
248/651-2157

## 62 ROMEO

**Village Barn**
186 S. Main St.
810/752-5489

**Romeo Antique Mall**
218 N. Main St.
810/752-6440

**Town Hall Antiques**
205 N. Main St.
810/752-5422

**Remember When Antiques**
143 W. Saint Clair St.
810/752-5499

## 63 ROYAL OAK

**Royal Oak Auction House & Gallery**
600 E. 11 Mile Road
248/398-0646

**Lovejoy's Antiques**
720 E. 11 Mile Road
248/545-9060

**Antique Connection**
710 E. 11 Mile Road
248/542-5042

**The White Elephant Antique Shop**
724 W. 11 Mile Road
248/543-5140

**Royal Antiques**
1106 E. 11 Mile Road
248/548-5230

**Trumbull's Antique Emporium**
112 E. 4th St.
248/584-0006

**Red Ribbon Antiques**
418 E. 4th St.
248/541-8117

**Antiques & Fine Jewelry by Helen**
107 S. Main St.
248/546-9467

**Pinks 'n' Lace**
1000 N. Main St.
248/543-3598

**Troy Street Antiques**
309 S. Troy St.
248/543-0272

**North Washington Antiques**
433 N. Washington Ave.
248/398-8006

**Antiques & Rare Old Prints**
516 S. Washington Ave.
248/548-5588

## 64 SAGINAW

**Salt Marsh**
220 N. Center Road
517/793-4861

**Antique Market Place**
418 Court St.
517/799-4110

**Little House**
418 Court St.
517/792-9622

**Antique Warehouse, Inc.**
1910 N. Michigan Ave.
517/755-4343

## 65 SAINT CLAIR

**Adam's English Antiques**
19717 9th Mile
810/777-1652

**Rivertown Antiques**
201 N. Riverside Ave.
810/329-1020

**Antique Inn**
302 Thornapple St.
810/329-5833

**Decades**
110 W. 4th St.
248/546-9289

**Dandelion Shop Antiques**
114 W. 4th St.
248/547-6288

**Delgiudice Fine Arts & Antiques**
515 S. Lafayette Ave.
248/399-2608

**Antiques on Main**
115 S. Main St.
248/545-4663

**Heritage Co. II Archl. Artifacts**
116 E. 7th St.
248/549-8342

**Yellow House Antiques**
125 N. Washington Ave.
248/541-2866

**Vertu**
511 S. Washington Ave.
248/545-6050

**Adomaitis Antiques**
412 Court St.
517/790-7469

**Dee Jays Antiques**
418 Court St.
517/799-4110

**Ron's Antiques**
12025 Gratiot Road
517/642-8479

**Jennifer's Trunk**
201 N. Riverside Ave.
810/329-2032

**John Moffett Antiques**
1102 S. 7th St.
810/329-3300

## 66 SALINE

**Attic Treasures**
10360 Moon Road
313/429-4242

**Saline Crossings**
107 E. Michigan Ave.
313/429-4400

**Pineapple House**
101 E. Michigan Ave.
313/429-1174

**Salt City Antiques**
116 W. Michigan Ave.
313/429-3997

## 67 SAUGATUCK

**Country Store Antiques**
120 Butler
616/857-8601

**Centennial Antiques**
3427 Holland St.
616/857-2743

**Fannie's Antique Market**
3604 64th St.
616/857-2698

**Taft Antiques**
240 Butler
616/857-2808

**Handled with Care**
403 Lake
616/857-4688

**Handled with Care — Everlasting**
3483 Washington Road
616/857-3044

## 68 SAULT STE MARIE

**Lagalerie Antiques**
1420 Ashmun
906/635-1044

## 69 SCHOOLCRAFT

### Norma's Antiques & Collectibles
231 Grand St.
616/679-4030
Open: Tues.–Sat. 10:30–6

Furniture, smalls and reference books, glassware and china, advertising, primitives, baskets, paper items, postcards, coins and jewelry.

### Prairie Home Antiques
240 N. Grand St. (Route 131)
616/679-2062
Open: Mon.–Tues. & Thurs.–Sat. 11–5, Sun. 12–5, Wed. by chance

Quality antiques in room settings. Furniture (1800–1950s), mirrors, art, textiles, china, children's items, antiques for your home and office.

### Ron's Grand Street Antiques
205 N. Grand St. (Route 131)
616/679-4774
Open: Tues.–Sat. 10–5, Sun. 12–5

A quality selection with an occasional hard-to-find item sprinkled in. Bridal registry and glass repair available.

## 70 SOUTH HAVEN

**Sunset Junque Antiques**
856 Blue Star Memorial Hwy.
616/637-5777

**Anchor Antiques Ltd.**
517 Phoenix St.
616/637-1500

**Black River Antiques & Gifts**
516 Phoenix St.
616/637-8042

**Antiques & Accents**
209 Center St.
616/639-1960

## 71 SOUTH LYON

**South Lyon Corner Store**
101 S. Lafayette St.
248/437-0205

**Cabbage Rose**
317 N. Lafayette St.
248/486-0930

**Pegasus Antiques & Collectibles**
105 N. Lafayette St.
248/437-0320

## 72 TECUMSEH

**Tecumseh Antique Mall**
112 E. Chicago Blvd.
517/423-6441

**Tecumseh Antique Mall II**
1111 W. Chicago Blvd.
517/423-6082

**L & M Antique Mall**
7811 E. Monroe Road
517/423-7346

**Wood's Antiques**
140 E. Chicago Blvd.
517/423-9545

**Hitching Post Antiques Mall**
1322 E. Monroe Road
517/423-8277

## 73 THREE RIVERS

### Links to the Past

52631 N. U.S. Hwy. 131
616/279-7310
Open: Mon.–Tues. & Thurs.–Sat. 10–6, Sun. 11–5

An entire house and connecting pole barn filled to the brim with quality antiques, thousands of collectibles and advertising memorabilia, plus six rooms of rare, used and collectible books, specializing in older children's books.

### Nettie Dee's Antiques

25 N. Main St.
616/273-9579
Open: Tues.–Sat. 10:30–5:30

Cherry, walnut, maple, oak and Victorian furniture; RS Prussia, Rubina, Nippon, Moser, cranberry, carnival & Steuben glass.

## 74 TRAVERSE CITY

### Walt's Antiques

M-37 (Old Mission Peninsula)
616/223-4123
Open: Mon.–Sat. 10–5:30, Sun. 12–5:30
Directions: Call for specific directions.

There's nothing romantic about livestock or farm implements, but the barns that house them—faded red or weathered gray—are another story.

Whether it's simply their sturdy architecture or nostalgia for a simpler country lifestyle, it seems that barns have been adapted very successfully as antiques shops.

From a distance, Walt's Antiques in Traverse City appears as quaint and untouched as when it was first built on Nelson Road in 1910. Primitives lie scattered across the yard and, in summer, among the flowers. The barn itself leans a bit, the windows are crooked, the road line seems to wander.

This unique shop is owned and operated by Walt and Susan Feiger. Susan, with the help of her mother, Marian Trager, first opened the barn to sell off family antiques and clear it of "junk," which the Feigers inherited when they bought the building stuffed to the rafters.

Even after the success of the initial sale, she had to be convinced by family members that she'd found her calling.

But by 1967 she was in business for the summer trade, and before long, her shop gained the enviable reputation as "the barn with everything."

Walt's barn has three floors crammed top to bottom. When you visit, give yourself plenty of time. You'll want to browse leisurely through the building and the fine antiques it holds.

A huge cabinet holds an assortment of butter pats, Limoges and early pressed glass. Another is filled with flow blue, Orientalia and a touch of stick sponge. Even jewelry—everything from Victorian to George Jensen and Taxco—has a place in the barn.

Walt Feiger, a license-plate collector who joined the business when he retired, is known across the country for his gas station memorabilia, slot machines and advertising signs. He does 30 percent of his business through interstate sales.

Although the barn and its inventory are absolutely vintage, the Feigers are state of the art antiques dealers. Susan does appraisals using a mini-cassette and the couple finds their computer invaluable as a research and advertising tool, especially when used with a digital camera that allows them to send photos of a gas pump or globe to a prospective customer anywhere around the world.

**Devonshire Antiques**
5085 Barney Road
616/947-1063

**Fascinations**
140 E. Front St.
616/922-0051

**Antique Company**
4386 W.S. Hwy. 31 N.
616/938-3000

**Wilson's Antiques**
123 S. Union St.
616/946-4177

**Antique Emporium**
565 W. Blue Star Dr.
616/943-3658

**Painted Door Gallery**
154 E. Front St.
616/929-4988

**Custer Antiques**
826 W. Front St.
616/929-9201

**Chum's Corner Antique Mall**
4200 U.S. Hwy. 31 S.
616/943-4200

### 75  UNION PIER

**Antique Mall & Village, Inc.**
9300 Union Pier Road
616/469-2555
Open: Daily 10–6
Directions: *From Indiana and Illinois:* Take I-94 to Union Pier Road, Exit 6, then west (right) onto Union Pier Road. The Antique Mall & Village is 500 feet from Exit 6 on the left, just past St. Julian Winery. *From northern Michigan:* Take I-94 to Union Pier Road, Exit 6, then turn left onto Union Pier Road. Antique Mall & Village is 100 feet from Exit 6, immediately turn left.

At the Antique Mall & Village, dealers from four states bring together some of the finest Victorian, primitives and collectibles for your shopping pleasure. The mall is the first installment of a complete village close to Lake Michigan in the heart of Harbor County. It is the area's largest, offering 15,000 square feet of quality antiques. They have patio dining when you need to replenish your energy for more shopping, offering sandwiches and salads.

**Plum Tree**
16337 Red Arrow Hwy.
616/469-5980

**Frog Forest Findings**
16100 York Road
616/469-7050

### 76  WATERFORD

**Great Midwestern Antique Emporium**
5233 Dixie Hwy.
248/623-7460

**Shoppe of Antiquity**
7766 Highland Road #M59
248/666-2333

### 77  WAYNE

**Heritage Colonial**
32224 Michigan Ave.
313/722-2332

**J. Wofford Co.**
32536 Michigan Ave.
313/721-1939

**Blue Willow Antiques**
34840 Michigan Ave.
313/729-4910

**Sanders Antiques**
35118 Michigan Ave.
313/721-3029

### 78  WILLIAMSTON

**Lyon's Den Antiques**
132 S. Putnam St.
517/655-2622
Open: Wed.–Sat. 11–5, Sun. 12–5, Thurs. til 8

Victorian and fancy oak furniture and flow blue are their specialities.

**Old Village Antiques**
125 E. Grand River Ave.
517/655-4827
Open: Tues.–Sat. 10–5

Specializing in cherry and walnut, fine glass and china, Wallace Nutting prints.

**Sign of the Pineapple Antiques**
137 E. Grand River Ave.
517/655-1905
Open: Tues.–Sat. 10–5, Sun. 1–5

Large mall with an emphasis on country, primitives, oak, Mission, Victorian, glassware and graniteware.

**Main Street Shoppe Antiques**
108 W. Grand River Ave.
517/655-4005

**Old Plank Road Antiques**
126 W. Grand River Ave.
517/655-4273

**Putnam Street Antiques**
122 S. Putnam St.
517/655-4521

**Antiques Market of Williamston**
2991 Williamston Road
517/655-1350

**Jolly Coachman**
115 W. Grand River Ave.
517/655-6064

**Corner Cottage Antiques**
120 High St.
517/655-3257

**Canterbury Antiques**
150 S. Putnam St.
517/655-6518

**Grand River Merchants**
2991 N. Williamston Road
517/655-1350

### 79  WYANDOTTE

**J & J Antiques**
1836 Biddle St.
313/283-6019

**Tony's Junk Shop**
1325 Fort St.
313/283-2160

**Yesterday's Treasures**
258 Elm St.
313/283-5232

**Thomas Antiques**
93 Oak St.
313/283-1880

**Lovejoy Antiques**
95 Oak St.
313/282-3072

**Etcetera Antiques**
99 Oak St.
313/282-3072

**Old Gray House Antiques**
303 Oak St.
313/285-2555

## 80 YPSILANTI

**Remington Walker Design Associates**
19 E. Cross St.
734/485-2164

**Jim MacDonald Antiques**
29 E. Cross St.
734/481-0555

**Renewed Interest Antiques**
33 E. Cross St.
734/482-4525

**Thomas L. Schmidt Antiques**
7099 McKean Road
734/485-8606

**Materials Unlimited**
2 W. Michigan Ave.
734/483-6980

**Schmidt's Antiques**
5138 W. Michigan Ave.
734/434-2660

**Griffin's Collectibles**
629 Lynne Ave.
734/482-0507

# Mississippi

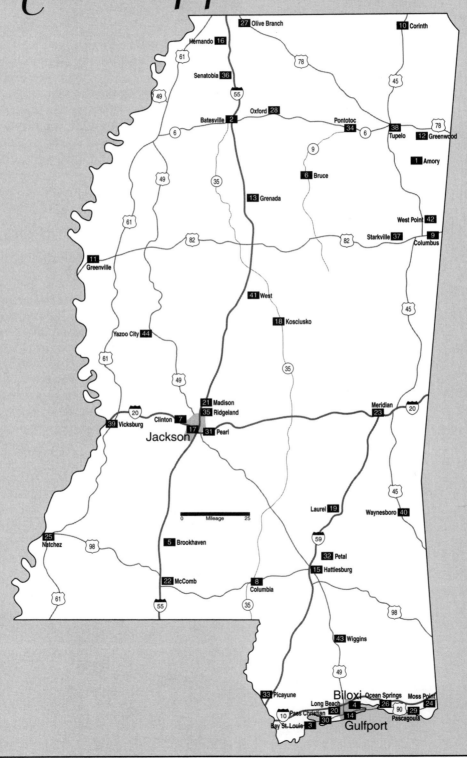

27 Olive Branch
10 Corinth
Hernando 16
78
45
61
Senatobia 36
49
55
Batesville 2    Oxford 28
Pontotoc 34    6    38 Tupelo
78
6
12 Greenwood
9
1 Amory
6 Bruce
35
13 Grenada
West Point 42
82
82    Starkville 37
9 Columbus
11
Greenville
61
41 West
45
18 Kosciusko
Yazoo City 44
35
61
49
21 Madison
35 Ridgeland    Meridian 23    20
20
Clinton 7
39 Vicksburg    17
31 Pearl
Jackson
45
Laurel 19    Waynesboro 40
0    Mileage    25
25    5 Brookhaven    59
Natchez    98
32 Petal
22 McComb    15 Hattiesburg
8
Columbia
35    98
61
55
43 Wiggins
49
33 Picayune    Biloxi    Ocean Springs    Moss Point
Long Beach    4    26    90    24
10 Pass Christian    20    29 Pascagoula
30    14
Bay St. Louis    3    Gulfport

# Mississippi

## 1 AMORY

**The Park Antiques**
109A S. Main St.
601/257-2299

**Jerry's Antiques & Collectibles**
300 N. Main St.
601/256-8790

**Amory Mini-Mall**
105 N. Main St.
601/256-8003

## 2 BATESVILLE

**Collector Antiques & Things**
111 Public Square
601/563-1916

## 3 BAY SAINT LOUIS

**Beach Antique Mall**
108 S. Beach Blvd.
601/467-7955

**Paper Moon**
220 Main St.
601/467-8318

**Lighthouse Antiques**
131 Main St.
601/467-1455

**Charter's Antiques**
125 Main St.
601/467-4665

**Cummings Antiques**
131 Main St.
601/467-1648

**Bay Shoppe Gallery, Inc.**
136 Main St.
601/466-2651

**Evergreen Antiques**
201 Main St.
601/467-9924

**M. Schon Antiques**
110 S. 2nd St.
601/467-9890

## 4 BILOXI

**Beauvoir Antique Mall & Flea**
190 Beuvoir Road
601/388-5506

**Memories Annex**
918 A St.
601/374-6708

**Nixon Antique Gallery Ltd.**
993 Howard Ave.
601/435-4336

**Tu J's Treasures Ltd.**
819 Jackson St.
601/435-5374

**Russenes**
128 Porter Ave.
601/432-0903

**Spanish Trail Books**
781 Vieux Marche Mall
601/435-1144

### Great Places to Stay

**The Father Ryan House Bed and Breakfast**
1196 Beach Blvd.
601/435-1189 or 1-800-295-1189

Circa 1841. National Register. One-time home and study of Father A. J. Ryan, poet laureate of the Confederacy. Private balconies overlooking white sand beaches and the Gulf. Nine rooms on 3 floors. Private bath. Period antiques. Pool and courtyard. Southern breakfast.

**The Old Santini House Bed and Breakfast**
964 Beach Blvd.
1-800-686-1146

The Old Santini House, listed on the National Register of Historic Places, was built on land purchased in 1828 by John Blight Byrne, a wealthy New Orleans merchant. Joseph Santini purchased the home in 1867, which remained in the family's hands until 1972. The simple but appealing design is perhaps the earliest example of the "American Cottage" in Biloxi. Extensive renovation has been done to the home to bring it to the present delightful decor, which reflects the Santini's business as an international importer.

Four guest rooms. Breakfast and afternoon appetizers are served.

## 5 BROOKHAVEN

**Brookwood Gifts & Antiques**
706 Hwy. 51 N.
601/833-3481

**This 'n' That**
1383A Union St. Ext. N.E.
601/835-1512

## 6 BRUCE

**Collins Antiques**
S. Tyson Road
601/983-7194

## 7 CLINTON

**Trash and Treasures**
590 Springridge Road
601/924-3224

**Brick Street Antiques**
312 N. Jefferson St.
601/924-5251

**Pette's Place**
300 Monroe
601/924-2147

**Cindy's**
406 Monroe
601/924-7078

## 8 COLUMBIA

**Neat Stuff**
919 High School Ave.
601/736-5061

**The Tiger Lily**
Main St.
601/731-2511

## 9 COLUMBUS

**Vintage Vignettes & Framery**
413 Main St.
601/327-5655

**Riverhill Antiques**
122 3rd St. S.
601/329-2669

**Love-Lincoln Carriage House**
714 3rd Ave.
601/328-5413

## Great Places To Stay

### Amzi Love Bed and Breakfast Inn
305 Seventh St. S.
601/328-5413

Circa 1848. National Register. Italian-style villa in historic district. Romantic English garden. Five bedrooms with baths. Home is steeped in history and features original furnishings and old scrapbooks. Southern breakfast.

### Liberty Hall
Armstrong Road
601/328-4110

Circa 1832. National Register. Nineteenth-century portraits are displayed, along with such interesting documents as the old planter's diary that recounts the trials of running a 6,000-acre plantation. Picnic lunches, dinner with advance reservations, hiking and fishing.

### 10 CORINTH

**Junkers Parlor Antiques**
2003 Hwy. 72 E.
601/287-5112

**Hammond House Antiques**
1004 Filmore St.
601/286-6786

## Great Places to Stay

### The General's Quarters
924 Filmore St.
601/286-3325

Circa 1872. Victorian home located in the historic district of old Civil War town. Suite contains 140-year-old canopy bed. Lounge on second floor, veranda, parlor and beautiful garden. Furnished with period antiques. Evening snack. Southern breakfast.

### Madison Inn
822 Main St.
601/287-7157

Turn-of-the-century house in downtown residential area. Four suites, with sitting room and private bath. Beautiful courtyard, aquarium, in-ground pool. Continental breakfast.

### Robbins Nest Bed and Breakfast
1523 Shiloh Road
601/286-3109

Circa 1869. Southern Colonial–style home surrounded by oak, dogwood and azaleas. Situated on two acres. Three guest rooms with antiques and private baths. Generous breakfast served on the back porch where guests may relax on antique wicker furniture.

### 11 GREENVILLE

**Dust & Rust**
603 Hwy. 82 E.
601/332-4708

**Lina's Interiors**
525 S. Main St.
601/332-7226

**Wilson's Junk Tique & Woodwork**
Hwy. 82 E.
601/335-7525

**Town & Country Antique Barn**
Hwy. 82 E.
601/335-2436

### 12 GREENWOOD

**Russell's Antique Jewelry**
229 Carollton Ave.
601/453-4017

**Warehouse Antiques**
229 Carollton Ave.
601/453-0785

**Olde World Antiques**
301 W. Market St.
601/455-9678

**Patsy's Hodge Podge**
511 Lamar St.
601/455-4927

**Heritage House Antiques**
311 E. Market St.
601/455-4800

**Finchers, Inc.**
512 W. Park Ave.
601/453-6246

**Antique Wholesalers**
527 W. Park Ave.
601/455-4401

**Corner Collection**
412 Walthall St.
601/453-8387

### 13 GRENADA

**Maw & Paws Antiques**
1079 Hebron Church Road
601/226-3672

**Donna's Antiques & Gifts**
N. Main St.
601/226-2595

### 14 GULFPORT

**Ronnie G's Antique & Furn. Restorations**
240 Courthouse Road
601/896-7391

**Artiques**
1130 Cowan Road
601/897-2273

**Old Things**
15415 Landon Road
601/832-6945

**Dear Hearts**
10425 Old High #49
601/832-6017

**Back in Time Antique Mall**
205 Pass Road
601/868-8246

**Handsboro Trading Post**
504 E. Pass Road
601/896-6787

**Ward Antique Brass**
711 E. Pass Road
601/896-5436

**Right Stuff Antiques**
1750 E. Pass Road
601/896-8127

# Mississippi

**Antique House**
1864 E. Pass Road
601/896-3435

**Circa 1909 Antiques**
2170 E. Pass Road
601/897-7744

**Alston's Antiques & Gifts**
2208 25th Ave.
601/868-3985

## 15 HATTIESBURG

**Early Settler Antiques & Collectibles**
5330 Hwy. 42
601/582-8212

**Calico Mall**
309 E. Pine St.
601/582-4351

**Tin Top Antiques**
1005 Bouie St.
601/584-7018

**Old High School Antiques**
846 N. Main St.
601/544-6644

**The Antique Mall**
2103 W. Pine St.
601/268-2511

**Riverwalk Marketplace**
5619 Hwy. 42
601/545-7001

### Great Places to Stay

## Tally House
402 Rebecca Ave.
601/582-3467

Circa 1907. National Register. Tally House has welcomed five Mississippi governors as overnight guests. The 13,000-square-foot home has an intriguing collection of antiques, cozy animals and birds to enjoy.

## 16 HERNANDO

**Buddy's Antiques**
151 Commerce
601/429-5338

**Harper's Antiques**
2610 Hwy. 51 S.
601/429-9387

### Great Places to Stay

## Shadow Hill
2310 Elm St.
601/449-0800

Originally opened as a tea room in 1923, this quiet country retreat is located on six acres and features large rooms, antiques, fireplaces and a wide front porch overlooking a deep, shaded lane.

## 17 JACKSON

## Interior Spaces
Maywood Mart
1220 E. Northside Dr., Suite 120
601/981-9820
Open: Mon.–Sat. 10–5:30

*Directions: If traveling north on I-55:* Take Exit 100. Go through the first stoplight on Frontage Road. Located on the right in Maywood Shopping Center. *If traveling south on I-55:* Take Exit 100. Go to the first stoplight. Turn left on Northside Drive. Then turn left on Frontage Road. Located on the right in Maywood Shopping Center.

Located in the metropolitan area of Jackson, Interior Spaces is an upscale antique market dealing with English, French, and American antiques. Beautifully displayed rooms entice the eye with assorted home accessories, original art, prints, mirrors, rugs, architectural elements and lamps. A wide price range makes this a "must see" stop for the discriminating buyer.

The staff includes several interior decorators, ready to assist you at your request. To complete your decorating needs, Interior Spaces offers an "in home" decorating service for a nominal fee.

**Oriental Shoppe**
110 Highland Village (I-55 N.)
601/362-4646

**Primos Annelle & Associates**
4500 Highland Village (I-55 N.)
601/362-6154

**Antique Mall of Richland**
731 Hwy. 49 S.
601/936-9007

**St. Martin's Gallery**
2817 Old Canton Road
601/362-1977

**Jim Westerfield Antiques**
4429 Old Canton Road
601/362-7508

**Stately Home Antiques**
737 N. State St.
601/355-1158

**Elephant's Ear**
3110 Old Canton Road
601/982-5140

**Interiors Market**
659 Duling Ave.
601/981-6020

**Oliver Antiques**
730 Lakeland Dr.
601/981-2564

**Jo's Antiques**
680 Commerce St.
601/352-3644

**Ax Antiques & Trading Post**
3953 Hwy. 80 E. (Pearl)
601/939-5887

**Kuntry Junkshun**
1135 Raymond Road
601/373-6503

**Caldwell Antiques**
1048 Old Brandon Road
601/939-4781

**Bobbie King Dressing Up**
667 Duling Ave.
601/362-9803

**C.W. Fewel & Co.**
840 N. State St.
601/355-5375

**High Street Collection**
1217 Vine St.
601/354-5222

**The Antique Market**
3009 N. State St.
601/982-5456

# *Mississippi*

## *Great Places to Stay*

### The Fairview Inn

734 Fairview St.
601/948-3429 or 1-888-948-1908
Rates: $100–$150, $15 each additional person
Directions: I-55 Exit 98A on Woodrow Wilson; left, first traffic light at North State; left, one block past second traffic light at Fairview Street. Inn is first property on left.

The Fairview Inn is Southern hospitality at its best. Constructed in 1908, at the turn of the century, Fairview is one of Jackson's landmark mansions and one of the few architecturally designed houses of that period remaining in the city. It was built for Cyrus C. Warren, vice president of the Warren-Goodwin Lumber Company, and was designed by the Chicago architectural firm of Spencer and Powers. Robert Closson Spencer was a prominent member of the Prairie School and a close associate of Frank Lloyd Wright. Walter Burley Griffin was his star employee.

Both the main house, whose front entrance facing Fairview Street is supported by modified Corinthian columns, and the carriage house facing Oakwood Street, are Colonial Revival, a style associated with the formality and elegance of Southern tradition. The classical detail and ordered proportions of the Palladian influence on Georgian architecture are also apparent in Fairview, and have caused it to be compared with Mount Vernon, although there are significant differences between the two structures. In recognition of its architectural character, Fairview was placed on the National Register of Historic Places in 1979.

The property was purchased in 1913 by Felix Gunter, president of the Jackson Board of Trade (forerunner of the Jackson Chamber of Commerce), and then by W. E. Guild, treasurer of the Finkbine Lumber Company, in 1921. In 1930, Fairview was purchased by D. C. Simmons, and has been a Simmons family home ever since. D. C. Simmons, associated for many years with Deposit Guaranty Bank and Trust Company and the Mississippi Baptist Hospital's Board of Trustees, lived in the house until his death in 1964, and his widow, Annie Belle Ferguson Simmons, continued to live in the house until her death in 1972. Their son, William J. Simmons, purchased the property from his parents' estate in 1972. He and his wife, Carol, are the present owners and residents.

The inn's eight guest rooms and suites are all elegantly decorated with antiques and reproductions, fine linens, and collectibles. Amenities include private baths, phones, data ports, voice mail, TV and VCR, sitting rooms, toiletries, and air conditioning. Some rooms have in-room Jacuzzis.

Each gourmet meal at the Fairview Inn is meticulously prepared by Chef Todd McClellan, a graduate of Johnson & Wales University. Fresh flowers, live music, and a five-course, five-star meal can make your evening one to remember.

The inn is a AAA Four Diamond Award–winning bed and breakfast and was recently chosen as one of four "dream vacations" by *Travel &*

*Leisure*. For a look inside Fairview Inn, visit them on the Internet at www.fairviewinn.com.

## 18  KOSCIUSKO

| Antiques & Interiors Mall | Peeler House Antiques |
|---|---|
| 301 W. Jefferson St. | 117 W. Jefferson St. |
| 601/289-3600 | 601/289-5165 |

### *Great Places to Stay*

### Redbud Inn

121 N. Wells St.
601/289-5086 or 1-800-379-5086

Circa 1884. National Register. Queen Anne–style Victorian two-story, listed on *Best Places to Stay in the South* and top-ten bed and breakfast inns in Mississippi. Furnished in period antiques. Antique shop. Tea room. Near downtown historic square. Southern breakfast.

## 19  LAUREL

| Southern Collections Mall | Antiques Mart |
|---|---|
| 317 Central Ave. | 427 Oak St. |
| 601/426-2322 | 601/425-0009 |

### *Great Places to Stay*

### The Mourning Dove Bed and Breakfast

556 N. Sixth Ave.
601/425-2561 or 1-800-863-3683

Circa 1907. National Register. Classic four-square one block from the Lauren Rogers Museum of Art and located in the historic district. Features two private cottages.

## 20  LONG BEACH

| Oak Leaf Shoppe | Doll Hospital |
|---|---|
| 410 Jeff Davis Ave. | 110 E. 5th St. |
| 601/868-9433 | 601/863-1024 |

### *Great Places to Stay*

### Red Creek Inn Vineyard & Racing Stable

7416 Red Creek Road
228/452-3080 or 1-800-729-9670

Red Creek Inn Vineyard & Racing Stable is a circa 1899 "raised French cottage" centrally located for antiquing in Biloxi and Ocean

Springs to the east, and Pass Christian and Bay St. Louis to the west. Located on 11 ½ acres of fragrant magnolias and ancient live oaks, you'll love swinging on Red Creek's 64-foot front porch, before hitting the nearby beaches, casinos, or historical sites—just minutes away!

## 21 MADISON

**Talk of the Town**
120 Depot Dr.
601/856-3087

**Inside Story**
2081 Main St.
601/856-3229

**Uptown Antiques Etc.**
111 Depot Dr.
601/853-9153

**Madison Antiques Market**
100 Post Oak St.
601/856-8036

## 22 McCOMB

**Traditions — Art & Antiques**
125 S. Broadway St.
601/249-3038

**J & E Antiques**
127 S. Magnolia St.
601/249-3309

**Bell Remnants, Inc.**
232 N. Railroad Blvd.
601/684-0529

**A.J. Sales**
205 E. Georgia Ave.
601/684-8249

**Whistle Stop Antiques**
228 N. Railroad Blvd.
601/249-3990

**Finders Limited**
239 Louisiana Ave.
601/684-5062

## 23 MERIDIAN

### Lincoln Ltd. Bed and Breakfast
601/482-5483 or 1-800-633-6477

Convenient to downtown Meridian. Home is filled with the host's collection of family heirlooms. Features a pre–Civil War mahogany-canopied bed, as well as a sun porch and patio.

**A & I Place**
2223 Front St.
601/483-9281

**Booker's Antiques**
Hwy. 19 S.
601/644-3272

**Cabin Antiques**
8343 Russell Topton Road
601/679-7922

**Z's Antiques**
1607 24th Ave.
601/482-0676

**Old South Antique Mall**
100 N. Frontage Road
601/483-1737

**Wayside Shop**
5523 Poplar Springs Dr.
601/485-2205

**House of Antiques & Collectibles**
1725 17th Ave.
601/485-5462

**Century House Antiques**
2101 24th Ave.
601/482-5504

## 24 MOSS POINT

**Fisher's Antiques**
5136 Elder St.
601/475-5731

**Pass-Point Antiques**
3806 Main St.
601/475-7863

## 25 NATCHEZ

**Antique Lantern**
145 Homochitto St.
601/445-9955

**As You Like It Silver Shop**
410 N. Commerce St.
601/442-0933

**H. Hal Garner Antiques**
610 Franklin St.
601/445-8416

**Simonton Antiques**
631 Franklin St.
601/442-5217

**Antique Mall**
700 Franklin St.
601/442-0130

**Natchez Antiques & Collectibles**
701 Franklin St.
601/442-9555

**Lower Lodge Antiques**
712 Franklin St.
601/442-2617

**Rendezvous Antiques & Gifts**
401 Main St.
601/442-9988

**Natchez Gun Shop**
533 S. Canal St.
601/442-7627

**Country Bumpkin**
502 Franklin St.
601/442-5908

**Antiquarian**
624 Franklin St.
601/445-0388

**Mrs. Holder's Antiques**
636 Franklin St.
601/442-0675

**Sharp Designs & Works of Art**
703 Franklin St.
601/442-5224

**Pippens Limited Antiques**
708 Franklin St.
601/442-0962

**Antiques — Washington Village**
824 Hwy. 61 N.
601/442-8021

**Tass House Antiques**
111 N. Pearl St.
601/446-9917

### *Great Places to Stay*

### Linden Bed and Breakfast
1 Linden Place
601/445-5472 or 1-800-1-LINDEN

Rising gracefully from the top of a gentle slope and set behind mossy oaks, this stunning mansion is the epitome of dignity, comfort, and hospitality. Linden is a Federal plantation home and has one of the finest collections of Federal furniture in the South. The home's front doorway was copied for Tara in *Gone with the Wind*.

Mrs. Jane Gustine Conner purchased the estate in 1849 and her descendants have lived in the home ever since. Today it is owned by Mrs. Jeanette Feltus, and her children are the sixth generation of the Conner family to reside there.

Linden's stately dining room is grand — a magnificent cypress punkah, painted white, hangs over the Hepplewhite banquet table, set with many pieces of family coin silver and heirloom china. On the walls are three Havell editions of John James Audubon's bird prints. Each of the seven bedrooms is furnished with antiques and canopied beds. All bedrooms have private baths and are centrally heated and air-conditioned. Most of the bedrooms open onto the galleries where old-fashioned rocking chairs welcome its guests to relax.

Linden has been home to many outstanding Mississippi statesmen such as Thomas B. Reed, first U. S. Senator from the then new state of Mississippi; Mrs. Margaret Conner Martin, wife of General W. T. Martin of Confederate fame; Michael Conner, Governor of Mississippi; and Mrs. Percy Quinn, wife of Senator Percy Quinn.

## Mark Twain Guest House
25 Silver St.
601/446-8023

Circa 1830. National Register. Three rooms, two rooms overlooking the Mississippi River and one with balcony and fireplace. Large shared bathroom. Entertainment downstairs in saloon on weekends. Near casino and restaurants.

### 26 OCEAN SPRINGS

**Temptations**
1508 Government St.
601/875-7896

**Clocksmith**
12401 Hanover Dr.
601/875-6613

**Artifacts European Antiques**
1202 Government St.
601/872-4545

**B.J. & Friends**
3100 Bienville Blvd.
601/872-0509

**Lumbee Antiques**
6510 Washington Ave.
601/872-2881

**Magnolia Antiques**
1013 Government St.
601/875-4404

**Old Biloxi Antiques**
6011 Washington Ave.
601/872-7110

### *Great Places to Stay*

## Oak Shade Bed and Breakfast
1017 La Fontaine
601/875-1050

Spacious and completely private retreat situated amid the quiet charm of old Ocean Springs. The room has a private entrance and a private bath. Library. Southern breakfast.

## Who's Inn
623 Washington Ave.
601/875-3251

Gallery rooms are furnished with art and sculpture by Southern artists. Handicapped accessible. Located in the center of downtown historic

district. Stocked refrigerator in each room, private baths, three blocks from beach, bikes available. Continental breakfast.

## The Wilson House Inn
6312 Allen Road
601/875-6933 or 1-800-872-6933

Circa 1923. Six guest rooms with private baths, white pine floors, fireplaces, 10-foot-wide wraparound porch, brick patio. One king bed, two queen beds, two full beds and one room with two twin beds. Southern breakfast.

### 27 OLIVE BRANCH

**Old Towne Antiques & Gifts**
9117 Pigeon Roost Road
601/893-2323

**Olive Branch Bazaar**
9119 Pigeon Roost Road
601/895-9496

**Meme's Attic**
9121 Pigeon Roost Road
601/895-8616

### 28 OXFORD

Directions: From I-55 South toward Jackson, Miss., exit onto Hwy. 6 West. At South Lamar, you have reached downtown Oxford's antique district.

## Bea's Antiques
1315 N. Lamar Blvd.
601/234-9405
Open: Mon.–Sat. 9–5

Antiques, used furniture, quilts, glassware, mirrors, pictures, lamps and much more. Bea's buys estates.

## The Bird in the Bush/The Oxford Collection
1415 University Ave. E.
601/234-5784
Open: Mon.–Sat. 9–5:30

A multidealer mall featuring affordable antiques and collectibles, nostalgic accessories, a variety of reproduction antiques, linens, quilts, and more.

## Creme de la Creme
319 N. Lamar Blvd.
601/234-1463
Open: Mon.–Sat. 10–5:30

A unique collection of shops featuring American, English, and French antiques and collectibles, distinguished home accessories, original art, children's furniture and gifts and a design and sew shop.

## Inside Oxford

1220 Jefferson Ave.
601/234-1444
Open: Mon.–Fri. 9–5:30, Sat. 10–5:30

French, English and American furniture both in the main showroom and in the warehouse. Oriental rugs, lamps, framed art, oil paintings and mirrors, chandeliers, accessories and gifts.

## Material Culture, Inc.

405 S. Lamar Blvd.
601/234-7055
Open: Tues.–Sat. 10–5, Mon. by appointment

Featuring all things Southern, plus early to mid-nineteenth century American furniture and decorative arts, antique Persian carpets, folk art, fine crafts, vintage linens, handcrafted jewelry, antique architectural elements and materials, quilts and silver.

| | |
|---|---|
| **Tommy's Antiques & Imports**<br>Hwy. 6 E.<br>601/234-4669 | **Ruffled Feathers**<br>Hwy. 6 W.<br>601/236-1537 |
| **Old House Juntiques**<br>Hwy. 30<br>601/236-7116 | **Weather Vane**<br>137 Courthouse Square<br>601/236-1120 |
| **Williams on the Square**<br>116 Courthouse Square<br>601/236-3041 | |

### *Great Places to Stay*

## Barksdale-Isom House

1003 Jefferson Ave.
601/236-5600 or 1-800-236-5696

Circa 1838. National Register. Constructed entirely of native timber cut from the grounds and handworked by Indian and slave labor. Classic example of planter-style architecture.

## Puddin Place

1008 University Ave.
601/234-1250

Circa 1892. Beautifully restored. Suite accommodations with private bath, fireplaces, antiques, collectibles and historic mementos. Short walk to historic town square, Ole Miss campus and Rowan Oak. Southern breakfast.

## The Oliver-Britt House

512 Van Buren Ave.
601/234-8043

Circa 1905. Greek Revival. Five second-floor bedrooms, all with private baths and antiques. Breakfast at Smitty's, an Oxford tradition, on weekdays. Southern breakfast.

## 29 PASCAGOULA

| | |
|---|---|
| **Samuels Antiques**<br>824 Denny Ave.<br>601/762-8593 | **Bernard Clark's White House Antqs.**<br>2128 Ingalls Ave.<br>601/762-3511 |
| **Wixon & Co. Jewelers**<br>1803 Jackson Ave.<br>601/762-7777 | **J & B Antiques**<br>3803 Willow St.<br>601/769-0542 |

## 30 PASS CHRISTIAN

## The Blue Rose Restaurant and Antiques

120 W. Scenic Dr.
601/452-7004

The Blue Rose Restaurant and Antiques in Pass Christian sits majestically on Scenic Drive across from the Pass Christian Yacht Harbor.

The house, built in 1848, was originally a 1½-story frame, five-bay coastal cottage with a gallery with square columns wrapped around three full sides of the house, and consoles carrying overhanging cornices over each bay. It has distinctive pilastered dormers and numerous rear ells attaching the former outbuildings and enclosing gallery.

Mr. Fitzpatrick, who built the home, was a merchant marine. He and his wife had four children, three girls and one boy. Their daughter Nettie was a nun and Kitty was the postmaster in the city of Pass Christian. Hugh was the supervisor for Beat 3 for many years and Lettie is believed to be a "ghost" at the Blue Rose. Lettie was mentally retarded and rarely allowed on the first floor of the house. It was rumored that at night, when everyone was asleep, Lettie would roam around the first floor with her terrier puppy. She died at the age of 11 or 12, of yellow fever. None of the other children had offspring and the house eventually went to a niece.

During World War II the house was converted into apartments and later sold to a man from Louisiana. The Blue Rose is now owned by Philip LaGrange, who is the fourth owner of the house in its history.

The house is listed on the National Register of Historic Places. The National Trust of Historic Preservation has described it as "the most significant antebellum home on the western portion of Pass Christian's beachfront."

The broad front porch is now glassed in with breathtaking views of the harbor and Gulf Coast waters. Interior areas are graced by stained glass, intricate woodwork, and high ceilings. The antique store, featuring fine antiques, estate silver and collectibles, is on the eastern portion of the house. The restaurant, featuring the finest cuisine on the Gulf Coast, is on the western portion of the house.

**Wicker 'n' Wood**
254 E. Beach — Hwy. 90
601/452-4083

**Old Community Antique Mall**
301 E. 2nd St.
601/452-3102

**Blue Rose Antiques**
120 W. Scenic Dr.
601/452-7004

### *Great Places to Stay*

## Inn at the Pass
125 E. Scenic Dr.
601/452-0333 or 1-800-217-2588

Circa 1879. National Register. On the beach of the Mississippi Gulf Coast. Victorian antiques, fireplaces, kitchenette, golf packages, restaurants and shops within walking distance. Original art in all rooms.

## 31 PEARL

**McClain's Antiques**
3834 York Road
601/679-5076

**Memory Lane Antique Mall**
413 N. Bierdeman Road
601/932-1946

## 32 PETAL

**Ruthie's Attic**
101 Pine St.
601/583-0429

## 33 PICAYUNE

**Pirates Plunder**
127 W. Canal St.
601/798-0885

**Pineros Antiques**
210 W. Canal St.
601/798-9615

**Edwards Antiques & Gallery**
335 W. Canal St.
601/798-3376

**Abundant Treasures**
111 N. Main St.
601/799-5871

**Just Stuff**
300 W. Canal St.
601/749-0461

**Nicholson Antique Trading Post**
73 Emmett Meitzler Road
601/798-7844

## 34 PONTOTOC

**Mason Jar Antique Mall**
34 Liberty
601/489-7420

**Court Square Antique Mall**
42 Liberty
601/488-8844

## 35 RIDGELAND

## Antique Mall of the South
367 Hwy. 51
601/853-4000
Open: Mon.–Sat. 10–6, Sun. 12–6
Directions: Located one mile north of I-55/County Road intersection (I-55 Exit 103). One mile north of Jackson.

This 14,000-square-foot antique mall is known to have the "finest quality antiques in the South." The inventory here will impress even the choosiest antique collector.

There is a distinct selection of furniture, including Early American, Country, Empire, Victorian, as well as "lots of oak." For collectors of fine glassware, they offer Fenton, flow blue, depression glass, and the finest cut-glass pieces around. Hummel collectors will be delighted to find a selection of their favorite figurines available here. The locomotive hobbyist searching for that new locomotive to add to his collection may just find it here among the dandy selections of trains and accessories.

For an outstanding representation of quality antiques and collectibles, a "must stop" on your antiquing trail is the 50-dealer Antique Mall of the South.

**Village Antiques**
554 Hwy. 51, Suite D
601/856-6021

**Copper Kettle**
637A Hwy. 51
601/856-7042

## 36 SENATOBIA

**Dot Mitchell Antiques**
123 Lively St.
601/562-4392

**Home Sweet Home**
220 W. Main St.
601/562-0027

### *Great Places to Stay*

## Spahn House
401 College St.
601/562-9853

Circa 1904. This gracious 15-room Southern mansion, situated on a picture-perfect shady street, is beautifully restored. Four guest rooms, Jacuzzi baths, common areas. Honeymoon package. Lunch or dinner. Southern breakfast.

## 37 STARKVILLE

**Back Roads Antiques**
Old Crawford Road
601/323-4763

**Gini's Attic Antiques**
1221 Old Hwy. 82 E.
601/323-8790

**Watson's Village Antiques**
1237 Old High, #82E
601/323-5526

**Tin Top Antiques**
891 Old West Point Road
601/323-2032

*Great Places to Stay*

## The Caragen House

1108 Hwy. 82 W.
601/323-0340

Circa 1890. Steamboat Gothic design, the only one of its kind in Mississippi. Located inside the city limits on 22 acres. Five bedrooms with private baths, king beds, and refreshment center.

### 38 TUPELO

**Red Door Antique Mall & Collectibles**
1001 Coley Road
601/840-6777

**Main Attraction**
214 W. Main St.
601/842-9617

**Chesterfield's**
624 W. Main St.
601/841-9171

**Murphey Antiques Ltd.**
1120 W. Main St.
601/844-3245

**Pam Antiques & Lamp Shop**
2229 W. Main St.
601/844-3050

**Rain Station Antiques**
202 S. Park St.
601/840-2030

**The Treasure Chest**
4097 W. Main St.
601/840-2015

**Cottage Book Shop**
214 N. Madison
601/844-1553

**Nostalgia Alley**
214 W. Main St.
601/842-2757

**George Watson Antiques**
628 W. Main St.
601/841-9411

**My Granny's Attic**
By appointment only
601/844-4614

**Skyline Antiques**
Old 78 E.
601/680-4559

**Peppertown Antiques**
Hwy. 78
601/862-9892

**Silver Web Antiques**
810 Harrison, #3
601/842-4022

*Great Places to Stay*

## The Mockingbird Inn

305 N. Gloster
601/841-0286

Seven guest rooms represent the decor from different corners of the world. Private bath and queen-size beds. Common rooms. Evening soft drinks, coffee, tea, bottled water and juices are complimentary. Southern breakfast.

### 39 VICKSBURG

## Yesterday's Treasures Antique Mall

1400 Washington St.
601/638-6213
Open: Mon.–Sat. 10–5, closed Sun.

A multidealer mall in historic downtown Vicksburg, offering furniture, glassware, Civil War relics, old books, pottery, quilts and linens, toys, collectibles, and much more!

**Old Feldhome Antiques**
2108 Cherry St.
601/636-0773

**Washington Street Antique Mall**
1305 Washington St.
601/636-3700

**River City Antiques**
1609 Levee St.
601/638-4758

**Yesterday's Treasures Antique Mall**
1400 Washington St.
601/638-6213

*Great Places to Stay*

## Balfour House

1002 Crawford St.
601/638-7113
Open: Year-round

Beneath the flickering glow of candlelight, elegant ladies and dashing Confederate officers danced one cold December evening in 1862, until a courier rushed in to announce that Union gunboats had been sighted on the Mississippi River. The officers bade their ladies a hasty good-bye and left to prepare for the defense of the city (an eventful night at Balfour House).

Each December, Balfour House is host to a gala evening of music and festive reenactment of the last grand ball before the siege of Vicksburg. Among Balfour House's other year-round accomplishments is its distinction as a National Register property and designated Mississippi landmark. Additionally, it is considered one of the finest Greek Revival structures in the state according to the Mississippi Department of Archives and History. This bed and breakfast establishment was certainly abuzz with activity during the siege of Vicksburg. In fact, and obviously so once you see, Balfour House became business headquarters for the Union Army after the fall of the city.

The 1982 restoration of the house complied obediently to the Secretary of the Interior's Standards for Rehabilitation, and the house's walls surrendered a cannonball and other Civil War artifacts. The three-story elliptical staircase and patterned hardwood floors were also restored in 1982. The work on these projects was honored with the 1984 Award of Merit from the state historical society.

With such a notable history, Balfour House would be a star stop for any Civil War, architectural or antique lover's tour of Vicksburg. Even so, the bed and breakfast offers delights matching the history of the home.

The bedrooms are authentically decorated, and upon stepping out of your guest room each morning, you are invited to partake of a full Southern-style breakfast which is always generous and hearty. During the day, you might enjoy following the guided tour of the home, which will enlighten you on all of its history and beauty.

## Annabelle Bed and Breakfast
501 Speed St.
601/638-2000 or 1-800-791-2000

Circa 1868. Located in Vicksburg's historic Garden District, this stately Victorian-Italianate residence is elegantly furnished with period antiques and rare family heirlooms. Private full baths. Southern breakfast.

## The Corners
601 Klein St.
601/636-7421 or 1-800-444-7421

Circa 1872. National Register. Original parterre gardens, a 70-foot gallery across the front with a view of the Mississippi River, double parlor, formal dining room and library. Five rooms with fireplaces and eight rooms with whirlpool tubs, private bath. Southern breakfast.

## Cedar Grove Mansion Inn
2200 Oak St.
601/636-1000 or 1-800-862-1300

Circa 1840. National Register. Greek Revival mansion overlooking the Mississippi River. Gardens, fountains and gazebos. Original antiques. AAA Four-Diamond rating. Gourmet candlelight dining and piano bar.

## Duff Green Mansion
1114 First East St.
601/636-6968 or 1-800-992-0037

Circa 1856. National Register. Used as a hospital for Confederate soldiers. Furnished with period antiques and reproductions. Honeymoon and anniversary package. Southern breakfast.

## Floweree
2309 Pearl St.
601/638-2704

Circa 1870. National Register. Fine example of Italianate architecture. Listed on Historic American Building Survey. Southern breakfast.

## The Stained Glass Manor
2430 Drummond St.
601/638-8893 or 1-800-771-8893

Circa 1906. National Register. The Stained Glass Manor, of Spanish design features 32 stained glass windows, fine oak paneling and a spectacular staircase. The interior glows from the light through the delicate panes of rose, salmon, rust, gold, blue and green.

## 40  WAYNESBORO

| Four Generations | Old French House |
|---|---|
| 124 Mississippi Dr. | 515 Mississippi Dr. |
| 601/735-5721 | 601/735-0353 |

## 41  WEST

### *Great Places to Stay*

## The Alexander House
11 Green St.
1-800-350-8034
Open: Year-round
Directions: From I-55, take Exit 164, between Jackson, Miss., and Memphis, Tenn. Go 3 miles off the interstate. Located on the second paved road to the right after leaving the interstate exchange.

*An incident from the rooms of the Alexander House as recounted by Ruth Ray and Woody Dinstel:*

## The Blinking Cat
Guests at the Alexander House often ask to photograph our rather elegant rooms and some of the more valuable or interesting antiques. We say, "Be our guests." One morning a guest was going through the rooms with a camcorder. She was in Miss Anne's room when she became excited and called everyone to her. She had a garbage can with an embossed cat as decoration in her viewfinder, and she cried out, "The cat blinked at me." We all gathered, but no one saw any blinking, no matter how hard we stared. A week or so later, this lady called from her home in Alabama to say when they showed the film on their television, the cat definitely blinked. Her husband even processed one frame that definitely showed the eyes closed! There is no streak of light across the frame. Needless to say, we have obtained a copy of the video, to show doubters the proof of the blinking cat.

Tucked lovingly into the heart of Mississippi is the town of West, which ironically is located east of Interstate 55. Among that town's historic buildings is the Alexander House. The unique events occurring in Miss Anne's room regarding "The Blinking Cat" are enough to entice the curious to spend a night or two peeping around corners to see embossed

# Mississippi

cats wink. Nevertheless, the opulent atmosphere and furnishings of this bed and breakfast will lure anyone with a taste to be pampered and surrounded by the uncommon and exquisite. That pampered feeling certainly comes from being luxuriously housed within the historic district of West. The Alexander House was constructed as early as 1880. In 1994, the owners, Ruth Ray and Woody Dinstel, opened the restored home in its period grandeur. As a guest, you will be treated to a complimentary, Southern-style (hearty portions) breakfast in the authentically furnished, two-story home.

Gourmet lunches and dinners are available by reservation.

## 42 WEST POINT

**Aunt Teek's**
743 E. Brame Ave.
601/494-2980

**Treasure Nook**
111 Commerce St.
601/494-1103

**Antique Mall**
415 Hwy. 45 N.
601/494-0098

**Once upon a Time Antiques**
910 Hwy. 45 Alt St.
601/494-7811

**Antiques on the Main**
123 E. Main St.
601/494-2010

**Wisteria**
411 E. Main St.
601/494-4205

## 43 WIGGINS

**Serendipity Shop**
203 E. Pine Ave.
601/928-5020

## 44 YAZOO CITY

**Main Street Antiques**
211 N. Main St.
601/746-9307

**Chesire Cat**
305 S. Main St.
601/746-8401

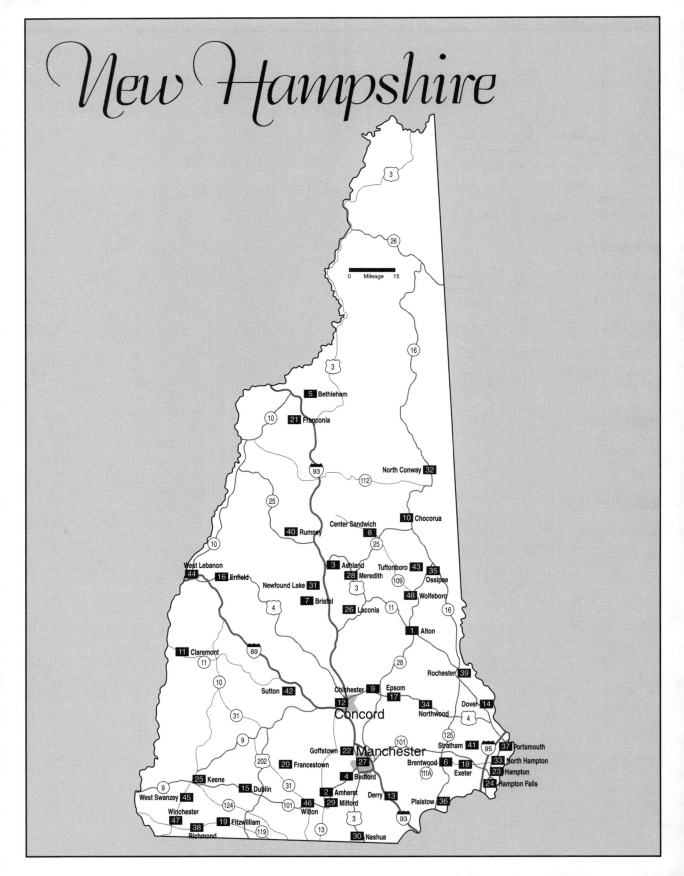

# New Hampshire

0 Mileage 15

3

26

16

**5** Bethlehem

**21** Franconia

10

93

**32** North Conway

25

112

**40** Rumney

Center Sandwich

**8**

**10** Chocorua

25

West Lebanon

**44**

**16** Enfield

**3** Ashland

Newfound Lake **31**

**28** Meredith

Tuftonboro **43**

**35** Ossipee

109

10

**7** Bristol

3

**48** Wolfeboro

**26** Laconia

11

16

4

**1** Alton

**11** Claremont

89

11

28

Rochester **39**

10

Sutton **42**

Chichester **9**

Epsom

**17**

**34** Northwood

Dover **14**

31

**12**

Concord

4

9

125

Stratham **41**

**95**

**37** Portsmouth

Goffstown **22**

Manchester

101

202

**20** Francestown

**27**

Brentwood **6**

**18**

**33** North Hampton

111A

Exeter

**23** Hampton

**25** Keene

**15** Dublin

**4** Bedford

**2** Amherst

Derry **13**

Plaistow **36**

**24** Hampton Falls

9

West Swanzey **45**

31

101

**46**

**29** Milford

Wilton

3

93

Winchester

**47**

**38**

**19** Fitzwilliam

124

119

13

**30** Nashua

Richmond

## 1 ALTON

**Cottontail Collectibles**
Main St. — Route 11
603/875-5456

**Homestead Place Antiques**
Jct. Routes 11 & 23
603/875-2556

## 2 AMHERST

### Needful Things
112 State Route 101A
603/889-1232
Open: Mon.–Sat. 10–5, Sun. 8–4

A quality group shop featuring 185 dealers.

### 101A Antique Center
141 State Route 101A
603/880-8422
Open: Mon.–Sat. 10–5, Sun. 9–5

Showcasing the wares of 175 dealers.

### Antiques at Mayfair
119-121 State Route 101A
603/595-7531
Open: Mon.–Sat. 10–6, Sun. 8–4, Thurs. until 8

One of the largest multidealer shops in the area; two large buildings filled with antiques and collectibles.

**Antique Gallery at Carriage Depot**
135 State Route 101A
603/594-0050

**Mori Books**
141 State Route 101A
602/882-2665

**Consignment Gallery**
74 State Route 101A
603/673-4114

**His & Hers Antiques**
96 State Route 101A
603/881-7722

**Treasures Antiques**
Route 122
603/672-2535

## 3 ASHLAND

**Antique House**
9 Highland
603/968-3357

## 4 BEDFORD

**Bell Hill Antiques**
Route 101
603/472-5580

## 5 BETHLEHEM

### Checkered Past Antiques
154 Guider Lane
603/444-6628
Open: Year-round, Mon.–Sat., 10–5; Sun., 12–4; closed Wed. Nov.–June
Email: kscope@ConnRiver.net
Directions: Located at the junction of Route 302 and I-93 (Exit 40), Checkered Past is easily accessible. When exiting off I-93 or traveling Route 302 East, turn left at the Adair Country Inn sign and take Guider Lane 4/10 of a mile to the end. When heading west on Route 302, immediately before the junction of I-93, turn right at the Adair Country Inn sign and follow Guider Lane 4/10 of a mile to the end.

In addition to Checkered Past's (what a great name!) ever-changing array of antiques, their heated 19th-century barn holds handcrafted, custom-made reproduction furniture.

**Curran's Antiques**
Main St.
603/869-2089

**Hundred Acre Wood**
Main St.
603/869-6427

**The Raven's Nest**
Main St.
603/869-2678

**3 of Cups**
Main St.
603/869-2606

### *Great Places to Stay*

### Wayside Inn
Route 302, P.O. Box 480
603/869-3364 or 1-800-448-9557
Open: Year-round; except Thanksgiving and Christmas
Directions: Take Exit 40 off I-93. Go east on Route 302 for 6³/10 miles. The inn is on the right side.

Wayside Inn has a long and interesting history. It began in 1832, when the main building was built as a boardinghouse for railroad workers (it sits across from the tracks). Around 1900 it became an inn for the general traveling public, and has remained open as such for nearly a century, making it the oldest continually operating inn in the area. The Victorian-style building holds an extensive collection of antiques and quilts, and offers guests 28 rooms, all with private baths. There is an award-winning restaurant and lounge for guests' dining pleasure, and the restaurant gives diners a rare opportunity to enjoy Swiss specialties.

## 6 BRENTWOOD

### Crawley Falls Antiques
159 Crawley Falls Road
603/642-3417
Directions: From Massachusetts: Take I-495 North to Exit 51B (Route 125). Follow Route 125 for approximately 16 miles. Look for the blinking light at the intersection of Routes 125 and 111A. Turn right at light, then make immediate left and go about 300 yards to shop parking lot. Shop is on the hill behind Lindy's Country Store. (From Route 101): Take Route 125 exit. South approximately 5 miles to Route 111A, left at blinking light.

Visit this fabulous 18th-century homestead where the barn shop is filled with antique furniture and decorative accessories — primitive and vintage. The shop also features linens, china, artists' signed teddy bears (some made specially for the shop), sewing machines, trunks, ephemera and a wide selection of smalls. Displays not only show off the fine pieces in this shop, but are also artfully arranged to help you visualize ways to decorate your own home. Owner Donna Judah has created a warm and inviting atmosphere at Crawley Falls, complete with a children's area and sitting porch. No matter what your collecting interests, you surely will find something to take home with you at this wonderful shop.

## 7 BRISTOL

**Remember When**
Route 104 - 52 Summer St.
603/744-2191

**New Hampton Antiques Center**
Route 104
603/744-5652

## 8 CENTER SANDWICH

### New England Antiques & Collectibles Festival
"A Show, Sale & Celebration of Old Time Living"
Sandwich Fairgrounds, Junctions 113 & 109
Call number below for dates.

New Hampshire's largest show, sale and celebration of old-time living features over 200 exhibitors of antiques and collectibles. Emphasis is placed on family fun, live entertainment and nostalgia. Great buys can be found on garden decorations, architectural details, Fiestaware, vintage toasters, radios, linens, tools, textiles, ephemera, robots, costume and Bakelite jewelry, '50s kitsch, dolls, art pottery, series books and country furniture. Interactive demonstrations include hearthside cooking, bee keeping, blacksmithing, and soap making. Vintage car, truck and motorcycle show, sale and swap held simultaneously on 22-acre fairgrounds in a quaint New England village.

For more information call New England Antique Show Management, 603/539-1900.

## 9 CHICHESTER

### Teachers' Antiques at Thunder Bridge
11 Depot Road
603/798-4314

Two floors of painted country items, flow blue and Shaker smalls.

**Austin's Antiques**
Route 4
603/798-3116

## 10 CHOCORUA

**Michael Dam Bookseller**
Route 16
603/323-8041

**Lucky Acres**
Route 16
603/323-8502

**Chocorua View Farm Antiques**
Route 16
603/323-8041

## 11 CLAREMONT

**La Deaus Annex**
38 Main St.
603/542-6352

**Farmor's Group Shoppes**
61 Main St.
603/542-2532

**Scottish Bear's Antiques, Inc.**
54 Pleasant St.
603/543-1978

**Antique Center**
66 Pleasant St.
603/542-9331

## 12 CONCORD

**House & House Collectibles**
1 Eagle Square
603/225-0050

**Ol Speedway**
374 Loudon Road
603/226-0977

**Interior Additions**
38 N. Main St.
603/224-3414

**B & M Trading Post**
176 S. Main St.
603/753-6241

**Whispering Birches Antiques**
185 S. Main St.
603/753-8519

**Not Necessarily Antiques**
182 King St.
603/796-2240

## 13 DERRY

**Derry Exchange**
13 1/2 Broadway
603/437-8771

**GRS Trading Post**
108 Chester Road
603/434-0220

**Antique & Used Furniture**
1 Pinkerton St.
603/437-4900

**Log Cabin**
182 Rockingham Road
603/434-7068

**Antique Store**
9 Grove St.
603/432-1070

## 14 DOVER

**Ubiquidous Antiques**
284 Central Ave.
603/749-9093

**Timeless Appeal**
83 Washington St.
603/749-7044

**Horse & Buggy Antiques**
34 Freshet Road
603/742-2989

## 15 DUBLIN

**Hedge House**
Main St. — Route 101
603/563-8833

**Seaver & McLellan Antiques**
Route 101
603/563-7144

**Peter Pap Oriental Rugs**
Route 101
603/563-8717

## 16 ENFIELD

### *Great Places to Stay*

## Mary Keane House

Box 5, Lower Shaker Village
603/632-4241 or 1-888-239-2153
Web site: mary.keane@valley.net
Open: Year-round
Directions: From I-89, take Exit 17. Bear right on Route 4 (east) for
1 1/2 miles. Turn right at the blinker light on Route 4A and go three
miles. The Mary Keane House is on the left in the heart of Lower
Shaker Village.

Mary Keane House is a late Victorian–style bed and breakfast located
in the heart of historic Lower Shaker Village on the shore of Mascoma
Lake. Expansive grounds, gardens, secluded beach and open and wooded
hiking trails protected by 1,200 acres of New Hampshire conservation
district provide a peaceful and serene setting for a relaxing and stress-
busting stay. Five spacious and light-filled one- and two-room suites (all
with private baths) provide for your pleasure, antiques and comfort,
elegance and whimsy. Watch the morning mist rise off the lake from
your own balcony or enjoy the sunset from the glider swing on the west
porch. The lakeside screened porch is the perfect spot to enjoy a summer
afternoon conversation, book or nap while the living room with fireplace
is the place to chase winter's chill. Full breakfast is served in the sunny
dining room. They'll even pack you a picnic lunch for the antique trail
or the hiking trail.

### *Interesting Side Trips*

## The Museum at Lower Shaker Village and Dana Robes' Workshop

Route 4A
For museum information call 603/632-4346
For Dana Robes' Wood Craftsmen information call 603/632-5385

Here in 1793 the Shakers established their Chosen Vale, a village of
quietly majestic buildings, gardens and fields. Today, the Shaker heritage
is preserved at the Museum at Lower Shaker Village and the Dana Robes'
Wood Craftsmen. Walking tours, exhibits, craft demonstrations,
workshops, special programs and events, and extensive gardens bring
new life to Shaker culture at the museum. Reproduction Shaker furniture,
and furniture inspired by Shaker design, is made by hand at Dana Robes'
workshop.

## 17 EPSOM

**North Wind Antiques**
1782 Dover Road
603/880-0966

**Epsom Trading Post**
Route #28
603/736-8843

**Center Epson Antiques**
100 Dover Road
603/736-9972

## 18 EXETER

## Peter Sawyer Antiques

17 Court St.
603/772-5279
Open: By appointment or by chance, but almost always open Mon.–
Fri, 8–5

Offering appraisal and conservation services, Peter Sawyer Antiques
specializes in important American clocks, particularly those of the New
England area. They also offer a selection of fine 18th- and 19th-century
New England furniture (emphasizing original state of preservation),
American paintings, watercolors, drawing and folk art.

**Decor Antiques**
11 Jady Hill Circle
603/772-4538

**Scotch Thistle**
92 Portsmouth Ave.
603/778-2908

# *New Hampshire*

## 19 FITZWILLIAM

### Rainy Day Books
Route 119
603/585-3448
Fax: 603/585-9108
Open: Early April–mid-November, Thurs.–Mon. 11–5, and by appointment/chance, closed Tues.–Wed.

Antiquarian books showcased in an antique setting in the center of New Hampshire — it's a true antique-lover's paradise! Rainy Day Books is a used and antiquarian bookstore housed in a 19th-century barn and adjacent house in Fitzwilliam, the antique center of the southern Monadnock region. There are five other antiquarian book shops within half an hour's drive of Fitzwilliam. Rainy Day has a general stock of over 30,000 books, and a good selection of old prints and maps. In addition to the general stock, they also have sizable collections in the following special areas: amateur radio, American History/Civil War, audio engineering, children's, computer technology, cookbooks, fiber arts, outdoors, polar/mountaineering, radar and antenna engineering, radio and wireless, royalty, steam engines, surveying, town histories, and transportation.

**Bloomin Antiques**
Route 12
603/585-6688

**Red Barn Antiques**
Old Richmond Road
603/585-3134

**Fitzwilliam Antiques**
Route 12
603/585-9092

## 20 FRANCESTOWN

**Mill Village Antiques**
195 New Boston Road
603/547-2050

**Stonewall Antiques**
532 New Boston Road
603/547-3485

## 21 FRANCONIA

**Colonial Cottage Antiques**
720 Blake Road
603/823-5614

### *Great Places to Stay*

### Blanche's Bed & Breakfast
351 Easton Valley Road
603/823-7061
Open: Year-round
Rates: $40–$85
Directions: *From I-93:* Take Exit 38 to Route 116 South for 5 miles. *From I-91:* Take Exit 17 to Route 302 East. Go 7 miles to Route 112 East, then go 9 miles to Route 116 North, then approximately 6 more miles to Blanche's.

Blanche's B&B gives guests a chance to relax in Victorian splendor while immersing themselves in an artistic atmosphere. Blanche's — named, by the way, for the family dog — is a restored 19th-century Victorian farmhouse with views of the Kinsman Ridge. The artistic atmosphere is prevalent in the numerous decorative paintings scattered throughout the house, and an artist's working studio on the premises featuring hand-painted canvas rugs. Steeped in the English B&B tradition, Blanche's offers antiques throughout, to compliment the cotton linens, down comforters, comfortable beds and great breakfast for the five guest rooms, one with private bath.

## 22 GOFFSTOWN

**Philip Davanza Clock Repair**
Addison Road
603/668-2256

**Griffin Watch & Antiques**
5 S. Mast St.
603/497-2624

**Country Princess Antiques**
191 Mast St.
603/497-2909

**Goffstown Village Antiques**
9 N. Mast St.
603/497-5238

## 23 HAMPTON

**H.G. Webber**
495 Lafayette Road
603/926-3349

**Berg Antiques**
835 Lafayette Road
603/929-4911

**Northeast Auctions**
694 Lafayette Road
603/926-8222

## 24 HAMPTON FALLS

**Antiques New Hampshire**
Route 1, Lafayette Road
603/926-9603

**Antiques One**
Route 1, Lafayette Road
603/926-5332

**Barn Antiques at Hampton Falls**
Route 1, Lafayette Road
603/926-9003

**Antiques at Hampton Falls**
Route 1, Lafayette Road
603/926-1971

## 25 KEENE

**Fourteenth Division Antiques**
95 Main St.
603/352-5454

**Good Fortune**
114 Main St.
603/357-7500

**Colony Mill Marketplace**
222 West St.
603/357-1240

## 26 LACONIA

**Agora Collectibles**
373 Court St.
603/524-0129

**Almost All Antiques**
100 New Salem St.
603/527-0043

**LKS Regional Flea Market & Antqs. Exch.**
38 Pearl St.
603/524-2441

**Barnless Bill Antiques**
30 Liscomb Circle
603/528-2443

**Glen & Ernie Antiques**
249 S. Main St.
603/524-2457

**Lake Village Antiques**
1073 Union Ave.
603/524-5591

## 27 MANCHESTER

**End of Trail Antiques**
420 Chestnut St.
603/669-1238

**Postcards from the Past**
571 Mast Road
603/668-5229

**Thistle Stop Antiques**
77 Pleasant St.
603/668-3678

**N.H. Bargain Mart**
334 Union St.
603/666-3644

**From out of the Woods Furniture**
394 2nd St.
603/624-8668

## 28 MEREDITH

**Etcetra Shoppe**
Route 25
603/279-5062

**Alexandria's Lamp Shop**
62 Main St.
603/279-4234

**Burlwood Antique Center**
Route 3
603/279-6387

**Gordon's Antiques**
Route 3
603/279-5458

**Old Print Barn**
Winona Road
603/279-6479

## 29 MILFORD

## The Alphabet Soup Co.

263 Union Square
603/673-1033
Open: Tues.–Sat. 10–4, Sun. 12–4

Antiques, painted furniture, statuary, garden and cottage.

## This Old Stuff

180 Elm St.
603/673-5454
Open: Mon.–Sun. 10–5, closed Wed.

One of the largest group shops in the area featuring 222 quality dealers.

**Elm Plaza Antique Center**
222 Elm St. (Route 101A)
603/672-7846

**Centurywood Antiques**
571 Elm St. (Route 101A)
603/672-2264

**New Hampshire Antique Co-op**
Elm St. (Route 101A)
603/673-8499

**Milford Antiques**
40 Nashua St.(Route 101A)
603/672-2311

**Golden Opportunities**
326 Nashua St. (Route 101A)
603/672-1223

**J.C. Devine, Inc.**
20 South St.
603/673-4967

**Simple Additions**
18 Middle St.
603/672-6179

## *Great Places to Stay*

## Zahn's Alpine Guest House

Route 13
603/673-2334
Fax: 603/673-8415
Rates: Single $56, double $65 includes tax
Web site: www.intercondesign.com/zahns
Directions: Zahn's Alpine Guest House is on a straight stretch of Route 13 with unimpeded visibility for almost a mile. On the left side (coming out of Milford, heading north) there is absolutely nothing at the roadside except the guest house's little cluster of signs (reflective at night), a lamp post (the only one), mail box, luminous green town-line marker, and the mouth of the driveway. The building itself is obscured by trees, but there are five yard lanterns.

Here's a twist that's a really nice change from the usual bed and breakfast. Bud and Anne Zahn have spent a lot of time in Austria, Bavaria and the South Tirol (northern Italy) over the past 30 years while importing antiques and leading bike/ski groups to Alpine Europe. Over the years they stayed primarily in small, out-of-the-way lodging places where the style of hospitality was quite different from anything stateside. They enjoyed this  European experience so much that they decided to re-create such a place in the states — and so Zahn's Alpine Guest House was born.

They chose pine post and beams for the outer structure, which not only gave the house the heavy, timbered look of old Alpine farmhouses, but lent itself perfectly to the deeply overhung roof (you don't have to close the windows when it rains), and the perimeter balcony. They shipped in a sea container full of antique farm furnishings, Alpine-authentic carpets, lampshades, wrought-iron lanterns and accessories. One of the high points that all guests comment on are the specially made mattresses and appropriate bedding that are exact replicas of the Alpine style. There are eight double rooms with private baths. One room has a conventional double bed. The others have European twin beds (three inches wider and six inches longer than usual). The top cover is an untucked, European-style comforter inside a sheeting cover. When these beds are pushed together, the effect is that of an oversized king-size bed, and the space between the mattresses is minimal.

The Stube (evening and breakfast room) is, as in Europe, at the

# New Hampshire

disposal of all the guests. Worth a visit just to examine something every American homeowner should consider is the Kachelofen — the hand-made-on-site, hand-decorated, two-ton tile oven. Almost all dwellings in Alpine Europe utilize these marvelous heaters which exploit masonry characteristics of "quick absorption, slow release of heat." The Zahns were fortunate to find a Bavarian master builder fairly nearby who could create one for the guest house. Antiquers' constitute a strong portion of the clientele at Zahn's due to the literally hundreds of antique shops located within 15-20 minutes of the house.

## 30 NASHUA

### House of Josephs Antiques & Collectibles
523 Broad St.
603/882-4118
Open: Tues.–Sun. 10–5
Directions: From Route 3 North, take Exit 6 and bear left off the ramp onto Route 130 West. From Route 3 South, take Exit 6 and bear right off the ramp onto Route 130 West. Either way, go approximately 3 miles. The shop is a big red barn on the right.

Housed in an actual, traditional red barn on Broad Street, this multi-dealer shop offers the discriminating antiquer an assortment of fine furniture, china, glass and collectibles. The shop has been in business for over 25 years, and holds a large selection of furniture and, among its many dealers, several who specialize in Oriental items, beer memorabilia, and glass pieces.

| | |
|---|---|
| **L. Morin Treasures**<br>191 W. Hollis St.<br>603/883-2809 | **Past & Present**<br>202 Main St.<br>603/880-7991 |
| **A A Antiques & Memorabilia**<br>214 Daniel Webster Hwy.<br>603/888-3222 | **Guerette Cosgrove Antiques**<br>85 W. Pearls<br>603/880-0966 |

## 31 NEWFOUND LAKE

### Great Places to Stay

### The Inn on Newfound Lake and Pasquany Restaurant
Route 3A
603/744-9111 or 1-800-745-7990 (reservations only)
Fax: 603/744-3894
Open: Daily 9–9
Rates: $55–$105
Directions: Take I-93 North (from Boston) to Exit 23. At the bottom of the ramp continue north on Route 104. At the small town of Bristol (approximately 6 miles) bear to the right (Route 3A). Continue on Route 3A approximately 6 miles, until you reach the inn, which is between the towns of Bristol and Plymouth.

The Inn on Newfound Lake has been welcoming travelers since 1840. Formerly known as the Pasquaney Inn, it was the midway stop on the stage coach route from Boston to Montreal and now is the only remaining inn on the lake — at one time there were seven or eight. Located on seven and a half acres of lush New Hampshire countryside, the inn hugs the shore of Newfound Lake, the fourth-largest lake in New Hampshire, and rated as one of the purest and cleanest bodies of fresh water in the world. As you can imagine, there is something to do outdoors in every season at the inn. Or if relaxation is what you're looking for, just kick back in one of the 31 extensively refurbished rooms. The main inn has 19 rooms, eleven with private baths and a common sitting room. Elmwood Cottage, which adjoins the main building by the veranda, contains 12 rooms, all with private baths and adjoining daybed rooms if needed. The cottage parlor has a full fireplace for added enjoyment. Besides the myriad outdoor activities and sports, indoor activities at the inn include shuffleboard, basketball, billiards, and table tennis, and a Jacuzzi and weight room.

When guests work up an appetite, they can go to the full-service Pasquaney Restaurant and tavern at the inn. The restaurant, complete with wood-burning stove, overlooks the lake for added atmosphere. Continental breakfast, lunch, dinner and Sunday brunch are available.

### The Cliff Lodge
Route 3A
603/744-8660
Directions: Take I-93 North to Exit 23. At the bottom of the ramp take Route 104 North. When you reach the town of Bristol (approximately 6 miles), bear right on Route 3. Head north on Route 3 about 4 miles to the lodge.

Here is a restaurant and cabins offering wonderful, casual country dining in a lodge perched on the side of a hill overlooking Newfound Lake. What better view could you ask for! It's a very romantic spot, and cabin rentals are available in the summer. A perfect weekend getaway, where you can enjoy the lake and surrounding countryside, eat great meals at your leisure, and never have to fight traffic!

## 32 NORTH CONWAY

| | |
|---|---|
| **Sedler's Antiques**<br>30 Kearsarge<br>603/356-6008 | **Antiques & Collectibles Barn**<br>Route 16<br>603/356-7118 |
| **Aunt Aggie's Attic**<br>Route 16<br>603/356-0060 | **Expressions by Robert N. Waldo**<br>Route 16<br>603/356-3611 |
| **Richard M. Plusch**<br>Route 16<br>603/356-3333 | **John F. Whitesides Antiques**<br>Route 16<br>603/356-3124 |

**North Conway Antiques & Collectibles**
3424 Main St.
603/356-6661

**Silk Road Trading Company**
135 McDonough St.
603/433-1213

## 33 NORTH HAMPTON

**North Hampton Antique Center**
1 Lafayette Road
603/964-6615

**John Piperhousentz**
Sandy Point Road
603/778-1347

## 34 NORTHWOOD

**Parker-French Antique Center**
1st New Hampshire Turnpike
603/942-8852

**R.S. Butler's Trading Co.**
1st New Hampshire Turnpike
603/942-8210

**White House Antiques**
1st New Hampshire Turnpike
603/942-8994

**Willow Hollow Antiques**
1st New Hampshire Turnpike
603/942-5739

**Country Tavern Antiques**
Route 4
603/942-7630

**Coveway Corner Antiques**
Route 4
603/942-7500

**The Hay Loft Antique Center**
Route 4
603/942-5153

**Town Pump Antiques**
Route 4
603/942-5515

## 35 OSSIPEE

**Lakewood Station Antiques**
Route 16
603/539-7414

**Dow Corner Shop**
133 Mountain Road
603/539-4790

**Red Pine Antiques**
Route 16
603/539-6834

**Mountain Road Antiques**
Norman Drew Hwy.
603/539-7136

**The Stuff Shop**
25 Water Village Road
603/539-7715

**Treasure Hunt**
465 Route 16
603/539-7877

## 36 PLAISTOW

**Plaistow Commons Antiques**
166 Plaistow
603/382-3621

## 37 PORTSMOUTH

**Antiques Etc.**
85 Albany St.
603/436-1286

**Trunk Shop**
23 Ceres St.
603/431-4399

**Moose America Rustic Antiques**
75 Congress St.
603/431-4677

**Olde Port Traders**
275 Islington
603/436-2431

**Margaret Carter Scott Antiques**
175 Market St.
603/436-1781

**Victory Antiques**
96 State St.
603/431-3046

## 38 RICHMOND

### The Yankee Smuggler Antiques

122 Fitzwilliam Road
603/239-4188
Fax: 603/239-4653
Open: Daily by chance or by appointment
Directions: Located 1/2 mile east of Route 32 (Richmond Four Corners). From I-91: Take Exit 28 (Northfield) to Route 10 to Winchester. Take a right on Route 119 and go 6 miles to Richmond Four Corners (blinking light). Yankee Smuggler is the sixth house on the left.

Ted and Carole Hayward are in their 40th year in the antique business and are still actively buying and selling quality country antiques, folk art and related accessories. Specializing in 18th- and 19th-century American country antiques with original painted surfaces, they carry large pieces of furniture like cupboards, tables, chests of drawers, desks, etc., as well as related accessories such as firkins, pantries, bowls, and picture frames, all in original paint — blue, red, green, mustard, and salmon, and grain, feather and sponge decorated. Visitors to the Yankee Smuggler can browse through two rooms in Ted and Carole's circa 1815 home, plus a large barn adjacent to the house.
For the collector or dealer who wants something special they are open year-round by chance or appointment, but they suggest visitors call ahead first — that way they can start a fresh pot of coffee!

## 39 ROCHESTER

**Elkins Trash & Treasures**
26 & 28 N. Main St.
603/332-1848

**Four Corners Antiques**
204 Estes Road
603/332-1522

**Signal St. Antiques**
5 Signal St.
603/335-0810

## 40 RUMNEY

**Courtyard Antiques**
Route 25
603/786-2306

**Willow Tree Antiques**
Route 25
603/786-2787

## 41 STRATHAM

**Compass Rose Antiques**
17 Winnicut Road
603/778-0163
Directions: Compass Rose is located 10 miles west of Portsmouth, just off Route 33.

This charming shop carries a wide range of antiques with a focus on accessories. A few select furniture pieces are available, but what's lacking in furnishings is made up in the enormous offering of smalls. They carry exquisite lighting fixtures, glass, china, jewelry and much, much more. Antique weapons are also included among their inventory. Owners Charles and Laurie Clark have been in business for seventeen years, and the shop is actually located at their home. All of their items are "really" old (nothing modern) antiques from the 1800s.

Among the Clarks' specialties are glass and china from the 1800s — "No Depression or collectibles," says Laurie. Charles is the antique weapons expert and is a licensed gun dealer. Lighting fixtures, mainly whale oil lamps and lanterns, are also his forte.

**The Wingate Collection**
94 Portsmouth, Route 108
603/778-4849

## 42 SUTTON

**Sutton Mills Antiques**
90 Main St.
603/927-4557
Open: Tues.–Sat. 10–6; Sun., 12–5; closed Mon.
Directions: From I-89 North and South: Take Exit 10 and follow 114 south for 4 miles. Turn right on Main Street and the store is ½ mile on the right.

Sutton Mills is located in 1,900 square feet of an old, 19th-century general store. This ten-dealer group features furniture, glass, old tools, estate and costume jewelry, coins and Americana.

## 43 TUFTONBORO

**Dow Corner Shop**
Route 171
603/539-4790

**Log Cabin Antiques**
Route 109A Ledge Hill Road
603/569-4249

## 44 WEST LEBANON

**Terry's Antiques**
Colonial Plaza-Airport Road
603/298-0556

**Colonial Antique Markets**
Route 12 A
603/298-7712

## 45 WEST SWANZEY

**Knotty Pine Antiques Market**
Route 10
603/352-5252

## 46 WILTON

**New England Antiques**
101 Intervale Road
603/654-5674

**Here Today**
71 Main St.
603/654-5295

**Noah's Ark**
Route 101
603/654-2595

## 47 WINCHESTER

**Latchkey Antiques**
4 Corners Plaza
603/239-6777

**Hearthside**
858 Keene Road
603/239-8697

## 48 WOLFEBORO

**The 44th Annual Wolfeboro Antiques Fair**
Brewster Academy, S. Main St.
Call number below for dates

Held for 44 continuous years, this show highlights 75 dealers in room settings and outdoors in a courtyard. Exhibitors offer high-quality antiques ranging from estate jewelry, Oriental rugs, quilts, books and prints to rustic, primitive and formal furniture, glass, paintings and silver. Located in Wolfeboro at Brewster Academy overlooking Lake Winnipesaukee and the Belknap Mountains. This picturesque community of New England white houses and country churches is also known as the "Oldest Summer Resort in America." This traditional antique fair and sale caters to tourists and summer residents alike.

For more information, call New England Antique Show Management, 603/539-1900.

**1810 House**
Route 28
603/569-8093

**Barbara's Corner Shop**
67 N. Main St.
603/569-3839

**Northline Antiques**
Northline Road
603/569-2476

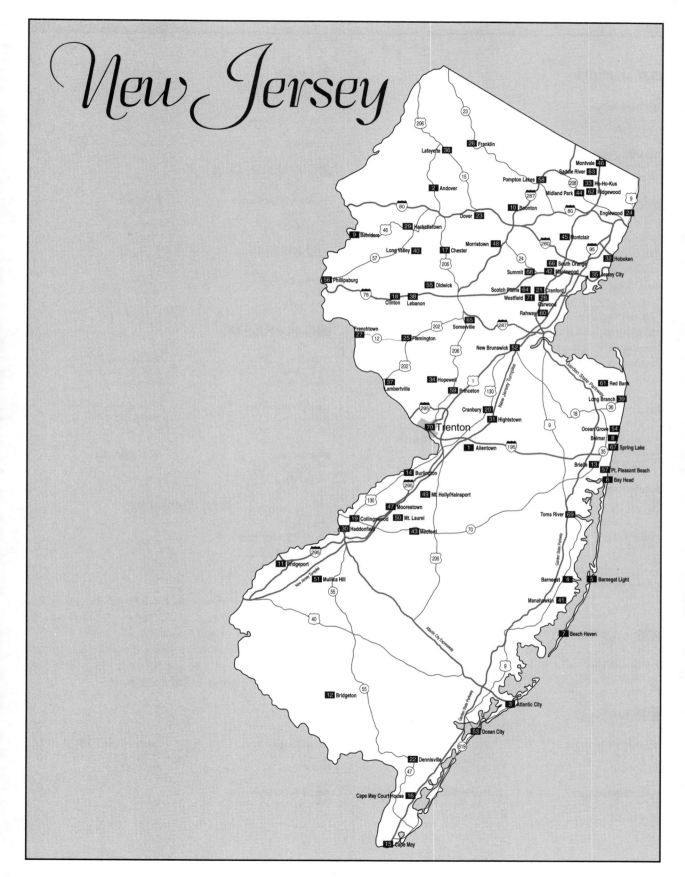

# New Jersey

23
206
26 Franklin
Lafayette 36
Montvale 46
Saddle River 63
15
Pompton Lakes 58
208
33 Ho-Ho-Kus
2 Andover
Midland Park 44
62 Ridgewood
80
287
9
10 Boonton
80
Dover 23
Englewood 24
46
29 Hackettstown
9 Belvidere
45 Montclair
280
Morristown 48
95
Long Valley 40
17 Chester
32 Hoboken
57
24
66 South Orange
206
Summit 68
42 Maplewood
56 Phillipsburg
55 Oldwick
35 Jersey City
Scotch Plains 64
21 Cranford
18 38
Westfield 71
28
78
Clinton Lebanon
Garwood
Rahway 60
Frenchtown
65
202
Somerville
27
287
25 Flemington
12
New Brunswick 52
206
61 Red Bank
37
34 Hopewell
Long Branch 39
Lambertville
202
1
59 Princeton
130
18
36
295
Cranbury 20
9
70 Trenton
31 Hightstown
Ocean Grove 54
Belmar 8
1 Allentown
67 Spring Lake
195
35
14 Burlington
Brielle 13
57 Pt. Pleasant Beach
295
6 Bay Head
49 Mt. Holly/Hainsport
130
47 Moorestown
Toms River 69
19 Collingswood
50 Mt. Laurel
30 Haddonfield
43 Medford
70
206
11 Bridgeport
295
Barnegat 4
5 Barnegat Light
51 Mullica Hill
55
Manahawkin 41
40
7 Beach Haven
12 Bridgeton
55
9
3 Atlantic City
53 Ocean City
22 Dennisville
619
47
Cape May Court House 16
15 Cape May

## 1 ALLENTOWN

**Mill House Antiques**
38 S. Main St.
609/259-0659

**Brown Bear's Antiques**
35 S. Main St.
609/259-0177

**The Artful Deposit**
46 S. Main St.
609/259-3234

## 2 ANDOVER

**Great Andover Antique Company**
124 Main St.
973/786-6384
Open: Wed.–Sun. 10–5, closed Mon. & Tues.

Housed within a 2500-square-foot building constructed in 1868 and extending to two floors are the offerings of Great Andover Antiques Company. The shop specializes in 18th- and 19th-century furniture, American pottery, textiles, jewelry, lighting, Edison players, Victrolas, radios, Victorian furniture and complete bedroom sets. A large collection of stained glass is displayed in the 1,000-square foot-former carriage house located on the property.

**3 Generations**
1 Gristmill Lane
201/786-7000

**Oriental Rugs & Antiques**
Hwy. 206
201/786-6004

**Scranberry Co-op**
Hwy. 206
201/786-6414

**Red Parrot Antiques**
118 Route 206
201/786-5007

**Vintage Sam's**
124 Main St.
201/786-7955

**Andover Village Shop**
125 Main St.
201/786-6494

**Country and Stuff**
127 Main St.
201/786-7086

**Andover's Mixed Bag**
131 Main St.
201/786-7702

## 3 ATLANTIC CITY

**Princeton Antiques**
2917 Atlantic Ave.
609/344-1943

**Bayside Basin Antiques**
800 N. New Hampshire Ave.
609/347-7143

## 4 BARNEGAT

**Barnegat Antique Country**
684 E. Bay Ave.
609/698-8967

**Goldduster**
695 E. Bay Ave.
609/698-2520

**First National Antiques**
708 W. Bay Ave.
609/698-1413

**Federal House Antiques**
719 W. Bay Ave.
609/698-5490

**Lavender Hall**
289 S. Main St.
609/698-8126

**Babes in Barnegat**
349 S. Main St.
609/698-2223

**Forget Me Not Shoppe**
689 E. Bay Ave.
609/698-4336

**Blaze of Glory**
307 Main St. S.
609/597-8416

## 5 BARNEGAT LIGHT

**Americana by the Seashore**
604 Broadway
609/494-0656

**The Sampler**
708 Broadway
609/494-3493

## 6 BAY HEAD

**Fables of Bay Head**
410 Main Ave.
732/899-3633

## 7 BEACH HAVEN

**Somewhere in Time**
118 N. Bay Ave.
609/492-3034

**Summerhouse**
412 N. Bay Ave.
609/492-6420

**Court's Treasure Chest**
1500 Long Beach Blvd.
609/494-0910

**House of Seven Wonders**
7600 Long Beach Blvd.
609/494-9673

**Wizard of Odds**
7601 Long Beach Blvd.
609/494-9384

**Age of Antiquities**
8013 Long Beach Blvd.
609/494-0735

### *Great Places to Stay*

**Amber Street Inn**
118 Amber St.
609/492-1611

The inn, built in 1885 as one of Beach Haven's original Victorian homes, was lovingly renovated and updated in 1991. Since then, the innkeepers, Joan and Michael Fitzsimmons, have worked to establish the inn's reputation as a casually elegant, comfortable and romantic seashore retreat. The inn's six well appointed rooms, all with private baths, welcome guests with their individual charm and decor.

## 8 BELMAR

**Unique Designs**
809 Main St.
732/681-2060

**Aajeda Antiques**
1800 Main St.
732/681-2288

**Belmar Trading Post**
1735 State Route 71
732/681-3207

*New Jersey*

## Great Places to Stay

include weather vanes, samplers and original painted furniture.

*Note: I've met up with George at several antique shows around the country. He's one of the nicest antique dealers in the business. At each of these shows, he always presents some very unusual pieces.*

### The Inn at the Shore
301 4th Ave.
732/681-3762

This stunning inn is located within sight of the Atlantic Ocean and Belmar's wide, beautiful beaches and boardwalk, and steps away from serene Silver Lake, home to the first flock of swans bred in America. Only a short walk from the inn to fine restaurants, marina, river, lake, boardwalk and beaches.

### 9 BELVIDERE

**Painted Lady**
16 Greenwich St.
908/475-1985

**Uncommon Market**
228 Mansfield St.
908/475-1460

**H & H Liquidating Co.**
427 Mansfield St.
908/475-4333

**Major Hoops Emporium Antiques**
13 Market St.
908/475-5031

### 10 BOONTON

**Cupboard**
410 Main St.
973/402-0400

**Boonton Antiques**
521 Main St.
973/334-4416

**Claire Ann's Antiques**
815 Main St.
973/334-2421

**Fox Hill Exchange**
900 Main St.
973/263-2270

**Elizabeth's Antiques Buying Center**
904 Main St.
973/263-9162

### 11 BRIDGEPORT

### Racoon Creek Antiques
20 Main St., Box 132
609/467-3197
Open: Thurs.–Sun. 12–5 or by appointment
Directions: *From the New Jersey Turnpike:* Take Exit 1 and go 5 miles west on 322. Follow the signs to 20 Main Street, Bridgeport. *From I-95:* Raccoon Creek Antiques is 30 minutes north of Wilmington, 30 minutes south of Philadelphia, and one mile from the base of Barry Bridge, which crosses the Delaware River on the "Jersey" side.

If you are in the market for truly "old" antiques, Raccoon Creek is an absolute must on your trek. George Allen has 11 years of accumulation and selected buying savvy in the field of Americana, quilts, pottery and folk art. "I deal in items that are pre-1860s," says George. "All my stock is pre–industrial age, everything handmade — absolutely no reproductions of any kind." Examples of just some of his Americana

### 12 BRIDGETON

**Kim Shell Gift Boutique**
404 Big Oak Road
609/451-4667

**Hudson House**
2012 Burlington Road
609/433-1414

**The Squirrel's Nest**
680 Shiloh Pike
609/455-6594

**Pony Point House/Candle Shop**
781 Shiloh Pike
609/451-6130

**Dutch Neck Village**
97 Trench Road
609/451-2188

### 13 BRIELLE

**Brielle Antique Center**
622A Green Ave.
732/528-8570

**Chappies Antiques**
406 Higgins Ave.
732/528-8989

**Relics**
604 Union Ave.
732/223-3452

### 14 BURLINGTON

### H. G. Sharkey & Company Antiques & Coffee House
306 High St.
609/239-0200
Open: Daily 8–8
Directions: From I-295, Burlington Exit 54, go to High Street. Located ½ block from the Delaware River.

Housed in a historical building, specializing in antique jewelry and collectibles. A coffee house is also located on the premises.

**Antique Row**
307 High St.
609/387-3050

### 15 CAPE MAY

**Bridgetowne**
523 Broadway
609/884-8107

**Curious Collectibles**
719 Broadway
609/884-5557

**Promises Collectables**
301 N. Broadway
609/884-4411

**Bogwater Jim Antiques**
201 S. Broadway
609/884-5558

**Studio Victorian Antiques**
607 Jefferson
609/884-0444

**Cape Island Antiques**
609 Jefferson
609/884-6028

**Finishing Touches**
678 Washington St.
609/896-0661

**Rocking Horse Antique Center**
405 W. Perry St.
609/898-0737

**Millstone Antiques & Collectibles**
742 Seashore Road
609/884-5155

**Nostalgia Shop**
408 Washington St.
609/884-7071

**Antique Doorknob**
600 Park Blvd.
609/884-6282

**Hazard Sealander Antiques**
479 W. Perry St.
609/884-0040

**Stephanie's Antiques**
318 Washington St.
609/884-0289

**Midsummer Night's Dream**
668 Washington St.
609/884-1380

### *Great Places to Stay*

## Abigail Adams Bed & Breakfast

12 Jackson St.
609/884-1371

Located just 100 feet from some of the widest beaches in Cape May, Abigail Adams' Bed and Breakfast by the sea offers a breathtaking view of the ocean from many of the charmingly furnished guest rooms. Wake up to the sound of the waves and to the aroma of fresh coffee brewing in the country kitchen. Breakfast is substantial and served in the 1891 Victorian hand-stenciled dining room.

## Bedford Inn

805 Stockton Ave.
609/884-4158
Web site: www.bbhost.com/bedfordinn

Just a half block to the beach and built in 1881 as a "mother-daughter" twin home, the beautifully restored Bedford Inn offers a warm and peaceful getaway. Innkeepers Alan and Cindy Schmucker have been welcoming guests to their home for more than 32 years. Enjoy the cozy fireplace in the Victorian parlor or laze away an hour or two on one of the old-fashioned verandas. Each room and "honeymoon" suite is furnished with authentic Victorian antiques and has a private bath.

## 16 CAPE MAY COURT HOUSE

**August Farmhouse**
1759 N. Route 9
609/465-5135

**Quilted Gull**
1909 N. Route 9
609/624-1630

**Mallard Lake Antiques**
1781 N. Route 9
609/465-7189

**Village Woodcrafter**
1843 N. Route 9
609/465-2197

## 17 CHESTER

**Chester Antique Center**
32 Grove St.
908/879-4331

**Delphinium's**
30 Main St.
908/879-8444

**Summerfield's Antique Furn. Warehouse**
44 Main St.
908/879-9020

**Pegasus Antiques**
98 Main St.
908/879-4792

**Marita Daniels Antiques**
127 Main St.
908/879-6488

**Black River Trading Co.**
15 Perry St.
908/879-6778

**Beauty of Civilization Vintage Boutq.**
30 Main St.
908/879-2044

**Postage Stamp**
38 W. Main St.
908/879-4257

**Aunt Pittypat's Parlour**
57 E. Main St.
908/879-4253

**The Chester Carousel**
125 Main St.
980/879-7141

**Chester House**
294 E. Main St.
908/879-7856

**Spinning Wheel Antiques**
76 Main St.
908/879-6080

## 18 CLINTON

**Arts Resale**
Hwy. 31
908/735-4442

**Memories**
21 Main St.
908/730-9096

**Weathervane Antiques**
18 Main St.
908/730-0877

**Paddy-Wak Antiques**
19 Old High #22
908/735-9770

## 19 COLLINGSWOOD

**Ashwell's Yesterday's Treasures**
738 Haddon Ave.
609/858-6659

**Collinswood Antiques**
812 Haddon Ave.
609/858-9700

**Unforgettables**
980 Haddon Ave.
609/858-4501

**Yesteryear Shop**
788 Haddon Ave.
609/854-1786

**Ellis Antiques**
817 Haddon Ave.
609/854-6346

## 20 CRANBURY

**Adams Brown Co.**
26 N. Main St.
609/655-8269

**Cranbury Collectibles**
60 N. Main St.
609/655-8568

**Cranbury Book Worm**
54 N. Main St.
609/655-1063

**David Wells Antiques**
60 N. Main St.
609/655-0085

*New Jersey*

## 21 CRANFORD

**Dovetails**
6 Eastman St.
908/709-1638

**Shirley Greens Antiques**
8 Eastman St.
908/709-0066

**Not Just Antiques**
218 South Ave. E.
908/276-3553

**Nancy's Antiques**
7 Walnut Ave.
908/272-5056

**Cobweb Collectibles & Ephemera**
9 Walnut Ave.
908/272-5777

## 22 DENNISVILLE

### *Great Places to Stay*

**The Henry Ludlam Inn**
1336 Route 47
609/861-5847
Open: Daily year-round
Directions: The inn is located on Route 47 in Dennisville. From Garden State Parkway: Go south to the second Ocean City exit. Turn right onto Route 631 for about two miles. Turn left on Route 610 and follow the road to the end. Turn right on Route 47. The inn is about one and a half miles on the right.

This National Historic Registry entry claims more than 250 years of history! Two wings of the house were built at different times, between 1740 and 1804. This Federal-style house offers guests five rooms, all with private baths. It is filled with period antiques and the Federalist style in decor helps put guests into a historical frame of mind. The inn is located near many antique shops, museums, the Cape May Zoo and county historical sites.

## 23 DOVER

**Peddler's Shop**
71 W. Blackwell St.
973/361-0545
Fax: 973/366-4147
Open: Wed. 2–7, Sat. 12–5, Sun. 9–5 or by appointment
Directions: The Peddler's Shop is located between Highway 46 and Highway 10. Take Exit 35 off of I-80 and take Mt. Hope Avenue. Cross Highway 46 and continue two blocks to Blackwell. Turn right and the Peddler's Shop is approximately five blocks on the right.

Since 1969 the Peddler's Shop has offered an unusual and rather distinctive array of items spread about its two floors of antiques. The shop is noted for its old lamps and lamp parts, furniture, glassware, dolls, trains, silver and books, and the largest watch fob collection in the East.

**At the Hop**
14 N. Morris St.
973/989-5225

**Sharp Shop**
34 W. Blackwell St.
973/366-2160

**Antiques Jungle**
12 W. Blackwell St.
973/537-0099

## 24 ENGLEWOOD

**Bizet Antiques & Unusual Finds**
6 S. Dean St.
201/568-5345

**Chelsea Square, Inc.**
10 Depot Square
201/568-5911

**Tony Art Gallery**
120 Grand Ave.
201/568-7271

**Antiques by Ophir Gallery**
12 E. Palisade Ave.
201/871-0424

**Elvid Gallery**
41 E. Palisade Ave.
201/871-8747

**Rose Hill Auction Gallery**
35 S. Van Brunt St.
201/816-1940

## 25 FLEMINGTON

**Antiques Emporium**
32 Church St.
908/782-5077

**55 Main Antiques**
55 Main St.
908/788-2605

**International Show Case**
169 Main St.
908/782-6640

**Furstover Antiques**
505 Stanton Station Road
908/782-3513

## 26 FRANKLIN

**The Munson Emporium**
33 Munsonhurst Road
973/827-0409

**The Iron Carriage Antique Center**
1 W. Blackwell St.
973/366-1440

**Corner Copia**
32 W. Blackwell St.
973/366-8999

**Jewel Spiegel Galleries**
30 N. Dean St.
201/871-3577

**Global Treasures**
120 Grand Ave.
201/569-5532

**Portobello Road Antiques**
491 Grand Ave.
201/568-5559

**Crown House Antiques**
39 E. Palisade Ave.
201/894-8789

**Royal Galleries Antiques**
66 E. Palisade Ave.
201/567-6354

**B & M Flemington Antiques**
24 Main St.
908/806-8841

**Main St. Antique Center Inc.**
156 Main St.
908/788-8767

**Popkorn Antiques**
4 Mine St.
908/782-9631

# New Jersey

## 27 FRENCHTOWN

**Brooks Antiques**
24 Bridge St.
908/996-7161

**Frenchtown House of Antiques**
15 Race St.
908/996-2482

**Jeanine-Louise Antiques**
8 Race St.
908/996-3520

## 28 GARWOOD

**Classic Antiques**
225 North Ave.
908/233-7667

## 29 HACKETTSTOWN

**Family Attic Antiques Ltd.**
117 Main St.
908/852-1206

**Whispering Pines Antiques**
77 State Route 57
908/852-2587

**Furnishings by Adam**
253 Main St.
908/852-4385

**Main Street Bazaar**
128 Willow Grove St.
908/813-2966

## 30 HADDONFIELD

**General Store**
37 Ellis St.
609/428-3707

**Two in the Attic**
3 Kings Court
609/429-4035

**Alice's Dolls**
9 Kings Hwy. E.
609/770-1155

**Owl's Tale**
140 Kings Hwy. E.
609/795-8110

**Post-Game Memories**
138 Kings Hwy E.
609/216-9881

**Haddonfield Gallery**
1 Kings Court
609/429-7722

**Adam's Antiques**
9 Kings Hwy. E.
609/770-1155

**Haddonfield Antiques**
9 Kings Hwy. E.
609/429-1929

**Hugh's Clock Shop**
33 Kings Hwy E.
609427-4444

**Sansone and Company**
24 Ellis St.
609/428-0962

## 31 HIGHTSTOWN

**Olde Country Antiques**
346 Franklin St.
609/448-2670

**Boat House Antiques**
161 E. Ward St.
609/448-2200

**Empire Antiques**
278 Monmouth St.
609/585-1266

**Timekeeper**
York Road
609/448-0269

## 32 HOBOKEN

**Fat Cat Antiques**
57 Newark St.
201/222-5454

**Sixth Street Antiques**
155 6th St.
201/656-5544

**Erie Street Antiques**
533 Washington St.
201/656-3596

**Mission Postion**
1122 Washington St.
201/222-5001

**Found in the Street**
86 Park Ave.
201/963-6494

**Hoboken Antiques**
511 Washington St.
201/659-7329

**House Wear, Inc.**
628 Washington St.
201/659-6009

**Little Cricket Antiques**
1200 Washington St.
201/222-6270

## 33 HO HO KUS

**Discovery Antiques**
618 N. Maple Ave.
201/444-9170

**Camelot Home Furnishings**
9 N. Franklin Turnpike
201/444-5300

**Porreca & Chettle**
620 N. Maple Ave.
201/445-7883

**Regal Antiques Ltd.**
181 S. Franklin Turnpike
201/447-5066

## 34 HOPEWELL

**H. Clark Interiors**
31 W. Broad St.
609/466-0738

**Ninotchka**
35 W. Broad St.
609/466-0556

**Hopewell Antique Center**
Hamilton Ave.
609/466-2990

**Your Aunt's Attic**
17 Seminary Ave.
609/466-0827

**Patsy's Antiques**
33 W. Broad St.
609/466-7720

**Antiques Etcetera**
47 W. Broad St.
609/466-0643

**Tomato Factory Antiques Center**
Hamilton Ave.
609/466-9860

**Hopewell Antique Cottage**
8 Somerset St.
609/466-1810

## 35 JERSEY CITY

**Cliff's Clocks**
400 7th St.
201/798-7510

**L & L Antiques**
1170 Summit Ave.
201/656-6928

## 36 LAFAYETTE

**Mill Mercantile**
11 Meadows Road
973/579-1588

**Silver Willow Inc.**
Meadows Road
973/383-5560

**Ivy Antiques**
Meadows Road
973/579-9602

**Lafayette Mill Antique Center**
Route 15
973/383-6057

**Lamplighters of Lafayette**
156 State Route 15
973/383-5513

**Sweet Pea's**
12 Morris Farm Road
973/579-6338

**37 LAMBERTVILLE**

## Stoneman of the Delaware

Located inside Lambertville Antique Market
Route 29
609/397-0456
Open: Wed.–Sun. 10–4
Directions: Located 1½ miles south of Lambertville on Route 29, River Road. Next to the Golden Nugget.

Stoneman of the Delaware is located inside the Lambertville Antique Market. Specializing in Civil War, Revolutionary, Colonial, Victorian, frontier through World War II and later; 1620–1960 historical collectibles, guns, parts, swords, bayonets, relics, coins, tokens, medals, arrowheads, marbles, old keys, jewelry, pottery, china, glassware and more. Don't miss museum case #36.

Additionally, the market offers more than 100 showcases packed with all types of antiques and collectibles.

## Lambertville Antique and Auction Center

333 N. Main St.
609/397-9374
Directions: From Philadelphia: take I-95 North into New Jersey. Exit at Route 29 North and follow 12 miles to Lambertville. Take a left at the light on Bridge Street. Take the next right onto Main Street and follow one mile to 333 North Main Street. The building will be on the left.

Year-round events including high-end arts and crafts, modern and general line auctions. Special events. Please call for information.

## Perrault-Rago Gallery

17 S. Main St.
609/397-1802
Open: Tues.–Sun. 12–5 (usually), call to confirm
Directions: From Philadelphia: take I-95 North into New Jersey. Exit at Route 29 North and follow 12 miles to Lambertville. Take a left at the light on Bridge Street. Take the next left onto South Main Street and follow one block to 17 South Main Street. The building will be on the right.

A memorable array of period furniture, decorative ceramics, metal, textiles and other accessories. Pottery, in particular, represents the finest "for sale" display in the country.

## David Rago Auctions, Inc.

333 N. Main St.
609/397-9374
Open: Mon.–Fri. 9–5:30
Directions: From Philadelphia: take I-95 North into New Jersey. Exit at Route 19 North and follow 12 miles to Lambertville. Take a left at the light on Bridge Street. Take the next right onto Main Street one mile. The building will be on the left.

Specializing in 20th-century Mission, Deco, and postwar decorative arts and furnishings. Consignments wanted.

**Jim's Antiques Ltd.**
6 Bridge St.
609/397-7700

**Bridge St. Antiques**
15 Bridge St.
609/397-9890

**Karen & David Dutch's Antiques**
22 Bridge St.
609/397-2288

**Stefon's Antiques**
29 Bridge St.
609/397-8609

**Mill Crest Antiques**
72 Bridge St.
609/397-4700

**Fran Jay Antiques**
10 Church St.
609/397-1571

**Porkyard Antiques**
8 Coryell St.
609/397-2088

**Coryell St. Antiques**
51 Coryell St.
609/397-5700

**Lambertville's Center Cy Antiques**
11 Klines Court
609/397-9886

**Peter Wallace Ltd.**
5 Lambert Lane
609/397-4914

**Charles King Ltd.**
36 S. Main St.
609/397-9733

**Golden Nugget Antique Flea Market**
State Hwy. #29
609/397-0811

**Prestige Antiques**
State Hwy. #29
609/397-2400

**JRJ Home**
7 N. Union St.
609/397-3800

**Yaroschuck Antiques**
10 N. Union St.
609/397-8886

**Artfull Eye**
12 N. Union St.
609/397-8115

**Lovrinics Fine Period Antiques**
15 N. Union St.
609/397-8600

**Robin's Egg Gallery**
24 N. Union St.
609/397-9137

**The Second Floor**
29 N. Union St.
609/397-8618

**Miller-Topia Designers**
35 N. Union St.
609/397-9339

**Garden House Antiques**
39 N. Union St.
609/397-9797

**Kevin Sives Antiques**
43 N. Union St.
609/397-4212

# New Jersey

**Meld**
53 N. Union St.
609/397-8487

**Best of France**
204 N. Union St.
609/397-9881

**Olde English Pine**
202 N. Union St.
609/397-4978

**Fox's Den**
7 N. Main St.
609/397-9881

## Great Places to Stay

### York Street House

No. 42 York St.
609/397-3007
Web site: www.virtualcities.com
Directions: Off I-95, Exit 1 Route 29, downtown Lambertville off Main Street.

This gracious 13-room manor house situated on three quarters of an acre of land was built in 1909 by George Massey as a 25th wedding anniversary gift for his beloved wife. Massey was one of the early industrialists who settled his family in the historical river village of Lambertville just after the turn of the century. In 1911, the home was featured as *House and Garden* magazine's Home of the Year, with all the modern conveniences including a central vacuum that still stands in the cellar. In 1983, the home became a designer showcase.

Today the York Street House will comfort and surround you with its elegant and comfortable atmosphere. The heart of the inn features a winding three-story staircase leading to six gracious guest rooms, some with queen-size canopy beds. From matching antique Waterford crystal sconces and chandelier in the sitting room, and cut glass doorknobs on the second floor to the original tile and claw-foot master bath with its leaded stained glass window, the preservation of details will delight you at every turn.

A gourmet breakfast is served in the oak-trimmed dining room with its built-in leaded glass china and large oak servers, looking out over the lawn and sitting porch. Feast your eyes on original art by Gilbert Bolitho, Jack B. Yeats, Rodriguez (Blue Dog), and Autorino.

The excitement starts two blocks away with antique shops, art galleries, bookstores and fine restaurants. Walk to New Hope, Pennsylvania, with its artful atmosphere, theater and gay clubs.

### 38 LEBANON

**Lebanon Antique Center**
U.S. Hwy. 22 E.
908/236-2851

### 39 LONG BRANCH

**Antiques & Accents**
55 Brighton Ave.
732/222-2274

**Hyspot Antiques & Collectibles**
61 Brighton Ave.
732/222-7880

**Take a Gander**
84 Brighton Ave.
732/229-7389

### 40 LONG VALLEY

**German Valley Antiques**
6 E. Mill Road
980/876-9202

**Tavern Antiques**
5 Will Road
908/876-5854

### 41 MANAHAWKIN

**Manor House Shops**
160 N. Main St.
609/597-1122

**The Shoppes at Rosewood**
182 N. Main St.
609/597-7331

**Cornucopia**
140 N. Main St.
609/978-0099

### 42 MAPLEWOOD

**Bee & Thistle Antiques**
89 Baker St.
973/763-3166

**Antiques by Greg Hawriluk**
48 Courter Ave.
973/378-9036

**Renaissance Consignment**
410 Ridgewood Road
973/761-7450

**Grey Swan**
411 Ridgewood Road
973/763-0660

### 43 MEDFORD

**Recollections**
6 N. Main St.
609/654-1515

**Spirit of '76**
49 N. Main St.
609/654-2850

**Regina's**
6 S. Main St.
609/654-2521

**Heather Furniture**
215 Medford Mount Holly
609/654-9506

**Toll House Antiques**
160 Old Marlton Pike
609/953-0005

**Yesterday & Today Shop**
668 Stokes Road
609/654-7786

### 44 MIDLAND PARK

### Brownstone Mill Antique Center

11 Paterson Ave.
201/445-3074 or 201/612-9555
Open: Wed.–Sat. 10:30–5, Tues. by appointment
Directions: Take Route 4 West or Route 287 North to Route 208; exit Goffle Road/Midland Park. Continue approximately 2 miles to the corner of Goffle Road/Paterson Avenue.

Features 20 unique shops under one roof.

**Tuc-D-Away Antiques**
229 Godwin Ave.
201/652-0730

**Time Will Tell**
644 Godwin Ave.
201/652-1025

**Blue Cow Antiques**
194 Westwood Ave.
732/747-7738

*New Jersey*

**G.F. Warhol & Co.**
18 Goffle Road
201/612-1010

**Blue Barn**
60 Goffle Road
201/612-0227

**Kingsway Antiques**
527 E. Main St.
609/234-7373

**Monique's Antiques**
400 Route 38 — Moorestown Mall
609/235-7407

**Her Own Place**
113 E. Main St.
609/234-2445

### 45 MONTCLAIR

**Threadneedle Street**
195 Bellevue Ave.
973/783-1336

**Sablon Antiques**
411 Bloomfield Ave.
973/746-4397

### 48 MORRISTOWN

**Americana Antiques**
411 Bloomfield Ave.
973/746-2605

**Past & Present Resale Shop**
416 Bloomfield Ave.
973/746-8871

**Associated Art**
31 Market St.
973/292-9203

**Morristown Antique Center**
45 Market St.
973/734-0900

**Gallery of Vintage**
504 Bloomfield Ave.
973/509-1201

**Ivory Bird Antiques**
555 Bloomfield Ave.
973/744-5225

**Marion Jaye Antiques**
990 Mount Kemble Ave.
973/425-0441

**Robert Fountain, Inc.**
1107 Mount Kemble Ave.
973/425-8111

**Antique Star**
627 Bloomfield Ave.
973/746-0070

**Buying Antiques**
629 Bloomfield Ave.
973/746-7331

**Fearicks Antiques**
166 Ridgedale Ave.
973/984-3140

**Bayberry Antiques**
Route 202 (Harding Township)
973/425-0101

**Milt's Antiques**
662 Bloomfield Ave.
973/746-4445

**American Sampler, Inc.**
26 Church St.
973/744-1474

**Coletree Antiques & Interiors**
166 South St.
973/993-3011

**William Martin Antiques & Home**
41 Church St.
973/744-1149

**Garage Sale**
194 Claremont Ave.
973/783-0806

### 49 MOUNT HOLLY/HAINSPORT

**Jackie's Antiques**
51 N. Fullerton Ave.
973/744-7972

**Earl Roberts Antiques & Interiors**
17 S. Fullerton Ave.
973/744-2232

## Country Antique Center

1925 Route 38
609/261-1924
Email: ca1925@aol.com
Open: Daily 10–5

**Noel's Place**
173 Glenridge Ave.
973/744-2156

**Station West Antiques**
225 Glenridge Ave.
973/744-9370

**Way We Were Antiques**
15 Midland Ave.
973/783-1111

Directions: *Traveling from I-295:* Take Exit 40 and travel east on Route 38 for 4.1 miles toward Mt. Holly. At the 8th light, take the jughandle to make a U-turn on Route 38. The shop's driveway is 50 feet from the U-turn on the westbound side of Route 38. *Traveling the New Jersey Turnpike:* Take Exit 5/Mt. Holly. After the tolls, turn right onto Route 541 toward Mt. Holly. At the 4th light bear right onto the Route 541/Mt. Holly Bypass. Continue on the bypass to the 3rd light (Route 38). Turn right onto Route 38 West and go 3 lights. The shop's driveway is 50 feet from the 3rd light. Country Antique Center is just 30 miles from Philadelphia on Route 38.

### 46 MONTVALE

**Antique Mall**
30 Chestnut Ridge Road
201/391-3940

**Discovery Antiques**
30 Chestnut Ridge Road
201/391-9024

**Knox Gold Corp.**
30 Chestnut Ridge Road
201/930-0323

**Lost & Found Antiques, Inc.**
30 Chestnut Ridge Road
201/391-0060

**Museum Shop**
30 Chestnut Ridge Road
201/573-8757

**Treasure Finders**
30 Chestnut Ridge Road
201/391-0006

The Country Antique Center celebrated its 10th anniversary in March of this year. When the "co-op" first opened its doors on March 1, 1989, it offered the wares of 28 dealers. Now, with the merging of two separate buildings into one, they are represented by more than 100 dealers from Pennsylvania and New Jersey, offering only antiques and collectibles in 8,000 square feet of browsing room. The dealers specialize in primitives, jewelry, cut glass, Depression, Heisey and Clevenger glass; Roseville pottery, dolls, furniture, postcards and paper products.

### 47 MOORESTOWN

**Country Peddler Antiques**
111 Chester Ave.
609/235-0680

**George Wurtzel Antiques**
69 E. Main St.
609/234-9631

**Carpet Bagger's Doll Hospital**
Creek Road
609/234-5095

**Bill's Bargains**
15 King St.
609-261-0096

*New Jersey*

**Center Stage Antiques**
41 King St.
609/261-0602

**Ebenezer Antiques**
2245 Route 38 @ Creek Road
609/702-9447

**Rupp's Antiques**
2108 Route 38
609/267-4848

**Abode Antiques**
99 Washington St.
609/267-1717

**Fox Hill Antiques**
2123 Route 38
609/518-0200

### 50 MOUNT LAUREL

**Collector's Express**
104 Berkshire Dr.
609/866-1693

**Creek Road Antique Centre, Inc.**
123 Creek Road
609/778-8899

### 51 MULLICA HILL

The story of Mullica Hill began in the late 1600s, when English and Irish Quakers moved to the area and began establishing plantations. This Quaker community centered on the south bank of Raccoon Creek and was called Spicerville, in honor of Jacob Spicer, a prominent landowner. Originally only the north bank of the creek was known as Mullica Hill, and it was named after the town's pioneering Finnish settlers — Eric, John, Olag and William Mullica — who first purchased land here in 1704. Two of the homes the Mullica family built are still standing on North Main near the creek, nearly 300 years later!

Prior to the American Revolution, Mullica Hill was a coach town of little more than two scattered clusters of houses north and south of the creek, two taverns and a grist mill. Four of these structures still remain today. The town's first real period of growth began around 1780 and continued until the 1830s. Commercial development sprang up primarily in Spicerville (South Main) and four of the town's first churches were built here. Although a blacksmith shop, schoolhouse and one of the town's two taverns were on the north side, this neighborhood remained mostly agricultural. However, the entire village became known as Mullica Hill, probably because the hill itself was the most notable feature in the entire town. Many of the buildings from this era are still standing on Main Street today.

In the late 1800s a small mill district was established along the Raccoon Creek raceway. A woolen mill and an iron foundry operated here for several decades until fire and competition from larger industrial centers caused the area to decline drastically. Today only the 18th-century gristmill remains — in a greatly altered state.

A second period of growth followed the Civil War and many noteworthy Victorian homes and public buildings were built throughout the entire village, including the town hall. Also, during this time Harrison Township established itself as one of the county's most productive agricultural areas. A railroad spur was built and very quickly the town became one of the nation's most active shipping points for agricultural commodities.

Throughout most of the 20th century Mullica Hill has served as the principal town and seat of government for Harrison Township, and its businesses catered to the needs of the surrounding farms. While agriculture today is still an important local industry, Mullica Hill's businesses are no longer so locally oriented. The town has emerged as a major antique and crafts center and is widely known for its nostalgic charm. Historic homes have been restored and the streets are now crowded with visitors from throughout the Eastern seaboard.

In 1991 the entire village of Mullica Hill was placed on the National Register of Historic Places and the New Jersey State Register of Historic Places. In 1992 Harrison Township established the village as a local historic district.

### The Warehouse
2 S. Main St.
609/478-4500
Open: Wed.–Sun. 11–5
Directions: *From I-95:* Take Commodore Barry Bridge and 322 East to Mullica Hill. *From the New Jersey Turnpike:* Take Exit 2 then 322 East to Mullica Hill. *From I-295:* Take Exit 11 then 322 East to Mullica Hill. The Warehouse is in the middle of town on Main Street.

This interesting, large, multidealer shop holds several divisions: an art gallery, jewelry store, candy store, furniture store, a large showcase shop, plus a cafe and tea room where you can recover when you realize that you've spent more than you should have! And it's all packaged in a Civil War–era building.

**Raccoon's Tale**
6 High St.
609/478-4488

**Elizabeth's of Mullica Hill**
32 N. Main St.
609/478-6510

**Kings Row Antiques**
46 N. Main St.
609/478-4361

**Murphy's Loft**
53 N. Main St.
609/478-4928

**The Country Christmas Shoppe**
86 N. Main St.
609/478-2250

**The Front Porch**
21 S. Main St.
609/478-6556

**Dolls, Toys, and Free Museum**
34 S. Main St.
609/478-6137

**Debra's Dolls**
20 N. Main St.
609/478-9778

**The Antique Center at Mullica Hill**
45 N. Main St.
609/478-4754

**The Queen's Inn Antiques**
48 N. Main St.
609/223-9433

**Carriage House Antiques**
62 N. Main St.
609/478-4459

**The Old Mill Antique Mall**
1 S. Main St.
609/478-9810

**The Sign of Saint George**
30 S. Main St.
609/478-6101

**Wolf's Antiques**
36 S. Main St.
609/478-4992

# New Jersey

**Deja Vu Antique & Gift Gallery**
38 S. Main St.
609/478-6351

**June Bug Antiques**
44 S. Main St.
609/478-2167

**Clock Shop**
45 S. Main St. (Rear Shop)
609/478-6555

**Lynne Antiques**
49 S. Main St.
609/223-9199

**The Treasure Chest**
50 S. Main St.
609/468-4371

**Antiquities at Mullica Hill**
43 S. Main St.
609/478-6773

**Sugar & Spice Antiques**
45 S. Main St.
609/478-2622

**Accesories**
46 S. Main St.
609/223-0100

**Jane "D" Antiques**
50 S. Main St.
No Phone

**Mullica Hill Art Glass**
53 S. Main St.
609/478-2552

## 52 NEW BRUNSWICK

**French Street Antiques**
108 French St.
732/545-9352

**Aaron Aardvark & Son**
119 French St.
732/246-1720

**Somewhere in Time**
115 French St.
732/247-3636

**Amber Lion Antiques**
365 George St.
732/214-9090

## 53 OCEAN CITY

**Joseph's Antiques**
908 Asbury Ave.
609/398-3855

**Sutton's Antiques**
1743 Asbury Ave.
609/399-0552

**B's Fantasy**
11th St.
609/398-9302

**Curiosity Shoppe**
1119 Asbury Ave.
609/407-1251

**Only Yesterday**
1108 Broadwalk
609/398-2869

## 54 OCEAN GROVE

### *Great Places to Stay*

## Cordova Hotel

26 Webb Ave.
732/774-3084 (in season); 212/751-9577 (winter)
Fax: 212/207-4720
Open: May 15–Sept. 30
Directions: Take the Garden State Parkway to Exit 100 (from the south) or Exit 100B (from the north), then go 15 minutes on Route 33 East to the end. Turn left for 100 feet then make an immediate right (Broadway) to the ocean. Turn left at the ocean and go to Webb. The inn is 1½ blocks from the beach.

This delightful century-old Victorian inn in historic Ocean Grove (listed in the National Register of Historical Places) has a friendly atmosphere with "Old World charm." At the Cordova you'll feel like a member of an extended family as you chat with your hosts or other guests over breakfast. Quiet and family oriented, the Cordova was selected by *New Jersey Magazine* as "one of the seven best places to stay on the Jersey Shore." Also featured in the travel guide *O'New Jersey* (1992). Full kitchen, living room, BBQ and picnic tables in a private garden are available for guests' use. Great for family gatherings!

Special weekday and 7-night rates, Saturday night wine and cheese parties, Murder Mystery weekends, Comedy Night, Food Fests, annual Choir Festival (2,000 voices), Tai Chi workshops, and work weekends (guests work/stay free) are especially popular. Call for details. The inn is near buses and trains.

## 55 OLDWICK

**Magic Shop**
60 Main St.
908/439-2330

**Collections**
Route 523
908/439-3736

## 56 PHILLIPSBURG

**Gracy's Manor**
1400 Belvidere Road
908/859-0928

**B & B Model A Ford Parts**
300 Firth St.
908/859-4856

**Michael J. Stasak Antiques**
376 River Road
908/454-6136

**Harmony Barn**
2481 Belvidere Road
908/859-6159

**Lil's**
103 Foch Blvd.
908/454-3982

**Jensen Antiques**
State Hwy. #57
908/859-0240

## 57 POINT PLEASANT BEACH

**The Time Machine**
516 Arnold Ave.
732/295-9695

**Wally's Follies Antiques**
626 Arnold Ave.
732/899-1840

**Snow Goose**
641 Arnold Ave.
732/892-6929

**Feather Tree Antiques**
624 Bay Ave.
732/899-8891

**Antiques Etc.**
1225 Bay Ave.
732/295-9888

**Fond Memories Antiques**
625 Arnold Ave.
732/892-4149

**Classy Collectibles**
633 Arnold Ave.
732/714-0957

**Clock Shop & Antiques**
726 Arnold Ave.
732/899-6200

**Company Store**
628 Bay Ave.
732/892-5353

**Antique Emporium**
Bay Ave & Trenton
732/892-2222

# New Jersey

**Ruddy Duck**
2034 Bridge Ave.
732/892-8893

**Bargain Outlet**
2104 Route 88
732/892-9007

## 58  POMPTON LAKES

**Charisma 7 Antiques**
212 Wanaque Ave.
973/839-7779

**Picker's Paradise**
269 Wanaque Ave.
973/616-9500

**Sterling Antique Center**
222 Wanaque Ave.
973/616-8986

## 59  PRINCETON

**Gilded Lion**
4 Chambers St.
609/924-6350

**Eye for Art**
6 Spring St.
609/924-5277

**Kingston Antiques**
4446 Route 27
609/924-0332

## 60  RAHWAY

**Royal Treasures Antique, Inc.**
69 E. Cherry St.
732/827-0409

**Ken, Antiques**
1667 Irving St.
732/381-7306

## 61  RED BANK

**Copper Kettle Antiques**
15 Broad St.
732/741-8583

**Tea & Vintage**
16 West St.
732/741-6676

**Antiques Associates**
205 W. Front St.
732/219-0377

**Monmouth Antiques Shoppes**
217 W. Front St.
732/842-7377

**Shore Antique Center**
300 High #35
732/295-5771

**Willinger Enterprises, Inc.**
626 Route 88
732/892-2217

**P.K.'s Treasures Ltd.**
229 Wanaque Ave.
973/835-5212

**Carrolls Antiques**
326 Wanaque Ave.
973/831-6186

**Girard Caron Interiors**
54 Constitution Hwy. W.
609/924-1007

**Tamara's Things**
4206 Quaker Bridge Road
609/452-1567

**East & West Chinese Antiques**
4451 Route 27
609/924-2743

**Tarnished Swan**
74 W. Cherry St.
732/499-7111

**Tower Hill Antiques & Design**
147 Broad St.
732/842-5551

**The Red Bank Antique Center**
195 W. Front St.
732/842-3393

**Gas Light Antiques**
212 W. Front St.
732/741-7323

**Antique Gallery**
27 Monmouth St.
732/224-0033

**Two Broad Antiques**
160 Monmouth St.
732/224-0122

**British Cottage Antiques**
126 Shrewsbury Ave.
732/530-0685

## 62  RIDGEWOOD

**Ridgewood Furniture Refinishing**
166 Chestnut St.
201/652-5566

**Marilyn of Monroe**
39 Godwin Ave.
201/447-3123

**Hahn's Antiques**
579 Goffle Road
201/251-9444

## 63  SADDLE RIVER

**Carriage House Antiques**
7 Barnstable Court
201/327-2100

**Richard Kyllo Antiques**
210 W. Saddle River Road
201/327-7343

## 64  SCOTCH PLAINS

**Antique Cottage**
1833 Front St.
908/322-2553

**Parse House Antiques**
1833 Front St.
908/322-9090

**Heritage Antiques Center**
364 Park Ave.
908/322-2311

**Heinemeyer's Collectibles & Antiques**
1380 Terrill Road
908/322-1788

## 65  SOMERVILLE

**Uptown Somerville Center**
Division St.
908/595-1294

**Gallery**
30 Division St.
908/429-0370

**Country Seat Antiques**
41 W. Main St.
908/595-9556

**Lone Arranger Outlet Store**
101 Shrewsbury Ave.
732/747-9238

**Irish Eyes Import**
1 Cottage Place
201/445-8585

**Then and Now**
419 Goffle Road
201/670-7090

**Ivory Tower, Inc.**
38 Oak St.
201/670-6191

**Baldini Ricci Galleries, Inc.**
24 Industrial Ave.
201/327-0890

**Oakwood Furniture Co.**
1833 Front St.
908/322-3873

**Gallerie Ani' Tiques**
Stage House Village — Park & Front
908/322-4600

**Seymour's Antiques & Collectibles**
1732 E. 2nd St.
908/322-1300

**Somerville Center Antiques**
17 Division St.
908/526-3446

**Incogneeto Neet-O-Rama**
19 W. Main St.
908/231-1887

## 66 SOUTH ORANGE

**Roberta Willner Antiques**
48 Crest Dr.
973/762-8844

**Aaltens Galleries Est. 1914**
461 Irvington Ave.
973/762-7200

**Carrie Topf Antiques**
50 W. South Orange Ave.
973/762-8773

## 67 SPRING LAKE

**Gallery III Antiques**
1720 State Hwy. #71
732/449-7560

**Spring Lake Antiques**
1201 3rd Ave.
732/449-3322

## 68 SUMMIT

**Plumquin Ltd.**
12 Beechwood Road
908/273-3425

**Summit Antiques Center, Inc.**
511 Morris Ave.
908/273-9373

**The Second Hand**
519 Morris Ave.
908/273-6021

**Charming Home**
358 Springfield Ave.
908/598-1022

**Country House**
361 Springfield Ave.
908-277-3400

**Remmey's Consignment**
83 Summit Ave.
908/273-5055

**Antiques & Art by Conductor**
88 Summit Ave.
908/273-6893

## 69 TOMS RIVER

**Antique Outlet**
552 Lakehurst Road
732/286-7788

**Main St. Antique Center**
251 Main St.
732/349-5764

**Piggy Bank**
2018 Route 37 E.
732/506-6133

**Bulldog Glass Co.**
10 W. Gateway
732/349-2742

## 70 TRENTON

### Conti Antiques & Figurines

52 Route 33 (1 mile off I-295, Exit 64)
609/584-1080 or 609/586-4531
Open: Mon.–Sat. usually 11–5; Sun. by appointment
Directions: Located on State Highway 33 between Robbinsville (Route 130) and Trenton. Also, Exit 64 off I-295. Two miles from Trenton, 8 miles from Bordentown, 12 miles from Hightstown, 15 miles from Princeton. Call before coming! Hours 11–5 unless on a house call or closed due to an estate appraisal. Call also for better directions.

Richard Conti has been in business 22 years, handling lots of smalls in his 1,400-square-foot shop. Most of his stock consists of furniture and figurines, which include Royal Doulton, Hummel, Boehm, Cybis, Ispanky, Precious Moments, Goebel and others. In addition to the shop and handling appraisals, Richard also holds auctions on an "as needed" basis.

**Greenwood Antiques**
1918 Greenwood Ave.
609/586-6887

**Armies of the Past Ltd.**
2038 Greenwood Ave.
609/890-0142

**Estate Galleries Ltd.**
1641 N. Olden Ave.
609/219-0300

**Canty, Inc.**
1680 N. Olden Ave.
609/530-1832

**Antiques by Selmon**
10 Vetterlein Ave.
609/586-0777

## 71 WESTFIELD

**Betty Gallagher Antiques, Inc.**
266 E. Broad St.
908/654-4222

**Westfield Antiques**
510 Central Ave.
908/232-3668

**Old Toy Shop**
759 Central Ave.
908/232-8388

**Linda Elmore Antiques**
395 Cumberland St.
908/233-5443

**Marylou's Memorabilia**
17 Elm St.
908/654-7277

**Back Room Antiques**
39 Elm St.
908/654-5777

**The Attic**
415 Westfield Ave.
908/233-1954

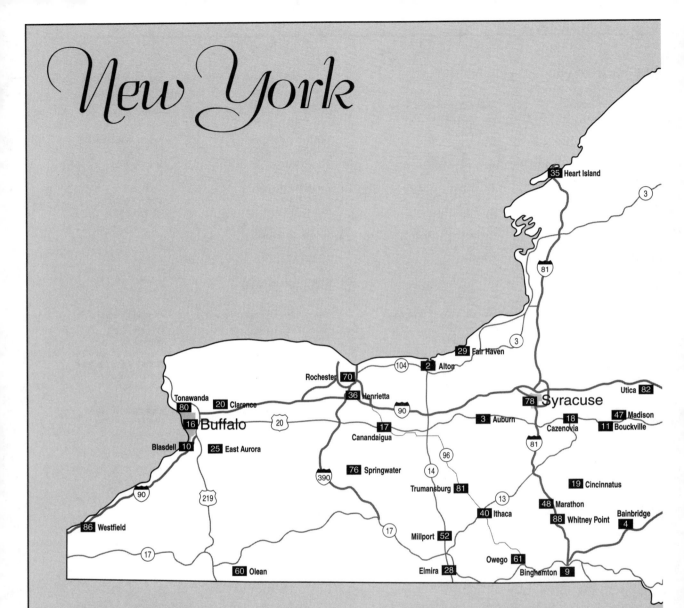

# New York

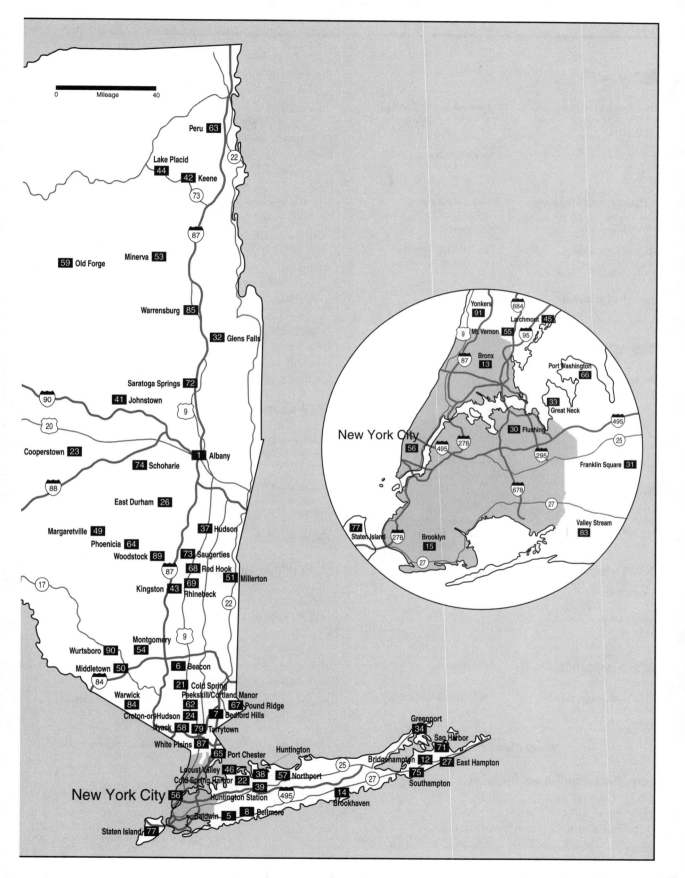

## 1 ALBANY

**Vince Kendrick Jewelers**
475 Albany Shaker Road
518/438-6350

**Zeller's**
32 Central Ave.
518/463-8221

**S & S Antique & Used Furniture Co.**
85 Central Ave.
518/462-3952

**Flamingo's '50s & '60s**
211 Lark St.
518/434-3829

**Yankee Peddler Thrift Shop**
265 Osborne Road
518/459-9353

**Daybreak Antique Clothing**
22 Central Ave.
518/434-4312

**Action Antiques**
85 Central Ave.
518/463-0841

**New Scotland Antiques**
240 Washington Ave.
518/463-1323

**Pocket Change Antiques**
4 Prospect Ave.
518/489-6413

## 2 ALTON

**Alton Antique Center**
8497 E. Ridge Road
315/483-2049
Open: Mon.–Sun. 10–5

Over 10,000 square feet of antiques and collectibles.

## 3 AUBURN

**Ward's Antiques**
56 E. Gennesee St.
315/252-7703

**Roesch's Antiques & Collectibles**
7255 Grant Ave.
315/255-0760

**Auburn Antiques**
33 Walnut St.
315/252-9701

**Fingerlake's Antiques**
104 Grant Ave.
315/252-4934

**Auburn Trading Post**
24 McMaster St.
315/258-9492

## 4 BAINBRIDGE

**Old Hickory Antique Center**
Route 7 at Gilford Road
607/967-4145

**Susquehanna Cafe & Antiques**
Route 7
607/967-4100

### *Great Places to Stay*

**Berry Hill Farms Bed and Breakfast**
242 Ward Loomis Road
607/967-8745 or 1-800-497-8745
Open: Year-round. Gardens open from 8 a.m. to dusk.
Directions: From I-88, take Exit 8, Bainbridge. Go west on Route 206

for about 4 miles to West Bainbridge. Turn right on State Route 17 toward Oxford. Go 2 $^3/_{10}$ miles. Turn right on Ward-Loomis Road. Go ¹/₂ mile to the top of the hill.

This secluded hilltop farm is surrounded by acres of woods and meadows. The 1820s farmhouse has been tastefully renovated, and is full of comfortable antiques. They have all the conveniences of home, and then some—flannel sheets, down comforters, extra pillows, fresh and dried flowers from the gardens and antiques everywhere.

The Berry Hill Farm gardens are already a local attraction. They are open to the public from May to October. Combined with the spectacular view, you'll find them a "bit of heaven," "a butterfly paradise," and "food for the soul."

Guided tours are available to ensure you experience everything that Berry Hill has to offer. Altogether, there are hundreds of species of plants, so you will always find something in bloom, something to smell, and something to taste. Many of the flowers and plants are dried here on the farm to be used for herbal teas, cooking and for their dried flower business. Berry Hill Farms is conveniently located to many antique shops and auctions in the area.

## 5 BALDWIN

**Baldwin Antiques Centre**
906 Merrick Road
516/867-9842

**Antique Quest**
87 Merrick Road
516/623-8351

**Artie's Corner**
754 Sunrise Hwy.
516/867-4297

## 6 BEACON

**Back in Time Antiques**
Located in Antiques and Uniques
346 Main St.
914/838-0623 or 914/737-8875

Back in Time Antiques features a nostalgic blend of antiques and collectibles, period furniture, unusual lamps, carnival and Depression glass, books, Limoges, jewelry, marbles and much, much more.

The shop is located among 30-plus other antique, specialty and art shops on busy Main Street.

**All That Jazz**
238 Main St.
914/838-0441

**Dickinson's Antiques**
440 Main St.
914/838-1643

**Cold Spring Galleries, Inc.**
324 Main St.
914/831-6800

**East End Antiques**
444 Main St.
914/838-9030

*New York*

**Early Everything**
470 Main St.
914/838-3014

**Tioronda Antiques**
15 Tioronda Ave.
914/831-3437

**Beacon Hill Antiques**
474 Main St.
914/831-4577

## 7 BEDFORD HILLS

**Raphael Gallery Paintings**
23 Depot Plaza
914/666-4780

**Bedford Salvage Co.**
2 Depot Plaza
914/666-4595

**Mark's Time**
132 Green Lane
914/242-0058

## 8 BELLMORE

**Antiques & Antiques**
111 Bedford Ave. N.
516/826-9839

**Austern's Antiques**
2970 Merrick Road
516/221-0098

**Ray's Antiques**
2962 Merrick Road
516/826-7129

## 9 BINGHAMTON

**Storekeeper**
95 Clinton St.
607/722-2431

**Clinton Mill Antique Center**
99 Clinton St.
607/773-2036

**Olde Breeze**
173 Clinton St.
607/724-2114

**Frog Alley**
300 Clinton St.
607/729-6133

**Interiors with Claudia**
310 Clinton St.
607/797-3200

**For Your Listening Pleasure**
368 Clinton St.
607/797-0066

**Mary Webster's Antique Frames**
12 Edwards
607/722-1483

**Buyers Unlimited**
140 Front St.
607/722-1725

**China Closet**
97 Clinton St.
607/724-3611

**Elysian Gems & Jewelry**
99 Clinton St.
607/724-0298

**Mad Hatter Antiques**
284 Clinton St.
607/729-6036

**Silver Fox Antiques**
304 Clinton St.
607/729-1342

**Rivers Twin Antiques**
352 Clinton St.
607/798-9395

**World Galleries**
591 Conklin Road
607/772-0900

**Antique Exchange**
22 Front St.
607/723-6921

**Bob Connelly & Sallie**
205 State St.
607/722-9593

## 10 BLASDELL

### *Great Places to Stay*

**Morning Glory Bed & Breakfast**
45 Kent St.
716/824-8989

## 11 BOUCKVILLE

**Cobblestone Store**
Corner Route 20 & 46
315/893-7670

**By-Gones-Hinmans Motel**
Route 20
No phone listed

**D & R Antiques**
Route 20
315/893-1801

**Gallery Co-Op**
Route 20
315/893-7752

**Jackie's Place**
Route 20
315/893-7457

**Stone Lodge Antiques**
Route 20
315/893-7270

**Bittersweet Bazaar**
Route 20
315/893-7229

**Bouckville Antique Corner**
Route 20
315/893-1828

**Depot Antiques**
Route 20
315/893-7676

**Elvira Stanton Antiques**
Route 20
315/893-7479

**Indian Opening Antique Center**
Route 20
315/893-7303

**Station House Antiques**
Route 20
315/893-7652

**Veranda Antiques & Art**
Route 20 & 12 B
315/893-7270

## 12 BRIDGEHAMPTON

**Beach Plum Antiques**
Main St.
516/537-7403

**Country Gear Ltd.**
Main St.
516/537-1032

**John Salibello Antiques**
Montauk Hwy.
516/537-1484

**Legendary Collections**
Montauk Hwy.
516/537-2211

**English Country Antiques**
Snake Hollow Road
516/537-0606

**Inez G. Macwhinnie**
Main St.
516/537-7433

**House of Charm Antiques**
Montauk Hwy.
516/537-3335

**Kinnaman & Ramaekers**
2466 Montauk Hwy.
516/537-3838

**Urban Archeology**
Montauk Hwy.
516/537-0124

**Ruby Beet's Antiques**
1703 Montauk Hwy.
516/537-2802

## 13  BRONX

**All Boro Estate Liquidators**
45 Bruckner Blvd.
718/402-8777

**Big Apple Antiques, Inc.**
430 E. 188th St.
718/220-4018

**T & I Thrift World**
3980 White Plains Road
718/519-6724

**Larry's Antiques**
2419 Eastchester Road
718/779-2304

**F & J Furniture**
1007 Tiffany St.
718/378-2038

## 14  BROOKHAVEN

**Brook Store**
378 S. Country Road
516/286-8503

**Delancy St. East**
2527 Montauk Hwy.
516/286-2956

## 15  BROOKLYN

**Horseman Antiques, Inc.**
351 Atlantic Ave.
718/596-1048

**In Days of Old Limited**
357 Atlantic Ave.
718/858-4233

**Atlantic Antique Center**
367 Atlantic Ave.
718/488-0149

**Circa Antiques Ltd.**
377 Atlantic Ave.
718/596-1866

**A Matter of Time**
380 Atlantic Ave.
718/624-7867

**Antiques and Collectibles Shop**
483 Atlantic Ave.
718/858-6903

**Easy Furniture, Inc.**
871 Broadway
718/574-6400

**Aaa-Abbey Merchandising Co., Inc.**
618 Coney Island Ave.
718/253-8830

**Antiques Plus**
744 Coney Island Ave.
718/941-8805

**Smitty's New & Used Furniture**
744 Coney Island Ave.
718/854-3052

**Town & Country Antiques**
352 Atlantic Ave.
718/875-7253

**City Barn Antiques**
362 Atlantic Ave.
718/855-8566

**Time Trader**
368 Atlantic Ave.
718/852-3301

**Times & Moments**
378 Atlantic Ave.
718/625-3145

**Assaf Antiques**
383 Atlantic Ave.
718/237-2912

**Antiques by Ruth**
507 Atlantic Ave.
718/382-3269

**Broadway Top Class Furniture**
1275 Broadway
718/452-1100

**Scottie's Gallery**
624 Coney Island Ave.
718/851-8325

**Bernstein's**
744 Coney Island Ave.
718/342-3564

**Tyler Antiques**
744 Coney Island Ave.
718/331-1533

**All Boro Furniture**
779 Coney Island Ave.
718/272-0559

**Northeast Furniture & Antiques**
779 Coney Island Ave.
718/272-4133

**Finders Keepers Antiques & Tag**
784 Coney Island Ave.
718/941-4481

**Yava Furniture**
832 Coney Island Ave.
718/693-3322

**Roy Electric Antique Light Co.**
1054 Coney Island Ave.
718/434-7002

**Astor Antiques**
1067 Coney Island Ave.
718/434-9200

**Attic**
220 Court St.
718/643-9535

**New You Zd**
1211 Flatbush Ave.
718/856-4819

**Bibilo Furniture Store**
502 5th Ave.
718/832-6696

**Colonial Global, Inc.**
6823 5th Ave.
718/748-4401

**Antiques & Decorations**
4319 14th Ave.
718/633-6393

**Park Hill Restoration**
375 Atlantic Ave.
718/624-0233

**Mel's Antique**
99 Smith St.
718/834-8700

**Grand Sterling Silver Co., Inc.**
4921 13th Ave.
718/854-0623

**TOP Cash Antiques**
2065 E. 33rd St.
718/382-4418

**Frank Galdi Antiques**
247 Warren St.
718/875-9293

**C.P. Galleries**
779 Coney Island Ave.
718/462-3606

**Flatbush Galleries**
779 Coney Island Ave.
718/287-8353

**Sciarrino Antiques**
830 Coney Island Ave.
718/462-8134

**Once upon a Time Antiques**
1053 Coney Island Ave.
718/859-6295

**Abbey Galleries**
1061 Coney Island Ave.
718/692-2421

**Charlotte's Nik Nak Nook Antiques**
1131 Coney Island Ave.
718/252-0088

**Action Furniture**
1171 Flatbush Ave.
718/284-2899

**People's Furniture**
1332 Flatbush Ave.
718/859-6850

**Juke Box Class & Vintage Slot**
6742 5th Ave.
718/833-8455

**Abboco**
8323 5th Ave.
718/238-6956

**South Portland Antiques**
753 Fulton
718/596-1556

**Gaslight Time Antiques**
5 Plaza St. W.
718/789-7185

**ACE New & Used Furniture**
575 Sutter Ave.
718/495-5711

**Discoveries**
8407 3rd Ave.
718/836-0583

**Dream Land Antiques**
619 Vanderbilt Ave.
718/230-9142

**Christmas Carol's**
492 Macon St.
718/919-9033

# 16 BUFFALO

| | |
|---|---|
| **Bailey's Furniture**<br>3191 Bailey Ave.<br>716/835-6171 | **Scotty's Furniture**<br>3112 Bailey Ave.<br>716/835-6199 |
| **Horsefeather's Architectural Antiques**<br>346 Connecticut St.<br>716/882-1581 | **Tres Beau Interiors**<br>489 Delaware Ave.<br>716/886-3514 |
| **C. Markarian & Sons, Inc.**<br>3807 Delaware Ave.<br>716/873-8667 | **Lete Antiques—Carl Stone**<br>65 Elmwood Ave.<br>716/884-0211 |
| **Eaton Galleries**<br>115 Elmwood Ave.<br>716/882-7823 | **Taylor Gallery**<br>125 Elmwood Ave.<br>716/881-0120 |
| **Assets Antiques**<br>140 Elmwood Ave.<br>716/882-2415 | **Jeffrey Thier Antiques**<br>152 Elmwood Ave.<br>716/883-2858 |
| **Source**<br>152 Elmwood Ave.<br>716/883-2858 | **MIX**<br>711 Elmwood Ave.<br>716/886-0141 |
| **Lots of Stuff**<br>2703 Elmwood Ave.<br>716/874-1164 | **Dana E. Tillou Gallery**<br>417 Franklin St.<br>716/854-5285 |
| **American Militaria Collector**<br>2409 Harlem Road<br>716/891-5200 | **Stock Exchange**<br>1421 Hertel Ave.<br>716/838-8294 |
| **Conley Interiors, Inc.**<br>1425 Hertel Ave.<br>716/838-1000 | **Just Browsin**<br>1439 Hertel Ave.<br>716/837-1840 |
| **Coo Coo U**<br>1478 Hertel Ave.<br>716/837-3385 | **Melange Vintage Clothing**<br>1484 Hertel Ave.<br>716/838-9290 |
| **A to Z Auction**<br>2150 William St.<br>716/896-3342 | **Antique Architectural Circus**<br>86 Vermont St.<br>716/885-5555 |
| **Antiques Americana**<br>5600 Main St.<br>716/633-2570 | **Jean's Creekview Antiques**<br>5629 Main St.<br>716/632-2711 |
| **Erie West Antiques & Collectibles**<br>10 Michael Road<br>716/677-2119 | **Attic Antiques & Collectibles**<br>550 Mineral Springs Road<br>716/822-0627 |
| **Antique Architectural Circus**<br>855 Niagra<br>716/885-5555 | **Antique Jewelry Trojners**<br>296 Roycroft Blvd.<br>716/839-5453 |
| **Gallery of Treasures**<br>2180 Seneca St.<br>716/826-3907 | |

## Great Places to Stay

**Beau Fleuve Bed & Breakfast Inn**
242 Linwood Ave.
1-800-278-0245

A grand, Stick-style Queen Anne Victorian in Buffalo's Linwood Historic Preservation District, the Beau Fleuve offers five tastefully decorated guest rooms featuring antique and heirloom beds, down bedding, and decorator linens. A unique handcrafted staircase and nine colorful stained glass windows reflect the Aesthetic Movement. Its signature motif, the sunflower, appears in the house in both wood carvings and art glass. The restored exterior is painted in authenic Aesthetic Movement colors. Continental or full breakfast is served by candlelight. House specialties include blueberry or raspberry pancakes, Belgian waffles, eggs benedict, french toast, or several varities of frittata.

# 17 CANANDAIGUA

| | |
|---|---|
| **Richard Cuddeback**<br>22 Leeward Lane<br>716/394-4097 | **Petticoat Junction Antiques**<br>103 Leicester St.<br>716/396-0691 |
| **Nostalgia Ltd.**<br>238 S. Main St.<br>716/396-9898 | **Kipling's Treasures**<br>116 S. Main St.<br>716/396-7270 |
| **Antiques Unlimited**<br>168 Niagara St.<br>716/394-7255 | **Harvest Mill**<br>40 Parrish St.<br>716/394-5907 |
| **Tall Pines Antiques**<br>3257 Routes<br>716/394-7230 | **Antique Center—30 Dealers**<br>47 Saltonstall St.<br>716/394-2297 |
| **Happy Clutter Antiques**<br>3735 State Route 5, #20<br>716/394-4199 | |

### *Nearby Antique Shopping (Farmington)*
*Farmington is 3 miles north of Canandaigua, 2 miles south of NYS Thruway at Exit 44.*

**Antique Emporium**
1740 Rochester Road (Route 332)
716/398-3997
Open: Mon.–Sun. 10–5

Over 18,000 square feet or rare collectibles and quality antiques. In addition there are 2 antique shops located nearby; Collectors Flea Market and the Antique Shop.

*New York*

## Great Places to Stay

### Sutherland House Bed & Breakfast
3179 State Route 21S
1-800-396-0375
Web site: www.sutherlandhouse.com

Sutherland House is an 1885 renovated Victorian centered on five private acres of quiet and solitude, surrounded by rolling farmland and mature trees. Don't forget to take a peek in the scrapbook that documents the transformation from haunted house to bed and breakfast.

### 18  CAZENOVIA

**Sally's Cellar**
58 Albany St.
315/655-3324

**Old Everlasting Antiques**
1826 Ballina Road
315/655-3212

**The Old Lamplighter Antiques**
3951 Number Nine Road
315/655-4991

**Amanda Bury**
97 Albany St., Route 20
315/655-3326

**Alexandra's Attic**
4010 Erieville Road
315/655-2146

**Web's Country House**
4031 Putnam Road
315/655-4177

### 19  CINCINNATUS

## Great Places to Stay

### Alice's Dowry B&B
2789 Route 26
607/863-3934
Web site: www.bbonline.com/ny/alicesdowry/

This beautifully restored Italianate Victorian offers two guest rooms with antique decor. In season, the one and a half acres provides the space to stroll and relax among the gardens or sit on the "Painted Lady" veranda in a wicker rocker. Full breakfasts, served on the sun porch at tables for two.

### 20  CLARENCE

**Christner's Antiques**
10715 Clarence Center Road
716/741-2826

**Antiques at the Barn**
9060 Main St.
716/632-6674

**Uncle Sam's Antiques**
9060 Main St.
716/741-8838

**VI & Sis Antiques**
8970 Main St.
716/634-4488

**Ruth's Antiques, Inc.**
9060 Main St.
716/741-8001

**Charles M. Fisher**
10255 Main St.
716/759-6433

**Kelly Schultz Antiques & Oriental**
10225 Main St.
716/759-2260

**Baumer Antiques**
10548 Main St.
716/759-6468

**Antique Emporium**
10225 Main St.
716/759-0718

**Antique Parlor**
10874 Main St.
716/759-2048

**Clarence Antiques Co-op**
11079 Main St.
716/759-7080

**Up Your Attic Vintage Clothing**
10255 Main St.
716/759-2866

**Muleskinner Antiques**
10626 Main St.
716/759-2661

**Clarence Hollow Antiques**
10863 Main St.
716/759-7878

**Antique World & Market Place**
10995 Main St.
716/759-8483

**Kelly's Antique Market**
11111 Main St.
716/759-7488

### 21  COLD SPRING

**Basso Brokerage Antiques**
12 Division St.
914/265-9650

**As Time Goes By**
72 Main St
914/265-7988

**Jacquie Antiques**
89 Main St.
914/265-7883

**Once upon a Time Antiques**
101 Main St.
914/265-4339

**Others Oldies**
169 Main St.
914/265-2323

**Dew Drop Inn Antique Center**
Route 9
914/265-4358

**38 Main**
38 Main St.
914/265-3838

**Tin Man**
75 Main St.
914/265-2903

**Sarabeck Antiques**
91 Main St.
914/265-4414

**Taca-Tiques**
109 Main St.
914/265-2655

**Ground Zero Antiques, Inc.**
290 Main St.
914/265-5275

**Rick Lawler Antiques**
168 Route 9
914/265-2231

### 22  COLD SPRING HARBOR

**M. Nash & Company, Inc.**
7 Main St.
516/692-7777

**Candle Wycke Antiques Ltd.**
147 Main St.
516/692-3106

**Arlene Coroaan Antiques**
7 Main St.
516/692-7777

**Huntington Antique Center**
129 Main St.
516/692-7777

**Lyman Thorne Enterprises Ltd.**
169 Main St.
516/692-2834

*New York*

## 23  COOPERSTOWN

The charming village of Cooperstown sits at the foot of Lake Ostego in the heart of the area made famous by author James Fenimore Cooper (1789–1851). The streets are lined with Victorian homes and storefronts decorated with hanging baskets and window boxes. The Fenimore House Museum includes the works of famed 19th- and 20th-century artists along with displays of Cooper memorabilia. Nearby, the Farmers' Museum, a living history center, re-creates a 19th-century village. This is the setting for one of the nation's premier sports shrines—the National Baseball Hall of Fame.

This red-brick facility traces its beginnings back to a discovery in a dust-covered attic near Cooperstown. Here was found an undersized, misshapen, homemade ball stuffed with cloth, believed to be the baseball used by Abner Doubleday in the first game. The baseball was purchased by Cooperstown resident Stephen C. Clark, who conceived the idea of displaying it along with other baseball objects. The one-room exhibition attracted such public interest that plans for a national museum were drawn up, and the official National Baseball Hall of Fame was officially opened in 1939 to commemorate the game's 100th anniversary.

### Cooperstown Antique Center

73 Chestnut St.
607/547-2435

General line of furniture and specializing in restored electrical lighting.

### *Great Places to Stay*

### Brown-Williams House

RR 1, Box 337
607/547-5569

Beautiful (c. 1825) Federal-style inn, located one and one half miles from Cooperstown, offers guests charm and tranquillity with the complete privacy of a "true country gentleman's estate." Immaculately kept, renovated by its owner to period Federal-Shaker style, the home offers a warm ambiance with its wood post and beam construction. Its generous center hall, great room and dining rooms all have beautiful hand-painted wall furnishings and stenciling.

### Nineteen Church Street B&B

19 Church St.
607/547-8384

This country home is located on a quiet street in the heart of Cooperstown. Built circa 1829, the bed and breakfast features stenciled floors and trompe l'oiel paintings. The Baseball Hall of Fame's back door is directly across the street. An easy walk to shopping and fishing, minutes by car or trolley to all the Cooperstown attractions, including Fenimore House, Farmers' Museum, golf, the opera house, antiquing and horseback riding.

## 24  CROTON-on-HUDSON

### *Great Places to Stay*

### Alexander Hamilton House

49 Van Wyck St.
914/271-6737
Fax: 914/271-3927
Directions: From Route 9, exit at Route 129. Go east to light at Riverside Avenue. Turn left onto Riverside for 1 block. Turn right on Grand Street. Go 1 block. Turn left onto Hamilton, which intersects Van Wyck right in front of #49. Go down the drive into the parking lot. Climb the porch steps and ring the bell.

Westchester's first bed and breakfast, the Alexander Hamilton House, circa 1889, is a stately Victorian home nestled on a cliff above the river, a short walk to the picturesque village of Croton-on-Hudson.

Note: The Bridal Chamber at the Alexander Hamilton House was rated 4 Kisses in *New York*'s Best Places to Kiss '92 & '94. Do you think five skylights, a king-sized bed, a Jacuzzi and a fireplace had anything to do with setting the mood?

## 25  EAST AURORA

**Fire House Antiques**
82 Elm St.
716/655-1035

**Barn Shoppe**
368 Mills Road
716/652-1099

**Roycroft Campus Antiques**
37 S. Grove St.
716/655-1565

## 26  EAST DURHAM

### *Great Places to Stay*

### Carriage House B&B

Box 12A, Route 145
518/634-2284

This small, family owned and operated business is located in the lower Catskill Mountains, with access to a host of nearby attractions, including five golf courses, a water park, horseback riding, and mountain summer festivals, as well as Howe's Caverns and Cooperstown.

*New York*

## 27 EAST HAMPTON

### Architrove, Inc.
74 Montauk Hwy., #3
516/329-229
Fax: 516/309-1155
Open: Daily 9–5 except Tues. & Wed. (call for appointment on those days)
Directions: Go 2 miles east of Wainslott on Route 27 (Montauk Hwy.) to the Red Horse Shopping Plaza.

This tasteful, upscale establishment offers the discriminating buyer the best in antique lighting fixtures, chandeliers, and sconces.

**Christina Borg, Inc.**
41 Main St.
516/324-6997

**Circle Antiques**
46 Main St.
516/324-0771

**Home James**
55 Main St.
516/324-2307

**Victory Gardens Ltd.**
63 Main St.
516/324-7800

**The Grand Alquistor**
110 N. Main St.
516/324-7272

**Antique Center of East Hampton**
251 Montauk Hwy.
516/324-9510

**Lars Bolander Antiques & Accessories**
5 Toilsome Lane
516/329-3400

**Pantigo House**
251 Pantigo Road
516/329-2831

**Country Green Antiques**
30 Race Lane
516/324-2756

**Maidstone Antiques**
512 Three Mile
516/329-7508

**Elaine's Room**
251 Partigo Road
516/324-4734

**Basil**
34 Park Place
516/324-4734

### *Great Places to Stay*

### East Hampton Point
P.O. Box 847
516/324-9191

Whether you arrive on your own boat and anchor in the beautiful marina or stay the weekend in one of the exquisitely designed country cottages or come to dine at the fabulous new indoor-outdoor restaurant, you'll experience East Hampton at its most romantic. The spacious one-bedroom and two-bedroom cottages are each individually decorated in a charming country manner with a large living/dining room complete with modern kitchen.

## 28 ELMIRA

**AAAAAA Antiques by Proper**
33 Brookline Ave.
607/734-0153

**Maple Avenue Antiques**
352 Maple Ave.
607/734-0332

**Mark Twain Country Antiques**
400 Maple Ave.
607/734-0916

**A Touch of Country House Shops**
1019 Pennsylvania Ave.
607/737-6945

**Michael Watts Antiques**
558 Riverside Ave.
607/733-9126

**Sturdivant Gallery**
912 Southport St.
607/733-1903

## 29 FAIR HAVEN

### *Great Places to Stay*

### Black Creek Farm
Mixer Road
315/947-5282
Fax: 315/947-5282
Open: Year-round for B&B. Antique shop open weekends 11–5, May 1–Sept. 15
Directions: From State Route 104, turn north on Route 104 A.
Go approximately 6 miles to Mixer Road, and turn left. The farm is ³/₄ mile down Mixer Road. From Oswego, N.Y., go west on Route 104 to Route 104A. Continue west through the village of Fair Haven to Mixer Road (about 2 miles). Turn right and go ³/₄ mile to Black Creek Farm.

This quiet, 20-acre farm is just 2 miles from Lake Ontario. Enjoy the tranquil surroundings of the fully restored 1888 Victorian farmhouse with four antique-filled, second-floor rooms. Two of these rooms have private baths.

You may "help yourself to the big outdoors by strolling the lawns and gardens, playing croquet, or exploring the country lanes on a bicycle-built-for-two." You may, however, prefer to simply take a nap in the hammock under the weeping birch trees.

Now available is a new guest house built beside the two-acre pond. Totally private and secluded, the guest house has everything you need for a romantic getaway.

The adjacent antique shop specializes in Victorian furniture, accessories, and collectibles. The owners refer to Black Creek Farm as "a 20-acre slice of serenity."

## Brown's Village Inn Bed and Breakfast and Antique Shop

Stafford St.

315/947-5817

Open: Tues.–Sun. 10–5

Directions: From Syracuse: Take Exit 34A, Route 481 North off the Thruway (Route 90). At Fulton, go west on Route 3 for about 14 miles to Route 104A. Take a left and follow into Fair Haven. The inn is on the 2nd street on the left after passing the state park.

Brown's Village Inn offers the perfect getaway near Fair Haven Beach. Fish the streams and lake for salmon, steelhead or trout; enjoy boating, swimming and cross-country skiing in winter. The inn's four guest rooms and two full baths offer all the comforts of home but without the responsibilities. For more private accommodations, a guest cottage is available.

Relax on the deck, walk to nearby shops and restaurants, stroll under the shade trees or enjoy the flowers in the yard.

## 30 FLUSHING

**Auctions Room Ltd.**
11641 Queens Blvd.
718/263-2274

**Comet Stamp & Coin Co., Inc.**
19207 Union Turnpike
718/479-0459

**Raymond's Antiques**
8603 Northern Blvd.
718/335-0553

**Ezra's Antiques**
4101 162nd St.
718/353-2603

**Feelings Antique Boutique**
4217 162nd St.
718/321-1939

**Peter Setzer Antiques**
4362 162nd St.
718/461-6999

**Antique Gallery**
3563 78th St.
718/478-1824

**Black Watch Rare Coins**
10412 Metropolitan Ave.
718/575-9779

**Old & New Shop, Inc.**
7130 Myrtle Ave.
718/381-8814

**Antique Shop**
15058 Northern Blvd.
718/886-8438

**M.P. Trading Co.**
4117 162nd St.
718/539-7019

**Queen's Collectibles**
4355 162nd St.
718/445-1316

**Rae's Antiques & Clocks**
4366 162nd St.
718/353-5577

**Golden Oldies Ltd.**
13229 33rd Ave.
718/445-4400

## 31 FRANKLIN SQUARE

## Di Salvo Galleries Ltd.

1015 Hempstead Turnpike

516/326-1090

Open: Tues.–Fri. 10–5, Sat. & Sun. 11–4

Directions: From Long Island Expressway: Take Exit 34 (New Hyde Park Road); go south approximately 3 to 4 miles. Make a right on Hempstead Turnpike. Proceed 1 ½ blocks. Di Salvo Galleries Ltd. is on the left.

Di Salvo Galleries is the brainchild of two very successful individuals who pooled their individual talents, experience and their general love for fine antiques into a thriving showroom gallery that attracts the novice collector, in addition to the most sophisticated individuals from the tri-state area.

One partner, Rosemarie Di Salvo, was formerly a legal professional specializing in estate and trust administration. For more than 20 years, Rosemarie liquidated estates with values ranging from $500,000 to millions of dollars. Through the years, Rosemarie developed close associations with appraisers, major auction houses and antique dealers. These relationships have proved invaluable as resources in obtaining wonderful selections of furniture and decorative accessories that are fresh to the market.

Annemarie Di Salvo is a designer who was formerly employed by a well-known Manhattan interior design firm specializing in residential design. Her projects included penthouse apartments in New York City, large beachfront homes in the Hamptons and country estates in New Jersey and Connecticut. Annemarie's background and experience lends itself very well to assisting clients with design projects and helping them to make the right purchasing decisions.

Annemarie is a New York University graduate with a certificate (interior design) in fine arts and antique appraisal studies; her speciality is in antique rugs and antique furniture.

The Di Salvo Gallery offers a wide variety of antique and vintage furniture, fine decorative accessories, art, porcelain, china, crystal, and antique and vintage linens. "Our inventory is selected based upon uniqueness and condition. Diversity is extremely important because our clients' needs run the gamut of singles and newlyweds setting up their first home, to the baby boomers who are the biggest segment of our client base. These clients are voracious in purchasing the same furniture styles that their parents or grandparents owned," explains Annemarie.

"Catering to the interior design community is our specialty, but we also welcome the general public."

**Estate Antiques**
967 Hempstead Turnpike
516-488-8100

## 32 GLENS FALLS

**Glenwood Manor Antiques Center**
Glenwood & Quaker Road
518/798-4747

## 33 GREAT NECK

**Charles Jewelers, Inc.**
62 Allenwood Road
516/482-6688

**Barbara Hart Yesteryears**
4 Bond St.
516/466-8748

*New York*

**Sabi Antiques**
112 Middle Neck Road
516/829-1330

## 34  GREENPORT

**Furniture Store**
214 Front St.
516/477-2980

**Cracker Barrel Antiques**
74365 Main Road
516/477-0843

**Primrose Lane**
74365 Main Road
516/477-8876

**Friendly Spirits Antiques**
311 Front St.
516/477-8680

**Greenport Antique Center**
74365 Main Road
516/477-0843

**Beall & Bell**
18 South St.
516/477-8239

## 35  HEART ISLAND

The legacy of Thousand Island's most tragic love affair can be found in Boldt Castle, a lavish, gilded-age mansion on Heart Island that dates back to the turn of the century. The castle motif is a monument to one man's love—hearts are carved in stone throughout the building and the island itself reshaped as a heart.

George Boldt, the owner of New York City's elegant Waldorf Astoria Hotel, decided to build a castle to symbolize his devotion to his young bride, Louise.

As a poor boy in Germany, George Boldt had gazed longingly at castles along the banks of the Rhine, so he commissioned workers to build a similar structure. The 120-room castle took form as the workers ferried blocks of stone and marble and exotic woods onto the island. Towns along the shoreline buzzed with excitement.

But before it was complete, the young Mrs. Boldt died suddenly. The wealthy millionaire ordered all work to come to a halt and never returned to the island. The castle that was to have been a place of great joy fell into disrepair.

In 1977, the Thousand Islands Bridge Authority acquired the property, and gradually began a restoration process that continues to this day. From the outside, the castle is an impressive structure. From the inside, parts are yet unfinished, in a sad way evocative of the affair. Visitors can walk the island, admire the carved-stone cherubs, stroll down marble hallways, examine handcrafted tile work and pause for a moment to consider lost dreams.

Today, Heart Island, near Alexandria Bay, is accessible by private craft and tour boats. For information, call 315/482-9724.

## 36  HENRIETTA

**Wanderer's Antiques**
3204 E. Henrietta Road
716/334-0224

## 37  HUDSON

Directions: Hudson is easily accessible from I-87 (15 minutes), I-90 (25 minutes), and the Taconic Parkway. Take a look inside some of Hudson's unique antique shops by visiting their web site at www.regionnet.com/colberk/hudsonantique.html.

With not a skyscraper or tall building in sight, Hudson is a conglomeration of architectural styles—Federal, Queen Anne, Greek Revival, Victorian and modern. It is a small city with a population of about 6,000 people. Within its downtown district over 40 antiques and collectibles shops are housed within the rich and diverse architecture of the river city. The city's grid design makes it readily accessible and its close proximity to New York draws weekend shoppers and tourists to explore the many offerings of Hudson. Most can be found on Warren Street along with many restaurants, diners, coffee shops and the newly renovated St. Charles Hotel.

**Americana Collectibles**
527 Warren St.
518/822-9026

**Antiques at 601**
601 Warren St.
518/822-0201

**Arenskjold Antiques Art**
537 Warren St.
518/828-2800

**The Armory Art & Antique Gallery**
State St. at N. 5th St.
518/822-1477

**Atlantis Rising**
545 Warren St.
518/822-0438

**The British Accent**
537 Warren St.
518/828-2800

**The Carriage House**
454 Union St.
518/828-0365

**The Clock Man**
541 Warren St.
518/828-8995

**Days Gone By**
530 Warren St.
518/828-6109

**Doyle Antiques**
711 Warren St.
518/828-3929

**Mark's Antiques**
612 Warren St.
518/766-3937

**David & Bonnie Montgomery**
526 Warren St.
518/822-0267

**Tom Noonan Antiques**
551 Warren St.
518/828-5779

**Northstar Antiques**
502 Warren St.
518/822-1563

**Past Perfect**
4 Park Place
518/822-1083

**Pavillion Style Est. 1980**
521 Warren St.
518/828-4750

**Quartermoon**
528 Warren St.
518/828-0728

**Relics**
551 Warren St.
518/828-4247

**Riverhill**
610 Warren St.
518/828-2823

**Jeremiah Rusconi**
By appointment only
518/828-7531

**Ecclectables**
2 Park Place
518/822-1286

**Fern**
554 Warren St.
518/828-2886

**Foxfire, Ltd.**
538 Warren St.
518/828-6281

**Judith Harris Antiques**
608 Warren St.
518/822-1371

**The Hudson Antiques Center**
536 Warren St.
518/828-9920

**Hudson Photographic Center**
611 Warren St.
518/828-2178

**Peter Jung Art & Antiques**
537 Warren St.
518/828-2698

**Kermani Oriental Rugs**
348 1/2 Warren St.
518/828-4804

**Larry's Back Room Antiques**
612 Warren St.
518/477-2643

**Vincent R. Mulford**
711 Warren St.
518/828-5489

**Savannah Antiques**
521 Warren St.
518/822-1343

**707 Antiques**
707 Warren St.
518/794-7883

**A. Slutter Antiques/20th Century**
556 Warren St.
518/822-0729

**Theron Ware**
548 Warren St.
518/828-9744

**Townhouse Antiques**
511 Warren St.
518/822-8500

**Uncle Sam Antiques**
535 Warren St.
518/828-2341

**Watnot Shop & Auction Service**
525 Warren St.
518/828-1081

**Benjamin Wilson Antiques**
513 Warren St.
518/822-0866

**K. West Antiques**
715 Warren St.
518/822-1960

## 38 HUNTINGTON

**Cracker Barrel Galleries, Inc.**
17 Green St.
516/421-1400

**Browsery Corner Shop**
449 E. Jericho Turnpike
516/351-9298

**Nannyberry's Antiques**
32 Macarthur Ave.
516/421-5491

**Ashbourne Antique Pine**
258 Main St.
516/547-5252

**John Gennosa Antiques**
51 Green St.
516/271-0355

**Antique & Design Center**
830 W Jericho Turnpike
516/673-4079

**Antiques and Jewels on Main**
293 Main St.
516/427-7674

**Estate Jewels of Huntington**
331 New York Ave.
516/421-4774

## 39 HUNTINGTON STATION

**Browsery Antiques**
449 E. Jericho Turnpike Road
516/351-8893

**Yankee Peddler Antqs. & Workshop**
1038 New York Ave.
516/271-5817

## 40 ITHACA

**Pastimes Antiques**
Dewitt
607/277-3457

**City Lights Antiques, Inc.**
1319 Mecklenburg Road
607/272-7010

**State Street Bargain House**
516 W. State St.
607/273-2303

**Asia House Gallery**
118 S. Meadow St.
607/272-8850

**Bogie's Bargains**
608 W. Seneca St.
607/272-6016

**Celia Bowers Antiques**
1406 Trumansburg Road
607/273-1994

### *Great Places to Stay*

**Log Country Inn B&B of Ithaca**
P.O. Box 581
1-800-274-4771
Web site: www.logtv.com/inn

Escape to the rustic charm of a log house at the edge of 7,000 acres of state forest. Awaken to the sound of birds and explore the peaceful surroundings. Easy access to hiking, cross-country trails, Cornell, Ithaca College, Corning Glass Center, wineries, and antique shops. Check out their photo gallery at their web site. It is called TODAY-AT LOG COUNTRY INN and is updated almost daily.

## 41 JOHNSTOWN

**Sir William Antiques**
Road Route 30A
518/762-4816

**Pillar**
222 N. Perry St.
518/762-4149

## 42 KEENE

### *Great Places to Stay*

**The Bark Eater Inn and Stable**
Alstead Hill Road
1-800-232-1607
Web site: www.tvenet.com//barkeater
Email: barkeater@tvenet.com
Open: All the time
Directions: From the south, take Exit 30 off I-87. Travel 17 miles west to Keene on Route 73. One mile west of Keene, heading toward Lake Placid, bear right onto Alstead Hill Road. The inn is 1/2 mile on the right. From the north, take Exit 34 off I-87. Proceed 25 miles south to Keene on Route 9 North. Turn right on Route 73, heading west. Bear right at the 1 mile point onto Alstead Hill Road.

A gracious 150-year-old farmhouse in the Adirondack Mountains is the setting for this unique cross-country ski center and riding stable.

Originally a stagecoach stopover, the rambling old inn with its 2 fireplaces, candlelight gourmet dinners, and graciously appointed accommodations offers a charming contrast to the vigorous outdoor activities that await you. Winter guests may choose cross-country or downhill skiing, bobsledding or ice climbing. If you're a beginner, Joe Pete Wilson (your host at Bark Eater) will assist you in your new adventure. You'll be in good hands; Joe Pete is a former Olympic and world competitor in nordic skiing, biathalon and bobsledding.

In summer, the inn is well known for its horseback-riding program, which includes polo. Well-trained horses, both English and Western, are available for the rank beginner to the expert. Enthusiasts can ride for hours on miles of logging trails and back roads. For you "city slickers," riding lessons are available.

They also offer less demanding sports like shopping, dining and porch rocking (soon to be an Olympic sport!).

After a full day, you may choose one of eleven sleeping facilities, including one hand-hewn log cottage, deep in the woods.

By the way, "bark eaters" was a derisive term applied by the Mohawks to their northern neighbors, the Algonquins. Loosely translated it means, "they who eat trees."

## 43 KINGSTON

### Zaborski Emporium
27 Hoffman St.
914/338-6464
Open: Tues.–Sat. 11–5, Sun. 1–5

Specializing in architectural antiques, hardware, lighting, and claw-foot tubs. The shop also carries a large selection of furniture, glassware, advertising items, and Lionel trains.

**Boulevard Attic**
400 Blvd.
914/339-6316

**John Street Jewelers**
292 Fair St
914/338-4101

**Catskill Mountain Antique Center**
Route 28
914/331-0880

**Stanz Used Items & Antiques**
743 Ulster Ave.
914/331-7579

**Vin-Dick Antiques**
Route 209
914/338-7113

**Skillypot Antique Center**
41 Broadway
914/338-6779

**Out Back Antiques**
72 Hurley Ave.
914/331-4481

**Lock Stock & Barrel**
Route 28
914/338-4397

**Wall Street Antiques**
333 Wall St.
914/338-3212

**Keystone Arts Antiques**
33 Broadway
914/331-6211

## 44 LAKE PLACID

### *Great Places to Stay*

### The Stagecoach Inn
Old Military Road
518-523-9474

Serving Lake Placid visitors since 1833, the inn is the quintessence of the Adirondacks. Five birch-trimmed fireplaces, antiques and Indian art make up the decor.

## 45 LARCHMONT

**Dualities Galleries**
2056 Boston Post Road
914/834-2773

**Interior Shop**
2081 Boston Post Road
914/834-6110

**Post Road Gallery**
2128 Boston Post Road
914/834-7568

**Antiques Consign Collectibles**
2134 Boston Post Road
914/833-1829

**Arti Antiques, Inc.**
2070 Boston Post Road
914/833-1794

**Briggs House Antiques**
2100 Boston Post Road
914/833-3087

**Woolf's Den Antiques**
2130 Boston Post Road
914/834-0066

**Thomas K. Salese Antiques**
2368 Boston Post Road
914/834-0222

## 46 LOCUST VALLEY

**Finer Things**
24 Birch Hill Road
516/676-6979

**Early & Co., Inc.**
53 Birch Hill Road
516/676-4800

**Rena Fortgang Interior Design**
27 Forest Ave.
516/759-7826

**Treasured Times**
49 Birch Hill Road
516/759-2010

**Oster Jensen Antiques**
86 Birch Hill Road
516/676-5454

**Country Cousin**
302 Forest Ave.
516/676-6767

## 47 MADISON

**Country Shop**
Route 20
315/893-7616

**Madison Inn Antiques**
Route 20
315/893-7639

**Grasshopper Antiques**
Route 20
315/893-7664

**Timothy's Treasures**
Route 20
315/893-7008

## 48 MARATHON

### Vosburg Antiques
7 Peck St.
607/849-4096
Open: Tues.–Sun. 10–6

Specializing in period antiques, displayed within a wonderful historical building.

**Antiques & Accents**
73 Cortland St.
607/849-3703

**Crosse's Antique Center**
Route 11
607/849-6605

**Goldilocks**
36 Main St.
607/849-6144

**Riverbend Antique Center**
79 Cortland St.
607/849-6305

**Yesteryear Shoppe**
20 Main St.
607/849-6471

## 49 MARGARETVILLE

### Kicking Stones Antiques
Main St.
914/586-1844
Open: Daily

Specializing in quality cupboards, country furniture, Mission, advertising, and an extensive collection of costume jewelry.

### Margaretville Antique Center
Main St.
914/586-2424
Open: Mon.–Sun. 10–5

Housed in the old Galli-Curci Theater, the shop features 20 dealers offering Victorian to primitives to funky '50s.

## 50 MIDDLETOWN

**7-11 Antiques**
7 W. Main St.
914/344-4289

**Attic**
101 Monhagen Ave.
914/342-2252

**Kaatskill Restoration & Antiques**
71 W. Main St.
914/343-6604

## 51 MILLERTON

**Old Mill of Irondale**
Route 22 NN
518/789-9433

**Millerton Antique Center**
Main St.
518/789-6004

**Junk-Atique**
Route 22
518/789-4718

**Country House Antiques & Interiors**
Main St.
518/789-3630

**Johnson & Johnson**
Route 22
518/789-3848

**Northeast Antiques**
Route 22
518/789-4014

## 52 MILLPORT

### Serendipity II
3867 Route 14
607/739-9413
Open: Year-round, Mon.–Fri. 10–5, Sat.–Sun. 11–4
Directions: Approximately 5 miles from Exit 52 North off Route 17. Located at the north end of Pine Valley, between Watkins Glen and Route 17.

Called "the little shop with the LARGE selection," this multidealer store offers a wide variety of glassware, especially depression and pressed glass. You'll also find an interesting assortment of furniture, lighting fixtures, books, and prints. They also offer a selection of sewing-related items.

But the most special service, and the one for which they are well known, is their dedication to attention and care given to their customers.

**Millport Mercantile**
4268 S. Main St.
607/739-3180

## 53 MINERVA

**Mountain Niche Antiques**
Route 28 N.
518/251-2566

## 54 MONTGOMERY

### Black Scottie Antiques
165 Ward St.
914/457-9343
Open: Daily 11–5, closed Wed. & Thurs.

Multidealer shop on 5 levels featuring antiques, collectibles, silverplate and sterling matching service.

**Clinton Shops**
84 Clinton St.
914/457-5392

**Olde Towne Antique & Used Shop**
110 Clinton St.
914/457-1030

**Montgomery Antique Mall**
40 Railroad Ave.
914/457-9339

**Guns & Collectibles**
1092 Route 17 K
914/457-9062

**Marilyn Quigley—Lamplighter Antiques**
70 Union
914/457-5228

**Red Rooster Antiques**
Clinton St.
914/457-4023

**Country Corner Antiques**
9 Bridge St.
914/457-5581

## 55 MOUNT VERNON

**Westchester Furniture Exchange**
78 W. 1st St.
914/668-0447

**Veneque Collection**
115 S. 4th Ave.
914/667-5207

**Westchester Furniture & Antique Center**
130 S. 4th Ave.
914/664-2727

**Trend Antique & Genesis Books**
154 S. 4th Ave.
914/664-4478

**Classic Furniture & Antiques, Inc.**
5 Gramatan Ave.
914/667-1651

**A. Aadams Unlimited**
19-21 Mount Vernon Ave.
914/668-0374

## 56 NEW YORK CITY

### Hugo, Ltd.

233 E. 59th St.
212/750-6877
Fax: 212/750-7346
Open: Call for current schedule or appointment
Directions: Located in the center of Manhattan, half a block from Bloomingdale's on 3rd Avenue and 59th Street.

Hugo, Ltd. offers its patrons the nation's leading collection of documented and authenticated 19th-century lighting and decorative arts.

With all offerings restored in-house to museum condition, this prestigious business prides itself on being a purveyor and consultant to the United States Senate and Treasury Department in Washington, D.C., as well as to the Metropolitan Museum of Art in New York City.

### Galleria Hugo

304 E. 76th St.
212/288-8444
Open: Mon.–Fri., some Sat.
Directions: Located in Manhattan's Upper East Side, between 1st and 2nd Avenues.

This highly respected establishment, like its counterpart, Hugo Ltd., offers the nation's leading collection of 19th-century documented and authenticated lighting. All in-house restoration is done using original finishes from that period — no plating or polishing.

Galleria Hugo is a supplier to major collections and museums.

### Cohen's Collectibles

110 W. 25th St., Shop 305
Phone and fax: 212/675-5300
Email: ephemera
Web site: KingCohen@MSN.com
Open: Daily 10–6
Directions: Going north on 6th Avenue, turn left onto 25th. The building is a few hundred feet further, on the left.

Located in the Chelsea Antique Building, Cohen's is the only open shop for "ephemera" in New York City.

The new and expanded shop buys and sells all types of airline and steamship nostalgia, sheet music, photographs, and autographs. For you photography buffs and postcard collectors, the shop offers over 4,000 photos and 5,000 postcards. This is also the place for Judaica and items pertaining to Black heritage.

### The Family Jewels Vintage Clothing Store

832 Ave. of the Americas
212/679-5023
Open: Daily 11–7
Directions: Located on the southeast corner of 29th Street and 6th Avenue (a.k.a. Avenue of the Americas).

Catering to men, women, and children, this store has been named one of the best vintage stores in the United States by *Vogue, In Style,* and *YM* magazines.

Filled with thousands of unique, one-of-a-kind antique wearables, the second-floor shop embraces every area from the lacy Victorian to the bell-bottomed '70s. They carry a head-to-toe, inside-out selection from sexy lingerie to overcoats, even vintage fabrics and linens.

International design houses including Dolce and Gabbana, Georgio Armani, Ralph Lauren, and Adrienne Vittadini have shopped there looking for "inspiration" for their own designs.

Costume designers, wardrobe supervisors, and photographers have dressed the likes of Cindy Crawford, Uma Thurman, David Bowie, and Rosie O'Donnell from this smashing specialty store.

**Hege Steen Flowers**
360 Amsterdam Ave.
212/496-2575

**More & More Antiques**
378 Amsterdam Ave.
212/580-8404

**Portobello Antiques**
190 Ave. of the Americas
212/925-4067

**A K F Trading Ltd., Inc.**
472 Ave. of the Americas
212/647-0410

**Icon Jewelry and Antiques**
472 Ave. of the Americas
212/647-0410

**Second Childhood**
283 Bleecker St.
212/989-6140

**Pierre Deux Antiques**
369 Bleecker St.
212/243-7740

**Clary & Co. Antiques Ltd.**
372 Bleecker St.
212/229-1773

**Kitschen**
380 Bleecker St.
212/727-0430

**Susan Parrish Antiques**
390 Bleecker St.
212/645-5020

**Avery Home, Inc.**
2 Bond St.
212/614-1492

**Il Buco**
47 Bond St.
212/533-1932

**B.M. Arts, Inc.**
367 W. Broadway
212/226-5808

**Antique Addiction**
436 W. Broadway
212/925-6342

**Antique Boutique**
712 Broadway
212/460-8830

**Agostino Antiques Ltd.**
808 Broadway
212/533-3355

**Jacob's Antiques**
810 Broadway
212/673-4254

**Abe's Antiques, Inc.**
815 Broadway
212/260-6424

**Howard Kaplan Antiques**
827 Broadway
212/674-1000

**Universe Antiques**
833 Broadway
212/260-9292

**David J. Air**
8 Beach St.
212/925-7867

**Niall Smith Antiques**
344 Bleecker St.
212/255-0660

**Distinctive Furnishings**
370 Bleecker St.
212/255-2476

**American Folkart Gallery**
374 Bleecker St.
212/366-6566

**Old Japan, Inc.**
382 Bleecker St.
212/633-0922

**Treasures & Trifles**
409 Bleecker St.
212/243-2723

**Rhubarb Home**
26 Bond St.
212/533-1817

**What Comes Around Goes Around**
351 W. Broadway
212/343-9303

**Paracelso**
414 W. Broadway
212/966-4232

**Alice Underground Ltd.**
481 Broadway
212/431-9067

**William Roland Antiques**
808 Broadway, Apt. 4J
212/260-2000

**Blatt Bowling & Billiard Corp.**
809 Broadway
212/674-8855

**Turbulence**
812 Broadway
212/598-9030

**Proctor Galleries**
824 Broadway
212/388-1539

**Philip Colleck of London**
830 Broadway
212/505-2500

**Hyde Park Antiques Corp.**
836 Broadway
212/477-0033

**David Seidenberg**
836 Broadway
212/260-2810

**Olden Camera & Lens Co., Inc.**
1265 Broadway
212/725-1234

**Penine Hart**
457 Broome St.
212/226-2761

**Gray Garden**
461 Broome St.
212/966-7116

**Henro, Inc.**
525 Broome St.
212/343-0221

**Tibet West**
19 Christopher St.
212/255-3416

**Shady Acres Antiques**
Clark St. Road
315/252-3740

**Classic Antique Iron Beds**
518 Columbus Ave.
212/496-8980

**Welcome Home Antiques Ltd.**
562 Columbus Ave.
212/362-4293

**Historical Materialism**
125 Crosby St.
212/431-3424

**Bernard & S. Dean Levy, Inc.**
24 E. 84th St.
212/628-7088

**84th St. Antiques Corp.**
235 E. 84th St.
212/650-1035

**Steve's Antiques**
206 W. 80th St.
212/721-2935

**Bijan Royal, Inc.**
60 E. 11th St.
212/228-3757

**David George Antiques**
165 E. 87th St.
212/860-3034

**Samuel Herrup Antiques**
12 E. 86th St.
212/737-9051

**Cheap Jack's Vintage Clothing**
841 Broadway
212/995-0403

**Estelle Stranger**
2508 Broadway
212/749-0393

**Paterae Antiques & Decorations**
458 Broome St.
212/941-0880

**Sammy's**
484 Broome St.
212/343-2357

**Essex Gallery Ltd.**
104 Central Park S.
212/757-2500

**Christopher Street Flea Market**
122 Christopher St.
212/924-6118

**La Belle Epoque Vintage**
280 Columbus Ave.
212/362-1770

**Golden Treasury**
550 Columbus Ave.
212/787-1411

**Crosby Antiques Studio**
117 Crosby St.
212/941-6863

**A I D S Thrift Shop, Inc.**
220 E. 81st St.
212/472-3573

**Better Times Antiques, Inc.**
201 W. 84th St.
212/496-9001

**L.J. Wender Chinese Fine Art**
3 E. 80th St.
212/734-3460

**Alex's Now & Then Collectibles**
256 89th St.
212/831-4825

**James Hepner Antiques**
130 E. 82nd St.
212/737-4470

**Heritage East, Inc.**
179 E. 87th St.
212/987-1901

**Once upon a Time Antiques**
36 E. 11th St.
212/473-6424

**Little Antique Shop**
44 E. 11th St.
212/673-5173

**William Albino Antiques**
55 E. 11th St.
212/677-8820

**Palace Galleries**
57 E. 11th St., 3rd Floor
212/228-8800

**Flores & Iva Antiques**
67 E. 11th St.
212/979-5461

**Maria Whitaker Ignez**
260 Elizabeth St.
212/941-6158

**Hebrew Religious Articles**
45 Essex St.
212/674-1770

**Columbus Circle Market**
58th & 8th
212/242-1217

**Charles G. Moore Americana Ltd.**
32 E. 57th St., 12th Floor
212/751-1900

**Megerian Rug Gallery**
262 5th Ave.
212/684-7847

**Sadigh Gallery & Ancient Art**
303 5th Ave.
212/725-7537

**Aaron Faber Gallery**
666 5th Ave.
212/586-8411

**Frederick P. Victoria & Son, Inc.**
154 E. 55th St.
212/755-2549

**James II Galleries Ltd.**
11 E. 57th St.
212/355-7040

**M.D. Flacks Ltd.**
38 E. 57th St.
212/838-4575

**Dalva Brothers, Inc.**
44 E. 57th St.
212/758-2297

**Abraham Moheban & Son Antique**
139 E. 57th St.
212/758-3900

**Big Apple Antiques, Inc.**
52 E. 11th St.
212/260-5110

**Kings Antiques Corp.**
57 E. 11th St.
212/255-6455

**Retro-Modern Studio**
58 E. 11th St.
212/674-0530

**Metro Antiques**
80 E. 11th St.
212/673-3510

**Zane Moss Antiques**
10 E. End Ave.
212/628-7130

**Tucker Robbins Warehouse**
366 W. 15th St.
212/366-4427

**Kermanshah Oriental Rugs**
57 5th Ave.
212/627-7077

**Alpine Designs, Inc.**
230 5th Ave.
212/532-5067

**Chan's Antiques & Furn. Co. Ltd.**
273 5th Ave.
212/686-8668

**Aaron's Antiques**
576 5th Ave.
1-800-447-5868

**Mercia Bross Gallery, Inc.**
160 E. 56th St. Gallery 8
212/355-4422

**Sheba Antiques, Inc.**
233 E. 59th St.
212/421-4848

**Sheila Toma Gallery**
24 W. 57th St., Suite 803
212/757-1480

**Vojtech Blan, Inc.**
6th Floor, 41 E. 57th St.
212/249-4525

**Alice Kwartler Antiques**
123 E. 57th St.
212/752-3590

**Golden Age Antique**
143 E. 57th St.
212/319-3336

**Nesle, Inc.**
151 E. 57th St.
212/755-0515

**Artifacts New York**
220 E. 57th St.
212/355-5575

**Iris Brown Antique Dolls, Est. 1967**
253 E. 57th St.
212/593-2882

**Regal Collection**
5 W. 56th St.
212/582-7695

**I. Freeman & Sons, Inc.**
60 E. 56th St.
212/759-6900

**J M S & Eva Ltd.**
160 E. 56th St., G8
212/593-1113

**Turner Antiques Ltd.**
160 E. 56th St. G2
212/935-1099

**New Era Fine Arts & Antiques**
164 E. 56th St.
212/751-3473

**A Repeat Performance**
156 1st Ave.
212/529-0832

**R. Anavian & Sons Gallery**
942 1st Ave.
212/879-1234

**Darrow's Fun Antiques**
1101 1st Ave.
212/838-0730

**Tamy's Antiques**
8 W. 47th St.
212/382-1112

**F. Namdar Jewelry & Antique Co.**
10 W. 47th St.
212/921-7990

**Ira Moskovitz Estate & Antique Jewelry**
10 W. 47th St.
212/921-7759

**Shans Premier Ancient Art**
31 W. 47th St., Suite 802
212/840-4805

**Antiques Corner, Inc.**
608 5th Ave.
212/869-1411

**Krishna Gallery Asian Arts, Inc.**
153 E. 57th St.
212/249-1677

**Lillian Nassau Ltd.**
220 E. 57th St.
212/759-6062

**Fil Caravans, Inc.**
301 E. 57th St.
212/421-5972

**Ralph M. Chait Galleries, Inc.**
12 E. 56th St.
212/758-0937

**Antique Interiors by Nushin**
160 E. 56th St.
212/486-1673

**John Salibello Antiques**
160 E. 56th St.
212/580-9560

**Windsor Antique, Inc.**
160 E. 56th St., G67
212/319-1077

**Newel Art Galleries Inc.**
425 E. 53rd St.
212/758-1970

**Charles P. Rogers Brass & Iron**
899 1st Ave.
212/935-6900

**Raphaelian Rug Co., Inc.**
1071 1st Ave.
212/759-5452

**N.S. Allan Ltd.**
Main Lobby at the Grand Hyatt
212/599-0620

**Expressions by Edith**
10 W. 47th St.
212/730-9584

**Galerie Spektrum**
10 W. 47th St.
212/840-1758

**Coin Dealer, Inc.**
15 W. 47th St., Booth #12
212/768-7297

**Euro Antiques & Gems**
36 W. 47th St.
212/997-5031

**Quilted Corner**
120 4th Ave.
212/505-6568

*New York*

**Anthony Frank Antiques**
124 E. 4th St.
212/477-1473

**Le Fanion**
299 W. 4th St.
212/463-8760

**Wyeth Et Daphney**
151 Franklin St.
212/925-5278

**Stardust Antiques**
38 Gramercy Park N.
212/677-2590

**Boca Grande Furnishings**
66 Greene St.
212/334-6120

**Back Pages Antiques**
125 Greene St.
212/460-5998

**Bars & Backbars of N.Y.**
49 E Houston St.
212/431-0600

**Cobweb**
116 W. Houston St.
212/505-1558

**Alphaville**
226 W. Houston St.
212/675-6850

**Jonathan Burden, Inc.**
632 Hudson St.
212/620-3989

**Chameleon Antiques**
231 Lafayette St.
212/343-9197

**Second Hand Rose**
130 Duane St.
212/393-9002

**Lost City Arts**
275 Lafayette St.
212/941-8025

**Rooms & Gardens, Inc.**
290 Lafayette St.
212/431-1297

**Old Print Shop, Inc.**
150 Lexington Ave.
212/683-3950

**Maximiliaan's Grnd Pianos & Fine Art**
200 Lexinton Ave., Main Floor
212/689-2177

**Sundown & Antiques**
143 W. 4th St.
212/539-1958

**Urban Archeology Co.**
143 Franklin St.
212/431-6969

**Mobiller**
180 Franklin St.
212/334-6197

**Niall Smith Antiques**
96 Grand St.
212/941-7354

**Alice's Antiques**
72 Greene St.
212/874-3400

**Charterhouse Antiques**
115 Greenwich Ave.
212/243-4726

**B-4 It Was Cool Antiques**
89 E. Houston St.
212/219-0139

**American Antique Firearms**
205 W. Houston St.
212/206-1004

**Uplift, Inc.**
506 Hudson St.
212/929-3632

**Kelter-Maice**
74 Jane St.
212/675-7380

**A & J 20th Century Designs**
255 Lafayette St.
212/226-6290

**Brian Winsor Art, Antiques**
272 Lafayette St.
212/274-0411

**Coming to America New York, Inc.**
276 Lafayette St.
212/343-2968

**J. Marvec & Co.**
946 Madison Ave.
212/517-7665

**Kim McGuire Antiques**
155 Lexington Ave.
212/686-0788

**The NY Doll Hospital, Inc.**
787 Lexington Ave.
212/838-7527

**Antique Salon**
870 Lexington Ave.
212/472-0191

**S. Wyler, Inc.**
941 Lexington Ave.
212/879-9848

**Deco Deluxe, Inc.**
993 Lexington Ave.
212/472-7222

**La Cadet De Gascogne**
1015 Lexington Ave.
212/744-5925

**Malvina Solomon**
1021 Lexington Ave.
212/535-5200

**Mood Indigo**
181 Prince St.
212/254-1176

**J. Dixon Prentice Antiques**
1036 Lexington Ave.
212/249-0458

**Tout Le Monde**
1178 Lexington Ave.
212/439-8487

**F.H. Coin & Stamp Exchange**
1187 Lexington Ave.
1-888-FHCoins

**Lands Beyond Ltd.**
1218 Lexington Ave.
212/249-6275

**Jerry Livian Antique Rugs**
148 Madison Ave.
212/683-2666

**Bolour**
595 Madison Ave.
212/752-0222

**Ronin Gallery**
605 Madison Ave.
212/688-0188

**Macklowe Gallery**
667 Madison Ave.
212/644-6400

**Mayfair & Company**
741 Madison Ave.
212/737-4776

**Imperial Fine Oriental Arts**
790 Madison Ave.
212/717-5383

**Lorraine Wohl Collection**
870 Lexington Ave.
212/472-0191

**Ellen Berenson Antiques**
988 Lexington Ave.
212/288-5302

**Nancy Brous Associates Ltd.**
1008 Lexington Ave.
212/772-7515

**Amy Perlin Antiques**
1020 Lexington Ave.
212/664-4923

**Bob Pryor Antiques**
1023 Lexington Ave.
212/861-1601

**Marckle Myers Ltd.**
1030 Lexington Ave.
212/288-3288

**Sylvia Pines Uniquities**
1102 Lexington Ave.
212/744-5141

**Garden Room**
1179 Lexington Ave.
212/879-1179

**Japan Gallery**
1210 Lexington Ave.
212/288-2241

**Las Venus**
163 Ludlow St.
212/982-0608

**Persian Shop, Inc.**
534 Madison Ave.
212/355-4643

**Anita De Carlo, Inc.**
605 Madison Ave.
212/288-4948

**F. Gorevic & Sons, Inc.**
635 Madison Ave., 2nd Floor
212/753-9319

**Lloyd Jensen Jewelers Ltd.**
716 Madison Ave.
212/980-3966

**America Hurrah Antiques**
766 Madison Ave.
212/535-1930

**Orientations Gallery**
802 Madison Ave.
212/772-7705

**Rosenblatt Minna Ltd.**
844 Madison Ave.
212/288-0250

**Devenish & Company, Inc.**
929 Madison Ave.
212/535-2888

**Stair & Company**
942 Madison Ave.
212/517-4400

**Florian Papp, Inc.**
962 Madison Ave.
212/288-6770

**Koreana Art & Antiques, Inc.**
963 Madison Ave.
212/249-0400

**Leigh Keno American Antiques**
980 Madison Ave.
212/734-2381

**Kenneth W. Rendell Gallery**
989 Madison Ave.
212/717-1776

**Rafael Gallery**
1020 Madison Ave.
212/744-8666

**Burlington Antique Toys**
1082 Madison Ave.
212/861-9708

**Guild Antiques II**
1089 Madison Ave.
212/717-1810

**Eagles Antiques, Inc.**
1097 Madison Ave.
212/772-3266

**Betty Jane Bart Antiques**
1225 Madison Ave.
212/410-2702

**Wicker Garden Antique Store**
1318 Madison Ave.
212/410-7000

**Barry of Chelsea Antiques**
154 9th Ave.
212/242-2666

**JAN Eleni Co.**
315 E.9th St.
212/533-4396

**Atomic Passion**
430 E. 9th St.
212/533-0718

**Bardith Ltd.**
901 Madison Ave.
212/737-3775

**Alexander Gallery**
942 Madison Ave.
212/472-1636

**Antiquarium Fine Ancient Arts**
948 Madison Ave.
212/734-9776

**Time Will Tell**
962 Madison Ave.
212/861-2663

**Leo Kaplan Ltd.**
967 Madison Ave.
212/249-6766

**Ursus Books Ltd.**
981 Madison Ave.
212/772-8787

**Edith Weber Antiques**
994 Madison Ave.
212/570-9668

**E. Frankel Ltd.**
1040 Madison Ave.
212/879-5733

**GEM Antiques**
1088 Madison Ave.
212/535-7399

**Guild Antiques II**
1095 Madison Ave.
212/472-0830

**Marco Polo Antiques**
1135 Madison Ave.
212/734-3775

**Carnegie Hill Antiques**
1309 Madison Ave., 2nd Floor
212/987-6819

**Frank Rogin, Inc.**
21 Mercer Sr
212/431-6545

**Something Else Antiques & Cllbls.**
182 9th Ave.
212/924-0006

**Archangel Antiques**
334 E. 9th St.
212/260-9313

**Upstairs Downtown Antiques**
12 W. 19th St.
212/989-8715

**Accents Unlimited**
65 W. 90th St.
212/799-7490

**John Rosselli International**
523 E. 73rd St.
212/722-2137

**Nelson & Nelson Antiques, Inc.**
445 Park Ave.
212/980-5825

**James Robinson, Inc.**
480 Park Ave.
212/752-6166

**Thomas**
41 Perry St.
212/675-7296

**Irreplaceable Artifacts**
14 2nd Ave.
212/473-3300

**Sapho Gallery, Inc.**
1037 2nd Ave.
212/308-0880

**Alexander's Antiques**
1050 2nd Ave., Gallery 43, 44, 45 & 85
212/935-9386

**Paul Stamati Gallery**
1050 2nd Ave., Gallery #38
212/754-4533

**Federico Carrera Antiques**
1050 2nd Ave., Gallery 18
212/750-2870

**Hadassa Antiques, Inc.**
1050 2nd Ave., Gallery 75
212/751-0009

**John Walker Antiques**
1050 2nd Ave.
212/832-9579

**Leah's Gallery, Inc.**
1050 2nd Ave., #42
212/838-5590

**Manhattan Art & Antiques Center**
1050 2nd Ave.
212/355-4400

**Natalie Bader**
1050 2nd Ave., Gallery 40A
212/486-7673

**Rita Facks/Limited Additions, Inc.**
1050 2nd Ave., G#94
212/421-8132

**Treasures & Gems**
250 E. 90th St.
212/410-7360

**Dixon Galleries, Inc.**
251 Park Ave. S.
212/475-6500

**Chinese Porcelain Co.**
475 Park Ave.
212/838-7744

**USED**
17 Perry St.
212/627-0730

**Rural Collections, Inc.**
117 Perry St.
212/645-4488

**Love Saves the Day**
119 2nd Ave.
212/228-3802

**AAA Silver Buyer**
1050 2nd Ave.
212/755-6320

**A.R. Broomer Ltd.**
1050 2nd Ave., Gallery 81
212/421-9530

**Estate Silver Co. Ltd.**
1050 2nd Ave. Gallery 65
212/758-4858

**Flying Cranes Antiques**
1050 2nd Ave., Gallery 55 & 56
212/223-4600

**Hoffman-Giampetro Antiques**
1050 2nd Ave., Gallery 37
212/755-1120

**Kurt Gluckselig Antiques**
1050 2nd Ave., Gallery #90
212/758-1805

**LES Gallery Looms, Inc.**
1050 2nd Ave., Gallery #59
212/752-0995

**Michael's Antiques & Jewelry**
1050 2nd Ave., Gallery #3
212/838-8780

**Nelson & Nelson Antiques, Inc.**
445 Park Ave.
212/980-5824

**Ostia, Inc.**
1050 2nd Ave.
212/371-2424

**J and P Timepieces, Inc.**
1057 2nd Ave.
212/980-1099

**R & P Kassai**
1050 2nd Ave., Gallery 1
212/838-7010

**Sidney Bell Fine Arts**
1050 2nd Ave., G16
212/486-0715

**Suchow & Siegel Antiques Ltd.**
1050 2nd Ave., Gallery 81
212/888-3489

**Treasures & Pleasures**
1050 2nd Ave.
212/750-1929

**Robert Altman**
1148 2nd Ave.
212/832-3490

**Fairfield Antique Gallery**
1166 2nd Ave.
212/759-6519

**David Weinbaum**
1175 2nd Ave.
212/755-6540

**Oaksmiths & Jones**
1510 2nd Ave.
212/327-3462

**James Lowe Autographs Ltd.**
30 E. 60th St., Suite 304
212/759-0775

**Paris to Provence**
207 E. 60th St.
212/750-0037

**GUY Regal Ltd.**
210 E. 60th St.
212/888-2134

**David Duncan Antiques**
227 E. 60th St.
212/688-0666

**A. Smith Antiques Ltd.**
235 E. 60th St.
212/888-6337

**Luxor Gallery**
238 E. 60th St.
212/832-3633

**William Lipton Ltd.**
27 E. 61st St.
212/751-8131

**Rover & Lorber NYC, Inc.**
1050 2nd Ave., G27
212/838-1302

**S. Elghanayan Antiques**
1050 2nd Ave., Gallery 6
212/750-3344

**Tibor Strasser**
1050 2nd Ave., G76
212/759-2513

**Time Gallery**
1050 2nd Ave., G54
212/593-2323

**Unique Finds, Inc.**
1050 2nd Ave., G36
212/751-1983

**A & R Asta Ltd.**
1152 2nd Ave.
212/750-3364

**Antique Accents**
1175 2nd Ave.
212/755-6540

**Elizabeth Street**
1190 2nd Ave.
212/644-6969

**Annex Antique Fair**
6th & 26th St.
212/243-5343

**Things Japanese**
127 E. 60th St.
212/371-4661

**Objets Trouves Ltd.**
217 E. 60th St.
212/753-0221

**Victor's Antiques Ltd.**
223 E. 60th St.
212/752-4100

**Brahms-Netski Antique Passage**
234 E. 60th St.
212/755-8307

**James Grafstein Ltd.**
236 E. 60th St.
212/754-1290

**Ann-Morris Antiques**
239 E. 60th St.
212/755-3308

**Naga Antiques Ltd.**
145 E. 61st St.
212/593-2788

**Dining Trade**
306 E. 61st St.
212/755-2304

**Town and Country Antiques**
306 E. 61st St.
212/752-1677

**Chrystian Aubusson**
315 E. 62nd St.
212/755-2432

**Objects Plus, Inc.**
315 E. 62nd St., 3rd Floor
212/832-3386

**Paris Antiques**
315 E. 62nd St.
212/421-3340

**Emporium Antique Shop Ltd.**
20 W. 64th St.
212/724-9521

**Schlesch & Gaza**
158 E. 64th St.
212/838-3923

**Rita Ford Music Boxes, Inc.**
19 E. 65th St.
212/535-6717

**Jean Hoffman Antiques**
207 E. 66th St.
212/535-6930

**Maya Schaper Cheese & Antiques**
106 W. 69th St.
212/873-2100

**Linda Morgan, Inc.**
152 E. 70th St.
212/628-4330

**Salander Oreilly Galleries, Inc.**
20 E. 79th St.
212/879-6606

**Godel & Co., Inc.**
39A E. 72nd St.
212/288-7272

**Lantiquaire & Connoisseur, Inc.**
36 E. 73rd St.
212/517-9176

**Eric Guy, Inc.**
503 E. 73rd St.
212/772-2326

**J. Mavec & Co.**
946 Madison Ave.
212/517-7665

**Epel & Lacoze Antiques, Inc.**
306 E. 61st St., 2nd Floor
212/355-0050

**Tender Buttons**
143 E. 62nd St.
212/758-7004

**Marvin Alexander, Inc.**
315 E. 62nd St.
212/838-2320

**OLD Versailles, Inc.**
315 E. 62nd St.
212/421-3663

**Wood & Hogan, Inc.**
305 E. 63rd St., 5th Floor
212/355-1335

**Harvey & Co. Antiques**
250 E. 60th St.
212/888-7952

**French & Co., Inc.**
17 E. 65th St.
212/535-3330

**Bizarre Bazaar Antiques Ltd.**
130 1/4 E. 65th St.
212/517-2100

**Margot Johnson, Inc.**
18 E. 68th St.
212/794-2225

**Victory Gardens Ltd.**
205 E. 68th St.
212/472-2472

**Leff Langham Art & Antiques**
19 E. 71st St.
212/288-4030

**George Glazer**
28 E. 72nd St.
212/535-5706

**Oriental Decorations**
253 E. 72nd St.
212/439-1573

**Hollis Taggart Galleries**
48 E. 73rd St.
212/628-4000

**Elliott Galleries**
155 E. 79th St.
212/861-2222

**Karen Warshaw Ltd.**
167 E. 74th St.
212/439-7870

*New York*

**Judith & James Milne, Inc.**
506 E. 74th St.
212/472-0107

**Treillage Ltd.**
418 E. 75th St.
212/535-2288

**Peter Roberts Antiques, Inc.**
134 Spring St.
212/226-4777

**Julian Antiques Restoration**
108 W. 25th St.
212/647-0305

**Design 18 Realty, Inc.**
979 3rd Ave., 4th Floor
212/753-8666

**D & D Building/Palisander Ltd.**
979 3rd Ave., Suite 818
212/755-0120

**Evergreen Antiques, Inc.**
1249 3rd Ave. (at 72nd)
212/744-5664

**Ghiordian Knot Ltd.**
1636 3rd Ave., Suite 169
212/371-6390

**China Importing Co. Ltd.**
28 E. 10th St.
212/995-0800

**Reymer-Jourdan Antiques**
29 E. 10th St.
212/674-4470

**E 'Epoque**
30 E. 10th St.
212/353-0972

**Ritter-Antik, Inc.**
35 E. 10th St.
212/673-2213

**Donzella 20th Century**
90 E. 10th St.
212/598-9675

**Regeneration Furniture, Inc.**
223 E. 10th St.
212/614-9577

**Renee Antiques, Inc.**
8 E. 12th St.
212/929-6870

**Waves**
110 W. 25th St., 10th Floor
212/989-9284

**Woodard Greenstien**
506 E. 74th St.
212/794-9404

**H.M. Luther, Inc.**
35 E. 76th St.
212/439-7919

**Classic Toys, Inc.**
218 Sullivan St.
212/674-4434

**Ultimate European Rugs & Oriental**
969 3rd Ave.
212/759-6000

**Nicholas Antiques**
979 3rd Ave.
212/688-3312

**Place Des Artes Corp.**
979 3rd Ave.
212/750-8092

**Gordon Foster Antiques**
1322 3rd Ave.
212/744-4922

**Caldonia Antiques**
1685 3rd Ave.
212/534-3307

**The Tudor Rose Antiques**
28 E. 10th St.
212/677-5239

**Bernd H. Goeckler Antiques, Inc.**
30 E. 10th St.
212/777-8209

**Karl Kemp & Associates Ltd. Antqs.**
34 E. 10th St.
212/254-1877

**Martell Antiques**
53 E. 10th St.
212/777-4360

**Robert Gingold Antiques**
95 E. 10th St.
212/475-4008

**Cheapside Inc.**
280 E. 10 th St.
212/780-9626

**Kentshire Galleries, Ltd.**
37 E. 12th St.
212/673-6644

**Dullsville, Inc.**
143 E. 13th St.
212/505-2505

**John Koch Antiques**
514 W. 24th St.
212/243-8625

**Tepper Galleries, Inc.**
110 E. 25th St.
212/677-5300

**Cherubs Antiques & Collectibles**
110 W. 25th St., 11th Floor
212/627-7097

**John Gredler Antiques & House of Art**
110 W. 25th St., Room 702
212/337-3667

**Lubin Galleries, Inc.**
110 W. 25th St.
212/924-3777

**Rocco, Vincent**
110 W. 25th St.
212/620-5652

**Vlasdimir's Antiques**
110 W. 25th St., Suite 207
212/337-3704

**Smith Gallery**
447 W. 24th St.
212/744-6171

**Old Paper Archive**
122 W. 25th St.
212/645-3983

**LES Deux, Inc.**
104 W. 27th St.
212/604-9743

**Sohell Oriental Rugs**
29 W. 30th St.
212/239-1069

**Kamall Oriental Rugs**
151 W. 30th St.
212/564-7000

**33rd Street Galleria**
100 W. 33rd St., 16th Floor
212/279-0462

**T & K French Antiques**
301 E. 38th St.
212/219-2472

**Lyme Regis Ltd.**
68 Thompson St.
212/334-2110

**Deco Jewels, Inc.**
131 Thompson St.
212/253-1222

**Forty Fifty Sixty**
108 W. 25th St., 4th Floor
212/463-0980

**Chelsea Antiques Building**
110 W. 25th St.
212/929-0909

**Cohen's Collectibles & Ephemera**
110 W. 25th St., 3rd Floor
212/675-5300

**Le Chateau**
110 W. 25th St.
212/741-7570

**Shirley Mariaschin & Jerry Spiller**
110 W. 25th St.
212/989-3414

**This 'n' That**
110 W. 25th St., Suite 613
212/255-0727

**Rene Kerne Antiques**
110 W. 25th St.
212/727-3455

**Garage Antique Show**
112 W. 25th St.
212/337-3704

**Lucille's Antique Emporium**
127 W. 26th St.
212/691-1041

**Metal Art Studio**
150 W. 28th St.
212/229-1130

**Ebison's Harounian Imports**
38 E. 30th St.
212/686-4262

**Joseph Solo Antiques**
1561 York Ave.
212/439-1555

**Pantry & Hearth**
121 E. 35th St.
212/889-0026

**Mary Efron Vintage**
68 Thompson St.
212/219-3099

**Legacy**
109 Thompson St.
212/966-4827

**Ellen Lane Antiques, Inc.**
150 Thompson St.
212/475-2988

**Stella Dallas**
218 Thompson St.
212/674-0447

**Lou Ficherea & Ron Perkins**
50 University Plaza
212/533-1430

**World Collectible Center**
18 Versey St.
212/267-7100

**Forty One**
41 Wooster St.
212/343-0935

**Sotheby's**
1334 York Ave.
212/606-7000

**Leo Design**
413 Bleecker St.
212/929-8466

**Second Hand Rose**
130 Duane St.
212/393-9002

**Garden Antiquary**
724 5th Ave., 3rd Floor
212/757-3008

**Roger Gross Ltd.**
225 E. 57th St.
212/759-2892

**Primavera Gallery**
808 Madison Ave.
212/288-1569

**Zero to Sixties**
75 Thompson St.
212/925-0932

**Pall Mall, Inc.**
99 University Plaza
212/677-5544

**Fountain Pen Hospital**
10 Warren St.
212/964-0580

**Interieurs**
114 Wooster St.
212/343-0800

**Kendra Krienke**
By appointment only
212/580-6516

**Arts & Antique Center**
160 E. 56th St., G7
212/229-0958

**Regeneration Furniture**
38 Renwick St.
212/741-2102

**Antiques Corner**
608 5th Ave.
212/869-1411

**Everett Collection, Inc.**
104 W. 27th St., 3rd. Floor
212/255-8610

**Antique Restoration by Julian**
108 W. 25th St., Suite #208
212/647-0305

### Great Places to Stay

## Incentra Village House

32 Eighth Ave.
212/206-0007

Incentra Village House, built in 1841, occupies two red-brick townhouses in New York's Greenwich Village Historic District. Offering an attractive alternative to Midtown's steel and glass, guests receive a warm welcome in the cozy double parlor which boasts two fireplaces, antique furniture, paintings, sculptures and a 1939 Steinway baby grand piano. To get to your room you'll wander down narrow corridors and up charming old stairways to one of twelve unique rooms. All studios and suites are pleasantly furnished and include a private bathroom, telephone, television and most include a working fireplace and kitchen or kitchenette. Each room is decorated according to cities that the founder lived in or to specific artwork or furniture in the room.

## 57 NORTHPORT

**Somewhere in Time Antiques**
162 Main St.
516/757-4148

**Top Notch Antiques**
76 Bayview Ave.
516/754-9396

**LEP Design & Consignment Shop**
160 Laurel Ave.
516/754-1831

**Harbor Lights Antique Boutique**
110 Main St.
516/757-4572

**Wild Rose Antiques**
189 Main St.
516/261-0888

**Country Shop**
171 Main St.
516/757-2362

**Scarlett's**
166 Main St.
516/754-0004

## 58 NYACK

## Lisa's Antiques

37 S. Broadway
914/358-7077
Fax: 914/358-1688
Open: Tues.–Sun. 12–6
Directions: *From New York City and New Jersey:* Take Pallisades Parkway North to Exit 4 (9 West). Go north on 9 West about 6 miles to the yellow blinking light. Bear right and proceed to the south end of the art, craft, and antiques Area. *From Upstate New York:* Take the New York Thruway South to Exit 11. Then go left on Route 59 (Main Street) to shopping area. *From Westchester and Connecticut:* Cross the Tappan Zee Bridge to the first exit (10). Follow the sign for South Nyack to Clinton Avenue. Go right 1 block to Broadway, then left to the shopping area.

Part of the Hudson Valley Emporium Mall, this antique and collectibles shop specializes in oak furniture, glassware, old toys, and sterling silver. Other specialty items include postcards, metal lunch boxes, and a selection of African American prints.

**Ramapo Collectors**
4 N. Broadway
914/353-3019

**Gene Reed Gallery**
77 S. Broadway
914/358-3750

**Antiques & Country Pine**
41B N. Broadway
914/358-7740

**Goldsmith's Treasure Mine**
79 S. Broadway
914/358-2204

**Elayne's Antiques & Collectibles**
6 S. Broadway
914/358-6465

**Remembrances**
37 S. Broadway
914/358-7226

**Towne Crier Antiques**
70 S. Broadway
914/358-5234

**Acorn Antiques & Collectibles**
142 Main St.
914/353-5897

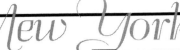
**Arlene Lederman Antiques**
142 Main St.
914/358-8616

**Decorative Arts & Antiques Nyack**
142 Main St.
914/353-1644

**J & J Antiques**
142 Main St.
914/353-3252

**Jo-Antiques**
142 Main St.
914/353-5154

**Old Business Antiques**
142 Main St.
914/358-7008

**S & M Antiques**
142 Main St.
914/353-4774

**Bruce Anderson Interior & Exterior**
145 Main St.
914/353-3992

**Allards**
167 Main St.
914/353-1884

**Ark Shop**
190 Main St.
914/358-1039

**CD Antiques**
142 Main St.
914/358-1704

**Hildegard's Antiques**
142 Main St.
914/353-2650

**Jeni Brandel's Antiques**
142 Main St.
914/353-3379

**Kuku Antiques**
142 Main St.
914/353-1130

**Room with a View**
142 Main St.
914/353-4072

**Vintage Gems & Antiques**
142 Main St.
914/353-2264

**Gloria Paul Antiques**
152 Main St.
914/358-1859

**Levesque Antiques**
170-2 Main St.
914/353-4050

**A Antique Center Upper Nyack**
366 Route 9 W.
914/358-3751

### 59 OLD FORGE

**Antiques & Articles**
Main St.
315/369-3316

**Wildwood Enterprises**
Main St.
315/369-3397

*Both of the above shops specialize in Adirondack antiques.*

### 60 OLEAN

**E-Lites Antiques, Inc.**
204 W. State St.
716/372-8661

**Jerry's Antique Co-op**
1217 N. Union St.
716/373-3702

**Olean Antique Center**
269 N. Union St.
716/372-8171

**Second Time Around**
126 Whitney Ave.
716/372-4308

### 61 OWEGO

**Hand of Man**
180 Front St.
607/687-2556

**Cracker Barrel Antiques & Gift**
202 Front St.
607/687-0555

**Sally's Place**
196 Front St.
607/687-4111

**Heritage Antiques**
36 John St.
607/687-3405

### 62 PEEKSKILL/CORTLAND MANOR

**Toddville Antique & Craft Center**
2201 Crompond Road
914/736-1117

**Garden Antiquary**
2551 Maple Ave.
914/737-6054

**Rose Cottage**
44 N. Division St.
914/737-1845

### 63 PERU

## American Pie Collectibles

29 Sullivan Road
518/643-0993
Web site: apc1@worldnet.att.net

A blast from the past; offering thousands of great collectibles from toys to movies, antiques and so much more. 24-hour mail order service.

**A Poor Man's Collectibles**
3023 Main St.
518/643-2016

### 64 PHOENICIA

**Hernandez Edom Antiques**
Route 28
914/688-2124

**Bethkens Antiques**
Woodland Valley Road
914/688-5620

**Phoenicia Antique Center**
Route 28
914/688-2095

**Antique Store**
Route 28
914/688-5654

### 65 PORT CHESTER

**Simon-World Arts**
168 Irving Ave.
914/934-0113

**Jack's Fabrics & Antiques**
33 S. Main St.
914/939-3308

**Nina's Antiques Collectibles**
191 Westchester Ave.
914/939-6806

**Greenberg's Antique Mall Port**
27 S. Main St.
914/937-4800

**House of Weltz**
26 Poningo St.
914/939-6513

### 66 PORT WASHINGTON

## Port Antique Center

289 Main St.
516/767-3313
Open: Tues.–Sat. 11–5, Sun. 12–5
Directions: Long Island Expressway to Exit 36 North Searingtown Road/Port Washington. Travel 4 miles north to Main Street. Left onto Main Street and go about 1 ½ miles down the hill to shop on your

right. Travel time by car is 40 minutes from Midtown Manhattan or 30 minutes by LIRR train.

This charming, quality multidealer shop is located in the heart of the Port Washington antiques district. Located one block from Port Washington Harbor, this shop offers a large selection of 19th- and 20th-century antiques and collectables.

Twenty-four dealers in the shop carry a wide variety of quality antiques including art pottery such as Roseville, Weller, Rookwood, Fulper and McCoy in addition to a wide variety of china and porcelain with a special accent on Chintz and Majolica. If glass is your passion, Port Antique Center offers a beautiful array including depression and elegant glass as well as art glass such as Tiffany and Loetz.

The store abounds in both fine and costume jewelry offering a wide selection of antique watches as well as an extraordinary collection of colorful Bakelite jewelry. Come browse and enjoy collections of silver, kitchenware, toys, vintage clothing and memorabilia. If you happen to visit during the spring, summer or fall, the Harbor Association hosts an Antique Street Fair on the last Sunday of each month from April to October. Port Antique Center is surrounded by other antique shops and restaurants all within walking distance of each other and beautiful Port Washington Harbor where you can stroll and relax in this beautiful bayside setting.

**Front Porch**
309 Main St.
516/944-6868

**Cat Lady Antiques**
164 Main St.
516/883-4334

**R.E. Steele Antiques**
165 Main St.
516/767-2283

**Nancy K. Banker Antiques**
279 Main St.
516/883-4184

**Pat Giles**
287 Main St.
516/883-1104

**Michael Mikiten**
287 Main St.
516/944-8767

**Red Door Antiques**
305 Main St.
516/883-5125

**Village Green**
306 Main St.
516/767-3698

**Baba Antiques & Collectibles**
292 Main St.
516/883-6274

## 67  POUND RIDGE

**Antiques & Tools Bus & Kitchen**
Scotts Corners
914/764-0015

**Petersons Antiques Ltd.**
26 Westchester Ave.
914/764-5074

**Antiques & Interiors, Inc.**
67 Westchester Ave.
914/764-4400

**Strap Hinge**
72 Westchester Ave.
914/764-1145

**Nancy Cody Antiques**
67 Westchester Ave.
914/764-4949

**Objects Trouvee, Inc.**
69 Westchester Ave.
914/234-7600

## 68  RED HOOK

**Broadway Antiques & Collectibles**
30 N. Broadway
914/876-1444

**Cider Mill Antiques**
5 Cherry St.
914/758-2599

**Victorian Corner**
19 W. Market St.
914/758-1011

**Anntex Antiques Center**
23 E. Market St.
914/758-2843

**Rock City Relics Antique Center**
Route 199 & 308
914/758-8603

### *Great Places to Stay*

### The Grand Dutchess
50 N. Broadway
914/758-5818

The Grand Dutchess is a Second-Empire Victorian mansion subtly updated to provide elegant and comfortable accommodations for the 20th-century traveler. An extensive collection of antique furniture and decoration provides the ambiance; firm queen-size beds provide the comfort; and a deliciously self-indulgent breakfast provides the sustenance.

### The Lombard's
R.D. 3, Box 79
914/758-3805

Peter and Peggy Anne Lombard were professionals in the Broadway theater and as a consequence they have developed a theatrical clientele and theater is a favorite subject at the breakfast table. Guests browse the family photo gallery (which includes two former American presidents) and often end up prowling the in-house antique parlor or the "primitive" room in the basement which boasts a huge original cooking hearth/fireplace. Barn and grounds are for exploring. Bikes are provided.

## 69  RHINEBECK

**Rhinebeck Antique Center**
7 W. Market St.
914/876-8168

**Hummingbird Jewelers**
20 W. Market St.
914/876-4585

**Gallery Shoppe**
9 Mill St.
914/876-2064

**Country Bazaar**
14 U.S. Hwy. 9 S.
914/876-4160

**Old Mill House Antiques**
144 U.S. Hwy. 9 N.
914/876-3636

## 70 ROCHESTER

**Treasure Hunters**
1434 Buffalo Road
716/235-5441

**Thomas R. Paddock Oriental Rugs**
342 East Ave.
716/325-3110

**Antiques & Old Lace**
274 Goodman St. N.
716/461-1884

**Yankee Peddler Bookshop, Vol II**
274 Goodman St. N.
716/271-5080

**Worldwide Antiques & Imports**
631 Monroe Ave.
716/271-3217

**James Jewelry**
1315 E Ridge Road
716/336-9960

**Antique & Colledtibles Co-op, Rochester**
151 Saint Paul St.
716/232-6440

**Walt's Place**
1570 Dewey Ave.
716/254-1880

**Eric Kase**
398 Westminster Road
716/461-4382

**Michael Latragna**
1275 Clover St.
716/442-0725

**Golden Oldies Antiques**
24 Bursen Court
716/266-2440

**Carousel Antiques**
3409 Saint Paul Blvd.
716/266-3420

**Jack Grecos Creekside Antiques**
1611 Scottsville Road
716/328-9150

**Chichelli Weiss Books & Antiques**
374 Meigs St.
716/271-3980

**Flower City Stamps and Coins**
1575 Dewey Ave.
716/647-9320

**Upstate Gallery Antiques**
16 Gardiner Park Drive
716/262-2089

**Village Gate Square**
274 Goodman St. N.
716/442-9061

**Marilyn's Antiques**
500 Lyell Ave.
716/647-2480

**Aries Antiques**
739 Monroe Ave.
716/244-7912

**Jewelry & Coin Exchange**
2000 Ridge Road W.
716/227-6370

**Warren Phillips Fine Art**
215 Tremont St.
716/235-4060

**Mission Oak Antiques**
378 Meigs St.
716/442-2480

**Newell Distributors**
39 Branford Road
716/442-8810

**International Art Acquisitions, Inc.**
3300 Monroe Ave.
716/264-1440

**Darcy's Adventures in the Past**
149 Monroe Ave.
716/262-4776

**Adventures in Past John**
149 Monroe Ave.
716/262-4776

**Household Sale by Mary Kay Roden**
20 Union Park
716/266-3524

**Bettiques**
1697 Monroe Ave.
716/442-2995

***Nearby Antique Shopping (Lima)***
***Lima is south of Rochester, 4 miles east of Exit I-390.***

### Crossroads Country Mall

7348 E. Main St. (Routes 5 & 20)
716/624-1993
Open: Daily 11–5, closed Tues.

One of the area's largest antiques centers with 7,000 square feet and 40 dealers featuring advertising, primitives, glass, silver, coins, folk art and more.

***Nearby Antique Shopping (Webster)***
***Webster is 6 miles east of Rochester.***

### Webster Antique Co-op

82 E. Main St.
716/265-3078
Open: Tues.–Sat. 11–5, Sun. 12–5

The largest antiques co-op in upstate New York, showcasing over 100 dealers within one building.

## 71 SAG HARBOR

**Carriage House Antiques**
34 Main St.
516/725-8004

**Diana's Place**
Main St.
516/725-4669

**Sage Street Antiques**
Sage St.
516/725-4036

**Madison House Antiques & Artifacts**
43 Madison St.
516/725-7242

**Ned Parkhouse Antiques**
Main St.
516/725-9830

**Carriage House Antiques**
34 Main St.
516/725-8004

## 72 SARATOGA SPRINGS

### Broadway Antiques Gallery

484 Broadway
518/581-8348
Open: Daily 11–6 and extended summer hours
Directions: From I-87, take either Exit 13N (from south) or Exit 15 (from north), and follow Route 9 to downtown. Broadway Antiques Gallery is 3 doors north of City Hall on the east side of Broadway in the center of downtown historic Saratoga Springs.

A cooperative effort of ten dealers brings you a wide variety of home furnishings and accessories. Over 3,000 square feet of antiques and unique gift items may be found in this shop.

*New York*

**Ye Olde Wishin' Shoppe**
353 Broadway
518/583-7782

**Saratoga Antiques**
727 Route 29 E.
518/587-3153

**Magnell's Antiques**
53 Old Schuylerville Road
518/587-8888

**Saratoga Antiques**
727 Route 29 E.
518/587-3153

**A Page in Time**
462 Broadway
518/584-4876

**9 Caroline Antiques & Collectibles**
9 Caroline St.
518/583-9112

**Regent St. Antique Center**
153 Regent St.
518/584-0107

## Great Places to Stay

## Chestnut Tree Inn

9 Whitney Place
518/587-8681
Open: April–November 1
Directions: From I-87, take Exit 13 North. Take Route 9 North to the 5th traffic light (Lincoln Avenue) and turn right. Take the 1st left onto Whitney Place. The inn is the 2nd house on the left.

Sample a more peaceful time in Saratoga's history at this fine traditional Victorian guest house. Situated conveniently near many of the city's attractions, the inn offers 10 rooms, most with private baths.

Continental breakfast is served each morning on the porch, and during July and August, guests may congregate there in the afternoons for wine, cheese, and crackers.

Sit and relax under what is reputed to be the last living chestnut tree in Saratoga.

## 73 SAUGERTIES

**Saugerties Antiques Center**
220 Main St.
914/246-8234

**Saugerties Antiques Gallery**
104 Partition St.
914/246-2323

**Peacock Antiques**
2769 Route 32
914/246-7070

**Fancy Flea**
50 Market St.
914/246-9391

**Acanthus**
112 Partition St.
914/247-0041

## 74 SCHOHARIE

**Cane Shoppe Antiques**
Barton Hill Road
518/295-8629

**Ginny's Hutch Antiques**
Route 30
518/295-7470

**Patent Country Shop & Antq. Emp.**
Route 145 East Cobleskill
518/296-8000

**Saltbox Antiques**
Stony Brook Road
518/295-7408

**Quest**
Vroman Road, Route 30
518/295-8805

## 75 SOUTHAMPTON

**Southampton Antique Center**
640 N. High
516/283-1006

**Elaine's Antiques**
9 Main St.
516/287-3276

**Bob Petrillo's Brouserie**
30 Main St.
516/283-6560

**Judi Boisson Antique American Quilts**
134 Mariners Dr.
516/283-5466

**Hampton Antiques**
116 N. Sea Road
516/283-3436

**Things I Love**
51 Jobs Lane
516/287-2756

**Croft Antiques**
11 S. Main St.
516/283-6445

**Old Town Crossing**
46 Main St.
516/283-7740

**Old Town Crossing Warehouse**
134 Mariners Dr.
516/287-4771

**John W. Nilsson, Inc.**
675 N. Sea Road
516/283-1434

## Great Places to Stay

## Caldwell's Carriage House

519 Hill St.
516/287-4720

Located in a historic shingled Colonial amid manicured lawns and lovely flower gardens, the Carriage House is one of the most unique accommodations in the Hamptons. Enter the suite through a private entrance leading to the sitting room with wide plank floors, window seat, and pull-out sofa. Full bath and efficiency kitchen on the ground level gives independence from the large bedroom above.

## 76 SPRINGWATER

## Canadice Farm Antiques

9034 Cratsley Hill Road
716/367-2771
Open: Sat. and Sun. 10–5 and by chance or appointment, Easter through Thanksgiving
Directions: From Route 390, exit at Avon/Lima. In Lima, turn right on 15A through Hemlock, then left on Route 20A. Go to County Road 37, then right and follow signs. From Rochester, go south on Route 65 (Clover Street). 65 becomes County Road 37 at Routes 5 and 20 (West Bloomfield). Continue south to Route 20A and follow signs. From Canandaigua, go west on Routes 5 and 20 to West Bloomfield. Turn left and follow County Road 37 to 20A in Honeoye.

Along with a full line of antiques, this store offers an appraisal service, expertise in interior design as well as landscape design. They'll even help you design the wedding of your dreams. One stop shopping!

## 77 STATEN ISLAND

**Harborview Antiques**
1385 Bay St.
718/448-4649

**Faban General Mercandise & Antq. Store**
147 Canal
718/727-2917

**Rainbow's End Gifts Antiques**
469 Port Richmond Ave.
718/273-3124

**New Drop Village Antiques**
517 & 519 Broadway
718/815-2526

**Hey Viv—Vintage Clothing**
125 Port Richmond Ave.
718/981-3575

**Richmond Consignments**
1434 Richmond Road
718/980-4333

## 78 SYRACUSE

**Cerenas Antiques & Home Furniture**
2111 Brewerton Road
315/454-5543

**Dacia of NY Vintage Furniture Shop**
2416 Court St.
315/455-2651

**Lilac House**
1415 W. Genesee St.
315/471-3866

**Dalton's Antiques**
1931 James St.
315/463-1568

**European Gallery & Frame Shop**
201 S. Main St.
315/458-6593

**AAAA Antiques & Appraisals**
101 Wells Ave. E.
315/458-8193

**Colella Galleries**
123 E. Willow St.
315/474-6950

**Karen's Deco-Craft**
2101 Brewerton Road
315/455-2214

**Shades of Yesteryear Antiques**
658 N. Salina St.
315/423-9810

**Antique Center of Syracuse**
1460 Burnet Ave.
315/476-8270

**Antique Underground**
247 W. Fayette St.
315/472-5510

**Dewitt Antique Jewelry & Coin Co.**
4621 E. Genesee St.
315/445-1065

**Antiques & Jewelry on Jefferson**
306 W. Jefferson St.
315/476-5926

**Boom Babies Vintage Clothing**
489 Westcott St.
315/472-1949

**Ace Enterprise**
1200 Butternut St.
315/475-8006

**Jerry Bonk Enterprises**
204 Rita Dr.
315/458-4649

**Antique Exchange**
1600 Block N. Salina St.
315/471-1841

**Cash Corner**
1101 N. Salina St.
315/475-4045

## Great Places to Stay

### Giddings Garden Bed and Breakfast
290 W. Seneca Turnpike
315/492-6389 or 1-800-377-3452
Open: Always
Directions: From Route 81, North or South, take Exit 16A (North 481 Dewitt). Stay on Route 481 to Exit 1 (Brighton Avenue/Rockcut Road). Bear right onto Rockcut Road to the top of the hill. Turn left at the light onto Brighton. At the light, turn right onto East Seneca Turnpike for 1 mile. Bed and breakfast is on the right, at the corner of Milburn Drive.

This elegantly restored Federal tavern, circa 1810, offers such tasteful amenities as in-room fireplaces, private baths, and poster beds.

Outside, the lush gardens and lily ponds offer more opportunity for peaceful pleasure.

In the morning, guests may start the day with a full gourmet breakfast followed by relaxation or antique hunting. For those who choose the latter, a local map and listings are available.

## 79 TARRYTOWN

**Treasure Trove**
19 N. Broadway
914/366-4243

**Remember Me Antiques**
9 Main St.
914/631-4080

**Carol Master Antiques**
15 Main St.
914/332-8441

**North Castle Antiques**
28 Main St.
914/631-1112

**Spencer Marks**
Main St.
914/332-1142

**Michael Christopher's**
Main St.
914/366-4665

**Sam Said**
80 S. Broadway
914/631-3368

**Virginia's**
13 Main St.
No Phone

**Tarrytown Art & Antique Center**
19 Main St.
914/524-9626

**Traeger's Antiques**
35 Main St.
914/631-8694

**Hank's Alley**
15 N. Washington St.
914/524-9895

## 80 TONAWANDA

**Bronstein Antiques**
4049 Delaware Ave.
716/873-7000

*New York*

## 81 TRUMANSBURG

### The Collection
9-11 Main St.
607/387-6579 or 607/273-3480
Open: Tues.–Sat. 11–5, Sun. 1–5, or by appointment
Directions: The Collection is 10 miles north of Ithaca, N.Y., on Route 96 North, 15 miles south of the New York Thruway, Geneva Exit, Route 96 South.

Featuring country Americana, 18th- and 19th-century country and formal furniture, primitives, quilts, folk art, early lighting, decorated stoneware and samplers. Insurance and estate appraisals.

**Ponzis Antiques**
9838 Congress St.
607/387-5248

### Great Places to Stay

### The Archway Bed and Breakfast
7020 Searsburg Road
607/387-6175 or 1-800-387-6175
Open: Daily
Directions: From New York State Route 96 in Trumansburg, go 1/2 mile south on 227 toward Watkins Glen. The bed and breakfast is on the corner of 227 and Searsburg.

Owner Meredith Pollard relates that when they were formerly listed as simply "The Archway," they kept getting orders for cookies! They would reply, "We don't do cookies, but we make great muffins!"

This particular bed and breakfast borders a public golf course.

## 82 UTICA

**Antiques & Such**
210 Bleecker St.
315/724-0889

**Antique Clothing Company**
252 Genesee St.
315/724-3262

**Comeskey Stamp & Coin**
701 Noyes St.
315/724-9616

**Mister Jack's Antiques & Furniture**
250 Genesee St.
315/735-3815

**AAA Vintage Furnishings**
337 Genesee St.
315/738-1333

**AA Jewelry Buyers & Swap Shop**
400 South St.
315/724-3525

## 83 VALLEY STREAM

**Central Antiques**
233 N. Central Ave.
516/825-1043

**Shure Barnette Antiques, Inc.**
904 Rockaway Ave.
516/825-9297

## 84 WARWICK

**Bearly Antiques**
18 Beverly Dr.
914/986-1996

**Clock Tower Antique Center**
65 Main St.
914/986-5199

**1809 House**
210 Route 94 S.
914/986-1809

**Antiques at the Clock Tower**
65 Main St.
914/986-5199

**Red Shutters**
34 Maple Ave.
914/986-5954

## 85 WARRENSBURG

**Barabara Ann-Tiques**
2 Elm St.
No phone listed

**Field House Antiques**
179 Main St.
518/623-9404

**Donegal Manor Antiques**
117 Main St.
518/623-3549

**Miller Art & Frame**
84 Main St.
518/623-3966

### Great Places to Stay

### The Merrill Magee House
2 Hudson St.
518/623-2449

From the inviting wicker chairs on the porch to the candlelit dining rooms, the inn offers the romance of a visit to a Victorian country home. Antiques, lace and fine linens are found in each of the individually decorated rooms along with handmade quilts and working fireplaces. Enjoy an intimate dinner in the award-winning dining room.

## 86 WESTFIELD

### Saraf's Emporium
58 E. Main St. (Route 20)
716/326-3590
Open: Mon.–Sat. 10–5, Sun. 1–5

Over 10,000 square feet of quality antiques from period furniture to '40s; fine art, early lighting, china, glass, jewelry, toys and Oriental carpets.

**Lakewood Antiques**
6940 Chestnut
716/326-6620

**The Leonards' Antiques**
E. Main St.
716/326-2210

**Antique Marketplace**
25 E. Main St.
716/326-2861

**Militello's Antiques**
31 Jefferson St.
716/326-2587

**Eley Place Antiques**
3 E. Main St.
716/326-2130

**Saraf's Emporium**
58 E. Main St.
716/326-3590

**Priscilla B. Nixon Antiques**
119 W. Main St.
716/326-3511

**Candelight Lodge Antiques**
143 E. Main St.
716/326-2830

**Landmark Acres—Antiques**
232 W. Main St.
716/326-4185

**Dorothea Bertram**
53 S. Portage St.
716/326-2551

**Vilardo Antiques**
7303 Walker Road
716/326-2714

**Mollard Antiques**
120 E. Main St.
716/326-3521

**Notaros Antiques**
161 W. Main St.
716/326-3348

**Arundel Antiques**
9 Market St.
No Phone

**J. Miller Antiques**
81 S. Portage St.
716/326-6699

**Monroe's Antiques & Collectibles**
69 E. Main St.
817326-3060

## 87 WHITE PLAINS

**Vintage by Stacey Lee**
305 Central Ave., Suite 4
914/328-0788

## 88 WHITNEY POINT

### Days Gone By

2659 Main St.
607/692-2713
Open: Wed.–Mon. 10–5 (closed Tues.)
Directions: *Traveling I-81 North:* Take Exit 8. Travel south on Route 26 to Route 11, and take a left. Take a right at the red light onto Main Street. *Traveling I-81 South:* Take Exit 8 to Route 11 and turn left. Turn right at 2nd light onto Main Street. The shop is in the old church between Aiello's and the Food King.

Nancy Jackson, owner of Days Gone By, is a girl after my own heart. Her antique shop is located in an old church. I've always wanted to own such a shop myself. The shop offers 20 quality dealers situated on three floors presenting everything from glassware to furniture, and primitives to collectibles. The staff is happy to assist you in finding something here or directing you to other local antique communities nearby.

## 89 WOODSTOCK

While Woodstock is famous for two rock concerts, one in 1969 and one in 1994, neither took place here. The first was held in Bethel, 50 miles southwest; the second in Sougerties, 10 miles northeast.

Yet Woodstock is a delightful artists' community, with galleries, antique shops and a selection of places to stop for lunch. Reminiscent of the '60s, long skirts, long hair and tie-dyed T-shirts are ubiquitous. At the center of town, you might find a reader of tarot cards, with a line of people patiently waiting a turn.

## 90 WURTSBORO

**Wurtsboro Wholesale Antiques**
203 Sullivan St.
914/888-4411

## 91 YONKERS

**M. O'Grady**
356 Riverdale Ave.
914/964-8836

**Mitchel's Antiques**
800 Yonkers Ave.
914/423-2600

**Lynn's Used Furniture**
26 Warburton Ave.
914/966-7075

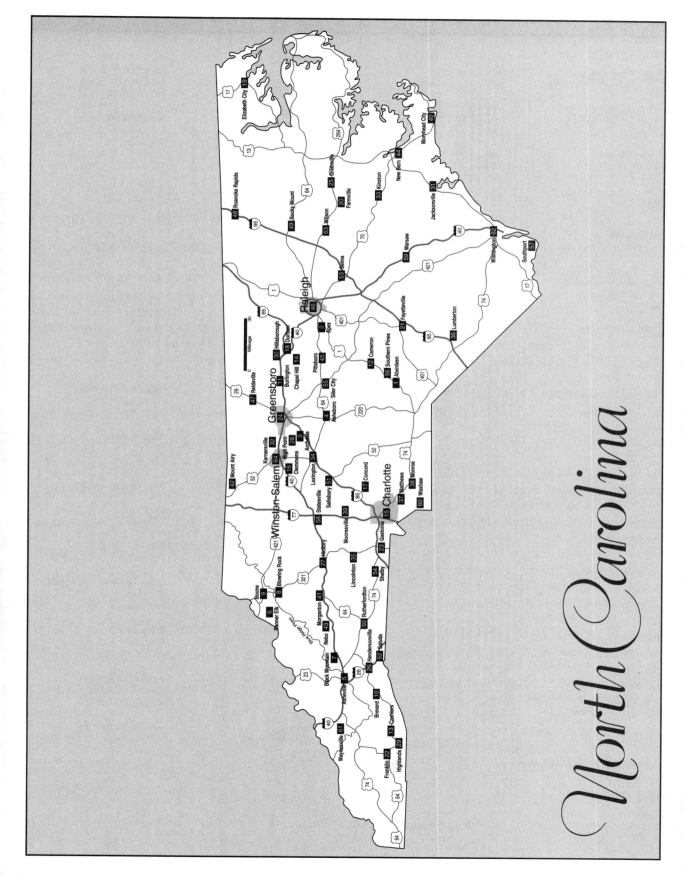

North Carolina

# North Carolina

## 1 ABERDEEN

**Cameron's Antique Station**
Hwy. 211 E. Ashley Heights
910/944-2022

**Honeycutt House**
204 E. Main St.
910/944-9236

**Cabbages & Kings**
111 W. Main St.
910/944-1110

**Town & Country Antique Mall**
1369 Sandhills Blvd. N.
910/944-3359

## 2 APEX

**Freewood Antiques**
541 New Hill Olive Chapel Road
919/362-6773

**Creative Expressions Gallery**
120 N. Salem St.
919/387-1952

**That Unique & Wonderful Place**
104 N. Salem St.
919/387-9550

**Olde Barn Antiques**
2708 Tingen Road
919/362-5266

## 3 ARCHDALE

### *Great Places to Stay*

### The Bouldin House Bed & Breakfast

4332 Archdale Road
910/431-4909 or 1-800-739-1816
Fax: 910/431-4914
Rates: $85–$95
Directions: Take Exit 111 off Interstate 85. Turn north on Route 311 toward High Point. Turn left on Balfour Drive. Turn right on Archdale Road. The Bouldin House is 2/10 mile on your left. Located four miles from downtown High Point, 20 minutes from Greensboro and 20 minutes from Winston-Salem.

The Bouldin House offers guests a graceful version of country living on the lush, green acres of a former tobacco farm at the edge of North Carolina's bustling Piedmont Triad area. It took nearly two years to restore this fine country home to its original beauty. Today, that beauty resonates in the wainscottting of the hallways, in the finely crafted oak paneling of the dining room and in the decorative patterns and designs of the hardwood floors. Each bedroom features a fireplace, modern bath, king-size bed and large closets. The bedrooms also have personalities reflected in their names: "Warm Morning Room," "Doctor's Den," "Weekend Retreat," and "The Parlor."

The inn is only minutes from elegant restaurants, historic sites, abundant sports and entertainment events, and America's largest concentration of furniture showrooms.

## 4 ASHEBORO

**Nostalgia**
111 N. Church St.
336/625-0644

**Holly House Antiques & Collectibles**
207 E. Pritchard St.
336/625-4994

**Collectors Antique Mall**
211 Sunset Ave.
336/629-8105

**Weathervane**
239 White Oak St.
336/625-2404

**Andorra's Antiques, Etc.**
305 Sunset Ave.
336/626-3699

**Cabin Creek Antiques**
3574 U.S. Hwy. 64 E.
336/626-0685

## 5 ASHEVILLE

### Fireside Antiques

30 All Souls Crescent
704/274-5977
Directions: Just one minute off I-40; take Exit 50B and the shop is located 1/4 mile on the left.

Fireside Antiques is a direct importer of European antiques featuring four galleries of fine antiques, gifts and Oriental porcelain. Specializing in English Georgian mahogany, English and Irish pine, walnut and French furniture of the 17th, 18th, and 19th centuries, this is a must-stop shop when traveling through Asheville.

**Pheasant on a Halfshell**
36 Battery Park Ave.
704/253-3577

**King-Thomasson Antiques, Inc.**
64 Biltmore Ave.
704/252-1565

**Chelsea's Gifts & Antiques**
6 Boston Way
704/274-4400

**Korth & Company**
30 Bryson St.
704/252-0906

**Catskill Antique Co.**
34 N. Lexington Ave.
704/252-2611

**House of Alexander**
54 N. Lexington Ave.
704/251-0505

**Mac's Antiques**
602 Haywood Road
704/255-7809

**Old but Good**
2614 Hendersonville Road
704/687-3890

**Lexington Park Antiques**
65 W. Walnut St.
704/253-3070

**Village Antiques**
755 Biltmore Ave.
704/252-5090

**Biltmore Antique Mall**
30 Bryson St.
704/255-0053

**Pals**
24 N. Lexington Ave.
704/253-0440

**Corner Cupboard Antique Mall**
49 N. Lexington Ave.
704/258-9815

**Jim Knapp Antiques**
503 Haywood Road
704/258-0031

**Interiors Marketplace**
2 Hendersonville Road
704/253-2300

**Asheville Antiques Mall**
43 Rankin Ave.
704/253-3634

*Great Places to Stay*

## Merry Heart Cabin

1-888-736-0423
Web site: www.bci.net/-merryheart

One hour east of Asheville, nestled in the Blue Ridge Mountains, is a place called Merry Heart Cabin.

Overlooking a forest glen, this refurbished 110-year-old log cabin is yours exclusively. Merry Heart is the perfect spot for both couples and families, the best get-away-from-it-all spot in North Carolina.

Just 8 miles north of Interstate 40 and five minutes away from beautiful Lake James, Merry Heart provides everything necessary for a peaceful alternative to the "hurry up and relax" syndrome often experienced during a typical vacation.

Perfect for families desiring a quality-time environment or for couples seeking a romantic love nest, Merry Heart has it all. It is also a beautiful "safe haven" for individuals who desire a time-out from life's busy pace.

Anything but a typical vacation cabin, Merry Heart recalls a simpler day in which a rich Southern culture took its time to enjoy the fullness of life. It is mood created when mankind and nature commune. Thus, Merry Heart Cabin accented by its unique miniature animal farm including 24-inch sheep from England, 20-inch goats from Nigeria, 42-inch cattle from Ireland,

34-inch donkeys from Sardinia, and others, has become a renewal and resting spot for hundreds over the past four years. Based upon the Bible scripture, "A merry heart doeth good like a medicine," the Smarts hope to offer a dose of serenity to those who visit the cabin and farm.

Proprietors Leslie and Connie Smart state it simply: "Here at Merry Heart our desire is to offer an atmosphere of recreation, whether you choose to spend time at our miniature-animal petting farm, horseback riding, rekindling your heart by the fire, soaking in your own private Jacuzzi or just enjoying the quiet intimacy of the quaint upstairs sleeping loft with beamed ceiling and spiral stairwell overlooking the living room with cozy fireplace."

Merry Heart is surrounded by breathtaking scenery as seen in the classic Michael Mann film *Last of the Mohicans*, which was filmed just a five-minute drive away from the cabin.

The cabin that is the centerpiece of Merry Heart was constructed in the 1800s of hand-hewn logs and unites old-time ambiance with the comfort of modern amenities such as air conditioning and gas heat.

From the rustic brick flooring to the high cedar-beamed ceiling, the cabin becomes a delightful home away from home.

Whether the guests have spent the day enjoying the nearby attractions or savoring a relaxing walk through the forest, a refreshing night awaits in the queen-size bed in the unique sleeping loft or the two twin beds located on the lower level.

For the convenience of the guests, the cabin has a fully equipped kitchen with all staples, microwave, digital coffee maker, etc. All linens are provided as well.

Be sure to climb the knoll located at Merry Heart, which provides a spectacular view over several ranges of the Appalachians, certain to enhance the peaceful mood created here. Often times guests are treated to views of the gentle deer which come to feed in the glen during the early evening.

For those who enjoy more rigorous activities, miles of exciting mountain biking and hiking trails are close by along "Old Highway 105" winding up to and overlooking the majestic Linville Wilderness Gorge area.

Hours of sightseeing are provided by such beautiful landmarks as Table Rock Mountain, Great Smokey Mountains National Park, Blue Ridge Parkway, Shortoff Mountain, Grandfather Mountain and Pisgah National Forest, to name a few.

Located about halfway between Statesville and Asheville, off I-40 and N.C. 126, Merry Heart Cabin is ideally situated to give access to western North Carolina's attractions and yet far enough away to provide a relaxing retreat.

## Chestnut Street Inn

176 E. Chestnut St.
1-800-894-2955

Chestnut Street Inn, located in the heart of the Liberty/Chester National Historic District, caters to those looking for an experience. The owner's love of people creates an inviting atmosphere to accompany the comfort and enchantment of the inn. Enjoy afternoon tea and crumpets, relax in the mountain breeze on one of the large porches, or take the five-minute walk to downtown Asheville for antiquing, sightseeing, or just selecting from several fine restaurants for dinner.

## The Inn on Montford

296 Montford Ave.
1-800-254-9509
Web site: innonmontford.com

The Inn on Montford was designed by Richard Sharp Smith, supervising architect for the Biltmore House. Today it is an elegant bed and breakfast furnished with English and American antiques dating from 1730 to 1910. Four exquisite rooms have private baths, queen-size beds, fireplaces and telephones.

## 6  BANNER ELK

**Finders Keepers**
Green Mansions Village/Hwy. 105
704/963-7300

**Marjon's Antiques**
10884 N. High, #1055
704/963-5305

**Mill Pond Arts & Antiques**
920 Shawneehaw Ave.
704/898-5175

**Susanna's Antiques**
Hwy. 105
704/963-8685

**Elk River Trading Post**
Hwy. 194
704/898-9477

## 7  BLACK MOUNTAIN

### Aly Goodwin: The N. E. Horton Antique Quilt Collection
100 Sutton Ave.
(inside Black Mountain Antique Mall)
704/669-6218
Open: Mon.–Sat. 10–5, Sun 1:30–5, year round
Directions: Located off I-40, 15 minutes east of Asheville. Headed east on I-40, take Exit 64. Turn left to Black Mountain; at traffic light, turn left, immediately pull to right and park. Approximately one mile from I-40.

Located in the Black Mountain Antique Mall, Aly Goodwin: The N. E. Horton Antique Quilt Collection specializes in antique quilts (c. 1780–1940) numbering over 300; as well as Southern pottery and folk art, furniture, Victorian antique paintings, linens, books, tools and much more. The 7,000-square-foot Black Mountain Antique Mall is noted as being North Carolina's year-round antique show!

**Treasures & Trivia**
106 Broadway St.
704/669-5190

**Hoard's Antiques**
121 Cherry St.
704/669-6494

**L.A. Glenn Co., Inc.**
109 Cherry St.
704/669-4886

**Cherry St. Antique Mall**
139 Cherry St.
704/669-7942

## 8  BLOWING ROCK

**Dreamfields of Blowing Rock**
Hwy. 105 Green Mt. Village
704/963-8333

**Antique Rug Buyers of Florida**
999 N. Main St.
704/295-7750

**Family Heirlooms**
1125 Main St.
704/295-0090

**Old World Galleries**
1053 N. Main St.
704/295-7508

**Blowing Rock Antique Center**
U.S. Hwy. 321 Bypass
704/295-4950

**Hanna's Oriental Rugs & Gifts**
1123 Main St.
704/295-7073

**Village Antiques**
1127 Main St.
704/295-7874

**Windwood Antiques**
1157 S. Main St.
704/295-9260

**Mystery Hill**
129 Mystery Hill Lane
704/264-2792

**Possum Hollow Antiques**
Opossum Hollow Road
704/295-3502

### *Great Places to Stay*

### Stone Pillar Bed & Breakfast
144 Pine St.
P.O. Box 1881
704/295-4141
Web site: blowingrock.com/northcarolina
Open: Daily 8–10
Rates: $65–$95
Directions: From I-40, Exit 123, to Hwy. 321 directly to Blowing Rock. At Sunset Drive turn left into town. At Main Street turn right to Pine Street (second street on right); turn right on Pine.

Nestled in the mountains of western North Carolina, just off the Blue Ridge Parkway, the town of Blowing Rock is home to Stone Pillar Bed & Breakfast. Located just 1/2 block from Main Street, the Stone Pillar provides a relaxing home-like atmosphere in an historic 1920s house. Six guests rooms, each with private bath, offer a tasteful blend of heirlooms and antiques, accented by a few touches of modern.

A full breakfast is created daily in the house kitchen and served family-style to the Stone Pillar's guests. The living/dining area, with its working fireplace, offers an opportunity to meet fellow guest.

If you want an action-packed day of frantic activity such as hiking, skiing, sight-seeing, antiquing or prefer to just relax and enjoy the peace and quiet and fresh mountain air, the high country area is the ideal place to enjoy your perfect getaway.

## 9  BOONE

**Antiques Unlimited Mall**
231 Boone Heights Dr.
704/265-3622

**Boone Antique Mall**
631 W. King St.
704/262-0521

**Hidden Valley Antiques**
Hwy. 105 S.
704/963-5224

**Loafer's Glory**
U.S. Hwy. 321
704/265-3797

**Unique Interiors**
240 Shadowline Dr.
704/265-1422

**Wilcox Emporium**
161 Howard St.
704/262-1221

**Blowing Rock Antique Center**
877 W. King St.
704/264-5757

**Marines Interiors, Inc.**
Hwy. 105 S.
704/963-4656

**Aunt Pymms Table Antiques**
U.S. Hwy. 421
704/262-1041

# 10 BREVARD

**John Reynolds Antiques**
6 S. Broad St.
704/884-4987

**Open Door Antique Mall**
15 W. Main St.
704/883-4323

**Brevard Antique Mall**
57 E. Main St.
704/885-2744

**Carolina Connection Antiques**
5 W. Main St.
704/884-9786

**Whitewater Gardens**
259 Rosman Hwy.
704/884-2656

# 11 BURLINGTON

## Lionheart Antiques

120 E. Front St.
336/570-0830 or 336/449-6595
Open: By appointment only
Directions: Off I-40 and I-85, between Raleigh and Greensboro, North Carolina. Take Exit 145 to downtown Burlington. Turn right on Main Street and continue for 2 blocks. Turn right on Front Street. Lionheart is on the left. Look for the lions.

From its beginning at the turn of the century, the building housing Lionheart Antiques has been a showcase for fine furniture and decorative pieces for the home. Today, with the focus on antiques, the 5,000-square-foot showroom presents mahogany and glass cases displaying porcelain, crystal, boxes and scientific instruments. In the Garden and Architectural Room, a complete Columbia, S.C., post office serves as a backdrop for cast-iron urns, fences, and gates from Europe. Many buying trips to Europe during the year keep the exciting and interesting pieces, from furniture to lamps and accessories, filling up the shop. Fair prices and a great variety is the reason shoppers return to Lionheart; or could it be because Boris, the Belgian shepard greets them at the door?

**Eric Lane Antiques**
2602 Eric Lane
336/222-1496

**Robert Hodgin Antiques**
346 S. Worth St.
336/229-1865

**Antiques Art**
309 Trollinger St.
336/229-1331

**Burlwood Farm Antiques**
4758 Friendship Patterson Mill
336/226-5139

# 12 CAMERON

**Aunt Bertie's**
Hwy. 24-27
910/245-7059

**Crabtree Antiques**
Hwy. 24-27
910/245-3163

**Crane's Creek Antiques**
Hwy. 24-27
910/245-4476

**Ferguson House Antiques**
Hwy. 24-27
910/245-3055

**McKeithen's Antiques**
Hwy. 24-27
910/245-4886

**McPherson's Antiques**
Hwy. 24-27
910/692-3449

**Old Greenwood Inn**
Hwy. 24-27
910/245-7431

# 13 CASHIERS

**Cobbies Interiors**
Route 64/Near Crossroads
704/743-2585

**Lyn K. Holloway Antiques**
Route 64 & 107
704/743-2524

**Trove Treasure**
Hwy. 64
704/743-9768

**Valley Gift Shop**
U.S. 64 W.
704/743-2944

**Wormy Chestnut Antiques**
Hwy. 64
704/743-3014

**Rosemary's Antiques, Etc.**
Hwy. 107
704/743-9808

**Cashiers East Antiques Mall**
Hwy. 107 S.
704/743-3580

**Not All Country Store**
Hwy. 107
704/743-3612

## *Great Places to Stay*

**Millstone Inn**
Hwy. 64 W.
1-888-645-5786
Web site: www.millstoneinn.com

The Millstone Inn is situated on a cool, breezy 3,500-foot hilltop overlooking the Nantahalah Forest. The wood exterior, exposed beam ceilings, and stone fireplace in conjunction with the period and antique furnishings project a truly rustic elegance. The magnificent trees, waterfalls and wonderful views provide a casual and beautiful setting. There are many hiking trails, a trout pond, wild flowers and colorful birds to enjoy. A delicious full breakfast is served in the dining room overlooking Whiteside Mountain.

# 14 CHAPEL HILL

**Patterson's Mill Country Store**
5109 Farrington Road
919/493-8149

**Whitehall at the Villa Antique**
1213 E. Franklin St.
919/942-3179

**Countryside Antiques, Inc.**
9555 U.S. Hwy. 15-501 N.
919/968-8375

# North Carolina

## *Great Places to Stay*

### The Inn at Bingham School
P.O. Box 267
919/563-5583

The inn is an award-winning restoration of a National Trust Property nestled among pecan trees and rolling farmland. Once a prestigious preparatory school for men, the inn is steeped in history. Offering a blend of old and new, you can select from five spacious guest rooms with modern private baths.

### **15** CHARLOTTE

### Blacklion Furniture, Gift & Design Showcases
10605 Park Road
704/541-1148
Directions: Conveniently located near SouthPark and Carolina Place Malls off I-485 at Hwy. 51.

Under one roof, in a convenient location, and in picturesque settings, Blacklion offers home decor from some of the most selective dealers in the Carolinas. A collection of distinctive show spaces feature old world antiques, over 2,382 works of art, lawn and garden accents, lamps and rugs, as well as gifts and accessories. Twenty-three interior designers are available for expressing ideas, inspiration and practical solutions to your decorating needs.

**Antique Kingdom**
700 Central Ave.
704/377-5464

**The Galleria Gifts & Interiors**
1401 Central Ave.
704/372-1050

**Circa Interiors & Antiques**
2321 Crescent Ave.
704/332-1668

**English Room**
519 Fenton Place
704/377-3625

**Queen City Antiques, Cllbls. & Jewelry**
3892 E. Independence Blvd.
704/531-6002

**Mary Frances Miller Antiques**
1437 E. Morehead St.
704/375-9240

**Karen's Beautiful Things**
8324 Pineville Matthews Road
704/542-1412

**Clearing House, Inc.**
701 Central Ave.
704/375-7708

**Crescent Collection Ltd.**
2318A Crescent Ave.
704/333-7922

**Tudor House Galleries, Inc.**
1401 East Blvd.
704/377-4748

**Consignment Corner**
3852 E. Independence Blvd.
704/535-3840

**Treasure House**
5300 Monroe Road
704/532-1613

**Treasures Unlimited, Inc.**
6401 Morrison Blvd.
704/366-7272

**Windwood Antiques**
421 Providence Road
704/372-4577

**Queen Charlotte Antiques Ltd.**
603 Providence Road
704/333-0472

**Gallery Designs Ltd.**
739 Providence Road
704/376-9163

**Antiques on Selwyn**
2909 Selwyn Ave.
704/342-2111

**Perry's at Southpark**
4400 Sharon Road
704/364-1391

**By-Gone Days Antiques, Inc.**
3100 South Blvd.
704/527-8717

**Metrolina Expo**
7100 Statesville Road
704/596-4643

**Thompson Antique Co.**
7631 Wilkinson Blvd.
704/399-1405

**Jenko's**
715 Providence Road
704/375-1779

**Colony Furniture Shops, Inc.**
811 Providence Road
704/333-8871

**Le-Dee-Das**
1942 E. 7th St.
704/372-9599

**Interiors Marketplace**
2000 South Blvd.
704/377-6226

**Chris' Collectibles**
7100 Statesville Road, B17
704/596-1592

**Dilworth Billiards**
300 E. Tremont Ave.
704/333-3021

## *Great Places to Stay*

### The Elizabeth Bed & Breakfast
2145 E. 5th St.
704/358-1368
Web site: www.bbhost.com/elizabethbnb

Built in 1923, this lavender-painted "lady" is in historic Charlotte's second-oldest neighborhood. European country-style rooms are beautifully appointed with antiques, ceiling fans, decorator linens and unique collections. Enjoy a delicious full breakfast, then relax in the garden courtyard or stroll beneath giant oak trees to convenient restaurants and shopping.

### The Homeplace Bed & Breakfast
5901 Sardis Road
704/365-1936

Built in 1902, this completely restored home sets on 2 1/2 wooded acres. The Homeplace has 10-foot beaded ceilings, eight fireplaces, front and back stairways, all in original heart-of-pine woodwork. While touring the grounds you will see "The Barnplace," a 1930s log barn that was moved to the property in 1991. Two guest rooms with private bath and a suite are available.

## 16 CLEMMONS

### *Great Places to Stay*

### Tanglewood Manor House Bed & Breakfast and Lodge
P.O. Box 1040
336/778-6370

Circa 1859 home located within walking distance of the beach, river, rodeo, ruins and winery. On site activities include downhill skiing.

## 17 CONCORD

**Irby's Antiques**
244 McGill Ave. N.W.
704/788-1810

**Clock & Lamp Shoppe**
250 McGill Ave. N.W.
704/786-1929

**Memory Shoppe**
885 Old Charlotte Road
704/788-9443

**Antique Market of Concord**
14 Union St.
704/786-4296

**21 Union Street—A Trading Co.**
21 Union St.
704/782-1212

**Six O One Trading Post**
4018 U.S. Hwy. 601 S.
704/782-1212

**Dennis Carpenter Repro Ford**
4140 U.S. Hwy. 29 S.
704/786-8139

**Annies Cane Shop**
5680 U.S. Hwy. 601 S.
704/782-4937

## 18 DURHAM

**Chelsea Antiques**
2631 Durham Chapel Hill Blvd.
919/683-1865

**Antiques 1**
4422 Durham Chapel Hill Blvd.
919/493-7135

**Original Illusions Antiques & Collectibles**
4422 Durham Chapel Hill Blvd.
919/493-4650

**Willow Park Lane**
4422 Durham Chapel Hill Blvd.
919/493-3923

**Attic Treasures**
2014 Granville Circle
919/403-8639

**Trash & Treasures**
2911 Guess Road
919/477-6716

**Antiques 1**
947 S. Miami Blvd.
919/596-1848

**James Kennedy Antiques Ltd.**
905 W. Main St.
919/682-1040

**White House Antiques**
3306 Old Chapel Hill Road
919/489-3016

**Twice Remembered**
4109 N. Roxboro Road
919/471-1148

**Sandpiper Antiques**
5218 Wake Forest Road
919/596-4949

**Finders Keepers**
2501 University Dr.
919/490-4441

**Maral Antiques & Interiors**
5102 Chapel Hill Road
919/493-7345

## 19 ELIZABETH CITY

**Pleasurehouse Antiques**
608 E. Colonial Ave.
919/338-6570

**Parker's Trading Post**
1051 U.S. Hwy. 17 S.
919/335-4896

**Pasquotank Antiques**
117 N. Water St.
919/331-2010

**Miller Antiques**
207 N. Water St.
919/335-1622

## 20 FARMVILLE

### The Hub Mall
104 S. Main St.
919/753-8560
Open: Mon.–Sat. 10–5:30
Directions: Off I-95 on Hwy. 264 East between Wilson, N.C., and Greenville, N.C.

If you believe all rooms should be comfortable, timeless, unpretentious, as well as beautiful, then you will want to shop at the Hub. There you can furnish your home with antiques of enduring value. Since the Hub Mall is an alliance of dealers, you will be more likely to find the piece you are seeking. Each shopping trip becomes an aesthetic experience as you search for craftsmanship, artistry and one of a kind items in this large historically restored building in downtown Farmville.

**Rememberings**
119 S. Main St.
919/753-7333

**Jackie's Ole House**
RR 1
919/753-2631

## 21 FAYETTEVILLE

**Warpath Military Collectibles**
3805 Cumberland Road
910/425-7000

**Craft Market**
5012 Cumberland Road
910/424-0838

**Antique & Gift Center**
123 Hay St.
910/485-7602

**David R. Walters Antiques**
1110 Hay St.
910/483-5832

**Harris Auction Gallery & Antique Mall**
2419 Hope Mills Road
910/424-0033

**Eastover Trading Co. Antique Mall**
Hwy. 301 N.
910/323-1121

**Country Junction**
Hwy. 87 S.
910/677-0017

**Antiques Unlimited of Eastover**
1128 Middle Road
910/323-5439

**Dimples & Sawdust Antique Dolls**
5409 Labrador
910/484-3655

**Tarbridge Military Collectibles**
5820 Ramsey St.
910/488-7207

**AA Antique Village**
5832 Ramsey St.
910/822-9822

**Unique Curtains & Antiques**
Stoney Point Road
910/424-1101

# North Carolina

## 22 FRANKLIN

**Smoky Mt. Antique Mall**
4488 Georgia Road
704/524-5293

**R & S Furnishing & Antique Mall**
354 E. Main St.
704/524-8188

**Friendly Village Antique Mall**
268 E. Palmer St.
704/524-8200

### Great Places to Stay

## Blaine House Bed & Breakfast and Cottage
661 Harrison Ave.
704/349-4230

Blaine House, situated in the beautiful mountains of western North Carolina, reflects the serenity that is reminiscent of homes of yesteryear. A true bed and breakfast, this 1910 home has been restored to its original state revealing beautiful oak floors and bead-board ceilings and walls. Guest rooms are immaculate, well-appointed and thoughtfully decorated with curios and relics to enhance their individual distinctiveness. Awake to the aroma of a chef's-choice breakfast that promises to be a truly memorable experience.

## 23 GASTONIA

**Past Time Antique Mall**
401 Cox Road
704/867-6535

**J & W Antiques**
181 W. Main Ave.
704/867-0097

**Willow Shoppe Ltd.**
1008 Union Road
704/866-9611

## 24 GREENSBORO

**Zenkes, Inc.**
210 Blandwood Ave.
336/273-9335

**Caroline Faison Antiques**
18 Battleground Court
336/272-0261

**Carlson Antiques & Gifts**
507 N. Church St.
336/273-1626

**Elm Street Marketplace**
203 S. Elm St.
336/273-1767

**Antiques & Accessories on Elm**
323 S. Elm St.
336/273-6468

**Browsery Used Book Store**
506 S. Elm St.
336/370-4648

**Browsery Antiques**
516 S. Elm St.
336/274-3231

**Dramore Antiques**
526 S. Elm St.
336/275-7563

**Unexpected Antique Shop**
534 S. Elm St.
336/275-4938

**Rhynes Corner Cupboard**
603 S. Elm St.
336/378-1380

**Edlins Antiques**
604 S. Elm St.
336/274-2509

**E. Freeman and Co.**
420 Eugene Court
336/275-8487

**Saltbox, Inc.**
2011 Golden Gate Drive
336/273-8758

**Skinner & Company**
2908 Liberty Road
336/691-1219

**Lavene Antiques**
4522 W. Market St.
336/854-8160

**O'Henry Antiques**
3224 N. O'Henry Blvd.
336/375-0191

**Cherry's Fine Guns**
3402 W. Wendover Ave., #A
336/854-4182

**Byerly's Antiques, Inc.**
4311 Wiley Davis Road
336/299-6510

## 25 GREENVILLE

**Cable & Craft at Woodside**
Allen Road
919/756-9929

**Woodside Antiques**
Allen Road
919/756-9929

**Artisan's Market**
2500 S. Charles St.
919/355-5536

**Tried & True, Inc.**
924 Dickinson Ave.
919/752-2139

**Dapper Dans**
417 S. Evans St.
919/752-1750

**Red Oak Show & Sell**
264 W. Farmville Hwy.
919/756-1156

**Greenville Antique Mall**
E. N.C. Hwy. 33
919/752-8111

**Now & Then Designs**
801 Red Banks Road
919/756-8470

**Johnsen's Antiques & Lamp Shop**
315 E. 11th St.
919/758-4839

## 26 HENDERSONVILLE

**Old & New Shop**
3400 Asheville Hwy.
704/697-6160

**Richard D. Hatch & Associates**
3700 Asheville Hwy.
704/696-3440

**Heritage Square Antiques**
Church & Barnwell
704/697-0313

**Antiques & Decorative Arts**
305 S. Church St.
704/697-6930

**Knight & Elliott**
909 N. Elm St.
336/370-4155

**Crumplers Antiques & Pottery**
442 N. Eugene St.
336/272-4383

**Posh**
5804 High Point Road
336/294-1028

**Spease House of Treasures**
350 McAdoo Ave.
336/275-2079

**Gallery Antiques**
801 Merritt Drive
336/299-2426

**Tyler-Smith Antiques**
501 Simpson St.
336/274-6498

**House Dressing**
3608 W. Wendover Ave.
336/294-3900

**Nancy Roth Antiques**
127 4th Ave. W.
704/697-7555

**Antiques, Etc.**
147 4th Ave. W.
704/696-8255

**Southern Pride Antiques**
1949 Startown Road
704/322-6205

**Antiques and More**
1046 3rd Ave. N.W.
704/326-9030

**Scottie's Jewelry & Fine Art**
225 N. Main St.
704/692-1350

**Days Gone By Antiques**
303 N. Main St.
704/693-9056

**Hickory Antiques Mall**
348 U.S. Hwy. 70 S.
704/322-4004

**L & L Antiques**
4025 U.S. Hwy. 70 S.
704/328-9373

**Calico Gallery of Crafts**
317 N. Main St.
704/697-2551

**Fourth & Main Antique Mall**
344 N. Main St.
704/698-0018

## 28 HIGH POINT

**Southern Comforts Antiques & Gifts**
628 Shawn Rachel Pkwy.
704/693-5310

**Wagon Wheel Antiques**
423 N. Main St.
704/692-0992

**Deep River Antiques**
2022 Eastchester Dr.
336/883-7005

**Wallace Antiques**
706 Greensboro Road
336/884-8044

**Village Green Antique Mall**
424 N. Main St.
704/692-9057

**Mehri & Co. of New York**
501 N. Main St.
704/693-0887

**Antique & Vintage Furnishings**
652 N. Main St.
336/886-5126

**Kathryn's Collection**
781 N. Main St.
336/841-7474

**Honeysuckle Hollow**
512 N. Main St.
704/697-2197

**South Main Antiques**
119 S. Main St.
704/693-3212

**North Main Antiques & Collectibles**
1240 N. Main St.
336/882-2512

**Elisabeth's Timeless Treasures**
1701 N. Main St.
336/887-3089

**Hendersonville Antiques Mall**
670 Spartanberg Hwy.
704/692-5125

**JRD's Classics & Collectibles**
102 3rd Ave. E.
704/698-0075

**Teague Pump Co., Inc.**
904 Old Thomasville Road
336/882-2916

**Randall Tysinger Antiques**
342 N. Wrenn St.
336/883-4477

### *Great Places to Stay*

## 29 HIGHLANDS

**A Country Home**
5162 Cashiers Road
704/526-9038

**Country Inn Antiques**
4th & Main/Highlands Inn
704/526-9380

## Melange Bed and Breakfast

1230 5th Ave. W.
1-800-303-5253
Web site: www.circle.net/~melange

**Home & Holiday**
4th St. on the Hill
704/526-2007

**Mirror Lake Antiques**
215 S. Fourth St.
704/526-2080

Melange is home to a blend of European and American cultures in a large New England Colonial home from the 1920s. The house, with its splendid gardens, received its opulent French character in the early sixties when structural changes were made to the interior. Marble mantels and ornate mirrors from Paris, crystal chandeliers from Vienna, and hand-painted porcelain accessories from Italy were imported. Fountains, Turkish tiles, a rose garden, colorful plants, enticing music, candles, old pictures, books and wonderful food underscore a cosmopolitan mind-set. Four-color theme-decorated rooms and a suite have private bath and Jacuzzi. Quiet and private. Paddleball court and fitness room. Less than a 20-minute walk to downtown Hendersonville and within a 30 minute drive to Biltmore Estate and Blue Ridge Parkway.

**C.K. Swann**
Hwy. 64 E.
704/526-2083

**Elephants Foot Antiques**
Hwy. 64 & Foreman Road
704/526-5451

**Hanover House Antiques**
Hwy. 64 E.
704/526-4425

**Juliana's**
Main St.
704/526-4306

**I'm Precious Too!**
E. Main St. at Leonard
704/526-2754

**Stone Lantern**
309 Main St.
704/526-2769

**Royal Scot, Inc.**
318 Main St.
704/526-5917

**Scudder's Galleries**
352 Main St.
704/526-4111

## 27 HICKORY

**Richard Guritz Antiques**
8 Mountain Brook Center
704/526-9680

**Fletcher & Lee Antiques**
10 Mountain Brook
704/526-5400

**Baker & Co. Antiques**
227 1st Ave. N.W.
704/324-2334

**Farm House Furnishings**
1432 1st Ave. S.W.
704/324-4595

**Great Things**
Wright Square
704/526-3966

**Collectors Cottage Antiques**
4164 Henry River Road
704/397-6386

**Norma's Antiques**
327 2nd Ave. N.W.
704/328-8660

### Great Places to Stay

## Colonial Pines Inn

541 Hickory St.
704/526-2060

Nestled on a secluded hillside just half a mile from Main Street, this gracious old home is surrounded by two acres of large rhododendron, hemlock, maple, and oak. Experience Highlands' clean, fresh air and enjoy lush views from wide porches. Sample berries from the garden, then visit the nature areas, ponds, fine boutiques and gourmet restaurants that are just a stroll away. Spacious suites and moderately priced rooms are filled with antique furnishings. A sumptuous breakfast is included and served in the dining room to the sounds of quiet classical, folk, or mountain tunes.

## Morning Star Inn

480 Flat Mountain Estates Road
704/526-1009

The Morning Star Inn is surrounded by waterfalls, gorgeous mountain scenery, trout-filled streams, and national forests. Prestigious golf courses and specialty and antique shops make this a couple's perfect getaway. The inn is on two private acres offering a gorgeous mountain view. Relax on the wicker-filled porch, enjoy wine and hor d'oeuvres in the large parlor with stone fireplace, and savor a gourmet breakfast in the sunroom.

## 30  HILLSBOROUGH

## Village Square Antiques & Auction

126 Antique St.
919/732-8799
Open: Wed.–Sat. 11–5, Sun. 1–5, closed Mon. & Tues.
Directions: Located I-85 Exit 164 & I-40 Exit 261 in the Daniel Boone Village.

Located in the "heart of North Carolina antique country," Village Square Antiques and Auctions is a jack-of-all-trades and master-of-ALL. The shop offers an outstanding selection of antiques such as depression glass, formal mahogany furniture, classic oak furniture, clocks, estate jewelry, carnival glass, lamps, chandeliers, old Fenton art glass, fine porcelain, Hawkes, Akro Agate children's dishes, sterling silver, cast iron and old tools, cut and elegant glass, oil paintings and prints, elegant mirrors, and the list could go on and on. All pieces are in the original finish or have been restored to their original beauty.

Village Square is both a retail and wholesale market, so dealers should definitely check this place out. L. B., the owner, has been known to give some deep discounts.

The shop also provides those "always needed" services of expert crystal repair, lamp repair and rewiring and chair caning. In addition, auctions are held periodically, but never on a set schedule.

Be sure to call ahead for auction dates.

**Court Square Shop**
108 S. Churton St.
919/732-4500

**Goldsmith & Precious Things**
116 Daniel Boone St.
919/732-6931

**Gatewood Antiques**
113 James Freeland Memorial Dr.
919/732-5081

**Hillsborough Antique Mall, Inc.**
387 Ja-Max Dr.
919/732-8882

**Yesterday's Treasures**
361 Ja-Max Dr.
919/732-9199

**House of Treasures #2**
383 Ja-Max Dr.
919/732-0709

**Hillside Antiques & Collectibles**
392 Ja-Max Dr.
919/644-6074

**Depot Antiques & Collectibles**
409 Village St.
919/732-9796

**Butner Antique Barn**
111 Antique St.
919/732-4606

## 31  JACKSONVILLE

**BJ's Antique Furniture**
333 Bell Fork Road
910/346-8693

**Jacksonville Antique Mall**
336 Henderson Dr.
910/938-8811

**Anchor Antiques & Lamp Shades**
117 S. Marine Blvd.
910/455-1900

**Basement**
237 S. Marine Blvd.
910/346-9833

## 32  KERNERSVILLE

**Collective Treasures**
4674 Kernersville Road
336/785-9886

**Curiosity Shoppe**
4710 Kernersville Road
336/785-4427

**Murphy's Keepsake**
231 N. Main St.
336/993-4105

**Main Street Collectibles**
321 N. Main St.
336/996-6969

**Shouse Antiques**
419 S. Main St.
336/996-5108

## 33  KINSTON

**Just Stuff**
121 E. Gordon St.
919/523-1515

**Antique Market**
Hwy. 70 W. Bypass
919/527-8300

**Claydel's Antiques**
1811 N. Queen St.
919/939-1710

*North Carolina*

## 34 LEXINGTON

**Candy Factory**
15 N. Main St.
336/249-6770

**Poor Boy Antiques**
1673 Old U.S. Hwy. 52
336/249-7226

**B & D Antiques**
1506 Winston Road
336/249-0745

**Link's Antique Shop**
2204 S. Main St.
336/249-9590

**Harry's Antiques**
3185 N. U.S. Hwy. 6
336/249-1716

## 35 LINCOLNTON

**Antiques & Art**
231 E. Main St.
704/735-5224

**Lincolnton Antique Mall**
2225 E. Main St.
704/732-3491

**Antiques & Collectibles**
333 E. Main St.
704/732-0500

**Cynthia Rankin Antqs. & Interiors**
U.S. 321 Hwy. Bypass
704/735-4400

## 36 LUMBERTON

**Antiques Limited**
215 N. Elm St.
910/738-4607

**Bell's Antiques**
2201 W. 5th St.
910/671-0264

**Lewis Durham Furniture**
307 W. 5th St
910/739-7327

**Somewhere in Time Antiques**
4420 Kahn Dr.
910/671-8660

## 37 MATTHEWS

**Town & Country Antiques**
11328 E. Independence Blvd.
704/847-2680

**Matthew's Antiques & Collectibles**
224 S. Trade St.
704/841-1400

**Antique Alley**
1325 Matthews Mint Hill Road
704/847-3003

## 38 MONROE

**Bloomin Furniture**
1401 N. Charlotte Ave.
704/289-4670

**Mary's Country Furniture & Antiques**
2502 Old Charlotte Hwy.
704/289-2367

**Crow's Nest Consignment Mall**
5811 Hwy. 74
704/821-4848

**Austin's Collectibles**
4108 Old Camden Road
704/282-0144

## 39 MOORESVILLE

**Twice Treasured Antique Mall**
132 S. Main St.
704/664-6255

## 40 MOREHEAD

**Seaport Antique Market**
509 Arendell St.
919/726-6606

**Coastal Treasures**
2210 Arendell St.
919/726-1570

**Sea Pony**
411 Evans St.
919/726-6070

**Cheeks Antiques**
727 Arendell St.
919/726-3247

**Ship & Shore Antiques**
4660 Arendell St.
919/726-0493

## 41 MORGANTON

**King's Depression**
1302 Bethel Road
704/437-7281

**Possibilities Antiques**
105 N. Sterling St.
704/433-0621

**Old Homestead Antiques**
2092 U.S. Hwy. 64
704/437-0863

**Dale's Antiques**
Hwy. 18
704/437-4464

**Dogwood Antiques**
402 S. Sterling St.
704/438-4138

**Southern Legacy**
106 W. Union St.
704/438-0808

## 42 MOUNT AIRY

Welcome to Mount Airy, also known as Mayberry, the birthplace of Andy Griffith. This small town was the model for the popular television series *The Andy Griffith Show*. While in the area you'll see such familiar sights as Pilot Mountain. In the downtown area, you can get a trim at Floyd's Barber Shop or go right next door for Andy's favorite pork-chop sandwich at Snappy Lunch.

### Mayberry Junction Antiques

1415 Fancy Gap Road
336/789-6743, 336/789-OPIE
Open: Fri.–Sat. 10–5, Sun. 1–5, on Mon. (May–October) 10–5
Directions: From Interstate 77 take Exit 100 (Mount Airy). Go east on 89 for 7 miles. Go under bridge, right onto 52 North Bypass. On 52 North go through two traffic lights. Take first left onto Fancy Gap Road. Look for Mayberry Junction billboard approximately 300 feet on the left.

At Mayberry Junction you'll experience true small-town hospitality. The coffee is always on the burner for you to enjoy as you're looking at anvils to wash boards, or simply finding one of many hometown treasures.

*North Carolina*

### 43  NEBO

#### *Great Places to Stay*

**Merry Heart Cabin**
1414 Merry Heart Lane
1-888-736-0423
Email: merryheart@hci.net
Web site: www.hci.net/~merryheart

For specific information, see Asheville #5.

### 44  NEW BERN

**Jane Sugg Antiques**
228 Middle St.
919/637-6985

**Tom's Coins & Antiques**
244 Middle St.
919/633-0615

**Middle Street Antique Market**
327 Middle St.
919/638-1685

**Elegant Days Antiques**
236 Middle St.
919/636-3689

**Cherishables**
712 Pollock St.
919/633-3118

**Will Gorges Antiques**
2100 Trent Blvd.
919/636-3039

**Seaport Antique Market**
504 Tryon Palace Dr.
919/637-5050

### 45  PITTSBORO

**Beggars & Choosers Antiques**
38 Hillsboro St.
919/542-5884

**52 Hillsboro St. Antiques**
52 Hillsboro St.
919/542-0789

**Edward's Antiques & Collectibles**
89 Hillsboro St.
919/542-5649

**Fields Antique Shoppe**
509 West St.
919/542-1126

### 46  RALEIGH

**Oakwood Antiques Mall**
1526 Wake Forest Road
919/834-5255
Open: Tues.–Sat. 10–6, Sun. 1–5,
closed Mon.
Directions: From I-40 at Exit 299
(Hammond Road/Person Street) going
toward downtown, go 3 7/10 miles to
Texaco canopy on the right side of the
street. Oakwood is located in the strip
with Texaco.

Inside the 10,000 square feet of

Oakwood Antiques Mall, more than 53 dealers have stuffed the aisles with a large variety of antiques and collectibles. No crafts or reproductions are allowed. Marvel at the extensive collection of furniture, glass, toys, deco and '50s memorabilia. The shop is know to display the largest selection of antique advertising items in North Carolina.

**Leet Antiques, Ltd.**
709 Hillsborough St.
919/834-5255
Fax: 919/834-9066
Open: Mon.–Fri. 10–6, Sat. 10–4
Directions: Going toward Raleigh on I-40 (East), take the Wade Ave. exit. Go down Wade Ave., take exit onto Glenwood Ave. (south). Go south on Glenwood to Hillsborough St., turn right onto Hillsborough (going west). Shop sits on south side of street between Boylan Ave. and Saint Mary's St.

Leet Antiques, Ltd. is a direct importer of English and French period antiques. Each item is hand-picked in Europe and no "container merchandise" is found in this exquisite shop. Instead, you will find majolica and Staffordshire, Oriental, crystal, colorful antique needlepoint rugs as well as a wide variety of gifts and accessories.

**City Antiques Market**
222 S. Blount St.
919/834-2489

**We've Lost Our Marbles Antiques**
406 Capital Blvd.
919/834-6950

**Gresham Lake Antique Mall**
6917 Capital Blvd.
919/878-9381

**Ordinary & Extraordinary**
115 W. Chatham — Ashworth Village
919/481-3955

**Carolina Antique Mall**
2050 Clark Ave.
919/833-8227

**Antiques Emporium**
2060 Clark Ave.
919-834-7250

**Acquisitions Ltd.**
2003 D Fairview Road
919/755-1110

**Antiques at Five Points**
2010 Fairview Road
919/834-4900

**Highsmith Antiques**
107 Glenwood Ave.
919/832-6275

**Aloma Crenshaw Antqs. & Interiors**
122 Glenwood Ave.
919/821-0705

**C & T Consignments**
122 Glenwood Ave.
919/828-2559

**Brideshead Antiques**
123 Glenwood Ave.
919/831-1926

**Ad Lib**
603 Glenwood Ave.
919/821-0031

**Gaston Street Antiques**
608 Gaston St.
919/821-5169

**Carolyn Broughton Antiques**
3309 Garner Road
919/772-8555

**Memory Layne Antiques Mall**
6013 Glenwood Ave.
919/881-2644

**O.C. Cozart Ltd. Antiques**
318 S. Harrington St.
919/828-8014

**Elisabeth's Space**
612 W. Johnson St.
919/821-2029

# North Carolina

**Shelton's Furniture Co.**
607 W. Morgan St.
919/833-5548

**Woody Biggs' Antiques**
509 Dixie Trail
919/834-2287

**Elaine Miller Collections**
2102 Smallwood Dr.
919/834-0044

**Carolina Collectibles**
11717 Six Forks Road
919/848-3778

**Classic Antiques**
319 W. Davie St.
919/839-8333

**Whitnee's Antiques**
1818 Oberlin Road
919/787-7202

**Woodleigh Place Interiors**
610 W. Peace St.
919/834-8324

**George R. McNeill Antiques, Inc.**
2102 Smallwood Dr.
919/833-1415

**Hillary's Interiors**
6301 Falls Road
919/878-6633

**Park Place Antiques at City Market**
135 E. Martin St.
919/821-5880

## 47 REIDSVILLE

**Uptown Antiques**
224 S.W. Market St.
336/349-4413

**Studebaker's of Rabbit Hill**
223 S. Scales St.
336/342-9400

**Auntie Q's Antique Mall**
211 S. Scales St.
336/349-5060

**Settle Street Station Antiques**
112 Settle St.
336/616-1133

## 48 ROANOKE RAPIDS

**Roanoke Valley Antiques**
Hwy. 158 W.
919/535-4242

**Odds & Ends**
1012 Roanoke Ave.
919/308-6960

**D & R Antiques**
518 Weldon Road
919/535-9172

**Past & Present Co.**
125 W. 9th St.
919/537-5843

**Curiosity Shop**
1346 Roanoke Ave.
919/535-1532

## 49 ROCKY MOUNT

**Carousel Antiques**
238 S.W. Main St.
919/442-5919

**Godwin's**
1130 S. Wesleyan Blvd.
919/972-8972

**Past 'n' Present**
120 Tarboro St.
919/446-1272

## 50 RUTHERFORDTON

**William & Mary Antiques**
Hwy. 74 W.
704/287-4507

**Pastimes Antique Mall**
803 S. Main St.
704/287-9288

**Victorian Lace Antique Mall**
202 N. Main St.
704/287-2820

**Fiddlesticks Antique Mall**
1201 Hwy. 221 S.
704/286-0054

## 51 SALISBURY

**Eighteen Thirty-Nine Antiques**
218 W. Cemetary St.
704/633-1839

**Salisbury Emporium**
230 E. Kerr St.
704/642-0039

**Lillian's Library & Antiques**
3024 S. Main St.
704/636-4671

**Livery Stable**
210 E. Innes St.
704/636-2955

**Beggar's Bazaar**
102 S. Main St.
704/633-5315

## 52 SALUDA

**The Little Store**
Main St.
704/749-1258

**The Brass Latch**
23 Main St. — Nostalgia Courtyard
704/749-4200

**Ryan & Boyle Antiques**
Main St.
704/749-9790

**A Gardener's Cottage**
Main St. — Nostalgia Courtyard
704/749-4200

## 53 SELMA

**TWM's Antique Mall**
211 J.R. Road
919/965-6699
Open: Mon.–Sat. 10–8, Sun. 10–6
Directions: Exit 97 off I-95 (Selma). Located at the junction of I-95 and U.S. 70A just south of J. R. Outlet Stores.

TWM's Antique Mall has a sterling silver tableware replacement service and also restores furniture.

## 54 SHELBY

**Ken's Antiques**
1671 E. Marion St.
704/482-4062

**Antique Outlet**
6300 Polkville Road
704/482-8542

**Bell's Antiques**
1502 New House Road
704/434-2254

**Millie's Back Porch**
1201 S. Post Road
704/487-4842

## 55 SILER CITY

### *Great Places to Stay*

**Laurel Ridge Bed and Breakfast**
Route 1, Box 116
1-800-742-6049

A contemporary but rustic post and beam home located on twenty-six forested acres bordering the Rocky River. Centrally located in the heart

# North Carolina

of North Carolina, the Triad (furniture market), Research Triangle Park, North Carolina Zoo and Seagrove Pottery are from 30 minutes to one hour away. A professional chef with 25 years' experience prepares the best breakfast in North Carolina using locally grown organic products.

## 56 SOUTHERN PINES

**Theater Antiques**
143 N.E. Broad St.
910/692-2482

**Thrifty Cobbler**
240 N.W. Broad St.
910/692-3250

**Gasoline Alley Antiques**
181 N.E. Broad St.
910/692-9147

**Down Memory Lane Collectibles**
795 S.W. Broad St.
910/693-1118

## 57 SOUTHPORT

**Curiosity Shop**
113 N. Howe St.
910/457-6118

**Second Hand Rose**
702 N. Howe St.
910/457-9475

**Antique Mall**
108 E. Moore St.
910/457-4982

**Waterfront Gifts & Antiques Ltd.**
117 S. Howe St.
910/457-6496

**Glass Menagerie Antiques**
1208 N. Howe St.
910/457-9188

**Northrop Antiques Mall**
111 E. Moore St.
910/457-9569

## 58 STATESVILLE

### Riverfront Antique Mall
1441 Wilkesboro Hwy.
1-800-856-2182
Open: Mon.–Sat. 10–8, Sun. 10–6
Directions: I-77 to I-40 West to Exit 150 (Route 115). Go north ¼ mile, mall is on the left.

North Carolina's largest antique mall featuring 350 dealers within 60,000 square feet.

**Duck Creek Antiques & Collectibles**
2731 Amity Hill Road
704/873-3825

**Westmoreland Antiques & Collectibles**
117 S. Center St.
704/871-1896

**Riverfront Antique Mall**
1441 Wilkesboro Road
704/873-9770

**Antique Market of Statesville**
114 N. Center St.
704/871-0056

**Shiloh Antique Mini-Mall**
Sharon School Road
704/872-2244

## 59 WARSAW

### Great Places to Stay

### The Squire's Vintage Inn
748 N.C. Hwy. 24 & 50
910/296-1831
Weekend specials for two available. Call for regular rates.
Directions: Located just off I-40 on Hwy. 24

The Squire's Vintage Inn is located in the heart of Dublin County in a rural, intimate setting surrounded by nature. Beautiful gardens and lakes adorn the property while winding brick sidewalks and rustic paths, flanked by tall pines and towering oak trees, provide the perfect walk through nature.

Twenty-four guests rooms are available at the inn with one king-size bridal suite. A continental breakfast is served to all guests in their rooms or it can be enjoyed in the sunken patio near the fountain shaded by pines.

The Peasant House, a two-bedroom, 1½-bath cottage with living room and kitchen, is also available by night, week or month. The country interior decor, brick patio, and fenced yard provide a setting for a pleasant and memorable stay.

### The Country Squire Restaurant
748 N.C. Hwy. 24 & 50
910/296-1727
Lunch: Mon.–Fri. 11:30–2, Sun. 12–2
Dinner: 5:30–until ?

The Country Squire Restaurant, located next door to the Squire's Vintage Inn, has been serving wonderful cuisine since 1961. Owner Iris Lennon has a unique way of making your dining experience a memorable one. Iris has her roots in Edinburgh, Scotland; however, she has lived many years along the coastline of Ayr where the beloved Scottish poet Robert Burns was born. Endowed with the natural charm of her Scottish ancestry, she makes each guest feel special.

The spacious Squire (seating 456) creates the impression of outdoor living as decor changes with the season. The restaurant is divided into themed room settings such as the Jester's Court. In the medieval period, the court jester was summoned to entertain the manor lord and his guests around tables ladened with the best from the manor's kitchens and cellars. The Jester's Court reflects this full tradition of warmth and conviviality through its rich exposed beams and traditional pine floors. The Mead Hall, a commodious room, reflects the region's earliest English heritage with its brick floors, murals, tapestries, rough-sawn paneling, and soft gas lighting.

Old cupboards, antiques, and fireplaces are strewn throughout the restaurant, creating a dramatic Colonial setting. With every serving of food, romance, history, legend and atmosphere from all over the world has been blended. The Country Squire always welcomes guests with reflections of good taste.

### 60 WAXHAW

**Red Barn Gallery**
103 S. Church St.
704/843-1309

**Byrum's Antiques**
101 Main St.
704/843-4702

**Ding-a-Ling Antiques**
103 E. North Main St.
704/843-2181

**The Rusty Hinge**
107 S. Main St.
704/843-4777

**Traders' Path Antiques**
516 E. South Main St.
704/843-2497

**The Junction**
100 E. South Main St.
704/843-3350

**Waxhaw Antique Mart**
101 W. South Main St.
704/843-3075

**Farmhouse Antiques**
103 Main St.
704/843-5500

**Sherlock's**
108 E. South Main St.
704/843-3433

**Victorian Lady**
8511 Prince Valiant Dr.
704/843-2917

### 61 WAYNESVILLE

**Magnolia Antique Mall**
322 Branner Ave.
704/456-5054

**Slow Lane Antiques**
71 N. Main St.
704/456-3682

**Thad Woods Antiques Mall**
780 Waynesville Plaza
704/456-3298

**Collector's Corner**
810 Delwood Ave.
704/452-2737

**Antiques of Today & Tomorrow**
241 N. Main St.
704/456-8832

### 62 WILMINGTON

**Floyd's Used Furniture, Antqs. & Auction**
2230 Carolina Beach Road
910/763-8702

**Michael Moore Antiques**
20 S. Front St.
910/763-0300

**Golden Goose**
27 S. Front St.
910/341-7969

**Unique Americana**
127 N. Front St.
910/251-8859

**Virginia Jennewein**
143 N. Front St.
910/763-3703

**Good Stuff**
5318 Carolina Beach Road
910/452-0091

**Antiques of Old Wilmington**
25 S. Front St.
910/763-6011

**About Time Antiques**
30 N. Front St.
910/762-9902

**Betty B's Trash to Treasure**
143 N. Front St.
910/763-3703

**Antiquity Ltd. of Wilmington**
1305 N. Front St.
910/763-5800

**Antiques & Collectibles on Kerr**
830 S. Kerr Ave.
910/791-7917

**Thieves Market**
6766 Market St.
910/392-9194

**Sentimental Journey Antiques**
6794 Market St.
910/790-5211

**Seven Seas Trading**
115 S Water St.
910/762-3022

**Cape Fear Antique Center**
1606 Market St.
910/763-1837

**Antiques & More**
6792 Market St.
910/392-3633

**Perry's Emporium**
3500 Oleander Dr.
910/392-6721

**McAllister & Solomon**
4402 Wrightsville Ave.
910/350-0189

### *Great Places to Stay*

**Rosehill Inn**
114 S. Third St.
1-800-815-0250
Web site: www.rosehill.com

Rosehill Inn offers travelers the warmth and security of returning home after a long day's journey. This beautiful house was built in 1848 by Henry Russel Savage, a prominent Wilmington businessman and banker. It was also the home of Henry Bacon, Jr., architect of the Lincoln Memorial in Washington, D.C. Rosehill Inn has been lovingly restored as an elegant, yet comfortable, bed and breakfast with an eclectic mix of antiques, fine linens, and beautiful gardens. Each of the large, luxurious guest rooms has been individually designed and decorated. The sparkling blue waters of the Atlantic Ocean, wide beaches, and world-class golf courses are within a 20-minute drive from the inn.

### 63 WILSON

**Fulford's Antique Warehouse**
320 Barnes St. S.
919/243-7727
Open: Mon.–Fri. 8–5, Sat. 8–3
Directions: Take I-95 to Hwy. 264 Exit. Follow into Wilson. Continue to Lodge Street taking a left. The shop is then on the right at the corner of Lodge and Barnes Streets.

Discover the treasures in the old Coca-Cola building, now Fulford's Antique Warehouse. With 28 years of family experience, the Fulfords have stuffed 67,000 square feet of their warehouse with an unimaginably enormous and varied collection of American, French, and English furniture, turn-of-the-century lighting, wrought iron furniture, tiger maple chests as well as a quaint selection of smalls. Across the street in the workshop, furniture repair and refinishing takes place.

# North Carolina

## Fulford's Antiques
2001 U.S. Hwy. 301 S.
919/243-5581
Directions: I-95 to Hwy. 264 Exit. Follow into Wilson, turn right on Forrest Hills Road at Golden Corral; continue to 301, turn left, next stoplight on right.

If you don't find what you're looking for at Fulford's Antique Warehouse, then at Fulford's Antiques you most assuredly will. Located in the old John Deere building, this shop offers an additional 7,000 square feet for "plowing around."

**Albury Eagle's Gallery, Inc.**
104 Douglas St.
919/237-9299

**Antique Barn & Hobby Shop**
2810 Forest Hills Road S.W.
919/237-6778

**Jean's Olde Store & Antiques**
2007 U.S. Hwy. 301 S.
919/234-7998

**Boone's Antiques, Inc.**
2014 U.S. Hwy. 301 S.W.
919/237-1508

**Bobby Langston Antiques**
2620 U.S. Hwy. 301 S.
919/237-8224

**Greater Wilson Antique Market**
4345 U.S. Hwy. 264
919/237-0402

**Marsha Stancil Antiques**
2020 U.S. Hwy. 301 S.W.
919/399-2093

**Boykin Antiques**
2013 Hwy. 301 S.
919/237-1700

### Great Places to Stay

## Miss Betty's Bed and Breakfast Inn
600 W. Nash St.
919/243-4447 or 1-800-258-2058

Wilson, the antique capital of North Carolina, is home to Miss Betty's Bed and Breakfast Inn which has been selected as one of the "Best Places to Stay in the South." Four exquisitely restored homes provide guests lodging amid Victorian elegance in downtown's historic setting. Browse for antiques at Miss Betty's or any of the other numerous shops in the area. The tranquil atmosphere of Wilson in eastern North Carolina is ideal for enjoying golf, tennis, or swimming. Don't dare leave town without sampling the famous eastern Carolina barbecue.

## 64 WINSTON-SALEM

**Pearl and Gearhart Antiques**
101 N. Broad St.
336/725-2102

**Brookstown Antiques**
1004 Brookstown Ave.
336/723-5956

**Brass Bed Antique Company**
451 W. End Blvd.
336/724-3461

**Extraordinary Goods**
1000 Brookstown Ave.
336/773-1220

**Memoirs Ltd.**
1148 Burke St.
336/631-9595

**Snob Consignment Shop**
465 W. End Blvd.
336/724-2547

**Karat Shop, Inc.**
420 Jonestown Road
336/768-3336

**Timeless Treasures**
3510 S. Main St.
336/785-2273

**Country Road Antiques**
901 S. Marshall St.
336/659-7555

**Kim Taylor & Co.**
114 Oakwood Dr.
336/722-8503

**Village Green Antiques**
114A Reynolda Village
336/721-0860

**Winston-Salem Emporium**
217 W. 6th St.
336/722-7277

**D & B Antiques**
2840 Waughtown St.
336/788-4309

**Cross Keys Antiques**
468 Knollwood St.
336/760-3585

**Larry Laster Old & Rare Books**
2416 Maplewood Ave.
336/724-7544

**Marshall St. Antique Mall**
901 S. Marshall St.
336/724-9007

**Reynolda Antique Gallery**
114 Reynolda Village
336/748-0741

**Alice Cunningham Interiors**
3120 Robinhood Road
336/724-9667

**Oxford Antiques & Gifts**
129 S. Stratford Road
336/723-7080

# Ohio

Conneaut 27

Ashtabula 5
33 Geneva
Perry 70
49 Madison
68 Painesville
89 Unionville

Toledo 87

80 90

Waterville 95  71 Perrysburg

Bowling Green 11

78

Sandusky

2

59 Milan

Cleveland

23

Willoughby 99
20  54 Mentor
42 Kirtland
17 Chardon
19 Chesterland
12 Burton
16 Chagrin Falls
57 Middlefield

Mesopotamia
55
41
Kinsman

Avon 8

44  422

11

85 Tiffin

32 Findlay

224

Peninsula 69
Cuyahoga Falls
29

Medina 53
Sharon Center 80  1 Akron
Wadsworth 92

Kent
40  76 Ravenna

76

Hubbard 39
Youngstown 101

80

Van Wert 91

Lima 45

68

23

Ashland 4  71

30

Mansfield 50

100 Wooster
250

88 Uniontown
Hartville 36  2 Alliance
15 Canton
30  Lisbon 46

62

25
Columbiana

76

93 Wapakoneta

33

63 Mt. Victory

4

39

Millersburg 61
62  18
Charm

83 Strasburg
64 New Philadelphia

Steubenville 82

127

31

Delaware 31

36

Coshocton
28

77

Piqua 73

68

36  90 Urbana

33

Powell 75
84 Sunbury
98 Westerville
Granville 34
66 Newark

16

Cambridge
13

70

Bellaire 10

9 Barnesville

3 Arcanum

86 Tipp City
Springfield 81

24 Clifton

Columbus 26

Norwich 67

102 Zanesville

30 Dayton

71

72 Pickerington
14 Canal Winchester
Lithopolis 47

270

7

Waynesville 96
Middletown 58  75
44 Lebanon

35 Hamilton
52 Mason

79 Shandon
West Chester 97

Miamitown 56  77
62 Montgomery
60 Milford

Reading

Cincinnati

21

275

65 New Richmond

37 Higginsport

Lancaster 43
22 Circleville
94 Washington Court House
6 Ashville

23

33

Marietta 51

48 Loveland

38 Hillsboro

50

20 Chillicothe

Athens 7

33

52

32

Portsmouth 74

52

0  Mileage  20

# Ohio

## 1 AKRON

Busy Akron gave the world Quaker Oats, Goodyear blimps, The All-American Soap Box Derby and, of course, rubber. Northeast Ohio's renowned "Rubber City" began as a nineteenth-century canal town. Within 100 years, it was a factory boom town. Dr. B. F. Goodrich's modest fire-hose plant had quietly launched Akron's rubber industry, but the burgeoning popularity of automobiles was assuring its prosperity.

**Annex Antiques & Consignment Shop**
1262 S. Cleveland Massillon Road
330/666-5544

**Antiques of Copley**
1463 S. Cleveland Massillon Road
330/666-8170

**Yellow Creek Barn**
794 Wye Road
330/666-8843

**Cuyahoga Valley Antiques**
929 N. Main St.
330/434-3333

**Jerome's**
451 W. Market St.
330/535-5700

**Courtyard Antiques**
467 W. Market St.
330/253-3336

**Stagecoach Antiques**
449 W. Market St.
330/762-5422

**Wizard of Odds II**
1265 S. Cleveland Massillon Road
330/666-1958

**Nanny's Antiques**
125 Ghent Road
330/865-1250

**Dreurey Lane Antiques**
7831 Main St.
330/882-6165

**Coventry Antiques & Crafts**
3358 Manchester Road
330/644-7474

**West Hill Antiques**
461 W. Market St.
330/762-6633

**Fish Market Antique Center, Inc.**
474 W. Market St.
330/535-7799

## 2 ALLIANCE

**Memory Lane Antiques**
20515 Alliance Sebring Road
330/823-8568

**Attic Treasures Antiques & More**
248 E. Main St.
330/823-8920

**Mack's Barn Antiques**
14665 Ravenna Ave N.E.
330/935-2746

**Aunt Polly's Country Store**
1930 S. Freedom Ave.
330/821-9136

**Alliance Antiques**
319 E. Main St.
330/821-0606

**Towne Hall Antiques**
12347 Marlboro Ave. N.E.
330/935-0114

**Bus Stop Antiques**
6727 Waterloo Road
330/947-2737

**New Baltimore Antique Center**
14725 Ravenna Ave. N.E.
330/935-3300

## 3 ARCANUM

**Smith's Antiques Store**
109 W. George St.
937/692-8540

**Stubblefield Antiques**
112 W. George St.
937/692-8882

**Staley's Antiques & Woodworking**
7 N. Sycamore St.
937/692-8050

## 4 ASHLAND

**The Gleaner**
1488 Ashland County Road #995
419/281-2849

**Antiques on Main**
143 W. Main St.
419/289-8599

## 5 ASHTABULA

**CJ's This 'n' That**
4616 Main Ave.
440/992-9479

**Trash & Treasures Barn**
5020 N. Ridge Road W.
440/998-2946

**The Way We Were**
1837 Walnut Blvd.
440/964-7576

**Country Cottage**
3616 N. Ridge Road E.
440/992-9620

**The Moses Antique Mall**
4135 State St.
440/992-5556

## 6 ASHVILLE

**The Barn**
5201 S. Bloomfield Royalton
614/983-2238

**South Bloomfield Antique Mall**
5004 Walnut St. N.
614/983-4300

## 7 ATHENS

**Lamborn's Studio**
19 W. State St.
614/593-6744 or 1-800-224-5567
Open: Mon.–Fri. 10:30–5:30, Sat. 10:30–5, Sun. 1–4
Directions: Downtown Athens

Located in a historically renovated building from the 1920s, Lamborn's offers fine antiques and collectibles scattered throughout the 5000-square-foot gallery that also features sculpture, prints, cards, stationery and local memorabilia.

Quality glassware, pottery and many fine old furniture pieces are available. Local artists exhibit hand-painted furniture and tiles, as well as jewelry made from antique beads and glass. Photography buffs will enjoy the photography studio, which houses a private collection of old cameras. This very unique store is tucked away in the downtown area and is within walking distance of many shops and eateries.

## The Refurniture Pod

16416 U.S. Route 50 E.
614/592-1949
Open: Hours vary, but appointments can be made by calling Lamborn's Studio at 614/593-6744.

Located just six miles from Athens, the Refurniture Pod is really an old barn built back in 1917. Inside, it's a furniture stripping and repair business — and a soon-to-be retail store specializing in furniture and collectibles.

As you might expect with this type of business, the hours of operation vary, but appointments may be made by calling Lamborn's Studio at the above number.

**Second Rose**
90 N. Court St.
614/592-4999

**Random House**
12 W. State St.
614/592-2464

**Canaanville Antiques**
16060 U.S. Hwy. 50
614/593-5105

## 8 AVON

**Country Heirs**
35800 Detroit Road
440/937-5544

**Country Side Antiques**
36290 Detroit Road
440/934-4228

**Jameson Homestead Antiques**
36675 Detroit Road
440/934-6977

**Woods & Goods**
36840 Detroit Road
440/934-6669

**Antique Gallery of Avon**
36923 Detroit Road
440/934-4797

**Sweet Caroline's**
37300 Detroit Road
440/934-4797

**Country Store**
2536 Stoney Ridge Road
440/934-6119

## 9 BARNESVILLE

## This Old House

118 N. Chestnut St.
740/425-4444
Open: Mon.–Sat. 10–5, Sun. Noon–5
Directions: Situated 6 miles south of I-70 at Exit 202, midway between Cambridge, Ohio, and Wheeling, W. Va.

This Old House, formerly known as the Smith House, was originally built in 1885 for Eli Moore, owner of the once-popular Moore's Opera House. A few years later, financial reverses forced him to sell to the Murphy family. A Murphy daughter married Carl Smith; thus the home became widely referred to as the Smith House.

This ten-room, Italianate-style brick home, listed on the National Register of Historic Places, features beautiful oak woodwork, fireplaces and ornate fretwood of the period. It provides the perfect setting for the presentation of fine antiques and gifts, such as pine furniture, lamps and shades, braided and woven rugs, Amish pictures and other wonderful decorative accessories.

**Antiques on the Main**
108 N. Chestnut St.
740/425-3406

**Barnesville Antique Mall**
202 N. Chestnut St.
740/425-2435

**East Main Flea Market**
511 E. Main St.
740/425-4310

## 10 BELLAIRE

**Collector's Corner**
3000 Belmont St.
740/676-8524

**Barn**
2095 Belmont St.
740/676-2613

### *Interesting Side Trips*

## Imperial Plaza

29th and Belmont St.
740/676-8300
Open: Mon.–Sat. 9–5, Sun. 8–4
Directions: Follow Ohio Route 7 south to 26th Street exit, three miles from I-470, four miles from I-70.

The Imperial Glass Factory was founded in 1901 with the goal of becoming the "most modern glass factory in America." The first glass was made for the mass market: jelly glasses with tin lids, pressed tumblers with horseshoe and star designs on the bottom, and assorted tableware.

The company later expanded and produced Nuart iridescent ware and imitation "Tiffany"-style lampshades. Later, Nucut Crystal, hand-pressed reproductions of early English cut-glass pieces, were made.

Hard times plagued the company during the Great Depression, but the Quaker Oats Company saved the company by ordering a premium piece which became the forerunner to the "Cape Cod" pattern.

In 1937, the famous Candlewick pattern was introduced. Imperial Glass was chosen by the Metropolitan Museum of Art, the Smithsonian Institution and Old Sturbridge Village to produce authentic reproductions of famous glass items for sale to discriminating collectors.

Today, though Imperial is no longer producing glassware, it has a new lease on life through the efforts of Maroon Enterprises, Inc., the new owners. Businesses are invited to locate within the complex of Imperial Plaza. Below is a sampling of some of the shops you will find inside Imperial Plaza:

Heritage House: Handmade quilts, baskets, braided rugs, plus other samples of handicrafts people would consider themselves fortunate to own are found here. Often crafts people can be observed at work preparing the many items made on the premises.

Glass Museum: On display in this museum are many, many authentic early glass pieces from a great number of manufacturers. In the Ohio Valley, glass-making thrived into the 1970s. Museum exhibits showcase local manufacturers and other famous makers.

Escott's Gallery: In addition to old and antique furniture, this gallery sells oil paintings, watercolors, sculptures in wood, bronze, terra cotta. Located in Escott's Gallery is Imperial Furniture Stripping/Refinishing. Repair services encompass resilvering mirrors, veneer, hand stripping and refinishing.

Flea Market: Each Sunday from 8–4 people flock to Imperial Plaza for the flea market.

The selling area is a hefty 40,000 square feet. Many bargains and treasures lurk throughout the flea market.

## 11 BOWLING GREEN

**Millikin Antique Mall**
101 S. Main St.
419/354-6606

## 12 BURTON

**Gordon's Antiques**
Route 87 — on the Square
440/834-1426

**Spring Street Antiques**
13822 Spring St.
440/834-0155

## 13 CAMBRIDGE

**Judy's Antiques**
422 S. 9th St.
740/432-5855

**Tenth St. Antique Mall**
127 S. 10th St.
740/432-3364

**Guernsey Antique Mall**
623 Wheeling Ave.
740/432-2570

**Penny Court**
637 Wheeling Ave.
740/432-4369

**Country Bits & Pieces**
700 Wheeling Ave.
740/432-7241

## 14 CANAL WINCHESTER

### The Iron Nail Collectibles, Crafts & Herbs

47 W. Waterloo St.
614/837-6047
Open: Mon.–Fri. 12–5:30, Sat. 11–5:30
Directions: Located 10 minutes from downtown Columbus, Ohio.
From I-70 East, take Route 33 East to Lancaster. Exit at Canal
Winchester–Gender Road. Then take a left on Waterloo Road across
from Winchester Shopping Mall. Another two miles to downtown
Canal Winchester. The shop is one block west of High and Waterloo in
a two-story brick house.

This very diversified shop derives its name from owner Peggy

Eisnaugle, whose last name means "iron nail" in Dutch-German.

The selection of antique headboards, mantelpieces, chests, chairs, and tables available here are sure to impress the discriminating antique shopper. The stock, however, is varied enough to meet the needs of those looking for more collectible items as well.

You'll find Raikes Bears and designer dolls by Virginia Turner. Interestingly, the Iron Nail also carries a line of fresh herbal products, edible and otherwise, many of which are from Peggy's own garden.

**Canal Country Coffee Mill**
154 N. High St.
614/837-4932

## 15 CANTON

**Somewhere in Time Antiques**
3823 Cleveland Ave. N.W.
330/493-0372

**Route 43 Antique Mall**
8340 Kent Ave N.E.
330/494-9268

**Oldies but Goodies**
101 Nassau St. W.
330/488-8008

**Treasure Trove Antiques**
4313 Tuscarawas St. W.
330/477-9099

**Andy's Antiques**
5064 Tuscarawas St. W.
330/477-3859

## 16 CHAGRIN FALLS

**Bell Corner Shop**
5197 Chillicothe Road
440/338-1101

**Chagrin Valley Antiques**
15605 Chillicothe Road
440/338-1800

**Market**
49 W. Orange St.
440/247-0733

**Chagrin Antiques Limited**
516 E. Washington St.
440/247-1080

**Martine's Antiques**
516 E. Washington St.
440/247-6421

**Hampton Antiques**
17578 Indian Hills Dr.
440/543-2530

**Erythea**
100 N. Main St.
440/247-1960

## 17 CHARDON

**Antiques on the Square**
101 Main St.
440/286-1912

**Steeplechase Antiques**
111 Main St.
440/286-7473

**Olden Dayes Shoppe**
129 Main St.
440/285-3307

**Elaine's Antiques & Stained Glass**
11970 Ravenna
440/285-8041

**Bostwick Antiques**
310 South St.
440/285-4701

**Wedgwood, Etc.**
By Appointment
440/285-5601

Claridon Antiques
13868 Mayfield Road
440/635-0359

## 18 CHARM

### *Great Places to Stay*

## Miller Haus Bed & Breakfast Inn
P.O. Box 129
330/893-3602
Open: Year-round
Directions: From Berlin, take State Route 39 East five miles to County Road 114; turn right on County Road 114, then right onto County Road 135. Signs will direct. From Sugar Creek, take State Route 39 West four miles to County Road 114; turn left on County Road 114, then right onto Count Road 135. Follow signs.

The unhurried atmosphere of the Amish community is charmingly captured at Miller Haus Bed & Breakfast Inn. Situated on 23 acres, it is one of the highest points in Holmes County. Needless to say, the view is spectacular.

Darryl and Lee Ann Miller, with son Teddy, and Lee Ann's mother, Ann, own and operate the inn. In fact, Darryl, a mason/carpenter by trade, and his uncle built the Miller Haus.

Here, you'll find all the comforts of home, and more. Each of the nine guest rooms has its own unique personality, carefully selected antiques, and a private bath. The sitting-living-dining-room area features a cathedral ceiling and a magnificent fireplace.

From the front porch you can watch Amish neighbors plow, plant and harvest crops, using horse-drawn equipment.

The inn is ideally situated in the country, but close enough to drive to area Amish restaurants, cheese factories, quilt shops, antique stores and other area tourist attractions.

Isn't it appropriate that the Miller Haus, which is a culmination of a love story that brought together an English girl and an Amish boy, came to be located in a town called Charm?

## 19 CHESTERLAND

The Second Time Around
11579 Chillicothe Road, Route 306
440/729-6555

Antiques of Chester
7976 Mayfield Road
440/729-3395

Furniture & More
12550 Chillicothe Road
440/729-0665

## 20 CHILLICOTHE

Tygert House
245 Arch St.
740/775-0222

Country Peddler Store
200 Burbridge Ave.
740/773-0658

Antiques on Main Street
145 E. Main St.
740/775-4802

Cellar Room Antiques
203 W. Water
740/775-9848

American Heritage Antiques
19 N. Paint St.
740/773-8811

## 21 CINCINNATI

## Drackett Designs & Antiques
9441 Main St. (Montgomery)
513/791-3868
Open: Tues.–Sat. 10–5 and by appointment
Directions: Interstate 71 north of Cincinnati to Cross County Parkway exit. After exiting, move to left lane and go north on Montgomery Road to Remmington Road. Turn right and they are on the corner of Remmington & Main. Parking lot behind house (also behind Montgomery Inn and across from Pomodori's Pizza).

Located in an historic home built in 1846, Drackett Designs & Antiques specializes in 18th- & 19th-century English antiques and accessories. The shop also offers interior design services.

Every Now & Then Antiques
430 W. Benson St.
513/821-1497

Special Things Antique Mall
5701 Cheviot Road
513/741-9127

Primitive Kitchen
9394 Butler Warren Lane Road
513/398-7139

Country Manor
7754 Camargo Road
513/271-3979

Latin Quarter
1408 Central Pkwy.
513/621-2300

Wooden Nickel Antiques
1410 Central Pkwy.
513/241-2985

Briarpatch
1006 Delta Ave.
513/321-0308

Markarian Oriental Rugs, Inc.
3420 Edwards Road
513/321-5877

Acanthus Antique & Decorative
3446 Edwards Road
513/533-1662

Boles Furniture
1711 Elm St.
513/621-2275

Phillip Bortz Jewelers
34 E. 4th St.
513/621-4441

Jamshid Antique Oriental Rugs
151 W. 4th St.
513/241-4004

Michael Lowe Gallery
338 W. 4th St.
513/651-4445

American Trading Co.
3236 W. Galbraith Road
513/385-6556

*Ohio*

**Peerson's Antiques**
4024 Hamilton Ave.
513/542-3849

**Shadow Box Mini-Mall**
3233 Harrison Ave.
513/662-4440

**Cheviot Trading Co.**
3621 Harrison Ave.
513/661-3633

**Covered Bridge Antique Mall**
7508 Hamilton Ave.
513/521-5739

**Bartoli Antiques**
7718 Hamilton Ave.
513/729-1073

**Treasures, Inc.**
1971 Madison Road
513/871-8555

**English Traditions**
2041 Madison Road
513/321-4730

**Duck Creek Antique Mall**
3715 Madison Road
513/321-0900

**Drackett Design & Antiques**
9441 Malin
513/791-3868

**Grosvenor Brant Antiques**
3407 Monteith Ave.
513/871-1333

**Regarding Books**
6095 Montgomery Road
513/531-4717

**Courtney's Corner**
7124 Montgomery Road
513/793-1177

**Aria's Oriental Rugs**
9689 Montgomery Road
513/745-9633

**Farr Furniture Co.**
8611 Reading Road
513/821-6535

**Glendale Antiques**
270 E. Sharon Road
513/772-0663

**Roth Furniture Co.**
1411 Vine St.
513/241-5491

**Mr. Furniture**
4044 Hamilton Ave.
513/541-1197

**Westwood Antiqs. & Fine Furniture**
3245 Harrison Ave.
513/481-8517

**Freeman Antiques**
7500 Hamilton Ave.
513/921-3222

**Teezer's Oldies & Oddities**
7513 Hamilton Ave.
513/729-1500

**Ferguson's Antique Mall**
3742 Kellogg Ave.
513/321-0919

**M.J. Nicholson Antiques**
2005 Madison Road
513/871-2466

**Federation**
2124 Madison Road
513/321-2671

**Greg's Antiques**
925 Main St.
513/241-5487

**Cannonball Express Antiques**
77175 Mile Road
513/231-2200

**Parlor Antiques by Benjamin**
6063 Montgomery Road
513/731-5550

**Architectural Art Glass Studio**
6099 Montgomery Road
513/731-7336

**Heriz Oriental Rugs**
9361 Montgomery Road
513/891-9777

**A.B. Closson Jr., Co.**
401 Race St.
513/762-5507

**Sales by Sylvia**
1217 Rulison Ave.
513/471-8180

**Springdale Coin & Antiques**
11500 Springfield Pike
513/772-2266

**Echos Past**
8376 Vine St.
513/821-9696

**Byrd Braman**
338 Ludlow Ave.
513/872-0200

**Mount Healthy Antiques Gallery**
7512 Hamiton Ave.
513/931-1880

**22  CIRCLEVILLE**

**The Country Wood Box**
7979 Bell Station Road
740/474-6617

**Brewer's Antique Mall**
105 W. Main St.
740/474-6257

**Gateway to Yesterday**
121 W. Main St.
740/474-4095

**Farm House Antiques**
29483 U.S. Route 23 S.
740/477-1092

**23  CLEVELAND**

**Ellen Stirn Galleries**
10405 Carnegie Ave.
216/231-6600

**Rastus Black Memorabilia**
510 Euclid Ave.
216/687-8115

**Larchmere Antiques**
12204 Larchmére Blvd.
216/231-8181

**Princeton Antiques**
12628 Larchmere Blvd.
216/231-8855

**Loganberry Books**
12633 Larchmere Blvd.
216/795-9800

**Heide Rivshun Furniture**
12702 Larchmere Blvd.
216/231-1003

**Shaker Square Antiques, Inc.**
12733 Larchmere Blvd.
216/231-8804

**Bingham & Vance Galleries**
12801 Larchmere Blvd.
216/721-1711

**Elegant Extras**
12900 Larchmere Blvd.
216/791-3017

**Treadway Gallery, Inc.**
2029 Madison Road
513/321-6742

**The Barn**
5201 S. Bloomfield Royalton
740/983-2238

**Peggy's Antiques**
109 E. Mound
740/474-4578

**Once Upon A Time Antiques**
130 W. Main St.
740/772-1164

**South Bloomfield Antique Mall**
U.S. Route 23
740/983-4300

**Attenson's Coventry Antiques**
1771 Coventry Road
216/321-2515

**Gwynby Antiques**
2482 Fairmount Blvd.
216/229-2526

**Paulette's Antiques**
12204 Larchmere Blvd.
216/231-8181

**Dede Moore**
12633 Larchmere Blvd.
216/795-9802

**R & S Antiques**
1237 Larchmere Blvd.
216/795-0408

**Ashley's Antiques & Interiors**
12726 Larchmere Blvd.
216/299-1970

**Mark Goodman Antiques**
12736 Larchmere Blvd.
216/229-8919

**Bayswater Antiques**
12805 Larchmere Blvd.
216/231-5055

**Bischoff Galleries**
12910 Larchmere Blvd.
216/231-8313

*Ohio*

**Studio Moderne**
13002 Larchmere Blvd.
216/721-2274

**Annie's**
10024 Lorain Ave.
216/961-3777

**Hommel's Furniture**
4617 Lorain Ave.
216/631-2797

**Century Antiques**
7410 Lorain Ave.
216/281-9145

**Artisan Antiques & Jewelry**
3095 Mayfield Road
216/371-8639

**Tudor House Antique Gallery**
5244 Mayfield Road
216/646-0120

**Ameriflag Antiques**
4240 Pearl Road
216/661-2608

**Ambrose Antiques**
1867 Prospect Ave. E.
216/771-4874

**Lee Fana Art Gallery**
845 S O M Cent
216/442-7955

**Yesterday's Treasures Antiques**
4829 Turney Road
216/441-1920

## 24 CLIFTON

**Weber's Antiques Americana**
Route 343 & Clay
937/767-8581

**Clifton Antique Mall**
301 N. Main St.
937/767-2277

## 25 COLUMBIANA

**Victorian Peacock**
139 N. Main St.
330/482-9139

**Philomeno's Antiques**
8 S. Main St.
330/482-0004

**Countryside Antiques**
16 S. Main St.
330/482-3259

**Blue Phoenix**
13017 Larchmere Blvd.
216/421-0234

**Metzgers—Ohio City**
3815 Lorain Ave.
216/631-5925

**Suite Lorain Antiques & Interiors**
7105 Lorain Ave.
216/281-1959

**Antique Emporium—Eldon Ebel**
7805 Lorain Ave.
216/651-5480

**June Greenwald Antiques**
3098 Mayfield Road
216/932-5535

**American Antiques**
3107 Mayfield Road
216/932-6380

**Oriental Rug Warehouse**
4925 Pointe Pkwy.
216/464-2430

**Wolf's Gallery**
1239 W. 6th St.
216/575-9653

**South Hills Antique Gallery**
2010 W. Schaaf Road
216/351-8500

**Last Moving Picture Co.**
2044 Unclid Ave., Suite 410
216/781-1821

**Weber's Antique Mall**
63 Clay
937/767-5060

**Historic Images Antiques**
8 S. Main St.
330/482-1171

**Stray Dog Antiques**
8 S. Main St.
330/482-1928

**Bunker Hill Antiques, Etc.**
24 S. Main St.
330/482-9004

**Vivian's Antiques & Collectibles**
24 S. Main St.
330/482-3144

**Glory Road Civil War Art**
103 S. Main St.
330/482-1812

**Columbiana Antiques Gallery**
103 S. Main St.
330/482-2240

**Main Street Antiques**
13 E. Park Ave.
330/482-5202

## 26 COLUMBUS

**Yesteryear Antiques & Fine Art**
268 S. 4th St.
614/224-4232
Fax: 614/221-6610
Directions: From I-70/71 traveling east, exit Fourth St., turn right four blocks, located at Main and Fourth. Traveling west, exit Third and Fourth St., cross Third, to Fourth, turn left on Fourth, four blocks down at Main and Fourth. Fourth is one-way.

Yesteryear Antiques & Fine Art is a veritable treasure trove that will surely delight even the most particular shopper. Owners John Blackburn and Gene Wagner, connoisseurs in their field, have assembled in their full-service store a collection of merchandise that is uncompromising in quality, workmanship, and artistry.

They offer the customer superior selections of furniture and accessories from this century and the last; lighting fixtures, cut crystal, bronzes, pottery, and oil paintings are but a few of the many exceptional pieces presented here.

They also offer appraisals, furniture refinishing and restoration, upholstery, and fabric selections. Upon request, they can ship your purchases anywhere in the U.S. or abroad.

**Midwest Quilt Exchange**
495 S. 3rd St.
614/221-8400

**Joseph M. Hayes Antiques**
491 City Park Ave.
614/221-8200

**Church on the Lane Antiques, Inc.**
1245 Grandview Ave.
614/488-3606

**Maggie's Place—Buy & Sell**
682 E Hudson St.
614/268-4167

**Gene's Furniture**
1100 N. High St.
614/299-8162

**Alexandra Pengwyn Books Ltd.**
2500 N. High St.
614/267-6711

**All Things Considered**
179 E. Arcadia Ave.
614/261-6633

**Minerva Park Furniture Gallery**
5200 Cleveland Ave.
614/890-5235

**Findley-Kohler Interiors, Inc.**
57 Granville St.
614/478-9500

**Biashara**
780 N. High St.
614/297-7367

**Downstairs Attic**
2348 N. High St.
614/262-4240

**Echoes of Americana**
3165 N. High St.
614/263-9600

*Ohio*

**Uncle Sam's Antiques**
3169 N. High St.
614/261-0078

**Antiques, Etc. Mall**
3265 N. High St.
614/447-2242

**Unique Treasures**
3514 N. High St.
614/262-5428

**Second Thoughts Antiques**
3525 N. High St.
614/262-0834

**Antique Mall on South High**
1045 S. High St.
614/443-7858

**Pritt's Antiques and Collectibles**
3745 Karl Road
614/261-8187

**Powell Antique Mart**
26 W. Olentangy St.
614/841-9808

**Vintage Jewels**
65 E. State St.
614/464-0921

**G.B. Antique Guns**
1421 Union Ave.
614/274-4121

**Antiques & Uniques**
247 W. 5th Ave.
614/294-9663

**Clintonville Antiques**
3244 N. High St.
614/262-0676

**Euro Classics**
3317 N. High St.
614/447-8108

**Antique, Etc.**
3521 N. High St.
614/262-7211

**Reserve Fine Area Rugs**
4784 N. High St.
614/447-9955

**Greater Columbus Antique Mall**
1045 S. High St.
614/443-7858

**David Franklin Ltd.**
2216 E. Main St.
614/338-0833

**German Village Furniture Co.**
960 Parsons
614/444-1901

**Thompson's Haus of Antiques**
499 S. 3rd St.
614/224-1740

**Myra's Antiques & Collectibles, Inc.**
2799 Winchester Pike
614/238-0520

### Interesting Side Trips

Travel U.S. Route 23 (High Street) to just north of downtown Columbus. The Short North Gallery District, bridging downtown and Ohio State University, is Columbus's Bohemia. Here galleries sell everything from fine art to folk art to kitsch. As you explore, you'll find vintage clothing stores, coffee houses and restaurants of every description. Don't miss the Gallery Hop, the first Saturday each month, when galleries and shops hold parties and open houses.

### 27  CONNEAUT

**Papa's Antiques & Military Collectibles**
1000 Buffalo St.
440/593-3582

**Ferguson Antique Shop**
282 E. Main Road, Route 20
440/599-7162

**Studio Antiques**
242 W. Main Road
440/599-7614

**The Furniture Doctor**
314 W. Main Road
440/593-4121

### 28  COSHOCTON

**C & M Collectibles**
603 S. Second St.
740/622-6776
Open: Mon.–Thurs. 12–5:30, by chance or appointment Fri.–Sun.
Directions: I-77 (N&S) Exit 65 (between Cleveland and Marietta), travel west approximately 20 miles, cross bridge, turn right on Second Street.

C & M Collectibles is a small Ma and Pa operation located within 1,200 square feet and a basement area. Customers often comment on how they are pleasantly surprised to find such excellent collectibles at this shop. The owners are very cautious not to mislead their customers; therefore, they make every effort to offer good smalls, glassware, toys, pottery pieces, small furniture pieces and more. Additionally, they purchase items from a variety of styles and periods in hopes that they will have something to offer each and every one of their customers.

**Coshocton Antique Malls**
315 Main St.
740/622-7792

### 29  CUYAHOGA FALLS

**House for Collectors**
2128 Front St.
330/928-2844

**Hidden Pearl**
2206 Front St.
330/928-8230

**Bill Holland & Associates**
2353 N. Haven Blvd.
330/923-5300

**Oakwood Antiques & Collectibles**
3265 Oakwood Dr.
330/923-7745

**Signature Gifts & Antiques**
2208 Front St.
330/922-4528

**Accent Antiques Gifts**
2204 Front St.
330/922-5411

**River Walk Antiques**
2237 Front St.
330/945-6898

**Silver Eagle Antiques**
2215 Front St.
330/929-0066

**Consignment Cottage**
2080 State Road
330/929-2080

### 30  DAYTON

Dayton has an extraordinary heritage of industry and invention. Daytonians devised the cash register and the automobile self-starter, which spawned the strong local presence of General Motors and NCR. The city's most clever sons were Orville and Wilbur Wright, the bicycle makers who elevated their skills to invent the airplane.

**Ginger Jar Antiques**
7521 Brandt Pike
937/236-6390

**Taylor & Mahan Emporium**
100 S. Clinton St.
937513/222-0999

**Then and Now**
436 E. 5th St.
937/461-5859

**Dorothy's Vintage Boutique**
521 E. 5th St.
937/461-7722

**Old World Antiques & Estate Jewelry**
4017 N. Main St.
937/275-4488

**Treasure Barn Antique Mall**
1043 S. Main St.
937/222-4400

**Park Avenue Antiques**
51 Park Ave.
937/293-5691

**House of Marks**
2025 Wayne Ave.
937/253-5100

**Arms Depot Gun Shop**
746 Watervliet Ave.
937/253-4843

### 31  DELAWARE

**J & D Furniture**
206 London Road
740/363-7575

**Corner Filling Station**
3770 U.S. Hwy. 42 S.
740/369-0499

**Katie's Gifts & Antiques**
2210 U.S. Hwy. 23 N.
740/363-5566

### 32  FINDLAY

Findlay was an active Underground Railroad center. In 1860, the local newspaper editor began publishing outrageously satirical letters signed by the fictitious Southern sympathizer Petroleum V. Nasby. These humorous Nasby Papers became so widely read that they helped sway national public opinion against slavery.

**Jeffrey's Antique Gallery**
11326 Allen Twp. Road #99
419/423-7500

**Blue House Antiques**
200 W. Lima St.
419/425-1507

**Bowman's Antiques**
303 E. Sandusky St.
419/422-3858

**Feathers Vintage Clothing**
440 E. 5th St.
937/228-2940

**Accents Antiques Etc.**
635 Kling Dr. & Patterson
937/298-7666

**Springhouse Antiques**
49 S. Main St.
937/433-2822

**Purple Pig**
23 Park Ave.
937/294-8197

**Ann's Furniture**
1917 E. 3rd St.
937/254-7214

**Good Ole Stuf**
621 Watervliet Ave.
937/254-9144

**Barn Antiques Gallery**
29 W. Whipp Road
937/438-1080

**Delaware Antiques Ltd.**
27 Troy Road
740/363-3165

**Crabtree Cottage**
4 W. Winter St.
740/369-0898

**Antiques Establishments**
3143 Crosshill Dr.
419/424-3699

**Kate's Korner**
540 S. Main St.
419/423-2653

**Am-Dia, Inc.**
16960 N. State Route 12 E.
419/424-1722

**Old Mill Antique Shop**
10111 W. U.S. Route 224
419/424-4012

### 33  GENEVA

**Geneva Antiques**
28 N. Broadway
440/466-0880

**Martha's Attic**
5501 Lake Road (Route 531)
440/466-8650

**Broadway Antiques & Collectibles**
71 N. Broadway
440/466-7754

### 34  GRANVILLE

**Lynne Windley Antiques**
226 Broadway E.
740/587-3242

**Greystone Country House Antiques**
128 S. Main St.
740/587-2243

**Our Place Antiques**
121 S. Prospect St.
740/587-4601

**Wee Antique Gallery**
1630 Columbus Road
740/587-2270

**Cream Station Antiques**
1444 Newark Granville Road
740/587-4814

*Great Places to Stay*

**The Porch House**
241 Maple St.
740/587-1995; 1-800-587-1995
Open: Year-round; reservations recommended. Please do not call after 9 p.m.
Directions: From I-70, go north on Route 37, nine miles to Granville. Turn right on Broadway. At the second light, turn right on South Pearl. The Porch House is on the corner of East Maple and South Pearl.

The Porch House, a turn-of-the-century home in historic Granville, offers charming guest rooms with private baths. The home is adjacent to one of Ohio's most visited bike paths and within short walking distance of village shops. A full country breakfast is served.

### 35  HAMILTON

**Grand Antiques**
1749 Grand Blvd.
513/895-5751

**Denny's Antiques**
119 Main St.
513/887-6341

**Garden Cottage**
8977 Princeton Glendale Road
513/942-1110

**Augspurger's Antiques**
315 Ludlow St.
513/893-1015

**The Brass Pineapple**
159 Millville Oxford Road
513/863-6166

## 36  HARTVILLE

**Hartville Antiques**
Ediston St. N.W.
330/877-8577

**Harville Coin Exchange**
1015 Edison St. N.W.
330/877-2949

**Past Memories**
751 Edison St. N.W.
330/877-4141

**Bennett's Antiques**
128 Erie Ave.
330/877-4336

**Bennett's Country Store**
106 E. Maple St.
330/877-6044

**Hartville Square Antiques**
107 W. Maple St.
330/877-3317

## 37  HIGGINSPORT

### *Great Places to Stay*

## J. Dugan Ohio River House Bed & Breakfast and Antiques
4 Brown St.
513/375-4395
Open: Year-round; call for reservations; antique shop is open most days 9–7 or by appointment
Directions: 35 miles east of Cincinnati, 7 miles west of Ripley, just ¼ mile off Highway 52. In Higginsport, turn south off Highway 52 onto Brown Street, in the center of town.

Situated high on a hill in the scenic River Hills area of Brown County, Ohio, and set back from town by the expansive grounds, J. Dugan Ohio River House treats its visitors to a quiet, secluded and exceptional river view.

J. Dugan Ohio House B & B was originally the home of J. Dugan, a merchant and river trader. The "four-brick-thick" tin-roofed house was built in 1830 from bricks handmade in the town. The adjacent all-brick warehouse, which now houses the apartments and antique business, once served as a coal unloading station and meat-packing house during its years of service in the river trade. The Dugan house was one of only a few houses in Higginsport that survived the great flood of 1937. After passing through many hands, not all of which treated this grand old house with the love and care it deserved, the Dugan home was purchased by Pat and Bob Costa in 1970, at which time, to use Bob's words, "there was only one pane of glass in any of the windows." After years of hard work by the Costas, the house was restored to its original splendor. The current owners, the Lloyds, purchased the property from the Costas and are continuing the restoration.

The Lloyds encourage travelers to "stop on by" for a visit in the antique shop and a tour of the house with its antique-furnished spacious rooms and several extensive collections of turn-of-the-century glassware. A seat on the terrace to watch the river traffic or moon rise grants you an escape and a vision of what life was like in a quieter time.

Bed and breakfast accommodations include outdoor riverside terrace, lovely grounds and antique-filled common and guest rooms. The J. Dugan

Ohio River House also has two furnished apartments with full kitchen available for overnight or longer stays. All overnight guests savor the complimentary full country breakfast.

The area surrounding the B & B offers public boat docks, great sightseeing outings, in addition to a multitude of antique shops within an hour's drive.

## 38  HILLSBORO

**Memory Lane Mall**
116 S. High St.
937/393-8202

**Fields Framing Antiques Art Gift**
921 N. High St.
937/393-5357

**Ayre's Antiques**
114 E. Main St.
937/393-1629

**Old Pants Factory Mall**
135 N. West St.
937/393-9934

## 39  HUBBARD

**Liberty Bell Antiques**
142 N. Main St.
330/534-3639

**Hubbard-Liberty Antique Mall**
5959 W. Liberty St.
330/534-9855

**Antiques & Things**
6138 W. Liberty St.
330/534-0880

## 40  KENT

**Hughes Antiques**
100 W. Crain Ave.
330/677-4489

**Dolphin Antiques**
135 Gougler Ave.
330/678-9595

**City Bank Antiques**
115 S. Water St.
330/677-1479

**Brown & Brown**
134 N. Willow St.
330/673-4396

## 41  KINSMAN

**The Hickory Tree**
8426 State St.
440/876-3178

**Antiques of Kinsman**
8374 Main St.
440/876-3511

## 42  KIRTLAND

**Yesteryear Shop**
7603 Chardon Road
440/256-8293

**Canterbury Station**
9081 Chillicothe Road
440/257-0321

## 43  LANCASTER

**Po Folks Antiques**
1016 Sugar Grove Road S.E.
740/681-9099

**Guthrie Place Antiques**
118 N. Columbus St.
740/654-2611

**Uniquely Yours Antiques**
139 W. 5th Ave.
740/654-8444

**Emporium—Downtown**
154 W. Main St.
740/653-5717

**Priscilla's**
156 W. Main St.
740/653-1355

**Lancaster Antique Emporium**
201 W. Main St.
740/653-1973

### 44 LEBANON

Brick sidewalks and broad avenues of fine old homes characterize this handsome southwestern Ohio town. Once the site of a Shaker settlement, Lebanon now has numerous antique and specialty shops featuring Shaker items. Collectors come from far and wide for Lebanon's January antique show and the annual holiday festival, which features a wonderful candlelight parade of horse-drawn antique carriages (Warren County Convention & Visitors Bureau, 1-800-617-6446).

At the Warren County Historical Museum, several rooms of fascinating antiques make its Shaker collection one of the world's largest and best known. Also popular is a collection of 19th-century storefronts assembled around a village green.

**A Gentler Thyme**
7 N. Broadway St.
513/933-9997

**Charles Gerhardt Antiques**
33 N. Broadway St.
513/932-9946

**Treasurer's Dust Antiques**
135 N. Broadway St.
513/932-3877

**Signs of Our Times**
2 S. Broadway St.
513/932-4435

**Broadway Antique Mall**
15 S. Broadway St.
513/932-1410

**Oh Suzanna**
16 S. Broadway St.
513/932-8246

**Garden Gate**
34 S. Broadway St.
513/932-8620

**The Cottage**
114 S. Broadway St.
513/933-9711

**Miller's Antique Market**
201 S. Broadway St.
513/932-8710

**Grandma's Attic**
9 E. Main St.
513/933-0082

**Linda Castiglione Antiques**
15 E. Main St.
513/933-8344

**Hunter's Horn**
35 E. Main St.
513/932-5688

**Captain Jack's**
35 E. Mulberry St.
513/932-2500

**Vice's Antiques**
519 Mound Court
513/932-7918

**Main Antiques**
31 E. Mulberry St.
513/932-0387

**Shoe Factory Antique Mall**
120 E. South St.
513/932-8300

**Sycamore Tree Antiques**
3 S. Sycamore St.
513/932-4567

### 45 LIMA

**Larry's Books**
1033 N. McClure Road
419/649-3420

**Uptown Antiques**
218 E. High St.
419/227-1814

### 46 LISBON

**Kiewall's Florist**
7735 State Route 45
330/424-0854

**Treasure Chest**
119 W. Lincoln Way
330/424-3016

**Treasures of Yesteryear**
343 W. Lincoln N. Ave.
330/424-0102

**New Lisbon Antiques**
120 S. Lincoln Ave.
330/424-1288

**Ye Olde Oaken Bucket Antiques**
38279 Adams Road
330/424-9914

### 47 LITHOPOLIS

**Lithopolis Antique Mart**
9 E. Columbus St.
614/837-9683

### 48 LOVELAND

**Hole in the Wall Antiques**
110 Broadway St.
513/683-7319

**Antique Market of Branch Hill**
392 Bridge St.
513/683-8754

**Path Through the Attic**
122 W. Loveland Ave.
513/683-5022

**Bike Trail Antiques**
124 W. Loveland Ave.
513/677-1224

**Loveland Antiques**
204 W. Loveland Ave.
513/677-0328

### 49 MADISON

**Colonel Lee's Antiques**
120 N. Lake St.
440/428-7933

**The Red Geranium**
120 N. Lake St.
440/428-7933

**Little Mountain Antiques**
7757 S. Ridge Road
440/428-4264

**Unionville Antiques**
7918 S. Ridge Road
440/428-4334

**Collector's Delight**
5813 N. Ridge Road
440/428-3563

### 50 MANSFIELD

**Cranberry Heart, Inc.**
1461 Ashland Road
419/589-0340

**Mid-Ohio Antiques Mall**
155 Cline Ave.
419/756-5852

**Mansfield Antique Mall**
1095 Koogle Road
419/589-5558

**The Antique Gallery**
1700 S. Main St.
419/756-6364

**Brantina's**
335 Park Ave. E.
419/524-5282

**Little Journey's Bookshop**
376 Park Ave. W.
419/522-2389

**Cricket House**
825 Park Ave. W.
419/524-7100

**Yesteryear Mart**
1237 Park Ave. W.
419/529-6212

### 51 MARIETTA

**Riverview Antiques**
102 Front St.
740/373-4068

**Fort Harmar Antiques**
154 Front St.
740/374-3538

**Stanley & Grass Vintage Furniture**
166 Front St.
740/373-1556

**Dollie Maude's Country Store**
176 Front St.
740/374-2710

**Tin Rabbit Antiques**
204 Front St.
740/373-1152

**Old Tool Shop**
208 Front St.
740/373-9973

**Dad's Advertising Collectibles**
118 Maple St.
740/376-2653

**Looking Glass**
187 Front St.
740/376-0113

### 52 MASON

**Dupriest Antiques**
207 W. Main St.
513/459-8805

**Route 42 Antique Mall**
1110 Reading Road
513/398-4003

**Something Old Something New**
4064 State Route 42
513/398-6036

### 53 MEDINA

**Moon & Star Antiques**
217 N. Court St.
330/723-9917

**Gramercy Gallery**
221 S. Court St.
330/725-6626

**Heirloom Cupboard**
239 S. Court St.
330/723-1010

**Unique Antiques & Collectibles**
602 W. Liberty St.
330/722-6666

**1894 Gift Co.**
1342 Medina Road
330/239-1311

**Country Collectibles**
2768 Pearl Road
330/723-1416

**Consignment Shop in Granny's Attic**
4184 Pearl Road
330/725-2277

**Creations of the Past**
44 Public Square
330/725-6979

**Chuck's Antiques**
7530 Tower Road
330/723-4406

**Brother's Antique Mall**
6132 Wooster Pike
330/723-7580

**Medina Antique Mall**
2797 Medina Road
330/722-0017

### 54 MENTOR

**Gold Coin & Card Outlet**
7292 Lakeshore Blvd.
440/946-0222

**Antique Center**
8435 Mentor Ave.
440/255-3315

**Garage Sale Store**
8510 Mentor Ave.
440/255-6296

**Mentor Village Antiques**
8619 Mentor Ave.
440/255-1438

**Maggie McGiggles Antiques**
8627 Mentor Ave.
440/255-1623

**Yesterday's**
8627 Mentor Ave.
440/255-7930

**Antique Dolls**
8920 Mentor Ave.
440/974-8600

### 55 MESOPOTAMIA

**Coffee Corners Antiques**
8715 Parkman-Mesopotamia Road
440/693-4376

**Beverly Tiffany Antiques**
7594 S. R 534
440/693-4322

**Fannie Mae Emporium**
8809 State Route 534
440/693-4482

### 56 MIAMITOWN

**Camille's Antiques**
State Route 128
513/353-9323

**Miamitown Antiques**
6655 State Route 128
513/353-4598

**An Added Touch**
6661 State Route 128
513/353-4144

**Vintage Antiques & Accents**
6737 State Route 128
513/353-2945

**Antiques & Things**
6755 State Route 128
513/353-1442

**Werts & Bledsoe Antique Mall**
6818 State Route 128
513/353-2689

**Merry's Go Round**
6828 State Route 128
513/353-1119

**Sweet Annie's Antiques & Accents**
6849 State Route 128
513/353-3099

**House of Antiques & Collectibles**
6850 State Route 128
513/353-9776

**Cade's Crossing Antiques**
6868 State Route 128
513/353-2232

### 57 MIDDLEFIELD

**Antiques of Middlefield**
14449 Old State Road (Route 600)
440/632-5221

**Country Collection Antiques**
15848 Nauvoo Road
440/632-1919

### 58 MIDDLETOWN

**Beauverre Studios**
4473 Marie Dr.
513/425-7312

**Dailey's Antiques**
32 S. Clinton St.
512/422-7277

**Fisher Antiques & Design**
1316 Central Ave.
513/422-0850

**Middletown Antique Mall**
1607 Central Ave.
513/422-9970

## 59 MILAN

**Kelly's Antiques**
32 Park
419/499-4570

**Crosby's Antiques**
4 Main St. N.
419/499-4001

**Sights & Sounds of Edison**
21 Main St. N.
419/499-3093

**Samaha Antiques**
28 Park
419/499-4044

**Betty Dorow Antiques**
29 Park
419/499-4102

**Milan Antique Quarters**
29 Park
419/499-4646

## 60 MILFORD

**Seibert's Antique Barn**
5737 Deerfield Road
513/575-1311

**Picket Fence Antiques**
5 Main St.
513/821-1500

**Village Mouse Antiques**
32 Main St.
513/831-0815

**Early's Antiques Shop**
123 Main St.
513/831-4833

**Backroom Antiques**
129 Main St.
513/831-5825

**Remember When Antqs. & Cllbls.**
413 Main St.
513/831-6609

## 61 MILLERSBURG

Ever see a McDonald's drive-through window designed for buggies? You'll find one in Millersburg, in the heart of Amish country. Ohio is proud to be home to the largest population of Amish people in the world. The Amish forswear modern conveniences, such as automobiles and electricity, in favor of a simpler way of life. In Amish country, women wear crisp white bonnets and long-sleeved dresses. Men wear simple black clothes and broad-brimmed hats. A few too many black buggies, and you have a traffic jam.

Most Amish in Ohio live in Geauga, Holmes, Trumbull, Tuscarawas and Wayne Counties. When you visit, keep an eye out for slow-moving buggies on the road. And be respectful of the privacy of these "plain people"—don't take close-up pictures.

For a look at Amish life firsthand, visit the Amish Farm and Home in Berlin, where you can see daily life among the Amish. Or head to Walnut Creek and Yoder's Amish Farm, an authentic working farm where you can enjoy seasonal events like the making of apple butter. Guides at Yoder's explain the history and customs of the Amish religion, and lead you on a tour of two houses and a barn. One house is typical of an Amish home from the late 1800s, with exposed wooden floors, simple furniture and such appliances as a pump sewing machine. The other is similar to a present-day Amish home, with running water and gas floor lamps.

Kidron's Amish and Mennonite communities join together for the annual Mennonite Relief Sale the first Sunday of August. Hundreds of collectors bid for the quilts, tools and folk art presented by members of more than 100 congregations. And while you're in Kidron, don't miss

Lehman's hardware store. There you'll find crockery, washboards, grist mills, copper and cast-iron kettles, water pumps—more than an acre's worth of nonelectric tools and appliances. Like quilts? Head next door to the Hearthside Quilt Shoppe.

Hungry? The Amish take as much pride in their food as in their crafts. Troyer's Genuine Trail Bologna, in Trails, sells the famous bologna in a country store near the factory where it's made. Try the out-of-this-world green moon cheese at Heini's Cheese Chalet in Berlin. Heini's sells more than 50 varieties of cheeses. At Guggisberg Cheese, near Charm, you can watch as Alfred Guggisberg's famous baby Swiss cheese is prepared each day from a secret recipe, in a factory that resembles a Swiss chalet. Across the road, at the Chalet in the Valley restaurant, you can sit down to a meal of Wiener schnitzel, bratwurst, freshly baked pies and Black Forest cake. As you eat, you'll be serenaded by yodelers and accordion players. If you prefer losing yourself in a nationally known peanut butter pie, try the Homestead Restaurant, where the menu of entrees also includes fried chicken and roast beef with mashed potatoes.

To soothe your sweet tooth, head for Burton and the sugar camp. You can buy candy and maple syrup from the camp at Burton Log Cabin. While you're in town, tour Century Village, a collection of historic buildings.

If you've never witnessed the Amish way of life, you may travel to Amish Country for the first time out of curiosity about a lifestyle unaffected by constantly changing surroundings. Once you've been there, you'll want to go back, again and again.

**Antique Emporium**
113 W. Jackson St.
330/674-0510

### *Great Places to Stay*

### Fields of Home Guest House Bed & Breakfast
7278 County Road 201
330/674-7152
Web site: www.bbonline.com/oh/fieldsofhome/
Open: Year-round; Sun. by reservations only.
Owned & operated by the Mervin Yoder family
Rates: $75–$125
Directions: From Berlin, take SR 39 west ½ mile to CR 201; turn right onto CR 201 at the Dutch Harvest Restaurant. Go north on CR 201 for 3 8/10 miles.

Talk about a room with a view! Fields of Home Guest House overlooks the beautiful Amish countryside near Millersburg, Ohio. Return to a simpler time — rolling hills, spring-fed ponds, the smell of freshly plowed soil, crickets singing, the clippity-clop of horses pulling black buggies — relax and enjoy an unhurried world of gentle people, where home is a quiet retreat, peaceful and cozy, and you're secure in the trust that tomorrow will be like today. This log cabin guest house offers all the

*Ohio*

accommodations of home and more; private baths with whirlpool tubs, fireplaces, kitchenettes, a large front porch with rocking chairs and beautiful views. A wonderful place to experience the simple pleasures of life.

## 62 MONTGOMERY

### Drackett Designs & Antiques
9441 Main St. (Montgomery)
513/791-3868
Open: Tues.–Sat. 10–5 and by appointment
Directions: Interstate 71 north of Cincinnati to Cross County Parkway exit. After exiting, move to left lane and go north on Montgomery Road to Remmington Road. Turn right and they are on the corner of Remmington & Main. Parking lot behind house (also behind Montgomery Inn and across from Pomodori's Pizza).

Located in an historic home built in 1846, Drackett Designs & Antiques specializes in 18th- & 19th-century English antiques and accessories. The shop also offers interior design services.

## 63 MOUNT VICTORY

**Newlands Antiques**
11262-11266 Lake View
937/842-3021

**Attic Treasures**
101 N. Main St.
937/354-5430

**Corbin Cottage**
111 S. Main St.
937/354-4330

**House of Yesteryear Antique Mall**
125 S. Main St.
937/354-2020

**Victory Corner Antiques**
305 Taylor St. E.
937/354-5475

## 64 NEW PHILADELPHIA

### Riverfront Antique Mall
1203 Front St.
1-800-926-9806
Open: Mon.–Sat. 10–8, Sun. 10–6
Directions: From I-77, take Exit 81. Go east on Route 39 to first light; right on Bluebell Drive, and follow to Riverfront Antique Mall.

Situated near the heart of Amish country, this mammoth antique mall proclaims itself to be "The Greatest Show in Ohio Seven Days a Week." Boasting 84,000 square feet and 350 dealers on one floor, the mall offers a 6,400-square-foot furniture showroom with another 6,000 square feet allotted to a "Rough Room," featuring unrestored and "as-is" finds.

Some of the finest dealers in the Midwest exhibit their wares in room settings or in showcases at Riverfront Antique Mall. Early advertising memorabilia, old dolls, telephones, cash registers, and toys are just a few

of the collectibles offered. Elegant glassware, pottery, lighting and lots of the unusual can always be found.

## 65 NEW RICHMOND

**A Loving Remembrance**
204 Front St.
513/553-9756

### *Great Places to Stay*

### Quigley House Bed & Breakfast
100 Market St.
513/553-6318
Open: Year-round
Rates: $85
Directions: Take 275 East to Exit 17, New Richmond (U.S. 52). Go 11 miles to New Richmond. Then go through 2 traffic lights. The next street to the right is Walnut. Make a right at the stop sign, then a left onto Market. Go 1 block, and the bed & breakfast is on the corner.

Quietly situated in the heart of historic New Richmond is the village's first bed and breakfast. Unique defines this lovely turn-of-the-century home which offers four spacious guest rooms with private baths, queen-size beds and decorative fireplaces. Guests will awaken to the aroma of freshly brewed coffee, served in the elegant dining room along with a deluxe continental breakfast. A lovely, large front porch invites you to reminisce and capture the nostalgia of this small river town.

Interests in the area include boating on the beautiful Ohio River with overnight mooring accommodations, restaurants, shops and golfing. Located just minutes away from River Downs Racetrack, River Bend Concert Center, Old Coney Island, Sunlight Pool, Riverfront Stadium and downtown Cincinnati.

## 66 NEWARK

**Arcade Korner Mall**
20 N. 4th St.
740/345-9176

**Loewendicks**
4248 Linnville Road S.E.
740/323-3127

**Park Place Antiques & Collectibles**
14 N. Park Place
740/349-7424

**American Antiques**
39 N. 3rd St.
740/345-0588

## 67 NORWICH

**White Pillars Antique Mall**
7525 E. Pike Road
740/872-3720

**Olde Trail Antiques**
7650 E. Pike Road
740/872-4001

**Kemble's Antiques**
55 N. Sundale Road
740/872-3507

**Antique Mall—Bogarts**
7527 East Pike Road
740/872-3514

# 68 PAINESVILLE

**Treasure Shop**
213 High St.
440/354-3552

**My Country Place**
2200 Mentor Ave.
440/354-8811

**A-1 Antique Buyers & Sellers**
1581 N. Ridge Road
440/352-3038

**Ye Olde Oaken Bucket**
776 Mentor Ave.
440/354-0007

**Windsor Antiques**
2200 Mentor Ave.
440/357-5792

**Miscellaneous Barn**
240 Mantle Road
216/354-5289

# 69 PENINSULA

**Antique Roost**
1455 Whines Hill Road
440/657-2687

**Downtown Emporium**
1595 Main St.
440/657-2778

**Innocent Age Antiques**
6084 N. Locust St.
440/657-2915

**Olde Players Barn**
1039 W. Streetsboro Road
440/657-2886

# 70 PERRY

**Main Street Antiques**
4179 Main St. (Narrows Road)
440/428-6016

**Dad's Old Store**
4184 Main St. (Narrows Road)
440/259-5547

# 71 PERRYSBURG

**Speck's Antique Furniture**
23248 Dunbridge Road
419/874-4272

**Perrysburg Antiques Market**
116 Louisiana Ave.
419/872-0231

**Jones & Jones Ltd. Antiques**
114 W. Indiana Ave.
419/874-2867

**Stony Ridge Antiques**
5535 Fremont Pike
419/837-5164

# 72 PICKERINGTON

**Olde Time Antiques**
12954 Stonecreek Dr. N.W.
614/759-7660

# 73 PIQUA

**Avenue & Alley Antiques**
312 E. Ash St.
937/778-1110

**World of Oz**
325 E. Ash St.
937/773-2130

**Apple Tree Gallery**
427 N. Main St.
937/773-1801

**Cheries Antiques & Fine Jewelry**
317 E. Ash St.
937/773-0779

**Memory Lane Antiques**
9277 N. County Road 25 A
937/778-0942

# 74 PORTSMOUTH

**Leading Lady Company**
620 Chillicothe St.
740/353-0700

**Oakery**
225 Harding Ave.
740/776-7481

**River Bend Antiques & Gifts**
440 2nd St.
740/354-3759

**Olde Towne Antique Mall**
541 2nd St.
740/353-7555

**Mr. Binn's Antique Shop**
604 2nd St. Ave.
740/353-2856

**Ratliff's Relics**
1608 Gallia St.
740/353-7409

**Shope Country**
537 2nd St.
740/353-4880

**Gay '90s Antiques**
543 2nd St.
740/353-6111

# 75 POWELL

**Depot Street Antiques**
41 Depot St.
614/885-6034

**Powell Antiques Center**
26 W. Olentangy St.
614/888-6447

**Lane Interiors Ltd.**
84 W. Olentangy St.
614/846-1007

**Manor at Catalpa Grove**
147 W. Olentangy St.
614/798-1471

**Windsor Ltd. Antiques**
9280 Dublin Road
614/761-7900

**Seasons Past Antiques**
38 W. Olentangy St.
614/431-1265

**Country Reflections**
87 W. Olentangy St.
614/848-3835

# 76 RAVENNA

Directions: Take Ohio Turnpike Exit 13A to Route 44S. Follow Route 44S into Ravenna. From I-76, use Exit 38B, Route 44N, and follow Route 44 north into Ravenna.

Ravenna, Ohio, is a town of antique shops, bed and breakfasts, and restaurants. Start on one end of Main Street and work your way, shop by shop, through town, occasionally taking a side street to reach a special place.

Begin at Copper Kettle Antiques. Spend some time admiring the tin ceilings and maple floors of this 1840 building. It still has its original central staircase, giving easy access to its 40 dealers in 6,000 square feet of space on two floors. You can browse through furniture, glassware, china, pottery, advertising memorabilia, Victrolas, primitives and tools, among other collectibles. Then wander next door to Hickory Way Antiques. They carry a wide variety of jewelry, furniture, paper items, glassware, leaded glass lamps, hand-

*Ohio*

painted lamp shades, Victorian lamps, primitives, and tools. Next is Farnsworth Antique Associates, a 12-dealer mall featuring pottery, upscale furniture, lighting items, and a general mixture.

Fourth on your list should be Timeless Treasure. Owners Linda and Jeff Nicolaus specialize in glass and china, and walnut, cherry, and mahogany furniture from the mid-1800s through the 1940s, which is beautifully displayed in room settings, making the shop one of the prettiest you've ever entered. Jeff designs and builds the mantels and shelves utilized in the shop and will take special requests to fill individual needs.

Next stop is Thyme Remembered. This unique shop blends a variety of old and new, country, primitives, and giftware in a quaint atmosphere.

By this time you will probably be ready for food, so you can start with Patricia's Family Tradition, just down the street on Main. They serve breakfast, lunch, dinner, sandwiches, and home-baked goods at reasonable prices. Or, you can hold on a little longer and make your way to Prospect Street and the Bello House Deli. They offer delicious soups, salads, and special sub sandwiches, served in an Italian villa-type setting. The atmosphere is friendly and the customers are treated like family.

A great way to work off that huge lunch is to head over to the Ohio Trader's Market & Antiques. Within 17,000 square feet, 40 dealers specialize in quality primitives, oak furniture, glassware, vintage clothing and furniture. The merchandise is neatly displayed in the friendly atmosphere of an old factory. People come not only to shop, but to admire the size of the building with gigantic windows.

The Upstairs Emporium, located on the second floor of the Ohio Trader's Mart, is a unique gift shop featuring one-of-a-kind decorator items from around the world, beautifully displayed amid silk flowers, concrete statuary, and fountains. The Emporium also features a year-round Holiday Shoppe overflowing with Christmas items. Move on and shop for a while at the Added Touch, located in an old house whose rooms are filled with the house specialty—the unusual in china, glass and furniture.

Your final stop for the day might be at the Rocking Horse Inn, where you can collapse for the night in comfort and homelike surroundings in one of its four guest rooms, complete with private baths. This bed and breakfast sits on land that was a part of the Western Reserve and the original platt of Ravenna. After buying the land in 1867, Rev. Edward Hubbell decided to build a grand home in the then-popular Stick style. Unfortunately, the construction got out of hand and was not completed until 1875 by Quincy Cook, who also built the mill on Main Street known today as Babcock Feed Mill, the oldest continuing operation in Ravenna. Following the death of Quincy's wife Charlotte in 1920, the house had several owners. The present owners, Jim and Carolyn Leffler, purchased the property in 1991 and opened it as the Rocking Horse Bed and Breakfast.

After a good night's sleep you're ready to spend the day at Ravenna's newest addition, the AAA I-76 Antique Mall with more than 400 dealers within 50,000 square feet. You can fill the car (most likely a U-Haul) on this antiquing adventure!

## AAA I-76 Antique Mall
4284 Lynn Road
1-888-476-8976
Directions: Convenience and accessibility make the AAA I-76 Antique Mall at Ravenna, Ohio, one of Ohio's best. Excellent visibility from I-76 at Exit 38B (State Route 44) make it a stopping point for many east-west cross-country travelers.

Arc-En-Ciel pottery, Cambridge glass, Cincinnati art pottery, Cowan pottery, Dagenhart glass, Erickson glass, Fenton art glass, Fostoria glass, Heisey glass, Hull pottery, Imperial glass, Lotus Ware, McCoy pottery, National cash registers, Nicodemus glass, Owens pottery, Peters & Reed pottery, Puriton pottery, Radford pottery, Rockwood pottery, Roseville pottery, Royal Copley, Shawnee pottery, Stanford pottery, Tiffin glass, Watt pottery, Weller pottery, Wheatley pottery, and Zanesville glass: what do all these items have in common? They were all made in Ohio and selections of these wonderful antiques and collectibles can be found at the newly opened AAA I-76 Antique Mall in Ravenna.

Ravenna has long been recognized as an antique mecca. This town is chock full of antique shops, bed and breakfasts and wonderful restaurants. The addition of AAA I-76 with 50,000 square feet and over 400 dealers will certainly lure travelers from nearby Interstate 76 to the charming town of Ravenna.

C. J. Hawley, owner of the new mall, is also an owner of the AAA I-70 Antique Mall in Springfield and says that this establishment will be similar in design to the Springfield mall.

Hours of operation are from 10–6 daily, according to Hawley, closing only three days of the year for Christmas, Thanksgiving and Easter.

**The Added Touch**
315 N. Chestnut St.
330/297-0701

**Copper Kettle Antiques**
115 E. Main St.
330/296-8708

**Farnsworth Antiques Associates**
126 E. Main St.
330/296-8600

**Hickory Way Antiques**
117 E. Main St.
330/296-5595

**Timeless Treasures Antiques**
129 E. Main St.
330/296-7800

**The Upstairs Emporium**
645 S. Chestnut St.
330/296-7050

**Thyme Remembered**
200 W. Main St.
330/296-0055

**The Ohio Trader's Market**
645 S. Chestnut St.
330/296-7050

### *Great Places to Eat*

## Bello House Deli
684 S. Prospect St.
330/297-6415
Open: Mon.–Fri. 11–2, Fri. & Sat. 5–8

**Patricia's Family Tradition**
250 W. Main St.
330/296-5201
Open: Daily 6:30–4

### Great Places to Stay

**Rocking Horse Inn**
248 W. Riddle Ave.
330/297-5720

## 77 READING

**Every Now & Then Antique Mall**
430 W. Benson St.
513/821-1497

**The Furniture Craftsman**
17 Pike St. (Rear)
513/554-0095

**Talk of the Town**
9019 Reading Road
513/563-8844

**Amazing Grace Antiques**
149 W. Benson St.
513/761-8300

**Millcreek Antiques**
100 Mill St. (Lockland)
513/761-1512

**Casablanca Vintage**
9001 Reading Road
513/733-8811

**Grand Antique Mall**
9701 Reading Road
513/554-1919

## 78 SANDUSKY

**Judee Hill Antiques & Appraisals**
809 Hayes Ave.
419/625-4442

**Now & Then Shoppe**
333 W. Market St.
419/625-1918

**Lake Erie Arts, Crafts & Gifts**
1521 Cleveland Road
419/627-0015

**Bay Window**
223 E. Market St.
419/625-1825

**Hobson's Choice Tiques-M-Porium**
135 Columbus Ave.
419/624-1591

## 79 SHANDON

**General Store & More**
4751 Cinti Brookvl Road
513/738-1881

**Red Door Antiques**
4843 Cinti Brookvl Road
513/738-0618

**Bruce Metzger Antiques**
4807 Cinti Brookvl Road
513/738-7256

## 80 SHARON CENTER

**Country Trader**
6324 Ridge Road
330/239-2104

## 81 SPRINGFIELD

**AAA I-70 Antique Mall**
4700 S. Charleston Pike (State Route 41)
937/324-8448
Directions: Convenience and accessibility make the AAA I-70 Antique
Mall at Springfield one of Ohio's best. Adjacent to the I-70 east-bound
off-ramp at Exit 59 (State Route 41).

Located in the heartland of America, AAA I-70 Antique Mall in
Springfield is truly one of Ohio's best. With two other antique malls within
two miles of their front door, as well
as the monthly Springfield Antique
Show & Flea Market, the area is
known as an "antique mecca"
boasting more than 150,000 square
feet of antiques and collectibles
within three modern malls.

AAA I-70 Antique Mall is a 30,000-
square-foot (a monster of a place), 250-dealer mall with a vast assortment
of antiques and collectibles displayed in a state-of-the-art, air-conditioned
single-floor building. Beautiful locked showcases display many smalls
such as R.S. Prussia, flow blue, Majolica, Weller, Roseville, toys, dolls
and much more.

A real treasure hunt of yesteryear's history, AAA I-70 Antique Mall is
one place where you can buy with confidence. The owners guarantee it
to be what they say it is or your money back.

**Old Canterbury Antiques**
4655 E. National Road
937/323-1418

**Central Ohio Antique Center**
1735 Titus Road
937/322-8868

**Deborah's Attic**
719 S. Limestone St.
937/322-8842

**Knight's Antiques**
4750 E. National Road
937/325-1412

**American Antiquities**
126 E. High St.
937/322-6281

**Mary's Variety Store**
42 W. High St.
937/324-5372

## 82 STEUBENVILLE

**Pottery City Antiques**
4th & Market
1-800-380-6933

**Antique Emporium**
2523 Sunset Blvd.
740/264-7806

**Yesterday Antiques & Collectibles**
159 N. 4th St.
740/283-2445

**Oldies but Goodies**
1939 Majestic Circle #250
740/282/3926

## 83 STRASBURG

Strasburg provides a convenient stop for antiquing travelers. Four antique shops, one mall, and one indoor Sunday flea market are all within one mile of Interstate 77, Exit 87, on Highway 250.

### Strasburg 77 Antiques & Collectibles

780 S. Wooster
330/878-7726
Open: Tues.–Sun. 11–5, and by chance or appointment
Directions: ¼ mile west of I-77 at Exit 87, State Route 250

Strasburg 77 Antiques & Collectibles is a treasure chest for those seeking interesting and unusual collectibles. The shop is packed with advertising memorabilia, old books and toys, bottles, tins, and those ever-popular Disney collectibles.

### Carol's Collection

840 S. Wooster
330/878-7898
Open: Tues.–Sun. 11–5
Directions: ¼ mile west of I-77 at Exit 87, State Route 250

Another great place to go for collectibles in Strasburg, Carol's Collection offers the usual in the way of collectibles such as bottles, advertising, books, etc. However, she loves to seek out and buy for her customers the unusual such as Indian arrowheads and relics, marbles and painted beer and soda bottles.

**Yesterday's Memories Antiques**
116 N. Wooster Ave.
330/878-7021

**Kandle Antiques**
1180 N. Wooster Ave.
330/878-5775

## 84 SUNBURY

**Pieces of the Past**
74 E. Cherry St.
614/965-1231

**Village Antiques**
5 S. Columbus St.
614/965-4343

**Coffee Antiques**
25 E. Granvill St.
614/965-1113

**Weidner's Village Square Antq. Mall**
31 E. Granvill St.
614/965-4377

**Sunberry Antique Mall**
20 S. Vernon
614/965-2279

**Cherry St. Antiques Center**
34 W. Cherry St.
614/888-6447

## 85 TIFFIN

**Deerfield Station**
60 Clay St.
419/448-0342

**The Gallery**
215 Riverside Dr.
419/447-1568

**That Old Log House Antiques**
1443 W. Seneca Ave.
419/447-0381

**Shumway Antiques**
94 N. Washington St.
491/447-8746

**Tiffin Town Antiques**
368 N. Washington St.
419/447-5364

## 86 TIPP CITY

**Kim's Furniture Store**
7505 S. County Road 25 A
937/667-3316

**Angel's Antiques**
27 E. Main St.
937/667-8861

**Venkin Antique Gallery**
14 E. Main St.
937/667-5526

## 87 TOLEDO

**Cobblestone Antiques Mall**
2635 W. Central Ave.
419/475-4561

**Leffler's Antiques**
2646 W. Central Ave.
419/473-3373

**The Station Shop**
130 W. Dudley
419/893-5674

**Custer Antiques & Investment Co.**
534 W. Laskey Road
419/478-4221

**Colour Your World**
414 Main St.
419/693-5283

**Cottage Antiques**
2423 N. Reynolds Road
419/536-3888

**Ancestor House Antiques**
3148 Tremainsville Road
419/474-0735

## 88 UNIONTOWN

**Wayside Antiques**
12921 Cleveland Ave. N.W.
330/699-2992

**Antique Mall Uniontown**
13443 Cleveland Ave. N.W.
330/699-6235

**Ashley's**
12980 Cleveland Ave. N.W.
330/699-5370

**Knic-Knac's Treasures**
22 S. Washington St.
419/447-5922

**Benkin & Company**
14 E. Main St.
937/667-5975

**Jezebel's Vintage Clothing**
15 N. 2nd St.
937/667-7566

**Keta's Antiques & Oriental Rugs**
2640 W. Central Ave.
419/474-1616

**Gold & Silver Lady**
5650 W. Central Ave.
419/537-9009

**Hyman's Red Barn**
922 Lagrange St.
419/243-9409

**The Gift Horse**
520 Madison Ave.
419/241-8547

**Frogtown Books, Inc.**
2131 N. Reynolds Road
419/531-8101

**Antique Barn**
1598 W. Sylvania Ave.
419/470-0118

**Colonial Antique Arts & Crafts**
13075 Cleveland Ave. N.W.
330/699-9878

**Antiques of Yesteryears**
13501 Cleveland Ave. N.W.
330/699-2090

 *Ohio*

## 89 UNIONVILLE

**The Green Door & Red Button**
6819 S. Ridge E. Route 84
440/428-5747

**Little Mountain Antiques**
7757 S. Ridge E. Route 84
440/428-4264

**Unionville Antiques**
Route 84
440/428-4334

## 90 URBANA

**Charlie Brown's Antiques**
4815 Cedar Creek Road
937/484-3535

**Kaleidoscope**
117 N. Main St.
937/653-8010

**Upper Valley Antiques**
3345 W. U.S. Hwy. 36
937/653-6600

## 91 VAN WERT

**Williman's Antiques**
115 S. Market St.
419/238-2282

**Years Ago Antique Mall**
108 W. Main St.
419/238-3362

**Heritage Coin & Antique Shop**
119 N. Washington St.
419/238-1671

## 92 WADSWORTH

**Wadsworth Antique Mall**
941 Broad St.
330/336-8620

**Lady Sodbuster Antiques**
121 E. Prospect St.
330/336-5239

**Antique Design**
112 Main St.
330/334-6530

**Country Trader**
6324 Ridge Road
330/239-2104

**William Hromy Antiques**
5958 Ridge Road
330/239-1409

## 93 WAPAKONETA

**Take It from the Top**
24 E. Auglaize St.
419/738-2421

**Antique Vault**
36 E. Auglaize St.
419/738-8711

**Antiques Etc.**
215 E. Auglaize St.
419/739-9382

**Rapunzel's**
115 W. Auglaize St.
419/738-3331

**Auglaize Antique Mall**
116 W. Auglaize St.
419/738-8004

**Brick Place**
202 W. Auglaize St.
419/738-5555

**Ivy Haus**
1321 Bellefontaine St.
419/739-9489

**Log Cabin**
408 S. Blackhoof St.
419/738-7578

**Purple Goose**
11539 Glynwood Road
419/738-7952

## 94 WASHINGTON COURT HOUSE

**Past & Present Memorabilias**
109 E. Court St.
740/333-3222

**This Old House**
427 E. East St.
740/335-8102

**Storage House**
153 S. Hinde St.
740/335-9267

**B & D Collectibles**
143 N. Main St.
740/335-8417

**Midland Mall**
153 S. Main St.
740/636-1071

## 95 WATERVILLE

**American Heritage Antiques**
17 N. 3rd St.
419/878-8355

**Waterville Antique Center**
19 N. 3rd St.
419/878-3006

**K & G Antiques & Etc.**
36 N. 3rd St.
419/878-7778

**Mill Race Antiques**
217 Mechanic St.
419/878-8762

## 96 WAYNESVILLE

Off I-71 at Exit 45, take Route 73 West to Waynesville, then U.S. Route 42 South to Lebanon. Waynesville is known for its antique shops. It is also know for its ghosts; the town's main street has been dubbed "America's Most Haunted." If you visit in October, take the Not-So-Dearly-Departed Tour. One stop will be the Hammel House Inn, where antiques and apparitions converge. If there are ghosts in nearby Lebanon, it's a safe bet they'll be at Pioneer Cemetery, eternal home of Sarah, Elizabeth, Mary, and Ann Harner. According to *Ripley's Believe It or Not*, the four sisters were simultaneously killed by a ball of lightning that came down the chimney of their farmhouse and struck them all, though each was in a different room.

**Highlander House**
22 S. Main St.
513/897-7900

**Remember When Antiques**
43 S. Main St.
513/897-2438

**Miscellany Collection**
49 S. Main St.
513/897-1070

**Bittersweet Antiques**
57 S. Main St.
513/897-4580

**Velvet Bear Antiques**
61 S. Main St.
513/897-0709

**Waynesville Antique Mall**
69 S. Main St.
513/897-6937

**My Wife's Antiques**
77 S. Main St.
513/897-7455

**Little Red Shed Antiques**
85 S. Main St.
513/897-6326

*Ohio*

**Olde Curiosity Shoppe**
88 S. Main St.
513/897-1755

**Baker's Antiques**
98 S. Main St.
513/897-0746

**Golden Pomegranate Antique Mall**
140 S. Main St.
513/897-7400

**Back in the Barn**
239 S. Main St.
513/897-7999

**Tiffany's Treasures**
273 S. Main St.
513/897-0116

**Silver City Mercantile Antiques**
1555 E. State Route 73
513/897-9000

**Cranberry Corner Antiques**
93 S. Main St.
513/897-6919

**Brass Lantern Antiques**
100 S. Main St.
513/897-9686

**Crazy Quilt Antiques**
211 S. Main St.
513/897-8181

**The Rose Cottage**
258 S. Main St.
513/897-1010

**Spencer's Antiques**
274 S. Main St.
513/897-7775

**Allen's Jewelry**
399 S. State St.
614/882-3937

**Mills Antique**
3790 E. Powell Road
614/890-7020

**Nestor's Antiques**
8999 Robinhood Circle
614/882-1939

## 99　WILLOUGHBY

**Somewhere in Time Antiques**
4117 Erie St.
440/975-9409

**Tiffany Rose Antiques**
4075 Erie St.
440/942-2065

**Market Square Antiques**
24 Public Square
440/975-1776

**Friends Antiques**
4119 Erie St.
440/946-1595

**Mr. Willoughby's Antiques**
14 Public Square
440/951-5464

## 97　WEST CHESTER

## Hidden Treasures Antiques

8825 Cincinnati Dayton Road
513/779-9908
Open: Tues.–Sat. 11–7, Sun. 1–6
Directions: I-75 to Cincinnati-Dayton Road. South approximately one half mile to 8825 Cincinnati-Dayton Road.

Located in a large historical home and barn, surrounded by a beautifully landscaped garden, Hidden Treasures Antiques is stacked from floor to ceiling with a fine selection of furniture, artwork, and accessories.

This family owned business prides itself in offering personal service and commitment to its customers as well as providing — you guessed it — "Hidden Treasures!"

**Van Skaik's Antiques**
9355 Cinti Colmbs Road
513/777-6481

**Memory Lane Antiques & Repair**
8872 Cincinnati-Dayton Road
513/777-8565

## 98　WESTERVILLE

**Springhouse Antique Mall**
2 N. State St.
614/882-2354

**Heart's Content Antique Mall**
9 N. State St.
614/891-6050

## 100　WOOSTER

## Norton's Antiques, Etc.

9423 Ashland Road
330/262-6439
Open: Daily by chance or by appointment
Directions: Halfway (10 miles) between Wooster and Ashland on State Route 250 in the village of New Pittsburg.

Inside Norton's Antiques, Etc., there are a host of small possibilities. In fact, Mr. Norton refers to the majority of his stock as a collection of smalls. From "primitives to Depression," his selections are worthy of your attention. He offers pottery, china, figurines, and glassware of all varieties. A wide selection of costume jewelry is also available. Norton's Antiques, Etc., located near Amish country in the village of New Pittsburgh, is an excellent reminder that, very often, good things do come in small packages.

**Uptown/Downtown Antique Mall**
215 W. Liberty St.
330/262-9735

**Green Room II Antiques**
1357 Old Columbus Road
330/264-7071

## 101　YOUNGSTOWN

**Kozak's Antiques & Appraisals**
1328 Elm St.
330/747-2775

**The Joshua Tree**
4059 Hillman Way
330/782-1993

**Now & Then Shoppe**
2618 Mahoning Ave.
330/799-8643

**Thomas E. Marsh Antiques**
914 Franklin Ave.
330/743-8600

**Home Classics**
15 W. McKinley Way
330/757-0423

**Twice-Loved Books**
19 E. Midlothian Blvd.
330/783-2016

**Antique Alley**
104 E. Midlothian Blvd.
330/783-1140

## 102 ZANESVILLE

**Log Hollow**
2825 Chandlersville Road
740/453-2318

**Allies Antiques**
524 Main St.
740/452-2280

**Elaine's Antique & Collectibles Mart**
531 Main St.
740/452-3627

**A Le Clara Belle**
4868 E. Pike Road
740/454-2884

**Christine's Unique Antique Mall**
28 N. 7th St.
614/455-2393

**Corner Cupboard Antiques**
1032 Linden Ave.
740/453-3246

**Olde Towne Antique Mall**
525 Main St.
740/452-1527

**Market St. Gallery**
822 Market St.
740/455-2787

**Seven Gables Antiques**
1570 S. River Road
740/454-1596

# Pennsylvania

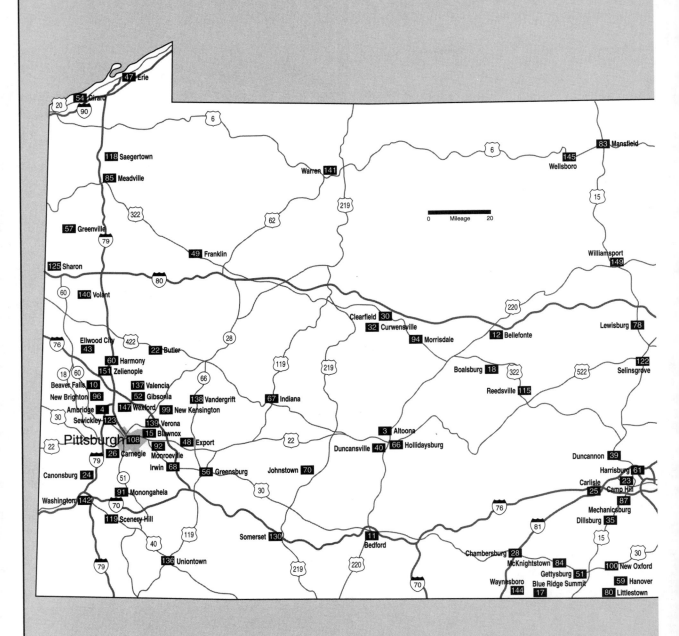

47 Erie

54 Girard
20
90

118 Saegertown

85 Meadville

57 Greenville
79

125 Sharon

60
140 Volant

76 Ellwood City
422
43
60 Harmony
18 60 151 Zelienople
Beaver Falls 10
137 Valencia
New Brighton 96
52 Gibsonia
Ambridge 4 147 Wexford
30 99 New Kensington
Sewickley 123
139 Verona
Pittsburgh 108 15 Blawnox
26 Carnegie 92
48 Export
22 Monroeville
79 Irwin 68
Canonsburg 24 56 Greensburg
51
91 Monongahela
Washington 142
70
119 Scenery Hill

40
119
136 Uniontown
79

6

6

83 Mansfield
145
Wellsboro

15

Warren 141

219

62

49 Franklin

80

Mileage
0        20

220

Clearfield 30
32 Curwensville
94 Morrisdale
12 Bellefonte

Lewisburg 78

28

119

219

66

138 Vandergrift
67 Indiana

3 Altoona
Duncansville 40 66 Hollidaysburg

22

Johnstown 70

30

Somerset 130

11
Bedford

219

220

Williamsport
149

Boalsburg 18
322
Reedsville 115

522

122
Selinsgrove

Duncannon 39
Harrisburg 61
Carlisle 23
25 Camp Hill
87
Mechanicsburg
Dillsburg 35

15

76

81

Chambersburg 28
McKnightstown 84
100 New Oxford
Gettysburg 51
59 Hanover
Waynesboro Blue Ridge Summit 80 Littlestown
144 17

70

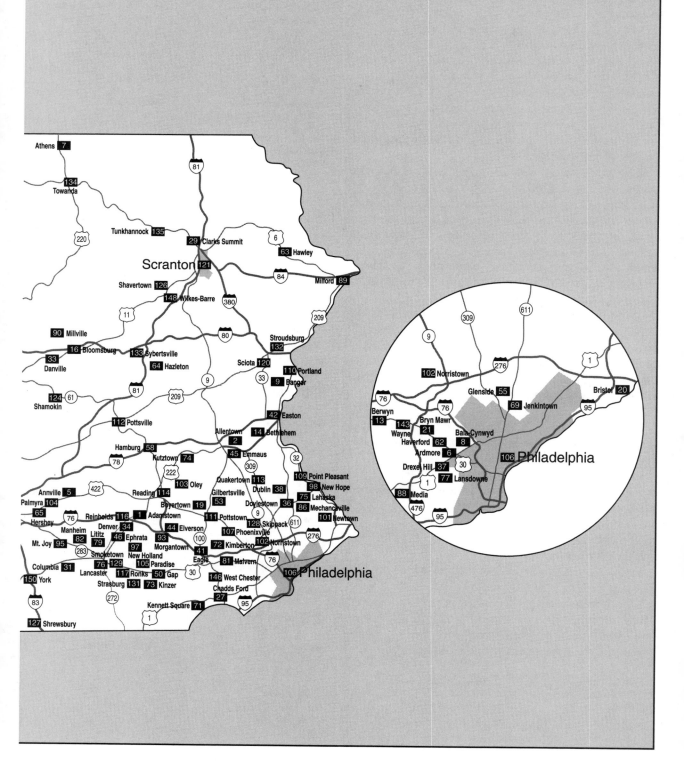

# Pennsylvania

## 1 ADAMSTOWN

What began as a temporary, stop-gap solution to a vacancy problem in a farmer's market has turned into the largest antique destination in the Northeast. Adamstown, Pa., began its reign as "Antiques Capital USA" in the early 1960s when Charles Weik, an antique dealer in the area, began holding flea markets in a place called Shupp's Grove on Sundays.

Shupp's Grove had long been a favorite spot for reunions, picnics, gospel singing, get-togethers and country-western music shows. The antiques offered at that time were excellent examples of Pennsylvania Dutch primitives, and there was already an established tradition of antiques shops in the area that were frequented by the Rockefellers, DuPonts, Barneses and Weygandts.

In the mid-1960s, Terry Heilman, resident manager of the former Renninger's Farmers' Market and himself an antiques collector, spent many of his Sundays at Shupp's. His farmers' market had a serious vacancy problem, so in the fall, when Shupp's Grove usually closed, Heilman began offering inside space at Renninger's to the antique dealers at Shupp's, which was all outdoors. They liked it, and by spring, the dealers wanted to stay. So Renninger's began the transformation from farmers' market to antique mall. Other ideas and things were added, and the idea grew — and grew — and grew.

Literally everything is for sale in what has become the Northeast's leading year-round antiques destination that pours hundreds of thousands of shoppers and visitors into this tiny town of 3,300. The range of objects runs from 18th to 20th century, sold by a true mixed bag of dealers: big firms, little dealers, co-ops, mom-and-pop operations, beginners, pros, you name it — indoor shops, outdoor groves, malls, farms, any and everywhere.

The anchor stores here are the original Renninger's, now called Renninger's Antique and Collector's Market, and the Black Angus Antiques Mall, both having been started over 25 years ago.

Renninger's has several hundred dealers. The Black Angus has 500. Both are open only on Sundays, and both have national reputations and followings.

Then there are the cooperatives, the fairly recent development in the antique world that has brought antiquing from its original "Sundays only" market to a daily retail-like level.

Antiques Alley in Adamstown has some of the best cooperatives on the East Coast, including South Pointe Antiques, General Heath's Antiques, Antiques Showcase at the Black Horse, and Adams Antique Market. Adamstown also has three yearly "Antiques Extravaganza" weekends that draw several thousand more dealers from all over the country. These special events are the last weekend in April, June and September.

**South Pointe Antiques**
Route 272 and Denver Road
717/484-1026

**General Heath's Antiques**
Route 272
717/484-1300

**Adamstown Antique Mall**
94 Lancaster Ave.
717/484-0464

**Greenwood Antique Center**
2455 N. Reading Road
717/335-3377

**Heritage Antique Center**
Route 272
717/484-4646

**Renninger's Antique Market**
Penn. Turnpike, Exit 21, Route 272
717/385-0104

**Stoudt's Black Angus**
Penn. Turnpike, Exit 21, Route 272
717/484-4385

**Oley Valley Architectural Antiques**
2453 N. Reading Road at Route 272
717/484-2191

**Friedman & Timmons Antiques**
Route 272
717/484-0949

**Country French Collection**
Route 272
717/484-0200

**Schupp's Grove**
Route 897 at Willow St.
717/484-4115

### *Great Places to Stay*

## Adamstown Inn Bed & Breakfast

62 W. Main St.
1-800-594-4808

Experience the simple elegance of the Adamstown Inn, a Victorian bed and breakfast resplendent with leaded-glass windows and door, magnificent chestnut woodwork, and Oriental rugs. All four guest rooms are decorated with family heirlooms, handmade quilts, lace curtains, fresh flowers and many distinctive touches which make your stay special.

## 2 ALLENTOWN

**Cottage Crafters**
4636 Broadway
610/366-9222

**Burick's Antiques**
880 N. Graham St.
610/432-8966

**Pete's Used Furniture & Antiques**
231 N. 7th St.
610/433-4481

**Camelot Collectibles & Antiques**
1518 W. Walnut St.
610/433-7744

**Golden Eagle Antiques**
1425 E. Gordon St.
610/432-1223

**Toonerville Junction Antiques**
522 W. Maple St.
610/435-8697

**Abe Ark Antiques**
1115 N. 22nd St.
610/770-1454

## 3 ALTOONA

**Johnny's Used Furniture & Antiques**
501 4th St.
814/944-3423

**T & L's Antiques**
3958 5th Ave.
814/946-5266

**Michelle's Antiques**
1546 Pleasant Valley Blvd.
814/943-6111

# Pennsylvania

## 4 AMBRIDGE

**Tom's Old Country Store**
511 Merchant St.
724/266-7215

**Nello's Taj Mahal**
1415 Merchant St.
724/266-5656

**Attic Attractions**
576 Merchant St.
724/266-3020

## 5 ANNVILLE

**Chris Machmer Antiques**
146 W. Main St.
717/867-4244

**Meadow View Antiques**
Route 322
717/838-9443

## 6 ARDMORE

**En Garde Antiques & Collectibles**
24 W. Lancaster Ave.
610/645-5785

**Daniel Wilson Antiques**
24 E. Lancaster Ave.
610/645-9533

**Ardmore Antiques & Oriental Rugs**
321 W. Lancaster Ave.
610/649-4432

## 7 ATHENS

**J & M Antiques**
122 N. Elmira St.
717/888-0650

### Great Places to Stay

## Failte Inn B&B and Antique Shop

Route 2, Box 323
717/358-3899
Rates: $65–$70
Directions: Highway 220 to the blinking light in the village of Uster, PA. Cross over the Susquehanna River bridge and turn left at end of bridge on SR 1043. Three miles to inn on right. From Towanda: turn left on SR 1043 after crossing James St. Bridge. From Athens: turn right on SR 1043 after crossing Susquehanna River bridge in downtown Athens.

Failte Inn is nestled in the Susquehanna Valley surrounded by the beautiful Endless Mountains of rural Pennsylvania. You can relax in the country atmosphere of rolling farmland, away from the noise of city traffic and the stress of busy lifestyles.

Enjoy the unhurried charm of yesterday in a turn of the century farmhouse decorated in the graceful elegance of the Victorian era. Escape to a quiet, well-stocked library, listen to fine music or play and enjoy the antique baby grand piano. Relax in front of warm fires in the library or parlor on a cold winter's day. Feel the cool mountain breezes beneath the paddle fans on the wide verandas during the lazy days of summer.

Enjoy a full country breakfast served in the elegantly appointed formal dining room or on the screened wraparound verandas overlooking 3 acres of green lawns, apple orchards and beautiful flower gardens (served 8 a.m. to 10 a.m.).

Join the innkeepers for a complimentary wine or brandy, coffee or tea accompanied by cheeses or homemade pastries in the historical, restored speakeasy dating from the days of prohibition.

Failte Inn offers 5 beautifully decorated guest rooms — each with its own private bath; Susan's Room on the ground floor, Catherine's Suite with sitting room, Mama's Room with Jacuzzi tub, Chelsea's Room with king-size bed, and Jennifer's Room, their most-selected room.

The Failte Inn antique shop specializes in glass and furnishings from the Victorian period.

## 8 BALA CYNWYD

**General Ecletic**
159 Bala Ave.
610/667-6677

**Something Beautiful to Buy**
333 Montgomery Ave.
610/667-2969

**Pieces of Tyme**
323 Montgomery Ave.
610/664-2050

## 9 BANGOR

**Tolerico's Antiques & Baseball Cards**
53 Broadway
610/588-5510

**Hartzell's Auction Gallery**
521 Richmond Road
610/588-5831

**Tolerico's Past Present Future**
13 N. Main St.
610/588-6981

**Expressions Thru Glass**
2242 Ridge Road
610/588-1490

## 10 BEAVER FALLS

## Leonard's Antiques & Uniques Mega-Mall

2586 Constitution Blvd.
724/847-2304 or 1-800-443-5052
Web site: leonards.antiqueshopper.com
Email: leonards@timesnet.net
Open: Mon.–Sat. 10–8; Sun. 10–6 (Open 362 days a year, closed Thanksgiving Day, Christmas Day and Easter Sunday, but open until midnight on New Year's Eve!)
Directions: Leonard's is located in the Chippewa Mall at the junction of Route 51 and Route 60, approximately 12 miles from the Ohio state line. From the Penn. Turnpike, take Exit 1A onto Route 60. Take Exit 15 off of Route 60 onto Route 51 at the Chippewa Mall.

Leonard's is the largest antiques mall in western Pennsylvania, with more than 300 dealers all under one roof, covering approximately 68,000 square feet. Inside this enormous mall, there are over a million-and-a-half items! It certainly lives up to its billing as a mega-mall! Of course,

# Pennsylvania

as you would expect in a space this large, they carry everything from pottery to china, primitives to paper, furniture to fine and costume jewelry. And what a great idea — staying open until midnight on New Year's Eve!

**Peggy Smith's Collections**
621 7th Ave.
724/843-2622

**Antique Emporium**
818 7th Ave.
724/847-1919

**Memory Lane Antiques**
456 Constitution Blvd., R 51
724/847-9910

**American & European Antiques**
601 Darlington Road
724/846-1002

## 11　BEDFORD

**Founders Crossing**
100 S. Juliana St.
814/623-9120

**Graystone Galleria**
203 E. Pitt St.
814/623-1768

**Lin's Touch of Elegance**
238 E. Pitt St.
814/623-2673

**Thomas Antiques**
Road 6 Box 21 Cumberland Road
814/623-5574

**Doug's Antiques**
112 N. Richard St.
814/623-7858

## 12　BELLEFONTE

**Times Past Antiques & Collectibles**
141 S. Allegheny St.
814/353-1750

**Hayloft Antiques**
660 Benner Pike
814/355-7588

## 13　BERWYN

**Circa Antiques & Decor**
712 Lancaster Ave.
610/651-8151

**McCoy**
722 W. Lancaster Ave.
610/640-0433

**Deja Vu**
11 Waterloo Ave.
610/296-2737

**And Antiques**
19 Waterloo Ave.
610/644-3659

**Anything & Everything Shop**
36 Waterloo Ave.
610/647-8186

## 14　BETHLEHEM

**C & D Guns, Coins & Antiques**
121 E. Broad St.
610/865-4355

**Sir Pack Rat**
99 W. Broad St.
610/974-8855

**Valley Antiques Gifts & Imports**
729 W. Broad St.
610/865-3880

**Yesterdays Ltd.**
2311 Center St.
610/691-8889

## 15　BLAWNOX

**Cottage Antiques**
231 Freeport Road
724/828-9201

**The Marlene Harris Collection**
238 1/2 Freeport Road
724/828-1245

**Mulberry Antiques**
262 1/2 Freeport Road
724/828-0144

**China Shop**
266 Freeport Road
724/826-8075

**Lotus Gallery**
309 Freeport Road
724/828-7588

**A Child's Heart**
334 Freeport Road
724/826-9192

**Blawnox Antiques**
340 Freeport Road
724/828-2224

**The Building Arts**
340 Freeport Road
724/828-6876

**Maple Hill Antiques & Lighting**
340 Freeport Road
724/826-9226

**Kirk's Antiques**
352 Freeport Road
724/828-7470

**Velvet Swing Antiques**
407 Freeport Road
724/828-4943

**B. Merry Interior Design**
1144 Freeport Road
724/781-6556

## 16　BLOOMSBURG

**Meckley's Books & Collectibles**
36 W. Main St.
570/784-3765

**Red Mill Antiques**
44 Red Mill Road
570/784-7146

**Hoffman's Antiques**
RR 4
570/784-9534

**Liberty Antiques**
RR 4
570/683-5419

## 17　BLUE RIDGE SUMMIT

### Wooden Horse Antiques
717/794-2717 (bus. day phone)
301/241-3460 (evening phone)
Open: By appointment only
Directions: If traveling on I-81, take Exit 3 (Greencastle, Penn./Route 16 East). Proceed east through Waynesboro (8 miles) and then to Blue Ridge Summit (6 miles). Go to the bottom of the mountain after Blue Ridge Summit. Wooden Horse is the third place on the right — there's a sign out front. If traveling Route 15, take the Emmetsburg/Route 140 West exit and proceed into Pennsylvania, where Route 140 West becomes Route 16 West. The shop is approximately 4 miles into Pennsylvania on the left — look for the sign out front.

The folks at Wooden Horse Antiques have been wholesaling to the antique trade for 25 years. They specialize in fancy oak and Victorian furniture and accessories; also country and period furniture and estate contents. Everything is sold in "as is" condition, but these folks look for and offer the "finer" pieces. In a recent conversation with Randy Sutton (the owner), he told me that he has been doing "quite a lot" with the finer circa 1900–1930s mahogany dining room and bedroom furniture. "Mostly ball and claw," he says. "I've also been fortunate to grab some outstanding estates lately." Dealers take note — you never know what might pop up in an estate. My suggestion is to make sure you stop to see Randy when traveling through Pennsylvania.

## 18 BOALSBURG

**Gates Antiques**
805 Boalsburg Pike
814/466-6333

**Serendipity Valley Farms**
122 E. Main St.
814/466-7282

## 19 BOYERTOWN

**Bashful Barn**
1 E. Philadelphia Ave.
610/367-2631

**Castle Hall Antiques**
5 E. Philadelphia Ave.
610/367-6506

**Homestead Antiques**
Route 73
610/367-6502

**Greshville Antiques**
Route 562
610/367-0076

**Boyertown Antiques**
1283 Weisstown Road
610/367-2452

## 20 BRISTOL

**Wilhelmina's**
369 Main St.
215/945-8606

**Another Time Antiques**
307 Mill St.
215/788-3131

**Place**
5 Pond St.
215/785-1494

## 21 BRYN MAWR

**Greentree Antiques**
825 W. Lancaster Ave.
610/526-1841

**Susan P. Vitale Antiques**
835 W. Lancaster Ave.
610/527-5653

**Sandy Demaio Antique Jewelry**
860 W. Lancaster Ave.
610/525-1717

## 22 BUTLER

**Bergbigler New & Used Furniture**
321 Center Ave.
724/287-0865

**Fox's Antiques**
160 Church Road
724/352-4500

**Thomas Antiques Shoppe**
424 S. Jackson St.
724/287-6839

**Ken's Antiques**
1251 Lake Vue Dr.
724/586-7271

**Antiques**
102 N. Main St.
724/282-2899

**William Smith Antiques**
102 N. Main St.
724/282-2899

**Arthur's Gift Shop**
126 N. Main St.
724/282-4000

**Store on Main**
108 S. Main St.
724/283-9923

**Alley Antiques**
125 S. Main St. (Rear)
724/283-6366

**Butler Antiques & Collectibles**
119 E. Wayne St.
724/282-7195

**Step Back in Time**
224 N. Washington St.
724/283-7509

## 23 CAMP HILL

**Rose Marie's Antiques**
2136 Market St.
717/763-8998

**Cordier Antiques**
307 N. 25th St.
717/731-8662

**Collector's World**
6 W. Main St.
717/763-8288

## 24 CANONSBURG

**Canonsburg Antique Mall I**
145 Adams Ave.
412/745-1333

**Houston Antiques**
22 Pike St.
412/745-2928

**Where the Toys Are**
45 W. Pike St.
412/745-4599

**Tri-State Antique Center**
47 W. Pike St.
412/745-9116

**Annabelle's Antiques**
51 W. Pike St.
412/746-5950

**Antique Junction**
2475 Washington Road
412/746-5119

**Route 19 Antique Mall**
2597 Washington Road
412/746-3277

**Canonsburg Antique Mall II**
99 Weavertown Road
412/745-1050

**Whiskey Run Antiques**
849 S. Washington Road
412/745-5808

## 25 CARLISLE

**Antiques by James L. Price**
831 Alexander Spring Road
717/243-0501

**Antiques on Hanover**
17 N. Hanover St.
717/249-6285

**Country Heritage**
24 N. Hanover St.
717/249-2600

**H & R Jewelry & Antiques**
33 N. Hanover St.
717/258-4024

**Baker's Antiques**
34 N. Hanover St.
717/258-1383

**Downtown Antiques**
152 N. Hanover St.
717/249-0395

**Northgate Antique Mall**
725th Hanover Manor #726N
717/243-5802

**Old Stone Tavern Antiques**
2408 Walnut Bottom Road
717/243-6304

# Pennsylvania

**The Antique Quilt Source**
385 Springview Road #D
717/245-2054

**Linden Hall Antiques**
211 Old Stonehouse Road
717/249-1978

## 26 CARNEGIE

**Heidelberg Antiques**
1451 Collier Ave.
724/429-9223

**Black Swan Art & Frame Gallery**
301 E. Main St.
724/276-3337

## 27 CHADDS FORD

### Olde Ridge Village Antique Shoppes
Route 202 & Ridge Road
610/459-0960
Open: Daily 10–5, 10–8 Thurs.
Directions: Route 202 & Ridge Road one mile south of Route 1. Traveling on Interstate 95 in the Wilmington, Del., area, take the Wilmington/West Chester Exit 8 north on Route 202. After crossing the PA border, travel two miles to the shop on the left. Coming from the PA Turnpike, take Exton Exit 23 south on Route 100. Exit onto Route 202 South and cross Route 1 (the shop is on the right one mile down).

Olde Ridge is a cooperative antique shop which is part of a twenty-store village of individually owned small shops and restaurants. Located in Pennsylvania's historic Chadds Ford, the shop is a 12-room, turn-of-the-century farmhouse filled with two floors of antiques and collectibles from about a dozen dealers. Displayed in room settings with country, Victorian and '30s–'40s furnishings, the shop also offers a number of showcases holding incredible antiques and collectibles. China, glassware, advertising and children's items are just a few of the specialities.

**Village Peddler**
Baltimore Pike
610/388-2828

**Diane's Antiques**
RR 1
610/388-3956

**Pennsbury Chadds Ford Antique**
RR 1
610/388-6480

**Frances Lantz Antique Shop**
Route 202 & State Line Road
610/459-4080

**Hillcrest Antiques**
31 E. Slate Hill Road
717/249-1987

**Heidelberg Antiques**
1550 Collier Ave.
724/429-9222

**Antique Reflections**
170 Fairville Road
610/388-0645

**Jane's Antiques**
RR 1
610/388-6730

**Aaron Goebel's Antiques**
Route 202 & Pyle Road
610/459-8555

**Wendy's Corner Antiques**
210 Wilmington W.
610/358-4077

**Joanne Rollins Antiques**
Pennsbury Chadds Ford
610/388-0959

**Antique Mall**
640 Baltimore Pike
610/388-1620

## 28 CHAMBERSBURG

**House of the Gabler**
71 N. Main St.
717/263-2202

## 29 CLARKS SUMMIT

### Carriage Barn Antiques
1550 Fairview Road
570/587-5405
Open: Mon.–Sun. 10–5
Directions: Off I-81 take Exit 59 and follow the signs.

Located in a beautifully restored barn, Carriage Barn Antiques is the largest antique store in northeastern Pennsylvania. Quality refinished furniture and unusual accent pieces. Featured in *Country Living Magazine*.

**Hawley Antiques Exchange**
Route 6
570/226-1711

## 30 CLEARFIELD

### Christopher Kratzer House Bed & Breakfast
101 E. Cherry St.
814/765-5024 or 1-888-252-2632
Open: Year round
Rates $55–$70
Directions: Traveling I-80: Take Exit 19 and follow the signs to Clearfield (322W). Turn left at the light before the Nichol Street bridge onto Front Street (Route 153 South). Continue along the river past Pine, Locust and Market Streets to the corner of Front and Cherry, across from the park and church.

This old (pre-1840) Greek Revival house is decorated with an eclectic mix of contemporary and antique pieces, artistically intermingled by innkeepers Bruce and Ginny Baggett. Bruce is a musician and Ginny is a printmaker, and the interior of the house reflects not only their interest in preserving history, but also their interests in art and music. Bruce has a collection of musical instruments and memorabilia of his more than 30 years in show business; he even entertains guests with songs at the piano in the music room! Ginny has filled the house with original artwork for sale and has installed an art gallery on the second floor.

**Brandywine River Antiques**
878 Baltimore Pike
610/388-2000

**Gateway Gallery**
643 Kriner Road
717/263-6512

**Heritage House Shoppes**
402 N. State St.
570/586-8575

# Pennsylvania

This is the oldest house in Clearfield, built by Christopher Kratzer, a noted lumberman, carpenter, architect, politician, and owner of the county's first newspaper. It is located in the Old Town Historic District and predates the Victorian era in which most of the other homes were built. The home overlooks the Susquehanna River and Witmer Park, and is within easy walking distance of shops, the public library, restaurants, a movie theater and the Clearfield County Historical Museum.

Guests have a choice of four rooms, two with views of the river and park, one with mahogany twin beds, the other with an antique queen-size spool bed. There is an upstairs sitting room that converts to a bedroom, and an additional bedroom with a private bath.

**Carousel Antiques**
404 W. 7th Ave.
814/765-8518

**Winter Barn Antiques**
Susquehanna Bridge Road
814/765-5248

## 31 COLUMBIA

**Restorations, Etc.**
125 Bank Ave.
717/684-5454

**C.A. Herr Annex**
35 N. 3rd St.
717/684-7850

**Partners Antique Center**
403 N. 3rd St.
717/684-5364

## 32 CURWENSVILLE

**Errigo's**
848 State St.
814/236-3403

## 33 DANVILLE

**Cloverleaf Barn Antiques**
120 McCracken Road
570/275-8838

**Rising Sun Antiques**
6 Mill St.
570/275-1776

**Wispy Willows**
419 Mill St.
570/275-1658

**Fleming Antiques & Lamps**
1609 Montour Blvd.
570/275-2081

## 34 DENVER

**Antique Showcase at Black Horse**
2222 N. Reading Road
570/336-3864

**Adams Antique & Cllbls. Market**
Route 272/2400 N. Reading Road
570/335-3116

**Heritage II**
Route 272
570/336-0888

**Covered Bridge Antiques**
Route 272
570/336-4480

**Lancaster County Antiques & Collectibles**
Route 272
570/336-2701

**Exit 21 Antiques & Collectibles**
Route 272
570/336-7482

**Adamstown Antique Gallery**
2000 N. Reading Road
570/335-3435

**J. S. Maxwell Jr./Virginia Caputo**
2350 N. Reading Road (Route 272)
570/336-2185

**Renninger's Antique Market**
Route 272
570/336-2177

**Lancaster County Antique Market**
2255 N. Reading Road
570/336-2701

## 35 DILLSBURG

**B & J Antique Mall**
14 Franklin Church Road
717/432-7353

## 36 DOYLESTOWN

**New Britain Antiques**
326 W. Butler Ave.
215/345-7282

**Nejad Gallery Fine Oriental Rugs**
1 N. Main St.
215/348-1255

**Y-Knot Shop**
New Galena Road & Route 313
215/249-9120

**Doylestown Antique Center**
3687 Old Easton Road
215/345-9277

**Renaissance Furnishings**
635 N. Main St.
215/348-3455

## 37 DREXEL HILL

**Brandywine House Antiques**
1201 Cornell Ave.
610/449-5208

**Spring House Antiques**
4213 Woodland Ave.
610/623-8898

## 38 DUBLIN

**Kramer's Rainbow Rooms**
104 Middle Road
215/249-1916

**Barr's Auction & Antique World**
2152 N. Reading Road
570/336-2861

**Shupp's Grove**
1686 Dry Tavern Road
570/484-4115

**Consignment Galleries**
470 Clemens Town Center
215/348-5244

**Dragon's Den of Antiques**
135 S. Main St.
215/345-8666

**Frog Pond**
128 W. State St.
215/348-3425

**Orchard Hill Collection**
4445 Lois Lane
215/230-7771

**Fields Antique Jewelers**
Landsdowne & Windsor Ave.
610/853-2740

**Ardmart Antique Village**
802 N. Lansdowne Ave.
610/789-6622

# Pennsylvania

## 39 DUNCANNON

### Old Sled Works
722 N. Market St.
717/834-9333
Open: Wed.–Sun. 10–5
Directions: Old Sled Works is located 1 mile off Route 11 and 15 or off Routes 22 and 322. The Works is approximately 15 miles northwest of Harrisburg.

Tradition and good family memories can often be the motivating factors in our lives as we ponder the age-old question of "What do I want to do when I grow up?" These factors were precisely the motivation behind Jimmy Rosen's Old Sled Works, an enormous, old, family-owned factory building in Duncannon, Penn., that now houses an antique mall, crafts center, sled museum, penny arcade, and soda fountain.

Flash back, if you will, to Jimmy's childhood (he's in his early 30s now). He grew up around the old factory, which his father owned, only then it was Standard Novelty Works. The factory produced not only wooden novelties like porch gates and swings, snow scooters, and sink protectors, but it also housed the Lightning Guider Sled Factory, which manufactured sleds — hundreds of thousands of sleds — from 1904 to 1988. In its heyday, the factory was one of the busiest and best-known makers of children's sleds in the country, turning out 1,600 to 1,800 sleds a day during the 1920s and 1930s, but the whole factory closed in 1990, a victim of high-tech toys and shopping malls.

So the Rosen family was left with an empty factory, but Jimmy could not accept its demise. As his drive, ambition and memories went into high gear, an idea began to emerge. Duncannon had lots of traffic — it's near Routes 11, 15 and 322 — but it was not tourist mecca, and it didn't have an established market for anything. Rosen had to create a draw for his town, and he chose antiques. But not just any antiques store or mall would do; this is where childhood memories kicked in.

In Jimmy's words, "I wanted to distinguish this [business] from most other antique malls in central Pennsylvania. Even though I'm set up in a historic old sled factory with over 125 great antique and craft vendors, I wanted something more for my customers. As a kid, I fondly remember playing in the arcades during my family's vacations in Miami Beach. Also, we lived close to Hershey Park, which I frequented. I would dream about having my own arcade and how great it would be to have a key to each machine so you could collect all the coins or play for free as many times as you wanted. Guys would think you were cool, and the girls would swoon, I suppose. Obviously, it was just a dream back then. However, when I opened the Old Sled Works, I had some extra space so I thought, 'This is the time and place for my arcade.' I wanted only electro-mechanical machines, like those I remember, and since most of my customers are roughly 35 to 64, I knew many would remember these older machines, too, and would be thrilled to relive their childhoods."

The old soda fountain isn't a museum, at least not in the "look but don't touch or use" sense. Everything works just fine, and on weekends everyone crowds the fountain to get some old-fashioned ice cream goodies, like fountain drinks, banana splits, malts, and milk shakes — oh yes, and to listen to the 1950s music from the old jukebox.

The complete soda fountain runs along the wall facing the games; counter, stools, freezers, ice cream dispensers, a life-sized soda jerk in full costume, signs, advertising, everything was lifted straight from the original setup. A small seating area forms an alcove at the end of the fountain counter complete with vintage 1950s furniture of chrome, vinyl and glass table tops.

The Old Sled Museum is a link between time past and time present. Jimmy wanted folks to know the history of the old factory building, which was a town landmark for nearly a century, so he put together exhibits covering the factory's 85 years. He has sleds displayed from each decade of operation, old catalogs and other advertising pieces, patent and trademark papers, tools, early printing and stenciling equipment and the original sled factory time clock. Many of the museum pieces are owned by the Old Sled Works, but several local collectors have donated or loaned items to the museum, including a valuable watch fob, sled advertising thermometer, and miscellaneous paper advertising. In 1992, the building became a registered historic site in Pennsylvania and now boasts a blue and gold marker on the grounds.

**Cove Barn**
10 Kinsey Road
717/834-4088

**Leonard's Antique Co-op**
1631 State Road
717/957-3536

**Peggy's Antique Shop**
2205 State Road
717/834-9379

## 40 DUNCANSVILLE

**Duncansville Antique Depot**
1401 2nd Ave.
814/696-4000

**Dodson's Antique Shop**
614 3rd Ave.
814/695-1901

**Creekside Antiques**
1031 3rd Ave.
814/695-5520

**Black Kermit**
1032 3rd Ave.
814/695-5909

**David Donnelly Antiques**
1224 3rd Ave.
814/695-5942

**Don's Antiques**
1324 3rd Ave.
814/696-0807

# *Pennsylvania*

## 41 EAGLE

### Little Bit Country
Route 100
(across from historic Eagle Tavern)
610/458-0363
Open: Mon.–Fri. 10–5; Sat. 11–7; Sun. 12–6
Directions: Little Bit Country is located just north, approximately 1 ½ miles, of the Pennsylvania Turnpike Exit 23, along Route 100 North.

This interesting shop, with a name that sounds suspiciously like a hit country song, carries a selection of antiques and primitives that varies. They also handle fabrics and gifts.

## 42 EASTON

**Dylan Spencer Antiques**
200 Northampton St.
610/252-6766

**Brick House Antiques**
1116 Northampton St.
610/515-8010

**Barry's New & Used Furniture**
500 Northampton St.
610/250-0220

**Eagle's Nest Antiques**
1717 Butler St.
610/258-4092

## 43 ELLWOOD CITY

**Marketplace on Main**
402 Lawrence Ave.
724/752-1201

**Gramma's House**
326 6th St.
724/758-4262

**Into Antiques**
RR 1
724/758-5127

## 44 ELVERSON

**Rosalind Lee's Antiques**
S. Chestnut St.
610/286-9869

**Chamberlain Antiques**
3601 Saint Peters Road
610/469-0894

**Tom E. Fisher**
11 E. Main St.
610/286-6618

## 45 EMMAUS

**Twin Jugs Consignments**
4033 Chestnut St.
610/967-4010

**The Tin Shop**
161 E. Main St.
(Macungie) No Phone

**Sweet Memories & Tea Room**
180 Main St.
610/967-0296

## 46 EPHRATA

Located in picturesque and well-known Lancaster County, home of the Pennsylvania Dutch, Mennonite and Amish communities, Ephrata was actually settled in 1732 by a German religious society under the leadership of Johann Beissel. The men and women formed the Society of the Solitary Brethren, a semimonastic order advocating celibacy and favoring common ownership of property, although neither marriage nor private ownership was prohibited. By 1740 the self-sufficient community consisted of 36 brethren and 35 sisters housed in a single building known as the Cloisters. At the height of its prosperity, the community numbered about 300 members. The hymns and experimental melodies of founder Johann Beissel that were published here were a major influence on American hymnology.

After Beissel's death in 1768, John Miller became the head of the community and was commissioned by the U.S. Congress to translate the Declaration of Independence into several European languages. In 1745 the second printing press in Pennsylvania was set up in Ephrata, and Continental money was printed there during the British occupation of Philadelphia. After the battle of Brandywine in 1777, the community buildings were used as hospitals. The Society of the Solitary Brethren declined after Miller's death, and today the Cloisters are maintained as a museum by the Pennsylvania Historical and Museum Commission.

Also today, the Route 272 corridor between Ephrata and Adamstown (in the vicinity of Exit 21 on the Pennsylvania Turnpike) is widely known as a flea market haven. Actually called "The Adamstown Antique Mile," it began as a strip of restaurants and motels easily accessible to the turnpike. This area is also the home of Pepperidge Farms, Inc.

**Summer House Antiques**
1156 W. Main St., Route 322
717/733-8989

**Goods Collectibles**
2460 W. Main St.
717/738-2033

**Grandma's Attic**
1862 W. Main St.
717/733-7158

**Antiques at Ephrata**
1749 W. Main St.
717/738-4818

**Olde Carriage House**
2425 W. Main St.
717/738-2033

**Mother Tucker's Antiques**
566 N. Reading Road
717/738-1297

**Three T's Antiques**
Route 272 South at 322
717/733-6572

**Clay House**
2465 W. Main St.
717/721-9400

# Pennsylvania

*Great Places to Stay*

## The Inns at Doneckers

318-324 N. State St.

717/738-9502

Open: Year-round except Christmas

Rates: $59–$185

Directions: From the Penn. Turnpike, take Exit 21 and take Route 222 South to the Ephrata exit. Turn right onto Route 322, which becomes Main Street in Ephrata. Go to the 4th traffic light and turn right onto State Street. The inns are about four blocks on the left.

There are four individual inn properties surrounding the Doneckers community here in Ephrata, each within walking distance of Doneckers Fashion Stores for the family and home, and a gourmet restaurant. Also within walking distance in the community is an artworks complex of more than 30 studios and galleries of fine art, quilts and designer crafts, and a farmer's markets. If that is not enough for you, the inns are just minutes from Adamstown's antique markets, a short scenic drive from Lancaster County's Amish farmland and attractions, and are convenient for a day trip to historic Gettysburg.

The four inns together offer 40 rooms (38 with private baths), each one furnished in antiques and hand-stenciled walls, and some rooms have fireplaces and Jacuzzis. Guests get to choose among the Guesthouse, the Historic 1777 House, the Homestead, and the Gerhart House.

### *A sampling of what you'll find at the Inns at Doneckers:*

## 1777 House at Doneckers

This late Georgian-style home, which takes its name from the year of its construction, was built by Jacob Gorgas, a clockmaker in the religious Ephrata Cloister community located in Lancaster County in 1777. Later, the house served as a tavern for travelers in Conestoga wagons on their way from Philadelphia to Pittsburgh. The house has been carefully restored, and the original stone masonry, tile flooring and many other authentic architectural details have been saved.

There are 12 guest rooms in this inn (some with fireplaces), all named for brothers and sisters of the Cloister. The adjacent Carriage House offers an additional two suites with lofts.

## The Guesthouse at Doneckers

Three turn-of-the-century Victorian homes have been artfully joined together to create the Guesthouse at Doneckers, offering 19 uniquely appointed rooms and suites. Fine antiques from Mr. Donecker's personal collection are used throughout the Guesthouse, as well as hand-stenciled walls and antique hooked rugs as art. A cheerful sunroom for relaxing has been added to complement the exisiting parlor, which is centrally located and used for games, reading and television viewing. Suites include a fireplace and/or oversized whirlpool bath for added luxury. Each room includes a private phone and air conditioning. Original Victorian features of the home have been retained, including inlaid wood floors and stained glass windows.

## The Homestead at Doneckers

Once the residence of the senior Mr. & Mrs. Donecker, this stately home has been restored to four charming suites and rooms, each with mini-refrigerator, remote-control cable color television, a fireplace and/or oversized whirlpool bath. Family antiques and local textiles have been used throughout the inn. The Homestead is a nonsmoking inn.

## The Gerhart House

Built in 1926 by local builder Alexander Gerhart, the home features the superior construction methods for which Gerhart was known: inlaid pine floors, frosted, beveled or stained glass and native chestnut doors and trim. The five rooms are perfect for a group to share, with a cozy living room as a shared common area. Many family reunions, getaways among friends, and small retreats have been hosted at the Gerhart House.

## 47   ERIE

**Antique Attractions**
202 E. 10th St.
814/459-0277

**Folly Antique Mall & Guns**
654 W. 26th St.
814/459-2503

**Dempsey & Baxter**
1009 E. 38th St.
814/825-6381

**Erie Antique Store**
1015 State St.
814/454-6256

**A Toy Collector**
1041 W. 31st St.
814/868-0592

**Antiques by Walker House**
1945 W. 26th St.
814/459-0880

**B. T. Antique Gallery**
400 Mill Creek Mall
814/866-8892

**Drumm's Toys & Antiques**
1012 Holland St.
814/455-5257

**Lee's Antiques**
601 W. 17th St.
814/455-9461

**Rage**
613 W. 26th St.
814/456-9931

**Antique Interiors by Dennis Pistone**
1209 State St.
814/455-6992

**Sherif's Imported Rugs**
3854 Peach St.
814/864-6460

**Dennis Pistone Antiques**
1207 State St.
814/454-1510

**Antique Buyer's Gallery**
411 E. 10th St.
814/898-1671

**Collector's Choice**
3421 W. Lake Road
814/838-6833

**Collector's Corner**
3020 Buffalo Road
814/899-5102

**Fine Antiques & Art by Linda**
1648 W. 8th St.
814/459-5927

**Tregler Gallery**
301 Cascade St.
814/454-0315

# Pennsylvania

## 48 EXPORT

### Schmidt's Springhouse Antiques
Route 66 at Pfeffer Road
724/325-2577 or 1-800-771-2684
Open: Tues.–Sat. 10–5, Sun. 1–5, closed Christmas, Thanksgiving, Easter
Directions: Located on the west side of Route 66, 5 miles north of Route 22 and 1 ½ miles south of Route 366.

A true Pennsylvania antiquing experience, Schmidt's Springhouse Antiques, owned by Betty and Ed Schmidt, is dedicated to providing a large variety of ready-to-display quality antique furniture, country, primitives, Empire, Victorian, oak and depression. Open since 1993, the shop provides 6,000 square feet and is expanding to over 10,000 square feet.

## 49 FRANKLIN

**Franklin Antique Mall & Auction**
1280 Franklin Ave.
814/432-8577

**Every Thing**
1335 Liberty St.
814/432-4460

**Knotty Pine Antiques**
304 2nd Ave.
814/432-4193

**Buttermilk Hill Antiques**
Buttermilk Hill
814/432-5691

**Haylett's**
338 Grant St.
814/432-5686

**Angus Antiques**
1581 Pittsburgh Road
814/432-3325

**Debence Downstairs Mall**
1261 Liberty St.
814/437-6550

## 50 GAP

**Mechanical Musical Memories**
5281 Lincoln Hwy.
717/442-8508

**Gap Village Store**
5403 Lincoln Hwy.
717/442-5263

## 51 GETTYSBURG

Don't ever accuse Southerners of being obsessive about the War Between the States, because there are probably not any folks more immersed in that era than the residents of Gettysburg, Pa.

There are probably only a handful of Americans who don't know something about this landmark battle of the American Civil War. It took place in July of 1863, and was the turning point of the war and the beginning of the end for the Confederacy. Here, General Robert E. Lee's Confederate army of 75,000 men and the 97,000-man Union army of General George G. Meade met — by chance — when a Confederate brigade, sent to the area for supplies, observed a forward column of Meade's cavalry.

Of the more than 2,000 land engagements of the Civil War, Gettysburg remains the single greatest battle of the war. It left us with names forever connected to battle: Seminary Ridge, Cemetery Ridge, Pickett's Charge. After the battle 51,000 casualties were counted, making Gettysburg the bloodiest battle of American history. Although the war raged for another two terrible and savage years, the Confederacy never recovered from the losses at Gettysburg, and Lee never again attempted an offensive operation of such proportions. The tide had turned at Gettysburg.

### T.T. & G.'s Antique Collectible Co-op
2031 York Road
717/334-0361
Open: Mon.–Sat. 9–4:30; Sun. 12–4:30
Directions: Located on U.S. 30, 7 miles west of New Oxford Square and 3 miles east of Gettysburg Square, on the south side of the highway.

T.T. & G.'s is 6,500 square feet of space in an old barn with 25 or more regular dealers. They carry everything from late 19th-century Victorian pieces (like Eastlake) to modern. They no longer operate an upholstery shop, but are opening a reproduction room for accessories and furniture. The wood types they handle include oak, mahogany, walnut and pine.

**Time Travel Antiques**
312 Baltimore St.
717/337-0011

**Antique & Collectibles & Curio Shop**
22 Carlisle St.
No phone listed

**Arrow Horse**
51 Chambersburg St.
717/337-2899

**Gettysburg Antiques & Collectibles**
54 Chambersburg St.
717/337-0432

**Keystone Country Furniture**
2904 Emmitsburg Road
717/337-3952

**Hope Springs Antiques**
2540 Mummasburg Road
717/677-4695

**Magic Town**
49 Steinwehr Ave.
717/337-0492

**Farnsworth House Inn**
401 Baltimore St.
717/334-8838

**Mel's Antiques & Collectibles**
103 Carlisle St.
717/334-9387

**Maggie's Another Place & Time**
52 Chambersburg St.
717/334-0325

**School House Antiques**
2523 Emmitsburg Road
717/334-4564

**Antique Center of Gettysburg**
7 Lincoln Square
717/337-3669

**Great Stuff**
45-47 Stienwehr Ave.
717/337-0442

**Fields of Glory**
55 York St.
717/337-2837

**Antiques & Collectibles Curio Shop**
22 Carlisle St.
No phone listed

## Great Places to Stay

### The Brafferton Inn
44 York St.
717/337-3423
Web site: www.bbhost.com/braffertoninn

In the historic town of Gettysburg the Brafferton Inn is one of its gracious landmarks. The elegant 1786 fieldstone home, listed on the National Registry of Historic Places, has been fully restored to include a private bath for each of the ten guest rooms. Featured in *Country Living,* the inn has exquisite antiques and original artistry throughout.

### Brickhouse Inn
452 Baltimore St.
1-800-864-3464
Web site: www.brickhouseinn.com

Located in Gettysburg's downtown historic district, guests of the Brickhouse Inn enjoy the comforts of today's living in a style reminiscent of the turn of the century. Throughout the 1898 brick home, family heirlooms and selected antiques combine Victorian grace with modern amenities. Superb hospitality, bountiful breakfasts, exceptional guest comfort and attention to detail are only the beginning of an unforgettable visit to this historic town.

### James Gettys Hotel
27 Chambersburg St.
717/337-1334

In 1787, the founder of Gettysburg, James Gettys, sold his first piece of land to John Troxell, Sr. In 1804, a tavern called Sing of the Buck was opened to accomodate those traveling to the western frontier of Pennsylvania and beyond. This structure has served as an inn, tavern or hotel for almost 200 years, and was used as a hospital for the wounded soldiers during the Battle of Gettysburg. In 1888, the third and fourth floors were added to accomodate the veterans as they returned to Gettysburg for the 25th anniversary of the battle. From 1888 to the late 1930s, the hotel could accommodate 250 guests a night. The hotel was later used as an apartment building and also as a youth hostel. In 1995, the building changed ownership to reopen as the James Gettys Hotel in September 1996. The building has had nine different names during its 193 years of existence and today each suite is named after a previous business or person who played a significant role in the hotel's history. The hotel offers 11 tastefully appointed suites, each with sitting area, kitchenette, bedroom, private bath, and all the comforts of home.

## 52 GIBSONIA

**Atlantic Crossing Antiques**
3748 Gibsonia Road
724/443-5858

**Allagheny Antiques**
5500 Molnar Drive
724/443-6425

**Jim's Antiques**
Route 8
724/443-4866

**Richland Antiques**
Route 8
724/443-8090

## 53 GILBERTSVILLE

**Shafer's Antiques**
1573 E. Philadelphia
610/369-1999

**Sutterby's Oak Furniture**
Zern's Market - Route 73
610/369-1777

## 54 GIRARD

**What Not Shop**
18 Main St.
814/774-4413

**Westaway's Antiques**
21 Myrtle St.
814/774-2829

**Heartland Antiques & Gifts**
10100 Old Ridge Road
814/774-0344

## 55 GLENSIDE

**Ludwig's Scattered Treasures**
221 W. Glenside Ave.
215/887-0512

**Kirkland & Kirkland**
Keswick Ave.
215/576-7771

**Yesterday and Today**
280 Keswick Ave.
215/572-6926

## 56 GREENSBURG

**J.A. Henderson Blacksmith, Inc.**
509 S. Main St.
724/838-7656

**Antique Treasures**
Route 22
724/837-4474

## 57 GREENVILLE

**Iron Bridge Shoppe**
108 Main St.
724/588-2455

**Country Store**
220 W. Methodist Road
724/588-9692

**Country Store**
133 Orangeville Road
724/588-5820

**J-Net Antiques & Gifts**
42 Shenango St.
724/588-6361

## 58 HAMBURG

**F & F Shop**
1 N. 4th St.
610/562-7687

## 59 HANOVER

**Nagengast Antiques**
37 Frederick St.
717/633-1148

## 60 HARMONY

**In Harmony**
250 Mercer St.
724/452-0203

**Olde Country House**
575 Perry Hwy.
724/452-0100

**Bee Four Collectibles**
Route 19 N.
724/452-0922

**J. Fox Antiques**
333 Perry Hwy.
724/452-4323

**Into Antiques**
280 Perry Hwy.
724/452-3210

**Finders Keepers**
657 Perry Hwy.
724/452-9960

**Bear Bottom Antiques**
Main St.
724/452-5270

## 61 HARRISBURG

**Antiques at Towne House Gallery**
242 North St.
717/238-4199

**Crafty Generations**
Strawberry Square
717/234-5521

**Doehnes Ox Box Shop**
N. Progress Ave.
717/545-7930

**Medina**
901 N. 2nd St.
717/233-0115

## 62 HAVERFORD

**Mock Fox**
15 Haverford Station Road
610/642-4990

**Chelsea House, Ltd.**
45 Haverford Station Road
610/896-5554

**French Corner Antiques**
16 Haverford Station Road
610/642-6867

**McClee's Galleries**
343 W. Lancaster
610/642-1661

## 63 HAWLEY

Natural resources have played an important part in the history of Hawley. The community was first inhabited in the late 18th century by pioneers who liked the potential of this area where three creeks converged. They settled, built a sawmill, and began sending lumber down the rivers to Philadelphia. The first child of the settlement was born in 1812; the first store opened in 1827; the Delaware & Hudson Canal, running from Honesdale to New York, was completed in 1828, and anthracite coal began moving on barges along towpaths through Hawley to the New York markets.

The area around Hawley saw great prosperity from the 1840s to the 1860s, with the economy continuing to be based around the coal industry to support businesses. In the 1920s, industries began to supplant Hawley's coal and lumber base, including fine cut glass, and silk and textile mills.

Another growth cycle began in 1925 with the introduction of hydroelectric power. The Pennsylvania Power & Light Company dammed the Wallenpaupack Creek and created the state's largest man-made lake, thus changing the focus of the area's industry. The Hawley region became an area of recreational and related business opportunities and continues in this field today.

**Timely Treasures**
475 Welwood Ave. (Route 6)
570/226-2838
Web site: www.timelytreasures.com
Open: Thurs.–Mon. 10–5, closed Tues. and Wed.

During the late 1800s, the building which now houses Timely Treasures was the town power plant. From this building power was made available to the residents of Hawley who chose to have electricity in their homes. An appropriate site for housing wonderful antiques, the shop has six rooms of antiques from the turn of the century through the 1950s. Their speciality is furniture (1850–1950s), but the owners also provide a nice selection of cut glass from the brilliant period, china, lamps, pottery (Roseville) and more.

**Castle Antiques & Reproductions**
515 Welwood Ave.
1-800-345-1667
Open: Mon.–Sat. 8:30–5
Directions: Hawley is located between Scranton and Milford, about 45 minutes from Scranton and about 30 minutes from Milford. *From Scranton:* Take 84E to Exit 6, go left onto Route 507. Go to the end, make a left onto Route 6, and go 1 1/2 miles. Castle Antiques is on the right. *From New York state or Milford, Pa.:* Take 84W to Pa. Exit 8 (Blooming Grove). Make a right onto Route 402. Go 5 miles to the end, make a left onto Route 6, and go 5 miles. Castle Antiques is on the right.

You really cannot miss this shop — it looks like a castle! Very appropriately named, Castle Antiques & Reproductions is housed in the historic landmark known as Sherman Mill. It was constructed in 1880 and is the largest bluestone granite building in North America.

The original water-powered mill sits in the picturesque Pocono Mountains, and the unusual stone architecture gives it the appearance of a castle. It was last purchased in 1989 and has undergone extensive renovations to return it to its original beauty. Now it offers 35,000 square feet of showroom space filled with treasures from around the world.

Some of the merchandise shoppers will find at the "Castle" includes American and imported furniture, lighting fixtures, statuary, bronzes, Tiffany-style lamps, and general merchandise, both old and new.

# Pennsylvania

**Barbara's Books & Antiques**
730 Hudson St.
570/226-9021

**Hawley Antique Center**
318 Main Ave.
570/226-8990

**Loft Antiques**
RR 590
570/685-4267

## 64  HAZLETON

**Remember When**
2 E. Broad St.
570/454-8465

**AAA Antiques**
163 Edgerock Dr.
570/455-8331

## 65  HERSHEY

**Canal Collectibles**
22 W. Canal St.
717/566-6940

**Ziegler's Antique Mall**
825 Cocoa Ave.
717/533-7990

### *Great Places to Stay*

## The Hen-Apple Bed & Breakfast

409 S. Lingle Ave.
717/838-8282
Open: Year-round
Rates: $55–$65
Directions: For specific directions to the Hen-Apple Bed & Breakfast, please call ahead. The innkeepers will provide excellent directions from your location.

A visit to the Hen-Apple is a chance to really enjoy the simple pleasures of country living. This bed and breakfast is a circa-1825 Georgian-style farmhouse situated on an acre of land on the edge of town. A "down home" atmosphere prevails, from the antique and reproduction furnishings to the full country breakfast. There are six guest rooms, all with private baths, plus three common rooms, a screened-in back porch, a front porch and a wicker room for guests to enjoy. Or take a stroll among the stand of old fruit trees, or snooze in the hammock or lawn chairs and play with the resident cat. And if and when you feel like exerting yourself, you'll be only minutes away from Hershey, Harrisburg, Gettysburg, Ephrata, Reading, antiques galore, auctions, crafts shops, Amish country, the Mt. Hope Winery, and so on and so on.

**Antiques & Collectibles**
202 Main Ave.
570/226-9524

**Decorators Den & Resale**
RR 6
570/226-0440

**Mariano's Furniture & Gifts**
1042 N. Church St.
570/455-0397

**Cocoa Curio Historical Militaria**
546 W. Chocolate Ave.
717/533-1167

## 66  HOLLIDAYSBURG

**Remember When**
1414 Allegheny St.
814/696-4638

**Burkholder's Antique Shop**
Route 22
814/695-1030

## 67  INDIANA

**Kemp's Old Mill Antique Shop**
Route 286 N. Box 170
724/463-0644

**Denise's Log Cabin Antique Mall**
Old Route 119 N. & 110
724/349-4001

## 68  IRWIN

## Antiques Odds & Ends

508 Lincoln Hwy. E., Route 30
724/863-9769
Open: Daily 11–5:30
Directions: Antiques Odds & Ends is located 1/2 mile off Pennsylvania Turnpike Exit 7 on Route 30 East

Antiques Odds & Ends is a husband-and-wife business. Vince and his wife have been partners for 27 years and were the "first in the state to open up an all-in-one antique shop." (I'm quoting Vince here, so figure this one out on your own.)

I've never personally met Vince, but he and I had a rather nice long chat (over the phone) about the antiques business. When he told me he had been in the "biz" for 27 years, I just had to pick his brain for some tips. This man has an incredible knowledge of antiques! We went on to discuss how sometimes it's very difficult to locate antique shops since most do not advertise. With a chuckle, Vince offered this very clever piece of advice: "A place of business with no sign, is a sign of no business."

Vince, thanks and here's your sign!

> ## Antiques Odds & Ends
> 3 large buildings covering 8,000 square feet
> Showcasing glassware, toys, clocks, lamps, primitives and more!
> One of the largest malls in the area.

**May's Antiques**
624 Main St.
724/863-1840

**Victoria's Looking Glass**
624 Main St.
724/863-1868

**Attic Treasures**
Route 993
724/863-0338

## 69  JENKINTOWN

**Hidden Treasure**
400 Leedom St.
215/887-4150

**Jeffrey Caesar Antiques**
214 Old York Road
215/572-6040

**Jenkintown Antique Guild**
208 York Road
215/576-5044

## 70 JOHNSTOWN

**Seven Gables Gifts & Antiques**
1404 Dwight Dr.
814/266-7117

**Curiosity Corner**
570 Grove Ave.
814/535-5210

**Greenwoods Antiques & Gifts**
3549 Menoher Blvd.
814/255-5057

**Always Antiques**
125 Truman Blvd.
814/539-0543

**Aardvark Antiques**
7 Bond St.
814/539-0185

## 71 KENNETT SQUARE

**Garrett Longwood**
864 S. Baltimore Pike Road
610/444-5257

**McLiman's**
806 W. Cypress St.
610/444-3876

**Clifton Mill Shoppes**
162 Old Kennett Road
610/444-5234

**Antiquus**
120 W. State St.
610/444-9892

**Kennett Square Jewelers**
123 W. State St.
610/444-5595

## 72 KIMBERTON

**Kimber Hall**
Hares Hill Road
610/933-8100

**Corner Cupboard Antiques**
Kimberton Road
610/933-9700

**Thorum's Antiques**
Prizer Road
610/935-3351

## 73 KINZER

### Old Kinzer Firehouse Antiques

3576 Lincoln Hwy. E. (U.S. Route 30)
717/442-1977 or 410/323-0445
Email: OKFrhsANTQ@aol.com

2,000-square-foot shop specializing in Mission and Victorian furnishings.

## 74 KUTZTOWN

### Greenwich Mills Antiques

1097 Krumsville Road
610/683-7866
Open: Weekends and by appointment
Directions: 2 ½ miles north of Kutztown along Route 737. Between Kutztown and I-78 (Exit 12).

Greenwich Mills Antiques, located in an old 1860s stone grist mill, is filled with local country furniture, primitives, textiles, art and collectibles. (One of my favorite places to shop.)

**Renninger's Antiques & Collectibles**
Noble St.
610/683-6848

**Louise's Old Things**
163 W. Main St.
610/683-8370

**Baver's Antiques**
232 W. Main St.
610/683-5045

**Bruce M. Moyer & Karen**
276 W. Main St.
610/683-9212

**Colonial Shop**
224 W. Main St.
610/683-3744

## 75 LAHASKA

**Oaklawn Metalcraft Shop**
5752 Route 202
215/794-7387

**Pickets Post**
5761 Route 202
215/794-7350

**Darby-Barrett Antiques**
5799 Route 202
215/794-8277

**Choate & Von Z.**
Route 202
215/794-8695

**Lahaska Antique Courte**
5788 York Road
215/794-7884

**Pfeifer Antiques**
5806 Route 202 York Road
215/794-7333

## 76 LANCASTER

**Chris's Buy & Sell**
201 W. King St.
717/291-9133

**Book Haven**
146 N. Prince St.
717/393-0920

**Pondora's Antiques**
2014 Old Philadelphia Pike
717/299-5305

**Olde Towne Interiors, Inc.**
224 W. Orange St.
717/394-6482

## 77 LANSDOWNE

**Good Old Days Antiques**
201 E. Plumstead Ave.
610/622-2688

**Clock Services**
2255 Garret Road
610/284-2600

**Ye Olde Thrift Shoppe**
213 W. Baltimore Ave.
610/623-3179

**Before Our Time Antiques**
54 W Marshall Road
610/259-6370

# Pennsylvania

**Ardmart Antique Mall**
State & Landsdowne
610/789-6622

**Attic Door**
8904 W. Chester Pike
610/446-6690

**Ann's Antiques & Curios**
213 W. Baltimore Pike
610/623-3179

## 78 LEWISBURG

**Lewis Keister Antiques**
209 Market St.
570/523-3945

**Brookpark Farms Antiques**
RR 45 W.
570/523-6555

**Lewisburg Roller Mills Marketplace**
517 Saint Mary St.
570/524-5733

## 79 LITITZ

**The Workshop**
945 Disston View Drive
717/626-6031

**House of Unusuals**
55 E. Main St.
717/626-7474

**Sylvan B. Brandt**
651 E. Main St.
717/626-4520

**Brickerville Antiques & Decoys**
117 N.E. 28th Diivisi Dr.
717/627-2464

## 80 LITTLESTOWN

**Second Chance Antiques**
4895 Baltimore Pike
717/359-4038

**Grandma Whitman's Country Cupboard**
40 N. Queen St.
717/359-4527

## 81 MALVERN

**Conestoga Antiques**
30 Conestoga Road
610/647-6627

**Nesting Feathers**
218 E. King St.
610/408-9377

**Henry Gerlach Jewelers**
414 S. State Road
610/449-7600

**Spring House Antiques**
4213 Woodland Ave.
610/623-8898

**Route 15 Flea Market**
Route 15
570/568-8080

**Victorian Lady**
RR 45 W.
570/523-8090

**Thomas K. Peper Antiques**
Stein Lane
570/523-8080

**Hardican Antiques**
34 E. Main St.
717/627-4603

**Garthoeffner Antiques**
122 E. Main St.
717/627-7998

**1857 Barn**
Route 322 & Route 501
717/626-5115

**Heritage Map Museum**
55 N. Water St.
717/626-5002

**Betty & Jack's Antiques**
31 W. King St.
717/359-4809

**King and Queen Antiques**
1 S. Queen St.
717/359-7953

**King Street Traders**
16 E. King St.
610/296-8818

**Station House Antiques Ltd.**
1 W. King St.
610/647-5193

**Steven's Antiques**
627 Lancaster Ave.
610/644-8282

## 82 MANHEIM

**Noll's Antiques**
1047 S. Colebrook Road
717/898-8677

**Exit 20 Antiques**
3091 Lebanon Road
717/665-5008

**Conestoga Auction Co., Inc.**
768 Graystone Road
717/898-7284

**Country Store Antiques & Museum**
60 W. Main St.
717/664-0022

## 83 MANSFIELD

**Country Trader**
9 N. Main St.
570/662-2309

**Mansfield Antique Shop**
763 S. Main St.
570/662-3624

**Tin Goose Gift Shop**
14 S. Main St.
570/662-3950

**Main St. Antiques Co-op**
17 N. Main St.
570/662-2444

**Times Remembered**
Route 6 W.
570/662-3474

## 84 McKNIGHTSTOWN

**Country Escape Bed & Breakfast**
275 Old Route 30
717/338-0611
Open: Year-round
Rates: $65–$80
Directions: From the square in Gettysburg, drive west on Route 30.
When you are 5 ⁴/₁₀ miles from the square, turn left at the small
McKnightstown sign onto Old Route 30. Country Escape is the last
house on the right in McKnightstown, just past the old post office.

As innkeeper Merry Bush describes it, this is a "laid back" bed and
breakfast. Her idea is to get people to relax and enjoy themselves and the
beautiful surroundings, but she does offer desktop publishing and faxing
services for you "type A" personalities who just can't unwind!

Country Escape offers queen-size beds and all the comforts of home
"amid the bucolic setting complete with mountain vistas and flower
gardens." After you've refreshed yourself with a good night's sleep and a
hearty breakfast, you can browse through the eclectic gift shop at the
inn, soak in the hot tub, or explore the many battle sites all around the
inn. The inn is located on the road where Confederate forces marched to
the battle of Gettysburg.

# Pennsylvania

## 85 MEADVILLE

**Troyer's Antiques**
Baldwin St. Extension
814/724-4036

**Marcia's Mercantile**
9006 Mercer Pike
814/724-8131

**Unger's Antique Shop**
1197 Pennsylvania
814/336-4262

**Artist's Gallery**
245 Chestnut St.
814/336-2792

**Pine Antique Shop**
988 Park Ave.
814/336-2466

**Tamarack Treasures**
Springs Road
814/333-2927

## 86 MECHANICSVILLE

**Buck House Antiques**
3336 Durham Road
215/794-8054

**Howard Szmolko Antique Shop**
5728 Mechanicsville Road
215/794-8115

## 87 MECHANICSBURG

**Alexander's Antiques**
6620 Carlisle Pike
717/766-5165

**Veronique's Antiques**
124 S. Market St.
717/697-4924

**White Barn Antiques**
973 W. Trindle Road
717/766-8727

**Dave & Annie Brown Antiques**
24 Hogestown Road
717/697-6880

**Rose's Odds & Ends**
123 E. Main St.
717/766-5017

**Mitrani & Company**
6 State St.
717/766-8367

**Country Gifts "n" Such**
5145 E. Trindle Road
717/697-3555

## 88 MEDIA

**Hometown Collection**
212 W. Baltimore Pike
610/565-9627

**Remember When Antiques**
21 W. State
610/566-7411

**Atelier**
36 W. State
610/566-6909

**Fitzgerald Group**
220 W. Baltimore Ave.
610/566-0703

**Antique Exchange of Media**
23 W. State
610/891-9992

## 89 MILFORD

**Ann East Gallery**
109 E. Ann St.
570/296-5166

**Schouppe's Antiques**
100 Bennett Ave.
570/296-6243

**AAA Quality Antiques**
100 Bennett Ave.
570/296-6243

**Forrest Hall Antique Center**
Broad & Hartford
570/296-4893

**Antiques of Milford**
216 Broad St.
717/296-4258

**Pear Alley Antiques**
220 Broad St.
717/296-8919

**Clockworks**
319 Broad St.
717/296-5236

**Pieces of Time**
Route 663 & Allentown Road
215/536-3135

**Judy's Antiques**
220 Broad St.
717/296-8626

**Elizabeth Restucci's Antiques**
214 Broad St.
717/296-2118

**110 East Catharine St.**
110 E. Catharine St.
717/296-4288

**Milford Antiques**
Route 663
215/536-9115

## 90 MILLVILLE

**Down on the Farm**
RR 1
570/458-4956

**Gay Fisk Ann Antiques**
Route 42
570/458-5131

**Cat's Pajamas Vintage Clothing**
Route 42
570/458-5233

## 91 MONONGAHELA

**Longwell House**
711 W. Main St.
724/258-3536

**Collectiques**
808 W. Main St.
724/258-4773

**Main Street Antiques**
800 W. Main St.
724/258-3560

## 92 MONROEVILLE

**Flowers in the Attic**
4713 Northern Pike
724/856-7001

## 93 MORGANTOWN

**Cinnamon Stick**
W. Main St.
610/286-7763

**Antique Collection**
238 W. Main St.
610/286-5244

**Treasure Hill**
W. Main St. Route 23
610/286-7119

**Morgantown Antique Center**
325 W. Main St.
610/286-8981

## 94 MORRISDALE

**Chris' Collectibles**
Allport Cut-off Road 1
814/342-3482

# Pennsylvania

## 95 MOUNT JOY

**White Horses Antique Market**
973 W. Main St.
717/653-6338

### Great Places to Stay

**Hillside Farm Bed & Breakfast**
607 Eby Chiques Road
717/653-6697
Email: hillside3@juno.com
Web site: www2.epix.net/~bblanco/hillside.htm/
Open: Year-round
Rates $60–$75
Directions: Traveling Route 283, take Salunga Exit. Turn right onto Spooky Nook Road and go 1¼ miles to Eby Chiques Road. Turn right and travel ¼ mile to Hillside. Hillside Farm is the first place on the right.

Everything about this charming bed and breakfast is a tribute to the farming area and all the bed and breakfast's immediate neighbors — dairy farms! Hillside Farm B&B is housed in an old (circa-1863) farmhouse, surrounded by an old barn and outbuildings; however, today's owners do not farm and have no farm animals except the barn cats. But they are surrounded by one of the largest areas of farmland left in Lancaster County, which is why it is so peaceful here.

Just a half mile down the road is one of the many Amish farms that dot the area, and a one-room schoolhouse. Innkeepers Deb and Gary Lintner can even arrange for guests to eat dinner with an Amish family (with advance reservations) and to see a modern milking at one of the other neighboring farms.

The B&B's "bottle theme" evolved from this dairy history and by an accidental discovery some few years ago. While Gary was cleaning some brush off a bank behind the barn, he noticed something shiny in the ground. Looking closer he discovered 21 unbroken antique milk bottles from different local dairies, most of which stopped operating in the late 1940s. These bottles are now displayed in the dining room.

Along with the bottles, Hillside is furnished with traditional furniture and other dairy antiques. The farmhouse is a 2½-story brick home featuring a standard design of four main rooms on each floor; although over the years, that design has been modified. Now the second floor features bedrooms, each with a view of the surrounding farmland. There are five guest rooms, three with private baths, and a hot tub for six on the porch.

Guests get a full breakfast, afternoon snacks, recommendations for dinner, and directions to all the antique shops and malls in the area! Then they can come back to the inn and relax on the balcony that overlooks Chiques Creek with a view of the mill dam and an old generator house. They can listen to the owls, bullfrogs and cows and watch rabbits, squirrels and woodchucks play in the yard and drift off to sleep with the sounds of nature and the country singing their own special lullaby.

## 96 NEW BRIGHTON

**Todd Antiques Plus**
920 3rd Ave.
724/847-0840

**Capo Furniture**
928 3rd Ave.
724/846-0721

**Pennypackers**
1010 3rd Ave.
724/843-3336

**Past and Presents**
1301 3rd Ave.
724/847-3006

**Our Barn Shoppe**
539 Harmony Road
724/847-9100

## 97 NEW HOLLAND

**Frank Cabanas Antiques**
1453 Division Hwy.
717/354-6564

**School House Antiques**
Main St. Route 23
717/455-7384

**Stew Country**
Route 322
717/354-7343

## 98 NEW HOPE

**Pink House**
W. Bridge St.
215/862-5947

**Hobensack & Keller**
57 W. Bridge St.
215/862-2406

**Bridge Street Old Books**
129 W. Bridge St.
215/862-0615

**Ferry Hill**
15 W. Ferry St.
215/862-5335

**Katy Kane, Inc.**
34 W. Ferry St.
215/862-5873

**Don Roberts Antiques**
38 W. Ferry St.
215/862-2702

**Kennedy Antiques**
6154 Lower York Road
215/794-8840

**Lehmann Antiques**
6154 Lower York Road
215/794-7724

**James Raymond & Co.**
6319 Lower York Road
215/862-9751

**Francis J. Purcell II**
88 N. Main St.
215/862-9100

**Crown & Eagle Antiques, Inc.**
Route 202
215/794-7972

**Gardner's Antiques**
Route 202
215/794-8616

**Ingham Springs Antique Center**
Route 202
215/862-0818

**Olde Hope Antiques**
Route 202
215/862-5055

**Hall and Winter**
429 York Road
215/862-0831

**Cockamamie's**
9A W. Bridge St.
215/862-5454

# *Pennsylvania*

## *Great Places To Stay*

### Pineapple Hill Bed & Breakfast

1324 River Road
215/862-1790 or 215/862-5273
Email: www.pineapplehill.com
Directions: For specific directions from your location, please call the innkeepers.

Enjoy the charm of a beautifully restored Colonial manor house built in 1790. Set on almost 6 acres, this Bucks County bed and breakfast rests between New Hope's center and Washington Crossing Park.

In the 1700s it was customary to place a pineapple on your front porch as a way of letting friends and neighbors know you were welcoming guests. Pineapple Hill continues this tradition by offering the same hospitality to their guests.

The 18-inch walls and original woodwork at the historically registered Pineapple Hill exemplify a craftsmanship long forgotten. On the grounds, the ruins of a stone barn enclose a beautiful hand-tiled pool.

Breakfast at Pineapple Hill is always the treat. A full gourmet breakfast is skillfully prepared and served in the common room each morning. Breakfast is served from 8–10 at individual candlelit tables. This room is available to use at your leisure — to watch a movie, read a book, or just curl up on a chilly evening in front of the fireplace.

Each of the spacious guest rooms is individually furnished with locally obtained antiques, collectibles, and original artwork. For your reading pleasure, all rooms are well stocked with books and magazines. Three of the guest rooms are accompanied by a separate living room with comfortable furnishings and cable televisions. Located on the second and third floors of the inn, all guest rooms at Pineapple Hill feature private baths for your comfort and convenience.

Pineapple Hill is located deep in the heart of antiquing territory, where treasure hunting at the local shops, auctions and flea markets is readily available. There are also art galleries, theater and speciality shops all nearby.

## 99 NEW KENSINGTON

**Jolar, Inc.**
879 5th Ave.
724/339-4766

**Bill's Antiques**
1152 7th St.
412/339-0559

**Gifts International**
2517 Leechburg Road
724/339-7075

**Howard F. Gordon Antiques**
3049 Bair Road
412/335-7164

## 100 NEW OXFORD

**Hart's Country Antiques**
2 Carlisle St.
717/624-7842

**Sarah's Antiques**
109 Carlisle St.
717/624-9664

**Rife Antiques**
4415 York Road
717/624-2546

**Center Square Antiques**
16 Center Square
717/624-3444

**Collectors Choice Antique Gallery**
330 W. Golden Lane
717/624-3440

**Storms Antiques & Collectibles**
1030 Kohler Mill Road
717/624-8112

**Bill's Old Toys**
19 Lincoln Way E.
717/624-4069

**Stonehouse**
100 Lincoln Way E
717/624-3755

**Lau's Antiques**
112 Lincoln Way E.
717/624-4972

**Remember When Shop**
4 Lincoln Way W.
717/624-2426

**Betty & Gene's Antiques**
110 Lincoln Way W.
717/624-4437

**New Oxford Antique Center**
333 Lincoln Way W.
717/624-7787

**Conewago Creek Forks**
1255 Oxford Road
717/624-4786

**Black Shutter Shoppes**
4335 York Road
717/624-8766

**Week's Antiques**
4335 York Road
717/624-7979

## 101 NEWTOWN

**Nostalgia Nook**
591 Durham Road
215/598-8837

**Temora Farm Antiques**
372 Swamp Road
215/860-2742

**Fountainview Antiques 'n' Things**
10 Center Square
717/624-9394

**New Oxford Antique Mall**
214 W. Golden Lane
717/624-3703

**Willow Way Enterprises**
390 Gun Club
717/624-4920

**Adam's Apple**
3 Lincoln Way
717/624-3488

**Keh'r Corner Cupboard**
20 Lincoln Way E.
717/624-3054

**Heartland Antiques & Gifts**
111 Lincoln Way E.
717/624-9686

**America's Past Antiques**
114 Lincoln Way E.
717/624-7830

**Oxford Hall Irish Too**
106 Lincoln Way W.
717/624-2337

**Oxford Barn**
330 Lincoln Way W.
717/624-4160

**Barry Click Antiques**
145 Newchester Road
717/624-3185

**Golden Lane Antique Gallery**
11 N. Water St.
717/624-3800

**Corner Cupboard**
4335 York Road
717/624-4242

**Hanging Lamp Antiques**
140 N. State St.
215/968-2015

**Miller & Co.**
15 S. State St.
215/968-8880

# Pennsylvania

## 102 NORRISTOWN

**Auntie Q's**
403 W. Marshall St.
610/279-8002

**Stephen Arena Antiques**
2118 W. Main St.
610/631-9100

## 103 OLEY

**Shadow Brook Farm Antiques**
Road 2, Box 17C
610/987-3349

**Oley Valley General Store**
Route 73
610/987-9858

## 104 PALMYRA

**Lenny's Antiques & Collectibles**
31 N. Railroad St.
717/838-4660

## 105 PARADISE

**Spring Hollow Antiques**
121 Mount Pleasant Road
717/687-6171

### *Great Places to Stay*

### Creekside Inn B&B
44 Leacock Road
717/687-0333
Web site: www.thecreeksideinn.com

This 1781 stone house is centrally located in the heart of Lancaster County and Amish country, peacefully situated on 2 acres along the Pequea Creek. From the porch, you can listen to the sounds of horse and buggy passing by as you retire from a busy day of antique shopping and sightseeing. A wide variety of dining choices are nearby, and the innkeepers can also arrange for you to have dinner in an Amish home.

The inn offers relaxing air-conditioned guest quarters appointed with antiques and Amish quilts. There are four second-floor rooms and a first floor suite, all with private in-room baths. Two of the bedrooms have working stone fireplaces. The warm and welcoming living room with its stone fireplace, or the lattice-enclosed porch with rockers, offer guests a chance to socialize and enjoy this countryside inn.

A full country breakfast, featuring home-baked treats, local Amish dishes, Lancaster County meats and farm fresh eggs and milk, is served each morning at 8:30 in the two dining rooms. After breakfast the innkeepers can help you plan your day and offer advice on how to see the "Undiscovered Lancaster County." This is a nonsmoking inn. Visa, MasterCard, Discover and personal checks are accepted. They can only accommodate children over 12 and they cannot accommodate pets.

Other nearby attractions include: Adamstown ("Antiques Capital of the USA"), 10 miles; Longwood Gardens, 30 miles; Hershey, 40 miles; and Gettysburg, 55 miles.

## 106 PHILADELPHIA

### Stoneman of the Delaware
Box 15309
215/322-1470

Stoneman of the Delaware is located in the Lambertville Antique Market in Lambertville, N.J. See listing under Lambertville, N.J., #37. When traveling in Philadelphia, you may reach Michael Barnes at the above number.

**Garden Gate Antiques**
8139 Germantown Ave.
215/248-5190

**Antiques at the Secret Garden**
12 E. Hartwell Lane
215/247-8550

**Watson 20th-Century Antiques**
307 Arch St.
215/923-2565

**Castor Furniture**
6441 Castor Ave.
215/535-1500

**Blum Chestnut Hill Antiques**
45 E. Chestnut Hill Ave.
215/242-8877

**Washington Square Gallery**
221 Chestnut St.
215/923-8873

**Schwarz Gallery**
1806 Chestnut St.
215/563-4887

**Stuart's Stamps**
1103 Cottman Ave.
215/335-0950

**David David Gallery**
260 S. 18th St.
215/735-2922

**McCarty Antiques**
7101 Emlen St.
215/247-5220

**Tyler's Antiques**
5249 Germantown Ave.
215/844-9272

**Chandlee & Bewick**
7811 Germantown Ave.
215/242-0375

**Porch Cellar**
7928 Germantown Ave.
215/247-1952

**Small's Antique Market**
7928 Germantown Ave.
215/247-1953

**Antique Gallery**
8523 Germantown Ave.
215/248-1700

**Harvey Wedeen Antiques**
8720 Germantown Ave.
215/242-1155

**Philadelphia Antique Center**
126 Leverington Ave.
215/487-3467

**Niederkorn Antique Silver**
2005 Locust St.
215/567-2606

**Antique Marketplace Manayunk**
3797 Main St.
215/482-4499

**Ida's Treasures & Gifts**
4388 Main St.
215/482-7060

**Bob Berman Mission Oak**
4456 Main St.
215/482-8667

**Philadelphia Trading Post**
4025-35 Market St.
215/222-1680

**Calderwood Gallery**
4111 Pechin St.
215/509-6644

**Ad Lib Antiques & Interiors**
918 Pine St.
215/627-5358

**Classic Antiques**
922 Pine St.
215/629-0211

**M. Finkel & Daughter**
936 Pine St.
215/627-7797

**G.B. Schaffer Antiques**
1014 Pine St.
215/923-2263

**Belle Epoque Antiques**
1029 Pine St.
215/351-5383

**Schaffer Antiques Since 1906**
1032 Pine St.
215/923-2949

**Sorger & Schwartz Antiques**
1108 Pine St.
215/627-5259

**Southwood House**
1732 Pine St.
215/545-4076

**Lock's Philadelphia Gun Exchange**
6700 Roland Ave.
215/332-6225

**Architectural Antiques Exchange**
715 N. 2nd St.
215/922-3669

**Hampton Court**
6th St. at Lombard
215/925-5321

**Den of Antiquities**
618 S. 6th St.
215/592-8610

**Charles Neri**
313 South St.
215/923-6669

**Mode Moderne**
111 N. 3rd St.
215/923-8536

**Calderwood Gallery**
1427 Walnut St.
215/568-7475

**Urban Artifacts**
4700 Wissachickon Ave.
215/844-8330

**Reese's Antiques**
930 Pine St.
215/922-0796

**Antiques & Interiors**
1010 Pine St.
215/925-8600

**Antique Design**
1016 Pine St.
215/629-1812

**Jeffrey L. Biber**
1030 Pine St.
215/574-3633

**First Loyalty**
1036 Pine St.
215/592-1670

**Kohn & Kohn**
1112 Pine St.
215/627-3909

**Keith's Antiques Ltd.**
7979 Rockwell Ave.
215/342-6556

**Classic Lighting Emporium**
62 N. 2nd St.
215/625-9552

**Scarlet's Closet**
261 S. 17th St.
215/546-4020

**Antiquarian's Delight**
615 S. 6th St.
215/592-0256

**Bob's Old Attic**
6916 Torresdale Ave.
215/624-6382

**Celebration Antiques**
416 South St.
215/627-0962

**Moderne Gallery**
159 N. 3rd St.
215/627-0299

**Eberhardt's Antiques**
2010 Walnut St.
215/568-1877

**Lumiere**
112 N. Third St.
215/922-6908

*Great Places to Stay*

**Ten Eleven Clinton**
1011 Clinton St.
215/923-8144
Email: 1011@concentric.net
Rates: $115–$175

Ten Eleven Clinton is an all-apartment bed and breakfast housed in an 1836 Federal-period townhouse in the heart of Philadelphia's historic, cultural and business districts. All the apartments have private baths and queen-size beds, and most have working fireplaces. Breakfast is served to each room and there is a flower-lined courtyard for guests to relax in in the summer.

Although the inn is located on a quiet residential street, guests will find themselves only a five-minute walk from the historic district and Independence Hall, the antique and jewelry districts, Chinatown, the Italian Market, South Street and the Academy of Music, just to name a few. Just a 10- to 15-minute walk brings guests to Penn's Landing Waterfront, the ferry to the New Jersey State Aquarium and Sony Entertainment Center, Rittenhouse Square, Center City shopping district and major department stores. Other area sites and attractions are only a short cab ride away.

## 107 PHOENIXVILLE

**Scioli's Antiques**
235 Bridge St.
610/935-0118

**Karl's Korner**
843 Valley Forge Road
610/935-1251

**Somogyi Antiques**
129 Route 113
610/933-5717

**Bridge Antiques Shop**
234 Bridge St.
610/917-9898

## 108 PITTSBURGH

**Dargate Galleries**
5607 Baum Blvd.
724/362-3558

**Etna Antiques**
343 Butler St.
724/782-0102

**Arsenal Antiques**
3803 Butler St.
724/681-3002

**Yesterday's News**
1405 E. Carson St.
724/431-1712

**Antique Gallery**
1713 E. Carson St.
724/481-9999

**Jess This 'n' That**
139 Brownsville Road
724/381-1140

**Lawrenceville Antiques**
3533 Butler St.
724/683-4471

**Antiques on North Canal**
1202 N. Canal St.
724/781-2710

**Antique Parlor**
1406 E Carson St.
724/381-1412

**Andtiques**
1829 E. Carson St.
724/381-2250

# Pennsylvania

**Make Mine Country**
190 Castle Shannon Blvd.
724/344-4141

**Mark Evers Antiques**
4951 Centre Ave.
724/633-9990

**Caliban Book Shop**
410 S. Craig St.
724/681-9111

**Antiques on Ellsworth**
5817 Ellsworth Ave.
724/363-7188

**Merryvale Antiques**
5865 Ellsworth Ave.
724/661-3200

**Crown Antiques & Collectibles**
1018 5th Ave.
724/422-7995

**Cottage Antiques**
231 Freeport Road
724/828-9201

**Four Winds Gallery, Inc.**
1 Oxford Center (Level 3)
724/355-0998

**Demetrius**
1420 W. Liberty Ave.
724/341-9768

**Southbery Antiques**
5179 Library Road
724/835-4750

**Tucker's Books**
2236 Murray Ave.
724/521-0249

**Classiques**
6014 Penn Circle S.
724/361-5885

**So Rare Galleries**
701 Smithfield St.
724/281-5150

**Edgewood Station Antiques**
101 E. Swissvale Ave.
724/242-6603

**Antique Prints**
5413B Walnut St.
724/682-6681

**Antiques of Shadyside**
5529 Walnut St.
724/621-4455

**Pittsburgh Antique Mall**
1116 Castle Shannon Blvd.
724/561-6331

**East End Galleries**
600 Clyde St.
724/682-6331

**B's South Park Antique Mall**
5710 Curry Road
724/653-9919

**Eons**
5850 Ellsworth Ave.
724/361-3368

**Kozloff & Meaders**
5883 Ellsworth Ave.
724/661-9339

**Crimes of Fashion**
4628 Forbes Ave.
724/682-7010

**Avenue Furniture Exchange**
6600 Hamilton Ave.
724/441-8538

**Joy's Antique & Estate Jewelry**
Clark Bldg./717 Liberty Ave.
724/261-5697

**Antique Exchange**
2938 W. Liberty Ave.
724/341-7107

**North Hills Antiques**
1039 McKnight Road
724/367-9975

**Aunt Nettie's Attic**
2010 Noble St.
724/351-2688

**Interior Accents**
6015 Penn Circle S.
724/362-4511

**Old Steuben Village**
6181 Steubenville Pike
724/787-8585

**Antiques Plus**
104 Swissvale Ave.
724/247-1016

**Four Winds Gallery, Inc.**
5512 Walnut St.
724/682-5092

**Angie's Antique Center**
701 Washington Road
724/343-5503

**Mastracci's Antiques**
802 Wenzell Ave.
724/561-8855

## 109 POINT PLEASANT

**Jacques M. Cornillon**
56 Byram Road
215/297-5854

**1807 House**
4962 River Road
215/297-0599

## 110 PORTLAND

**Long Ago Antiques**
Delaware Ave.
570/897-0407

**Graystone Collectiques**
511 Deleware Ave.
570/897-7170

## 111 POTTSTOWN

**Shaner's Antiques & Collectibles**
403 N. Charlotte St.
610/326-0165

**St. Peter's General Store**
Saint Peters Road
610/469-1000

## 112 POTTSVILLE

**Dave & Julie's Then & Now**
16 N. Centre St.
570/628-2838

**Bernie's Antiques**
313 W. Market St.
570/622-7747

## 113 QUAKERTOWN

**Allegheny City Stalls**
940 Western Ave.
724/323-8830

**River Run Antiques**
River Road (166)
215/297-5303

**Portland Antiques & Collectibles**
Delaware Ave.
570/897-0129

**Bill's Carpet Shop**
1359 Farmington Ave.
610/323-9210

**Curious Goods**
556 N. Centre St.
570/622-2173

## Quakertown Heirlooms

141 E. Broad St.
215/536-9088
Jim & Linda Roth, Owners
Open: Daily 10–5, Fri. til 7, closed Sun.
Directions: From the PA Turnpike: Quakertown Exit Route 663 North to 313 East about 1 ¹/₂ miles. One block after railroad tracks on left corner. From I-78: Route 309 South to 313 East. Same as above.

Quakertown Heirlooms is an eclectic antique consortium featuring antiques, classic furniture, elegant glass, primitives, collectibles, treasured tomes, and nostalgia. Visa/MasterCard/personal checks accepted.

# Pennsylvania

**Trolley House Emporium**
108 E. Broad St.
215/538-7733

**Curio Corner**
200 E. Broad St.
215/536-4547

**Quaker Antique Mall**
70 Tollgate Road
215/538-9445

**Grandpa's Treasures**
137 E. Broad St.
215/536-5066

**Pat & Louis Curiosity Shop**
513 W. End Blvd.
215/536-8248

## 114 READING

**Ray's Antiques & Refinishing**
401 N. 5th St.
610/373-2907

**Search Ends Here Antiques**
RR 6
610/777-2442

**Alternative Furnishing Antiques**
3728 Lancaster Pike
610/796-2990

**White's Store Front**
304 N. 5th St.
610/374-8128

**Weaver's Antique Mall**
3730 Lancaster Pike
610/777-8535

**Berks County Antique Center**
Route 222
610/777-5355

**Memories**
622 Penn Ave.
610/374-4480

## 115 REEDSVILLE

**Old Woolen Mill Antiques**
RR 1
717/667-2173

**Dairy Land Antique Center**
Route 665
717/667-9093

## 116 REINHOLDS

**General Heath's Antiques**
Route 272/Seoudeburg Road
717/484-1300

**Clock Tower Antiques**
Cocalico Road
717/484-2757

### *Great Places to Stay*

## Brownstone Corner B&B

590 Galen Hall Road
717/484-4460 or 1-800-239-9902
Directions: For specific directions from your location, please call the innkeepers.

Located in northeastern Lancaster County, Brownstone Corner is situated on seven acres amid the farms and old German towns of the "Pennsylvania Dutch."

The so-called Pennsylvania Dutch are not Dutch at all, but are the descendants of German (Deutsch) Mennonite and Amish settlers who emigrated here in the 1700s.

It was one of these descendants who, between 1759 and 1790, built the present three-story brownstone structure.

Today, this unique house still maintains its original Colonial charm. Inside, the wide-plank wooden floors, lofty windows, and family antique furnishings create a warm, cozy feeling.

The house is sheltered by large, age-old sycamore trees, and the property is surrounded by mature blue spruce and fir trees which afford the guests the privacy they deserve.

Guests are invited to relax in the comfortable setting of the living room where one can read literature about the Old Order Amish, find information on local attractions and activities, or sit back and watch TV or videos.

Start your day with a full, family-style breakfast in the large country kitchen with the ambiance of Colonial America. Fresh fruit, juice, freshly baked quiche or souffles, home-baked breads and cakes, homemade jellies, and fresh brewed coffee and assorted teas are just an example of the country fare that awaits you after a restful night in this tranquil setting.

Lancaster and Berks Counties offer numerous diverse popular attractions. Among the many reasons people come to this area are to visit Amish farms, antique hunting, shopping at nearby discount factory outlets, or to simply get away from the hectic city life.

## 117 RONKS

## Ja-Bar Enterprises

2812 Lincoln Highway E.
717/393-0098 (business office)
717/687-6208 (shop)
Open: Varies according to the season!
Directions: Traveling U.S. Route 30 East out of Lancaster, Pa., cross Pa. Route 896. Continue 1 1/2 miles east to Ronks Road. The shop is located 200 feet east of the intersection, directly across from the Miller's Smorgasbord in the heart of Pennsylvania Dutch Country.

The personalities of owners Jack and Barbara Wolf (especially Jack's), make these shops what they are — fun! Jack is known as Mr. Fun in Lancaster County, also as Mr. Tree — he's been a top tree surgeon for almost 50 years, while Barbara keeps things climbing smoothly in the office of the tree-cutting business.

Together they now have Ja-Bar Enterprises, an eclectic place they bill as "fun shops." They divide their stock into Jack's Junque and Barb's Bric-a-brac and have it scattered about in a collection of small shops that has something for everyone: collectibles, military items, farm items, toys, household items, plus the mainstay of hats and canes. Seems like Jack started collecting hats and canes some 30 years ago and kept his collection on display in the basement of their home. When Barbara gently suggested one day that Jack sell his collection at a public sale, he decided right then that he would open an antique shop. Now he collects and sells his favorites. "I love wood," Jack says, in explanation of his passion for canes and walking sticks. "And hats always have fascinated me." When you catch Jack at the shop, you never know which hat he'll be wearing. He's been known to dress up as a clown and hand out balloons to kids of

# *Pennsylvania*

all ages; on some days he may be decked out in his chef's hat, dishing up some edible treats from the Dutch Hutch outdoor kitchenette that serves fried sweet bologna sandwiches, pork roll sandwiches, hot dogs and drinks.

## The Antique Market-Place
2856 Lincoln Highway E.
717/687-6345
Open: Daily 10–5
Directions: The Antique Market-Place is located 5 miles east of Lancaster in Soudersburg, across from Dutch Haven, and 2 miles west of Paradise! From the Pennsylvania Turnpike, go south on Route 222 about 18 miles to Route 30. Go east on Route 30 about 8 miles. The mall is about 5 miles east on Lancaster on Route 30.

This is an interesting shop, full of great pieces and knowledgeable dealers, who operate the store themselves. There are 35 dealers in this large yellow building, all of whom have been there since 1981. In fact, the Antique Market-Place was one of the first full-time antique cooperatives in the area. In the mall's 7,000 square feet you will find country and primitive furniture, glassware, linens, old tools, salts, old games, toys, miniatures, quilts, silver, lamps, china, collectibles, and antique jewelry, among other things.

**Dutch Barn Antiques**
3272 W. Newport Road
717/768-3067

**Country Antiques**
2845A Lincoln Hwy. E.
717/687-7088

## 118 SAEGERTOWN

**Memory Lane Antiques & Collectibles**
211 Grant
814/763-4916

**McQuiston's Main St. Antiques**
440 Main St.
814/763-2274

**Richard J. Sheakley**
RR 1
814/763-3399

## 119 SCENERY HILL

**Heart of Country Antiques**
Route 40
724/945-6687

**Little Journeys**
Route 40
724/945-5160

**Pepper Mill**
Route 40
724/945-5155

## 120 SCIOTA

### Halloran's Antiques
Fenner Ave.
570/992-4651
Open: 12–4 Sat. and 9–5 Sun., open weekends year-round, open daily 11–4 during July and August, also open by chance or by appointment
Directions: Traveling I-80, take Exit 46A. Travel south approximately 9 miles and take the exit marked "Route 209 South Lehighton." Take the first exit (Sciota). At the bottom of the exit ramp, make a right turn, then take the second left onto Fenner Avenue. Go one block to Halloran's Antiques. Look for the two red barns on the right.

Halloran's has two barns full ... sort of like "three bags full," only larger! These folks specialize in the purchase of complete local estates and have a great selection of "the unusual" in antiques. They also offer an excellent selection of antique American brass and copper, old holiday items and kitchen gadgets. Halloran's is a family-run business that has been in its same location for over 18 years, so you know that they know what they're doing.

**Collectors Cove Ltd.**
Route 33
570/421-7439

**Yestertiques Antique Center**
Route 209 & Bossardsville
570/992-6576

**Whispers in Time Antiques**
Fenner Ave.
570/992-9387

## 121 SCRANTON

**Sacchetti Enterprises**
1602 Capouse Ave.
570/969-1779

**Originally Yours**
1614 Luzerne St.
570/341-7600

**Alma's Antiques**
921 S. Webster Ave.
570/344-5945

**N.B. Levy's Jewelers**
120 Wyoming Ave.
570/344-6187

**Garth T. Watkins Antiques**
409 Prospect Ave.
570/343-1741

**Wildflower Antiques**
1365 Wyoming Ave.
570/341-0511

## 122 SELINSGROVE

**Dutch Country Store**
6B S. Hwy. 11 #15
570/743-4407

**Gaskin's Antiques**
300 S. Market St.
570/374-9275

**Kinney's Antiques**
412 W. Pine St.
570/374-1395

# Pennsylvania

## 123 SEWICKLEY

**Nickelodeon Antiques**
433 Beaver St.
724/749-0525

**Natasha's**
551 Beaver St.
724/741-9484

**Antiquarian Shop**
506 Beaver St.
724/741-1969

**Sewickley Traditions**
555 Beaver St.
724/741-4051

## 124 SHAMOKIN

From a space carved out of rugged, raw wilderness, Shamokin went from a wilderness settlement to the "home" of coal in America. The current town of Shamokin encompasses 400 acres of what used to be mountain forests surrounding a narrow river valley of almost impenetrable swamp, densely covered with pine, hemlock, laurel and rocks, where a tortuously winding river flowed.

The first settlers came in the mid-1700s, with the Old Reading Road that opened in 1770, running through what is now Shamokin in its route between Sunbury and Reading. The town was laid out in 1835, but didn't start growing until 1838, when the western section of the Danville and Pottsville Railroad was completed. By 1839 Shamokin actually looked like a small village, and by 1890 its population was just over 14,000.

Coal was first discovered in Shamokin in 1790, when Isaac Tomlinson picked some pieces out of the earth and took them into a neighboring county for a blacksmith to try. But the ore was not put to practical use until 1810. From this small beginning coal emerged as an industrial weapon, and played a big part in the Industrial Revolution and in the industrial development of Shamokin. By 1889 more than 2.5 million tons of the black rock were being mined by 12,085 men and boys in Shamokin. At the peak of the industrial movement based on coal, Shamokin's population had grown to 16,879. But as the coal industry declined, so did the town's populace, and by the 1990 census there were only 9,184 residents in the town.

### Odds & Ends Store
415 N. Shamokin St.
570/648-2013
Open: Mon.–Sat. 10–5 or by appointment, closed Sun. except by appointment
Directions: From Harrisburg, Pa., go east on I-78 to I-81. Go north on I-81 to Exit 35/Route 901/Mt. Carmel. Go north on Route 901 to Shamokin, Pa. (approx. 16 miles). At the second traffic light in Shamokin City, turn left onto Shamokin Street.

This shop has over 8,000 square feet of show space and display area in which they offer shoppers everything from primitive and country pieces to items of the 1960s. An enormous selection of antique glassware, pottery and other various collectibles can also be found here.

## 125 SHARON

**Honey House Antiques**
71 N. Sharpsville Ave.
724/981-2208

**Tannie's Antiques**
141 E. State St.
724/347-4438

**Treasure Chest**
110 S. Sharpsville Ave.
724/981-1730

## 126 SHAVERTOWN

**Quilt Racque**
183 N. Main St.
570/675-0914

**The Bay Window Shops**
100 E. Overbrook Road
570/675-6400

## 127 SHREWSBURY

**Shrewsbury Antique Center**
65 N. Highland Dr.
717/235-6637

**Olde Towne Antiques Shrewsbury**
10 N. Main St.
717/227-0988

**Full Country Antiques & Collectibles**
21 N. Main St.
717/235-4200

**Another Time**
49 N. Main St.
717/235-0664

**Antiques on Shrewsburg Square**
2 N. Main St.
717/235-1056

**Sixteen N. Main Antiques**
16 N. Main St.
717/235-3448

**Antique Sounds**
4 S. Main St.
717/235-3360

**Village Studio Antiques**
13 N. Main St.
717/227-9428

## 128 SKIPPACK

**Remains to Be Seen**
4022 Skippack Pike
610/584-5770

**Nostalgia**
4034 Skippack Pike
610/584-4112

**Thorpe Antiques**
4027 Skippack Pike
610/584-1177

**Snyder Antiques**
4006 Skippack Pike
610/584-6454

# Pennsylvania

## 129 SMOKETOWN

### Great Places to Stay

**Homestead Lodging**
184 E. Brook Road (Route 896)
717/393-6927
Open: All year
Tour buses available daily; children welcome; MasterCard/Visa
accepted/No pets allowed.
Directions: Take Route 30 to Route 896 North. The Homestead is
located one mile on the left. From the Pennsylvania Turnpike, take
Exit 21 to Route 222 South to Route 30 East to Route 896 North. Go
one mile and the inn is on the left.

Here's a place in the country where guests can enjoy clean country air,
good country cooking, and interesting country company. Located in the
heart of Lancaster County, the Homestead is right in the middle of Amish
country. As a matter of fact, guests can hear the clippity-clop of Amish
buggies as they go by. There is even an Amish farm down the lane from
the inn. But that's not all that's nearby. The inn is located within walking
distance of restaurants, and is minutes from farmer's markets, quilt,
antique and craft shops, outlets, auctions and museums. All rooms have
private baths, color TV, refrigerator, queen or double beds, individually
controlled heating and cooling. Complimentary continental breakfast
served each morning.

## 130 SOMERSET

**Somerset Antique Mall**
113 E. Main St.
814/445-9690

**Somerset Galleries**
152 W. Main St.
814/443-1369

**Shoemaker's Antiques**
398 W. Patriot St.
814/443-2942

**Bryner's Antiques & Clock Repair**
RR 6
814/445-3352

**Exit 10 Antiques**
RR 7
814/445-7856

## 131 STRASBURG

**William Wood & Son Old Mill**
215 Georgetown Road
717/687-6978

**Iron Star Antiques**
53 W. Main St.
717/392-5175

**James W. Frey, Jr.**
209 W. Main St.
717/687-6722

**Sugarbush Antiques**
832 May Post Office Road
717/687-7179

**Spring Hollow Antiques**
121 Mt. Pleasant Road
717/687-6171

**Antiques & Uniques**
1545 Oregon Pike
717/397-9119

**Beech Tree Antiques**
1249 Penn Grant Road
717/687-6881

**Strasburg Antique Market**
207 Georgetown Road
717/687-5624

## 132 STROUDSBURG

**Eleanor's Antiques**
809 Ann St.
570/424-7724

**Lavender and Lace**
350 Main St.
570/424-7087

**Ibi's Antiques**
517 Main St.
570/424-8721

**Olde Engine Works Market Place**
62 N. 3rd St.
570/421-4340

## 133 SYBERTSVILLE

**Angie's Antiques & Collectibles**
Main St.
570/788-4461

**A Country Place**
Route 93
570/788-2457

## 134 TOWANDA

**Martin's Antiques**
Bailey Road
570/265-8782

**Foster Hall Antiques & Gifts**
512 Main St.
570/265-3572

**Jac's Antiques & Collectibles**
417 State St.
570/265-6107

## 135 TUNKHANNOCK

**Harry's Wood Shop**
RR 6
570/836-2346

**La Torres Antiques**
RR 6
570/836-2021

**Old Store**
RR 6
570/836-6088

**Village Antique Mall**
RR 6
570/836-8713

**Country Classics Gift Shoppe**
19 E. Tioga St.
570/836-2030

**Bygones Antiques & Collectibles**
8 W. Tioga St.
570/836-5815

**Marcy A. Rau Antiques**
11 E. Tioga St. (Route 6)
570/836-3052

## 136 UNIONTOWN

**Country Stroll Antiques & Collectibles**
RR 119 S.
724/438-2700

## 137 VALENCIA

**Larry Fox Antiques**
124 Mekis Road
724/898-1114

**Wagon Wheel Antiques**
Route 8
724/898-9974

## 138 VANDERGRIFT

**Odyssey Gallery Antiques**
110 Grant Ave.
724/568-2373

**Grant Ave. Express Antiques**
124 Grant Ave.
724/568-2111

**Vantiques**
140 Lincoln Ave.
724/567-5937

## 139 VERONA

**Allegheny River Arsenal, Inc.**
614 Allegheny River Blvd.
724/826-9699

**Ages Ago Antiques**
722 Allegheny River Blvd.
724/828-9800

**Three Antiques**
760 Allegheny River Blvd.
724/828-8140

## 140 VOLANT

**Volant Mills**
Main St.
724/533-5611

**Leesburg Station Antiques**
1753 Perry Hwy.
724/748-3040

**Something Different**
RR 19
724/748-4134

**Wayne's World**
RR 19
724/748-3072

## 141 WARREN

**McIntyre's Antiques**
334 Pennsylvania Ave. W.
814/726-7011

**Steppin' Back Antiques**
1208 Pennsylvania Ave. E.
814/726-9653

**Antiques Kinzua Country**
102 Pennsylvania Ave. W.
814/726-0298

## 142 WASHINGTON

**Antiques Downtown**
88 S. Main St.
724/222-6800

**Old Pike Antique Center**
438 E. National Pike
724/228-6006

**Krause's**
97 W. Wheeling St.
724/228-5034

## 143 WAYNE

**Wilsons Main Line Antiques**
329 E. Constoga
610/687-5500

**Golden Eagle Antiques**
201 E. Lancaster Ave.
610/293-9290

**Old Store**
238 E. Lancaster Ave.
610/688-3344

**Pembroke Shop**
167 W. Lancaster Ave.
610/688-8185

**Knightsbridge Antiques Ltd.**
121 N. Wayne Ave.
610/971-9551

## 144 WAYNESBORO

**Andy Zeger Antiques**
32 E. Main St.
717/762-6595

**Antique Market**
86 W. Main St.
717/762-4711

## 145 WELLSBORO

**Etc. Antiques Station**
5 East Ave.
570/724-2733

**Country Owl Florist**
15 Queen St.
570/724-6355

**Stefanko's Has Good Stuff**
RR 6
570/724-2096

## 146 WEST CHESTER

**Woman's Exchange**
10 S. Church St.
610/696-3058

**My Best Junk**
622 E. Gay St.
610/429-3388

**Sunset Hill Jewelers**
23 N. High St.
610/692-0374

**Baldwin's Book Barn**
865 Lenape Road
610/696-0816

**T. Newsome & Morris Antiques**
106 W. Market St.
610/344-0657

**Herbert Schiffer Antiques, Inc.**
1469 Morstein Road
610/696-1521

**Fleury Olivier, Inc.**
708 Oakbourne Road
610/692-0445

**Palma J. Antiques**
1144 Old Wilmington Pike
610/399-1210

**R.M. Worth Antiques**
1388 Old Wilmington Pike
610/388-2121

**H.L. Chalfant Antiques**
1352 Paoli Pike
610/696-1862

**My Best Junk**
500 N. Pottstown Pike
610/524-1116

**Coldren Monroe Antiques**
723 E. Virginia Ave.
610/692-5651

### *Great Places to Stay*

### The Bankhouse Bed & Breakfast

875 Hillsdale Road
610/344-7388

The Bankhouse B&B is an 18th-century "bankhouse" nestled in a quiet country setting overlooking a field and pond. The rooms are charmingly decorated with country antiques, stenciling, folk art and handmade quilted wall hangings. The Bankhouse is ideally located; you can reach either Philadelphia (downtown or airport) and Lancaster within 45 minutes.

# Pennsylvania

## 147 WEXFORD

**Wexford General Store Antique Center**
150 Church Road
724/935-9959

**Ruth Arnold Antiques**
End of Baur Road off English
724/935-3217

**Scharf's Antiques**
511 Wallace Road
724/935-3197

**Foster's Antique Shop**
181 Route 910
724/935-2206

**North Hills Antique Gallery**
251 Church Road
724/935-9804

**Antique Treasures of Wexford**
10326 Perry Hwy. Route 19
724/934-8360

**Red Chimney Antiques & Millies**
Warrendale Bakerstown Road
724/935-1990

## 148 WILKES-BARRE

**A.A.G. International**
1266B Sans Souci Pkwy.
570/822-5300

**Penn Floral & Antiques**
235 Scott St.
570/821-1770

## 149 WILLIAMSPORT

**Cillo Antiques & Coins**
11 W. 4th St.
570/327-9272

**Canterbury House Antiques**
315 S. Market St.
570/322-2097

**Lycoming Creek Trading Co.**
RR 4
570/322-7155

**Edmonston's Old Style Furniture**
2705 Euclid Ave.
570/323-1940

**Harrar House**
915 W. 4th St.
570/322-2900

**Do Fisher Antiques & Books**
345 Pine St.
570/323-3573

**D. Keller Merchant**
152 W. 4th St.
570/322-7001

## 150 YORK

**The York Antiques Fair**
Jim Burk Antique Shows
3012 Miller Road
Washington Boro, Pa. 17582
717/397-7209
*For information on show dates
call the number listed above*

**Antique Center of York**
190 Arsenal Road
717/846-1994

**Pantry Antiques**
314 Chestnut St.
717/843-5383

**Leon Ness Jewelry Barn**
2695 S. George St.
717/741-1113

**York Tailgate Antiques Show**
Barry Cohen, Manager
P.O. Box 9095
Alexandria, Va. 22304
703/914-1268
*For information on show dates
call the number listed above*

**Bernie's What-Nots**
7129 Carlisle Pike
717/528-4271

**Antique Fishing Tackle Shoppe**
133 N. Duke St.
717/845-4422

**Almost Anything**
500 Hanover Road
717/792-4386

**Paul L. Ettline**
3790 E. Market St.
717/755-3927

**Dec-Art Antiques**
1419 W. Market St.
717/854-6192

**Kennedy's Antiques**
4290 W. Market St.
717/792-1920

**J & J Plitt Furniture & Antiques**
2406 N. Sherman St.
717/755-4535

**Thee Almost Anything Store**
324 W. Market St.
717/846-7926

**Dennis's Antiques**
1779 W. Market St.
717/845-2418

**Wish-'n'-Want Antiques**
4230 N. Susquehanna Trail
717/266-5961

**Olde Factory Antique Market**
204 S. Sumner St.
717/843-2467

### *Great Places to Stay*

**Friendship House Bed and Breakfast**
728 E. Philadelphia St.
717/843-8299

Although the house was built in 1897, it wasn't until June 1992 that it was opened to the public as Friendship House Bed and Breakfast. The master room, or Philadelphia Room, is of country decor with a private bath connected. The Rose Room has a taste of Victorian with black, pinks, and white. Finally, the Young at Heart Room is decorated with toys, a school desk, and a single, metal bed. Just off this room is the original bath, complete with the original tub and wainscoting. Breakfast is served in the spacious and bright country kitchen, or outside in the private yard. A perfect place to stay while attending the York antiques shows.

## 151 ZELIENOPLE

**Andrea's**
110 N. Main St.
724/452-4144

**Thru Time**
107 E. New Castle St.
724/452-2270

**Main Street Antiques**
204 S. Main St.
724/452-8620

**Vanwhy's Antiques**
300 S. Main St.
724/452-0854

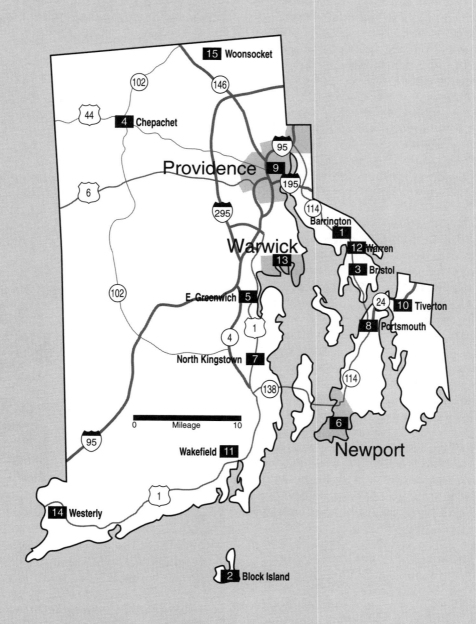

# Rhode Island

15 Woonsocket

102

146

44

4 Chepachet

Providence

95

9

195

295

114

Barrington

1

12 Warren

Warwick

13

3 Bristol

102

E. Greenwich 5

24

10 Tiverton

8 Portsmouth

4

1

North Kingstown 7

138

114

Mileage
0        10

6

95

Newport

Wakefield 11

1

14 Westerly

2 Block Island

# Rhode Island

## 1 BARRINGTON

### The Stock Exchange & The Annex

57 Maple Ave. & 232 Wascca Ave.
401/245-4170

Open: Tues.–Sat. 10–4, Thurs. open until 7, Sun. 12–4, closed Mon.
Directions: *From Route 95 North or South:* Take 195 East to Barrington Exit/Route 114 South. Follow Route 114 for 8 miles. Coming into the center of Barrington, the Town Hall will be on your left. Take a right at the light onto Maple Avenue. The Stock Exchange is the 5th building on the right. *From Newport:* Cross the Mt. Hope Bridge into Bristol, bear left after the bridge onto Route 114 North, pass through the center of Bristol, then the center of Warren and over two small bridges into Barrington. At the 4th light turn left onto Maple Avenue. The Stock Exchange is the 5th building on the right. The Annex is two blocks away; just continue past the Stock Exchange on Maple Avenue, at the corner of West Street take the first left at Vienna Bakery. Then two blocks down turn left onto Wascca Avenue.

The proprietor, Jennifer LaFrance, has developed the Stock Exchange, established in 1977, into Rhode Island's premiere consignment store for fine home furnishings and antiques. Enjoying another successful year, the Stock Exchange found itself bursting at the seams. With no room to expand at the original location, Jennifer opted to open a second location within the same town. The Annex, just two blocks away, offers a larger selection of fine furniture and features a cozy reading nook with an ever changing variety of pre-owned books. The perfect place to spend a rainy afternoon.

The Stock Exchange & Annex continues to consign and sell countless household items, including but not limited to: furniture, lamps, linens, china, silver, crystal, glassware, pictures, rugs, tools, pots and pans. Jennifer loves to keep the store interesting and diverse, so they welcome a wide range of consignable items at affordable prices. Attorneys, estate planners, trust officers and realtors have come to realize what a valuable asset the store can be. The Stock Exchange & Annex specializes in buying and removing entire households and estates. Jennifer and her staff invite you to visit and wander through five floors and two locations of fine home furnishings and antiques. Jennifer guarantees you will be planning your next visit before you leave.

**Hearts & Flowers Antiques**
270 County Road
401/247-0770

**House of Windsor**
233 Waseca Ave.
401/245-7540

**Antique Depot**
40 Maple Ave.
401/247-2006

**Barrington Place Antiques**
70 Maple Ave.
401/245-4510

## 2 BLOCK ISLAND

Block Island is one of Rhode Island's scenic wonders. This rustic and pristine island was rated one of the twelve best unspoiled areas in the Western Hemisphere. A short ferry ride brings you to a place where you can enjoy spectacular vistas from awe-inspiring bluffs. It is ideal for visitors seeking lighthouses, delightful inns, and peace and quiet.

### The Island Exchange

Ocean Ave.
401/466-2093

Open: June 15–Labor Day, 7 days a week, 1–5; Labor Day–June 15, open most Sat., Sun., and Mon. holidays, 1–5
Directions: To reach Block Island by ferry: *From Route 95 North*, take Exit 92; turn right on Route 2, and proceed to Route 78 (Westerly Bypass). Follow Route 78 to end; go left on Route 1, and travel east to Narragausett. Exit at sign for Block Island Ferry, turn right, then right again onto Route 108, then right to Galilee. *From 95 South*, Exit 9 onto Route 4 South, to 1 South, to Narragausett and to Route 108 South, to Galilee.

This uniquely located shop brings to its customers furniture, china, glassware, collectibles and housewares. Items may be antique or merely secondhand, according to Dodie Sorensen, the store owner. However, the selection is varied with new pieces arriving daily.

At any one time, there are items belonging to 300-350 consignors in addition to store-owned specialties such as pine, maple, cherry and oak furniture, white ironstone and wonderful old utilitarian crockery (mixing bowls are the favorite). Turnover is fast and the shop changes noticeably from week to week especially in the spring, fall and summer.

Dodie relates a charming story of determination regarding the shop. "Even though the Island Exchange is on an island at sea, there is always a way to get that special item home. A few years ago, a couple bought a huge spinning wheel and the matching yarn winder, but they were traveling on their sailboat. The resourceful husband had a taxi bring the items to the marina dock where he loaded them into a borrowed dinghy and then towed it behind his own dinghy out to the sailboat at its mooring in the harbor. Safely stowed away, the spinning wheel sailed away to its new home, leaving a harbor full of astonished spectators behind."

## *Great Places to Stay*

### The 1661 Inn & Hotel Manisses
One Spring St.
1-800-MAN-ISSE
Email: biresorts@aol.com

The Hotel Manisses was built in 1872 as the ideal holiday destination and today still retains its stature as a premier hotel on the island. The hotel's seventeen rooms and parlors have been furnished with Victorian antiques. All of the rooms provide private baths, and in addition, a number of rooms feature a luxurious whirlpool tub. A Victorian landmark, the hotel boasts of an elegant dining room, known as one of the finest places to dine on the island. The Top Shelf Bar, located in the parlor, is celebrated for its tableside flaming coffees.

### 3 BRISTOL

**Stickney & Stickney Antiques**
295 Hope St.
401/254-0179

**Gift Unique**
458 Hope St.
401/254-1114

**Center Chimney**
39 State St.
401/253-8010

**Alfred's Annex**
331 Hope St.
401/253-3465

**Dantiques**
676 Hope St.
401/253-1122

**Jesse-James Antiques**
44 State St.
401/253-2240

## *Great Places to Stay*

### Williams Grant Inn
154 High St.
1-800-596-4222

Just two blocks from Bristol's unspoiled harbor you'll find the Sea Captain's House that Deputy Governor William Bradford granted to his grandson in 1808. Mary and Mike Rose restored and remodeled the five-bay Colonial/Federal house, turning it into a gracious, beautifully appointed inn decorated with traditional and folk art. Breakfasts are always a treat, with home-baked goodies, fresh fruit and perhaps Mike's huevos rancheros or Mary's pesto omelets.

### 4 CHEPACHET

**Harold's Antique Shop**
1191 Main St.
401/568-6030

**Stone Mill Antique Center**
Main St.
401/568-6662

### 5 EAST GREENWICH

**Hill & Harbour Antiques**
187 Main St.
401/885-4990

**Gallery 500**
500 Main St.
401/885-6711

**Country Squire Antiques**
Main St.
401/885-1044

**Shadow of Yesteryear**
307 Main St.
401/885-3666

**Antique Boutique**
527 Main St.
401/884-3800

### 6 NEWPORT

**What Not Shop**
16 Franklin St.
401/847-4262

**Exotic Treasures**
622 Thames St.
401/842-0040

**Courtyard Antiques**
142 Bellevue Ave.
401/849-4554

**Patina**
26 Franklin St.
401/846-4666

**Ramson House Antiques**
36 Franklin St.
401/847-0555

**Alice Simpson Antiques**
40 1/2 Franklin St.
401/849-4252

**Lee's Wharf Eclectics**
5 Lees Wharf
401/849-8786

**Renaissance Antiques**
42 Spring St., #7
401/849-8515

**Nautical Nook**
86 Spring St.
401/846-6810

**Michael Westman**
135 Spring St.
401/847-3091

**Forever Yours**
220 Spring St.
401/841-5290

**Prince Albert's Victorian**
431 Thames St.
401/848-5372

**Newport Book Store**
116 Bellevue Ave.
401/847-3400

**Bellevue Antiques**
121 Bellevue Ave.
401/846-7898

**Newport China Trade**
8 Franklin St.
401/841-5267

**J.B. Antiques**
33 Franklin St.
401/849-0450

**A & A Gaines**
40 Franklin St.
401/849-6844

**Smith Marble, Ltd.**
44 Franklin St.
401/846-7689

**Lamp Lighter Antiques**
42 Spring St., #5
401/849-4179

**New England Antiques**
60 Spring St.
401/849-6646

**Harbor Antiques**
134 Spring St.
401/848-9711

**Drawing Room**
152 Spring St.
401/841-5060

**Armory Antique Center**
365 Thames St.
401/848-2398

**Aardvark Antiques**
475 1/2 Thames St.
401/849-7233

# Rhode Island

*Great Places to Stay*

## Castle Hill Inn & Resort

590 Ocean Dr.
401/849-3800
Web site: www.castlehillinn.com

Castle Hill is located on a 40-acre peninsula at the west end of Newport's world-renowned Ocean Drive. The inn offers guests the romance, seclusion, and extraordinary beauty of a private oceanfront resort. An elegantly restored Victorian mansion overlooking Narragansett Bay and quaint beach cottages nestled along the coastline provide an enchanting escape from the outside world.

## Inn at Shadow Lawn

120 Miantonomi Ave.
1-800-352-3750
Web site: www.bbhost.com/innatshadowlawn

From the moment you step through the door you know there's something special about the Inn at Shadow Lawn. A quiet place, yet convenient to Newport's attractions, the Inn at Shadow Lawn reflects the grace and style of Newport's yesterday while providing the modern comforts of today.

## 7  NORTH KINGSTOWN

**Lavender & Lace**
4 Brown St.
401/295-0313

**Apple Antiques**
11 Burnt Cedar Dr.
401/295-8840

**Lillian's Antiques**
7442 Post Road
401/885-2512

**Lafayette Antiques**
814 Ten Rod Road
401/295-2504

**Wickford Antique Center II**
93 Brown St.
401/295-2966

**Antique Center**
1121 Ten Rod Road
401/294-9958

**Mentor Antiques**
7512 Post Road
401/294-9412

## 8  PORTSMOUTH

**Stock & Trade**
2771 E. Main Road
401/683-4700

**Caron & Co. Antiques & Decor**
980 E. Main Road
401/683-4560

**Eagle's Nest Antique Center**
3101 E. Main Road
401/683-3500

## 9  PROVIDENCE

In Providence, scores of 18th-century homes line Benefit Street's "Mile of History." The most famous are the palatial Gilded Age Newport mansions that were once the summer "cottages" of New York's wealthiest families.

**Benefit Street Gallery**
140 Wickenden St. FL 1
401/751-9109

**Providence Antique Center**
442 Wickenden St.
401/274-5820

**Alaimo Gallery**
301 Wickenden St.
401/421-5360

**Eastwick Antiques**
434 Wickenden St.
No phone listed

**Angell Street Curiosities**
183 Angell St.
401/455-0450

**Lee Hartwell**
141 Elmgrove Ave.
401/273-7433

**Carole's Antiques**
219 Lenox Ave.
401/941-8680

**Boulevard Antiques**
773 Blackstone Blvd.
401/273-4934

**Providence Antique Center**
442 Wickenden St.
401/274-5820

**Doyle's Antiques**
197 Wickenden St.
401/272-3202

**This & That Shoppe**
236 Wickenden St.
401/861-1394

**Antiques at India Point**
409 Wickenden St.
401/273-5550

**Antiques & Artifacts**
436 Wickenden St.
401/421-8334

**Robert's Gallery**
777 Westminister St.
401/453-1270

**Forgotten Garden**
60 Gano St.
401/453-3650

**Jerry's Gallery**
5 Traverse St.
401/331-0558

**Philip Zexter Antiques**
460 Wickenden St.
401/272-6905

*Great Places to Stay*

## Charles Hodges House

19 Pratt St.
401/861-7244

In the heart of Providence's east side, the Charles Hodges House is an impressive Federal home built by a coal merchant in 1850. Wide pine floors set off the extensive decor of the 19th-century antique furnishings and memorabilia. Two rooms accommodate guests in cozy comfort. Breakfast is served on a huge oak table that came from the state capitol, or, in good weather, on the flower-laden porch under a spreading ash tree. Visitors are one block from Benefit Street, which features some of America's finest Colonial architecture.

## 10 TIVERTON

**Past & Presents Tearoom**
2753 Main Road
401/624-2890

**Country Cabin**
3964 Main Road
401/624-2279

**Peter's Attic**
3879 Main Road
401/625-5912

## 11 WAKEFIELD

**Olde Friends Antiques**
355 Main St.
401/789-1470

**Dove & Distaff Antiques**
365 Main St.
401/783-5714

## 12 WARREN

**Fortier's Antiques**
Route #136
401/247-2788

**Country Antique Shop**
382 Market St.
401/247-4878

**Water Street Antiques**
149 Water St.
401/245-6440

**Crosstown Antiques**
309 Market St.
401/245-9176

**Warren Antique Center**
5 Miller St.
401/245-5461

**Tony Cellar**
23 Market St.
401/245-2020

## 13 WARWICK

**Clock Shop**
667 Bald Hill Road
401/826-1212

**Antique Haven**
30 Post Road
401/785-0327

**Apponaug Village Antiques**
3159 Post Road
401/739-7466

**Antique & Decorating Warehouse**
626 Warwick Ave.
401/461-0008

**Golden Heart Antiques**
1627 Warwick Ave.
401/738-2243

**Brown Dog Antiques**
334 Knight St.
402/826-1007

**Riklyn Collectibles**
2260 W. Shore Road
401/738-3939

**Pontiac Mill Antiques**
334 Knight St.
401/732-3969

**Pre-Amble Consignments**
2457 Post Road
401/739-8886

**Golden Era Antiques**
858 W. Shore Road
401/738-2518

**Aable Antiques**
1615 Warwick Ave.
401/738-6099

**Emporium**
1629 Warwick Ave.
401/738-8824

**Treasure Barn Antiques**
334 Knight St.
401/736-9773

## 14 WESTERLY

**Mary D's Antiques & Collectibles**
3 Commerce St.
401/596-5653

**Riverside Antiques**
8 Broad St.
401/596-0266

**Frink's Collectables**
271 Post Road
401/322-4055

**Buried Treasures**
12 Canal St.
401/596-6633

## 15 WOONSOCKET

**The Corner Curiosity Shoppe**
279 Greene St.
401/766-2628

**Main Street Antiques & Collectibles**
32 Main St.
401/762-0805

**L'Antiques & Decoys**
489 Diamond Hill Road Route 114
401/767-3336

**Vazinan's Antique Marketplace**
101 Main St.
401/762-9661

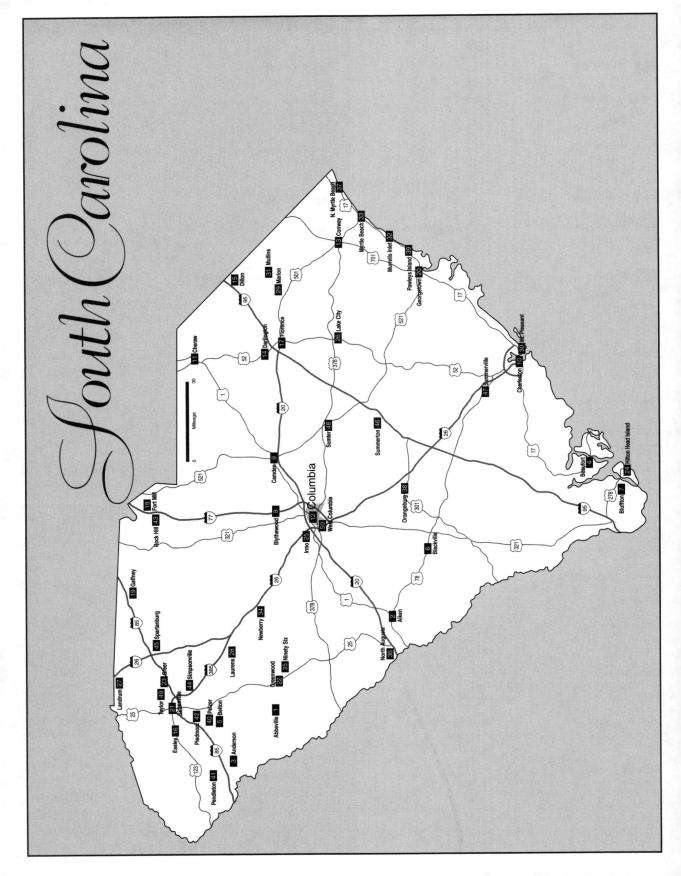

# South Carolina

## 1 ABBEVILLE

**Edith's Decor House & Attic Antiques**
Court Square
864/459-5222

**Emporium**
115 Trinity St.
864/459-5388

**Bagwell's Furniture Warehouse**
130 Trinity St.
864/459-5861

**Collectors Antique Mall Abbeville**
300 S. Main St.
864/459-5935

**Miriam's Southern Accents**
128 Trinity St.
864/459-5995

## 2 AIKEN

### Aiken Antique Mall

112-114 Laurens St. S.W.
803/648-6700
Cpen: Mon.–Sat. 10-6; Sun. 1–6
Directions: Two doors from the intersection of State Hwys. 1 and 78

Fifty dealers fill 13,000 square feet in this old department store building. A variety of antiques such as kitchen items, period furniture, cut glass, art glass, crystal, silver, primitives, painted furniture, vintage books and Civil War relics may be found here. One dealer specializes in old hunting and fishing collectibles with a large quantity of old fishing lures. Another dealer is a local artist and historian, displaying prints and paintings that are historically correct.

### Swan Antique Mall

3557 Richland Ave. W.
803/643-9922
Open: Mon.–Sat.10–5:30, Sun. 1–5
Directions: From I-20, exit onto Highway 1 and go 4 miles into Aiken.

With 150 dealers and 22,500 square feet, this easily accessible mall carries all types of antiques and collectibles. They offer their customers very good prices, friendly service, a country cafe serving wonderful country cooking. The house specialty is chicken and dumplings.

**York Cottage Antiques**
809 Hayne Ave. S.W.
803/642-9524

**Sanford Oaks Ltd.**
Laurens St. S.W.
803/641-1168

**Antique Mall—Market Place**
343 Park Ave. S.W.
803/648-9696

**Memory Lane Antiques**
2483 Williston Road
803/652-3096

## 3 ANDERSON

**Brookgreen Courts**
311 N. Main St.
864/225-3126

**Bee Hive**
510 N. Main St.
864/225-2377

**Belinda's Antique Mall & Jewelry**
711 S. Main St.
864/224-0938

**Highland House Interiors**
1307 North Blvd.
864/226-4626

**Eason's Antiques & Linens**
2711 Whitehall Ave.
864/226-0415

**Avenue of Oaks Antiques**
2409 S. Main St.
864/225-8530

**McDowell's Emporium**
104 Oak Dr.
864/231-8896

## 4 BEAUFORT

**Rhett Gallery**
901 Bay St.
843/524-3339

**Michael Rainey Antiques**
702 Craven St.
843/521-4532

**Consignors Antique Mall**
913 Port Republic St.
843/521-0660

**Bellavista Antiques & Interior**
206 Carteret St.
843/521-0687

**Chitty & Co.**
208 Carteret St.
843/524-7889

**Sturdy Beggar**
900 Port Republic St.
843/521-9006

**Past Time**
205 Scott St.
843/522-8881

**Den of Antiquity**
330 Hwy. 170 W.
843/521-9990

## 5 BELTON

**Ox Yoke Antiques**
3023 Hwy. 29 N.
864/261-3275

## 6 BLACKVILLE

**Parrott's Antiques & Gifts**
108 Lartigue St.
803/284-3670

## 7 BLUFFTON

**Barrett L. Antiques**
Hayward St.
843/757-6630

**Stock Farm Antiques**
Hwy. 46
843/757-2511

## 8 BLYTHEWOOD

### Blythewood Antiques

206 Blythewood Road
803/754-1116
Open: Tues.–Sat. 10–6, closed Sun.–Mon.
Directions: Take Exit 27 off I-77

Blythewood Antiques is located in a house with rooms set up for show of antique furniture, glassware, collectibles, linens and more.

# South Carolina

## The Root Cellar

10500 Wilson Blvd.
803/754-7578
Open: Tues.–Sat. 10–6, closed Sun.–Mon.
Directions: The Root Cellar is located at Exit 24, just 1 mile off I-77 on Hwy. 21/Wilson Road.

The Root Cellar holds 3,000 square feet of antique and collectible consignments, including furniture, dolls, china, lamps, old toys, linens, fine art, handpainted furniture and crystal.

## Heart's Desire

162 Langford
803/691-8833
Open: Tues.–Fri. 10–5:30; Wed. 10–1:30, Sat. 10–5, closed Sun.–Mon.
Directions: Take Exit 24 off I-77. Heart's Desire is located 3 miles from I-77 at Hwy. 21 and Langford Road

Heart's Desire is a delightful, magical gift and antique shop housed in a spacious home built in 1875. Their antiques range from dolls to jewelry to furniture and more, while their gifts include baskets, florals and gifts for home and garden.

## 9  CAMDEN

Established in 1732, Camden is the oldest inland city in South Carolina and was the major British garrison of Lord Cornwallis. The Battles of Hobkirk Hill and Camden were fought in the vicinity and twelve other Revolutionary War battles took place nearby. The Camden area is also known for the fine horses trained and bred here and for its beautiful homes. The world-famous "Colonial Cup," a day of steeplechase and flat racing, takes place around Easter.

## Wartime Collectibles

539 Dekalb St.
803/424-5273
Open: Tues.–Fri.10:30–6, Mon. and Sat. by chance
Directions: From I-20, take Exit 92 or 98, at the intersection of U.S. Hwy. 1 and State Route 521

This shop specializes in military memorabilia, both foreign and domestic from World Wars I and II, as well as the Civil War. All items are authentic and guaranteed. You will also find included in the inventory many old toys.

**Camden Antiques Exchange**
818 Broad St.
803/424-1700

**Camden Antique Mall**
830 Broad St.
803/432-0818

**Granary Antiques**
830 Broad St.
803/432-8811

**Antiques on Broad**
2513 Broad St.
803/424-1338

**South's Treasures**
538 Dekalb St.
803/432-7709

**Boykin Furniture Co.**
922 Broad St.
803/432-4386

**Timley Treasures**
845 Broad St.
803/424-0171

**Dusty Bin Antiques**
2606 Broad St.
803/432-3676

**Fancy That Antiques**
914 Market St.
803/425-5111

**Pine Burr Antiques**
1004 Tickle Hill Road
803/432-4636

## 10  CHARLESTON

Her charm and beauty have long proven to be irresible. You'll see it in the lacy trim of her breezy piazzas and feel it in the spirit of her rich heritage. A port city steeped in history, it has barely changed since its founding in 1670.

Here you'll find the very best of the South. A genteel nature, so inviting, so gracious and an indomitable strength that has proudly withstood great fires, earthquakes, pirate rouges, the Civil War and hurricanes with little more than a bat of an eye.

Indeed, the Charleston area is a place that visitors rarely want to leave. In 1995, *Glamour* magazine rated the area one of the top-ten travel destinations in the U.S., and *Condé Nast* readers rated it fourth as a destination in a list of its top-ten cities. With a metro population of over 500,000, this aristocratic Colonial port boasts 73 pre-Revolutionary buildings, 136 from the late 18th century and more than 600 others built prior to the 1840s. Come wander along cobblestone streets, smell the sea breezes, explore antique shops and boutiques and treat yourself to the delicious fresh seafood. Come experience the Charleston area—her streets, her homes, her people.

## Period Antiques

194 King St.
843/723-2724
Open: Mon.–Sat. 10–5
Directions: Take I-26 to its end in Charleston and take the King Street exit. Turn right onto King Street and continue about a mile to the heart of downtown Charleston. Period Antiques is at 194 King Street on the left.

An interesting, unusual and changing selection of choice American and European antiques can be found at Period Antiques, including furniture, paintings, mirrors and decorative accessories — a small shop full of treasures.

**Zinn Rug Gallery**
269 E. Bay St.
843/577-0300

**Acquisitions**
273 E. Bay St.
843/577-8004

**Charleston Rare Book Co.**
66 Church St.
843/723-3330

**Church Street Galleries**
100 Church St.
843/937-0808

**Second Fling Antiques**
7440 Cross Country Road
843/552-6604

**Goat Cart**
18 E. Elliott St.
843/722-1128

**152 A.D. Antiques**
152 King St.
843/577-7042

**Ginkgo Leaf**
159 King St.
843/722-0640

**Livingston and Sons**
163 King St.
843/723-9697

**Decorator's Alley**
177 1/2 King St
843/722-2707

**D. Bigda Antiques**
178 King St.
843/722-0248

**Jack Patla Co.**
181 King St.
843/723-2314

**Joint Ventures Estate Jewelry**
185 King St.
843/722-6730

**George C. Birlant & Co.**
191 King St.
843/722-3842

**Architrave Antiques**
193 King St.
843/577-2860

**Jean Keegan**
196 King St.
843/723-3953

**Elysia Antiques**
200 King St.
843/853-8502

**A. Zola**
202 King St.
843/723-3175

**Century House Antiques**
85 Church St.
843/722-6248

**Trio Ltd.**
175 Church St.
843/853-9966

**Nazan**
4501 Dorsey Ave.
843/745-0005

**Chicora Antiques, Inc.**
154 King St.
843/723-1711

**Estate Antiques**
155 King St.
843/723-2362

**Moore House Antiques**
161 1/2 King St.
843/722-8065

**Helen Martin Antiques**
169 King St.
843/577-6533

**Poppe House, Inc.**
177 King St.
843/853-9559

**English Patina, Inc.**
179 King St.
843/853-0380

**John Gibson Antiques**
183 King St.
843/722-0909

**Carolina Prints**
188 King St.
843/723-2266

**D & D Antiques**
192 King St.
843/853-5266

**The Silver Vault**
195 King St.
843/722-0631

**Verdi Antiques & Accessories**
196 King St.
843/723-3953

**Petterson Antiques**
201 King St.
843/723-5714

**A'Riga IV**
204 King St.
843/577-3075

**Riddler Page Rare Maps**
205 E. King St., Suite 102
843/723-1734

**Granny's Goodies**
301 King St.
843/577-6200

**James Island Antiques**
2028 Maybank Hwy.
843/762-1415

**Antiquities Historical Galleries**
199 Meeting St.
843/720-8771

**Flynn's**
Old Market 188 Meeting
843/577-7229

**D & M Antiques**
4923 Rivers Ave.
843/744-6777

**Architectural Elements**
1011 Saint Andrews Blvd.
843/571-3389

**Tanner's Collectibles**
1024 Savannah Hwy.
843/763-0199

**Antique Mall**
2241 Savannah Hwy.
843/766-8899

**Shalimar Antiques**
2418 Savannah Hwy.
843/766-1529

**Carpenter's Antiques**
1106 Chuck Dawley Blvd. (Mt. Pleasant)
843/884-3411

**Goat Cart**
18 E. Elliott St.
843/722-1128

## 11 CHERAW

**Antique Imports, Inc.**
92 Powe St.
843/537-5762

**L & M Antiques**
RR 1
843/623-7307

**Cheraw Furniture Refinishing**
133 Second St.
843/379-3562

**Golden & Associate Antiques**
206 King St.
843/723-8886

**Croghan's Jewel Box**
308 King St.
843/723-6589

**Terrace Oaks Antique Mall**
2037 Maybank Hwy.
843/795-9689

**Seymour Antique Center**
1066 E. Montague Ave.
843/554-5005

**Peacock Alley Antiques**
9 Princess St.
843/722-6056

**Brass & Silver Workshop**
758 Saint Andrews Blvd.
843/571-4302

**Grey Goose Antique Mall**
1011 Saint Andrews Blvd.
843/763-9131

**Livingston & Sons Antiques, Inc.**
2137 Savannah Hwy.
843/556-6162

**Roumilliat's Antique Mall**
2241 Savannah Hwy.
843/766-8899

**Attic Treasures**
2024 Wappoo Dr.
843/762-0418

**Architrave Antiques**
153 King St.
843/577-2860

**Red Torii Oriental Antiques**
197 King St.
843/723-0443

**Thomas Antique Co.**
92 Powe St.
843/537-3422

**Sentimental Journey**
242 2nd St.
843/537-0461

**Expressions**
129 Main St. (12 mi. W.)
843/623-6668

# South Carolina

## 12 COLUMBIA

**Ole Towne Antique Mall**
2956 Broad River Road
803/798-2078

**Amick's Bottles & Collectibles**
6420 Garners Ferry Road
803/783-0300

**Past & Present, Inc.**
8105 Garners Ferry Road
803/776-6807

**Mais Oui Ltd.**
929 Gervais St.
803/733-1704

**Chic Antiques**
602 Huger St.
803/765-1584

**B & M Enterprises, Inc.**
3510 Phillips St.
803/799-6153

**Balloonyville USA**
141 S. Shandon St.
803/771-4555

**Ole Towne Antique Mall, Inc.**
8724 Two Notch Road
803/736-7575

**Non E Such**
2754 Devine St.
803/254-0772

**Wolfe's Antiques**
7001 Patricia Dr.
803/783-6327

**Heirloom Antiques & Collectibles**
6000 Garners Ferry Road
803/776-3955

**Ole Towne Antique Mall**
7748 Garners Ferry Road
803/695-1992

**City Market Antiques Mall**
701 Gervais St.
803/799-7722

**Mary Clowney Antiques & Interiors**
1009 Gervias St.
803/765-1280

**Columbia Antique Mall**
602 Huger St.
803/765-1584

**Antique Mall**
1215 Pulaski St.
803/256-1420

**BC Treasure Barn**
2515 Two Notch Road
803/799-7366

**Charlton Hall Galleries, Inc.**
912 Gervais St.
803/779-5678

**Olde Towne Antique Mall**
2918 Broad River Road
803/772-5057

## 13 CONWAY

**Hidden Attic Antiques Mall**
1014 4th Ave.
843/248-6262

**Kingston Antiques**
326 Main St.
843/248-0212

**Trader John Antiques**
2197 Hwy. 501 E.
843/248-9077

## 14 DARLINGTON

Built around a courthouse square, the mural on the side of the courthouse is a graphic reminder of the country's colorful past. The town really comes alive on Labor Day weekend when the "Granddaddy of them all," the Mountain Dew Southern 500 stock car race is held.

**Scarlett's Antiques**
500 E. Broad St.
843/393-4952

**H & M Plunder Shop**
512 S. Main St.
843/393-4888

## 15 DILLON

**Chris's Pack House**
Hwy. 9
843/774-6144

**House of Willow Antiques**
2806 Hwy. 9 W.
843/841-3040

**Breeden's Old Stuff**
201 Harrison St.
843/774-6321

## 16 EASLEY

**Main Street Market**
203 W. Main St.
864/855-8658

**King's Things Antiques**
1001 Pelzer Hwy.
864/859-0313

**Adam's Attic Antiques**
223 W. Main St.
864/859-4996

**Wilma's Antiques**
4225 Calhoun Memorial Hwy.
864/220-1055

## 17 FLORENCE

### Red Brick House
1005 S. Cashua Dr.
843/669-4860
Open: Thurs.–Sat. or by chance
Directions: From I-95, take Exit 157 and travel east to the first red light. Turn right on Cashua and the shop is three miles further on the left.

Owner David Robinson can help shoppers in several ways. He can sell you something from his 7,000 square feet of antiques (mostly furniture). He can refinish a piece for you in his shop on the premises. He can help you pick out a gift from the line of gift items he carries. Is that what they mean by one-stop shopping?

**Ann's Patchwork Palette**
105 S. Franklin Dr.
843/665-1944

**Grapevine Antiques Collectibles, Etc.**
2138 3rd Loop
843/629-9745

**Antique Market & Etc.**
1356 James Jones Ave.
843/665-1812

**Hodge's Furniture Shop**
Hwy. 52 N.
843/669-7391

**Hamilton House Antiques**
549 W. Evans St.
843/665-7161

**Trading Post**
217 N. Irby St.
843/673-0332

## 18 FORT MILL

**Antique Mall of the Carolinas**
3700 Ave. of the Carolinas
803/548-6255

**Antiques on Main**
233 Main St.
803/802-2242

**Antique & Garden Shop**
229 Main St.
803/547-7822

# 19 GAFFNEY

**Vassey's Antiques**
1084 N. Green River Road
864/461-8111

**Pieces from the Past**
2105 Cherokee Ave.
864/489-4668

# 20 GEORGETOWN

## Tosh Antiques
802 Church St.
843/527-8537
Open: Mon.–Sat. 10–5, Sun. by chance
Directions: Located on Hwy. 17 in downtown Georgetown

Everything is of fine quality here. You'll find Victorian furniture, pieces from occupied Japan, primitives, as well as Roseville, sterling silver, and brilliant cut glass.

**Hill's Used Furniture & Antiques**
4161 Andrews Hwy.
843/546-6610

**Clement's Carolina**
803 Front St.
843/545-9000

**Grandma's Attic**
2106 Highmarket
843/546-2607

# 21 GREENVILLE

## The Corner Antique Mall
700 N. Main St.
864/232-9337
Open: Mon.–Sat. 10–5, closed Sun.
Directions: The Corner Antique Mall is located on U.S. Hwy. 276, where it intersects with Main Street. However, traveling I-85, take Exit 51 and travel north on I-385 to Exit 42, which is Stone Avenue. Turn right and go to the "Corner" at Stone and Main.

This 5,000-square-foot "corner" of the antique world is packed with treasures, including advertising collectibles, books and magazines, art, china, glassware, pottery, jewelry, dolls and figurines, vintage clothing, some furniture and accessories, and many more collectibles and antiques.

**Little Stores of West End**
315 Augusta St.
864/467-1770

**Brown Street Antiques, Inc.**
115 N. Brown St.
864/232-5304

**Penny Farthing Antiques**
93 Cleveland St.
864/271-9370

**Reedy River Antiques**
220 Howe St.
864/242-0310

**Antiques Associates**
633 S. Main St.
864/235-3503

**Accents Unlimited, Inc.**
520 Mills Ave.
864/235-4825

**Greenville Furniture Exchange, Inc.**
113 Poinsett Hwy.
864/233-3702

**William Key Interiors**
909 E. Washington St.
864/233-4329

**Greystone Antiques**
1501 Augusta St.
864/242-2486

**All That Jazz**
1547 Wade Hampton Blvd.
864/292-3900

**Southern Estate Antiques**
415 Mauldin Road
864/299-8981

**Bedding World Antiques**
236 Wade Hampton Blvd.
864/242-0908

**Gallery at Park & Main**
605 N. Main St.
864/235-8866

**Robbin's Rarities, Inc.**
2038 Laurens Road #C
864/297-7948

**North Country Treasures**
110 Poinsett Hwy.
864/271-4030

# 22 GREENWOOD

**Brewington Antiques**
1215 Montague Ave.
864/229-3086

**Bud's Antiques**
803 Ninety Six Hwy.
864/227-8999

**Rainbo Antiques**
2720 Hwy. 25 S.
864/227-1921

**Mackey's**
1728 Montague Ave.
864/223-3400

**Memories Antique Shop**
626 Lowell Ave.
864/229-6353

# 23 GREER

**Pot Luck Antiques**
2013 Hwy. 101 S.
864/877-1818

**Cooper Furniture Co.**
214 Trade St.
864/877-2761

**Mercantile on Trade**
230 Trade St.
864/801-1300

**Coach House Antiques**
401 Johnson Road
864/879-2616

**West Gerald Interiors**
711 W. Wade Hampton Blvd.
864/879-2148

**Ralph's Antiques & Auctions**
116 Bright Road
864/879-3073

# 24 HILTON HEAD ISLAND

**Decorator's Wholesale Antiques**
1 Cardinal Road #5
843/681-7463

**Low Country Collectibles**
32 Palmetto Bay Road
843/842-8543

**Bargains & Treasures**
4 Archer Road, #E
843/785-7929

**Interiors—Kay Buck a Rare Find**
Village at Wexford, #E6
843/686-6606

**Annie's Attic of Consigned**
20 Palmetto Bay Road
843/686-6970

**Guggenheim's**
20 Dunnigans Alley
843/785-9580

# South Carolina

**Michael & Co. Antiques**
26 Arrow Road
843/686-3222

**Ruth Edward's Antiques**
8 Beach Lagoon Road
843/671-2223

**Nearly New**
27 Arrow Road
843/785-7911

**Swan House Antiques Gallery**
7 Bow Circle
843/785-7926

## 25 IRMO

**Broad River Antiques**
7232 Broad River Road
803/749-6909

**Farmhouse Antiques**
1300 Old Dutch Fork Road
803/732-6287

**Dutch Fork Antiques**
1000 Dutch Fork Road
803/781-7174

## 26 LAKE CITY

Established in 1732, tobacco was introduced in the late 1800s. The market was established in 1889 and has grown to become one of the largest in the state. The crop is saluted every September during the town's Tobacco Festival. Dr. Ronald E. McNair, one of the astronauts aboard the Space Shuttle *Challenger*, was born and buried here.

**Gloria's Antiques & Gifts**
116 E. Main St.
843/394-8360

**Oakdale Antiques**
3831 W. Turbeville
843/659-2210

## 27 LANDRUM

### Landrum Antique Mall
221 Rutherford Road
864/457-4000
Open: Mon.–Sat. 10–5, closed Sun.
Directions: From I-26, take Exit 1 and the shop is located 1 mile off of the interstate

There's lots in a relatively small space here, so browse slowly and don't miss a thing! Fifty dealers have filled 10,000 square feet with early 1900s furniture, collectibles, silver, chandeliers, rugs, china and estate jewelry.

**My Favorite Shop**
203 E. Rutherford St.
864/457-4840

**Lasting Impressions**
227 E. Rutherford St.
864/457-4697

**Bloomsbury Cottage Antqs. & Interiors**
204 E. Rutherford St.
864/457-3111

## 28 LAURENS

This town is named for Revolutionary War statesman Henry Laurens, who was imprisoned in the Tower of London for his patriotism. The courthouse square was purchased in 1792 for two guineas (about $21).

It was in this vicinity that Andrew Johnson, 17th President of the United States, once operated a tailor shop.

**Treasure House Antiques**
Dial Place Road
864/682-5915

**Jeff's Antiques & Furniture**
Hwy. 221 S.
864/682-8079

**Harper House**
101 Wayside Dr.
864/984-7945

**Hall Antiques**
Hwy. 221
864/984-0315

**Palmetto Antiques & Auction**
106 E. Main St.
864/984-3011

## 29 MARION

**Antiques Dujour**
231 N. Main St.
843/423-3366

**Judy's Antiques**
329 N. Main St.
843/423-5227

**Theodosia's**
724 N. Main St.
843/423-7693

**Swamp Fox Antiques & Books**
326 Main St.
843/423-0819

**Cuckoo's Nest**
403 N. Main St.
843/423-1636

## 30 MOUNT PLEASANT

**Linda Page's Thieves Market**
1460 Ben Sawyer Blvd.
843/884-9672

**Pleasant Antiques**
616 Coleman Blvd.
843/849-7005

**Victoria & Thomas Trading Co.**
803 Coleman Blvd.
843/849-7230

**Mike's Antiques, Inc.**
401 Johnnie Dodds Blvd.
843/849-1744

**Carpentier's Antiques & Restoration**
1106 Chuck Dawley Blvd.
843/884-3411

**Lowcountry Antique Mall**
630 Coleman Blvd.
843/849-8850

**Sweet Magnolias**
976 Houston Northcutt Blvd.
843/856-9131

**Tomorrow's Treasures & Antiques**
113 Pitt St.
843/881-2072

## 31 MULLINS

**Southern Treasures**
155 S. Main St.
843/464-6425

**Patsy's Antiques**
302 S. Main St.
843/464-2066

## 32 MURRELLS INLET

### Wachesaw Row Antique Mall
4650 Hwy. 17 S.
843/651-7719
Open: Mon.–Sat. 10–5
Directions: Located between Georgetown and Myrtle Beach on Hwy. 17 Bypass

This seven-dealer mall carries a little bit of everything including American, French, and English furniture and accessories, primitives, paintings, prints, china and glassware. They also offer a selection of coins, guns, and sports memorabilia.

**Golden Image Game Room**
2761 Hwy. 17
843/651-0338

**Tillie's Attic**
3692 Hwy. 17
843/651-1900

**Memories Antiques**
4763 Hwy. 17 Bypass
843/651-7888

**Legacy Antique Mall**
3420 Hwy. 17
843/651-0884

**A & G Furniture**
3974 Hwy. 17
843/651-3777

**Long Bay Trading Co.**
4771 Hwy. 17 Bypass
843/357-1252

## 33 MYRTLE BEACH

**Peggy's Antiques & Collectibles**
1040 Hwy. 17 S.
843/238-1442

**Collectibles Mall**
4011 Hwy. 501
843/236-1029

**Socastee Trading Post**
8569 Hwy. 544
843/236-2244

**Noah & Friends**
1307 Celebrity Circle
843/448-8105

**Myrtle Beach Antiques Mall**
1014 Hwy. 501
843/448-4762

**Fox & Hounds Antiques Mall**
4015 Hwy. 501
843/236-1027

**Joseph Bridger Fine Antiques**
5311 N. Kings Hwy.
843/449-4171

## 34 NEWBERRY

**Leslie's Main Street Antiques & Auctions**
934 Main St.
803/276-8600

**Trader John's**
11213 S.C. Hwy. 121
803/276-0432

**Antiques and SoForths**
1213 Main St.
803/276-1073

## 35 NINETY SIX

**Burnett House**
118 Main St. N.W.
864/543-3236

**Mainly Antiques**
101 Main St. N.E.
864/543-3636

## 36 NORTH AUGUSTA

In 1833, the Charleston-Hamburg Railroad ended its 138-mile rail line, then the longest steam-operated railroad in the world, at the small town of Hamburg, near the present-day town of North Augusta. Chartered by the state in 1906, North Augusta was once a foremost winter resort frequented by the very wealthy. Magnificent old Victorian cottages and imposing churches are reminders of the city's past.

**Plunder Valley Antiques**
207 Belvedere Clearwater Road
803/279-1200

**Peddler's Way**
4631 Jefferson Davis Hwy.
803/593-4447

## 37 NORTH MYRTLE BEACH

**Junktique**
204 Hwy. 17 N.
843/249-7443

**Cottage Antiques of Cherry Grove**
621 Sea Mountain Hwy.
843/249-7563

**B & B Antiques**
1604 Hwy. 17 S.
843/361-0101

**Curious Mermaid**
1669 Old Hwy. 17 N.
843/280-0050

## 38 ORANGEBURG

**Browsabout Antiques & Accents**
1036 Broughton St.
803/536-2182

**Something Different**
1041 Broughton St.
803/536-0710

## 39 PAWLEYS ISLAND

**Elizabeth Taylor Satterfield**
42 N. Causeway
843/237-8701

**Traddrock Antiques & Design**
2176 S. Kings Hwy.
843/237-9232

**McElveen Design, Antiques & Furniture**
13302 Ocean Hwy.
843/237-3326

**Mary Frances Miller Antiques**
Hammock Shop/Hwy. 17
843/237-2466

**Harrington Altman Limited**
10729 Ocean Hwy.
843/237-2056

**Classic Consignments, Inc.**
11195 Ocean Hwy.
843/237-8355

## 40 PELZER

**Pelzer Antique Market**
19 Main St.
864/947-5558

**Sue's Antiques & Collectibles**
6633 Hwy. 29 N.
864/947-2039

## 41 PENDLETON

**Pendleton Antique Co.**
134 E. Main St.
864/646-7725

**Pendleton Place Antiques**
651 S. Mechanic St.
864/646-7673

## 42 PIEDMONT

**P & N Antiques International**
100 Piedmont Road
864/295-3134

**Papa's Book Haven Antiques**
2510 River Road
864/269-5700

## 43 ROCK HILL

In northern York County, this rapidly expanding city is the county's newest and largest. It was named for a cut made through white flinty rock during construction of the Columbia to Charlotte railroad. The Catawba Cultural Center at 1536 Tom Steven Road., in the small town of Catawba about 10 miles southeast of Rock Hill, has exhibits and videos about the Catawba Indian Nation. A craft store, which features the distinctive Catawba pottery and nature trail, is also open.

**Antique & Garden Shoppe**
609 Cherry Road
803/327-4858

**Upcountry Antiques & Handcraft**
1449 Ebenezer Road
803/324-5503

**Reid Antiques**
2641 India Hook Road
803/366-4949

**Collectibles on Main**
427 E. Main St.
803/366-8337

**Antique Mall**
104 S. Oakland Ave.
803/324-1855

**Pix Designer Warehouse**
147 W. Oakland Ave.
803/325-1116

## 44 SIMPSONVILLE

**Cudds Zoo Antiques**
101 E. Curtis St.
864/963-2375
Open: Mon.–Sat. 10–5 and by appointment
Directions: Located three miles off I-385 on Main Street

This shop carries mostly glass: Depression, pressed, cameo, and art. There is also a small quantity of quality furniture. The owner does chair recaning.

**Hunter House Antiques & B&B**
201 E. College St.
864/967-2827

**Satterfield's Antiques**
106 W. Curtis St.
864/967-0955

## 45 SPARTANBURG

**John Morton Antiques**
160 E. Broad St.
864/583-0427
Directions: Follow the Spartanburg exits off either I-26 or I-85. John Morton Antiques is located in downtown Spartanburg.

This shop specializes in period, regional and country furniture and accessories, and has a furniture restoration service attached.

**South Pine Antique Mall**
856 S. Pine St.
864/542-2975
Open: Mon.–Sat. 10–6, closed Sun.
Directions: Take Exit 585 off Interstate 85. Located five miles south of the interstate on Pine Street.

This 6,000-square-foot mall encompasses a variety of furniture, glassware, lamps, mirrors, pictures and collectibles. Several quality period pieces as well as '40s mahoganys may also be found here.

**Old Southern Trading Co.**
1926 Boiling Springs Road
864/578-1025

**Town & Country Antiques & Cllbls.**
2929 Boiling Springs Road
864/578-0970

**Yesterday's Treasures**
2306 Chesnee Hwy.
864/542-9888

**Chestnut Galleries Antiques**
144 Chestnut St.
864/585-9576

**C.W. Trantham Trading Co.**
360 Dogwood Club Road
864/542-2311

**Ballard's Sales Co.**
8521 Fairforest Road
864/582-4852

**Bye-Gone Treasures**
169 E. Main St.
864/542-1590

**Nan's Antiques & Collectibles**
330 E. Main St.
864/585-6039

**Shades of the Past Antique Mall**
512 E. Main St.
864/585-1172

**Prissy's Antique Mall**
914 E. Main St.
864/582-1032

**Treasures of Time**
155 W. Main St.
864/573-7178

**Jeanne Harley Antiques**
910 S. Pine St.
864/585-0386

**Rickinghall Antiques Warehouse**
400 Westbrook Court
864/583-7221

## 46 SUMMERTON

Fishermen particularly love this town on the north shore of Lake Marion. Antique stores and beautiful historic homes and buildings enhance its charm. Stop for freshly ground grits at Senn's Grist Mill on Cantey Street on Saturdays from 8:30 to noon.

**Antiques, Etc.**
103 Main St.
803/485-8714

**Antique Mall**
123 Main St.
803/485-2205

### 47 SUMMERVILLE

## Country Store & Antiques
1106 Main St.
843/871-7548
Open: Mon.–Sat. 10–5:30, Sun. 1–5 in Oct.–Dec.
Directions: Country Store is located ½ mile from I-26 at Exit 199A.

These folks have been in business for 13 years, and their motto is "Where Customers Are Friends." The shop's 2,000 square feet are filled with primitives, oak furniture and pottery. They also carry a line of gifts including All God's Children by Martha Holcomb.

**Missy's Memories Antiques**
127 S. Main St.
843/871-5334

**Carriage House Collectables**
1213 S. Main St.
843/873-5704

**Early Traditions**
100 W. Richardson Ave.
843/851-1627

**Antiques 'n' Stuff**
128 E. Richardson Ave.
843/875-4155

**People Places & Quilts**
129 W. Richardson Ave.
843/871-8872

**Town Fair Antiques**
131 E. Richardson Ave.
843/873-3462

**Granny's Attic**
71 Trolley Road
843/871-6838

**Remember When**
301 Trolley Road
843/821-1018

**Adell's**
211 W. Richardson Ave.
843/871-8249

**North & South Gun Shop**
113 S. Main St.
843/821-7524

### 48 SUMTER

Named for Revolutionary War hero General Thomas Sumter, this progressive city was settled around 1740.

Visit Sumter's antique row: seven shops on Broad Street less than one mile from Highways 15, 521, 378 and 76, and 15 miles from I-20 and I-95.

**T. J. Player**
202 Broad St.
803/778-1173

**Why-Not Antiques**
202 Broad St.
803/778-1173

**Broadstone Manor Antiques**
204 Broad St.
803/778-1890

**Estate Antiques Gifts and Clocks**
210 Broad St.
803/773-4214

**Keepsakes and Collectibles**
408 Broad St.
803/773-2235

**Sumter Antique Mall**
719 Broad St.
803/778-0269

**Gingerbread House**
205 Broad St.
803/775-9716

### 49 TAYLOR

**Spinning Wheel Antiques**
3228 Wade Hampton Blvd.
864/244-3195

**Danny's Antique Mall**
4949 Wade Hampton Blvd.
864/848-7316

**Buncombe Antiques Mall**
5000 Wade Hampton Blvd.
864/268-4498

**Way Back When Antique Mall**
5111 Wade Hampton Blvd.
864/848-9839

### 50 WEST COLUMBIA

## 378 Antique Mall
620 Sunset Blvd.
803/791-3132
Open: Mon.–Sat. 10–5, Sun. 1:30–5:30
Directions: From I-26, take the Hwy. 378 exit, go 2⁸/₁₀ miles (Hwy. 378 and Sunset Blvd. are one and the same).

With more than 50 dealers in 20,000 square feet of space, and 10 years in business, visitors can expect to find just about everything they are looking for at the 378 Antique Mall. They feature furniture from the 1800s to the early 1900s, glassware, lamps, framed art, military items, vintage jewelry, country collectables, dolls, porcelains, chandeliers, silver, art glass and cameo glass.

**Harvest Moon**
351 Meeting St.
803/739-0637

**Rudy's Upper Deck**
511 Meeting St.
803/739-9191

**De Ja Vu Antiques**
615 Meeting St.
803/926-0021

**Boltinhouse Jewelers**
3015 Platt Springs Road
803/794-1466

**Westbank Antique Mall**
118 State St.
803/796-9764

**State Street Antiques**
131 State St.
803/791-0008

**Old Mill Antique Mall**
310 State St.
803/796-4229

**Treasure Aisles Bazaar**
1217 Sunset Blvd.
803/791-5777

**Park's Furniture Antiques**
3131 Sunset Blvd.
803/791-4071

**Dewey's Antiques**
3740 Sunset Blvd.
803/794-9075

**Eau Gallie Interiors**
3937 Sunset Blvd.
803/926-9370

**Attic Treasures**
620 Sunset Blvd.
803/796-1882

**Dewey's Antiques**
3745 Sunset Blvd.
803/794-9075

# Tennessee

Reelfoot Lake 72
Troy 84
Obion 67
Sharon 76
Paris 69
155
45W
45E
Dyersburg 27
Trenton 83
51
70
Henning 39
Covington 22
Brownsville 9
Jackson 42
40
Selmer 74
64
45
22
13
Clarksburg 13
Clarksville 14
24
Cross Plains 23
65
48
Erin 29
Ashland City 4
Greenbrier 36
Goodlettsville 35
Gallatin 32
Hendersonville 38
Old Hickory 68
Carthage 11
56
79
641
70
Waverly 87
Dickson 25
Madison 56
Nashville 65
Hermitage 40
Lebanon 51
Hickman 41
Alexandria 1
Buffalo Valley 10
Smithville 79
231
Brentwood 7
Franklin 31
Nolensville 66
Arrington 3
College Grove 17
Murfreesboro 64
Woodbury 88
McMinnville 60
Columbia 19
41
55
56
13
48
Mt. Pleasant 63
Shelbyville 77
Wartrace 86
Manchester 58
Lewisburg 53
Lawrenceburg 50
Pulaski 71
Tullahoma 85
24
43
31
65
Fayetteville 30
64
Arlington 2
Bartlett 6
Memphis 61
Cordova 21
Germantown 34
Collierville 18
40

Mileage 0 — 30

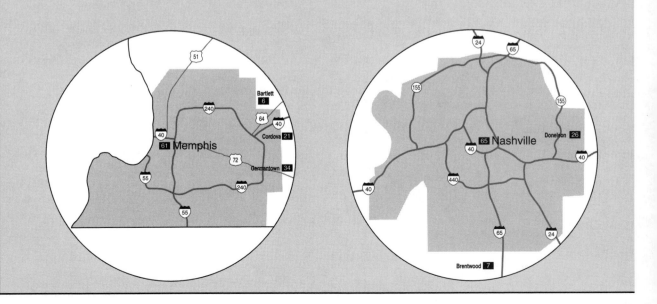

51
Bartlett 6
240
64
40
40
Cordova 21
Memphis 61
72
Germantown 34
55
240
55

24
65
155
155
Nashville 65
Donelson 26
40
40
40
440
40
65
24
Brentwood 7

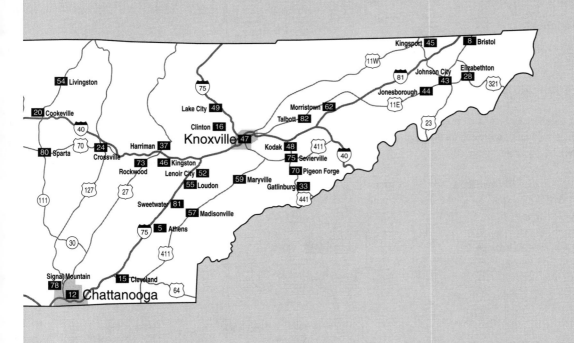

54 Livingston

20 Cookeville

75

Lake City 49

Clinton 16

40

70 80 Sparta

24 Harriman 37 Knoxville 47

Crossville 73 46 Kingston

Rockwood Lenoir City 52

127 55 Loudon

27 Sweetwater 81

111 57 Madisonville

30 75 5 Athens

411

Signal Mountain 15 Cleveland

78 64

12 Chattanooga

Kingsport 45 8 Bristol

11W

81 Johnson City Elizabethton

Jonesborough 44 43 28

11E 321

23

Morristown 62

Talbott 82

Kodak 48 411

75 Sevierville

70 Pigeon Forge

59 Maryville

Gatlinburg 33

441

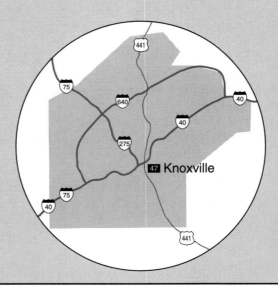

441

75 40

640

40

275

47 Knoxville

75

40

441

*Tennessee*

## 1 ALEXANDRIA

**Judy's Antiques**
Hwy. 70
615/529-1008

Antiques, collectibles, advertising, pitchers and lamps.

## 2 ARLINGTON AREA

**Lamb Crossing Antiques**
11022 Hwy. 70
901/867-0404
Fax: 901/867-0929
Open: Daily Mon.–Fri. 10–4, Sat. 10–2:30, Sun. 1–5 (closed last Sun. of the month)
Directions: Traveling I-40, take Exit 20. Go north on Canada Road for 2 miles to Hwy. 70. Turn right and continue 3 miles. The store is on the left just after the Arlington city limits sign.

This store opened in March of 1997. It's a quaint little shop, located in an old store, and filled with an eclectic blend of country and unusual items. Make sure you stop by on your way to Memphis.

### *Great Places to Eat*

**Bozo's**
Hwy. 70 (approximately 20 miles from Memphis)
901/294-3400

Bozo's menu becomes apparent about a half mile away — barbeque! About the time you see the cloud of hickory smoke hovering over the restaurant, you start smelling all that sizzling pork. Bozo's is one of west Tennessee's landmarks, having been open every day except Sundays since 1923!

There is absolutely nothing about the decor to inspire a sense of elegance or upscale atmosphere — tired wood paneling, formica-topped tables, wooden chairs, a well-scuffed linoleum floor, pale green stools lined up at gray counters, a Chevrolet clock on the wall. The only reason you go to Bozo's is for some of the best food you'll ever eat. They serve shrimp, chicken, salads, and steak, but the house specialty is pork, especially something called a "white and brown pulled pig plate." It's succulent white meat from the inside of the shoulder, and crustier brown meat from the outside, pulled into shreds and hunks and heaped on a plate along with saucy barbeque beans and sweet cole slaw. You can also get chopped plates and barbeque sandwiches, and sauce on the side. Nobody does it better!

## 3 ARRINGTON

**DH Interiors**
4812A Hwy. 96
615/395-4630
Open: Mon.–Sat. 10–5, Sun. 1–5, closed Wed.

One of my favorite antique shops and a delightful owner as well, this multidealer shop will have a lot of your favorite things. Country furnishings and accessories, garden and architectural pieces and unusual stuff is what you'll find here. The best part — the prices are unusually good.

**Mar-Jac's Bygone Days**
4812C Hwy. 96
615/395-4493

## 4 ASHLAND CITY

**B J's Attic**
108 N. Main St.
615/792-7208

**Saint Elsewhere Antiques**
110 N. Main St.
615/792-9337

**Ruth Ellen's Antiques**
202 N. Main St.
615/792-1915

## 5 ATHENS

**Ourloom**
804 S. White St.
423/745-6055

**Antiques Unique**
Hwy. 30 W.
423/745-5941

**Gene's Olde Country Shoppe**
813 S. White St.
423/745-2254

**Cottage Antiques & Gifts**
15 W. Washington Ave.
423/745-8528

**Piedmont Antique & Interior Design**
104 N. White St.
423/745-2731

**Hughes Furniture Company**
316 N. White St.
423/745-2183

## 6 BARTLETT

**Upstage Antiques**
6214 Stage Road
901/385-0035
Open: Mon.–Wed. 10–6, Thurs.–Sat. 10–8, Sun. 12–6

**The Antique Gallery**
6044 Stage Road
901/385-2544
Open: Mon.–Sat. 10–6, Sun. 1–5
Directions: On I-40, Exit 12 and travel north on Sycamore View to Stage Road. Turn right onto Stage Road and left at the first light between McDonald's and KFC.

Dealer space of 35,000 square feet may seem imposing, but the only overwhelming thing about the Antique Gallery is the positive response of its visitors. From abounding friendliness to the pride expressed in the displays of the 150 dealers, shoppers delight in taking part in this group shop. Although extremely spacious, the gallery is always full, but never overcrowded, as owner Robert Bowden and manager Eric Triche strive to maintain an "airy" feeling.

Booths are inviting with excellent dealer presentation of the merchandise. Boasts Mr. Bowden, "The prices offered in the Gallery are fantastic, the best in the area, and because of the fairness in pricing, collectors are drawn here from all regions of the country." Dealers are offered even better pricing through discounts.

Within such immenseness you would not expect the diversity the Antique Gallery provides. Offerings include most any familiar name: Nippon, Hummel, Dresden, Wedgwood, Roseville, Hull, McCoy, Royal Doulton, Limoges — to name a few — and also an array of categories like Depression glass, carnival glass, crystal, silver, and flow blue. The selection in furniture is equally diverse. Many other collectibles are also part of the inventory. Showcases highlight the small and often rare items.

Include the family in this stop and dine in the Serendipity Tea Room any day, except Sunday, from 11 a.m. to 2 p.m. Menu items are freshly made and include soups, salads, sandwiches, and deliciously different biscuits. Twenty-eight specialty teas are also offered. Private parties and receptions can be held in the Serendipity Tea Room after 6 p.m. If you find any of the furnishings inviting, they too are for sale.

## 7 BRENTWOOD

**Ivy Crest Gallery**
1501 Franklin Road
615/377-0676

**Gallery of Cool Springs**
7104 Crossroads Blvd., #115
615/661-5435

**Alcove Antiques**
9825 Concord Road
615/776-5152

## 8 BRISTOL

**Oak Door Antiques**
1258 Hwy. 126
423/968-7177

**Ruth King Antiques**
618 State St.
423/968-9062

**Mary Ann Stone Antiques**
610 State St.
423/968-5181

**States Alternative Antiques**
105 17th St.
423/764-3188

**Antiques Unlimited**
620 State St.
423/764-4211

### Great Places to Stay

**New Hope Bed & Breakfast**
822 Georgia Ave.
423/989-3343 or 1-888-989-3343
Open: Daily
Rates $70–$130
Directions: From I-81, take Exit 3 onto Commonwealth Avenue. Turn left onto State Street (downtown Bristol) and pass under the large sign. At the second light after the sign turn right onto Georgia Avenue and go five blocks. The inn is on the right, on the corner of Georgia and Pine.

The New Hope Bed & Breakfast is an 1892 Victorian that wraps its guests in a cloud of turn-of-the-century memories. The house exudes an atmosphere of Victorian elegance, complete with furnishings that are a mixture of antique and period. Located in an historic neighborhood, guests can stroll the streets on guided walking tours. The large wrap-around porch is the setting not only for morning or afternoon relaxation, but where breakfast is served in good weather. The private baths are large and inviting, with robes provided for after-bath enjoyment.

## 9 BROWNSVILLE

**Mid-Town Auction**
230 S. Church St.
901/772-3382
Auction Dates: First Sun. of the month at 10 a.m.
Directions: Off I-40

This little country auction has some surprising results. They always manage to have something that I want. The merchandise varies from sale to sale; sometimes early primitive pieces; sometimes rough; sometimes Depression. You just never know so, you have to be there. They usually have lots of glass and advertising items; Roseville and other potteries and old prints can almost always be found. A great dealer auction!

## 10 BUFFALO VALLEY

**Buffalo Valley Antiques**
18560 Buffalo Valley Road
615/858-6071
Open: Mon.–Wed. 9–3, Thurs.–Sun. 10–4
Directions: Take Exit 268 from I-40

A large selection of primitives, glassware, iron, and much more in an early 1900s general store and bank.

# *Tennessee*

## 11  CARTHAGE

**The Specialty Shop**
209 3rd Ave. W.
615/735-8441

**Massey's Country Antiques**
336 Defeated Creek Hwy.
615/774-3146

**Carthage Antique Mall**
110 W. 3rd Ave.
615/735-1590

**Windy Hill Antiques**
Hwy. 70 N.
615/735-2561

**Shirley's Antiques**
47 Cookeville Hwy.
615/735-9887

## 12  CHATTANOOGA

### East Town Antique Mall
6503 Slater Road
423/899-5498 or 423/490-0121
Open: Daily 10–6 and Sat. 9–8 during daylight savings
Directions: From I-75: Take Exit 1 or 1B ½ mile south of the junction of I-24 and I-75 (one mile north of the Georgia state line). *Traveling south*, take Exit 1, turn right, then turn right at the first red light. *Traveling north*, take Exit 1B, turn right at the second red light. The mall is behind Cracker Barrel.

This upscale mall, opened 10 years ago by John and Carol Hudson, allows antiques and collectibles only — no reproductions. "We stress quality," says Carol, "and we discourage damaged merchandise." With more than 300 booths and showcases, you can imagine the diversity of items you will find here. An abbreviated list includes the largest selection of American art pottery, two dealers who specialize in advertising memorabilia, several Depression and elegant glass  dealers, one dealer who carries R.S. Prussia and art glass, one dealer who has specialized in pressed glass for more than 25 years, two dealers who carry American, German, Russian and Japanese military collectibles (all authentic), several dealers whose display of American and English dinnerware includes many hard-to-find patterns, one dealer who offers a huge array of signed cast iron, including a complete set of Griswold skillets from the smallest to the largest, another dealer who specializes in Torquay and who is part president of the collector's club, several toy and cowboy memorabilia dealers, one dealer who specializes in Nippon, another who carries many hard to find primitive items. The mall is also home to many retired modern collectibles such as Department 56, David Winder, Lladro, Royal Doulton, Wedgwood, Hummel, Disney Classics and others.

They keep a "Want List" for customers looking for special items, and

with the new expansion of 12,000 square feet, the Hudsons have added a large selection of fine furniture in all styles. There are several motels and restaurants at East Town's exit, so plan to spend the night to explore all that Chattanooga has to offer.

**Coates Antiques**
520 Ashland Terrace
423/870-1880

**Cooper's Antiques & Decor**
3210 Brainerd Road
423/629-7411

**Chase Dacus Collection**
3214 Brainerd Road
423/622-1715

**Marie's Antiques**
6503 Slater Road
423/899-4607

**Temple & Co. Antiques**
1816 Broad St.
423/265-9339

**Chattanooga Antique Mall**
1901 Broad St.
423/266-9910

**McCracken Bros.**
2622 Broad St.
423/266-0027

**High Point Antiques**
1704 Cummings Hwy.
423/756-9566

**Davis's Trading Post**
3627 Cummings Hwy.
423/821-0061

**Dacus Antiques & Fine Furniture**
2422 S. Hickory
423/622-2220

**Norma Jean's Antiques**
3829 Hixson Pike
423/877-5719

**Barnyard Antiques, Etc.**
7160 Lee Hwy.
423/899-3913

**Furniture Barn**
39 E. Main St.
423/265-1406

**Berning House Antiques & Dolls**
605 Marlboro Ave.
423/624-4436

**Lambs & Ivy Antiques**
249 Northgate Mall
423/877-6871

**Lowe's Antiques**
4000 Ringgold Road
423/633-2902

**Junque Nique Shop**
6009 Ringgold Road
423/894-7817

**Cross the Years**
6503 Slater Road
423/892-4193

**Antiques on the Southside**
Corner of 14th & Williams
423/265-3003

**Antiques & Country Decor**
3813 Dayton Blvd.
423/870-3687

**Antiques on the Southside**
1401 Williams St., #C
423/265-3003

**Clement's Carnahan, Inc.**
2420 S. Hickory St.
423/698-2800

**Dacus Antiques**
3214 Brainerd Road
423/622-1717

**Fanny's Antiques & Fancies**
3202 Brainerd Road
423/624-6421

**Galleries at Southside**
1404 Cowart St.
423/267-8101

**Status Symbol**
1707 Cummings Hwy.
423/267-3001

# Tennessee

## Great Places to Stay

### Adams Hilborne
801 Vine St.
423/265-5000

Located at the cornerstone of the Fort Hood Historic District, this majestic Romanesque Victorian mansion is built in castlelike proportions of native mountain stone. The Adams Hilborne is lavished with fine antiques, original artwork, and exquisite fabrics in all the oversized guest suites.

### 13 CLARKSBURG

**Oma's Antik Haus**
3375 Hwy. 22
901/986-3018

### 14 CLARKSVILLE

### Carter's Cabin
3650 Hwy. 41A
931/358-9707

Quality antiques including furniture, Dresden, lamps, clocks and accessories at affordable prices. Dealers welcome.

### Pedigo's Madison Street Antiques
1461 Madison St.
931/553-0420
Open: Mon.–Sun. 1–5

Antique furniture, pottery, R.S. Prussia, Nippon, Limoges, Roseville, McCoy, Hull, costume jewelry, old books, lamps, and more.

**East Gate Antiques**
321 Drinkard Dr.
931/551-9572

**High Street Antique Mall**
40 High St.
931/553-4040

**Ragin Cajun Antiques**
210 Kraft St.
931/552-0545

**Madison Street Antiques**
1461 Madison St.
931/553-0420

**Alcock's Heritage Hill Antiques**
416 N. 2nd St.
931/648-3989

**Traditions**
131 Franklin St.
931/551-9800

**Cherry Station Antiques & More**
212 Warfield Blvd.
931/648-4830

**The Emporium**
739 Madison St.
931/645-1607

**Granny's Antiques**
924 Providence Blvd.
931/648-0077

**D.R. Marable Sales Antiques**
1303 Tylertown Road
931/551-3259

**Saint John's Antiques**
128 University
931/503-1515

**Betty's Antiques Market**
152 Kraft St.
931/648-9201

**Country Junction**
140 Lafayette Road
931/645-9349

**Hidden Treasures Antiques**
208 Kraft St.
931/645-2345

**Sango Antiques**
3484 Hwy. 41A
931/358-3545

**Salem Place Antiques**
1761 Hwy. 48
931/645-3943

**Carousel Antiques**
161 Kraft St.
931/645-8122

**Cracklin' Rose Flea Market**
1218 College St.
931/905-0029

**Homespun Corner**
1214 College St.
931/552-4422

**Wildflower Antiques**
I-24 at Exit 11 (at Homeplace Rest.)
email: cosy@usit.net

## Great Places to Eat

### The Rose Garden Tearoom
512 Madison St.
931/906-1000
Open: Mon.–Sat. 9–5 (shop), Mon.–Sat. 11:30–3:30 (tearoom)

Enjoy a delicious breakfast or lunch in a beautiful Victorian setting; homemade sandwiches, salads, casseroles, and desserts.

### 15 CLEVELAND

**Carousel**
80 Church St. N.E.
423/339-3934

**Antiques Parlour**
208 Grove Ave. N.W.
423/476-6921

**Treasures Forever**
151 Inman St. S.E.
423/478-2711

**Boardwalk Uniques & Antiques**
251 Inman St. N.E.
423/478-1010

**Presswood's Vintage Antiques**
3350 Ocoee St. N.
423/479-4460

**Carolyn's Antiques & Oriental**
464 1st St. N.W.
423/472-5000

**Lace Emporium**
2065 Collins Dr. N.W.
423/476-5836

**Westside Shop**
2910 Harrison Pike
423/339-9838

**Cleveland Furniture Sales**
220 Inman St. S.W.
423/472-0099

**Reflections**
94 Mikel St. N.W.
423/559-0140

**Lamps & Things**
702 17th St. N.W.
423/339-3963

**Yesterday's Treasures**
2101 Dalton Pike S.E.
423/476-1808

### 16 CLINTON

**Clinton Antique Mall**
317 N. Main St.
423/457-3110

**Market Place Antiques**
333 Market St.
423/463-8635

# Tennessee

## Leon Tywater & Sons Auction Company

Hwy. 31 A
615/790-7145 or 615/368-7772
Call for auction dates
Directions: 30 miles south of Nashville on 31A

There are lots of reasons to attend Leon & Andy's (that's Leon's son) auction. One being, that for an auction to be located so far out in the sticks, they sure have some "good stuff." I honestly don't know where they get their merchandise, but I can tell you this — it is exceptional. If you are into early American (as I am), then this is the sale for you. The last time I attended the auction I purchased an 1800s plantation desk, a cannonball rope bed, a cherry sideboard (pegged), a mantle with original mustard paint and I let a fabulous sugar chest get away. But, if this isn't reason enough to encourage you, then this most assuredly will. Leon's wife is a wonderful cook! Leon too! They start cooking about a week in advance of the sale. Leon smokes the barbeque, and his wife makes homemade sandwiches, pies (several kinds), cakes and fried pies. But, my favorite is the chocolate cake — "it's to die for." The last time I talked to Leon he told me to call first and he would have her bake me a whole one. Well, get ready, Leon, as soon as this book goes to print I'm on my way, so preheat the oven.

**Stonekirk Antiques**
8327 Horton Hwy.
615/368-7528

## **18** COLLIERVILLE

Collierville has over 13 shops and malls, all within a short distance of each other. Most of the shops are located on the historic town square however, two wonderful malls can be found as you enter Collierville on Poplar. These two malls are listed below.

*Directions to Collierville:* From I-240, take the Poplar Avenue exit for Germantown. Continue on Poplar through Germantown. Collierville is located approximately 10 minutes from Germantown. To reach the town square, continue on Poplar to the third light past Abbington Antique Mall. Turn right on Main Street. A historic town square marker is located in front of the bank on your right to indicate its location.

## Sheffield Antiques Mall

708 W. Poplar Ave.
901/853-7822
Open: Mon.–Thurs. 10–5, Fri.–Sat. 10–8, Sun. 12–6
Directions: Located behind Wendy's on the left.

Sheffield Antiques Mall is Collierville's largest antique haven. With over 150 quality dealers you are sure to find many treasures here. The mall is represented by some of the best dealers in the Memphis area, offering a wonderful selection of French, English and American antiques.

Lunch in the Garden Room Cafe located within the mall. Open for lunch 11–2, Tuesday–Saturday, the Cafe features gourmet soups, salads, sandwiches and desserts. A sampling of the sumptuous menu includes Hot Ham Delights, Crab Toasties Florentine, Faccacia Rueben, Napa Valley Chicken Salad, Shrimp and Crab Louis, Caribbean Tuna Salad and Gorgonzola Potato Salad. The dessert menu includes Sweet German Chocolate Pie (the best), Cream Cheese Clouds and Fruit Cobbler.

## Abbington Antiques Mall

575 W. Poplar Ave.
901/854-3568
Open: Mon.–Sat. 10–6, Sun. 12–6
Directions: Located across the street from Wal-Mart on Poplar

Abbington Antiques, since its very beginning, has been known for exceptional antiques. Presenting distinctive pieces for the discerning customer is the desire of the dealers who make Abbington what it is today. With a focus on decorating for the home or office, an unusual offering of architectural iron, sewing collectibles, Regina music boxes, phonographs, radios, lamps, mirrors, statuary, candles, antique tools and more is available. The furnishings offered by the shop are of excellent style and quality and are often sought after by decorators from the Memphis area.

**DeSheilds Lighting, Inc.**
451 Hwy. 72
901/854-8691

**White Church Antiques & Tea Room**
196 N. Main St.
901/854-6433

**Old Towne Antiques & Gifts**
521 W. Poplar Ave.
901/854-7063

**Past & Presents**
307 W. Poplar Ave.
901/853-6454

**Roseview Antique Mall**
112 U.S. Hwy. 72 E.
901/854-1462

## Unique Antiques & Auction

449 U.S. Hwy. 72 W. #3
901/854-1141
Web site: www.uniqueauctions.com
Auction held third Sun. of every month at 1 p.m.

Offering a huge selection of the finest American and European antiques, fine furnishings and decorative items.

*Tennessee*

**Listed below are the shops located
around the historic town square.**

## Center Street Antiques
198 S. Center St.
901/861-3711
Open: Mon.–Sat. 10–5, Sun. & evenings by appointment
Directions: From I-240, take Poplar Avenue exit for Germantown.
Continue on Poplar through Germantown to Collierville, take a right
(east) on Hwy. 72. At the first traffic light, turn left on Center Street.

Located one block south (across the railroad tracks) of Collierville's
historic town square, Center Street Antiques is the newest addition to the
town's growing collection of antique shops. Filled with a unique
assortment of English, Continental, American, primitive and Victorian
furniture, there's something for everyone. The great selection of
architectural pieces, gardenware, vintage lighting, china, antique toys
and collectibles is sure to inspire the decorator in you. With each new
dealer, the list of fabulous finds continues to grow.

**Town Square Antique Mall**
118 E. Mulberry St.
901/854-9839

**Not Forgotten**
94 N. Main St.
901/854-8859

**Sentimental Journey Antiques**
118 N. Main St.
901/853-9019

**Liberty Tree Antiques**
120 N. Main St.
901/854-4364

**English Country Antiques**
102 E. Mulberry St.
901/853-3170

**Remember When Antiques**
110 E. Mulberry St.
901/853-5470

**Shepherd's Store**
122 E. Mulberry St.
901/853-8415

**Antique Marketplace of Collierville**
88 N. Main St.
901/854-8859

### 19 COLUMBIA

## Accents and Antiques of Columbia
37-38 Public Square
119 Nashville Hwy. — Hwy. 31
931/380-8975
Fax: 931/380-8975
Open: Mon.–Sat. 10–5, Sun. 1–5
Directions: From I-65: Take Exit 46, then turn left onto Hwy. 412. At
the end of the highway, take a left onto Hwy. 31. Follow the road until
the 2nd light. Accents and Antiques is on the right.

Owner Debbie Harris has been in business six years and has over 7,000
square feet of general antiques and collectibles. She offers the very needed
service of lamp repair, so when your lighting treasures burn out, you
know where to go.

## Berry's Antiques
1402-B Hampshire Pike
931/540-8313
Open: Mon.–Sat. 10–5

Furniture, Fiesta, carnival, Fostoria, Candlewick, Blue Willow,
Depression, Roseville, vaseline, cranberry, Fenton, and head vases.

## Bill's Attic
1106 Hampshire Pike
931/380-0733

Hundreds of old license plates, old bottles, old tools, kitchen items,
advertising and collectibles.

**Sewell's Antiques**
217 Bear Creek Pike/Hwy. 412
931/388-3973

**Memory Shop Antiques**
1564 Bear Creek Pike/Hwy. 412
931/388-4131

**High Attic Antiques**
216 W. 8th St.
931/381-2819

**Uptown Antiques**
220 W. 8th St.
931/388-4061

**Moore's Antiques & Etc.**
910 S. Garden St.
931/388-4289

**Steely's Corner**
201 E. 9th St.
931/388-7101

**Golden Ivy**
I-65, Columbia Exit 46
931/840-9909

### 20 COOKEVILLE

**A-1 Clock Shop & Antiques**
8 S. Washington
931/526-1496

**Broadway Antiques**
247 W. Broad St.
931/520-1978

**Cookeville Antique Mall**
1095 Bunker Hill Road
931/526-8223

**Attic Window**
1281 Bunker Hill Road
931/528-7273

**Cedar Street Antiques**
44 S. Cedar Ave.
931/528-9129

**Cherry Creek Antiques**
5589 Cherry Creek Road
931/526-7834

**Fiesta Plus**
380 Hawkins Crawford Road
931/372-8333

**City Square Antiques**
8 S. Washington
931/526-6939

**Antique Vault**
26 W. Broad St.
931/528-3388

## 21 CORDOVA

### Antique Market of Cordova

1740 Germantown Pkwy.
901/759-0414
Open: Mon.–Sat. 10–6, Sun. 1–5
Directions: Traveling I-40 just east of Memphis, take the Germantown exit, which will be Germantown Parkway. Turn south and stay on Germantown Parkway through two red lights. The market is located at the third red light on the southeast corner where Dexter Road intersects with Germantown Parkway. Look for the big red Antiques sign. Turn left on Dexter Road and make an immediate right into the Dexter Ridge Shopping Center parking lot. Located in the corner of the center. Only about 1 mile from I-40.

Within this quality, upscale market you'll find pieces from Victorian to primitive to Deco. A charming shop to explore, the shop is known for its quality glassware and pristine furnishings. One dealer specializes in old radios and lamps. Garden accessories are a favorite among locals so you are sure to find wonderful pieces available at all times.

### Sign of the Goose

9155 Rocky Cannon
901/756-0726
Open: By appointment only

The Sign of the Goose is a "must see" for anyone who likes antiques, old homes, history, or just a good story.

The shop itself is located at the unique, two-story log house where Bill and Sylvia Cochran live. Sylvia actually uses her entire house as an informal showroom — but call first, because this is a by-appointment-only arrangement.

The house/shop began as an 1810 log home in Kentucky. In the 1970s a man had disassembled, tagged, numbered and hauled the logs to Tennessee, where he planned to rebuild it. But he decided not to finish the project, and that's how Sylvia first saw her family's future home: as a skeletal framework and a pile of old logs. She knew she could turn it into a wonderful home, and after much discussion with her family, Sylvia realized she would get her chance when husband, Bill, gave her a box of Lincoln Logs for their 16th anniversary!

The Cochrans moved the entire home — as it was — to their 20-acre homesite in Cordova near Memphis. The house was already atypical of log homes of its period, with its original 2,000 square feet and full second floor with high ceilings. And it was ideal for raising five children, who not only had a big, tough home, but acres of woods and ponds and outdoor delights to explore and enjoy. After reconstructing it, bringing it up to modern standards, adding a new porch and balcony across the front, and a kitchen addition to the back, the Cochrans had their dream house.

The rough, strikingly colored walls and plank flooring are an ideal and authentic setting for Sylvia's collection of American country furniture. She's been antiquing for 20 years, and has amassed an enormous wealth of pieces, accessories, and knowledge to share with customers.

An interesting note: During the Cochran's building process, they discovered a secret hidey-hole where an early 19th-century deed of sale was found. It had been stuffed into a chink in one of the giant timbers. Now it hangs, carefully framed, on one of the log walls. Be sure to look for it as you browse through the country American antiques and architectural pieces.

### *Great Places to Stay*

### The Bridgewater House Bed & Breakfast

7015 Raleigh LaGrange Road
901/384-0080

A romantic step back into history awaits you when you walk into this Greek Revival home, which has been magnificently converted from a schoolhouse into a lovely, elegant dwelling filled with remembrances of travels, antiques, family heirlooms and Oriental rugs. The living room has 12-foot bookcases flanking a 200 to 250-year-old Adams mantel with an ornate three-section mirror reminiscent of a figure head on a ship's bow. The Bridgewater House has the original hardwood floors cut from five different trees on the property. There are enormous rooms, high ceilings, leaded glass windows and deep hand-marbled moldings.

## 22 COVINGTON

### Brooks Auction

Court Square
901/475-1744

Brooks' Auction, located on the Court Square in Covington, has been a monthly outing for us since 1994. Brad Brooks, the auctioneer, was raised in the auction business and schooled by his father from a very young age. The auctions are held the third Saturday night of each month at 6:30 sharp. The merchandise ranges from top of the line, fine quality, home or showroom ready, to some interesting fixer-uppers. You just need to be there to see what crosses the auction block.

Tip for glass collectors: Brad always has some very nice glassware; Depression, Roseville, etc. I would say he has an excellent picker.

*Tennessee*

## That Certain Touch

Located on the town square
901/475-9100
Open: Mon.–Sat. 9–5, closed Sun.

That Certain Touch is a fantastic new mall owned and operated by Danny Moon. Danny formerly was located on Highway 51 N., but due to increased business he has moved to a new location and expanded to include new dealers. You will always find the unique and unusual at That Certain Touch and the merchandise will always be displayed in a manner which will give you useful ideas for your home. Danny himself is always most helpful in providing ideas on arranging your purchases.

**Main Street Antiques**
650 U.S. Hwy. 51 S.
901/475-6181

**Six Oaks Antiques, Inc.**
4095 Hwy. 59 E.
901/476-3135

**Town Square Antique Mall**
Located on the town square
No phone listed

## 23 CROSS PLAINS

## G. Skipper Antiques

4604 E. Robertson Road
615/654-3307
Open: Tues.–Fri. 10–5, Sat. by chance

Antiques, collectibles, Tennessee handmade baskets, and willow furniture.

## Red River Antique Mall

8759 Hwy. 25 at I-65, Exit 112
615/654-7799

Over 80 booths featuring antiques, collectibles, furniture, glassware and more.

**Graves Market Antiques**
Hwy. 25
615/654-4800

**Ima Jean's**
Hwy. 25
615/654-3287

### *Great Places to Eat*

## Thomas Drugs

Downtown Cross Plains
4 miles off I-65 on Hwy. 25
615/654-3877
Open: Mon.–Fri. 8–6, Sat. 8–12

An old-time soda fountain with delicious milkshakes, ice cream sundaes, and ice cream. They also serve lunch and have neat gifts.

## The Robin's Nest

8402 Cedar Grove Road
615/654-3797

Enjoy a wonderful family experience; apples, apple cider, homemade jams and jellies, a bakery and deli to feed hungry antiquers.

## 24 CROSSVILLE

## Stonehaus Winery, Inc.

2444 Genesis Road
Exit 320, I-40
931/484-WINE (9463)
Fax: 931/484-9425
Open: Mon.–Sat. 9–6, Sun. 12–5 (Reduced hours during the winter months)
Directions: Stonehaus Winery is located at I-40 Exit 320 (Genesis Road), just across the interstate from Vanity Fair Shopping Mall.

Grapes, vineyards, and award-winning wines are not the things that one generally thinks of when the state of Tennessee is mentioned, but the Stonehaus Winery in Crossville, Tenn., will be producing from 80,000 to 100,000 bottles of wine this year. A wide selection of premium wines are available, including reds, whites, rose and blushes to suit the most discriminating palates.

The entire wine process is accomplished at Stonehaus, from the crushing and pressing of grapes to the fermentation, aging and bottling.

A gift shop situated in the adjoining building features many fine items from which to choose. Stroll through the shop and sample the homemade fudge. From there you can enter the cheese pantry where over 40 varieties of domestic and imported cheese, homemade bread and gourmet foods are available. From the winery you can visit the Stonehaus Antiques Shop located on the property, featuring eleven rooms of quality antiques such as quilts, glassware, furniture and more.

**Antique Village Mall**
I-40 Exit 320 Genesis Road
931/484-8664

**Rose of Sharon**
2238 Peavine Road
931/484-5221

**Crossville Collectibles**
314 Old Homestead Hwy.
931/456-7641

**Cumberland Mt. General Store**
6807 South York Hwy.
931/863-3880

**Crossville Antique Mall**
Hwy. 127 N.
931/456-8768

**Finders Keepers Treasures**
100 West Ave. S.
931/456-5533

**Page's Furniture**
302 Rockwood Ave.
931/456-0849

**Grandma's Attic**
371 Hwy. 68
931/456-5699

**Stonehaus Antique Shop**
2444 Genesis Road (located on the winery property)
931/456-5540

# *Tennessee*

Dickson can probably best be compared to some type of rubber ball or toy that keeps bouncing back every time after being flattened! The town wasn't actually chartered until 1873, although there were settlers in the immediate area long before then. In 1883, just ten years later, the town charter was revoked over some kind of argument about whiskey, and they didn't get it back until 1899. In the meantime, the town burned down! Then there was another fire in 1893 that destroyed all but three of the downtown buildings. Another fire in 1905 wiped everything out again! That's why there is very little 19th-century architecture in the town today. On the other hand, Dickson is almost a perfect personification of mid-century America — the 1950s, with nighttime cruising down the main streets in '50s hot rods and classics, even down to the drive-in theater that's been open since 1950!

They also have an Old-Timers Day, held the first Saturday in May since its beginning in 1958! It starts with a parade and goes on to lots of crafts, a flea market, plenty of food and entertainment that includes a liars' contest and a seniors' talent contest that's wide open to whatever kind of talent the old-timers want to show off.

## Ox-Yoke Antique & Gift
1901 Hwy. 46 S.
615/446-6979
Open: Mon.–Sat. 10–5 and by appointment
Directions: Take I-40 to Exit 172 onto Hwy. 46. The red-brick store is about 1³/₄ miles north at the red light.

Mr. and Mrs. Yates have been very busy and inventive over the last 30 years. Their building has housed four very different types of businesses — and they have owned and operated all of them! First they opened a service station in 1967; years later it became a fabric store. Then it was a steak house for the next 13 years, and in 1991, they transformed it into an antique store. Mrs. Yates, with her eye for display, carries a lot of oak, walnut and pine furniture, all kinds of collectibles including glassware, pottery, some 1950s ware, silverplate, lamps, and a nice array of jewelry.

## Hamilton Place
202-210 N. Mulberry St.
615/446-5255
Open: Mon.–Sat. 9–5

Within nearly 9,000 square feet of space filled with forty-eight booths, Hamilton Place antique mall is simply packed with wonderfully unique items. Owners Jim and Ruby Reynolds remodeled and air-conditioned the historic old Roger L. Hamilton Super Market, owned by her parents, in developing the mall, which covers half a block.

Hamilton Place is filled with booths offering mostly antiques and collectibles (including "David Winter Cottages," "Hamilton Collection

Dolls," and "Boyds Bears") woodcrafts, silk and dried floral items, linens, lace, brass, home accessories, "Tennessee and English" gift baskets, books, ceramics, porcelain, porcelain dolls, framed prints, custom curtains and accessories and more.

There is a bridal registry, layaway and an item locator service, plus all credit cards are accepted. The Reynolds also have a bed and breakfast (see below). If you like to shop, you'll love Hamilton Place— "Refreshingly Different Products at Friendly Prices."

## Old Timer's Antique Mall
134 N. Main St.
615/446-2387
Open: Mon.–Sat. 10–5, Sun. 1–5

Over 40 vendors and two floors filled with an incredible treasury of antique furniture, glassware and collectibles.

**Nana's Attic**
208 W. College St.
615/441-6032

**Antique Thimble**
4504 Hwy. 70 E.
615/797-2993

**Haynie's Corner**
101 S. Main St.
615/446-2993

**Main St. Antiques Mall**
131 N. Main St.
615/441-3633

**Hamilton Place**
202 N. Mulberry St.
615/446-5255

**Behind Times Antiques**
105 W. Railroad St.
615/441-1864

**Our Place**
1065 Old Hwy. 48
615/789-4557

### *Nearby Antique Shopping (Centerville)*

## Broken Kettle Antiques
204 E. Public Square
931/729-9866
Open: Mon.–Fri. 9–4, Sat. 12–3

Depression glass, Blue Ridge, jadite, cast iron.

### *Great Places to Stay*

## Deerfield Country Inn
170 Woodycrest Close
615/446-3325
Directions: *From Nashville:* Travel west on Interstate 40 approximately 35 miles to Exit 172. Exit right onto Hwy. 46. Go about two miles to the first red light. Turn left onto Pomona Road and drive to its end (about two miles) then turn left onto West Grab Creek Road. Go ¹/₄ mile to Woodycrest Road (first road on your right). Turn right and go to the end of the road (about ¹/₂ mile). Turn left onto

Woodycrest Close. The inn is on your right amid a grove of trees. *From Memphis:* Travel east on Interstate 40 to Exit 172 — then refer to the directions above.

The Deerfield Country Inn is a newly constructed, stately, six-columnar Georgian Colonial home that blends Old South charm with modern-day amenities.

Fancy yourself as Scarlet or Rhett as you saunter to the spacious front porch and enter a foyer spotlighting a grand circular staircase. Impressive antiques, Oriental rugs and chandeliers augment your sense of opulence as you ramble through the main rooms. An open, airy kitchen accented with Quimper pottery and Longaberger baskets engenders a warm, welcoming ambiance.

The large first- and second-story verandas in front and two sizeable decks on the lower level at the rear entice enjoyment of a serene, rustic setting. Savor bountiful breakfasts or succumb to decadent desserts. You can always burn the calories by exploring 57 acres of shady paths and rolling hills, bicycling or playing a game of croquet.

Guest Room 1 is the Susie Lucille Room. Named for the late mother of Jim Reynolds, this cozy room overlooks the field of dreams from the upstairs veranda facing southeast — the front of the house. The room is decorated with Laura Ashley wallcovering and accessories. Of special interest is the ornate double-iron bed and a dresser acquired from the estate of former Tennessee Governor Frank Clement. Guest Room 2 is the Pearl Margaret Room. This generous-sized room — named in honor of the late mother of Ruby Hamilton Reynolds — faces northwest and boasts an antique twin-bedded suite and doll collection. Guest Room 3 is the Mulberry Room. Stretch out and unwind on the carved bed in this roomy space. Sit in one of the antique chairs by the large bay window facing northwest and listen to birds singing in the trees. This room is decorated with Eastlake antiques, old-fashioned purses and a compelling collection of books, pictures and memorabilia of the Royal family — acquired during the years your hosts lived in England. This is a great getaway for those who want to experience Southern hospitality and peaceful seclusion.

Deerfield Country Inn is conveniently located just minutes from I-40 and downtown Dickson. Stroll along historic Main Street and exchange hearty greetings with the locals. Hunt for treasures at many area antique shops. Tap your toes to a live country music show downtown on Saturday night. Take afternoon tea and nibble on tarts at a charming area tea room. Enjoy a Southern-cooked meal or a fine dinner at one of several restaurants.

Your gracious hosts at Deerfield Country Inn are well traveled and have lived abroad periodically. Since they're familiar with many cultures, you'll find them easy to talk to. As owners of an antique mall, they're happy to share their collectibles savvy. And because Jim's an accomplished carpenter and Ruby's an interior decorator, things aren't always the same at the inn!

## 26 DONELSON

**A's Antiques**
2615 Lebanon Road
615/874-0201

**Raggs & Riches**
2744 Lebanon Road
615/872-9798

## 27 DYERSBURG

### Walton's Antique Mall
2470 Lake Road (behind McDonald's)
901/287-7086
Open: Mon.–Sat. 10–5, Sun. 1–5
Directions: Exit 13 off I-155. Located behind McDonald's.

This 12,000-square-foot mall of 25 dealers offers the antiquer an eclectic selection of antique furnishings and accessories including garden and architectural pieces, Victorian, primitive, old toys, pottery, nice glassware, linens and old books, just to name a few. If you miss this mall you'll be passing up the opportunity to purchase some of the best and most unusual early collectibles around. Bill Walton, the owner, has a "nose" for finding rarities; old grape crushers, trunks and boxes, great advertising pieces (much to choose from), early toys, quilts, old coffee grinders, tools, farm tables and more. You never know what he'll find next! I highly recommend a stop at Walton's Antique Mall.

**Dyersburg Antique Gallery**
2004 E. Court St.
901/285-0999

**Days Gone By**
913 Forrest St.
901/285-2704

**Babe's**
Court Square
New business

### *Great Places to Stay*

### Aunt Ginny's Bed & Breakfast
520 Sampson Ave.
901/285-2028
Rates: Single $65, double $75 (massage $35 half hour, $50 full hour)

Aunt Ginny's Bed & Breakfast is a Victorian farmhouse, built in 1886, decorated with country antiques and collectibles, which create a homey atmosphere. Located in one of historic Dyersburg's fine old neighborhoods, it is about 18 miles from Reelfoot Lake and across the Mississippi River from Casino Aztar Riverboat.

Enjoy the shaded Victorian porch, the country feel of the garden and the outdoor hot tub. Inside you won't feel confined to your room. You can watch cable TV or read a book in the den, converse in the parlor, or enjoy the outside while still inside

# Tennessee

in the atrium. For the ultimate in relaxation, you may arrange for a half hour or a full hour of therapeutic massage. Both of your hosts are licensed in therapeutic massage.

Each of the rooms has a private bath.

A continental breakfast of coffee, juice, homemade bread and jams, muffins and/or coffee cake is served each morning in the atrium and outside, weather permitting.

## 28 ELIZABETHTON

**Antique & Curio Corner**
441 E. Elk Ave.
423/542-0603

**Antiques on Elk**
509 E. Elk Ave.
423/542-3355

**Duck Crossing Antique Mall**
515 E. Elk Ave.
423/542-3055

**Sycamore Shoals Antiques**
1788 W. Elk Ave.
423/542-5423

**Rasnick's Antiques**
Hwy. 19 E. Bypass
423/543-2494

**Antique Mall**
Hwy. 19 E.
423/542-6366

**Maude's Antiques**
Hwy. 19 E. Bypass
423/543-1979

## 29 ERIN

### Jitterbug Cafe, Antiques & Collectibles

Court Square
931/289-5588
Open: (shop) Mon.–Fri. 10:30–5 (lunch) Mon.–Fri. 10:30–2, supper on Fri. night

Great food, antiques and collectibles from fun to funky.

**J.J. Nave Antiques**
8 N. Church St.
931/326-5764

## 30 FAYETTEVILLE

### Magnolia Mall Antiques

121 S. Main St.
931/433-9987
Open: Mon.–Sat. 9:30–4:30

Over 50 booths on three levels in a century-old building including furniture, glassware, collectibles, old tools and more.

### Mockingbird Antique Mall, Ice Cream Parlor & Deli

100 E. College St.
931/438-0058
Open: Mon.–Sat. 10–5

Antiques, collectibles, ice cream, banana splits, sandwiches and specials of the day.

**Fayetteville Antique Mall**
112 College St. E.
931/433-1231

**Cobblestone Collectibles**
209 College St. E.
931/433-4778

**Wyatt Antiques**
301 Elk Ave. N.
931/433-4241

**Clark Antique & Collectibles**
3011 Huntsville Hwy.
931/438-0377

**Davis Antiques**
201 Mulberry Ave.
931/433-1036

**Tennessee Antiques**
2939 Huntsville Hwy.
931/433-6084

## 31 FRANKLIN

The town of Franklin was officially established in 1799 in Williamson County, which was one of the wealthiest counties in the state by the mid-1800s, and still is today. The town itself, as well as the surrounding area, is full of historic homes and antebellum plantations, most of which have been restored. Two in particular are often mentioned in connection with Franklin, the Carter House and Lotz House.

The Carter House had the great misfortune to be caught exactly in the middle of the battlefield of one of the worst battles of the Civil War — the Battle of Franklin. The Carter family huddled in the cellar of their house while 35,000 soldiers fought in an area roughly two miles long by one mile wide … all centered around the house. According to area historians, there were more generals (12 total) either killed or wounded here than in any other battle in the history of warfare, and the Carter House is the most battle-damaged site in the country, with evidence of over 600 cannonball and bullet holes, 203 in one structure alone! All of this damage was done in the space of a five-hour battle, two-thirds of which was fought in total darkness.

Ironically, just across the street from this amazing relic is the Lotz House. During the same battle, the Lotz family hid in the basement of the Carter House with the Carter family, but the Lotz House has no battle scars! Presumably, Mr. Lotz, who was an extraordinarily skilled woodworker, repaired the damages to his home. The house is now a museum containing the South's largest privately-owned collection of Civil War memorabilia for public display.

# Tennessee

## Franklin Antique Mall

Winner of *Tennessean's* Reader's Choice Award and former nominee of the Commerical Historical Preservation Award
251 Second Ave. S.
615/790-8593

In 1980, Joan and Archie Glenn opened the Franklin Antique Mall as their dream. Little did they know how successful the activity at the old "icehouse" would become, as what started out as 35 booths grew through three expansions to more than 100 dealers and 14,000 square feet. Located 20 miles south of Nashville, in a huge, handmade brick structure, the multilevel building, constructed in 1870, originally became a flour mill and was more widely known as Williamson County's Icehouse at the turn of the century.

It has now become home to one of the area's most charming malls. Inside among the wood and brick decor, collectors will find one of the South's biggest collections of furniture, from Early American to Victorian

and turn of the century pieces in solid cherry, walnut, mahogany and oak. There is an ample supply of chests, tables, desks, beds, bookcase, sets of chairs and even a Jackson Press or two. There is a wide array of glassware from all periods, pottery, china, books, quilts, linens, clocks and pictures, and a booth of old lamps and replacement parts. Each booth is a treasure chest of nostalgia that collectively is an antique buff's bonanza.

The Franklin Antique Mall, multiple past winner of the *Tennessean's* Reader's Choice Award and former nominee of the Commerical Historical Preservation Award, just celebrated its 20th anniversary last year. The mall is now owned and operated by Amanda Glenn Pitts and Shawn Glenn since the death of their mother, Joan.

"The Mall With It All," as dubbed by *Nashville Magazine,* is located at the corner of Second Avenue South and South Margin Street in Franklin and is open 10–5, Monday through Saturday and 1–5 on Sunday.

## Clementine's Antiques

210 Second Ave. S.
615/599-5406

You could say that Clementine's Antiques, Franklin's newest antique mall, is a mirror of the historic town in which it is located. The outstanding selections are offered inside an 1880s Folk Victorian home which was a prefab house ordered from a Sears & Roebuck catalog at a cost of $500.

Within this beautifully decorated home are the wares of eight dealers

offering period antiques, country furnishings (particularly in original paint), period Tennessee pieces, historical architectural elements, antique garden accessories, rare and unusual collectibles, formal furnishings and shabby-chic decor. A must-stop on your antiquing adventure, not just for the incredible offerings, but to say "hello" to the owners.

## Harpeth Antique Mall

Exit 65 from I-65
Alexander Plaza, behind McDonalds
615/790-7965
Open: Mon.–Sat. 10–6, Sun. 1–6

12,000 square feet of quality furniture, china, estate jewelry, fine glass, pottery, carnival glass, books, and collectibles.

## Heritage Antique Mall

Alexander Plaza, next to Harpeth
615/790-8115
Open: Mon.–Sat. 10–6, Sun. 1–6

Specializing in English, primitives, American and architectural antiques.

## Country Charm Mall

301 Lewisburg Ave.
615/790-8908
Open: Mon.–Sat. 10–5:30, Sun. 12–5

A nice selection of affordable antiques and collectibles, especially glassware, china and primitives.

## Rebel's Rest

A Civil War Museum and Artifact Shop
212 S. Margin St.
615/790-7199
Open: Mon.–Sat. 10–6, Sun. 1–5

Largest selection of quality investment-grade Civil War and Indian War artifacts and memorabilia for sale and display.

## Tennessee

### J J Ashley's
119 S. Margin St.
615/791-0011
Open: Mon.–Sat. 10–5, Sun. 1–5

Antiques and authentic reproductions located in the old Franklin Railroad Depot. Specializing in American, French and English furniture.

### Heirloom Antiques
Margin St. (Barn)
615/791-0847
Open: Mon.–Sat. 10–5, Sun. 1–5

A barn full of antiques, architectural elements, old paintings, furniture (refinished and in the rough).

### Antiques on Second Avenue
236 Second Ave.
615/791-6159
Open: Mon.–Sat. 10–5, Sun. 1–5

Discover wonderful antiques and collectibles from fine furnishings to old toys in a circa-1820s home.

### Antiques of Franklin
230 Franklin Road (Behind Magnolia's Restaurant)
615/591-4612
Open: Mon.–Sat. 10–5, Sun. 1–5

Over 50 dealers, 15,000 square feet. Located in the historic "Factory at Franklin."

### Battleground Antique Mall
232 Franklin Road
615/794-9444
Open: Mon.–Sat. 10–5, Sun. 1–5

Specializing in French, English, American, primitive antique furniture, Civil War artifacts and dolls.

### Hood's Retreat Antiques
117 First Ave.
615/591-7819
Open: Mon.–Sat. 10–5, Sun. 12–5, closed Wed.

Specializing in architectural, garden, primitives and collectibles.

### Rustic House Antiques
111 Bridge St.
615/794-7779
Open: Mon.–Sat. 10–5, Sun. 1–5

Specializing in historical architectural and Early American painted furniture.

### Winchester Antique Mall
113 Bridge St.
615/791-5846
Open: Mon.–Sat. 10–5, Sun. 12–5

Charming two-story antique mall with a wide selection of antiques and collectibles.

### Riverside Antiques
144 Bridge St.
615/591-4089
Open: Mon.–Sat. 10–5, Sun. 1–5

A complete line of glassware, pottery, sports collectibles and advertising.

### Savannah West
343 Main St.
615/791-0159
Open: Sat. 10:30–6, weekdays by chance or appointment

Continental antiques flavored with influences of the West and Southern Coastal Regions.

### Magic Memories
345 Main St.
615/794-2848
Open: Mon.–Sat. 10–5

Antiques, estate jewelry, accessories and Civil War relics.

### Patchwork Palace American Legacy
340 Main St.
615/790-1382
Open: Sat. 9:30–5

Antiques, primitives, 300–400 fine antique quilts, folk art, collectible bears and Santas.

# Tennessee

## Walton's Antique & Estate Jewelry
410 Main St.
615/790-0244
Open: Mon.–Sat. 10–5

Specializing in fine antique handmade jewelry.

## Legacy Antiques
420 Main St.
615/791-5770
Open: Mon.–Sat. 10:30–4

Quality 18th- and 19th-century period furniture and accessories.

## The Iron Gate
412 Cummins St.
615/791-7511
Open: Mon.–Sat. 10–5, Sun. 1–5

Stroll in the courtyard and sample the gourmet Italian coffee. Specializing in European pine.

## Yarrow Acres
434 Main St.
615/591-7090
Open: Mon.–Sat. 10–5, Sun. 12–5

Gifts for the gardener, folk art and country antiques.

## The Junktique Shop
227 Franklin Road
615/790-6544
Open: Thurs.–Sat. 10–4:30

Junk, antiques and collectibles.

### *Great Places to Stay*

Historic Franklin has numerous bed and breakfasts. For a complete listing along with brochures, contact the Franklin Chamber of Commerce at 615/794-1225

## 32 GALLATIN

**Antiques & Uniques**
111 Main St.
615/452-6227

**Antiques on Main**
117 W. Main St.
615/451-0426

**Gallatin Antiques**
913 S. Water St.
615/452-4373

**On the Square Antiques**
116 N. Water St.
615/230-5673

**The Odd & End Store**
460 S. Water St.
615/451-1118

## 33 GATLINBURG

**Morton's Antiques**
409 Parkway
423/436-5504

### *Great Places to Stay*

## Butcher House in the Mountains
1520 Garrett Lane
423/436-9457

Nestled within the pristine beauty of the Smoky Mountains, and secluded from any commercial area, is Butcher House in the Mountains — a favorite hideout for artists, photographers, hikers, and guests with a palate for uniquely different cuisine. Hugh, a former executive, is now the "Muffin Man," creating fresh delicacies every morning. Gloria, an Italian Yankee from the North, and Hugh a Southerner, can create riotous conversations in the morning. Breakfast time is party time! Italian hospitality is found here in abundance just like a European gourmet meal.

The indescribable view of a 6,000-foot mountain range as far as the eye can see will greet you each morning. AAA calls the view "spectacular."

## 34 GERMANTOWN

## Anderson Mulkins Antiques
9336 Poplar Ave. (Hwy. 72)
901/754-7909
Open: Tues.–Sat. 10–5
Directions: From Memphis, take I-240 and exit at Germantown. Go 8 miles to 9336 Poplar Avenue (Poplar is also Hwy. 72 and Hwy. 57) and the shop is on the left side, at the corner of Johnson Road and Poplar Avenue. The address is on the mailbox. The shop is between Germantown and Collierville, 4 miles either way.

The Mulkins and family really know antiques. They have been in the retail business (antiques) since 1906 — more than 90 years! — and the business is still family owned and operated. Shoppers at Anderson's will find furniture and accessories, but they specialize in dining room chairs. Over the past 90 years they have forgotten more than most people ever know! It's worth a stop just to talk to them and hear what they have to say, not only about antiques, but about the life and times they have experienced firsthand — a life that most of us would call "antique" itself!

# Tennessee

## 35   GOODLETTSVILLE

**Fanny's Sugar Barrell**
112 Old Brick Church Pike
615/859-7319

**Antique Corner Mall**
128 N. Main St.
615/859-7673

**Sweet Memories**
400 N. Main St.
615/851-9922

**One Man's Treasure**
429 N. Main St.
615/859-7734

**Main Street Antique Mall**
120 N. Main St.
615/851-1704

**Goodlettsville Antique Mall**
213 N. Main St.
615/859-7002

**Rare Bird Antique Mall**
212 S. Main St.
615/851-2635

## 36   GREENBRIER

**Ox Yoke**
2141 Hwy. 41 S.
615/643-0843

**Little Bit of Everything**
2616 Hwy. 41 S.
615/643-8029

**Sanders Antiques & Restoration**
2606 Hwy. 41
615/329-1017

## 37   HARRIMAN

**Wright's Antiques**
2120 S. Roane St.
423/882-6060

**Adkisson's Antiques**
503 N. Roane St.
423/882-3165

**Out of the Past Antiques**
1310 S. Roane St.
423/882-9756

**Harriman Antique Mall**
1611 S. Roane St.
423/882-8930

## 38   HENDERSONVILLE

**Antique Gallery/Treasure Hut Antiques**
115 Dunn St.
615/824-0930

**Hendersonville Antique Mall**
339 Rockland Road
615/824-5850

**Tuttle Bros. Antiques**
691 W. Main St./Hwy. 31 E.
615/824-7222

## 39   HENNING

A great many people know about Henning, Tenn., because of one man, his book, and the movie. The man of course is Alex Haley, and the book and movie is *Roots*. But there is more to Henning than Alex Haley. It is a town of interesting history and homes, a community intermingled with black and white, and a town that is now striving to preserve its heritage and become a source for future generations.

Although unknown to a lot of people in the West Tennessee area, Henning is the home of a Choctaw Indian Reservation. Each fall and summer the reservation sponsors an Indian Festival. Thousands of people from across the country flock to this tiny town to participate in the celebration and to learn more about the Choctaw culture. (For information on the Choctaw Indian Festivals call Cubert Bell at 901/738-2951.)

### J & A Antiques & Collectibles
236 Graves St., Hwy. 87 E. (1/2 mile off Hwy. 51)
901/738-5367

John and Aliene Richards handle the general spread of collectibles, particularly smalls, glassware and costume jewelry, but they also specialize in one item you don't find often — old marbles! They also know how to make do in a pinch, as this funny story shows: "We loaded up to do a flea market in Arkansas and went over the evening before," say Aliene. "The van was full to within 12 inches of the ceiling. When we arrived, there were no motels available and we had to set up at daybreak, so we slept on top of the tables in the van. When we got up at daybreak to start setting up, John had lost his glasses somewhere in the van during the night, and couldn't see to begin setting up! After much searching, we finally found his glasses, but we haven't had to sleep on tables since that show, and don't plan to do so again!"

### Kitty & Tony Ables
140 N. Main St.
901/738-2381

Kitty and Tony Ables have been personal friends of mine for a long time. We talk almost daily about this crazy antiques business and offer opinions to each other as to why something does or does not sell. Of course we have all the answers to this perplexity, so one would think we should be wealthy just for offering all this advice. But, until the world learns that we have the answers to all their problems, we probably should keep doing what we hope is best— selling antiques.

Kitty and Tony have a knack for finding some of the best early authentic pieces. Their eye for style and detail have enabled them to grab the attention of some very influential people. They travel the country to attend the finest antique shows such as Heart of Country in Nashville and Marilyn Gould's shows. Several times a year, Kitty and Tony open their home to unloading sales. People come from ten states just to attend these sales, mostly because the Ables' have gained a reputation for selling quality, authentic antiques. If you are traveling through Tennessee near Memphis, you can call anytime to let Kitty know you're in the area and would like to stop by. Her home is always open to fellow antiquers.

# Tennessee

Scoggin's Collectibles
114 S. Main St.
901/738-5405

Peas 'n' Pod
105 Moorer
901/738-2959

## 40 HERMITAGE

Spring Valley Antiques
4348 Lebanon Road/Hwy. 70
615/889-0267

Hermitage Antique Mall
4144 Lebanon Road #B
615/883-5789

## 41 HICKMAN

**Antique Malls of Tennessee**
2 Sykes Road (at Gordonsville Hwy.)
615/683-6066
Fax: 615/683-6067
Open: Call ahead for hours
Directions: Approximately 45 miles east of Nashville on I-40. From I-40 take Exit 258 (Carthage — Gordonsville Exit). Go south (right) 2 miles to Hickman.

Historic downtown Hickman was once a bustling 23-store metropolis. Because the railroad ran through town, it was almost chosen as the county seat. Unfortunately, the Cumberland River ran through the nearby town of Carthage and due to ever-increasing commercial boat traffic, Carthage won the bid for county seat. This doomed Hickman's commercial growth. The tomato cannery finally closed, the once internationally famous mule trading went by the wayside, the infamous "hotel on the hill" closed or burned, the grainery closed and one by one, all the businesses ceased to exist. Only the bank of Hickman remained until it surrendered to the 1930s crash, along with the town's general store which survived well into the 1980s.

By 1996, only the bank and general store complex remained in its original state, the last remaining evidence of a once-thriving business center. In May of 1996, Larry and Penny Bartlett, while visiting the area, chanced upon these two historic buildings. They fell in love with and purchased these buildings on their visit. Windows were broken out and/or boarded up, no electricity in the bank, no floors or ceilings — in other words, a shell. The general store was in better condition, but still needed extensive restoration. Penny asked Larry, "How long will it take to get it open for our antique mall!" Larry responded, "About three months." Two years later, the store was finally opened. The Bartletts were not in a position to hire the work done, so Larry quit his job in California and began the restoration himself. Seven days a week, ten to twelve hours a day, definitely a labor of love, the results of this painstaking work is evidenced by the now completely restored complex.

The mall consists of many collectibles of various types, as well as antique furniture and artifacts in the more upscale range. No new items,

and reproductions are consistently purged. The second floor of the bank is dedicated to art, from signed limited editions to fine oils, once again, of the vintage type. The art gallery also consists of various unique objets d'art and statuary. They have commissioned a famous artist in Venice, Italy, to create an exclusive masterpiece for display. Truly, one of the best examples of revitalization in the area.

## 42 JACKSON

**Yarbro's Antique Mall**
350 Carriage House Dr.
901/664-6600
Open Mon.–Sat. 10–5, Sun. 1–5
Directions: Visible from I-40. Call for directions.

With its recent relocation, this mall promises even more dealers with more selections than ever before. They carry a general line of antiques including Victorian furniture and accessories and many flow blue pieces. One dealer specializes in country furniture.

**Brooks Shaw's Old Country Store and Casey Jones Village**
Casey Jones Village
901/668-1223 or 1-800-748-9588
Fax: 901/664-TOUR
Station Inn reservations 1-800-628-2812
Open: summer 6–10, winter 6–9
Directions: Casey Jones Village is located nearly midpoint between Nashville and Memphis on I-40 and Hwy. 45 Bypass, Exit 80A, in Jackson, just 90 seconds off the interstate. Look for the original 50-foot caboose sign.

At the Old Country Store and Casey Jones Village, visitors can shop, eat, sleep and get a dose of history all at the same time. An extremely popular tourist stop, the entire place is perfectly suited for little folks and big people alike, especially if they are into trains. At the Old Country Store, visitors can eat in an enormous restaurant with buffet setting, then stroll through 6,000 square feet of gifts, confections, collectibles and souvenirs, then dive into the 1890s ice cream parlor for dessert while gazing at 15,000 Southern antiques on display. If that's not enough, the historic home of Casey Jones is right next door, along with a railroad museum and train store, complete with a Lionel dealer on the premises. You can climb aboard Engine #382, then take a mini–train ride and then play miniature golf. At this point you should be ready to fall asleep, and the Casey Jones Station Inn is conveniently right there, offering 50 train-themed rooms. You can choose to sleep in a rail-car suite or a caboose. Kids of all ages will love it!

# Tennessee

## I-40 Antique Mall
2150 Hwy. 70
901/423-4448
Open Mon.–Sat. 9–6, Sun. 1–5
Directions: Take Exit 87 off I-40. You can see the mall from the exit.
Next door to the Citgo gas station.

Large antique mall featuring antiques, collectibles, primitives, glassware, old toys, pedal cars, Fenton, Roseville, Hull, and McCoy.

**Trading Post**
116 W. Chester St.
901/424-9511

**Yesterday's Antiques**
212 N. Liberty St.
901/427-2690

**Tara Antiques**
205 S. Shannon St.
901/422-3935

**I-40 Antique Mall**
2150 U.S. Hwy. 70 E.
901/423-4448

**Old South Antique Mall**
1155 Rushmeade Road
901/664-9692

### Great Places to Stay

## Highland Place Bed & Breakfast
519 N. Highland Ave.
901/427-1472
Fax: 901/422-7994
Open: year-round, 7 a.m.–10 p.m. (office hours)
Directions: From I-40 traveling either from Memphis or Nashville, take Exit 82A onto Highland Avenue (also Hwy. 45 South). The inn is just 3 3/10 miles south of I-40 on Highland Avenue, between Arlington and West King Streets in the North Highland Historical District, five blocks from downtown Jackson.

There's plenty to do and see in and around Jackson, but the layout of this particular B&B suggests you carefully choose your traveling companion — it is a romantic delight and should be especially considered for those intimate little getaways you occasionally indulge in!

Highland Place has four guest rooms, with an arrangement flexible enough to have one's own multiple-room suite. The Louis Room has a sitting area, antique vanity and king-size bed, with an authentic claw foot bathtub with solid brass plumbing and handheld shower. The Butler Suite boasts a queen-size cherry bed with feather mattress and a sitting area with working table (great for corporate travelers) and private bath. The Hamilton Suite offers an antique walnut dresser and a custom-built walnut queen-size canopy bed, a working fireplace (very nice for romance), and just across your own private hall, a bath with a tub large enough for two. The newest addition (as of yet unnamed) is a suite with skylight, feather mattress on a queen-size bed, and a private bath with a waterfall shower for two!

## 43 JOHNSON CITY

**Granny's Attic**
200 N. Commerce St.
423/929-2205

**Antiques & Heirlooms**
126 W. Main St.
423/928-8220

**Antique Village**
228 E. Main St.
423/926-6996

**Memory Lane Antiques & Mall**
324 E. Main St.
423/929-3998

**Youngdale Antiques**
214 Mountcastle Drive
423/282-1164

**Country Peddler**
1121 N. Roan St.
423/975-0935

**Curiosity Shop**
206 E. 8th Ave.
423/928-3322

**American Pastimes Antique Market**
217 E. Main St.
423/928-1611

**Town Square Antiques**
234 E. Main St.
423/929-3373

**Antiques Antiques Antiques**
125 W. Market St.
423/928-8697

**Finishing Touch**
158 Austin Springs Road
423/915-0395

## 44 JONESBOROUGH

This is Tennessee's oldest town, chartered in 1779. Its history has been colorful and exciting, and today the town is a perfect window to the past. Among the many things to do and see in Jonesborough is a stop at the Visitor's Center, where you can become acquainted with the town and its history; a visit to the Washington County History Museum; shopping in the numerous antique and specialty stores in the historic districts; and visits to the annual festivals held in July (Historic Jonesborough Days), August (Quilt Fest, with classes and exhibits), November and December (holiday arts and crafts and celebrations), and the big event in Jonesborough — the National Storytelling Festival in October. The National Storytelling Association, based in Jonesborough, has been holding this festival every year since 1973. Visitors can hear tall tales, Jack tales, Grandfather tales, anecdotes, legends, myths and more, while getting a glimpse of the oral tradition that has entertained and informed Americans for more than 200 years!

**Mauks of Jonesborough**
101 W. Main St.
423/753-4648

**Old Town Hall**
144 E. Main St.
423/753-2095

**Jonesborough Antique Mart**
115 E. Main St.
423/753-8301

**Trading Post Antiques**
1200 W. Main St.
423/753-3661

# Tennessee

## Great Places to Eat

### The Parson's Table
102 Woodrow Ave.
615/753-8002
Open for lunch and dinner weekdays.
Sunday buffet 11:30–2
Directions: From Knoxville, take I-81 to Exit 23 (Hwy. 11-E). Traveling south, take 181 to the Jonesborough exit. The restaurant is behind the courthouse off Main Street.

This lovely Gothic structure was once the First Christian Church in Jonesborough, and has been a temperance hall, lecture room, and woodworking shop.

Carefully preserving its history while enhancing its Victorian origin, Chef Jeff Myron and his wife, Debra, have converted the architectural landmark into a soul-satisfying restaurant. The fare is continental, or as they say, "refined South, with a little bit of French, and a whole lot of love."

The heavenly selections include crepes, rack of lamb dijonaise, roast duckling a'l'orange, with a choice of sinful desserts such as "Parson's Passion" and "Devilish Chocolate Ecstasy."

## 45 KINGSPORT

**The Antique Mall**
9951 Airport Pkwy.
423/323-2990

**Antiques I-81**
9959 Airport Pkwy.
423/323-0808

**Anchor Antiques**
137 Broad St.
423/378-3188

**Adams Company & Friends**
231 Broad St.
423/247-9775

**Country Square Antiques**
635 Fairview Ave.
423/378-4130

**Village Antiques**
4993 Hwy. 11 W.
423/323-2287

**Smith Sholal's Antiques**
315 Beulah Church Drive
423/239-6280

**Amanda's Antiques**
115 Broad St.
423/245-1423

**Haggle Shop Antique Mall**
147 Broad St.
423/246-6588

**Colonial Antique Mall**
245 Broad St.
423/246-5559

**Pittypat's Country Interiors**
2633 Fort Henry Drive
423/247-2244

**Toy Train Antiques**
214 E. Market St.
423/245-8451

## 46 KINGSTON

### Kingston Antique Mall
719 N. Kentucky St.
423/717-0088
Open Mon.–Sat. 10–6, Sun. 1–6

Featuring a large selection of furniture, Roseville, glassware, pedal cars, tools and fishing items.

**Babe's Antiques**
215 Roan St.
423/717-1166

## 47 KNOXVILLE

### Campbell Station Antiques
620 Campbell Station Road
423/966-4348
Open: Daily Mon.–Sat. 10–6, Sun. 1–6
Directions: From I-40 and I-75, take Exit 373. Turn south and go 200 yards. The shop is on the left in Station West Center next to Cracker Barrel.

Established in 1983, this 35-dealer mall has several specialties to tempt shoppers. In its 10,000 square feet of space you'll find vintage linens and clothing from the Victorian era through the 1960s, sterling serving pieces, fine porcelains such as flow blue, Dresden and Limoges. Dealers in the mall specialize in period furniture (American, Country and French) and one dealer travels to Europe to buy.

A large selection of clocks from the 1820s–1920s are offered at Campbell Station in addition to architectural accents such as mantles, columns, stained glass and garden accents. The shop specializes in rare and hard to find books and offers a search service to its many customers from around the U.S.

**Farragut Antique Mall**
101 Campbell Station Road
423/671-3630

**B E L Antiques**
5520 Brier Cliff Road
423/688-2664

**Antiques Plus**
4500 Walker Blvd.
423/687-6536

**Time Trader**
720 Broadway
423/521-9660

# Tennessee

**Broadway Bargain Barn**
1305 N. Broadway St.
423/524-5221

**Marty's Antiques & Collectibles**
1313 N. Broadway St.
423/522-6466

**South Fork Furniture**
712 N. Central St.
423/525-0513

**French Market Shops**
4900 Chambliss Ave.
423/558-6065

**The Bottom Antiques & Collectibles**
3701 Chapman Hwy.
423/579-4202

**Gateway Antiques**
5925 Chapman Hwy.
423/573-2663

**Chapman Hwy. Antique Mall**
7624 Chapman Hwy.
423/573-7022

**Fever**
133 S. Gay St.
423/525-4771

**Sullivan Street Market**
118 E. Jackson Ave.
423/522-2231

**Kingston Pike Antique Mall**
4612 Kingston Pike
423/588-2889

**Dominick's Antique Galleries**
5119 Kingston Pike
423/584-1513

**Antiques, Inc.**
5121 Kingston Pike
423/588-5063

**West End Antique Market**
5613 Kingston Pike
423/588-1388

**Incurable Collector**
5805 Kingston Pike
423/584-4371

**Northern Friends**
1507 9th Ave.
423/546-5400

**Wildwood Gallery & Frames**
2924 Sutherland Ave.
423/546-3811

**Attic Antiques on Broadway**
1313 N. Broadway St.
423/524-2514

**Key Antiques**
133 S. Central St.
423/546-2739

**Chance's Antiques**
1509 N. Central St.
423/522-0311

**South Knox Collectibles Mall**
3615 Chapman Hwy.
423/577-6252

**Colonial Antique Mall**
4939 Chapman Hwy.
423/573-6660

**Crossroads Antiques**
7100 Commercial Park Dr.
423/922-9595

**Blair House Antiques**
210 Forest Park Blvd.
423/584-8119

**Jackson Ave. Antique Market Place**
111 E. Jackson Ave.
423/521-6704

**Carpenter Clock & Watch Repair**
4612 Kingston Pike
423/584-2570

**Antiques and Accents**
5002 Kingston Pike
423/584-5918

**Garrison Collection**
5130 Kingston Pike
423/558-0906

**Sequoyah Antiques Exchange**
5305 Kingston Pike
423/588-9490

**Calloway's Lamps Shades & Gifts**
5714 Kingston Pike
423/588-0684

**Bearden Antique Mall**
310 Mohican St.
423/584-1521

**Appalachian Antiques**
11312 Station West Dr.
423/675-5690

**A True North, Inc.**
611 Worcester Road
423/675-7772

**Homespun Craft & Antique Mall**
11523 Kingston Pike
423/671-3444

**Broadway Antiques**
2310 N. Broadway St.
423/546-3303

**Vieux Carre Antiques**
1204 N. Central St.
423/544-7700

## 48  KODAK

**Dumplin Valley Antiques & Collectibles**
340 W. Dumplin Valley Road
423/932-7713
Open: Fri. 10–6, Sat. & Sun. 9–6
Directions: Traveling I-40, Exit 407. Turn south on Hwy.66 toward Gatlinburg. Turn right on the first road, which is Dumplin Valley Road. Continue 1 mile. Shop is on the right.

Most of us save the top of our wedding cake, the dress, or flowers as a momento of our wedding day. But Jane Carson saved the entire church! The little church in which Jane and her husband, William, were married was built in 1839. Over the past 158 years it has sheltered many members of the faith (including  Jane herself) and hosted hundreds of weddings. So, when Jane heard that her little church was being torn down to build a new one, she bought it, had it moved, and opened an antique shop in it.

Today, instead of preachers and pews, you'll find depression glassware, china, pottery, lamps, late 1800s and early 1900s furniture and more. Two dealers specialize in Fostoria, china and wood and tin advertising items.

## 49  LAKE CITY

**Valley Antiques**
808 N. Main St.
423/426-9445

## 50  LAWRENCEBURG

**Lawrenceburg Antique & Auction**
266 N. Military Ave.
931/762-6695

**Flea Market Shop**
46 Public Square
931/762-6963

**Bill Moore Silver Matching**
310 Mohican St.
423/584-7642

**ESA US Antique Market**
1549 Coleman Road
423/588-1233

**Carriage House II**
34 & 38 Public Square
931/766-0428

**Gibb's Antiques & Collectibles**
2310 Pulaski Hwy./Hwy. 64
931/762-1441

**Clover Leaf Antiques**
4449 Waynesboro Hwy./Hwy. 64
931/762-5658

**Market Place Antique Mall**
34 Public Square
931/762-1619

## 51 LEBANON

Directions: Take I-40 to the Lebanon Exit 238, go north on Hwy. 231 to find the town square area and south to find everything else.

It's difficult to picture the now bustling public square in Lebanon as once vacant, but that was the scene before its transformation. Originally, Lebanon was an active town, with business held inside its buildings and outside in the square. Time, as in many small towns, took its toll as movement to the perimeter of town, rather than the center, became the trend. Lebanon was fortunate in that, one by one, its wonderful structures in the public square area were purchased or leased and revived to become the center of activity once again. As crafters and antiquers occupied the old buildings, public interest grew, and so did that of professionals who also wanted to become a part of the newly created, active center of town. Now the town, built in 1819, has experienced a rebirth and has undergone a facelift so that passersby, too, can share their proud heritage.

### Tennessee Treasures
Public Square
615/443-2136
Open: Mon.–Sat. 10–5

There's no telling what you'll encounter at Tennessee Treasures, but you can be reasonably assured that if Grandma had one, this shop does too! Although their specialty is kitchen items, you'll find a unique garden section with old plows, wheelbarrows, garden utensils, and gifts related to gardening. Also a part of the offerings are upscale furniture, unusual vintage clothing, and handmade Country American Christmas ornaments. There's even a birthing chair that breaks down to be carried in a bag by a midwife. Stop in, you never know when you'll catch a sale in progress!

### In Cahoots!
123 Public Square
615/444-8037
Open: Tues.–Sat. 10–6, Sun.–Mon. by chance

If you're searching for old drugstore or five-and-dime store merchandise, visit In Cahoots! They also carry antique and vintage furniture, or for something a little different see their hand-painted children's furniture. As an added surprise, In Cahoots! includes a full-service doll shop that performs minor repairs or redresses and cleans dolls. Madam Alexander, Lee Middleton, Susan Wakeen, and antique and vintage dolls are just part of their line.

### Rainbow Relics
27 Public Square
615/449-6777
Open: Mon.–Sat. 9–6, Sun. 1–6

Originally a bank that was torn down and then rebuilt around its old vaults in 1977, it become home to Rainbow Relics and now houses antiques, including furniture — especially oak, primitives, linens, and glassware. Also offered are collectibles of art glass by Boyd and Marble Mountain Creations, which are limited-edition pieces made from Georgia marble in the shape of, for example, cars, tractors, and trains.

### Cuz's Antique Center
140 Public Square
615/444-8070
Open: Mon.–Sat. 9–5, Sun. 11–5

Dubbed a "center" because it spans three buildings, Cuz's is the largest collection of merchandise in the area. Inventory includes not only fine examples of American, English, and French antiques, but also wonderful reproductions of such pieces. Cuz's also carries furniture, glassware, and bronzes. As you would expect, their selection includes oil paintings, stained glass windows, and a tremendous selection of jewelry, both estate and modern. For the pocket-knife collector, Cuz's is also the home of the Fightin' Rooster Cutlery Company.

### Off the Square Cafe
109 S. Cumberland St.
615/444-6217

If all of your searching for treasures has created an appetite, stop at the Off the Square Cafe, located inside the Tennessee Treasures Antique Mall. Try one of their specialty sandwiches like the homemade apple and grape chicken salad or the Cajun roasted beef. If a sandwich is a little heavy, try one of the thick and hearty homemade soups prepared daily, or have half a sandwich and a cup of soup. Whatever you choose, just save room for one of their homemade desserts!

### Coach House Antiques
Public Square
615/443-1905

In the early days, Coach House Antiques was the town lawyer's office. It would be interesting to know the kinds of legal problems the town's folk had back in the 1800s. But today, throughout this historic building, the only decisions to be made are those of a "selective" nature. The shop carries a general line of antiques — everything from antique furnishings to collectibles.

## Bonnie Blue Antiques

107 S. Cumberland
615/453-1158

What once was the men's store of Lebanon has now transformed into a chapter from *Gone with the Wind* collectibles and memorabilia. Victorian furnishings and accessories, vintage clothing and exquisite glassware are also offered at Bonnie Blue.

## Downtown Antique Mall

112 Public Square
615/444-4966

Downtown Antique Mall once sparkled with diamonds and jewels as the town jewelry shop. Today it's no different. For the past 15 to 20 years, this shop has furnished its customers with jewels of a different nature. This 2-story building houses some of the best American furnishings in the area as well as outstanding glassware.

## Denise's Timeless Treasures

146 Public Square
615/443-4996

For the past 70 years this store has been a favorite with women. It began life as a shoe store and now houses fine antiques, particularly from the Victorian period. In addition, the shop stocks accessories to compliment the furnishings as well as pretty stationery for your writing table.

## Southern Rose Antiques

105 Public Square
615/444-3308

Isn't it amazing how some things were just meant to be? Southern Rose was once a furniture warehouse and it still is today. This shop is filled to the brim with furniture from all styles and periods. Most likely you can spot pieces which appeared there over 100 years ago when they were sold as new.

## Ophelia's Antiques

107 Public Square
615/443-0783

A hodgepodge, fun place to shop, Ophelia's carries antiques and collectibles covering many periods. Glassware, china, furniture, linens, prints and more can be found at this antique "stop."

**Antique Attic**
610 S. Cumberland
615/449-7376

**Antique Doctor**
113 S. Cumberland
615/444-9964

**Granny's Playhouse Antiques**
11537 Stewart's Ferry Pike
615/444-0189

**The Emporium**
109 Public Square
615/449-9601

## 52 LENOIR CITY

**Buttermilk Road Antiques**
144 Antique Lane
423/376-5912

**John Farmer Sales**
105 W. Broadway
423/986-5144

**Valley Antiques**
I-75, Exit 76, 11020 Hotchkiss Valley Road
423/986-6636

**"Good" win's Antiques**
9900 White Wing Road/Hwy. 321
423/986-3396

## 53 LEWISBURG

## King's Antiques

1104 W. Cedar St.
931/359-3086
Open: Daily except Sun.

Featuring pattern glass, fine china, oak and walnut furniture, old lamp parts.

**Antique Mall of Lewisburg**
131 E. Commerce St.
931/359-9400

## 54 LIVINGSTON

**A Different Drummer**
106 E. Broad St.
No phone listed

**Court Square Emporium**
108 N. Court Square
931/823-6741

**Livingston Trade Center**
203 S. Goodposture St.
931/823-2898

## 55 LOUDON

**Shirley's Charm Shop**
407 Grove St.
No phone listed

**Log Cabin Antiques**
Horn Springs Road
615/444-1200

**Town Creek Antiques**
101 Short St.
615/453-9552

**Allen's Antiques**
103 E. Broadway
423/986-2724

**Victoria's Antique Mall**
1200 W. Broadway
423/988-7957

**Twin Lakes Antiques**
11827 Hwy. 321 S.
423/986-8082

**Zpast Antique Warehouse**
313 S. Church St.
931/823-8888

**Antique Market**
116 N. Court Square
931/823-4943

**Helen's Now and Then**
521 E. Main St.
931/823-1626

**Sisters**
Mulberry St.
423/458-8027

*Tennessee*

**Brick Box**
400 Mulberry St.
423/458-0850

**Carroll's Bargain Box**
854 Mulberry St.
423/458-6320

**Warehouse Antiques Collectibles & Gifts**
1034 Mulberry St.
423/458-3412

### 56 MADISON

**Always Antiques**
505 S. Gallatin Road
615/860-3400

**Madison Antique Mall**
320 S. Gallatin Road
615/865-4677

### 57 MADISONVILLE

**Ye Ole Towne Antiques & Collectibles**
203 Tellico St.
423/442-5509

### 58 MANCHESTER

**Top of the Hill Antiques**
5751 Cathey Ridge Road
931/728-2610

**Antiques-a-Rama**
626 Hillsboro Blvd.
931/723-4209

**Somewhere in Time**
324 Ragsdale Road
931/728-8987

**Charlie's Trading Post**
Hwy. 41 & 53
No phone listed

**Schuler's Antiques**
4870 McMinnville Hwy.
931/723-2692

### 59 MARYVILLE

**Boone's Barn Antiques Collectibles**
2408 N.W. Lamar Alexander
423/681-0877

**Law's Interiors, Inc.**
306 S. Washington St.
423/982-0321

**General Store**
411 Mulberry St.
423/458-6433

**Sweet Memories Antique Mall**
930 Mulberry St., Suite 104
423/458-2331

**Judy's Antiques**
100 Steekee Creek Road
423/458-4211

**Dusk Catcher's**
101 Harris St.
615/865-7333

**Two Ps in a Pod**
266 Warren St.
423/442-6607

**Lester's Antiques**
707 Gowen Road
931/728-2669

**North Side Clocks**
2032 MacArthur/Hwy. 55
931/728-4307

**Antique World**
410 Woodbury Hwy.
931/728-4007

**Johnson's Hwy. 55 Fleamarket**
Hwy. 55
931/723-0740

**Back in Time Antiques**
504 Odell
423/983-7055

**Memories of the Past Antiques**
931 E. Broadway Ave.
423/982-2810

### 60 McMINNVILLE

This is one of the strangest and most fun places to visit that you're likely to run across! McMinnville is the "Nursery Capital of the World," has the second largest cavern system in the country, a bed and breakfast in a fabulous old Victorian mansion, and one of the few remaining cheese factories still in the state. And on top of all this, it has antiques. Is this a combination or what!

There really are between 400 and 500 nursery growers (trees, plants, that kind of nursery) in the area. This is evidently the only place in the world that has such a perfect combination of climate and soil. This industry began in the 1800s when the area was widely known for its apples and especially for the apple brandy that was produced. The apple tree business grew and evolved into this enormous industry that is now world famous.

Cumberland Caverns are open to the public May through October. They were discovered in 1810 and are now a national landmark.

**McMinnville Antique Mall, Inc.**
2419 Smithville Hwy.
931/668-4735
Open: Mon.–Sat. 9–5, Sun. 1–5
Directions: Take Exit 111 (Manchester) off I-24, Hwy. 55, or take Silver Point Exit off of I-40, Hwy. 56. The shop is one mile past McDonald's on Hwy. 56 North off of Hwy. 70 South.

Pay close attention, because this gets confusing. Barbara Oliver owns the mall, and Susan is Barbara's daughter and Charlotte is Barbara's daughter-in-law. Susan went to work at this mall, and she and Charlotte decided they wanted to own it. So they asked Barbara to buy it so they could run it. Barbara agreed, and bought the mall, Susan and Charlotte manage it, and Barbara has her own shop elsewhere. Susan and Charlotte have 28 dealers in the McMinnville Antique Mall, offering a variety of furniture, Depression and other glassware, as well as pottery and a multitude of other items. It's not confusing if you're just going there to shop . . .

**Antiques on Main**
123 E. Main St.
931/473-1032

**Somewhere in Time**
2419 Smithville Hwy.
931/668-4735

**Antiques on High**
301 S. High St.
931/473-0922

**B & P Lamp Supply**
843 Old Morrison Hwy. 55
931/473-3016

**The Collection Mall**
216 E. Main St.
931/473-1666

# Tennessee

## Great Places to Stay

### Historic Falcon Manor

Winner of the 1997 Great American Home Award for outstanding home restoration by the National Trust for Historic Preservation

2645 Faulkner Springs Road

931/668-4444

Web site: FalconManor.com

Email: FalconManor@FalconManor.com

Directions: *From I-24:* Take Manchester Exit 111 east to McMinnville. DO NOT go into the business district. Keep going straight on Hwy. 70 S. Bypass. At the fifth traffic light, turn left onto Faulkner Springs Road. The mansion is at the end of the road, 1 ³/₁₀ miles from the Bypass. *From I-40:* Take Exit 273 S. and go straight through Smithville. In McMinnville, turn left onto Hwy. 70 S. Bypass, then left at the second light onto Faulkner Springs Road.

In the year 1896, wealthy entrepreneur Clay Faulkner constructed the solid brick mansion now known as Falcon Manor. He promised to build his wife "the finest home in the county" if she would move next to the mill outside McMinnville where he made Gorilla jeans.

But the building looked more like the victim of a terrorist bombing than the finest house in the county when George McGlothin bought it at an auction in 1989. Faulkner's mansion had been converted into a hospital and nursing home in the middle part of this century.

George and Charlien McGlothin spent 4 ¹/₂ years completing the restoration, doing about 95 percent of the work themselves. With both the mansion's decor and their extensive collection of Victorian antiques, the McGlothins have authentically re-created Clay Faulkner's 1890s home. Local octogenarians who remember the mansion in its heyday say Falcon Manor is even more beautiful than it was in Faulkner's time.

Historic Falcon Manor took first prize in the bed and breakfast category of the 1997 Great American Homes Awards. The National Trust added the B&B category just to pay tribute to "a type of establishment that has not only supported countless building rescues but also introduced their many visitors to the pleasures of living, if only temporarily, in old house."

"George decided we would just work on restoring it as we had time and then retire there," remembers Charlien. "It didn't take us long, though, to realize that this place has a friendly elegance and warmth that draws people to it.

"Even when we were just beginning the restoration, folks were stopping to ask for tours. We concluded this would always be a public place, whatever our intentions, so we made it official by opening Historic Falcon Manor as a bed and breakfast in 1993."

In addition to giving B&B guests an opportunity to "relive the peaceful romance of the 1890s," the mansion is open for tours each day at 1 p.m. "This is a favorite getaway for honeymooners, couples celebrating birthdays and anniversaries, and folks who just want to escape the stress of modern life," George observed. "History buffs, antique collectors, and people who've been involved in home restoration projects themselves take a special delight in experiencing the place. Of course, with the Victorian theme being so popular, we play host to lots of weddings as well."

The spacious guest rooms boast rich colors and museum-quality antiques. A sweeping staircase beckons guest to explore the mansion, while the 100-foot-long, wraparound gingerbread veranda invites them to rock in the shade of century-old trees and sip Falcon Manor's signature pink lemonade. McMinnville is located halfway between Nashville and Chattanooga, making it an ideal base for a Tennessee vacation.

In 1995, the McGlothins opened the Victorian Gift Shop in the original smokehouse. Their lastest project, a 200-seat Victorian Carriage House dining room, is the site for elegant weekend meals by reservation.

The mansion was listed on the National Register of Historic Places in 1992, and it was designated as a historic site on Tennessee's Heritage Trail in 1996.

## 61  MEMPHIS

### Satterfield's Home Accessories

2847 Poplar Ave., Suite 102

901/324-7312

Directions: *From I-40:* Take I-40 to Sam Cooper Blvd. And turn left on Tillman. Take a right on Poplar Avenue, then a left on Humes. *From I-240:* Exit at Poplar Avenue and then head toward downtown west.

Satterfield's is a distinctive decorator shop filled with treasures from around the world. Some of its wares include Majolica, Spelter, porcelain and crystal. They also have a large selection of oil paintings, mirrors and bronzes.

| | |
|---|---|
| **Pinch Antique Mall** | **Cottage Antiques & Gifts** |
| 430 N. Front St. | 2330 S. Germantown Road |
| 901/525-0929 | 901/754-5975 |
| | |
| **David's Antiques** | **Crump-Padgett Antique Gallery** |
| 3397 Lamar Ave. | 645 Marshall Ave. |
| 901/566-0953 | 901/522-1155 |
| | |
| **Springer's Antiques** | **Cottage House Mall** |
| 5050 Park Ave. | 4701 Summer Ave. |
| 901/681-0025 | 901/761-5588 |
| | |
| **Broken Spoke Collectiques** | **Savannah's Fine Antiques** |
| 6445 Summer Ave. | 2847 Poplar Ave., Suite 104 |
| 901/377-7974 | 901/452-7799 |
| | |
| **Chip 'n' Dale's** | **Chip 'n' Dale's** |
| 3475 Summer Ave. | 3457 Summer Ave. |
| 901/452-8366 | 901/452-5620 |

*Tennessee*

**Palladio Antique & Interior Marketplace**
2169 Central Ave.
901/276-3808

**Antique Warehouse**
2563 Summer Ave.
901/323-0600

**Bo-Jo's Antique Mall**
3400 Summer Ave.
901/323-2050

**Common Market, Inc.**
364 S. Front St.
901/526-4501

**Crocker Galleria**
2281 Central Ave.
901/274-1515

**House of Yesteryear**
1692 Madison Ave.
901/276-0416

**Madison Antiques**
1964 Madison Ave.
901/728-5520

**Second Hand Rose**
2129 Central Ave.
901/276-4600

**Vance Boyd Antiques & Collectibles**
171 S. Cooper St.
901/726-4652

**Antique Mall of Midtown**
2151 Central Ave.
901/274-8563

**Bill Rick's Antiques**
733 S. Cooper St.
901/725-9635

**Buckley's Antiques**
1965 Madison Ave.
901/726-5358

**Consignments**
2300 Central Ave.
901/278-5909

**Flashback, Inc.**
2304 Central Ave.
901/272-2304

**Idlewild House**
149 Union Ave.
901/527-9855

**Market Central**
2215 Central Ave.
901/278-0888

**Union Avenue Antique Mall**
1652 Union Ave.
901/276-0089

## 62 MORRISTOWN

**A-Z Repeat 'n' More**
5968 W Andrew Johnson Hwy.
423/581-2623

**Dianne's Place Antiques**
1040 Buffalo Trail
423/318-0700

**Bacon's Antiques & Collectibles**
413 N. Cumberland St.
423/581-7420

**Farm House Antiques**
148 W. Main St.
423/581-1527

**Yesterday — Antiques & Uniques**
128 E. Morris Blvd.
423/586-9273

**Johnny's Antiques**
415 E. Converse Ave.
423/587-4750

**Radio Center Antiques**
1225 S. Cumberland St.
423/586-4337

**Olde Towne Antique Mall**
181 W. Main St.
423/581-6423

## 63 MT. PLEASANT

**GG's Antique Mall**
119 N. Main St.
931/379-5737
Open: Mon.–Sat. 10–5, Sun. 1–5

Antiques, furniture, primitives, china, glassware, old planters, rugs and copies of Tennessee handmade circa-1800s furniture.

**The Etagère**
111 N. Main St.
931/379-9068

### *Great Places to Eat*

**Lumpy's Malt Shop**
On The Square

A nifty '50s flashback … a time and place where Fats is still a singer. Lumpy's is an authentic malt shop where you can remember the great days of the '50s, eat a meal, drink a vanilla soda and listen to Elvis on the jukebox. Along with the 1952 soda fountain, there is a wide array of memorabilia and antiques. All this serves to remind us of days when life seemed much simpler. Lumpy's is an experience you don't want to miss.

**Duck River Orchards**
1-800-964-4043

Unusually good mouth-watering food is a "given" at Duck River Orchards. Whether you are looking for special cappuccino and a fresh, hot homemade doughnut, a gourmet gift basket for someone special, homemade fudge, bakery products or home-grown peaches and apples, this is the place to stop.

### *Great Places to Stay*

**Academy Place Bed & Breakfast**
301 Goodloe St.
931/379-3198 or 1-888-252-1892

Lavender in color, this Colonial/ Victorian is furnished with many family antiques and memorabilia. Academy Place, c. 1835 and 1904, offers quiet relaxation, rocking on the porches, soothing in the hot spa or snoozing on queen beds in tastefully decorated rooms. Full breakfast awaits you each morning in the turn of the century dining room. Randall and Faye Wyatt, innkeepers.

# *Tennessee*

## 64 MURFREESBORO

Located in the heart of Tennessee, Murfreesboro's location is the geographical center of the state, and home to Middle Tennessee State University and the Stones River National Battlefield. The location of the Nissan U.S.A. motor manufacturing plant and its close proximity to Nashville has made Rutherford County one of the fastest growing in the state.

### Antique Centers I & II

2213-2219 S. Church St.
615/896-5188 (I) or 615/890-4252 (II)
Open: Mon.–Sat. 9–5; Sun. 10–5
Directions: From I-24 (25 miles southeast of Nashville) take Exit 81B at U.S. 231 Murfreesboro. Turn onto the access road in front of Burger King. The Centers are next to Cracker Barrel.

The Antique Center has been at the same location since its beginning in 1973. The 30,00- square-foot building was divided into two shops at that time and has continued as such, therefore, giving it the name "I & II." Antique Center I has 40 dealers, three of whom have been with the center since 1973. Antique Center II has 30 dealers. Both shops carry a wide selection of furniture to meet the needs of both decorator and first-time buyers. Several dealers specialize in Depression glass, elegant glassware such as Fostoria, Cambridge, Tiffin, Heisey, Carnival and art glass. Showcases highlight pottery such as Roseville, Hull, Weller, Watt, sterling silver, holiday collectibles, black memorabilia, toys and dolls. Antique Center II specializes in chandeliers. The chandeliers have been refurbished and are ready to go into the home. They range in size from 18 inches to 6 feet, and from one bulb to 12 or more as well as gas light fixtures. Delivery and shipping is available.

### Keepsake Antiques Mall

2349 S. Church St.
615/890-4125
Open: Mon.–Sat. 9–5, Sun. 1–5

Keepsake Antiques Mall is one of Murfreesboro's largest antique malls offering hundreds of dealers in a 21,000-square-foot facility. Voted #1 antique mall in Rutherford County by the *Daily News Journal* two years running. Offering fine antiques, glassware, toys, collectibles, iron, estate jewelry and more.

### Smotherman's Antique Wholesalers

Rockvale
615/274-2830
Open: Call for appointment

Randy and Belinda Smotherman specialize in 18th- and 19th-century antique furniture and garden accessories. They particularly love Tennessee furniture and have often found wonderful Tennessee sugar chests and cupboards. Wholesale to dealers only.

**Chick's Antique Shop**
516 S. Church St.
615/893-2459

**Antiques Unlimited**
2303 S. Church St.
615/895-3183

**Forty-One-"0"-Six Antiques**
4106 E. Main St.
615/563-3282

**Premise Antiques**
Broad St.
615/896-2112

**Yesteryear Civil War Relics**
3511 Old Nashville Hwy.
615/893-3470

**Magnolias**
229 River Rock Blvd.
615/848-2905

## 65 NASHVILLE

### Heart of Country Antiques Show

Opryland Hotel
Richard E. Kramer & Associates
427 Midvale Ave.
St. Louis, MO 63130
1-800-862-1090
Call for dates

Every year Nashville's Opryland Hotel plays host to the Heart of Country Antiques show, an award-winning event managed by Richard E. Kramer & Associates of St. Louis, Missouri. The eighteen-year-old antiques show boasts representation from thirty-six states, and some of its more than 175 dealers have been with the production the entire eighteen years! Just the fact that dealers travel to Nashville to participate in the show from as far away as California and New York serves as testimony to the show's success.

The Heart of Country is a three-day show that is held each year in February and again in October. Prior to each show is a preview party held the night before opening day. Since the dealers are all chosen because they not only have interesting merchandise, but because they also passed the "friendly test," the preview party serves as a way to bring them together with live music, food, and guest speakers on special topics of interest to the collectors of the old and desirable.

Dick and Libby Kramer, founders and managers of Heart of Country, work diligently to ensure the event is rewarding for the dealer and the buyer. The show's name is synonymous with its offerings—American Country. From the large, as in Country cupboards and decorated Sheraton pieces, to the small, as in game boards and dolls' quilts, Heart of Country pleases all who attend. It is a collector's paradise.

Heart of Country seems to be defining what is "in" in collecting, as dealers take note of the best-selling items. Some collectibles seem to never lose their appeal, like architectural items and miniatures. This year's show pointed to a general interest in garden accessories and architectural pieces for practical use or for accent.

## Antique Merchants Mall
2015 8th Ave. S.
615/292-7811
Open: Mon.–Sat. 10–5, Sun. 1–5
Directions: The Antique Merchants Mall is located in the heart of Nashville's "Antique District." It is five minutes south of downtown Nashville. *Traveling from Memphis:* follow I-40 to I-65 South, then take Exit 81 (Wedgewood). Take a right and go to the traffic light and take a left at 8th Avenue South. The mall is the third business on the right. *From the Opryland/Airport area:* Take I-40 West to I-440 West to I-65 North toward Nashville, Exit 81 (Wedgewood). Take a left at the exit and go to the traffic light, which is at 8th Avenue South. At 8th Avenue South take a left, and the mall is the third business on the right.

For 20 years the Antique Merchants Mall has been Nashville's premier source for antiques and collectibles. It has been in business since 1977, making it one of the oldest antique malls in the Middle Tennessee area. It has over 40 dealers in about 6,000 square feet of space, with some dealers specializing in American, French, and English furniture. Shoppers will also find porcelains, china and crystal, as well as booths filled with pottery, silver, furniture, paintings, Depression glass, and one dealer with over 12,000 out-of-print, rare and collectible books.

## Belle Meade Interiors Market
5133 Harding Road
Belle Meade Galleria
615/356-7861
Open: 10–5:30, Mon.–Sat.
Directions: Belle Meade Interior Market is located in the heart of Belle Meade on Harding Road between Belle Meade Mansion and Cheekwood.

Belle Meade Interiors Market is a gallery of shops filled with American, English, French and other European fine antiques and objets d'art. Many of Nashville's premier designers are a part of Belle Meade Interiors Market and many of Nashville's talented local artists display their works there. Visitors will find a wealth of unique accessories and furnishings for the home. Belle Meade Interiors Market acts as direct importers of many one-of-a-kind pieces, wrought iron, garden and architectural elements.

**Oriental Shop**
2121 Bandywood Dr.
615/297-0945

**The Gallery of Belle Meade**
Belle Meade Shopping Center
615/298-5825

**Antique & Flea Gallery**
4606 Charlotte Pike
615/385-1055

**Curiosity Shop**
996 Davidson Dr.
615/352-3840

**Downtown Antique Mall**
612 8th Ave. S.
615/256-6616

**Art-Deco Shoppe & Antique Mall**
2110 8th Ave. S.
615/386-9373

**American Classical II Antiques**
2116 8th Ave. S.
615/297-5514

**Van-Garde Alternative Clothing**
2204 Elliston Place
615/321-5326

**Ted Leland, Inc.**
3301 W. End Ave.
615/383-2421

**Temptation Gallery**
2301 Franklin Road
615/297-7412

**Little Antique Shop**
6017 Hwy. 100
615/352-5190

**Marymont Plantation Antique Shop**
6035 Hwy. 100
615/352-4902

**Streater Spencer**
6045 Hwy. 100
615/356-1992

**Calvert Antiques**
6518 Hwy. 100
615/353-2879

**Cinnamon Hill Antiques & Interiors**
6608 Hwy. 100
615/352-6608

**Polk Place Antiques**
6614 Hwy. 100
615/353-1324

**Green Hills Antique Mall**
4108 Hillsboro Road
615/383-4999

**Tennessee Antique Mall**
654 Wedgewood Ave.
615/259-4077

**Crystal Dragon Antqs. & Collectibles**
4900 Charlotte Pike
615/383-2189

**White Way Antique Mall**
Edgehill & Villa Place
615/327-1098

**Pia's Antique Gallery**
1800 8th Ave. S.
615/251-4721

**Cane Ery Antique Mall**
2112 8th Ave. S.
615/269-4780

**Elders Book Store**
2115 Elliston Place
615/327-1867

**Made in France, Inc.**
3001 W. End Ave.
615/329-9300

**Germantown Antiques**
1205 4th Ave. N.
615/242-7555

**Courtyard Gate Antiques**
2504 Franklin Road
615/383-0530

**Tony Brown Antiques**
6027 Hwy. 100
615/356-7772

**Evelyn Anderson Galleries**
6043 Hwy. 100
615/352-6770

**Spaulding Antiques**
6608 Hwy. 100
615/352-1272

**Ro's Oriental Rugs, Inc.**
6602 Hwy. 100
615/352-9055

**Pembroke Antiques**
6610 Hwy. 100
615/353-0889

**Harpeth Gallery**
4102 Hillsboro Road
615/297-4300

**Cinemonde**
138 2nd Ave. N.
615/742-3048

**Wedgewood Station Antique Mall**
657 Wedgewood Ave.
615/259-0939

# *Tennessee*

**Forsyth's Antiques**
2120 Crestmoor Road
615/298-5107

**Belmont Antiques**
3112 Belmont Blvd.
615/383-5994

**Dealer's Choice Auction**
2109 8th Ave. S.
615/383-7030

**Fairbank's Antique & Furniture**
7330 Charlotte Pike
615/352-4986

**Glenn's Antiques Gallery**
2919 Nolensville Road
615/832-5277

**Artifacts**
105 Heady Dr.
615/354-1267

**Magnolia House**
1516 8th Ave.
615/259-0002

**Auntie's Attic**
2506 8th Ave.
615/292-4381

**Annabell Lynn's Antiques**
5001 Alabama Ave.
615/297-7355

**Always Antiques**
505 Gallatin Road
615/860-3400

**Davishire Interiors**
2106 21st Ave. S.
615/298-2670

**Ejvind's Antiques**
2108 8th Ave. S.
615/383-2012

**Gatti's Antiques**
6264 Nolensville Road
615/834-4582

**Amici**
6518 Hwy. 100
615/298-4201

**Classics International**
427 Chestnut St.
615/400-6625

**Virginia Parker**
1016 8th Ave.
615/742-0985

**Belle Meade Antiques Market**
4336 Kenilwood Dr.
615/832-8800

**Estelle's Antiques**
601 8th Ave.
615/259-2630

## 66　NOLENSVILLE

### Gattis Antiques

6264 Nolensville Road
615/834-4582

Specializing in blue and white stoneware, old Fenton glass, graniteware, pottery, pattern glass, primitives, and loads of smalls. In business 31 years.

**Honeysuckle Antiques**
7291 Nolensville Road
615/776-5806

**The Daisy Chain**
7289 Nolensville Road
615/776-3439

## 67　OBION

**Obion Antiques**
223 E. Palestine St.
901/536-3905

**Depot Antiques**
Palestine St.
901/536-5886

## 68　OLD HICKORY

**CJ & J's Antiques**
2005-B Hadley Ave.
615/847-5599

**Honey Pumpkin Antiques**
22nd and Hadley Ave.
615/847-5495

## 69　PARIS

### Market Street Antique Mall

414 N. Market St.
901/642-6996
Open: Mon.–Sat. 10–6, Sun. 1–5

The largest antique mall in the area (60,000 square feet). I won't even attempt to list what you will find in this mall, just plan to spend the day. Cafe located inside the mall serving great country cooking.

**Old Depot Antique Mall**
203 N. Fentress St.
901/642-0222

**Grapevine Mall**
114 W. Washington St.
901/642-7850

## 70　PIGEON FORGE

See Sevierville, #75, for antiquing in Pigeon Forge.

### *Great Places to Stay*

### Hiltons Bluff Bed and Breakfast

2654 Valley Heights Dr.
1-800-441-4188

This romantic hilltop hideaway is a beautiful two-story cedar inn with covered decks, oak rockers and nature's ever-changing mountain views. Decorated with country quilts and lace, the ten guest rooms—honeymoon suites feature deluxe king beds, waterbeds and heart-shaped Jacuzzi. Elegant country living minutes from the heart of Pigeon Forge and the Great Smoky Mountains National Park.

## 71　PULASKI

**Harmony Farms Gifts & Antiques**
211 N. 1st St.
931/424-5937

**Bee-Line This & That**
705 N. 1st St.
931/424-5120

**Mama's Cedar Chest**
Hwy. 64
No phone listed

**Kevin Walker Antiques**
110 N. 2nd St.
931/424-1825

**Bunker Hill Antiques**
145 Bunker Hill/Bryson Road
931/732-4500

## 72　REELFOOT LAKE

History records that Reelfoot Lake was created, in part, by a series of severe earthquakes during the winter of 1811–1812. The quakes were said to be so severe that a man could not stand on his feet during them. Landslides swept down bluffs, large areas of land were uplifted, and still larger areas sank.

*Tennessee*

Over the years, one of these sunken areas filled with water and became known as Reelfoot Lake.

Reelfoot Lake lies in the northwest corner of Tennessee in Lake and Obion Counties. It contains approximately 25,000 acres, 15,000 of which are water. The area has an excellent reputation for hunting and fishing. It harbors numerous shore and wading birds, as well as the American bald eagle.

### The Quilt Lady
Hwy. 21
901/253-0001

A large selection of antique quilts, most from Tennessee.

### Eagle Tree Gallery
Southwest Indian Art
Edgewater Beach Road
901/253-8652

Featuring museum-quality Hopi Kachinas, pottery, paintings and jewelry.

#### *Great Places to Eat*

### Boyette's
Hwy. 21
901/253-7307

Boyette's Dining Room has been serving fine food at Reelfoot Lake since 1921. Boyette's first opened as a country grocery store that sold sandwiches and lunches to fishermen and hunters with just a few seats for eating. Presently Boyette's seats 300 people and has three private dining areas. Boyette's specializes in fish dinners, fried chicken and Tennessee country ham.

### 73 ROCKWOOD

### O' Those Were the Days Antique Mall
224 W. Rockwood St.
423/354-9629

### Something Olde 'n' Something New
Magnolia Tea Room
215 W. Rockwood St.
Open: Mon.–Fri. 10–6, Sat. 10–5, Sun. 1–5

**The Happy Box**
239 W. Rockwood St.
423/354-6100

**Rockwood Mini-Mall**
221 W. Rockwood St.
423/354-8121

### 74 SELMER

**Kennedy's Antique World**
160 W. Court Ave.
901/645-6357

**King's Antiques**
Hwy. 45 S.
901/645-5581

**Memory Lane**
124 W. Court Ave.
901/645-7734

### 75 SEVIERVILLE

### Riverside Antique and Collectors Mall
1442 Winfield Dunn Pkwy. (Hwy. 66)
423/429-0100
Fax: 423/428-5221
Open: Daily 9–6, with extended summer hours
Directions: From I-40, take Exit 407 (Gatlinburg, Sevierville, Hwy. 66). Go south five miles and the mall is located on the right side of the highway. Look for the huge light-gray building with a dark red roof.

I once spent four hours in this mall looking for nothing but blue and white dishes. The selection was great. One dealer had an entire wall filled with every imaginable pattern and maker. The great thing about this mall is its diverse selection. While I was looking for dishes, David was  preoccupied with the "man things." This mall has a lot to offer for the man in your life: matchbox cars, fishing equipment, old tool boxes, sports memorabilia, Indian relics and collectible knives.

Riverside Antique Mall encompasses 35,000 square feet, so I could burn up a lot of paper mentioning the usual hodgepodge of items most malls of this size offer. Instead I think I'll tell you about some of the unusual things you'll find here. For starters, they stock over 400 reference-book titles, including *Leggetts' Antiques Atlas* (so if you've borrowed the one you're reading, stop by and get your own). They have a huge handmade basket section, row after row of showcases housing many rare items and a nice country candy counter with all sorts of varieties of candies and dried fruits (recommended for snacking on down the road). The mall is decorated with hundreds of advertising signs which really sets the mood for shopping the minute you walk in the door. And, since I've mentioned advertising signs, I probably should tell you they have much to offer in that section as well.

Even after spending over four hours at Riverside, I still don't think we saw everything. It is one of the most interesting and clean (especially the bathrooms) antique malls I have ever been in. On our next trip to the Great Smoky Mountains, I am going to allow more time for Riverside Antique and Collectors Mall.

# Tennessee

## Riverside Cutlery Co.
1442 Winfield Dunn Pkwy.
423/453-9558
Located inside the Riverside Antiques and Collectors Mall

Grudgingly, but with a smile, I wheeled into the parking lot of another antique mall, but this one was the largest of any we had already been to. As we entered the building I was immediately struck with a sense of amazement because this one was different. The first thing to catch my eye was a nice display of Indian artifacts and Remington bronzes. As I looked over the gigantic selection of reference-book titles, I saw, out of the corner of my eye, a huge antique and collectible knife department. I was truly on a mission now. I had to see those knives, touch them, hear the "walk and talk" of precision steel. As I peered deep into these well-lit, neatly arranged showcases, I heard someone say, "May I show you something?" Yes, all of them, I thought. There were knives of all kinds — Case, Boker, Remington, Ka-Bar, Winchester, Queen, bargain knives, limited editions, commemoratives, and so much more. I told this nice young man about my personal collection of knives, a story I am sure he has heard many times before from others. He told me about this great catalog called, appropriately, Riverside Cutlery Co., which was mailed out free to over 700 avid collectors like myself. He had me put my name on the mailing list right there so I could be sure to get the next mailing. I was really amazed at the quality of antique and collectible knives that I found hidden within the pages. The next thing that caught my eye was a wall full of fine antique firearms — Winchesters, Colts, Remingtons, military and Western firearms, I couldn't believe the amount of great items. I was really impressed with the amount of fine merchandise to choose from in this knife department as well as the entire mall. As I decided what to buy (my wife was waiting on me for a change!), this fine Riverside employee told me if I ever decided to sell my collection to give him a call. He said they also buy collections, large or small! I left Riverside knowing that on my next trip to the Smoky Mountains, I would bring some of my knives and maybe do some trading!

## Memory Lane Antique Mall
1838 Winfield Dunn Pkwy.
423/428-0536
Open: Daily 9–5:30, March–October; 9–5 November–February
Directions: From I-40, take Exit 407. The mall is 4 1/2 miles off I-40 on the right off 66 or Winfield Dunn Parkway.

The outside of this place is deceiving. It looks much smaller than it really is and, in fact, even though it's larger when you get inside, I still can't figure out how that much glassware could fit into that size space. (That's almost a tongue twister.) Memory Lane's unusually large glass selection consists of Tiffany, Daum, Loetz, French Cameo, along with Austria and German pieces. If you are looking to add to your Depression glass collection you'll probably find it here. The various dealers who

display in the shop carry a huge offering of such pieces. The furniture, though limited, is in excellent condition.

**Wagon Wheel Antiques**
131 Bruce St.
423/429-4007

**Family Antiques**
2093 Chapman Hwy.
423/428-6669

**Antiques of Chapman Hwy.**
2121 Chapman Hwy.
423/428-3609

**Wears Valley Antique Gallery**
3234 Wears Valley Road
423/453-5294

**Tudor House Antiques & Collectibles**
1417 Winfield Dunn Pkwy.
423/428-4400

**Heartland Antiques & Collectibles**
1441 Winfield Dunn Pkwy.
423/429-1791

**Olden Days Antiques & Collectibles**
1846 Winfield Dunn Pkwy.
423/453-7318

**Action Antique Mall**
2189 Winfield Dunn Pkwy.
423/453-0052

## 76 SHARON

**Willow Creek Collectibles**
5117 Hwy. 45 S.
901/456-2433

## 77 SHELBYVILLE

Directions: Take I-24 to the Beech Grove Road/Shelbyville Exit 97, go west on Hwy. 64, then turn right at Hwy. 41A/Madison Street. Hwy. 231, which intersects with Hwy. 41A, leads to the town square.

Shelbyville is known for three things: one well known, two almost unheard of. The first thing is its international designation as the "Walking Horse Capital of the World." The second thing is its almost unknown title of Pencil City, because the town is the center of the American pencil-making industry! The third thing is that the Shelbyville town square, laid out in 1809, was used as a prototype for town squares all over the South and Midwest.

Synonymous with Shelbyville, in most people's minds, is "The Celebration," the largest and most renowned walking horse show in the world. The show is held each year in late summer for the 10 days ending on the Saturday night before Labor Day.

Other area attractions that will be interesting to visitors are the towns of Wartrace and Bell Buckle, the Jack Daniel's and George Dickel distilleries, and perhaps unknown but worth a stop, the family owned and operated Tri-Star Vineyards and Winery just north of Shelbyville.

## Judy's Jewels Antiques & Collectibles
730 N. Main St.
931/685-4200
Open: Daily

Judy's Jewels are found within her wonderful collection of antiques, a love that grew out of an affection for her mother's beautiful, old things.

*Tennessee*

Among her treasures are Persian rugs, bronzes, pictures, glassware, and a fabulous collection of fine porcelain that include R.S. Prussia, Nippon, Royal Bayreuth, and Beleek. An exquisite selection of furnishings are available as well.

## The Antique Marketplace
208 Elm St.
931/684-8493

The Antique Marketplace is the largest antique mall and auction house in Shelbyville. Over 100 quality dealers occupy what once was the old Coca-Cola bottling plant. Come take a step back in time with Cavigny and Mike House and enjoy an old-fashioned bottled Coke and a sample of homemade fudge. The mall offers an eclectic array of wonderful antiques from which to choose; furniture, excellent Depression glassware, costume jewelry, pottery, Blue Ridge, primitives and garden accessories. Special services are also offered such as furniture stripping, sandblasting, framing, chair caning and lamp repair. A monthly auction is held on the second Friday of each month. Call to be added to their list.

## Ole Grapevine Antique Shoppe
113 Depot St.
931/684-1068

Connie and Eddie Murray invite you to visit Shelbyville's oldest antique shop (est. 1975) at their new location — 2 doors off Shelbyville's historic square. Step back in time, browse through their collections of walking horse memorabilia, *Old Blue Ribbon* magazines, a variety of antique furniture, primitives, lots of smalls, jewelry, fishing items and all kinds of lamps and gardening accessories. They also offer chair caning, picture framing and lamp repair.

## 78 SIGNAL MOUNTAIN

**Antique Stations**
1906 Taft Hwy.
423/886-7291

**Aunt Polly's Parlor**
3500 Taft Hwy.
423/886-4705

**The Log Cabin Herbs & Antiques**
4111 Taft Hwy.
423/886-2663

**Woody's Goodies**
4702 Taft Hwy.
423/886-4095

**Church's Antique & Access**
1819 Taft Hwy.
423/886-9636

## 79 SMITHVILLE

### Fuston's Antiques
123 W. Market St.
615/597-5232
Open: Mon.–Sat. 9–5
Directions: Traveling I-40 east from Nashville or west from Knoxville, take Exit 273 and travel south on Hwy. 56 approximately 12 miles to the first red light. At the light turn right and go two blocks to the courthouse square. Go halfway around the courthouse and turn right onto Main Street. Go to the red light and turn left onto College Street. Go one block. The shop is located on the corner of Walnut Street and South College Street.

Fuston's is a breathtaking, awe-inspiring, ocular odyssey of 25 years of accumulation. The store holds the most amazing collection of antique and collectible glassware, antique clocks and music boxes, china and lamps — both oil and electric. But the "shop" is in reality a total of five buildings all crammed with loads of furniture and everything else. Mr. Fuston has over 25,000 square feet of merchandise to choose from. Two of the buildings were, until fairly recently, the 1930s era Fuston's Five and Dime (his since the 1950s). An amazing place and an owner to match — don't miss it!

## 80 SPARTA

**Country Treasures**
447 W. Brockman Way
931/836-3572

**Jongee's Antiques & Gifts**
137 S. Young St.
931/836-2822

**Liberty Square Antiques**
1 Maple St.
931/836-3997

## 81 SWEETWATER

**Bottle Shop**
121 County Road 308
423/337-0512

**Country Store**
121 County Road 308
423/337-6540

## 82 TALBOTT

**Alpha Antique Mall**
6205 W. Andrew Johnson Hwy.
423/581-2371

## 83 TRENTON

**Carol's Antique Mall**
148 Davy Crockett
901/855-0783

**Virginia's Antiques**
209 W. Eaton St.
901/855-0261

**Bill Hamilton's Antiques**
203 W. Huntingdon St.
901/855-9641

## 84 TROY

**Troy Antique Mall**
1104 N. U.S. Hwy. 51 S.
901/536-4211

## 85 TULLAHOMA

**Keepsake Antiques & Collectibles**
310 S. Anderson St.
931/455-8612

**Ole World Antiques**
321 S. Anderson St.
931/455-7666

**Memories Antique & Mall**
117 W. Lincoln St.
931/455-3992

**Lincoln Street Antiques**
212 E. Lincoln St.
931/454-9391

**Davicki House**
407 S. Jackson St.
931/393-4549

**Good Ole Days Antiques**
803 E. Lincoln St.
931/455-2026

**Tullahoma Art & Antiques**
114 N. Collins St.
931/455-0777

**Rose Cottage Antiques**
203 S. Jackson St.
931/455-2049

## 86 WARTRACE

Directions: Take I-24 to the Beech Grove Road/Shelbyville Exit 97. Take Hwy. 64 directly to Wartrace.

This antique hamlet is known as the "cradle of the Tennessee walking horse," because walking horses were first bred here in the 1930s. The town gets its name from the Native American trail that passed through the town that was used as a war path or war "trace" (the designation for wilderness roads during the 1600s and 1700s).

### *Great Places to Stay*

**The Log Cabin Bed & Breakfast**
171 Loop Road
931/389-6713
Open: Year-round

Emily Pomrenke is kinda (that's Southern for "kind of") special to us. She was one of the early supporters of the *Antiques Atlas*. Shortly after our commitment to this huge undertaking, Emily called to express her interest and excitement in a three-hour phone conversation. The conversations continued to the point that we decided to go meet her in person. The Log Cabin is out in the country on a small paved road where everybody waves when they pass. It was easy to spot — the marker on the road led us up the driveway to the cabin on the hill. It was just as I had pictured it — a wonderful getaway with an informal atmosphere.

Each of the three guest rooms has its own theme. The Heart of Texas Room, the one most requested by horse enthusiasts who stay with Emily while competing in the nearby Shelbyville horse shows, is decorated in Texas memorabilia. The Swing by the Window (there really is one) has a springtime appeal. The Family Room, synonymous with its intent (to welcome a family) has plenty of sleeping space.

**Walking Horse Hotel and Shops**
101 Spring St.
931/389-7050 or 1-800-513-8876
Open: Year-round

While we were in Wartrace visiting Emily, we happened upon a magnificent structure that immediately drew us in. It came as no surprise that we weren't the only ones mystified by the Walking Horse Hotel. The owner, John Garland, was inside, steadily working on the hotel's renovation. He, too, had happened upon the hotel, which was in desperate need of repair, but, captivated by its history and charm, decided to purchase it and move to Wartrace from his home in Oregon. We understood his enthusiasm. The Walking Horse was, in its day, a first-class hotel. In the 1930s Middle Tennessee was fast becoming "the walking horse capital of the world." The hotel's "claim to fame" was credited to the breeding and boarding of "Strolling Jim," a high-stepping horse who won the first World Grand Championship Title in 1939. The champion trainer was Floyd Caruthers, who owned both the hotel and the stables. Strolling Jim is still at home as his final resting place is in the backyard of the hotel.

Today, the Walking Horse Hotel has been restored to its grandeur with seven guest rooms, six occupying the third floor. Specialty shops adorn the second-floor level offering a barber shop, candy shop, and framing studio, along with several gift shops. The restaurant located on the main floor serves delicious Southern cuisine.

**Ledford Mill Bed & Breakfast**
Route 2
931/455-2546 or 454-9228
Open: Year-round

This is another story of someone who came to visit and decided to stay. In December 1995, Dennis and Kathleen Depert bought the mill and moved from their home on an island in Puget Sound off the coast of Washington state to the tiny town of Wartrace. The Deperts have converted the mill into a wonderful bed and breakfast inn with three special accommodations all having access to the gardens, waterfall and creek. The mill's original machinery is highlighted in each room, where early 1900s furnishings are arranged within a spacious old factory setting. Visitors to the gift shop on the main floor are quite taken with the floor-to-ceiling mural in sepia tones, depicting an old mill delivery wagon. Kathleen drew her inspiration for this from an old photograph. The main

*Tennessee*

floor also includes a lobby, old-time kitchen and breakfast room overlooking the falls.

Ledford Mill is still one of the best-kept secrets on the Tennessee backroads. It is not unusual that a Nashville, Chattanooga or Huntsville traveler, taking a different turn, will discover the mill tucked in its secluded hollow and decide to stay the night. One guest was heard to say recently that "this is not your daily grind."

## 87 WAVERLY

You could spend a day or two in Waverly just poking around in the various museums and odd places in town. The town was founded in 1838 and named for one of the founding families. There is a barely changed 1948 movie house that's still operating on the square and a 1960s drive-in theater just down the highway, owned by the same family. There's Mr. Pilkington's World-o-Tools Museum just past the Farmers Co-op (be sure and call first to make sure Mr. Pilkington is there). Collecting tools was just a hobby for Mr. P. in the 1950s, but now he has about 25,000 old and unique tools, primarily from the 20th century, but lots from the 1800s and even earlier. Also on the square is the Humphreys County Museum, open whenever the Chamber of Commerce is open, because they're both in the same building.

### Nolan House
375 Hwy. 13 N.
931/296-2511
Open: March–December (office hours 9–7)
Rates: $50–$75
Directions: *From I-40:* Take Exit 143 (Hwy. 13 North) past Loretta Lynn's Dude Ranch, approximately 14 miles. At the Waverly town center, follow Hwy. 13 North across the viaduct. At the top of the viaduct turn left at the first house. *From U.S. 70 East or West:* Follow the Hwy. 13 North signs across the viaduct. At the top of the viaduct turn left at the first house.

The Nolan House offers a little bit o' Ireland in the rural Tennessee countryside. This National Register home was built after the Civil War by Irishman James Nicholas Nolan, who stayed in Waverly after the war and became a very successful businessman. It remained in the Nolan family for 109 years, until the last family member died in 1979. The current owners, Linda and Patrick O'Lee, are keeping the Irish legacy alive by offering spacious guests rooms, decorated with antiques. The warm ambiance of the spacious Great Room is the setting for breakfast served on fine china. Country living at its most gracious includes day trips to Nashville, Memphis, state parks with hiking, canoeing, swimming, golfing, visiting historic Civil War sites, and, of course, antique shopping.

Legend has it that Jesse James hitched his horse in front of the Nolan House.

## 88 WOODBURY

**Academy Antiques**
115 S. McCrary St.
615/563-8509

**Old Feed Store Antique Mall**
310 W. Water St.
615/563-2108

**Saltbox Gallery Antiques**
6737 McMinnville Hwy.
615/563-4113

**Emma's Antique Mall**
953 S. McCrary St.
615/563-4161

**Red Rooster Antiques**
217 W. Main St.
615/563-8790

**Wilma's House**
7228 McMinnville Hwy.
615/563-5666

# Vermont

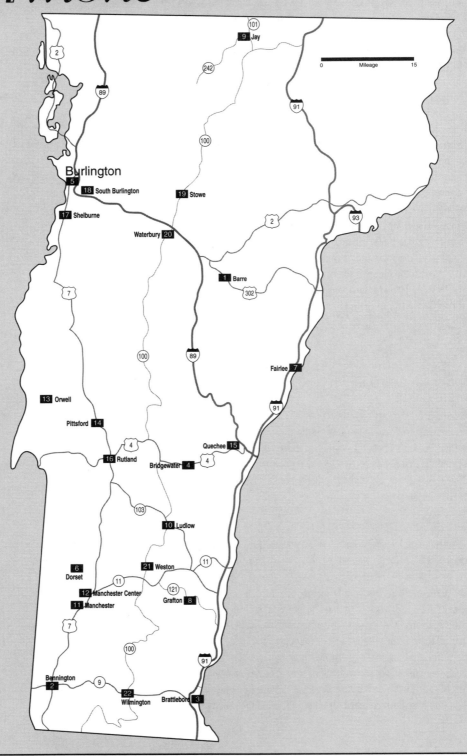

Mileage
0       15

2

101
9 Jay

242

89

91

100

Burlington
5
18 South Burlington
19 Stowe

17 Shelburne

2

93

Waterbury 20

7

1 Barre

302

100

89

Fairlee 7

13 Orwell

91

Pittsford 14

4
16 Rutland    Bridgewater 4    4    Quechee 15

103

10 Ludlow

11

6    21 Weston
Dorset

11
12 Manchester Center    121
11 Manchester    Grafton 8

7

100

91

Bennington
2    9
22
Wilmington    Brattleboro 3

# Vermont

## 1　BARRE

### East Barre Antique Mall
133 Mill St.
(East Barre)
802/479-5190
Open: Daily 10–5
Directions: Located just off the junction of U.S. Route 302 East &
Route 110 on Mill Street in the heart of East Barre. Bear right at the
fork and up the hill.

East Barre Antique Mall is a group shop located in the center of East
Barre, Vermont. Besides a general line of antiques, they offer the largest
selection of antique furniture in the area, antique silver, glassware, framed
prints, sports items, primitives and collectibles. The largest and cleanest
shop in central Vermont, with over 12,000 square feet, featuring items
tastefully displayed throughout making it easy to spot your favorite pieces.

**Red Wagon Antiques**
1079 S. Barre Road
802/479-3611

**Everything under the Sun**
Barre Road
802/479-2563

## 2　BENNINGTON

**Four Corners East**
307 North St.
802/442-2612

**Antique Center at Camelot Village**
60 West Road
802/447-0039

**Molly Stark Antiques**
Route 9 E.
802/442-2129

**Pentimento**
359 Main St.
802/442-8550

## 3　BRATTLEBORO

**Village Farm Antiques**
Green River Village
802/254-7366

**Richter Gallery**
111 Main St.
802/254-1110

**Black Mountain Antique Center**
Route 30
802/254-3848

**Kit Barry Antiques**
109 Main St.
802/254-3634

## 4　BRIDGEWATER

### Bridgewater Mill Antique Centre
Old Mill Marketplace
Route 4
802/672-3049
Open: Daily 10–6
Directions: Take I-91 North to Exit 9 (Hartland). Take Route 12 North
to Route 4 West, which goes to Bridgewater. The Old Mill Marketplace
is situated on the left side of Route 4. Bridgewater is 10 miles west of
Woodstock and 15 miles east of Killington.

The Bridgewater Antique Centre is located on the third floor in the Old
Mill Marketplace, a 150-year-old woolen mill turned antique shop. With
over 100 quality dealers in 8,000 square feet, the Centre features a large
assortment of antique furniture, glassware, and collectibles. They also
have an impressive selection of Victorian furniture, oak dressers and tables,
reconstructed pie safes, jelly and corner cupboards, dry sinks, harvest
tables, and armoires.

Shipping arrangements can be made in-house for delivery of large
furniture anywhere in the United States. United Parcel Service (UPS)
shipping is available for smaller pieces.

**Red Horse**
Route 4
802/672-3220

## 5　BURLINGTON

**Underground Antiques**
96 Church St.
802/864-5183

**Architectural Salvage Warehouse**
212 Battery St.
802/658-5011

**Bygone Books**
31 Main St.
802/862-4397

**Calliope Music**
202 Main St.
802/863-4613

**Miss Pickle's Attic**
151 Battery St.
802/865-4788

## 6　DORSET

**Marie Miller American Quilts**
Main St.
802/867-5969

**Carlson Antiques**
On the Village Green/Route 30
802/867-4510

## 7　FAIRLEE

**Vollbrecht Antiques**
Main St.
802/333-4223

**Paper Americana**
Main St.
802/333-4784

## 8　GRAFTON

### *Great Places to Stay*

### Brandywine Bed and Breakfast and Antiques
Main St.
802/843-2250
Open: 7 days a week
Directions: Located 8 miles off of Route 91 North, Exit 5. Brandywine is
25 minutes from Manchester University and 30 minutes from Mount
Salow as well as Straton Mountain; 45 minutes south of Ludlow, Vt.,
and 1 hour south of Ruthana.

*Vermont*

Located in the center of Vermont's most charming village, Brandywine wraps you in the peace of enjoying gorgeous surroundings in a country-formal atmosphere.

It's a wonderful place to relax, or if you are looking for activity, you can enjoy many sports and hobbies right in town. The surrounding area offers many miles of fabulous hiking trails, biking, tennis, and beautiful streams for fishing. Guests can take a horse-drawn carriage ride through the charming village

or enjoy a picnic lunch on one of the beautiful covered bridges located on the property. For those who enjoy golf, there are several outstanding courses in the immediate area.

Built in the 1830s, this spacious village inn is on the National Historic Register. It is beautifully furnished with period antiques, and is as comfortable as it is elegant.

For those in love with the sport of antiquing, there is a 25 by 50-foot post and beam barn filled with a fabulous array of antiques for sale. The two floors of treasures are sure to please those who enjoy finding a bargain. From primitive through refined, you will discover one of Vermont's most interesting, eclectic antique shops.

Brandywine is always delighted to have families with children and offers accommodations for your cat, dog or horse.

### 9  JAY

**The Tickle Trunk**
Jay Village
Box 132
802/988-4731
Open: Thurs.–Sun. 11–5 (7 days a week at holiday times)
Directions: One mile from Jay Peak Ski Resort. At main intersection in Jay Village on Route 242 and Crossroads. From I-19, Exit 27 to Newport. 30-minute drive to Jay via Route 105 to Route 101 to Route 242.

The Tickle Trunk, as the name implies, is noted for trunks. They also specialize in clocks, primitives, Victorian furniture, vintage clothing, costume jewelry from the '40s up, and numerous other wonderful antiques and collectibles.

### 10  LUDLOW

**Village Barn**
126 Main St.
802/228-3275

**Cool-Edge Collection**
Route 100 N.
802/228-4168

**Needham House**
Route 100 N.
802/228-2255

### 11  MANCHESTER

**Clarke Comollo Antiques**
Route 7 A
802/362-7188

### 12  MANCHESTER CENTER

**Center Hill Past & Present**
Center Hill
802/362-3211

**Cachet**
Route 11
802/362-0058

**Carriage Trade Antique Center**
Route 7A N.
802/362-1125

**Brewster Antiques**
Route 30
802/362-1579

**Maiden Lane**
Elm St.
802/362-2004

**Judy Pascal Antiques**
Elm St.
802/362-2004

**Equinox Antiques**
29 Historic Main St.
802/362-3540

### 13  ORWELL

**Brookside Farms Country Inn and Antique Shop**
Hwy. 22 A
802/948-2727

Listed on the National Register of Historic Places, this restored 1789 farmhouse and the 1843 Greek Revival mansion is located on a 300-acre estate. Both the farmhouse and the mansion are decorated in 18th- and 19th-century furnishings. An antique shop is located on the property as well.

### 14  PITTSFORD

**Tuffy Antiques**
Route 7
802/483-6610

**Rutland Antiques**
Route 7
802/483-6434

### 15  QUECHEE

**Quechee Gorge Village**
Route 4
802/295-1550

**Antiques Collaborative, Inc.**
Waterman Place/Route 4
802/296-5858

## 16 RUTLAND

### Park Antiques, Inc.
75 Woodstock Ave.
802/775-4184
Open: Daily except Mon. 10–5
Directions: Located ¼ mile east on Route 4 from Route 7

Park Antiques, Inc., is the home of an ever-changing stock of furniture (Victorian and oak), primitives, collectibles, jewelry, stoneware, paintings, china, glassware and more.

**Conway's Antiques & Decor**
90 Center St.
802/775-5153

**The Gallery of Antiques & Cllbls.**
Route 4
802/773-4940

**Trader Rick's**
407 West St.
802/775-4455

**Treasure Chest**
Route 4 E. (Shops at Mendon W.)
802/775-0310

## 17 SHELBURNE

### Vincent Fernandez Oriental Rugs and Antiques
Route 7
802/985-2275
Open: Mon.–Sat. 10–5
Directions: On Interstate 89 take Shelburne exit, travel south on Route 7, shop is six miles on the left across from the Shelburne Museum.

Rugs have been used in homes in America since the 17th century. Oriental rugs during the early periods were sometimes used on a table rather than on the floor. At Vincent Fernandez Oriental Rugs and Antiques, the offerings are spectacular. You're sure to find something to enhance any decor. This shop always carries an excellent selection of antiques.

### Shelburne Village Antiques
Route 7 — On the Green
802/985-1447
Open: Mon.–Sat. 10-5, also most Sun.
Directions: Located on Route 7, six miles from I-89 in the heart of Shelburne Village. Within walking distance of Shelburne Museum.

A unique collection of New England furniture and decorative accessories, along with a complete line of Americana, folk art and primitives invitingly beckons the traveler to stop and shop.

### Black Hawk
2131 Route 7 — On the Green
802/985-8049
Open: Mon.–Sun. 10–5
Directions: Traveling I-89, south to Shelburne Village. Black Hawk is a 5-minute walk from the Shelburne Museum.

Black Hawk, located in an historic 19th-century storefront, is known for its American antiques and accessories.

**Somewear in Time**
2131 Route 7
802/985-3816

**Burlington Center for Antiques**
1966 Shelburne Road
802/985-4911

**Champlain Valley Antique Center**
1991 Shelburne Road
802/985-8116

**It's About Time Ltd.**
3 Webster Road
802/985-5772

### *Interesting Side Trips*

### Shelburne Museum
Route 7
802/985-3346
Open: From late May to late Oct., 10–5 every day. From late Oct. to late May, 1 p.m. guided tour daily.
Directions: From I-89, take Exit 13 to Route 7 south to Shelburne.

Described as New England's Smithsonian, Shelburne Museum is located in the heart of Vermont's scenic Champlain Valley. It was founded in 1947 by Electra Havemeyer Webb, a pioneer collector of American folk art. Mrs. Webb became captivated by the sometimes unexpected beauty of utilitarian objects that exemplified "the ingenuity and craftsmanship of the preindustrial era."

The 37 exhibit buildings, situated on 45 scenic acres, house 80,000 objects of art, artifacts, and architecture spanning 3 centuries of American culture.

At first glance the museum looks like a well-preserved historic village, but look again — the Adirondack-style hunting lodge sits near a turn-of-the-century paddle-wheel steamboat, which in turn borders a collection of community buildings and historic houses that date back to the 18th and 19th century.

The contents in some of these architectural treasures document the era of the particular building, but others serve as galleries for diverse collections to be enjoyed in a friendly and informal way.

The Shelburne Museum is a lively and intriguing combination of art and history that promises visitors a veritable patchwork of America's past.

# Vermont

## 18 SOUTH BURLINGTON

**Ethan Allen Antique Shop**
32 Beacon St.
802/863-3764

**New England Import Rug Gallery**
930 Shelburne Road
802/865-0503

## 19 STOWE

### Rosebud Antiques at Houston Farm

2850 Mountain Road
802/253-2333
Open: Wed.–Sun. 9–5, closed Mon. & Tues.
Directions: Exit 10 (Stowe) off I-89. Take 100 North. At the crossroads in the village take Mountain Road (108) 2 miles. Shop is on the right.

Visiting with this shop owner by phone was quite a treat. This quaint little shop, attached to an 1850s home, is ten minutes from a ski resort. As you might surmise, they specialize in sports antiquities: skiing, fishing, snow shoes, etc. They also have a wonderful collection of children's antique sleds. Old chocolate and ice cream molds are another hard-to-find item from the past featured in this shop.

**Belle Maison**
1799 Mountain Road
802/253-8248

**Stowe Antiques Center**
51 S. Main St.
802/253-9875

### *Great Places to Stay*

### Bittersweet Inn

692 S. Main St. (Route 100)
802/253-7787

The 18th-century brick farmhouse and converted carriage house provides comfortable lodging, private baths, a friendly warm atmosphere, and courteous service by your host and hostess. Bittersweet Inn is located on the south edge of Stowe Village, just a half-mile walk from the center of town, and just minutes away from the ski lifts and cross-country touring centers. Hiking and bike trails abound.

### Brass Lantern Inn

717 Maple St.
1-800-729-2980
Web site: www.stoweinfo.com/saa/brasslantern

Warm your hearts at the Brass Lantern Inn in picturesque Stowe, Vermont. From the cozy fireplaces and soothing whirlpool tubs to the handmade quilts and spectacular mountain views, this charming restored farmhouse and carriage barn defines romance. Exquisite cuisine, glorious shopping and outdoor recreation nearby. Hearty country breakfast prepared with local Vermont products and produce. The inn is AAA Three Diamond approved.

## 20 WATERBURY

### Early Vermont Antiques

Route 100 N.
802/244-5373
Open: Daily 10–5 year-round
Directions: From I-89, take Exit 10, onto Route 100. The shop is directly across from Ben and Jerry's Ice Cream Store.

This shop is the perfect place to stop if you're hot because they are located directly across the street from Ben & Jerry's Ice Cream Store. Once you cool off with all that ice cream (it's absolutely wonderful, you know), cross the street to visit Barbara at Early Vermont. This fabulous group shop offers the finest in early American antiques. Tastefully displayed throughout the shop you will find early furnishings, glass, collectibles, and accessories often native to the Vermont area.

**Sugar Hill Antiques**
Route 100
802/244-7707

## 21 WESTON

### Weston Antiques Barn

Route 100
802/824-4097
Open: Mon.–Fri. 10–5, Sun. 11–4 during Nov.–May; Mon.–Sat. 10–5, Sun. 11–4 during June–Oct.
Directions: The Weston Antiques Barn is located on Route 100, 1 mile north of historic Weston Village.

This 25-dealer shop offers a wide array of furniture, pottery, glass, paintings, books, metals and textiles. A great source for collectors, decorators, and anyone looking for something unique to treasure.

### The Vermont County Store

Route 100
802/362-2400
Open: Mon.–Sat. 9–5, closed Sun.

Known in all 50 states through the Voice of the Mountains mail order catalog, here you will rediscover products you thought had long disappeared such as penny candy, Vermont Common Crackers, and flour-sack towels, as well as many other useful and practical items. Interspersed with the merchandise are hundreds of artifacts from the past — it's like shopping in a museum. A visit you'll remember long after you get home.

## Left Bank Antiques
Route 9 and 100
802/464-3224
Open: Thurs.–Mon. 11–5, closed Tues. and Wed.
Directions: Located at the Junction of Routes 9 and 100 (at the light).

Roseville pottery, chandeliers and lighting, early 1900s furniture, old trunks and a multitude of glassware are only a few of the examples of fine antiques you will find in this eight-dealer shop.

**Royle's Bazaar**
W. Main St.
802/464-8093

**Etcetera Shop**
Route 9 W.
802/464-5394

**Yankee Pickers**
Route 100
802/464-3884

**Pine Tree Hill Antiques**
21 Warnock Road
802/464-2922

**Sugar House Antique Center**
W. Main St.
802/464-8948

### *Great Places to Stay*

## The Inn at Quail Run
106 Smith Road
1-800-343-7227
Web site: www.sover.net/~dvalnews/quailrun.html

Off the beaten track and nestled in the woods, yet only three and a half miles from Mt. Snow, Quail Run is located on fifteen pristine wooded acres and offers a spectacular view of the Mt. Snow Valley. As a family oriented inn, children of all ages and well-behaved pets are welcome. The inn has eleven recently renovated guest rooms, all with private bath and several with gas fireplaces. There is a two-room suite as well as a four-room, four-bath cottage, complete with kitchen and living room. A full country breakfast is served each morning.

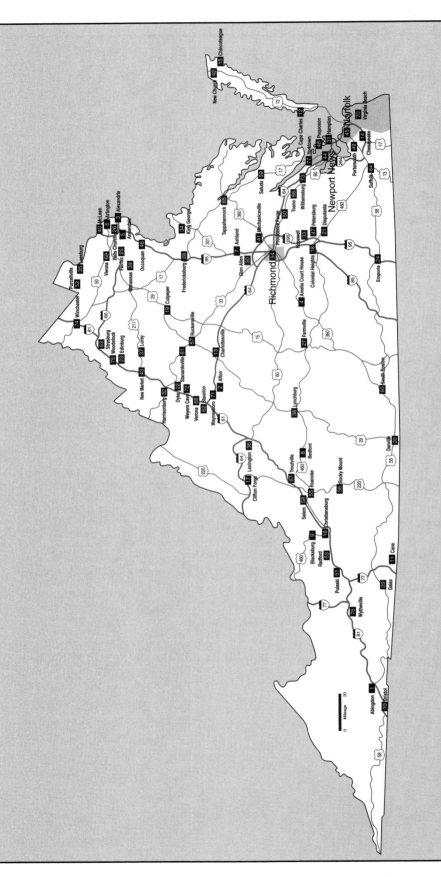

Virginia

# Virginia

## 1 ABINGDON

**Court Street Collectibles**
104 Court St. N.E.
540/628-3500

**Storyteller's Antiques**
173 E. Main St.
540/628-8669

**Highland Antique Mall**
246 W. Main St.
540/676-4438

**Garden Artifacts**
272 W. Main St.
540/628-9686

**Brandy Wine Antiques**
477 W. Main St.
540/676-3944

**J & R Furniture & Design**
108 W. Main St.
540/628-2369

**Abingdon Mercantile & Frames**
130 S. Wall St.
540/628-2788

### *Great Places to Stay*

**River Garden Bed and Breakfast**
19080 N. Fork River Road
540/676-0335 or 1-800-952-4296
Open: Daily, year-round
Rates: $60–$65
Directions: Exit 17 off I-81 in Virginia following signs to Abingdon, and the road becomes Cumings Street. Continue on Cumings Street to Valley Street (dead end), and take a left on Valley Street. At Russell Road (dead end) turn right. Go to Highway 19 North. Turn right on 19 North (Porterfield Highway). At Route 611 (North Fork River Road) turn right. River Garden is 2 ½ miles on the right.

The River Garden Bed and Breakfast, located on the bank of the Holston River, and seated at the base of Clinch Mountain, provides a beautiful, welcome sight for travelers. Each room has its own private bath. Rooms are furnished with antique and period furniture, complete with full, queen, or king beds. To make the stay feel more homey, guests are welcome to share the kitchen area, living room, den, and dining room. Enjoy the deck from each room, which overlooks the Holston River. With private entrances, guests are invited to come and go as they please. Full breakfast is served each morning by the delightful hosts, Carol and Bill Crump.

**Maplewood Farm B&B**
20004 Cleveland Road
540/628-2640

Maplewood Farm is truly a naturalist's haven. The 66-acre horse farm, originally part of a king's grant, has high wooded land with hiking trails and a lake stocked with bass and sunfish. The home, circa 1880, is a beautifully renovated farmhouse shaded by old maple trees, hence the name Maplewood Farm. Two guest rooms and a two-bedroom suite all include private baths. Full breakfasts are served in the Garden Room or on an outside deck overlooking the lake and meadow.

## 2 AFTON

**Whitehouse Antiques**
2621 Greenfield Road
540/942-1194
Open: Daily 10–5
Directions: Exit 99 from I-64 (Waynesboro/Afton exit). Exit 107 from I-64 (Crozet exit). U.S. Route 250 to State Route 6 on the east side of Afton Mountain.

With a building over 100 years old as home and Virginia's famous Blue Ridge Mountains as landscape, Whitehouse Antiques presents fine American antiques in room settings. Specializing in furniture from country to formal, many pieces are local antiques selected from area estates. Decorative and accessory "smalls," also available, provide distinctive touches to any decor.

**Antiques @ Afton**
State Route 6
540/456-6515

## 3 ALEXANDRIA

**Belgravia Fine Art**
411 Cameron St.
703/548-7702

**Reunions**
1719 Centre Plaza
703/931-8161

**Bird-in-the-Cage Antiques**
110 King St.
703/549-5114

**Antiques on King Street**
917 King St.
703/739-9750

**French Country Antiques**
1000 King St.
703/548-8563

**Iron Gate Antiques**
1007 King St.
703/549-7429

**King Street Antiques**
1015 King St.
703/549-0883

**Random Harvest**
1117 King St.
703/548-8820

**Banana Tree**
1223 King St.
703/836-4317

**Odds & Ends Antique Shop**
1325 King St.
703/836-6722

**Micheline's Antiques**
1600 King St.
703/836-1893

**Cambridge Classics**
210 N. Lee St.
703/739-2877

**Old Town Antiques**
210 N. Lee St.
703/519-0009

**Teacher's Pet Antiques**
210 N. Lee St.
703/549-9766

**Times Juggler**
210 N. Lee St.
703/836-3594

**Trojan Antiques**
210 N. Lee St.
703/549-9766

**Trojan Antiques Too**
216 N. Lee St.
703/836-5410

**Reflections Antiques**
222 N. Lee St.
703/683-6808

**Alexandria Coin Sales**
6550 Little River Turnpike
703/354-3700

**Trojan Three**
320 Prince St.
703/548-8558

**Thieves Market Antiques Center**
8101 Richmond Hwy.
703/360-4200

**Lenore & Daughters Antiques**
130 S. Royal St.
703/836-3356

**James Wilholt Antiques**
150 N. Saint Asaph St.
703/683-6595

**Old Colony Shop**
222 S. Washington St.
703/548-8008

**Donna Lee's Cllbls. & Rare Book Shop**
419 S. Washington St.
703/548-5830

**Sumpter Priddy III, Inc.**
601 S. Washington St.
703/299-0800

**Antiques of Essence**
5801 Duke St.
703/642-8831

**Alexandria's House of Antiques**
124 S. West St.
703/836-3912

**Boxwood Antiques & Fine Art**
303 Cameron St.
703/518-4444

**European Concepts**
1009 King St.
703/739-8885

**Lloyd's Row**
119 S. Henry St.
703/684-1711

### 4   AMELIA COURT HOUSE

**Amelia Antique Mall**
Church St.
804/561-2511

**Jodenes Antiques**
12710 Patrick Henry Hwy.
804/561-3333

**Jerry's Now & Then**
Court St.
804/561-5075

**Presidential Coin & Antique Co.**
6550 Little River Turnpike
703/354-5454

**Cavalier Antiques**
400 Prince St.
703/836-2539

**Jane's Antiques**
8853 Richmond Hwy.
703/360-1428

**Seaport Traders Arts & Antiques**
1201 N. Royal St.
703/684-2901

**Icon Gallery**
101 N. Union
703/739-0700

**Brocketts Row Antiques & Fine Art**
303 N. Washington St.
703/684-0464

**Studio Antiques & Fine Art**
524 N. Washington St.
703/548-5188

**Frances Simmons Antiques**
619 S. Washington St.
703/549-1291

**Alan Marschke's Gallery**
687 S. Washington St.
703/548-0909

**Antique Warehouse**
8123 Richmond Hwy.
703/360-4700

**Curzon Hill Antiques**
108 S. Columbus St.
703/684-0667

**Hulda's Antiques**
1518 Belle View Blvd.
703/765-5159

**Washington Square Antiques**
689 S. Washington St.
703/836-3214

**Cindy Garrett Antiques**
13241 Mount Olive Lane
804/561-3999

**Emerson Antique Mall & Cllbls.**
19720 Patrick Henry Hwy.
804/561-5276

### 5   ANNANDALE

**Heart's Desire**
7120 Little River Turnpike
703/916-0361

**Antique Medley**
7120 Little River Turnpike
703/354-6279

**Chris' Collectibles**
7120 Little River Turnpike
703/941-0361

**Chrystal Mint**
7120 Little River Turnpike
703/256-6688

**The Cottage**
7120 Little River Turnpike
703/256-6688

**Dlove's Antiques**
7120 Little River Turnpike
703/256-6688

**French Connection**
7120 Little River Turnpike
703/256-6688

**Guinevere's Journey**
7120 Little River Turnpike
703/941-0130

**Joan's**
7120 Little Rive Turnpike
703/256-6688

**Kabul Antiques & Jewelry**
7120 Little River Turnpike
703/642-8260

**Lady Randolph's**
7120 Little River Turnpike
703/750-1609

**Misty Memories**
7120 Little River Turnpike
703/642-1052

**Osbourne House**
7120 Little River Turnpike
703/256-6688

**Peggotly Antiques & Collectibles**
7120 Little River Turnpike
703/642-5750

**Shamma's Antiques**
7120 Little River Turnpike
703/750-6439

**Southerland**
7120 Little River Turnpike
703/256-6688

**Krueger's Antique Plus**
7129 Little River Turnpike
703/941-3644

**Bill Siaz**
7120 Little River Turnpike
703/256-6688

**Christian Deschamps**
7120 Little River Turnpike
703/256-6688

**The Clock Works**
7120 Little River Turnpike
703/256-6688

**David's Place**
7120 Little River Turnpike
703/256-6688

**Figaro Gallery**
7120 Little River Turnpike
703/354-3200

**Gene's Antiques**
7120 Little River Turnpike
703/256-6688

**Henry's Antiques**
7120 Little River Turnpike
703/256-6688

**JR's**
7120 Little River Turnpike
703/256-6688

**Kim's Country House**
7120 Little River Turnpike
703/256-6688

**Mary's Antiques**
7120 Little River Turnpike
703/256-6688

**The Old Crank**
7120 Little River Turnpike
703/256-6688

**Past Pleasure Antiques**
7120 Little River Turnpike
703/256-6688

**Rags to Riches**
7120 Little River Turnpike
703/941-0130

**Showcase Antiques**
7120 Little River Turnpike
703/941-0130

**Vintage Radio**
7120 Little Rive Turnpike
703/256-6688

# Virginia

**Virgilian Fine Arts, Antiques & Collectibles**
7120 Little River Turnpike
703/256-6688

**Grammie's Collectibles**
7129 Little River Turnpike
703/642-3999

**And Antiques**
7129 Little River Turnpike
703/941-7360

**Ken's Antiques**
7129 Little River Turnpike
703/750-5453

## 6  ARLINGTON

**Granny's Attic**
3911 Lee Hwy.
703/812-0389

**Corner Cupboard**
2649 N. Pershing Dr.
703/276-0060

**Book Ends**
2710 Washington Blvd.
703/524-4976

**Consignments Unlimited**
2645 N. Pershing Dr.
703/276-0051

**Something Unique**
933 N. Quincy St.
703/807-2432

**Home Artifacts**
2836 Wilson Blvd.
703/812-8348

## 7  ASHLAND

**Billy's Collectibles**
12083 Washington Hwy.
804-798-9414

**Brumble's Antiques**
10449 Design Road
804/752-5871

### *Great Places to Stay*

### Henry Clay Inn
114 N. Railroad Ave.
1-800-343-4565

Enjoy the small-town atmosphere of Ashland and take advantage of its central location to the historic areas of Richmond, Williamsburg, Charlottesville and Fredericksburg. This 15-room Georgian Revival inn is furnished in antique reproductions with private baths and other amenities.

## 8  BEDFORD

**Elizabeth N. Gladwell & Associates**
124 S. Bridge St.
540/586-4567

**Hamilton's**
155 W. Main St.
540/586-5592

**Stoney Creek Antiques**
Route 460 W.
540/586-0166

**Bedford Antique Mall**
109 S. Bridge St.
540/587-9322

**Bridge Street Antiques**
201 N. Bridge St.
540/586-6611

**Granny's Antiques & Etc.**
Route 460 E.
540/586-6861

**Olde Liberty Antique Mall**
802 E. Washington St.
540/586-3804

## 9  BLACKSBURG

**Other Times Ltd.**
891 Kabrich St.
540/552-1615

**Heirlooms Originals**
609 N. Main St.
540/552-9241

**Grady's Antiques**
208 N. Main St.
540/951-0623

**Whitaker's Antiques**
1102 Progress St.
540/552-1186

## 10  BRISTOL

**Antiques on Commonwealth**
57 Commonwealth Ave.
540/669-1886

**Abe's Antiques**
411 Commonwealth Ave.
540/466-6895

**Art History & Antiques**
42 Piedmont Ave.
540/669-6491

**Pete Moore Antiques**
1615 W. State St.
540/669-2333

**Bristol Antique Mall**
403 Commonwealth Ave.
540/466-4064

**Frank's Antiques**
413 Commonwealth Ave.
540/669-4138

**Heritage Antiques**
625 State St.
540/669-9774

## 11  CANA

### Thelma Lou's Antiques & Collectibles, Inc.
Route 1, Box 43-A
Hwy. 52 N.
540/755-2858
Directions: Located in Cana, Va., between Mt. Airy, N.C., Andy Griffith's hometown, and the Blue Ridge Parkway at Fancy Gap, Va., on Scenic Hwy. 52. *From I-77 South in Virginia:* Take Exit 8, turn left go ½ mile to Hwy. 52. Turn right, go approximately 7 miles. On your right next to Nance Interiors. *From I-77 North in North Carolina:* Take Exit 100 onto Route 89. Turn right. Go 7¼ miles to Hwy. 52 Bypass North. Go 6½ miles. On left next to Nance Interiors.

Thelma Lou's is a wonderful collectibles shop offering *Gone with the Wind, Wizard of Oz* and *Mayberry* collectibles, plus a large selection of Madame Alexander, Seymour Mann and other dolls. In addition to the collectibles, there are thirty quality dealers with a nice variety of furniture, glassware, cookie jars, carnival glass, bottles, old paints and more.

**Antique House**
Hwy. 52
540/755-4700

**Van Noppen T P Antiques**
Hwy. 52
540/755-4382

**Mountain Side Antiques**
Hwy. 52
540/755-3875

# *Virginia*

## 12 CAPE CHARLES

**Charmers Antique**
211 Mason Ave.
757/331-1488

### *Great Places to Stay*

**Bay Avenue's Sunset Bed & Breakfast**
108 Bay Ave.
757/331-2424
Open: All year
Rates: $75–$85
Directions: From Route 13 traffic light, go west 2 miles on Route 184 to Chesapeake Bay. Turn right, 4th house.

Unwind under the spell of a bygone era in a 1915 Victorian home nestled directly on Chesapeake Bay. This recipient of AAA's 3 diamond rating and American Bed and Breakfast Association's 3 crown "Excellent" Award offers accommodations with individual decor including the Victorian Room (period wallpaper, window seat, pedestal sink, old claw-foot tub), Sheena Room (extra-large contemporary with a touch of the rain forest), the Courtney Room (white wicker furniture, bay view), and the Abigail Room (Colonial in decor). The common area provides a view of the bay from 3 windows. Sitting back in a rocker on the west-facing front porch is a delightful way to soak in the sunset. The nearby historic district is host to several quaint antique and specialty shops.

## 13 CHARLOTTESVILLE

**Aaron's Attic**
1700 Allied St.
804/295-5760

**First Street Antiques**
107 N. 1st St.
804/295-7650

**Stedman House**
201 E. High St.
804/295-0671

**1740 House Antiques & Fine Art**
3449 Ivy Road (Route 250 W.)
804/977-1740

**Consignment House Unlimited**
121 W. Main St.
804/977-5527

**Oyster House Antiques**
219 E. Main St.
804/295-4757

**Deloach Antiques**
1211 W. Main St.
804/979-7209

**Heartwood Books**
59 Elliewood Ave.
804/295-7083

**Court Square Antiques**
216 4th St.
804/295-6244

**Eternal Attic**
2125 Ivy Road
804/977-2667

**Ming-Quing Antiques**
111 Main St.
804/979-8426

**20th Century Art & Antiques**
201 E. Main St.
804/296-6818

**Daniel Chenn Gallery**
619 W. Main St.
804/977-8890

**1817 Antique Inn**
1211 W. Main St.
804/979-7353

**Jefferson Coin Shop**
301 E. Market St.
804/295-1765

**The Antiquers Mall**
Route 29 N.
804/973-3478

**Kenny Ball Antiques**
Ivy Commons
804/293-1361

### *Great Places to Stay*

**The Inn at Monticello**
Hwy. 20 S.
1188 Scottsville Road
804/979-3593

The Inn at Monticello is a charming country manor house built circa 1850. The property has the quiet atmosphere of a lovely, classic getaway spot, enhanced by a bubbling brook, flowers and trees, with lovely mountain views. Guest rooms, each with private bath, are uniquely decorated in period antiques and fine reproductions, all coordinated with the elegance and comforts befitting a romantic country inn. Gourmet breakfasts are outstanding.

**The Inn at the Crossroads**
P.O. Box 6519
804/979-6452
Web site: www.crossroadsinn.com

Registered as a Virginia Historic Landmark, the inn has been welcoming travelers since 1820. Located on four acres in the foothills of the Blue Ridge Mountains, it is a charming four-story brick building with timber framing and an English kitchen on the lower level. Its simple Federal style is characteristic of the public houses of that period. Separate from the main building, a two-room cottage offers guests that honeymoonlike escape.

## 14 CHESAPEAKE

**American Antiques at Blue Ridge**
1505 Blue Ridge Road
757/482-7330

**Cal's Antiques**
928 Canal Dr.
757/485-1895

**Maria's Antiques & Collectibles**
3021 S. Military Hwy.
757/485-1799

**Second Wind**
1117 E. Market St.
804/296-1413

**Renaissance Gallery**
By appointment only
804/296-9208

**Way Back Yonder Antiques**
916 Canal Dr.
757/487-8459

**Fran's Antiques**
3017 S. Military Hwy.
757/485-1656

**Chesapeake House Antiques**
3040 S. Military Hwy.
757/487-2219

**T-N-T Treasures**
3044 S. Military Hwy.
757/485-3927

**Now & Then Shop**
3112 S. Military Hwy.
757/485-1383

**Quiet Shoppe Saddlery**
3935 Poplar Hill Road
757/483-9358

## 15  CHINCOTEAGUE

### Great Places to Stay

### Island Manor House
4160 Main St.
757/336-5436

The Island Manor House, built in 1848, was the grand home of Nathaniel Smith, the island's first doctor, who tended troops during the Civil War. Beautifully restored in Federal style, the inn offers eight lovely guest rooms, six with private baths, furnished with antiques to provide a warm and comfortable ambiance. Noteworthy is the Garden Room, where guests relax by the fireplace amid collections of antiques, fine art, and rare books.

### The Watson House
4240 Main St.
1-800-336-6787

Featured on The Learning Channel's *Romantic Escapes*, the Watson House is a recently restored Victorian country home built in the late 1800s by David Robert Watson. Nestled in the heart of Chincoteague, it is within walking distance of favorite shops and restaurants. Guest rooms are tastefully and individually decorated with charming Victorian and country antiques, nostalgic pieces, wicker and many other special touches.

## 16  CHRISTIANSBURG

**Cambria Emporium**
596 Depot St. N.E.
540/381-0949

### Great Places to Stay

### The Oaks Victorian Inn
311 E. Main St.
540/381-1500
Open: Year-round
Directions: *From I-81:* Take Exit 114. At the bottom of the ramp, turn left if approaching from the south, and right if approaching from the north. You are on Main Street, and so is the Oaks. Continue for approximately 2 miles to fork at Park and Main Streets, bear right on Park, then left into the Oaks' driveway. *From the Blue Ridge*

*Parkway:* Take Route 8 (MP 165) through Floyd to Christiansburg. Route 8 becomes Main Street. Follow earlier directions.

Situated atop the highest hill in town, the Oaks is the focal point of the East Main Street Historic District in Christiansburg, Va. The home was designed by a New York architect. Construction began in 1889 and was completed in 1893 for Major W. L. Pierce, who built the magnificent Queen Anne Victorian for his wife and seven children. It remained in the Pierce family for 90 years, then was purchased by the Hardies in 1982. Preserving the original floor plan and elegant interior, the home was extensively restored and renovated, including the addition of  modern bathrooms and other amenities. Tom and Margaret Ray bought the home on September 21, 1989, and converted it to one of the premier bed and breakfast facilities in the nation.

The Oaks is a relaxing place — in perfect harmony with an elegant, gracious atmosphere. Guests awake to the aroma of freshly ground, perked coffee and a newspaper. All rooms have a queen- or king-size bed, and private bathrooms — modern and stocked with plush towels, fluffy terry robes and toiletries.

The garden gazebo houses a new hydro-jet hot tub. Breakfast is always generous. Each day the menu varies with delightful specialties such as curried eggs served in white wine sauce with shitake mushrooms, raisin/ Granny Smith apple or broccoli/lemon quiche, shirred eggs in spinach nests, rum raisin French toast or whole wheat buttermilk pancakes in praline syrup with toasted pecans and maple cream, and fluffy omelets with surprise fillings and sauces. Oven-fresh breads accompany the entree — spicy pear, French apple and banana muffins, cranberry and pumpkin tea breads and Southern buttermilk biscuits. Sausage, bacon and ginger-braised chicken breast are favorites.

### Evergreen The Bell-Capozzi House
201 E. Main St.
540/382-7372 or 1-800-905-7372
Email: evegrninn@aol
Web site: www.bnt.com/evergreen
Directions: For specific directions from your location, please call the innkeepers.

Fully called Evergreen The Bell-Capozzi House, this Southwestern Virginia bed and breakfast graces the hills of Christiansburg. Guests will be surprised that the house's lavish facade hides an in-ground heated pool in the backyard, replete with lounge chairs, gazebo, rose garden, and fish pond.

After a good workout in the pool, you can settle into comfort in a poster bed in one of the large bedrooms, each individually decorated with captivating works of talented local artists.

Yes, there is a *Gone with the Wind* bedroom in this Victorian mansion. It features a king-size, four-poster bed along with a desk and comfortable chairs. Scarlett O'Beara and Rhett Bearler complete the theme. Among the home's 17 rooms are five guest quarters, all with heart pine floors, original light fixtures, and private baths.

Fireplaces warm the two parlors. The formal library converts easily into a conference room that can accommodate 12 people. Innkeepers, Rocco, transplanted from Corning, N.Y., and Barbara, a native of Virginia, whose great-grandfathers fought in the Civil War, restored and decorated the house "for comfort" without altering it. Guests call it a "relaxed elegance."

Your hosts cook up a traditional Southern breakfast with homemade biscuits, country ham, cheese grits, silver dollar pancakes, fresh fruit, locally made jams and jellies, and apple butter, and growing in fame, Mill Mountain coffee and tea.

Tea time arrives in style at 5 p.m. in the library during winter months with scones, cookies, cake, and small sandwiches. Summer guests are served on the porches, humming with rockers and swings.

Two blocks away are the Montgomery Museum and Lewis Miller Regional Art Center. The 204-year-old city of Christiansburg is the county seat for Montgomery County. Nearby Virginia Tech is a premier depository of American Civil War history and home base for noted Civil War historian James I. Robertson, Jr.

When you're finished scouting out the Civil War archives, you can canoe or raft the Little and New Rivers, play bocce ball on Evergreen's lawn, fish Claytor Lake and the rivers, golf at Round Meadow or Virginia Tech, hike the Appalachian Trail and George Washington–Jefferson National Forest, horseback ride at Mountain Lake, or play tennis at several convenient sites. At Evergreen, when you aren't swimming, you can try your hand at puzzles, bridge, or the 1887 Bechstein concert grand piano.

## 17 CLIFTON FORGE

**Mary's Antiques & Collectibles**
608 Main St.
540/863-8577

**Dews Etc.**
420 E. Ridgeway
No phone

**Always Roxie's**
622 Main St.
540/862-2999

## 18 COLONIAL HEIGHTS

**Blue and Gray Relic Shop**
2012 Boulevard
804/526-6863

**Friendly Hearth Antiques**
17002 Jefferson Davis Hwy.
804/526-1900

**T J's Corner**
17100 Jefferson Davis Hwy.
804/526-3074

## 19 CULPEPER

### Country Shoppes Of Culpeper
10046 James Monroe Hwy. (U.S. 29 N.)
540/547-4000
Open: Mon.–Sat. 9–6, Sun. 12–5
Directions: Located on U.S. Hwy. 29 (James Monroe Hwy.) 2 mi. south of Culpeper, Va., and 35 mi. west of I-95/Route 3 Fredericksburg exit.

One hundred dealers have stuffed this 15,000-square-foot mall full of antique furniture, accessories, collectibles, glassware, jewelry, and so much more. Unique gifts and gourmet foods enhance the selection. Daily additions to vendor's wares increase possibilities and variety.

**Ace Books & Antiques**
120 W. Culpeper St.
540/825-8973

**Minute Man Mini-Mall**
746 Germanna Hwy.
540/825-3133

**Barter Post at Davis Street**
179 E. Davis St.
540/829-6814

**Leonard's Antiques & Collectibles**
10042 James Monroe Hwy.
540/547-4104

## 20 DANVILLE

**Pike's End Antiques**
103 Franklin Turnpike
804/836-2449

**John's Antiques**
2011 N. Main St.
804/793-7961

**Majestic Interiors**
127 Tunstall Road
804/792-2521

**Westover Antiques**
2720 Westover Dr.
804/822-0443

**Judy Adkins Antiques**
230 Lamberth Dr.
804/822-2257

**Finders Antique House**
1169 Piney Forest Road
804/836-6782

**Antiques Cellar English Imports**
643 Tunstall Road
804/792-1966

## 21 DISPUTANTA

**Antiques Junction**
10020 County Dr.
804/991-2463

**Kathy's Hideway Antiques**
10032 County Dr.
804/991-2061

**Mule Shed**
10026 County Dr.
804/991-2115

**Yesterday's Treasure**
9909 County Dr.
804/991-3013

# Virginia

## 22 DYKE

### Great Places to Stay

**Cottages at Chesley Creek Farm**
P.O. Box 52
804/985-7129

Chesley Creek Farm is situated on 200 acres in the Blue Ridge Mountains, 28 miles northwest of Charlottesville. There are two cottages on the property, Creek House and Laurel Wood. All dishes and utensils necessary for preparing meals are provided with gas BBQ grills on the deck. All towels and linens are furnished.

## 23 EDINBURG

**Richard's Antiques**
14211 Old Valley Pike
540/984-4502

## 24 EMPORIA

**Dutchman's Treasures**
135 E. Atlantic St.
804/634-2267

**Reid's of Emporia**
408 S. Main St.
804/634-6536

## 25 FAIRFAX

**Culpeper Shoppe**
11821 Lee Hwy.
703/631-0405

**My Home Shop**
12501 Lee Hwy.
703/631-0554

**Fairfax Antique Mall**
10334 Main St.
703/591-8883

## 26 FALLS CHURCH

**Falls Church Antique Co. Ltd.**
260 W. Broad St.
703/241-7074

**Old Market Antiques**
442 S. Washington St.
703/241-1722

**Place Where Louie Dwells**
431 N. Maple Ave.
703/237-5312

## 27 FARMVILLE

**Granny's Attic**
Hwy. 15 N.
804/392-8699

**Suzi's Antiques**
235 N. Main St.
804/392-4655

**Poplar Hall Antiques**
308 N. Main St.
804/392-1658

**Mottley Emporium**
518 N. Main St.
804/392-4698

## 28 FREDERICKSBURG

Long before Union and Confederate cannons fired across the rolling hills, Fredericksburg was already rich in Colonial and Revolutionary history. George Washington grew up at Ferry Farm, where legend has it that he swung an axe against a cherry tree. Patriots like Thomas Jefferson and James Monroe knew Fredericksburg well. In four of the Civil War's bloodiest battles, armies under Lee and Grant fought to decide the course of our nation.

History is still alive today in more than 350 original 18th- and 19th-century buildings all contained within a 40-block national historic district. The buildings house antique and gift shops as well as many fine restaurants.

### Caroline Square
910-916 Caroline St.
540/371-4454
Open: Mon.–Sat. 10–5, Sun. 12–5
Directions: From I-95, take the Fredericksburg-Culpeper exit to Route 3 which becomes William Street in Fredericksburg. Turn right at Caroline Street. Or from I-95, take the Massaponax-Fredericksburg exit onto Route 1 which jogs to the left to become Jefferson Davis Hwy., then left onto Caroline Street.

A rich collection of the past awaits you in this court of shops featuring fifty dealers. Choose from antique furniture and collectibles, quilts, dolls, as well as Shaker furniture. Most shops welcome special orders.

**Neat Stuff**
109 Amelia St.
540/373-7115

**Picket Post**
602 Caroline St.
540/371-7703

**Bonannos Antiques, Inc.**
619 Caroline St.
540/373-3331

**Beck's Antiques & Books**
708 Caroline St.
540/371-1766

**Morland House Antiques**
714 Caroline St.
540/373-6144

**Blockade Runner**
719 Caroline St.
540/374-9346

**Pavilion, Inc.**
723 Caroline St.
540/371-0850

**Future Antiques**
820 Caroline St.
540/899-6229

**Busy B's Treasures**
822 Caroline St .
540/899-9185

**Antique Corner Fredericksburg**
900 Caroline St.
540373-0826

**Upstairs Downstairs Antiques**
922 Caroline St.
540/373-0370

**Antique Court of Shoppes**
1001 Caroline St.
540/371-0685

**Willow Hill Antiques**
1001 Caroline St.
540/371-0685

**Fredericksburg Antique Gallery**
1023 Caroline St.
540/373-2961

*Virginia*

**Past And Present**
5099 Jefferson Davis Hwy.
540/891-8977

**Gold Rooster Consignment**
4010 Lafayette Blvd.
540/898-4349

**Amore Antiques, Collectibles & Gifts**
1011 Princess Anne St.
540/372-3740

**Sophia Street Antiques**
915 Sophia St.
540/899-3881

**Gary L. Johnson Antiques**
1005 Sophia St.
540/371-7141

**Liberty Park Antiques**
208 William St.
540/371-5309

**Century Shop**
202 Wolfe St.
540/371-7734

**Consignment Junction Ltd.**
2012 Lafayette Blvd.
540/898-2344

**Antique Village**
4800 Plank Road
540/786-9648

**Virginians Antiques, Inc.**
2217 Princess Anne St.
540/371-2288

**She-Kees Antique Gallery**
919 Sophia St.
540/899-3808

**Country Crossing**
106 William St.
540/371-4588

**Fredericksburg Antique Mall**
211 William St.
540/372-6894

**Southern Heritage Antiques**
107 William St.
540/371-0200

### *Great Places to Stay*

## Richard Johnston Inn
711 Caroline St.
504/899-7606

This elegant bed and breakfast was constructed in the mid- to late 1700s and served as the home of Richard Johnston, mayor of Fredericksburg from 1809 to 1810. The inn still reflects all the grace and charm of a past era, while providing all the amenities necessary for the traveler of today. The seven bedrooms and two suites have been decorated with antiques and reproductions and all have private baths.

### 29  GALAX

**Vernon's Antiques**
Hwy. 58
540/236-6390

**L & H Antiques**
Main St.
No phone listed

**Antique Apple**
118 S. Main St.
540/236-0881

**Robert's Gift Gallery**
203 S. Main St.
540/238-8877

### 30  GLEN ALLEN

**Dixie Trading Co.**
9911 Brook Road
804/266-6733

**Dick & Jeanette's Antiques**
10770 Staples Mill Road
804/672-6138

**Treasures, Inc.**
9915 Greenwood Road
804/264-8478

**Wigwam Reservation Shops**
10412 Washington Hwy.—Route 1
804/550-9698

**Singletree Antiques**
10717 Staples Mill Road
804/672-3795

### 31  HAMPTON

**Odessey Village & Old Village Books**
26 S. King St.
757/727-0028

**Victorian Station**
36 N. Mallory St.
757/723-5663

**Free City Traders**
22 Mellen St.
757/722-3899

**CC & Co.**
1729 W. Pembroke Ave.
757/727-0766

**Poquoson Antique Shop**
969 N. King St.
757/723-0501

**Return Engagements**
18 E. Mellen St.
757/722-0617

**The Way We Were Antiques**
33 E. Mellen St.
757/726-2300

**Chuck's Anything Shop**
3927 Kecoughtan Road
757/727-0740

### 32  HARRISONBURG

**Bea's Bears & Variety Shop**
Hwy. 724
540/434-3337

**Villager Antiques**
673 N. Main St.
540/433-7226

**Rolling Hills Antique Mall**
779 E. Market St.
540/433-8988

For a great place to stay while visiting in the Harrisonburg area, see New Market, #43.

### 33  HOPEWELL

**Bargain Bazaar**
201 E. Broadway Ave.
804/458-1122

**Curio Shop**
501 N. 7th Ave.
804/458-7990

**Junk Shop**
3305 Oaklawn Blvd.
804/458-3473

**Hamilton's Civil War Relic**
257 E. Broadway Ave.
804/458-6504

**AAA Antiques**
2602 Oaklawn Blvd.
804/452-0967

### 34  KING GEORGE

**End-of-Lane Antiques**
9553 James Madison Pkwy.
540/755-9838

**Swamp Fox Antiques**
9553 James Madison Pkwy.
540/775-5534

**Shadyview Antiques**
9294 Lambs Creek Church
540/775-0506

## 35 LEESBURG

Travel south on U.S. 15 to Leesburg, described by the National Register as "one of the best preserved, most picturesque communities in Virginia."

The Loudoun Museum in downtown Leesburg displays artifacts chronicling the area's colorful history from the Colonial era to the 20th century. Take a walking tour past more than fifty historic structures, and enjoy summer Sunday evenings with the music from the Bluemont Concert Series on the courthouse lawn.

**Loudoun Antiques Marketplace**
850 Davis St. S.E. (Route 15 S.)
703/777-5358

**Leesburg Downtown Antique Center**
27 S. King St.
703/779-8130

**Leesburg Antique Emporium**
32 S. King St.
703/777-3553

**Loudoun Street Antiques**
3 Loudoun St. S.W.
703/779-4009

**K & L Market St. Antiques**
5 E. Market St.
703/443-1827

**Catheran C. Johnston Antiques**
101 S. King St.
703/777-3337

**Uncle Sam's Attic Antiques**
2 Loudoun St. S.W., #B
703/777-5588

**Leesburg Antq. "Court of Shoppes"**
Route 15, 2.5 Miles
703/777-7799

**Leesburg Antique Gallery**
7 Wirt St. S.W.
703/777-2366

**Spurgeon-Lewis Antiques**
219 W. Market St.
703/777-6606

**Crafters Gallery**
9 W. Market St.
703/771-9017

**Preston's Antiques**
1 Loudoun St. S.W.
703/777-6055

**My Wit's End**
12810 James Monroe Hwy.
703/777-1561

## 36 LEXINGTON

**Lexington Antique & Craft Mall**
Hwy. 11
540/463-9511

**Lexington Antiques**
25 W. Washington St.
540/463-9519

**A. Fairfax Antiques**
13 W. Nelson
540/463-9885

### *Great Places to Stay*

### Inn at Union Run

325 Union Run Road
1-800-528-6466
Web site: www.virtualcities.com/ons/va/r/var1602.htm

This 1883 manor house is located on a creekfront mountainside three miles from historic Lexington and is situated on ten picturesque acres with views of the Allegheny and Blue Ridge mountain ranges. Located along the Union Run Creek, where the Union Army camped during and after the Battle of Lexington, the inn's name is derived from the Civil War event. The inn offers eight spacious guest rooms, all with private baths, and six with Jacuzzis. The common area and the guest rooms are filled with authentic period antiques, including Meissen porcelain, Venetian glass and furniture collections. Many of these antiques are from the estate of S. S. Kresege, Helena Reubenstein, Henry Wadsworth Longfellow and Winston Churchill.

## 37 LURAY

**Woods Antiques**
Hwy. 211 E.
540/743-4406

**Mama's Treasures**
22 E. Main St.
540/743-1352

**Zib's Country Connection**
24 E. Main St.
540/743-7394

**P. Buckley Moss Gallery**
Mimslyn Inn-Main St.
540/743-5105

**Wanda's Wonders**
Hwy. 340 S.
540/743-4197

**James McHone Antiques**
24 E. Main St.
540/743-9001

**Luray Antique Depot**
49 E. Main St.
540/743-1298

## 38 LYNCHBURG

**James River Antiques Lynchburg**
503 Clay St.
804/528-1960

**Scarlett's Treasures Antique Mall**
1026 Main St.
804/528-0488

**Langhorne-Stokes Antiques**
1421 Main St.
804/846-7452

**Saks Ally**
172 Norfolk Ave.
804/846-4712

**Time & Again Antiques**
2909 Old Forest Road
804/384-4807

**Wildwood Antique Market**
195 Old Timberlake Road
804/525-0207

**Dee's Antiques**
1724 Lakeside Dr.
804/385-4008

**Sweeney's Curious Goods**
1220 Main St.
804/846-7839

**Redcoat Gallery & Antiques**
1421 Main St.
804/528-3182

**Jackson's Antiques**
2627 Old Forest Road
804/384-6411

**Lynchburg Florist & Antiques**
3224 Old Forest Road
804/385-6566

# Virginia

*Great Places to Stay*

## 1880s Madison House Bed and Breakfast

413 Madison St.
1-800-828-6422
Web site: www.bbhost.com/1880s-madison

The 1880s Madison House is an elegantly restored Victorian bed and breakfast whose nine-color painted exterior testifies to something wonderful within. The bed and breakfast opened in Lynchburg in 1990 and is located in the Garland Hill Historic District, one of five historic districts in the city. The home retains its authentic Victorian appeal throughout the house, and offers many amenities including warm, soft robes.

## 39  MANASSAS

Travel east on U.S. 50, west on U.S. 15 and east on I-66 to Manassas, an important Civil War site.

Step back in time at Rohr's, an old-time variety store and museum with tin ceilings, penny candy and displays of antique toys, household and business items.

Take the walking trail at Manassas National Battlefield Park — scene of two Civil War battles known in the South as First and Second Manassas — that leads to Henry Hill with a panoramic view of the battlefield where Confederate Gen. Thomas "Stonewall" Jackson earned his nickname. The driving tour will take you to key points of interest in the fields. The visitor center of the 5,000-acre battlefield park features exhibits, a slide presentation and a map program explaining movements of the opposing armies on an intricate scale model of the battlefield.

**Delisle Antiques**
9115 Center St.
703/330-1160

**Roger's Antiques**
7217 Centreville Road
703/368-3366

**Wicker Place Antiques**
7305 Centreville Road
703/361-8622

**Don Mattingly Antiques**
7217 Centreville Road
703/368-2252

**Law's Antique Center**
7208 Centreville Road
703/330-9282

**Manassas Treasures**
9023 Centreville Road
703/368-8222

**Law's Antique Complex**
7209 Centreville Road
703/631-0590

**Silk Purse**
7217 Centreville Road
703/369-7817

**Cunningham Antiques**
7217 Centreville Road
703/335-6534

**First Impressions**
8388 Centreville Road
703/369-5696

**Lilian's Antiques**
7217 Centreville Road
703/361-7712

**Sam's Coins & Decoys**
7208 Centreville Road
703/361-3199

**Traditions**
7618 Centreville Road
703/361-4303

## 40  MCLEAN

**Lilly Parker Antiques, Inc.**
1317 A Chain Bridge Road
703/893-5298

**East and Beyond Ltd.**
6727 Curran St.
703/448-8200

**Abbott Gallery & Framing**
6673 Old Dominion Drive
703/893-2010

**Yorkshire Furniture Co.**
7312 Centreville Road
703/361-4697

**Solovey Jewelers, Inc.**
1475 Chain Bridge Road
703/356-0138

**Folk Art Gallery**
6216 Old Dominion
703/532-6923

**Lights Fantastic**
6825 Tennyson
703/356-2285

## 41  MECHANICSVILLE

## Mechanicsville Antique Mall

7508 Mechanicsville Turnpike
804/730-5091
Open: Daily 10–5
Directions: Once on I-295 take Exit 37B; from the Main 360 take first right (Business 360)

In August 1997, Mechanicsville Antique Mall was voted the 2nd Best Antique Mall in Richmond by *Richmond Magazine*. This comes as no surprise since this 30,000-square-foot mall is jam packed with over 100 booths and 25 showcase galleries featuring the best in early American, Victorian, golden oak, art pottery, art glass, toys and clocks. The mall even offers clock repair. Be sure to check out Hanover Auction House, adjacent to the antique mall. For information on fine quality estate auctions, call 1-800-694-0759.

**Antique Village**
10203 Chamberlayne Road
804/746-8914

**Maplewood Farm Antiques**
10203 Chamberlayne Road
804/730-0698

**Governor's Antiques Ltd.**
Polegrain Road
804/746-1030

**Whitings Old Paper at Village**
6700 Chamberlayne Road
804/746-4710

## 42  NEW CHURCH

**Bluewater Trading Co.**
6180 Lankford Hwy.
757/824-3124

**Worchester House**
Lankford Hwy.
757/824-3847

## 43  NEW MARKET

**New Market Battlefield Civil War Museum**
9500 Collins Dr.
540/740-8065

**B & B Valley Antiques**
9294 N. Congress St.
540/740-8700

**Elliot's Shenandoah Antiques**
9298 N. Congress St.
540/740-3827

**Paper Treasures**
9595 S. Congress St.
540/740-3135

**Benny Long's Antiques**
9386 N. Congress St.
540/740-3512

**Antiques by Burt Long**
345 Old Valley Pike
540/740-3777

## Great Places to Stay

### Cross Roads Inn Bed and Breakfast

9222 John Sevier Road
540/740-4157
Open: Year-round
Rates: $55–$100
Directions: Take Exit 264 (New Market) off I-81. Go east on Route 211 through town ¾ mile.

Cross Roads Inn features bedrooms with English floral wallpapers and tasteful antiques, including four-poster and canopy beds with cozy down comforters. Each bedroom has a private bath.

Gourmet breakfast, included with your room, is served in the sunny breakfast room, or on the terrace. Served with your breakfast are home-baked European breads and muffins as well as gourmet Austrian coffee.

Their Austrian tradition of hospitality includes your first cup of coffee in your room if you desire, and afternoon coffee/tea with Mary-Lloyd's famous strudel.

## 44 NEWPORT NEWS

**Lorraine's**
758 J Clyde Morris Blvd.
757/596-1886

**Fine Arts Shop**
10178 Warwick Blvd.
757/595-7754

**Chameleon**
10363 Warwick Blvd.
757/596-9324

**Denbigh Antique & Collectible Mall**
13811 Warwick Blvd.
757/875-5221

**Brill's Antiques**
10527 Jefferson Ave.
757/596-5333

**Another Man's Treasure**
10239 Warwick Blvd.
757/596-3739

**Plantiques Hilton Village**
10377 Warwick Blvd.
757/595-1545

**Deb's Antiques & Collectibles**
13595 Warwick Blvd.
757/886-0883

## 45 NORFOLK

**Anne Spencer Antiques**
505 Botetourt St.
757/624-9156

**Nero's Antiques & Appraisals**
1101 Colonial Ave.
757/627-1111

**Gale Goss Country French Antiques**
1607 Colley Ave.
757/625-1211

**Nick Nack's Collectibles & Antiques**
1905 Colonial Ave.
757/533-9545

**Hollingsworth Antiques**
819 Granby St.
757/625-6525

**Nineteenth-Century Antiques**
1804 Granby St.
757/622-0905

**Country Boy's Antiques**
1912 Granby St.
757/627-3630

**A Touch of Mystery**
2412 Granby St.
757/622-7907

**A Niche in Tyme**
9631 Granby St.
757/588-1684

**Merlo's**
131 W. Olney Road
757/622-2699

**Carriage House Antiques**
110 W. 21st St.
757/625-4504

**Grapevine of Ghent**
122 W. 21st St.
757/627-0519

**International Antiques Importers Co.**
240 W. 21st St.
757/624-9658

**Palace Antiques Gallery**
300 W. 21st St.
757/622-2733

**Ghent Antique & Consignment Emporium**
517 W. 21st St.
757/627-1900

**Scott & Company**
537 W. 21st St.
757/640-1319

**Di-Antiques**
5901 E. Virginia Beach Blvd.
757/466-1717

**A Touch of Mystery**
333 Waterside Drive
757/627-9684

**Fran's Fantasies Granby St. Antique**
1022 Granby St.
757/622-6996

**Grey Horse Antiques**
1904 Granby St.
757/626-3152

**David's Antiques**
2410 Granby St.
757/627-6376

**Decades Art & Antiques**
2608 Granby St.
757/627-0785

**Wooden Things II**
2715 Monticello Ave.
757/624-1273

**G. Carr Ltd. Art & Antiques**
522 W. 20th St.
757/624-1289

**Fairfax Shop**
120 W. 21st St.
757/625-5539

**Richard Levins Garfields**
122 W. 21st St.
757/622-0414

**Morgan House Antiques Gallery**
242 W. 21st St.
757/627-2486

**Primrose**
400 W. 21st St.
757/624-8473

**Norfolk Antique Co.**
537 W. 21st St.
757/627-6199

**Monticello Antique Shop**
227 W. York St.
757/622-4124

**Nautical Antiques & Furniture**
6150 E. Virginia Beach Blvd.
757/461-2465

## 46 OCCOQUAN

**Country Hollow**
210 A Commerce St.
703/490-1877

**Commerce Street Gallery**
204 Commerce St.
703/491-9020

## Virginia

**Heart of Occoquan**
305 Mill St.
703/492-9158

**Future Antiques**
407 Mill St.
703/491-5192

**Victoria's Past Tyme**
308 A Poplar Alley
703/494-6134

### 47  PETERSBURG

**Hall's Antiques**
12 W. Bank St.
804/861-6060

**White Oak Antique & Gift Shop**
24118 Cox Road
804/861-9127

**Woody's Antiques**
3 W. Old St.
804/861-9642

**John Reads Row**
102 W. Old St.
804/732-5690

**Cockade Antiques**
1 W. Old St.
804/861-2417

### 48  POQUOSON

**Joanne's This That & the Other**
798 Poquoson Ave.
757/868-4770

**Antiques East**
476 Wythe Creek Road
757/868-9976

**Shoppe on Wythe Creek**
501 Wythe Creek Road
757/868-9751

### 49  PORTSMOUTH

**Prison Square Antiques**
440 High St.
757/399-4174

**Mount Vernon Antique Shop**
258 Mount Vernon Ave.
757/399-6550

**Old Schoolhouse Antiques**
4903 Portsmouth Blvd.
757/465-3145

**Sisters**
308 Mill St.
703/497-3131

**Sloan's Antique Gallery**
407 Mill St.
703/494-5231

**Village Jaile Shoppe**
20829 Chesterfield Ave.
804/526-7073

**America Hurrah Antiques**
406 N. Market St.
804/861-9659

**Estate Treasures & Antiques**
9 W. Old St.
804/732-3032

**Coin Exchange**
104 W. Old St.
804/861-6449

**Martin-Wilson House**
326 Wythe Creek Road
757/868-7070

**Candlelight Antiques & Designs**
499 Wythe Creek Road
757/868-8898

**Olde Towne Sales**
719 High St.
757/399-4009

**Jems from Jennie**
Poplar Hill Shopping Center
757/484-9581

**Prison Square Antiques**
327 High St.
757/399-4174

### 50  PROVIDENCE FORGE

*Great Places to Stay*

**Jasmine Plantation Bed and Breakfast Inn**
4500 North Courthouse Road
804/966-9836 or 1-800-NEW-KENT
Open: Year-round
Directions: Halfway between Williamsburg and Richmond, the inn is located 2.4 miles south of I-64 at Exit 214. Or from Route 60, go north on State Route 155 for 1 $^4/_{10}$ miles.

A great place to relax between antiquing days is this 1750s farmhouse offering 6 rooms with antique decor. Enjoy the afternoon sitting on the front porch or experiencing nature along the 47 acres of walking trails. Don't pass up the complimentary full "skip lunch" country breakfast.

### 51  PULASKI

**Upstairs Downstairs**
27 Main St. W.
540/980-4809

**Around the World Antiques**
86 W. Main St.
540/980-8389

**Colony of Virginia Ltd.**
61 W. Main St.
540/980-8932

### 52  PURCELLVILLE

**Noni's Attic**
148 N. 21st St.
540/338-3489

**Swanson & Ball Antiques & Collectibles**
142 N. 21st St.
540/338-7077

**Mary Ellen Stover**
120 N. 21st St.
540/338-3823

**Where the Attic Bird Sings**
21st & Main St.
540/338-5474

**The Petite Emporium**
105 E. Main St.
540/338-2298

**Ray E. Fields III**
120 Main St.
540/338-3829

**Iron Gate Antiques**
151 W. Main St.
540/338-6636

**Carousel/Finders Keepers**
144 N. 21st St.
540/338-9075

**Nick Greer Antique Restoration**
Route 711
540/338-6607

**Clark & Palmer**
108 N. 21st St.
540/338-7229

**Irene Mary Antiques & Collectibles**
Corner 21st & Main St.
540/338-1999

**End of the Rainbow**
121 E. Main St.
540/338-5913

**Preservation Hall**
111 N. 21st St.
540/338-4233

**Samuel S. Case Antiques**
120 W. Main St.
540/338-2725

## 53 RADFORD

**Once upon a Time**
221 1st St.
540/633-3987

**Uncle Bill's Treasures**
1103 Norwood St.
540/633-0589

**Grandma's Memories Antqs. Shop**
237 1st St.
540/639-0054

## 54 RICHMOND

### Midlothian Antiques Center
Coolfield Road
804/897-4913
*and*
### West End Antiques Mall
6504 Horsepen Road
804/285-1916
Open: Mon.–Sat. 10–6, Sun. 12–6 for both locations

Antiques Centers, Inc., with its two locations, makes finding your treasure even easier. These centers have a combined 160 dealers and 36,000 square feet of merchandise. Choose from a huge selection of country, formal, or vintage wicker furniture, quilts, linens, glassware and books. You may also want to check their framed collectibles, woodblock prints and pewter.

**Berry's Antiques**
318 W. Broad St.
804/643-1044

**Antique Boutique & Delectable Collectibles**
1310 E. Cary St.
804/775-2525

**World of Mirth**
2925 W. Cary St.
804/353-8991

**Johnson's Antiques**
5033 Forest Hill Ave.
804/231-9727

**Antique Exchange**
6800 Forest Hill Ave.
804/272-2990

**Kim Faison Antiques**
5608 Grove Ave.
804/282-3736

**Hampton House**
5720 Grove Ave.
804/285-3479

**Glass Lady**
7501 Iron Bridge Road
804/743-9811

**Shamburger's Antiques**
5208 Brook Road
804/266-8457

**Bygones Vintage Clothing**
2916 W. Cary St.
804/353-1919

**Distinctive Consignments Ltd.**
3422 W. Cary St.
804/359-3778

**Vintage Antique & Art Co.**
5047 Forest Hill Ave.
804/233-1808

**Exile**
822 W. Grace St.
804/358-3348

**Robert Blair Antiques**
5612 Grove Ave.
804/285-9441

**Chadwick Antiques**
5805 Grove Ave.
804/285-3355

**Jahnke Road Antique Center**
6207 Jahnke Road
804/231-5838

**Robin's Nest**
6925 Lakeside Ave.
804/553-1061

**Civil War Antiques**
7605 Midlothian Turnpike
804/272-4570

**Tudor Gallery Estate Jewelry & Antiques**
113 S. 12th St.
804/780-0020

**Barbara L. Gordon Antiques**
8211 Bevlynn Way
804/288-5155

## 55 ROANOKE

**12 E. Campbell Antiques**
12 Campbell Ave. S.W.
540/343-7946

**Continental Antiques**
1809 Franklin Road S.W.
540/982-5476

**White House Galleries**
4347 Franklin Road S.W.
540/774-3529

**Carriage House**
5999 Franklin Road S.W.
540/776-0499

**Howard R. McManus**
11 S. Jefferson St.
540/344-2302

**BoLily Antiques**
124 Kirk Ave. S.W.
540/343-0100

**Bargain Corner Antique Shop**
3804 Melrose Ave. N.W.
540/366-1278

**Webb's Antiques**
3906 Old Garst Mill Road
540/774-3790

**Kirk's**
312 2nd St. S.W.
540/344-8161

**Now & Then Shop**
3133 Williamson Road N.W.
540/366-1905

**Russell's Yesteryear**
117 Campbell Ave. S.E.
540/342-1750

**Bradley's Antiques**
101 E. Main St.
804/644-7305

**Halcyon-Vintage Clothing**
117 N. Robinson St.
804/358-1311

**Antiques Warehouse**
1310 E. Cary St.
804/643-1310

**Kaleidoscope**
7501 Iron Bridge Road
804/743-9811

**Sandra's Cellar**
109 Campbell Ave. S.W.
540/342-8123

**John Davis Antiques**
4347 Franklin Road S.W.
540/772-7378

**Home Place Antiques**
5348 Franklin Road S.W.
540/774-0774

**Sissy's Antiques**
2914 Jae Valley Road
540/427-1712

**Bob Anderson Antiques**
617 S. Jefferson St.
540/343-7008

**Bob Beard Antiques**
105 Market Square S.E.
540/981-1757

**Olde Window Glass Co.**
4026 Melrose Ave. N.W.
540/362-3386

**Roanoke Antique Mall**
2302 Orange Ave. N.E.
540/344-0264

**Trudy's Antiques**
2205 Williamson Road N.E.
540/366-7898

**Happy's**
5411 Williamson Road N.W.
540/563-4473

*Virginia*

## 56 ROCKY MOUNT

**Spinning Wheel Antiques**
Route 220
540/489-5355

**Blue Ridge Antique Center**
Route 220-20100 Virgil H Goode Hwy.
540/483-2362

## 57 RUCKERSVILLE

**Archangel Antiques & Fine Art**
Route 29 S.
804/985-7456

**Country Store Antique Mall**
Route 29
804/985-3649

**Early-Time Antiques & Fine Art**
Route 29 N.
804/985-3602

**Green House Shops**
Route 29 N. & 33
804/985-6053

**Red Fox Antiques**
Route 29 N.
804/985-2080

**Antique Collectors**
Route 29 N. & 33
804/985-8966

**Lawson's Antiques—Collectibles**
Route 33 E.
804/985-1070

## 58 SALEM

### Wright Place Antique Mall

27 W. Main St.
540/389-8507
Open: Mon.–Sat. 10–6, Sun. 12:30–6

Step back in time at Wright Place Antique Mall located in the middle of downtown historic Salem. Enjoy a cup of coffee or a cold drink while you browse.

The mall offers a distinctive collection of beautiful furniture including: oak, walnut, mahogany, cherry & primitive. Tables, chairs, beds, kitchen cabinets, rockers, bookcases and secretaries. Railroad items: dishes, lanterns, nails, locks, paper items, etc. Advertising: Coke items, signs, neons, smoking items, bottles, etc. Books: history, novels, Civil War, science novels, books for all ages. Quilts, rugs, linens, license plates, crocks, toys, dolls, clocks, cookie jars, McCoy, Hull, Watt pottery, Weller, Roseville, art, pictures, statues, jewelry, iron items, lamps, glass chandeliers, hurricane, etc. Glassware: cut glass, Depression, Fenton, china, carnival glass, etc.

Antique in one of the nation's most beautiful settings, and take home memories to last a lifetime. Experience a sunrise from the Blue Ridge Parkway or the Appalachian Trail, two of America's most-revered scenic byways, both winding their way through the Roanoke Valley. Enjoy the sights, sounds and smells of the farmers' markets in Roanoke, Salem and Vinton as they come to life almost every morning with their offerings of produce, flowers, baked goods and handmade items.

No visit would be complete without exploring all the shopping options which one will find at every turn. From antiques to outlets, and million-square-foot malls to boutiques in historic settings, there is something to satisfy every taste and need.

After indulging in the area's many attractions and shops, tempt your taste buds by enjoying a sumptuous meal in one of the many area restaurants. The valley has long held an excellent reputation for its wide variety of outstanding dining facilities. Delight in old-fashioned, down-home Southern cooking or a romantic candlelit dinner for two.

There's history, architecture, whimsy and excitement all over the valley. You'll meet some of the friendliest, most hospitable people in the world, who welcome the opportunity to share the area with you.

*Note: Plenty of lodging is available for over-nighters who need to spend just one more day in beautiful, historic Salem.*

**Christopher Gladden Bookseller**
211 S. College Ave.
540/389-4892

**Eddy Street Antiques**
1502 Eddy St.
540/389-9411

**Salem Market Antiques**
1 W. Main St.
540/389-8920

**Virginia Showcase Antiques**
4 E. Main St.
540/387-5842

**Green Market Antique Mall**
8 E. Main St.
540/387-3879

**Elite Antique & Consignments**
17 W. Main St.
540/389-9222

**Olde Curiosity Shoppe Antique Mall**
27/29 E. Main St.
540/387-2007

**Olde Salem Stained Glass Art**
120 E. Main St.
540/389-9968

**Auntie Em's Antiques & More**
514 W. Main St.
540/389-2294

**Antique Lamp Shop**
1800 W. Main St.
540/389-3163

**Red Barn Antiques**
4506 W. Main St.
540/380-4307

**Guthrie's Antiques**
221 E. 6th St.
540/389-3621

**Antique Mall 50-Plus Shops**
27 W. Main St.
540/389-2484

### Great Places to Stay

### The Inn at Burwell Place

601 W. Main St.
540/387-0250 or 1-800-891-0250
Rates $70–$110 (includes full breakfast and private bath)
Directions: From I-81 southbound, take Exit 140 (Route 311) south 1 1/4 miles to East Main Street; turn right on East Main Street and go through downtown Salem, 1 mile. The inn is on the right.

This spacious mansion was built in 1907 by Samuel H. McVitty, a local industrialist, on a summit overlooking Salem and the Southwest Roanoke Valley. Mr. McVitty built the mansion on land purchased from Mr. Nathaniel Burwell (pronounced Burr-ell) a prominent Salem landowner, civic leader, state assemblyman and gentleman justice of the County Court.

In 1915, McVitty sold the mansion to Lewis E. Dawson, whose family lived there until 1971. The Dawsons made major renovations and an addition to the house in 1925. The house was home to six Dawson children and their families during this period. It was the site of many parties, weddings, and family gatherings.

During the 1970s and the 1980s the mansion was used as an architect's office and the YWCA.

Each guest room has its own bathroom with vintage 1920s fixtures and a queen-size 4-poster bed. A wide hallway connects the second-floor bedrooms. Antique walnut and cherry furnishings adorn each room.

Downstairs, the expansive common area consists of a living room, sun porch (complete with 6 by 8-foot antique carousel), two dining rooms and a massive wraparound front porch, an ideal place for reading and watching television. The common area has been the scene of many weddings, receptions, parties and business meetings reminiscent of yesteryear. Within a short walk from the inn is a restored park and duck pond (circa 1890); historic downtown Salem, with numerous antique shops, gift boutiques, restaurants and coffee shops.

The inn serves a full breakfast consisting of the chef's choice of Eggs Benedict, hash browns, fruit compote, a special fruit-juice blend, fresh baked muffins or fruit breads, coffee and teas. Another popular entree is French toast prepared with fresh apple-cinnamon bread.

## 59  SALUDA

**The Shops at Saluda Market**
Route 17 & 33
804/758-2888

**Urbanna Antique Gallery**
124 Rappahannock Ave.
804/758-2000

**Trimble's Antiques**
Hwy. 17
804/758-5732

**Courthouse Antiques**
S-17 Bypass
804/758-4861

## 60  SOUTH BOSTON

**Z's Antiques**
Hwy. 58 W.
804/572-6741

**Miss W. & Sis Art All Nations**
206 Main St.
804/575-0858

**Crystal Hill Antiques**
1902 Seymour Dr.
804/575-8810

**Van's Barnyard Antiques**
Hwy. 716 Airport Road
804/572-4754

**My Brother's Place Antique Mall**
234 S. Main St.
804/572-8888

## 61  STANARDSVILLE

**Towne Shops**
121 W. Main St.
804/985-8222

**J & T Antiques**
317 Main St.
804/985-7299

**Trader Mike's Antiques**
313 E. Main St.
804/985-6440

## 62  STAUNTON

**Turtle Lane**
10 E. Beverly St.
540/886-8591

**Warehouse Antiques & Collectibles**
26 W. Beverly St.
540/885-0891

**Memory Makers**
15 Middlebrook Ave.
540/886-5341

**Once upon a Time Clock Shop**
25 W. Beverly St.
540/885-6064

**Honeysuckle Hill**
100 E. Beverly St.
540/885-8261

**Jolly Roger Haggle Shop**
27 Middlebrook Ave.
540/886-9527

## 63  STRASBURG

**Sullivan's Country House Antiques**
Hwy. 55 & I-81 Exit #296
540/465-5192

**Heritage Antiques**
102 Massanutten Manor Circle
540/465-5000

**Strasburg Emporium**
110 N. Massanutten St.
540/465-3711

**Tiques**
114 Orchard St.
540/465-4115

**River Gallery**
208 W. King St.
540/465-3527

**Wayside of Virginia, Inc.**
108 N. Massanutten St.
540/465-4650

**Vilnis and Company Antiques**
305 N. Massanutten St.
540/465-4405

**Emmart's Antiques Classics**
28814 Old Valley Pike
540/465-5040

## 64  SUFFOLK

**Holly Bluff Antiques**
2697 Bridge Road
757/484-4246

**Judy's Treasures**
723 Carolina Road
757/934-7624

**Carolyn's Country Charm**
3093 Godwin Blvd.
757/934-2868

**Nansemond Antique Shop**
3537 Pruden Blvd.
757/539-6269

**Now & Then Antiques**
6140 Whaleyville Blvd.
757/986-2429

**Once upon a Time Antiques**
2948 Bridge Road
757/483-1344

**Southern Gun Works**
109 Cherry St.
757/934-1423

**Attic Trunk**
167 S. Main St.
757/934-0882

**Willow's**
800 W. Washington St.
757/934-2411

## 65  TAPPAHANNOCK

**A to Z Antiques**
608 Church Lane
804/443-4585

**Hoskin's Creek Table Co.**
1014 Church Lane
804/443-6500

**Antiques Place**
804 Church Lane
804/443-6549

**Mayhew's Antiques**
205 Queen
804/443-2961

**Queen Street Mall 2**
227 Queen
804/443-2424

**Nadji Nook Antiques**
Queen & Cross St., Route 360
804/443-3298

## 66 TOANO

**Charlie's Antiques**
7766 Richmond Road
757/566-8300

**Pocahonta's Trail Antiques**
7778 Richmond Road
757/566-8050

**Colonial Antique Center**
7828 Richmond Road
757/566-8720

**J & L Treasure Chest**
7880 Richmond Road
757/566-1878

**King William Antiques**
7880 Richmond Road
757/566-2270

## 67 TROUTVILLE

**Buffalo Creek Antiques**
941 Lee Hwy. S.
540/992-5288

**Troutville Antique Mart**
941 Lee Hwy. S.
540/992-4249

**Kelly's Real Deal**
1411 Lee Hwy. S.
540/992-5096

**Harris Antiques**
2240 Roanoke
540/992-5225

## 68 VERONA

**Factory**
I-81 Exit 227
540/248-1110

**Pat's Antique Mall**
5505 Lee Hwy.
540/248-7287

**Verona Flea Market**
Hwy. 11
540/248-3532

**Wilson Gallery**
4719 Lee Hwy.
540/248-4292

**Village Antique**
Route 11 (Mount Sidney)
540/248-7807

**Dusty's Antique Market**
Route 11 (Mount Sidney)
540/248-2018

## 69 VIENNA

**Finders Keepers**
131 N.W. Church St.
703/319-9318

**Now and Then**
131 N.W. Church St.
703/242-3959

**Village Antiques**
120 Lawyers Road N.W.
703/938-0084

**Vienna Bargains**
128 Maple Ave. E.
703/255-6119

**Twig House**
132 Maple Ave. E.
703/255-4985

**Cameo Coins & Collectibles**
444 Maple Ave. E.
703/281-7053

**Cabbage Rose**
213 Mill St.
703/242-2051

**Pleasant Street Antiques**
115 Pleasant St. N.W.
703/938-0003

**Furniture Center**
126 Maple Ave. E.
703/938-1714

## 70 VIRGINIA BEACH

**Colonial Cottage Antiques**
3900 Bonney Road
804/498-0600

**Mary's Attic**
3900 Bonney Road
804/498-0600

**Pat's Antiques**
3900 Bonney Road
804/463-1252

**Pelican Bay**
3900 Bonney Road
804/481-4445

**Hard Timz & Sunshine**
244 London Bridge Shop
804/463-7335

**Something Unique**
1600 Independence Blvd.
804/363-9512

**Echoes of Time Antiques**
320 Laskin Road
804/428-2332

**Shutter Door Antiques**
968 Laskin Road
804/422-6999

**La Galleria, Inc.**
993 Laskin Road
804/428-5909

**Garden Gallery**
1860 Laskin Road
804/428-8427

**Chesapeake Antiques & Collectibles**
210 24th St.
804/425-6530

**Rudy's Antiques**
3324 Virginia Beach Blvd.
804/340-2079

**Eddie's Antique Mall**
4801 A Virginia Beach Blvd.
804/497-0537

**Barrett Street Antique Center**
2645 Dean Drive
757/463-8600

**Christy's Antiques**
6353 Indian River Road
757/424-8770

## 71 WAYNESBORO

**Annetteque's Antiques**
305 12th St.
540/949-7670

**Apple Acres Antiques**
1432 Lyndhurst Road
540/949-8522

**Ladd Framing Shop**
Route 340 S.
540/943-6287

**Unique Andteek**
Hwy. 340 N.
540/949-4983

**Village Showcase**
601 Shenandoah Village Dr.
540/932-7599

**Tommy's Olde Town Used**
208 Arch Ave.
540/949-5559

**Someplace Else**
430 N. Commerce Ave.
540/942-9888

**The Silent Woman Antiques**
139 N. Wayne Ave.
540/949-4483

**Treasures 'n' Things**
141 N. Wayne Ave.
540/942-3223

**Stuart's Draft Antique Mall**
Route 340 S. (4 mi. S. of Waynesboro)
540/946-8488

## 72 WEYERS CAVE

**Rocky's Antique Mall**
Hwy. 11
540/234-9900

**Ace Antiques**
Hwy. 11
540/234-9079

# *Virginia*

**Blue Ridge Antiques**
Hwy. 11
540/234-0112

## 73 WILLIAMSBURG

**London Shop**
1206 Jamestown Road
757/229-8754

**Old Chickahominy House**
1211 Jamestown Road
757/229-4689

**Shaia Oriental Rugs**
1325 Jamestown Road
757/220-0400

**TK Oriental Antiques**
1654 Jamestown Road
757/220-8590

**Hamilton's Book Store**
1784 Jamestown Road
757/220-3000

**Quilts Unlimited**
Merchants Square
757/253-0222

**J.L. McCandlish Antiques Art**
1915 Pocahontas Trail
757/259-0472

**Peacock Hill**
445 Prince George St.
757/220-0429

**Attic Collections**
2229 Richmond Road
757/229-0032

**R & M Antiques**
5435 Richmond Road
757/565-3344

**Lamplighter Shoppe Ltd.**
6502 Richmond Road
757/565-4676

**Things Unique**
6506 Richmond Road
757/564-1140

**Oriental Textile Arts**
Village Shop
757/220-3736

**Williamsburg Antique Mall**
500 Lightfoot Road
757/565-2587

### *Great Places to Stay*

## Applewood Colonial B&B
605 Richmond Road
1-800-899-2753

"An 'Applewood' a day, for a memorable stay," says innkeeper Fred Strout. This Flemish bond–brick home was built in 1929 by the construction manager for the Colonial Williamsburg restoration and features many finely crafted Colonial details of the 18th century. Antiques and 20th-century comfort throughout the house are accented by the owner's unique apple collection.

Guests enjoy a full breakfast served by candlelight in the elegant dining room.

## Williamsburg Sampler B&B
922 Jamestown Road
1-800-722-1169

The Sampler is the finest 18th-century plantation-style Colonial located in the Architectural Corridor Protection Distric of Williamsburg. Proclaimed by Virginia's governor as the 1995 Inn of the Year ("I call its significance to the attention of all our citizens"). Guest rooms have king-

or queen-size four-poster beds, TV and private bath. Additionally, suites have wet bar/refrigerator, fireplace and TV.

## 74 WINCHESTER

## Betty's Antiques
127 Morgan Mill Road
540/667-8558
Open: Wed.–Sat. 12–5, Sun.–Tues. by chance or appointment
Directions: Take Exit 315 from I-81 onto Route 7. The shop is east of Winchester.

Established in 1973, the shop specializes in refinished American oak furniture. Pieces such as bedroom suites, dressers, and round tables are just a few of the many quality antiques available here.

**Past and Present**
1121 Berryville Ave.
540/678-8766

**Boscawen Gold & Silver**
41 W. Boscawen St.
540/667-6065

**Kimberly's Antiques & Linens**
135 N. Braddock St.
540/662-2195

**Glover's Antiques**
422 S. Cameron St.
540/662-3737

**Stone Soup Gallery/Old Downtown Mall**
107 N. Loudoun St.
540/722-3976

**Winchester Antiques & Collectibles**
1815 S. Loudoun St.
540/667-7411

**Clay Hill Antiques**
2869 Middle Road
540/662-3623

**Millwood Crossing Shops**
381 Millwood Ave.
540/662-5157

**Doll House Antiques**
618 S. Cameron St./by appointment
540/665-0964

**50 West Antiques**
2480 Northwestern Pike
540/662-7624

**Wrenwood Antique Gallery**
39 W. Piccadilly St.
540/665-3055

**Cecil Antiques**
522 N. Sunnyside St.
540/667-0787

**Applegate Antiques & Art**
1844 Valley Ave.
540/665-1933

## 75 WOODSTOCK

**Valley Treasures**
660 N. Main St.
540/459-2334

**Spring Hollow Antiques**
322 S. Main St.
540/459-3946

*Great Places to Stay*

## River'd Inn

1972 Artz Road
540/459-5369 or 1-800-637-4561
Lodging available daily, $150–$325 per night includes full breakfast.
Restaurant open Wed.–Sun. 5–9 p.m., Sun. brunch served 11–2
Directions: I-81 to Route 11, just north of Woodstock take SR 663 2 $\frac{1}{10}$
miles.

The River'd Inn offers luxurious accommodations nestled in the heart of Virginia's Shenandoah Valley. Spacious bedrooms feature antique furnishings, fireplaces and private baths with whirlpool tubs. Beautiful views from decks and porches. Gourmet restaurant, open to the public, features French-based cuisine. Fine selection of beer, wine, and spirits available. Outdoor pool with hot tub. Situated on 25 forested acres with gardens, mountain views, and paths to the Shenandoah River. Numerous attractions including Civil War sites, antique and gift shops, wineries, golf, skiing, hiking, canoeing, picnicking, and more nearby. Easy access from Interstate 81. Handicapped accessible dining and lodging.

## 76 WYTHEVILLE

**Old Fort Antique Mall**
I-81 Exit # 80
540/228-4438

**Snoopers, Inc.**
I-81 Exit # 80
540/637-6441

## 77 YORKTOWN

**High Cotton Ltd.**
3630 George Washington Mem. Hwy.
757/867-7132

**Scott's Corner Antiques**
4827 George Washington Mem. Hwy.
757/898-1404

**Galleria Antique Mall**
7628 George Washington Mem. Hwy.
757/890-2950

**Swan Tavern Antiques**
300 Main St.
757/898-3033

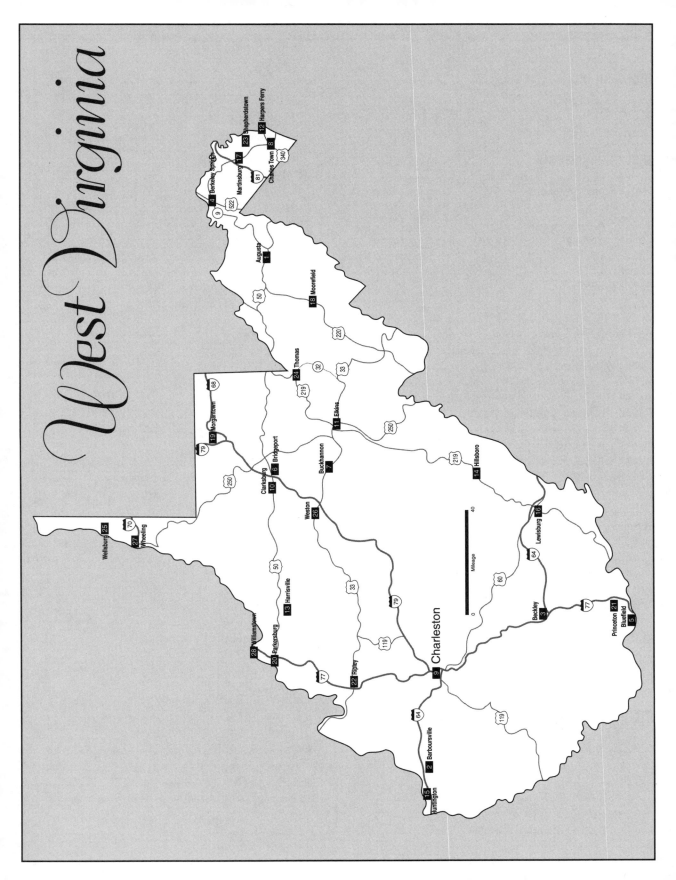

# West Virginia

## 1  AUGUSTA

**Dan's Antiques**
Route 50
304/496-8187

**Smith's Antiques**
Route 50
304/496-9474

## 2  BARBOURSVILLE

### Miller House Antiques

1112 Main St.
304/736-0845 or 304/523-6064
Open: Tues.–Sat. 10–5, Sun.–Mon. By appointment
Directions: From I-64, take the Barboursville Exit. Continue for 2 miles into downtown Barboursville. The shop is located on Main Street in the historic downtown area.

The William Clendenim Miller home was built in 1852 out of "Barboursville brick," made on site. It served as the town post office from 1840 to 1860, and W. C. Miller, who was postmaster, would read letters to the townspeople from his porch or the parlor. On July 14, 1861, the Civil War's first skirmish of Barboursville took place within sight of the home, and Miller's son, John William, took a little double-barreled pistol and joined the Confederate forces. During the second skirmish the 2nd Virginia Cavalry (Union) was ordered to attack the house on rumors that it was the headquarters of Confederate Brig. A.S. Jenkins. Union Duty Sergeant Braxton P. Reeves was killed and his body placed on the porch of the Miller House until it could be retrieved by the Union.

In the early 1900s the home was purchased from the Miller family and used as a college boarding house.

In 1914 John W. Miller, son of the original owner, bought back his birthplace (he was born there in 1845) for obvious sentimental reasons.

Today, the house is an antique shop and is decorated with period furniture, china, paintings, quilts, etc. All are for sale. There are 11 rooms, each with a fireplace. The house is on a daily scheduled walking tour of historic Barboursville.

## 3  BECKLEY

**Beckley Antique Mall**
268 George St.
304/255-6825

## 4  BERKELEY SPRINGS

### Berkeley Springs Antique Mall

100 Fairfax St.
304/258-5676
Open: Thurs.–Tues. 10–5, closed Wed.
Directions: From Route 70, take Highway 522 South and follow it straight for 7 miles to the heart of downtown Berkeley Springs.

Berkeley Springs offers visitors a general line of antiques from 30 dealers in 6,500 square feet of space housed in a 1910 building.

**Curiosity Shop**
101 N. Washington St.
304/258-1634

**Antique House**
312 N. Washington St.
304/258-9420

## 5  BLUEFIELD

If a taste of coal culture piques your interest, head for West Virginia's southernmost border. Bluefield, off I-77, is the scene of much coal history, both past and present. The downtown overlooks an extensive network of railroad tracks, often loaded with car after car of glittering black rock. The Eastern Regional Coal Archives are housed in the Craft Memorial Library and include coal company records, diaries, oral histories and displays of miners' tools and industry artifacts.

**Second Time Around**
1715 Bluefield Ave.
304/325-9855

**Landmark Mini-Mall**
200 Federal St.
304/327-9686

**Antiques at the Old Trade Post**
1204 Augusta St.
304/325-2554

### *Interesting Side Trip*

A few miles northwest of Bluefield on U.S. 52 is Bramwell, once considered the richest town in the United States. As many as 14 millionaires resided there in the early 20th century during the height of the coal boom. Tours are available in May and December, or can be pre-arranged anytime. Today the town's late 19th-century fairy-tale architecture of turrets, gables, slate and tile roofs, leaded and stained glass, ornate woodwork and wide porches are a well-preserved reminder of West Virginia's Gilded Age.

## 6  BRIDGEPORT

### Shahady's Antiques

214 E. Main St.
304/842-6691 or 1-800-252-0766
Open: Tues.–Sat. 10–5
Directions: Traveling I-79, take Exit 119 (Bridgeport/Clarksburg, W.Va.) to Route 50 East 1½ miles to downtown Bridgeport

Shahady's carries the largest diversified inventory in the tri-state area, with 500 pieces of furniture in stock, ranging from the 1800s to the 20th century. They also handle stoneware, lighting fixtures and glassware, plus architectural antiques, both retail and wholesale to the trade.

**Grey Fox Farm Antiques**
RR 1, #39 A
304/842-4219
Open: Mon.–Sat. 11–3
Directions: From I-79, take Exit 119. Turn left and go east on Route 50 for several miles. Turn right onto Route 58 and go a half mile to the stop sign. Turn left on Route 26. The shop is located 2 9/10 miles farther on the right.

The shop is actually located in the barn of Grey Fox Farm. They (the shopkeepers) specialize in carefully selected 18th- and 19th-century furniture, as well as offering a wide selection of decorative accessories and gifts.

### 7  BUCKHANNON

**Buckhannon Antique Mall**
Clarksburg Road
304/472-9605

**Franklin Trash & Treasury Antiques**
Clarksburg Road
304/472-8738

**Antiques Etc.**
4 E. Main St.
304/472-1120

### *Great Places to Stay*

**Post Mansion Inn B&B**
8 Island Ave.
1-800-301-9309

The Post Mansion, one of the oldest bed and breakfasts in Upshur County, was constructed in 1860 and remodeled of prison-cut stone in 1892 for Senator William Post. Being the largest example of a native cut-stone house in Upshur County, the home has fondly been called the "mansion" or "castle." The house contains thirty rooms, five of which are guest rooms, five baths, old wood staircases, stained glass windows, and porches. The inn is located on six acres of land with the Buckhannon River bordering both the front and rear.

### 8  CHARLES TOWN

**Wooden Shoe**
222 W. Washington St.
304/725-1673

**Grandma's Treasures**
615 E. Washington St.
304/728-2199

### 9  CHARLESTON

**Hale St. Antiques & Collectibles Mall**
213 Hale St.
304/345-6040
Open: Tues.–Sun. 11–5
Directions: From I-64 East, take the Lee Street exit and turn right onto Hale Street.

This antique mall is located in a historic hardware and paint store, and is the largest antiques shop in Charleston. Its three floors are filled with a variety of furniture, glassware and collectibles.

**South Charleston Antique Mall**
4800 MacCorkle Ave. S.W.
304/766-6761
Open: Mon.–Sun. 10-whenever
Directions: From I-64 take Exit 54 to U.S. Route 60 which is also MacCorkle Ave. One light west of Thomas Hospital.

One of West Virginia's antique malls, this market is a must-stop on the antiquing trail; over 18,000 square feet.

**Alex Franklin Ltd.**
1007 Bridge Road
304/342-8333

**Attic Antiques**
313 D St.
304/744-8975

**Capital Flea Market**
Route 114 S.
304/342-1626

**Tiny Tim's**
5206 MacCorkle Ave. S.E.
304/768-8111

**Trophy Design**
418 Virginia St. W.
304/346-3907

**Tiki's Antique. Gallery**
1312 Watts St.
304/346-6160

**Belle's Antiques**
4270 Woodrums Lane
304/744-5435

**Kanawha Coin/Antiques**
707/712 Fife
304/342-8081

**Split Rail Antiques**
2580 Benson Dr.
304/342-6084

### 10  CLARKSBURG

Clarksburg, the birthplace of General Thomas "Stonewall" Jackson, was the adopted home of thousands of immigrant laborers after the Civil War and, thanks to the discovery of gas and oil, a manufacturing center for glass, tin and zinc.

Two monuments mark the town's heritage. A likeness of "Stonewall" sits astride a bronze horse on the courthouse plaza, and, nearby, a heroic sculpture represents the Belgian, Czech, Greek, Hungarian, Irish, Italian, Romanian and Spanish immigrants who flocked to the region beginning in the 1880s.

**Kollage**
1625 Buckhannon Pike
304/622-8137

**Red Wheel Antiques**
600 Southern Ave.
304/622-2192

**Briar Patch Antiques**
Route 20 S.
304/623-1213

**West End Antiques**
97 Milford St.
304/624-7600

**Carney's Fine Antiques**
315 Spring Ave.
304/622-1317

## 11 ELKINS

### Bittersweet Books & Antiques

212 Davis Ave.
304/636-6338 or 1-800-417-6338
Open: Mon.–Sat. 10–5, Sun. by appointment or chance
Directions: Bittersweet is accessible from Highways 250, 33 and 219, all of which lead to historic downtown Elkins.

Bittersweet Books and Antiques specializes in paper, as well as carrying a general line of antiques. Their paper goods include sheet music, postcards, magazines, trade cards, and old and rare books.

**S and S Company**
204 Findley St.
304/636-2366

**Justine's Antiques Etc.**
Old Seneca Road
304/636-2891

**Granny's Attic**
427 Kerens Ave.
304/636-4121

**Mrs. McGillicuddy's Antiques**
203 4th St.
304/636-9356

### Great Places to Stay

### The Warfield House Bed & Breakfast

318 Buffalo St.
1-888-636-4555
Open: All year
Rates: $65–$75 includes a complimentary full breakfast. Children 12 and older welcome. Absolutely smoke-free residence.
For specific directions to the Warfield House Bed and Breakfast, call the innkeepers.

The Warfield House Bed & Breakfast provides the traveler with comfort, warm hospitality, and good food, all in an elegant turn-of-the-century setting. Whether you're looking for a mountain retreat or an activity-packed vacation you will find it in the beautiful mountains of West Virginia. The quaint town of Elkins is the perfect central location for year-round outdoor recreation and the Warfield House is the perfect "home base" from which to explore.

Built in 1901 by a local bank executive, Harry Ridgely Warfield and his wife, Susan Stadtler, the grand shingle and brick house was listed on the National Register of Historic Places in 1997. The spacious rooms

display an abundance of woodwork, beautiful stained glass, and period fixtures. The foyer opens to an interior vestibule where an oak staircase, bathed in rich hues from the two-story stained glass window on the landing, rises to four large guest rooms on the second floor. Two of these four rooms currently have private baths but a planned renovation to the rear porch will allow another bath to be added, thus equipping all the guest rooms with private baths in the near future. The fifth bedroom, over the kitchen wing, is accessed by its own private staircase and has a private bath.

Guests are welcome to make use of the parlor, library, and dining room on the first floor to relax, read, eat, or plan their next excursion. After a full breakfast of fresh fruit, home-baked breads and pastries, and hot entree served family style at the massive oak table, you may choose a day trip to Blackwater Falls State Park, Canaan Valley Resort, Cass Scenic Railroad, Spruce Knob/Seneca Rocks Recreation Area, the historic Swiss Village of Helvetia or Rich Mountain Battlefield.

If you choose instead to stay close to home, a five-minute walk to downtown Elkins will bring you to cozy restaurants, an artists' gallery, and of course, several terrific antique shops. Among our favorites is Bittersweet Books and Antiques, specializing in old and rare books, ephemera, and a general line of antiques.

The bed and breakfast cannot accommodate your pets but their dog, "Boo" and cat, "Red" welcome your attention.

## 12 HARPERS FERRY

The town of Harpers Ferry is perhaps livelier today than it was in 1859, when abolitionist John Brown staged his raid on the United States Arsenal there, setting off a chain of events that resulted in the Civil War. Undoubtedly more beautiful than ever, its historic section is polished and maintained as a national historic park, and is part of the Civil War Discovery Trail.

### Hodge Podge

144 High St.
304/535-6917
Open: Mon.–Fri. 10–5, Sat.–Sun. 10–6
Directions: Hodge Podge is located on Highway 340 in downtown historic Harpers Ferry.

Hodge Podge handles small antiques, gifts, collectibles, and Civil War items—a true "hodgepodge" of merchandise!

**Stone House Antiques**
108 Potomac St.
304/535-6688

**Washington St. Antiques**
1080 Washington St.
304/535-2411

## Great Places to Stay

**Ranson Armory House Bed & Breakfast**
690 Washington St.
304/535-2142

Ranson Armory House Bed & Breakfast is located in historic Harpers Ferry at the confluence of the Potomac and Shenandoah Rivers. The original dwelling, dating from the 1830s, was built by the Federal government to house U.S. Armory staff. It was enlarged in the 1890s with Victorian architectural features. The spacious rooms are furnished with antiques and family heirlooms and have mountain views.

### Interesting Side Trip

Wind along the cobblestone streets of Harpers Ferry to the town of Bolivar, where shops feature a remarkable collection of antiques including Civil War memorabilia and local crafts.

### 13  HARRISVILLE

A short detour off U.S. Highway 50 South on West Virginia Route 16 takes you to quaint Harrisville, where Berdine's Five & Dime, the nation's oldest five and dime, still operates after 80 years on Court Street. Its solid oak cabinets and glass bins offer penny candy, small toys and practical household items.

**The Upper Room**
201A E. Main St.
304/643-2599

**Barb & Ben's Antique Shop**
1012 E. Main St.
304/643-2977

### 14  HILLSBORO

On the literary front, Hillsboro is the birthplace of Pearl S. Buck, one of the world's best-loved authors. Her family home, the Stulting House, is open for tours, and contains original furnishings and memorabilia. Among its annual events is Author's Day in August, dedicated to keeping the Nobel- and Pulitzer Prize-winning writer's spirit alive.

While in Hillsboro, step back in time at the Hillsboro General Store, and stop for a bite to eat at the popular little Country Roads Cafe.

**Hillsboro General Store**
Route 219
304/653-4414

## Great Places to Eat

**Country Roads Cafe**
Route 219
304/653-8595
Open: Tues.–Fri. 11–9, Sat. & Sun. 8–9

The modern incarnation of Country Roads Cafe is serving up home-cooked meals with fresh-baked desserts. Breakfast, lunch and dinner specials are regular features. This 100-year-old establishment still possesses a ladder from its earliest years as a general store. Furnishings are antique, and visitors can buy antique wire-made frames, mirrors, and numerous other small delights.

### 15  HUNTINGTON

**Antique Center, Inc.**
610 14th St. W.
304/523-7887

**Adams Avenue Antique Mall**
1460 Adams Ave.
304/523-7231

**Collectors Store Antique Mall**
1660 Adams Ave.
304/429-3900

**Stouffer's Shady Business**
845 8th Ave.
304/697-8905

**Bus Barn Antiques Mall**
402 18th St. W.
304/429-3485

**Hattie and Nan's Antq. Market Place**
521 14th St. W.
304/523-8844

**Mark's Antiques**
600 14th St. W.
304/525-3275

**Pieces of the Past**
606 14th St. W.
304/522-7892

**Bob's Second Hand**
619 14th St. W.
304/523-6854

**Lucky Penny**
1404 Washington Ave.
304/522-1777

**Lewis' Antiques & Collectibles**
720 14th St. W.
304/522-0444

**Memories of the Heart**
1408 Adams Ave.
304/697-5301

**A Touch of Country**
418 9th St.
304/525-2808

**Mimmi's Collectors Dolls**
544 6th Ave.
304/522-4841

**Central City Antique Mall**
611 14th St. W.
304/523-0311

**Classics Antiques & Interiors**
1337 5th Ave. W.
304/697-3416

**Adell's Antiques**
444 W. 14th St.
304/529-1177

### 16  LEWISBURG

**Antiques**
120 E. Washington St.
304/647-3404

**Peddlar's Alley Antiques**
123 E. Washington St.
304/645-4082

# West Virginia

*West Virginia*

## *Great Places to Stay*

### Lynn's Inn Bed & Breakfast
Route 4, Box 40
1-800-304-2003
Open: Year-round
Rates: Seasonal
Directions: Lynn's is located 1 ½ miles north of I-64 (Exit 169) on U.S. Highway 219.

This is a switch from the majority of bed and breakfasts because, instead of being a former farm, this is a working farm — they actually raise beef cattle. The inn itself is a former tourist home built in 1935 and furnished with original antiques. There are four guest rooms, all with private baths and two sitting rooms. Guests are served a full country breakfast, and there is a large porch with rockers and ferns to help folks enjoy a true country weekend.

### General Lewis Inn
301 E. Washington St.
1-800-628-4454

The General Lewis is a unique blend of the old and the new, created and operated by the Hock family since 1928. The eastern end of the building, including the dining room, the kitchen and a suite of rooms on the first floor plus two bedrooms and a suite on the second floor, was a brick residence built in the early 1800s by John H. Withrow. Mr. and Mrs. Randolph Hock purchased it from Withrow's daughter. Walter Martens, a well-known West Virginia architect who designed the Governor's Mansion in Charleston, designed the main section and the west wing according to their plans. The Hock family spent many years gathering antiques from Greenbrier and adjourning counties to furnish the inn. Spool and canopy beds, chests of drawers, china, glass, old prints and other memorabilia are throughout the home.

## 17 MARTINSBURG

Incorporated in 1778, Martinsburg later flourished as a railroad town, home to the B & O Railroad engine shop. Coveted by both sides in the Civil War, the Union army held it for 32 months, the Confederate for 16.

Old Town Martinsburg offers a variety of antique shops specializing in primitives, Victorian, dolls, linens and unusual accessories.

**Manor House Antiques**
242 S. Queen St.
304/263-5950

**Little Shop Antiques**
563 N. Queen St.
304/267-1603

**Affordable Antiques & Furniture**
556 N. Queen St.
304/263-9024

**Blue Ridge Country Antqs. & Intrs.**
204 S. Queen St.
304/263-4275

## *Great Places to Eat*

### Market House Grill
100 N. Queen St.
304/263-7615

To dine at the historic Market House Grill is considered an "eating adventure," with both continental and Cajun fare their specialty — quite out of the ordinary for the location.

## *Interesting Side Trips*

### The Apollo Civic Theatre
128 E. Martin St., P.O. Box 519
304/263-6766

The Apollo Civic Theatre has the distinction of being the oldest live performance stage in West Virginia. Call for a complete listing of shows, times and ticket prices.

## 18 MOOREFIELD

## *Great Places to Stay*

### McMechen House Inn
109 N. Main St.
1-800-298-2466

Innkeepers Bob and Linda Curtis invite you to return to the mid-1800s. Imagine a time of delicate antebellum grace backdropped against roaring political activity. The McMechen House is a splendid romantic home built in 1853 by Samuel A. McMechen, a local merchant and political activist. The three-story brick home features Greek Revival style and is located in the center of Moorefield Historic District. During the Civil War the house served as headquarters to both the Union and Confederate forces as military control of the valley changed hands.

Here you will find excellent food, spacious rooms, friendship, and generous hospitality. Tour local wineries or shop the antique and gift shops. Catch a community play or ride the Potomac Eagle (seasonal) or just simply relax on one of the inn's spacious porches. Cradled in the historic South Branch Valley and surrounded by the majestic mountains of the Potomac Highlands, you can enjoy a myriad of river sports — fishing, canoeing, or kayaking.

*West Virginia*

## 19 MORGANTOWN

**Bittersweet Antiques**
431 Beechurst
304/296-4602

**Dale's Oldtiques**
Stewartstown Road
304/599-9074

**Sally's Alley**
1389 University Ave.
304/292-9230

## 20 PARKERSBURG

Antique shops in the region frequently carry a broad selection of vintage regional glass. Maher's Antiques in Parkersburg offers glass, plus a selection of crocks with A.P. Donagho's Excelsior Pottery signature, recalling the days when homes throughout the Midwest stored food in the Parkersburg company's pots.

**Maher's Antiques**
1619 Saint Mary's Ave.
304/485-1331

**Pure & Simple Antiques & Cllbls.**
60 Schultz St.
304/422-3117

## 21 PRINCETON

**Hobby Shop Antiques**
305 Mercer St.
304/487-1990

**Olde Towne Shoppe**
929 Mercer St.
304/425-3677

**A-Z Trading Center**
509 Roger St.
304/425-4365

## 22 RIPLEY

### Blue Ribbon Antiques
Route 33
304/372-5006
Open: Tues.–Sat. 9–4, closed Sun.–Mon.
Directions: Take Exit 138 off I-77. The shop is 2 miles west of the Ripley Exit on Route 33.

Here's one for a rainy day or for the serious browser. Housed in a 200-year-old, seven-room farmhouse, the shopkeeper describes Blue Ribbon Antiques as being "floor to ceiling, wall to wall; the old house is literally bulging with antiques and glassware."

**Country Place**
111 Court St. S.
304/372-5048

**Millie's Antiques**
1 Starcher Place
304/372-1859

## 23 SHEPHERDSTOWN

Just a few miles northeast of Martinsburg lies Shepherdstown, one of the oldest towns in West Virginia, established in the 1730s as Mechlenberg. Today, it's a quaint town of wooden storefronts and tree-lined streets, where specialty shops, charming restaurants, small inns and cultural programs of Shepherd College fill the town with visitors.

The eclectic 1930s Yellow Brick Bank, the Olde Pharmacy Cafe, complete with original pharmaceutical trappings, and Ye Olde Sweet Shoppe offer historic settings and good food.

**Matthews & Shank Antiques**
139 W. German
304/876-6550

### *Great Places to Stay*

### Stonebrake Cottage
P.O. Box 1612
304/876-6607

Stonebrake Cottage is a darling Victorian country home located at the edge of the owner's 145-acre farm. It is unique because the guests occupying the cottage have the exclusive use of the entire cottage for their stay. The cottage will sleep up to six people in one part and is decorated throughout with early American antiques.

## 24 THOMAS

### Eagle's Nest I & II
Route 32
304/463-4186 or 304/463-4113
Open: Daily 10–5
Directions: Both Eagle's Nests are located on Route 32 in Thomas, 37 miles from Elkins.

These two stores carry collectibles, antiques and good junque. They also claim to have the best selection of handmade dolls and crafts in West Virginia. After you're through admiring the familiar, the strange and the remarkable, have a refreshment at their coffee bar while you decide what to take home from the shop.

## 25 WELLSBURG

True to its beginnings as a late 18th-century port, Wellsburg's downtown wharf still welcomes vintage river boats such as the *Mississippi Queen* in July and the *Delta Queen* in October. For each visit, the town puts on a party, with bands, food, artisans and boat tours.

Wellsburg's downtown national historic district features specialty shops, riverside greens and restaurants. A short drive from downtown you'll find Drover's Inn, an authentic 1848 country inn with handcrafted furnishings, an Old English–style pub and a restaurant famous for its home-cooked buffet.

# West Virginia

**Wellsburg Flower Shop, Inc.**
600 Charles St.
304/737-3380

**Watzman's Old Place**
709 Charles St.
304/737-0711

## 26 WESTON

**Ethel's Antiques & Collectibles**
107 Main Ave.
304/269-7690

## 27 WHEELING

Wheeling is the historical and commercial hub of the northern Panhandle. From its earliest days as a pre-Revolutionary outpost and stop along the National Road's path to the western frontier, to its 18th- and 19th-century role as a port of entry, through its boom and bust Victorian era as the center of glass, steel and textiles, Wheeling has preserved and persevered.

Independence Hall in downtown Wheeling has served as an 18th- and 19th-century customs house, as the capital of the restored government of West Virginia, and later as the state capital for the new state of West Virginia. Today, it serves as a center for art and a showcase for the state's history, and is part of the Civil War Discovery Trail.

The city's most distinctive historic landmark, the 1849 Wheeling Suspension Bridge, dazzles visitors at night with its brilliant necklace of decorative lights. The oldest major long-span suspension bridge in the world, the bridge is a designated National Historic Landmark.

Just blocks from downtown, Wheeling's Centre Market District is listed on the National Register of Historic Places. It's also high on the list for shoppers seeking antiques, traditional crafts, gourmet and specialty food items and unique gifts. Restaurants and a Victorian-style confectionery will rejuvenate the weary shopper.

The Old Town neighborhood on Main Street in north Wheeling also offers shoppers the opportunity to visit another era. Shops located in historic townhouses and mansions offer fine works of art, antiques and Victorian decorations and accents. Unique restaurants provide a relaxing respite.

**Northgate Antiques & Interiors, Inc.**
735 Main St.
304/232-1475

**Downtown Wheeling Antiques**
1120 Main St.
304/232-8951

**Raggedy Ann's Country Store**
740 Charles St.
304/737-1518

**A Penny Saved Antique & Cllbls.**
230 Main Ave.
304/269-3258

**Outdoor Store**
1065 Main St.
304/233-1080

**Antiques on the Market**
2265 Market St.
304/232-1665

## 28 WILLIAMSTOWN

Since 1905, Williamstown's Fenton Art Glass Company has been producing the finest in original art glass. On a free plant tour, you'll see molten glass born in fiery hot furnaces begin its unique journey on the way to becoming tomorrow's heirlooms. Under the persuasion of master craftsmen using century-old tools and techniques, beautiful Fenton glassware takes shape amid a constant, roaring baptism of fire. For a nominal fee, visit the company's glass museum to view one-of-a-kind glass pieces, including Fenton's original carnival glass, and to watch a video on the history of Fenton Glass.

**Williamstown Antique Mall**
439 Highland Ave.
304/375-6315

# Largest Malls

## ALABAMA

### Birmingham
**Riverchase Antique Gallery**
3454 Lorna Road
205/823-6433
36,000 sq. ft. — 146 dealers

### Heflin
**The Willoughby St. Mall**
91-A Willoughby St.
205/463-5409
35,000 sq. ft.

### Huntsville
**HartLex Antique Mall**
1030 Old Monrovia Road
205/830-4278
60,000 sq. ft. — 300 dealers

### Mobile
**Mobile Antique Gallery**
1616 S. Beltline Hwy.
334/666-6677
21,000 sq. ft.

### Montgomery
**Montgomery Antique Galleries**
1955 Eastern Blvd.
334/277-2490
20,000 sq. ft. — 50 dealers

**SouthEast Antiques & Collectibles**
2530 E. South Blvd.
334/284-5711
15,000 sq. ft. — 40 dealers

### Northport
**Anne Marie's Antique Emporium**
5925 Hwy. 43
1-888-333-1398
30,000 sq. ft.

### Vernon
**Falkner Antique Mall**
Courtsquare
205/695-9841
14,000 sq. ft. — 60 dealers

### Winfield
**Between a Rock & a Hard Place**
Hwy. 78 W.
205/487-2924
72,000 sq. ft. plus monthly auctions

## CONNECTICUT

### Collinsville
**The Collinsville Antiques Co.**
Rt. 179
860/693-1011
17,000 sq. ft. — 2 floors

### East Hampton
**Old Bank Antiques**
66 Main St.
860/267-0790
6,000 sq. ft. — 3 floors

### Old Saybrook
**Essex Saybrook Antiques Village**
345 Middlesex Turnpike (Rt. 154)
860/388-0689
120 dealers

**Essex Town Line Antiques Village**
985 Middlesex Turnpike (Rt. 154)
860/388-5000
10,000 sq. ft.

**Old Saybrook Antiques Center**
756 Middlesex Turnpike (Rt. 154)
860/388-1600
125 dealers

### Putnam
**The Antiques Marketplace**
109 Main St. & Rt. 44
860/928-0442
22,000 sq. ft. — 300 dealers

### Stamford
**Antique & Artisan Center**
69 Jefferson
203/327-6022
22,000 sq. ft. — 100 dealers

**Stamford Antiques Center**
735 Canal St.
1-888-329-3546
135 dealers

### Stratford
**Stratford Antique Center**
400 Honeyspot Road
203/378-7754
200 dealers

## DELAWARE

### Lewes
**Heritage Antique Market**
130 Hwy. One
302/645-2309
10,500 sq. ft.

## FLORIDA

### Chipley
**Historic Chipley Antique Mall**
1368 N. Railroad Ave.
850/638-2535
10,000 sq. ft. — 50 dealers

### Deerfield
**Hillsboro Antique Mall & Tea Room**
1025 E. Hillsboro Blvd.
954/571-9988
32,000 sq. ft. — 200 dealers

### Havana
**Havana's Cannery**
115 E. 8th Ave.
850/539-3800
16 shops — over 125 dealers

### High Springs
**High Springs Antique District**
From I-75 Exits 78, 79, 80 or Hwy. 441
1-888-454-7655 Visitor Info

### Jacksonville
**Avonlea Antique Center**
11000 Beach Blvd.
904/645-0806
100,000 sq. ft. — 180 dealers

### Lake City
**Britannia Antiques**
U.S. 90, 1/2 mile W. Of I-75
904/755-0120
15,000 sq. ft.

**Webb's**
I-75 at Exit 80
904/758-9280
150,000 sq. ft. — 1,000 booths

### Micanopy
**Smiley's**
I-75 at Exit 73, Rd. 234
342/466-0707

### Mount Dora
**Renninger's**
20651 U.S. Hwy. 441
352/383-8393
200 dealers

### St. Augustine
**Lovejoy's Antique Mall**
1302 N. Ponce de Leon Blvd. (U.S. 1)
904/826-0200
144 dealers

### St. Petersburg
**Antique Exchange**
2535 Central Ave.
813/321-6621
100 dealers

### Tampa
**Gaslight Antiques**
3616 Henderson Blvd.
813/870-0934
Half a city block — 3 huge stores

## GEORGIA

### Byron
**The Big Peach Antiques & Collectible Mall**
119 Peachtree Road
912/956-6256
40,000 sq. ft. — 200 dealers

### Chamblee
**Broad Street Antique Mall**
3550 Broad St.
770/458-6316
20,000 sq. ft.

**Moose Breath Trading Company**
5461 Peachtree Road
770/458-7210
20,000 sq. ft.

### Gainesville
**Gainesville Antique Gallery**
131 Bradford St.
770/532-4950
25,000 sq. ft.

### Kennesaw
**Big Shanty Antique Mall**
1720 N. Roberts Road
770/795-1704
50,000 sq. ft. — 150+ dealers

### Macon
**Old Mill Antique Mall**
155 Coliseum Dr.
912/743-1948
35,000 sq. ft.

### Marietta
**Dupre's Antique Market**
17 Whitelock Ave. N.W.
770/428-2667
Over 17,000 sq. ft.

### Perry
**Perry's Antiques & Cllbls. Mall**
351 General Courtney Hodges Blvd.
912/987-4001
100+ dealers

### Ringgold
**Gateway Antiques Center**
4103 Cloud Springs Road
706/858-9685
40,000 sq. ft. — 300 dealers

### Rome
**Heritage Antiques**
174 Chatillon Road
706/291-4589
10,000 sq. ft. — 37 dealers

### Roswell
**Roswell Antique Gallery**
10930 Crabapple Road
770/594-8484
30,000 sq. ft. - 245 dealer spaces

# *Largest Malls*

## Savannah
**Jere's Antiques**
9 N. Jefferson St.
912/236-2815
30,000 sq. ft.

## Tifton
**Sue's Antique Mall**
I-75 at Exit 23
912/388-1856
10,000 sq. ft. — No reproductions

## *INDIANA*

## Anderson
**Anderson Antique Mall**
1407 Main St.
765/622-9517
30,000 sq. ft. — four floors

## Bloomington
**Bloomington Antique Mall**
311 W. 7th St.
812/332-2290
120+ dealers

## Centerville
**Webb's Antique Malls**
200 W. Union St.
765/855-5542
100,000 sq. ft. — 600+ dealers

## Chesterton
**Yesterday's Treasures Antique Mall**
700 Broadway
219/926-2268
30,000 sq. ft. — 100+ dealers

## Evansville
**Franklin St. Antique Mall**
2123 W. Franklin St.
812/428-0988
21,000 sq. ft.— Historic Building

## Ft. Wayne
**Karen's Antique Mall**
1510 Fairfield
219/422-4030
18,000 sq. ft. — 65+ dealers

## Indianapolis
**Fountain Square Antique Mall**
1056 Virginia Ave.
317/636-1056
14,000 sq. ft. — 70+ dealers

**Manor House Antique Mall**
5454 U.S. 31 S.
317/782-1358
20,000 sq. ft. — 140 dealers

**Southport Antique Mall**
2028 E. Southport Road
317/786-8246
29,000 sq. ft. — 210 dealers

## Knightstown
**Knightstown Antique Mall**
136 W. Carey St.
765/345-5665
city block of merchandise

## LaPorte
**Coachman Antique Mall**
500 Lincolnway
219/326-5933
23,000 sq. ft. — 100 dealers

## Muncie
**Off Broadway Antique Mall**
2404 N. Broadway
765/747-5000
½ acre under one roof — 70+ dealers

## Nappanee
**Borkholder Dutch Village**
CR 101
219/773-2828

## Plainfield
**Gilley's Antique Mall**
5789 E. U.S. Hwy. 40
317/839-8779
7 buildings — 400+ booths

## Westfield
**R. Beauchamp Antiques**
16405 Westfield Blvd.
217/867-3327
15,000 sq. ft.

**Westfield Antique Mall**
800 E. Main St., Hwy. 232
317/867-3327
17,000 sq. ft.

## *KENTUCKY*

## Corbin
**Past Times Antique Mall**
135 W. Cumberland Gap Pkwy.
606/528-8818
14,000 sq. ft. — 95 dealers

## Georgetown
**Georgetown Antique Mall**
124 W. Main St.
502/863-1275
4 buildings, 6 floors — 100+ dealers

## Harrodsburg
**The Antique Mall of Harrodsburg**
540 N. College St. (Hwy. 127)
606/734-5191
Over 130 dealers

**North Main Center Antique Mall**
520 N. Main St.
606/734-2200
22,000 sq. ft.

## Lexington
**Boone's Antiques of Kentucky**
4996 Old Versailles Road
606/254-5335
27,000 sq. ft.

**Country Antique Mall Inc.**
1455 Leestown Road
Meadowthorpe Shopping Center
606/233-0075
14,000 sq. ft. — 60 dealers

## Louisville
**Louisville Antique Mall**
900 Goss Ave.
502/635-2852
72,000 sq. ft.

**Swan Street Antique Mall**
947 E. Breckinridge St.
502/584-6255
30,000 sq. ft. — 125 dealers

## Mt. Sterling
**Monarch Mill Antiques**
101 S. Maysville St.
606/498-3744
Over 13,000 sq. ft.

## Newport
**471 Antique Mall**
901 E. 6th St.
606/431-4753
20,000 sq. ft. — 2 floors

## *MAINE*

## Auburn
**Orphan Annie's Antiques**
96 Court St.
207/782-0638
3 warehouses

## Brewer
**Center Mall**
39 Center St.
207/989-9842
12,000 sq. ft. — 55 dealers

## Kennebunkport
**Antiques USA**
RR 1
207/985-7766
Over 200 dealers — One of largest in state

## Wells
**Wells Union Antique Center**
1755 Post Road
207/646-6996
9 buildings

## York
**York Antiques Gallery**
Rte. 1
207/363-5002
4 floors — 80 dealers

## *MARYLAND*

## Baltimore
**"Howard Street" Antique District**
Over 20 shops

**Antique Warehouse at 1300**
1300 Jackson St.
410/659-0662
15,000 sq. ft. — 35 dealers

## Cambridge
**Packing House Antique Mall**
411 Dorchester
410/221-8544
60,000 sq. ft. — 140 dealers

## Easton
**Sullivan's Antique Warehouse**
28272 St. Michaels Road
410/822-4723
4 large buildings

## Ellicott
**Shops at Ellicott Mills**
8307 Main St.
410/461-8700
100 dealers

## Frederick
**Antique Station**
194 Thomas Johnson Dr.
301/695-0888
New section "mile long"

## Hanover
**AAA Antiques Mall**
2659 Annapolis Road
410/551-4101
58,000 sq. ft.

## *MASSACHUSETTS*

## Boston
**"Charles St." Antique District**
Over 20 shops

## Cambridge
**Antiques on Cambridge Street**
1076 Cambridge St.
617/234-0001
100 dealers

**Cambridge Antique Market**
201 Monsignor O'Brien Hwy.
617/868-9600
5 floors — 150 dealers

## Dennis
**Antiques Center Warehouse**
243 Main St., Route 6A
508/385-5133
2 buildings — 235 dealers

# Largest Malls

### Georgetown
**Sedler's Antique Village**
51 W. Main St.
978/352-8282
10,000 square feet, — 30 shops

### Sandwich
**Sandwich Antiques Center**
131 Route 6A
508/833-3600
Over 150 dealers

### Southampton
**Southampton Antiques**
172 College Hwy. (Route 10)
413/527-1022
3 large barns with five floors

### Sturbridge
**Showcase Antique Center, Inc.**
Entrance to Old Sturbridge Village
508/347-7190
160 dealers

## *MICHIGAN*

### Allen
**Antique Capital**
Hwy. 12
120,000 sq. ft. — 260 dealers

**Allen Antique Mall**
9011 W. Chicago St.
517/869-2788
"Michigan's Largest" — 260+ dealers

### Bay City
**Bay City Antiques Center**
1010 N. Water St. at Third
517/893-1116 or 888/893-0251
53,000 sq. ft. — 3 floors

### Clinton
**First Class Antique Mall**
112 E. Michigan Ave.
517/456-6410
15,000 sq. ft.

### Flint
**Reminisce Antiques & Collectibles**
3124 S. Dort Hwy.
810/744-1090
15,000 sq. ft. — 50 dealers

### Grand Haven
**West Michigan Antique Mall**
13279 168th Ave.
616/842-0370
12,000 sq. ft. — 75 dealers

### Holland
**Tulip City Antique Mall**
3500 U.S. Hwy. 31
616/786-4424
30,000 sq. ft. — 200 dealers

### Lansing
**Mid Michigan Mega Mall**
15487 U.S. Hwy. 27
517/487-3275
230 dealers

### Lowell
**Flat River Antique Mall**
212 W. Main St.
616/897-5360
40,000 sq. ft. — 5 floors

### Muskegon
**Downtown Muskegon Antique Mall**
1321 Division St.
616/728-0305
12,000 sq. ft.

### Niles
**Niles Michigan**
4 malls - 300 shops
80,000 sq. ft.

### Saginaw
**The Antique Warehouse**
1910 N. Michigan at Genesee
517/755-4343
30,000 sq. ft. — 70 dealers — lunchroom

### Schoolcraft
**Norma's Antiques & Collectibles**
231 Grand (U.S. Hwy. 131)
616/679-4030
Over 10,000 sq. ft. — 3 floors

### Union Pier
**Antique Mall & Village Inc.**
9300 Union Pier Road
616/469-2555
15,000 sq. ft. — 4 buildings

## *MISSISSIPPI*

### Biloxi
**Beauvoir Antique Mall**
190 Beauvoir Road
601/388-5506
Huge building — 50+ dealers

### Hattiesburg
**Old High School Antiques**
846 N. Main St.
601/544-6644
4 stories — 50+ dealers

### Natchez
**Natchez Antique District**
Located on Franklin St.
12 plus shops

## *NEW HAMPSHIRE*

### Amherst
**101-A Antiques & Collectibles Center**
141 State Route 101A
603/880-8422
175+ dealers

**Needful Things/Antiques & Collectibles**
112 State Route 101A
603/889-1232
185 dealers

### Meredith
**Burlwood Antique Center**
Route 3
603/279-6387
170 dealers

### Milford
**New Hampshire Antique Co-op**
Elm St. — Route 101A
603/673-8499
280 dealers

### West Swanzey
**Knotty Pine Antique Market**
Route 10
603/352-5252
300 antique shops under one roof

### Wilton
**Noah's Ark**
Route 101
603/654-2595
234 dealers

## *NEW JERSEY*

### Andover
**Great Andover Antique Company**
124 Main St.
973/786-6384
2 huge buildings

### Dover
**The Iron Carriage Antique Center**
1 W. Blackwell
973/366-1440
30,000 sq. ft. — 100 dealers

### Haddonfield
**Haddonfield Antique District**
Kingo Hwy. E.
7 shops within 2 blocks

### Hopewell
**Tomato Factory Antique Center**
Hamilton Ave.
609/466-9860
Shops in old 2-story canning factory

### Lebanon
**Lebanon Antique Center**
U.S. Hwy. 22 E.
908/236-2851
5 acres

### Manahawkin
**The Shoppes at Rosewood**
182 N. Main St.
609/597-7331
Group in Victorian neighborhood

## *NEW YORK*

### Brooklyn
**Brooklyn Antique District**
Atlantic Ave.
12 shops

### Clarence
**Downtown Clarence**
Main St.
14+ shops

### Hudson
**5 historic walking blocks of antique shops**

## *NORTH CAROLINA*

### Asheville
**Fireside Antiques**
30 All Souls Crescent
704/274-5977
4 galleries of antiques

### Boone
**Wilcox Emporium**
161 Howard St.
704/262-1221
60,000 sq. ft., plus 3 new large showrooms

### Charlotte
**Black Lion Furniture**
**Gift & Design Showcases**
10605 Park Road
704/541-1148

### Gastonia
**J & W Antiques**
181 W. Main St.
704/867-0097
28,000 sq. ft.

### Hendersonville
**Hendersonville Antique District**
Downtown Main St.
Multiple shops — all within blocks

### Statesville
**Riverfront Antique Mall**
1441 Wilkesboro Hwy.
800/856-2182
60,000 sq. ft.

# Largest Malls

## Wilson
**Fulford's Antique Warehouse**
320 Barnes St. S.
919/243-7727
67,000 sq. ft.

## OHIO

### Bellaire
**Imperial Plaza**
29th & Belmont St.
614/676-8300
40,000 sq. ft.

### Findlay
**Jeffrey's Antique Gallery**
11326 Township Road 99
419/423-7500
40,000 sq. ft.

### Medina
**Medina Antique Mall**
2797 Medina Road
330/722-0017
52,000 sq. ft.

### New Philadelphia
**Riverfront Antique Mall**
1203 Front St.
1-800-926-9806
96,400 sq. ft. — 350 dealers

### Ravenna
**AAA I-76 Antique Mall**
4284 Lynn Road
1-888-476-8976
50,000 sq. ft. — 450 dealers

**Ravenna Antique District**
The entire town of Ravenna offers many antiquing possibilities.

Springfield
*AAA I-10 Antique Mall*
4700 S. Charleston Pike
(State Route 41)
513/324-8448
150,000 sq. ft. — 250 dealers

## PENNSYLVANIA

### Adamstown
**Renninger's Antique Market**
PA Turnpike, Exit 21, Route 272
717/385-0104
Several hundred booths

**South Pointe Antiques**
Route 272 & Denver Road
717/484-1026
135 dealers

**Stoudt's Black Angus**
PA Turnpike, Exit 21, Route 272
717/484-4385
Over 500 booths

## Beaver Falls
**Leonard's Antqs. Uniques Mega Mall**
2586 Constitution
704/847-2304
68,000 sq. ft. — 300 dealers

### Export
**Schmidt's Springhouse Antiques**
Route 66 at Pfeffer Road
724/325-2577
10,000 sq. ft.

### Irwin
**Antiques Odds & Ends**
508 Lincoln Hwy. E. (Route 30)
724/863-9769
8,000 sq. ft. — 3 large buildings

### Sciota
**Halloran's Antiques**
Fenner Ave.
717/992-4651
3 barns full

## RHODE ISLAND

### Barrington
**The Stock Exchange & The Annex**
57 Maple Ave. & 232 Wascca Ave.
401/245-4170

### Newport
Aardvark Antiques
475 ½ Thames
401/849-7233
65,000 sq. ft.

**Armory Antique Center**
365 Thames St.
401/848-2398
8,000 sq. ft. — 125 dealers

### Portsmouth
**Eagles Nest Antique Center**
3101 E. Main Road
401/683-3500
124 dealers

### Warren
**Warren Antique Center**
5 Miller St.
401/245-5461
Located in old theater — 4 levels —
100+ dealers

## SOUTH CAROLINA

### Aiken
**Aiken Antique Mall**
112-114 Laurens St. S.W.
803/648-6700
13,000 sq. ft. — 50 dealers

## Swan Antique Mall
3557 Richland Ave. W.
803/643-9922
20,000 sq. ft.

### West Columbia
**378 Antique Mall**
620 Sunset Blvd.
803/791-3132
20,000 sq. ft.

## TENNESSEE

### Bartlett
**Antique Gallery**
6044 Stage Road
901/385-2544
35,000 sq. ft. — 150 dealers

### Chattanooga
**East Town Antique Mall**
6503 Slater Road
423/899-5498
30,000 sq. ft. — over 300 booths and showcases

### Cordova
**Antique Market of Cordova**
1740 N. Germantown Pkwy., Suite 18
901/759-0414
8,500 sq. ft. — 30+ dealers

### Franklin
**Franklin Antique Historic District Area**
251 Second Ave. S.
615/599-5406
14,000 sq. ft. — 100 dealers

### Knoxville
**Antiques Plus**
4500 Walker Blvd.
423/687-6536
12,000 sq. ft.

**Campbell Station Antiques**
620 Campbell Station Road
423/966-4348
10,000 sq. ft.

### Lebanon
**Lebanon Antique District**
Downtown Lebanon
"Public Square"

### Morristown
**Olde Town Antique Mall**
181 W. Main St.
423/581-6423
15,000 sq. ft.

### Murfreesboro
**Antique Centers I & II**
2213-2219 S. Church St.
615/896-5188
30,000 sq. ft.

## Sevierville
**Riverside Antique & Collectible Mall**
1442 Winfield Dunn Pkwy.
423/429-0100
35,000 sq. ft.

### Shelbyville
**The Antique Marketplace**
208 Elm St.
931/684-8493
100+ dealers

### Smithville
**Fuston's Antiques**
123 W. Market St.
615/597-5232
25,000 sq. ft.

## VERMONT

### Barre
**East Barre Antique Mall**
133 Mill St.
802/479-5190
12,000 sq. ft.

### Quechee
**Quechee Gorge Village**
Route 4
1-800-438-5565
450 dealers

## VIRGINIA

### Culpeper
**Country Shoppes of Culpeper**
10046 James Monroe Hwy.
540/547-4000
15,000 sq. ft. — 100+ dealers

### Mechanicsville
**Mechanicsville Antique Mall**
7508 Mechanicsville Turnpike
804/730-5091
30,000 sq. ft. - 100 booths

### Richmond
**West End Antiques Mall**
6504 Horsepen Road
804/285-1916
Combined 36,000 sq. ft. — 160 dealers

## WEST VIRGINIA

### Charleston
**Hale Street Antiques**
213 Hale St.
304/345-6040
3 full floors